BRITISH BUSINESS AND PROTECTION 1903–1932

British Business and Protection 1903–1932

Andrew Marrison

CLARENDON PRESS · OXFORD
1996

Oxford University Press, Walton Street, Oxford OX2 6DP
Oxford New York
Athens Auckland Bangkok Bombay
Calcutta Cape Town Dar es Salaam Delhi
Florence Hong Kong Istanbul Karachi
Kuala Lumpur Madras Madrid Melbourne
Mexico City Nairobi Paris Singapore
Taipei Tokyo Toronto
and associated companies in
Berlin Ibadan

Oxford is a trade mark of Oxford University Press

Published in the United States
by Oxford University Press Inc., New York

British Library Cataloguing in Publication Data
Data available
Marrison, Andrew.
British business and protection, 1903–1932
/ Andrew Marrison. p. cm.
Includes bibliographical references and index.
1. Protectionism—Great Britain—History. 2. Great Britain—
Commercial policy. 3. Free trade—Public opinion—History.
4. Public opinion—Great Britain—History. 5. Businessmen—Great
Britain—Attitudes—History. I. Title.
HF2046.M368 1995   95-37703
382'.73' 0941—dc20
ISBN 0-19-820298-9

1 3 5 7 9 10 8 6 4 2

Typeset by Pure Tech India Ltd., Pondicherry
Printed in Great Britain
on acid-free paper by
Bookcraft Ltd., Midsomer Norton, Avon

To my Mother and Father

Preface

In recording my debts and my thanks, it is not easy to know where to start and where to end. The following list can only be incomplete. My thanks and appreciation are due to those who have read draft chapters of the present work, and contributed substantially to its improvement: Janet Blackman; Steve Broadberry; Richard Davenport-Hines; Don McCloskey; Bob Millward; Rudra Mukherjee; Ted Musson; Alan Sykes; and three anonymous referees from OUP. I would also like to thank those with whom I have discussed aspects of my argument and the subject more generally, or who have helped in other, more particular, ways: Kenneth D. Brown; Peter Cain; Forrest Capie; the late Professor W. H. Chaloner; Phil Cottrell; John Chartres; Nick Crafts; Peter N. Davies; Douglas Farnie; James Foreman-Peck; Rick Garside; Leslie Hannah; David Jeremy; the late Professor A. H. John; Ian Kershaw; Clive Lee; Norman McCord; Joe Melling; Charles Munn; Keith Nield; Avner Offer; Dilwyn Porter; Michael E. Rose; John Saville; and John Wilson. In ways no doubt far more important to me than memorable to them, Theo Barker, A. W. Coats, and Kenneth Morgan offered encouragement that was, and is still, much appreciated. Other valued contributions were made by the participants in research seminars held at the Universities of Durham, Exeter, Hull, Liverpool, Warwick, and Manchester.

My thanks are also due to the librarians, archivists, and staffs of those institutions holding the manuscript and other collections on which this study is mainly based. These are listed in the bibliography, but it is proper to record them here: Birmingham University Library; the British Library; the Bodleian Library, Oxford; the Brotherton Library, University of Leeds; the British Library of Political and Economic Science, London; Cambridge University Library; Churchill College Library, Cambridge; the Guildhall Library, London; the House of Lords Record Office; Hull University Library; the John Rylands University Library, Manchester; Leeds Central Reference Library; Macclesfield Public Library; Manchester Central Reference Library; the Public Record Office; Sheffield University Library; and the Modern Records Centre, University of Warwick. It was a pleasure to do research in all these libraries, but I am conscious of the fact that I was unduly intrusive upon the time of the staff at the British Library of Political and Economic Science and at Sheffield University Library; and, especially, upon that of Richard Storey at the Modern Records Centre at Warwick.

I am grateful to the secretaries of the following chambers of commerce for permission to consult their records: the Associated British Chambers of

Commerce, Birmingham Chamber of Commerce, Hull Chamber of Commerce, Leeds Chamber of Commerce, London Chamber of Commerce and Industry, Nottingham Chamber of Commerce, and Sheffield Chamber of Commerce. Particular thanks are due to the Secretaries and Assistant Secretaries of the Birmingham and Nottingham Chambers, who allowed me to conduct research in their own offices, in conditions of comfort and hospitality which were quite remarkable. For future researchers into the underwritten history of chambers of commerce, let me be wicked enough to suggest the week before Christmas!

Crown-copyright material in the Public Record Office is quoted with the permission of the Controller of Her Majesty's Stationery Office. I would like to acknowledge the permission of the Clerk of Records of the House of Lords and Anthony and Sir Simeon Bull for permission to quote from the papers of Sir William Bull. For permission to quote from other copyright material, I am most grateful to Elizabeth Boyd Adams of the Association of British Chambers of Commerce (papers of the Associated Chambers of Commerce of the United Kingdom and the Association of British Chambers of Commerce); Lord Addison (papers of Christopher, Viscount Addison); the Trustees of the Beaverbrook Foundation (papers of Sir Patrick Hannon); the Bodleian Library (papers of Lord Asquith and Oxford and of Sir Laming Worthington-Evans); G. C. Robin Booth of London Chamber of Commerce and Industry (papers of London Chamber of Commerce); the British Library (Arthur Balfour Papers); Cambridge University Press; Alistair Cooke, OBE and Conservative Central Office (papers of the Conservative Research Department); Lord Croft (Henry Page Croft Papers); Professor Phyllis Deane; J. A. Hyde of the Confederation of British Industries (CBI Predecessor Archive); Professor D. N. McCloskey; Dr. B. R. Mitchell; the Fellows and Librarian of New College, Oxford (papers of Alfred, Viscount Milner); the University of Birmingham (Austen and Joseph Chamberlain Papers); the University of Sheffield (W. A. S. Hewins Papers); and the Earl of Swinton (papers of the Sir Philip Cunliffe-Lister, First Earl of Swinton). I apologize to the owners of any collections whom I have been unable to contact or whose copyright I have unconsciously infringed.

I am most grateful to the Editor of Manchester University Press for permission to reproduce an abbreviated and modified version of my chapter, 'The Development of a Tariff Reform Policy during Joseph Chamberlain's First Campaign', which originally appeared in W. H. Chaloner and B. M. Ratcliffe (eds.), *Trade and Transport: Essays in Economic History in Honour of T. S. Willan* (Manchester University Press, 1977); to Frank Cass and Co. Ltd. and the Editors of *Business History* for permission to reproduce an abbreviated and modified version of parts of my article, 'Businessmen, Industries and Tariff Reform in Great Britain, 1903–1930', originally published in volume 25 (1983) of that journal; and to the Editor of *Agricultural History Review* for permission to reproduce a highly abbreviated version of my article, 'The Tariff Commission, Agricultural Protection and

Food Taxes, 1903–1913', which originally appeared in volume 34 (1986) of that journal. These appear in Chapters 1, 2, and 7 of the present work respectively. To Tony Morris and his staff at OUP, all of whom possess the unusual combination of enthusiasm and patience, I also extend my thanks.

I would also like to express my gratitude to those who were kind enough to lodge and feed an itinerant scholar. In an age when scholarly research is too often an uncomfortable balance between subsidizing out of the family income and unseemly predatory strikes upon one's friends, Eric Hobsbawm is not the only historian who fully understands the world of the tramping artisan. Grateful thanks are due to Mel and Margaret Cayzer; Richard Cust and Anne Hughes; Ian Kershaw again; Philip Marr; Keith and Julie Maunders; John and Kathy Moore; my mother- and father-in-law; and my father and mother. I persist in the optimistic belief that the last-mentioned were not the only ones who were always pleased to see me.

In time-honoured fashion, I leave acknowledgement of my greatest debts until last. Theo Balderston has read successive drafts and re-drafts of the chapters in this volume as they have appeared, has read the whole manuscript about three times, and has subjected me to the merciless discipline of trying to divine his handwriting. Beyond such technical matters of record, his friendship and encouragement cannot be overstated. If this book proves to have any merit, then he, at least, will have absolutely no need to read it. If Theo has had to suffer too frequently my intrusions upon his time, the same can scarcely be said of Christine, Tom, and Rosie. They have put up with my absence, both mental and physical, my irritability, and my preoccupation. I will not enquire too closely into whether they consider the end result worth it, but I will promise to try to be a bit better in future.

Manchester, 1995

A. M.

Contents

List of Figures

List of Tables

Abbreviations

ABCC	Associated British Chambers of Commerce (formerly ACCUK)
ACCUK	Associated Chambers of Commerce of the United Kingdom (subsequently ABCC)
ACM (VT)	Agricultural Committee Minutes (verbatim typescript) [Tariff Commission]
ACP	Austen Chamberlain Papers
AGM	Annual General Meeting (several organizations, as relevant)
Agricultural Report	*The Tariff Commission*, iii. *Report of the Agricultural Committee* (London, 1906)
AIA	Abnormal Importations Act (1931)
ARC	Agricultural Research Committee (CRD)
BBC	Balfour of Burleigh Committee
BCCJ	*Birmingham Chamber of Commerce Journal*
BCU	British Commonwealth Union
BDH	British Drug Houses Ltd.
BdI	*Bund der Industriellen*
BEA	British Engineers' Association
BEAMA	British Electrical and Allied Manufacturers' Association
BEPO	British Empire Producers' Organisation
BIDCo	Bankers' Industrial Development Company
BITA	British Iron Trade Association
BMA	British Manufacturers' Association
BSA	British Small Arms Company Ltd.
CCA	Central and Associated Chambers of Agriculture of the United Kingdom
CCJ	[London] *Chamber of Commerce Journal*
CCR	Committee for Civil Research
CdI	*Centralverband deutscher Industriellen*
Cotton Report	*Report of the Tariff Commission*, ii. *The Textile Trades*, 1: *The Cotton Industry* (London, 1905)
CRD	Conservative Research Department
DNB	*Dictionary of National Biography*
EDU	Empire Development Union
EEC	Economic Emergency Committee (FBI)

EEU	Empire Economic Union
EIA	Empire Industries Association
EEF	Engineering Employers' Federation
Engineering Report	*Report of the Tariff Commission*, iv. *The Engineering Industries, including Structural, Electrical, Marine and Shipbuilding, Mechanical and General Industrial Engineering* (London, 1909)
EPA	Employers' Parliamentary Association
FBI	Federation of British Industries
FCSDA	Fine Cotton Spinners' and Doublers' Association
FPC	Fiscal Policy Committee (FBI)
FPEC	Fiscal Policy Enquiry Committee (FBI)
FTL	Free Trade League
GATT	General Agreement on Tariffs and Trade
GEC	General Electric Company Ltd.
GKN	Guest, Keen, Nettlefolds Ltd.
GPC	General Purposes Committee (several organizations, as relevant)
HP	Hewins Papers
Hull CC	Hull Chamber of Commerce
ICA	Imperial Commercial Association
ICI	Imperial Chemical Industries Ltd.
IDAC	Import Duties Advisory Committee
ILP	Independent Labour Party
Iron and Steel Report	*Report of the Tariff Commission*, i. *The Iron and Steel Trades* (London, 1904)
ISTC	Iron and Steel Trades' Confederation
ITC	Imperial Tariff Committee (Birmingham)
JCP	Joseph Chamberlain Papers
LCC	London Chamber of Commerce
Leeds CC	Leeds Chamber of Commerce
MFN	Most Favoured Nation
NCC	Nottingham Chamber of Commerce
NCIC	National Council of Industry and Commerce
NFISM	National Federation of Iron and Steel Manufacturers
NFU	National Farmers' Union
NUM	National Union of Manufacturers
Pottery Report	*Report of the Tariff Commission*, vii. *The Pottery Industries* (London, 1907)
PRO	Public Record Office
SIA	Safeguarding of Industries Act (1921)
SIMA	Scottish Iron Manufacturers' Association

SMT	Securities Management Trust Ltd.
TAC	Tariff Advisory Committee
TCM(P)	Tariff Commission Minutes (printed)
TCM(VT)	Tariff Commission Minutes (verbatim typescript)
TCP	Tariff Commission Papers
TRL	Tariff Reform League
TUC	Trades' Union Congress
UBC	Unionist Business Committee
UEP	United Empire Party
UWC	Unionist War Committee
Woollen Report	*Report of the Tariff Commission*, ii. *The Textile Trades*, 2: *Evidence on the Woollen Industry* (London, 1905)

Introduction

This study is concerned principally with that frontier where the worlds of business and politics collide. Specifically, it seeks to explore the objectives and strategies of protectionist businessmen, and the organizations through which they were pursued, in a period during which conflict over the tariff was a dominant theme of British politics. It is not, essentially, concerned with the question of whether there was an economically valid case for some measure of Tariff Reform in the period between 1900 and 1932. Nevertheless, it would seem useful to start with a discussion of that question. Protectionists are often dismissed simply as 'rent-seekers', the success of their policies seen as inimical to the wider public good. But to approach the historical record with such stylized preconceptions both obscures and distorts. The Tariff Reformers recognized truths and tendencies to which their adversaries were blind. Even if we conclude that their prescriptions were misguided, inappropriate, or worse, we will at least have located their concerns within the longer-run pattern of British economic development.

I

When, in 1958, Albert Imlah published his brilliant and influential *Economic Elements of the Pax Britannica*, he made a direct association between the dismantling of the Corn Laws, the Navigation System, and Britain's other protective devices, and the international boom of the 1850s and 1860s. Though he appreciated that there were other forces working for expansion in the mid-Victorian years, the weight of his analysis was clear:

The new policy proved wonderfully suitable to [Britain's] national needs and interests. Industries thrived and multiplied, commerce expanded at a rate beyond past precedent, and her people enjoyed a period of unwonted prosperity and social peace. Moreover, the fact that the markets of this giant among the trading nations of the day were opened freely to the products of other lands promoted economic development throughout the world and eased international tensions.[1]

This association had long been stressed by Free Trade polemicists—the establishment of the Cobden Club itself was a celebration of the link and the memory. As one Conservative complained in the 1930s, '[i]t was not too well appreciated . . . how fortunate Free Trade was in its allies and in the moment of its

---

[1] A. H. Imlah, *Economic Elements in the Pax Britannica* (Cambridge, Mass., 1958), 114 and ch. 6.

introduction; it came, as they used to say in the Greek tragedies, *enkairios*.[2] The mid-Victorian boom, with its associated transport improvements and gold discoveries, did for the reputation of the Manchester School what a similar boom in the 1950s and 1960s was to do for the Keynesians.[3]

Imlah's work lent academic detachment to the association. In doing so, it fitted well with a prevailing historiography of the Industrial Revolution, whiggish and self-congratulatory in tendency, 'optimistic' to some, 'neutralist' to others, which saw Britain in the 1850s as standing on a pinnacle of industrial development and leadership.[4] At the same time, it enhanced the stature of those studies, less specifically economic in their handling, which examined the romance of the Free Trade movement, its connections with the Board of Trade and the statistical movement, and the class politics of the Anti-Corn Law League.[5]

Writing after Imlah, other economic historians were more doubtful. J. R. T. Hughes, in his study of the 1850s, considered that Free Trade '*probably* stimulated relatively inefficient industries into greater productivity . . . but it is not certain how much of the improvement was due exclusively to Free Trade'.[6] Using Hughes' data, Roy Church looked for evidence that rising British imports held the key to prosperity in the export sector, via world trade expansion, and did not find it.[7] But, ironically, it was a former student of Imlah, Donald McCloskey, who made the most profound revision. The effects of Free Trade on British national income were much more marginal than had hitherto been assumed, and, given the effect of deteriorating terms of trade, on balance harmful. Commenting on earlier studies, McCloskey observed that:

Historians have adopted the contemporary view of the matter. The correlation between rising national income and the move to free trade, the apparent significance for the distribution of income of removing high duties on food and the intense involvement of Britain in the international economy have been the elements in a demonstration that commercial policy had a substantial effect on the size and distribution of British national income in the nineteenth century. The depth of analysis, to be sure, has left something to be desired, for free trade has not been isolated from other factors influencing national income, the effects on distribution have been treated in purely qualitative terms and the argument has been bound together by an unsupported conviction that foreign trade was crucial to Britain's economic welfare . . . Historians have naturally if not always correctly assumed that it matters economically how a great issue of economic policy such as this is

[2] D. Walker-Smith, *The Protectionist Case in the 1840s* (Oxford, 1933), 88.

[3] See R. C. O. Matthews, 'Why has Britain had Full Employment since the War?', *Economic Journal*, 78 (1968), 555–69.

[4] D. C. Coleman, *History and the Economic Past* (Oxford, 1987), ch. 5.

[5] F. E. Hyde, *Mr. Gladstone at the Board of Trade* (1934); L. Brown, *The Board of Trade and the Free Trade Movement 1830–42* (Oxford, 1958); N. McCord, *The Anti-Corn Law League 1838–1846* (1958).

[6] J. R. T. Hughes, *Fluctuations in Trade, Industry and Finance 1850–1860* (Oxford, 1960), 9, 36–68.

[7] R. A. Church, *The Great Victorian Boom 1850–1873* (Houndmills, 1975), 59–65.

resolved, the more so as the historical study of the issue has been left largely to political rather than economic historians.[8]

If economic historians today doubt whether Free Trade made a great deal of difference to the performance of the mid-Victorian economy, what of the later period—the 1880s, when Fair Trade caused a ripple in British politics, and the 1900s, when Joseph Chamberlain's Tariff Reform dominated them? Political historians have mined a rich vein. Clearly, Tariff Reform was a political presence which affected elections, shaped alliances and schisms, determined governments.[9] Clearly, also, it was a *Weltanschauung*, which could be dissected and analyzed, placed in the context of parallel streams of Unionist philosophy.[10] Indeed, historians have long recognized that, in its implications for public finance and the struggle between individualism and collectivism, Tariff Reform lay near the centre of almost every political development between the 1880s and the 1930s.[11] Study of the economic implications of the Tariff Reformers' schemes is, however, much less developed.

This is unfortunate because the period concerned is of particular importance, is even perhaps a crucial stage, in Britain's long-term economic development. Whilst econometric studies have demonstrated that aggregate productivity growth rates in the British economy did not decelerate markedly until the 1890s or 1900s, they have not seriously modified the more traditional analysis of *industrial* retardation relative to Germany and the US.[12] Indeed, one of the

[8] D. N. McCloskey, 'Magnanimous Albion: Free Trade and British National Income, 1841–1881', in D. N. McCloskey (ed.), *Enterprise and Trade in Victorian Britain* (1981), 155–72; for slightly different estimates, see D. A. Irwin, 'Welfare Effects of British Free Trade: Debate and Evidence from the 1840s', *Journal of Political Economy*, 96 (1988), 1142–64. Also C. H. Lee, *The British Economy since 1700* (Cambridge, 1986), 118.

[9] P. Fraser, 'Unionism and Tariff Reform: The Crisis of 1906', *Historical Journal*, 5 (1962), 149–66; and *Joseph Chamberlain*, (1966), chs. 10–12; S. H. Zebel, 'Joseph Chamberlain and the Genesis of Tariff Reform', *Journal of British Studies*, 7 (1967), 131–57; N. Blewett, 'Free Fooders, Balfourites, Whole Hoggers. Factionalism within the Unionist Party, 1906–10', *Historical Journal*, 11 (1968), 95–124; and *The Peers, the Parties and the People*, (1972); J. Amery, *Life of Joseph Chamberlain*, v., vi. *Joseph Chamberlain and the Tariff Reform Movement* (1969); R. A. Rempel, *Unionists Divided*, (Newton Abbot, 1974); A. Sykes, 'The Confederacy and the Purge of the Unionist Free Traders, 1906–1910', *Historical Journal*, 18 (1975), 349–66; and *Tariff Reform in British Politics, 1903–1913* (Oxford, 1979); P. M. Kennedy, *The Rise of Anglo-German Antagonism, 1860–1914* (1980), IV; E. H. H. Green, 'Radical Conservatism: The Electoral Genesis of Tariff Reform', *Historical Journal*, 28 (1985), 667–92; and 'Radical Conservatism in Britain, 1900–1914', unpubl. Ph.D. thesis, Univ. of Cambridge, 1985.

[10] See, *inter alia*, B. Semmel, *Imperialism and Social Reform* (1960); R. J. Scally, *The Origins of the Lloyd George Coalition* (Princeton, 1975), esp. ch. 4; A. Summers, 'The Character of Edwardian Nationalism: Three Popular Leagues', in P. Kennedy and A. Nicholls (eds.), *Nationalist and Racialist Movements in Britain and Germany before 1914* (1981), 68–87; A. L. Friedberg, *The Weary Titan* (Princeton, 1988); F. Coetzee, *For Party or Country* (New York, 1990).

[11] See e.g. its incursion into the themes contained in P. F. Clarke, *Lancashire and the New Liberalism* (Cambridge, 1971), and M. Cowling, *The Impact of Labour* (Cambridge, 1971).

[12] For a recent summary of the large amount of research into economic and industrial growth rates and productivity trends in the period 1870–1914, see S. Pollard, *Britain's Prime and Britain's Decline* (1989), ch. 1.

leading British exponents of total factor-productivity analysis has suggested that Britain's problem in the 1880s may simply have been that growth rates *did not accelerate*, whereas elsewhere they did.[13] This fits nicely with the views of earlier historians, who discerned a 'second industrial revolution' based on applied science and scientific management in which Britain no longer led, and with those of recent business historians who dwell upon Britain's failure to emulate the American transition to the large-scale integrated company and her lack of a managerial revolution.[14] Economic historians have also long been aware of the more competitive conditions facing British exporters from the 1880s onwards, as nominal tariff levels rose in the 'Great Depression', as the development of indigenous industries abroad led to import substitution, and as export rivals began to contest their dominance of neutral markets. Based extensively on contemporary comment, some early studies were considerable exaggerations, but later ones were more judicious.[15]

Whilst we should be wary of any teleological approach, many historians have located the origins of Britain's relative economic decline squarely in the period 1880–1914. Whether the prevailing economic policy was appropriate is clearly a question of considerable interest to historians, as well as having been the issue which fired a controversy which shaped politics right into the 1930s. Yet there has only been one attempt to calculate the overall effect that a Chamberlainite policy, had it been implemented, would have had. Mark Thomas used input-output analysis to suggest that, when analyzed using the concepts of effective protection and optimum tariffs, Tariff Reform did indeed have some potential for raising growth rates. His findings were briefly reported in the *Journal of Economic History*, but otherwise his work has made a regrettably small impact.[16]

That most economic historians have been more cautious is understandable. In one of the best introductions to the economic aspects of Tariff Reform, intended primarily for students, Peter Cain considered that 'the many-faceted nature of the tariff problem probably explains why . . . modern historians have shied away from tackling it in depth'.[17] Indeed, if the intention was to construct a counterfactual model with which to estimate the relative benefits of Free Trade and protection, not least of the problems would be to determine the time period in question. A balance sheet drawn up to demonstrate the probable effects of

[13] i.e. N. F. R. Crafts. For a good summary, see N. F. R. Crafts, S. J. Leybourne, and T. C. Mills, 'Britain', in R. Sylla and G. Toniolo (eds.), *Patterns of European Industrialization* (1991), esp. 141.

[14] D. S. Landes, *The Unbound Prometheus* (Cambridge, 1969), 196, 239–358; A. D. Chandler, *Scale and Scope* (Cambridge, Mass., 1990), 3; B. Elbaum and W. Lazonick (eds.), *The Decline of the British Economy* (Oxford, 1986).

[15] R. J. S. Hoffman, *Great Britain and the German Trade Rivalry, 1875–1914* (Philadelphia, 1933); cf. D. H. Aldcroft (ed.), *The Development of British Industry and Foreign Competition, 1875–1914* (1968).

[16] M. Thomas, 'An Input-Output Approach to the British Economy, 1890–1914', *Journal of Economic History*, 45 (1985), 460–3.

[17] P. Cain, 'Political Economy in Edwardian England: The Tariff-Reform Controversy', in A. O'Day (ed.), *The Edwardian Age* (1979), 35.

Tariff Reform by 1913 would scarcely be adequate to test the Tariff Reformers' vision of the future. If they had stated their views openly, which they could not, the more advanced Tariff Reformers would without doubt have been willing to accept short-term losses in the interests of what they regarded as a superior long-term development path. But, over time, the effects of tariffs are notoriously difficult to calculate, and would in any case be swamped in the specific historical context by the First World War. Indeed, even where the issues can be pinned down more precisely, they are scarcely less intractable. To assess the effects of the tariffs that *were* implemented in 1932 in the containable period prior to the outbreak of war might be thought to be relatively simple, but it is not. Forrest Capie has recently observed that no consensus has emerged on this issue, and that 'conclusions have as often been asserted as demonstrated'.[18]

Another factor that has almost certainly contributed to this professional cautiousness is that economic historians have been influenced by the general presumption in favour of Free Trade held by economists, both during the contemporary debate and since. The consequence has probably been to discourage revisionism because it carries in this case more than its due measure of notoriety, and to make more acceptable superficiality and mere assertion as long as it conforms to orthodoxist belief. In the academic as well as the public mind, protectionism was and still is often associated with venality, improper support of vested interests, graft, and corruption. Orthodox economics thus reinforces an acceptable public position—as Duncan Burn noted long ago, the result was that economists could indulge in large generalizations based on simple logical precepts elevated to axioms, without any enquiry into specific industrial and trading structures and conditions.[19] It might be observed that the body of theory on international trade and commercial policy has never been designed to analyze a historical condition where the rest of the world was protectionist and Britain was not. But nor is it easy for the economic historian to make up this deficiency. As Burn again noted, the detailed knowledge of industrial structure and trading conditions necessary to make a judgement on the likely effect of protection on even a single industry is immense.[20] If applied economists at the time eschewed such study, it is unlikely that the modern historian would find the exercise possible. We are forced back to judgements according to the larger precepts, and those are governed by prevailing concepts of intellectual legitimacy.

---

[18] F. Capie, *Depression and Protectionism* (1983), 105. In addition to Capie himself, those who have gone beyond mere assertion include H. W. Richardson, *Economic Recovery in Britain, 1932–39* (1967), 236–65; J. Foreman Peck, 'Tariff Protection and Economies of Scale: The British Motor Industry before 1939', *Oxford Economic Papers*, 31 (1979), 237–57; and 'The British Tariff and Industrial Protection in the 1930s: An Alternative Model', *Economic History Review*, 34 (1981), 132–9; B. Eichengreen, 'The Macroeconomic Effects of the British General Tariff of 1932' (mimeograph, 1979); M. Kitson and S. Solomou, *Protectionism and Economic Revival* (Cambridge, 1990).
[19] D. Burn, *Economic History of Steelmaking 1867–1939* (Cambridge, 1940), 322–4.
[20] Ibid. 99–102, 314–15, 322.

Against this background, few economic historians have devoted much attention to Tariff Reform; such verdicts as have been made have mostly been in passing, the product of study in adjacent areas, and have often reflected the times in which they were delivered. Though a Free Trader in the contemporary debate, Clapham was well aware by the 1930s of the dangers of dogmatism. Of the Fair Trade movement of the 1880s, he wrote that 'its strength lay less in its economics, though they were not negligible, than in its sense of a changing world and in its nationalism'.[21] If he was influenced in this by the lurch towards autarky and protectionism in the inter-war years, S. B. Saul was perhaps contrarily influenced by the expansive world economy of the 1950s: Tariff Reform was 'as much irrelevant as a positive danger'.[22] In the optimistic 1960s, the decade of the Kennedy Round, one searches almost in vain for any academic discussion of the possible validity of the Tariff Reform case. The one significant exception was seven brief pages by Aldcroft and Richardson. Whilst they doubted the wisdom of a return to general protectionism, they perceived with some sagacity that 'infant-industry duties [on the newer industries] would not have required an overall departure from free trade'.[23]

In the 1970s and 1980s, some economic historians became more sensitive to the constraints which British institutions, particularly inherited company structure and the capital market, placed upon economic performance, and more concerned about a possibly dichotomy of interest between the industrial and financial sectors.[24] To an extent, this brought them more into contact with at least the *objectives*, if not the prescriptions, of the more sophisticated Tariff Reformers. But, at the same time, econometric studies seemed almost to deny that the late-nineteenth-century British economy *had* any problems, and Mrs Thatcher's decade seemed to see no dangers in the collapse of manufacturing and the rise of a service-based economy. In consequence, Tariff Reform was little subjected to detailed scrutiny from fresh perspectives. Cain used mostly long-familiar arguments to conclude that Chamberlain's policy was 'inappropriate'.[25] Even Sidney Pollard, ideally placed to make telling comparisons between Britain and Germany and with a greater natural sympathy for the manufacturing interest and for the economics of Friedrich List, concluded with some reluctance that 'industrial protection could not have made much difference one way or the other'.[26]

That economic historians have, on the whole, avoided detailed analysis of the implications of the tariff controversy may not be surprising, but it is unfortunate.

---

[21] J. H. Clapham, *An Economic History of Modern Britain*, ii. (Cambridge, 1932), 251.

[22] S. B. Saul, *Studies in British Overseas Trade 1870–1914* (Liverpool, 1960), 165.

[23] D. H. Aldcroft and H. W. Richardson, *The British Economy 1870–1939* (1969), 77–84.

[24] See e.g. the essays in B. Elbaum and W. Lazonick (eds.), *Decline of the British Economy*.

[25] P. Cain, Political Economy, 52.

[26] S. Pollard, *Britain's Prime*, 242–3.

As well as bearing closely on the formulation of budgetary, social, and imperial policy, all subjects of perennial interest to a wide range of scholars, Tariff Reform carried substantial implications for at least three topics central to the study of British economic growth in the long run: industrial efficiency; industrial structure and export orientation; and the relationship between the financial and industrial sectors. Time and again, historians working in these areas seem to have *implicit* positions on Tariff Reform, but these are almost never openly acknowledged.

II

The more sophisticated Tariff Reformers argued that protection would promote industrial efficiency by limiting the disruptive effects of imports on the domestic market, thus stimulating investment. Free Traders countered this with standard, well-worn assertions of the relation between monopoly and inefficiency. Theirs was a static comparison of the effects of the alternative policies which missed the implicit dynamism and developmental logic of the Tariff Reformers' arguments. As Pollard concedes, 'no one looking at the debate at the time can believe that the manufacturers' main argument, that it was better to preserve industrial power for the future, as opposed to enjoying a high level of real incomes through cheap imports today, received adequate consideration'.[27] Whilst the 'import invasion' scares of the 1890s and 1900s were in certain respects exaggerated, the emphasis of the more sophisticated Tariff Reformers was on future trends, trends which they held to be irreversible under the prevailing conditions of trade and exchange. As Jha has perceptively noted, the Tariff Commission was the pioneering analyst of Britain's relative industrial decline.[28]

A search through the literature of modern economic history does not yield plentiful evidence, at least openly stated, of the belief that protection would have encouraged inefficiency in British industry. This is presumably because economic historians are well aware that the tariff was projected as a means of encouraging efficiency, and there are plausible arguments on both sides. Alfred Marshall knew and feared that his own formulation of the concept of 'increasing returns' might be used to generalize the case for an 'infant industry' duty, widely accepted since J. S. Mill, to any situation where costs fell as output increased.[29] By the late nineteenth century, Britain too had her infant industries, as well as having industries which, though nominally 'mature', could still profit by emulating best practice abroad. Hence it is possible for Newton and Porter, evidently

[27] Ibid.
[28] R. H. Heindel, *The American Impact on Great Britain 1898–1914* (New York, 1968 edn.), ch. 7–9; W. E. Minchinton, 'E. E. Williams: "Made in Germany" and after', *Vieteljahrschrift für Sozial-und Wirtschaftsgeschichte*, 62 (1975), 229–42; N. Jha, *The Age of Marshall* (2nd edn., 1973), 61.
[29] A. C. Pigou (ed.), *Memorials of Alfred Marshall* (1925), 449; N. Jha, *Age of Marshall*, 46, 51.

sympathetic to the idea, to interpret Tariff Reform as a valid attempt to introduce a policy of industrial modernization and regeneration.[30]

But almost immediately the problems multiply. Could a tariff have effected change within the firm, producing greater market stability which induced capital expenditure and managerial change? Or would it have required a strategic hand to re-shape the whole industry, in some precursor to the feeble rationalization movement of the inter-war period? If the latter, we are immediately conscious that our argument becomes anachronistic: few contemporary Tariff Reformers thought British industry so broken that it required wholesale restructuring, whilst most Free Traders would have found the idea of accelerated trustification repugnant. If the inter-war steel industry was obdurate in the face of such changes, the Edwardian would have offered even sterner resistance.

Economic historians have been less uncertain in their assessment of the relationship between trade policy, the prosperity of the staple export industries, and the export-orientation of the British economy as a whole.[31] By the late nineteenth century, Britain's manufactured exports were dominated by textiles, especially cotton, where at its peak the British industry exported 80 per cent of its output,[32] by semi-finished iron and steel, where exports typically constituted some 40 per cent of output,[33] and by a fairly narrow range of heavy engineering products and ships. The vulnerability of the British economy to any policy which threatened to affect the staple export sector adversely was highlighted by Saul, whose painstaking researches reconstructed the elegant completeness and symmetry of the world multilateral payments system, with Britain regnant at its centre.[34] Saul's analysis has been extremely pervasive, and it is superficially reinforced by study of tariff politics in many countries, which demonstrates conflict between export-orientated and home-market-orientated pressure groups. Protection would have acted negatively on the export trades, and contemporaries well appreciated this.

Free Traders rested their case on the dogma that the free operation of comparative advantage promoted the best of all possible worlds. The proof of this was a familiar and elementary exercise in comparative statics which ignored

---

[30] S. Newton and D. Porter, *Modernization Frustrated* (1988), esp. ch. 1. Though more circumspect, E. H. H. Green's recent *The Crisis of Conservatism: The Politics, Economics and Ideology of the British Conservative Party, 1880–1914* (1994) might also be placed in this category. It is gratifying to note that Green's treatment of the Tariff Commission essentially accepts the analysis contained in my 'British Businessmen and the "Scientific Tariff": A Study of Joseph Chamberlain's Tariff Commission, 1903–1921', unpubl. Ph. D. dissertation, Univ. of Hull, 1980.

[31] A. E. Kahn, *Great Britain in the World Economy* (New York, 1946), 65–72, highlighted the precariousness of this structure.

[32] P. Deane and W. A. Cole, *British Economic Growth 1688–1959* (Cambridge, 2nd edn., 1967), 187 Table 43.

[33] S. Tolliday, *Business, Banking, and Politics: The Case of British Steel 1918–1939* (Cambridge, Mass., 1987), 23.

[34] S. B. Saul, *British Overseas Trade*, esp. ch. 3.

the developmental implications of particular trading configurations. Comparative advantage has seldom seemed so advantageous from the standpoint of economists in poorer countries locked into export dependence on a few low-technology primary products. And it could be the case that, under Free Trade, comparative advantage was doing much the same thing to the late nineteenth-century British economy.

The Tariff Commission stressed the sharp decline in the proportion of British exports destined for the 'principal protected countries', or advanced industrial economies, and the rising proportion going to the underdeveloped and developing countries as a whole.[35] Increasingly, in the twentieth century, as the third world has found to its cost, the main expansion in world trade has been the 'inter-trade' of manufactures between advanced industrial economies.[36] This trend was scarcely in its infancy before 1914, but hindsight yields significant glimpses of its conception, especially in the area of product and production technology, and also, probably, product quality. In most, if not all of those areas of product innovation, product design, and production technology which were to be the growth areas of advanced twentieth century economies—including light engineering and machine tools, motor vehicles, and agricultural machinery; scientific and optical instruments; electrical engineering and supply; dyestuffs, fine chemicals, and pharmaceuticals—Britain experienced less development than Germany and the USA. Clearly, Britain's success as an export economy in the long run depended, at least in part, on a more vigorous development of these industries, and their ability to participate in 'inter-trade' with similar products from other advanced industrial economies.

This, of course, reverberates on the efficiency issue and the effect of the domestic market upon it. In doing so, it raises the question, seldom broached in today's literature, of whether a judicious application of 'infant-industry' protection might not have proved expedient. This is particularly important because, in some of the 'newer' industries, the appearance of initial weakness seems to have been quite specifically located. Yet, in their search for long-run causes of Britain's industrial 'disease', economic historians have neglected the possibility that short bursts of deterioration might have an enduring and compounding legacy. As Alfred Chandler has written, with a common sense which confounds much loftier analysis:

The failure in light machinery is understandable. American first movers established themselves so quickly in Britain that local firms hardly had a chance to get started. The invaders' experience with the American system of manufacturing [ie. standardization and

---

[35] *Report of the Tariff Commission*, ii. *The Textile Trades*, 1: *The Cotton Industry*, (1905), tables 18–19, paras. 50–1. Following the Board of Trade, the Commission defined the 'principal protected countries' to include Germany, Holland, Belgium, France, Italy, Austria, and the USA.

[36] H. G. Grubel and P. J. Lloyd, *Intra-Industry Trade* (1975), 40–5; A. Maizels, *Growth and Trade* (Cambridge, 1970), 81, 91–2, 109.

interchangeability], reinforced by their impressive scale economies in production and their proved efficiencies in marketing made them all but invincible.[37]

The onslaught was scarcely slower in electrical machinery, where foreign firms had less of a head start, but where nevertheless two-thirds of British output was made by foreign subsidiaries by 1914, or in organic chemicals, where by the mid-1880s the 'glowing potential' of early British advances had already been eclipsed by German investment in giant plants, managerial structures, and marketing organizations.[38]

The bulk of Britain's late-nineteenth-century exports was of course in more traditional products. In some, such as steel and woollens, there was by 1900 sufficient import penetration for the efficiency problem to have relevance. In others, such as cotton, this was not the case, since imports were negligible. As regards the foreign markets for these products, most economic historians would agree that, to some extent, the return to protection abroad after 1870 damaged Britain's export prospects. But the majority would argue that Britain's adherence to Free Trade minimized the damage in two ways. Firstly, it allowed Britain to maintain a network of most-favoured-nation treaties with foreign countries, and secondly, together with the large export of capital which was so largely its child, it allowed and promoted the full flowering of the multilateral system of settlements.[39]

Both these arguments, albeit in different ways, leave unconsidered the nature of the markets in question. MFN treaties only ensured that British exporters were not disadvantaged in relation to rival exporters. Thus their position in the classic 'neutral' market, with little or no manufacturing industry, was unimpaired except for the price effect on volume of what tariff they still did have to face. But, even with MFN arrangements, Britain's position in the home market of more advanced industrial countries, or countries in which some manufacturing activity was emerging, was scarcely so fortunate, since the minimum tariffs faced in such cases were still determined largely unilaterally by national need. It might be objected that, even so, the tariff faced by Britain under an MFN treaty would have been no higher than if she had possessed any other commercial policy. Had not Germany's minimum tariff been settled in negotiation with other protectionist countries? Britain simply collected the advantage. But in fact Britain merely collected reductions on goods considered important by other countries when they sat down to negotiate bilateral treaties. Given the immense complexity of tariff schedules, there was considerable scope for denying advantage to third parties.[40]

---

[37] A. D. Chandler, *Scale and Scope*, 275.

[38] Ibid. 276, 278.

[39] S. B. Saul, *British Overseas Trade*, chs. 3–4.

[40] Charles Follett, 'The Most Favoured Nation Clause', 23 Nov. [1904], 6/1/8, TCP. See also Lansdowne, Foreign Secretary, in *Parliamentary Debates, House of Lords*, 19 Feb. 1904, 4th Ser. cxxx, 433. The most famous case of what Follett called 'evasion by classification' was cl. 103 of the German tariff of 1902, relating to imports of transhumance cattle and designed to favour Switzerland.

Here, almost certainly, was a lost opportunity. As a market, Britain was hugely more important than was any of the trading partners with which any protectionist country sat down to negotiate commercial treaties in the decades before 1914.[41] It is both interesting and significant that, when Britain abrogated her treaty with Germany in order to uphold Canada's right to grant her a unilateral preference, Berlin issued yearly an imperial decree to continue Britain's access to the MFN treatment to which she was no longer formally entitled.[42] No country was so much to be feared for her power of retaliation as was Britain. If she had used that power, it is likely that the tariffs she faced would have been lower. It is ironic that one of the objections to Balfour's compromise policy of retaliation was based on the fear of foreign reprisals.[43] Retaliation, of course, was not only in Balfour's mind. Since the 1880s Fair Traders had used the euphemisms 'one-sided Free Trade' and 'true Free Trade'. Though they seldom receive much attention in academic studies of the pre-war controversy, retaliation and reciprocity were integral to the Chamberlainite scheme of Tariff Reform, as worked out in the Tariff Commission's enquiries into iron and steel and cotton.[44]

If the MFN system served Britain best in neutral markets, those markets were in many ways the least useful ones in the incentives and opportunities they gave for exploiting new technologies and new products. The multilateral system is held up by Saul as being of benefit precisely because it allowed the greater cultivation of such markets. Taking the tariff levels facing Britain from the highly protectionist industrial economies as given, Saul argues that the UK could offset mounting imports from Germany and the US by increased attention towards the developing countries.[45] Whilst this is obviously true, many of those countries, especially India and Latin America, though perhaps less so Canada and Australia, were a poor substitute. Again, the quality of the market has been left unconsidered. It was certainly not always the case that Britain possessed positive advantages in those markets, though this was clearly true in some—the purchasing policy of the Indian civil service, or consumer sentiment in Canada and Australia, for example, resulted in a high propensity to import British goods.[46] But American automobiles, agricultural machinery, sewing machines, and so on

[41] In 1913 the value of Britain's imports was 15,704.5m *Reichsmarks*; the corresponding figure for the USA was 7,525.3m; for France, 6,521.3m; and for Russia, 2,967.9m. See *Statistik des Deutschen Reichs*, vol. 339, 318–20.

[42] As well as commercial considerations, Berlin appreciated the danger of fuelling anti-German feeling in Britain. See P. M. Kennedy, *Anglo-German Antagonism* 261–5; 'Preference and the New Canadian Tariff Arrangements with France, Germany and the United States', Tariff Commission Memorandum 41 (7 May 1910), 11–12.

[43] A. J. Balfour, *Economic Notes on Insular Free Trade* (1903); H. Cox, *Mr. Balfour's Pamphlet: A Reply* (1903), 30–1; J. Sturgis, *The Prime Minister's Pamphlet* (1903), 24.

[44] See below, ch. 5.

[45] S. B. Saul, *Studies, British Overseas Trade*, ch. 3.

[46] Tariff Reformers made much of comparative per capita imports of British goods into Empire and foreign countries during the controversy. See e.g., W. J. Ashley, *The Tariff Problem* (1903), 143–5.

found ready markets even in those countries,[47] and in such innovative products Britain was, even in the colonies, increasingly peripheralized, being limited to the supply of less-sophisticated electrical-engineering goods, for example.[48] All too often, Saul's escape corridor locked Britain in, ever more firmly, to the supply of low-technology, low-value-added products to the world beyond Europe and the USA. Elsewhere in his writings, Saul has emphasized the importance of market differences in explaining the differential development of the American and British mechanical engineering industries in the late nineteenth century, whereby Britain maintained her superiority in many low-volume, craft-skill-intensive branches of heavy engineering, such as marine steam engines, shipbuilding, and textile machinery, whilst the USA forged ahead in the application of mass-production techniques in light engineering and volume-produced locomotives. His stress on the importance of demand factors and the nature of the market would seem quite compatible with the argument being advanced here.[49] It fits less well with his belief in the unqualified benefits of the multilateral system.

Other consequences of Britain's high export-orientation are more hidden. The dependence on low-income markets may have blunted or constrained the need for technological advance even in the staple industries themselves. Certainly, in Latin America, the British cotton industry could not exert its superiority over its German and Swiss competitors in fine cloth because the *peons* exercised demand at the bottom end of the market; the US industry, which did attempt to supply higher-quality goods designed according to the tastes and pockets of its own home market, and using production technologies such as the Northrop loom and state-of-the-art printing machinery, was relatively unsuccessful south of the Rio Grande.[50]

Furthermore, the strict price-constraints often imposed by low-income markets suggest that the value-added content of many manufactured exports was probably low. This was at a time when the large part of Britain's visible import surplus was in raw materials, a matter of some discomfort to the Tariff Reformers.[51] If these two characteristics are put together, then Britain's need for such large raw-materials imports was in part due to the fact that a high proportion of her manufactured exports had a low value-added content, so that she was re-exporting the raw material and not much more. The cotton industry's

---

[47] W. H. Becker, *The Dynamics of Business-Government Relations: Industry and Exports, 1893–1921* (Chicago, 1982), ch. 1; and 'American Manufacturers and Foreign Markets, 1870–1900: Business Historians and the "New Economic Determinists" ', *Business History Review*, 47 (1973), 466–81.

[48] I. C. R. Byatt, *The British Electrical Industry 1875–1914* (Oxford, 1979), 168–70.

[49] S. B. Saul, 'The Market and the Development of the Mechanical Engineering Industries in Britain, 1860–1914', *Economic History Review*, 20 (1967), 111–30.

[50] A. J. Marrison, 'Great Britain and her Rivals in the Latin American Cotton Piece Goods Market, 1880–1914', in B. M. Ratcliffe (ed.), *Great Britain and Her World 1750–1914* (Manchester, 1975), 319–48.

[51] H. H. Asquith at Cinderford, 8 Oct. 1903; repr. in his *Trade and the Empire* (1903), 15.

obsession with 'margins', the difference between raw cotton and finished product prices, is a strong example.[52] Obviously, Britain's high trade-to-income ratio was inevitable under her free trade system, but it was made unusually high by a unilateral free trade stance which skewed her trade towards low-income partners.

More importantly, the very size of Britain's vast export trade in 1905–1913 made it almost inevitable that it was fragmented between a multiplicity of often very small markets with immensely varied and sometimes capricious tastes. In making difficult the effort to standardize production, this compounded the technological effect. It could also give rise to a conflict between streamlining overseas-marketing effort, perhaps by centralized selling agencies, and satisfying the 'perverse specifications [and] . . . unreasonable demands' of foreign customers.[53] Such 'unreasonable' requirements were of course not necessarily imposed only by purchasers from less-developed countries, but it is significant that it was precisely in those countries that the traditional export house : import house structure, at its best in handling simple, low-value goods, survived longest.[54] Hence it is no surprise that, in his attempt to rehabilitate Britain's export-marketing performance, Stephen Nicholas concentrates on the export of 'newer' products which required direct selling, overseas branches, and agency arrangements.[55]

Such methods of marketing, which at their most advanced yielded considerable economies of scale in distribution, were most typically associated with the large companies that represent the ideal of Chandlerian analysis. Sharing this ideal, Lazonick has argued that 'as individualistic managers in a highly competitive and vertically specialized structure [British manufacturers] were powerless to alter the organizational constraints' that barred the way to vertical integration, mass-production technologies, and corporate structures. Britain was relatively slow to make the transition from competitive and family capitalism to corporate capitalism. It is, however, by no means accepted that the Chandlerian paradigm represents the only successful transition path to the advanced twentieth-century economy. There has been vigorous criticism of Lazonick's specific claim that the failure to move to the integrated spinning and weaving firm represented some

---

[52] On value-added content in cotton manufacturing, see D. A. Farnie, *The English Cotton Industry and the World Market, 1815–1896* (Oxford, 1979), 26. There was also a huge increase in coal exports between 1850 and 1913 (22 times by volume, and from $2\frac{1}{2}$% to 10% of total British exports by value). See H. S. Jevons, The British Coal Trade (Newton Abbot, 1969 edn.), 675.

[53] P. L. Payne, *British Entrepreneurship in the Nineteenth Century* (2nd edn., 1988), 52.

[54] F. E. Hyde and S. Marriner, 'The Economic Functions of the Export Merchant', *Manchester School*, 20 (1952), 215–26. See also, more generally, G. Porter and H. C. Livesay, *Merchants and Manufacturers: Studies in the Changing Structure of Nineteenth-Century Marketing* (Baltimore, 1971).

[55] S. J. Nicholas, 'The Overseas Marketing Performance of British Industry, 1870–1914', *Economic History Review*, 37 (1984), 489–506. See also, however, the more pessimistic studies in R. P. T. Davenport-Hines (ed.), *Markets and Bagmen: Studies in the History of Marketing and British Industrial Performance 1830–1939* (1986).

kind of failure in the pre-1914 British cotton industry. Furthermore, the broader Chandler thesis has been questioned, both in a number of case studies, for instance of Philadelphia textiles and of Pittsburgh and Sheffield steel, and in more general criticisms which seek to refute the universalism of the thesis and its applicability to Europe.[56] Whilst this is not the place to review these criticisms and qualifications, they are clearly well-founded. That being said, it is at least true that the development of a corporate aspect was prominent in the development of advanced capitalist economies up to at least the late 1960s, and was clearly, at least in the context of the time, an appropriate form of business organization for a significant number of important, high-growth, high-technology industries. Furthermore, the precise dependent relationships between a large corporate sector and satellite small- and medium-sized, personally-managed firms have not as yet been studied in detail by business historians. And, not infrequently, the development paths offered as alternatives to the Chandlerian model involve an element of 'niche' positioning, this suggesting a displacement from the mainstream and implying a limit to capital and employment growth. Niche positioning may be a viable long-term strategy for the individual firm, but it is less certain that a national economy's industrial structure could consist predominantly of 'niche' industries and yet as a whole stay fully competitive abroad. Thus, the relatively slow development of the large-scale firm and the corporate ideal in Britain remains a significant historical question, and it should not be assumed prematurely that this question is unrelated to the broader issue of Britain's industrial and economic performance. Today, small enterprise may be fashionable in post-Reagan America and post-Thatcher Britain, but industrial structure in the export sectors of the high-growth economies of South East Asia suggests that the future may well look back upon 'niche' industries in the West as 'survivors'—from the point of view of the national economy, a 'second best' solution.

Lazonick's analysis has not been entirely successful in identifying immovable constraints upon the development of large-scale and the corporate form, and in certain of its aspects it is not entirely novel, but it does remedy the neglect that

[56] A. D. Chandler, *The Visible Hand: The Managerial Revolution in American Business* (Cambridge, Mass., 1977), and *Scale and Scope*; W. Lazonick, 'Competition, Specialization, and Industrial Decline', *Journal of Economic History*, 41 (1981), 31–8; P. Scranton, *Proprietary Capitalism: The Textile Manufacture at Philadelphia, 1800–1885* (Cambridge, 1983); J. N. Ingham, *Making Iron and Steel: Independent Mills in Pittsburgh, 1820–1920* (Columbus, Ohio, 1991); R. Lloyd-Jones and M. J. Lewis, 'Personal Capitalism and British Industrial Decline: The Personally Managed Firm and Business Strategy in Sheffield, 1880–1920', *Business History Review*, 68 (1994), 364–411; B. Supple, 'Scale and Scope: Alfred Chandler and the Dynamics of Industrial Capitalism', *EcHR*, 44 (1991), 500–14; L. Hannah, 'Scale and Scope: Towards a European Visible Hand?', *Business History*, 33 (1991), 297–309. For an overview, see J. F. Wilson, *British Business History, 1770–1994* (Manchester, 1995), 3–10 and *passim*. For reviews of the specific debate on cotton textiles, see W. Mass and W. Lazonick's partisan, 'The British Cotton Industry and International Competitive Advantage: The State of the Debates', *Business History*, 33 (1991), and A. J. Marrison, 'Indian Summer, 1870–1914', in Mary B. Rose (ed.), *The Lancashire Cotton Industry: A History since 1700* (Perston, 1995), ch. 9.

features relating to the corporate structure have received in the debate on British economic retardation. It is therefore ironic that, in the words of his critics, 'Lazonick has always preferred the United States as exemplar'.[57] Contemporary Americans, muckrakers, lawyers, economists, and corporate managers alike, had little doubt that the US tariff encouraged market devices, large scale, and combination.[58] British observers, Free Traders and Tariff Reformers alike, concurred. Today, more aware of the complexity of the forces behind giantism,[59] we might doubt the primacy of the association, but not its direction. If the tendency towards large-scale and monopolistic domination of markets was to Lazonick desirable, British Free Trade stands as an identifiable constraint on such developments.[60] At the very least, Lazonick's institutional approach emphasizes by omission that there has been little speculation, still less study, of the extent to which Britain's unique tariff heritage, and the legacy of this for the industrialist's participation in politics, inhibited the emergence of corporate and corporatist attitudes and institutions.

The third theme of major interest to modern economic historians into which the tariff question deserves closer incorporation is the role of overseas lending and the financial sector in British economic development. Probably the dominant strand of opinion has accepted, and still accepts, that Britain's rapid and unique build-up of foreign assets was beneficial to the domestic economy, and that Free Trade facilitated the process of accumulation. This follows in the tradition of Imlah, though it does perhaps neglect that the foundations on which the process was built, whether they were mercantile or industrial, were laid in a protectionist rather than a Free-Trade period of British history. Whilst such a position has the strength of recognizing that the manufacturing sector has never dominated the aggregate British economy, it does tend to make the assumption that all forms of economic activity are equally beneficial, indistinguishable in a developmental context.

Clive Lee has argued that 'when the real revolution in manufacturing occurred in the late nineteenth century', Britain no longer led it—rather, her 'main hold on the international system, and rôle within it, was firmly secured as a financier not a manufacturer'. In similar vein, but perhaps more controversially, Rubinstein has argued that 'Britain was *never* fundamentally an industrial and manufacturing economy; rather, it was *always*, even at the height of the industrial

[57] G. Saxonhouse and G. Wright, 'Stubborn Mules and Vertical Integration: The Disappearing Constraint', *Economic History Review*, 40 (1987), 92.

[58] F. Pierce, *The Tariff and the Trusts* (New York, 1907); J. Jenks and W. E. Clark, *The Trust Problem* (New York, 4th edn., 1920), ch. 4.

[59] C. H. Lee, 'Corporate Behaviour in Theory and History: I. The Evolution of Theory', *Business History*, 32 (1990), 22–4, 24–7, 29–30.

[60] H. W. Macrosty, *The Trust Movement in British Industry*, (1907), 3, 342; A. Marshall, *Industry and Trade* (London, 1919; 1927 edn.), 851.

revolution, essentially a commercial, financial, and service-based economy whose comparative advantage always lay with commerce and finance.'[61]

This argument is an important corrective, but it is not necessary to agree with Rubinstein that previous writers have displayed a 'manufacturing fetishism', misplaced on account of the unimportance of manufacturing decline (a matter on which Rubinstein himself displays some ambivalence) in a more general economic decline which Rubinstein disputes. Nor should his argument be taken to support the position that there was an inevitability in the relative decline of British manufacturing, and that the process is thereby rendered somehow unsurprising. Firstly, the assertion of comparative advantage in services is almost certainly too global—it is hard to argue that *any other nation* had a comparative advantage in manufacturing at the height of Britain's classic industrial revolution. Secondly, and more importantly, it is necessary to avoid the element of *post hoc ergo propter hoc* argument that lies in too hasty a resort to the concept of 'comparative advantage'. In the Ricardian model, comparative advantage based on factor endowments can be easily understood, and indeed regarded as fixed. But in the real world of modern capitalism, where foresight and strategy, education and skill, finance and importable technology are all significant variables, it is not so fixed. *Ex-post*, it might be argued that Britain must have had a comparative advantage in finance or in manufacturing—though even this is likely to be the outcome of dubious averaging in the sense that neither of these sectors was monolithic and undifferentiated. But, *ex-ante*, that comparative advantage was not pre-determined by some natural strengths or deficiencies among British businessmen or their workers; it could change, or be changed, and it does not follow that a vibrant financial sector necessarily imposed limitations on Britain's manufacturing progress. Rubinstein points, for his own purposes, to the effectiveness of American and European tariffs in fostering their manufacturing industry in the nineteenth century.[62] If the comparative advantage of British finance was due in some part to the fact that British capital was welcomed freely in the markets of the world whereas British manufactures were discriminated against by high and specifically-tailored tariffs, our point will be more readily understood. The process whereby Britain's lead in manufacturing was eroded cannot in some way be defined away as axiomatic or definitional: it still has autonomy and significance as a subject for discussion, as does the British manufacturing sector's limited ability to stay at the forefront as the locus of production tilted towards the science-based and mass-produced goods of the 'second industrial revolution'.

Many economic historians remain uneasy in the view that the sectoral origins of income and product are of little consequence for long-run development and

---

[61] C. H. Lee, *British Economy*, 124; W. D. Rubinstein, *Capitalism, Culture and Decline in Britain, 1750–1990*, (1993), 24 (Rubinstein's emphasis).

[62] W. D. Rubinstein, *Capitalism, Culture and Decline*, 76–7.

competitivity. This unease surfaces in a narrower manifestation: a dispute over whether Britain's large capital exports before 1914 hindered industrial development. Some of those who share Lazonick's 'institutional' persuasion criticize the capital market for preventing the more rapid development of the 'new' industries. Kennedy has constructed a hypothetical alternative, a less export-orientated British economy with a lower foreign-to-home investment ratio, but one, he maintains, which would have retained its importance in world markets because of its greater competitive vitality.[63] Kennedy's bold approach has come in for stringent criticism,[64] and most dissenters from orthodoxy are more circumspect in their treatment.

An intuitive suspicion of a situation where, in the late nineteenth century, around half of Britain's total investment fund went abroad cannot just be ascribed to an unseemly predilection for populist economics. Furthermore, that suspicion is not as easily confounded as might appear on the surface. The demonstration that, after about 1870, net new foreign lending was never as large as dividends and was interest remitted home is insufficient.[65] It is playing with words to claim that Britain in fact was a capital importer when the whole culture of an important section of investors was suffused with cosmopolitanism. Nor, too, is it safe to be influenced by demonstrations that the risk-adjusted rate of return was higher on foreign assets[66]—it is the long-term effect of the allocation process rather than its short-term rationality that is pertinent here. Most importantly, it is not adequate to argue that Britain's capital export had no deleterious effects because there is no strong evidence of a capital shortage at home,[67] for two reasons. Firstly, the home market was conditioned by an income distribution and consumption patterns that were themselves shaped by the fact that there was indeed a large capital export and a substantial, but almost entirely unstudied, rentier class.[68] And secondly, Britain's export of capital in itself influenced the exchange rate. Though one or two scholars have made suggestive comments in this area, there has been no detailed work to examine whether a strong balance of payments, strong not *because* of industrial strength, but *in spite* of increasing industrial weakness, simply left the British manufacturer prey to attack in both

---

[63] W. P. Kennedy, *Industrial Structure, Capital Markets and the Origins of British Economic Decline* (Cambridge, 1987), chs. 4–5.

[64] D. N. McCloskey, comments on W. P. Kennedy, 'Economic Growth and Structural Change in the United Kingdom, 1870–1914', *Journal of Economic History*, 42 (1982), 117–18. See also his review of Kennedy, *Industrial Structure*, in *Economic History Review*, 42 (1989), 141–3.

[65] S. Pollard, 'British Capital Exports, 1870–1914: Harmful or Beneficial?', *Economic History Review*, 38 (1985), 493–4.

[66] M. Edelstein, *Overseas Investment in the Age of High Imperialism* (New York, 1982), esp. ch. 5.

[67] S. Pollard, loc. cit., 501.

[68] For significant beginnings, see L. E. Davis and R. A. Huttenback, *Mammon and the Pursuit of Empire* (Cambridge, 1986), esp. ch. 7; R. C. Michie, 'The Social Web of Investment in the Nineteenth Century', *Revue internationale de histoire de la banque*, 18–19 (1979); P. J. Cain and A. G. Hopkins, *British Imperialism: Innovation and Expansion, 1688–1914* (1993), 182–9.

home and overseas markets at a time when he might have hoped for the protection of devaluation to offset the fact that the technological lead was passing to others.[69]

Thus, some switch to home investment might have altered sectoral income distribution in the British economy, almost certainly by evening it out a little and transferring it northwards and away from rentiers. Such effects would have had consequences for aggregate savings, consumption patterns, and growth, but have never seriously been considered by economic historians. They might also have had effects in changing the balance between portfolio and direct investment by British investors, for in the long run it is not necessary, or even probable, that manufacturing strength and overseas lending are mutually antagonistic. Like the efficiency problematic, such issues require prior determination before a verdict can be delivered safely on Tariff Reform.

Closely related to this is the impact of Tariff Reform on the British financial sector itself. Banking, finance, and insurance were important in themselves as sources of profit and providers of employment: indeed, advances in aggregate analysis have revealed the limited degree to which industry ever predominated in Britain's economic past. Historians have long had a fairly clear idea of the 'mind of the City' and its close blood-ties with the 'Treasury View'.[70] But the recent opening of bank archives has also added depth to our understanding of the sociology of the banking community, and scholars have uncovered a 'gentlemanly capitalism', a network of interest and association which ensured that the concerns of the City were never far from the minds of Britain's legislators.[71]

It is not sufficient to argue that Tariff Reform would have damaged the City. If there were corresponding benefits in the industrial sector, the important question is by how much the City would have been damaged. Obviously, the protestations of those who stood to be affected cannot easily be taken at face value. It is almost certainly fanciful, historically implausible, to argue that a Chamberlainite policy would have spelt doom for the City. Any marked change in economic policy will carry with it disadvantages as well as advantages, losses as well as benefits. To argue that the policy was inappropriate simply because there *were* disadvantages is insufficient, and recent work has acknowledged this. Of course, if Tariff Reform had destroyed the export industries, it would have been a disaster. If it had resulted in the extinction of the City of London it would have had few supporters south of the Trent. The important issue is one of scale and degree. Commentating upon the sympathy of some leading City figures for Chamberlain around 1906, Cain and Hopkins observe that:

[69] See R. C. O. Matthews, C. H. Feinstein, and J. C. Odling-Smee, *British Economic Growth, 1856–1973* (Oxford, 1982), 455–6.

[70] S. G. Checkland, 'The Mind of the City', *Oxford Economic Papers*, 9 (1957), 261–78.

[71] P. J. Cain and A. G. Hopkins, *British Imperialism: Innovation and Expansion, passim.*

the [tariff] issue was not regarded as one of outstanding importance by most prominent men in the City: the movement away from free trade proposed by the Tariff Reformers was probably too small to change either the pattern or the volume of world commerce very much and, in any case, the City was far more interested in keeping the gold standard than in maintaining free trade.[72]

This evaluation is important, not least because of the sense of scale and perspective that it introduces. Indeed, it is salutary to remember that when, in the inter-war years, London was replaced as the world's financial centre, it was New York, labouring under the historical fetters of Morrill, McKinley, and Dingley, and crushed under the contemporary deadweight of Fordney-McCumber and Hawley-Smoot, which came nearest to replacing it. In truth, the shipping and merchanting sectors of the British economy were probably more vulnerable to Tariff Reform than the bankers and investors of the City—they were certainly more vociferous in denouncing it.

III

When Tariff Reform became an issue of practical politics in 1903, its principal proponents were almost certainly more fired by the imperial dimension than by considerations of domestic protectionism. Whilst many industrialists professed support for imperial preference, their real enthusiasm for the duties on foodstuffs that were its necessary corollary was often lukewarm, and they were often doubtful that the dominions would extend concessions of real value to Britain when they were intent on fostering domestic industry and on improving their treaty relations with foreign powers. The accusation that within the imperial thrust was a desire for the 'easy sell' is thus perhaps overdrawn. The multilateral system, on the other hand, is seldom portrayed in the same manner. At the same time that Cain asserts that imperial preference would have provided 'bolt holes for traditional industries', he also sees Tariff Reform as undermining a beneficial multilateral system.[73] Since British industry's role in the multilateral system was to provide exports to underdeveloped and developing nations, the multilateral system may have provided precisely the same 'bolt holes' for the traditional industries that would have been so damaging had imperial preference been introduced.

Even so, the potential economic benefits from preference would seem to have been limited. As was recognized by contemporaries, and has been repeated by historians, only 20 per cent of Britain's food imports came from the Empire at the time Chamberlain launched his crusade, and only 40 per cent of her manufactured exports went to it.[74] In a static situation, there was obviously a

---

[72] Ibid. 218.
[73] P.J. Cain, 'Political Economy', 49–50.
[74] M. Balfour, *Britain and Joesph Chamberlain* (1985), 285–6.

danger, both for Britain and her imperial partners, that raising these proportions would represent 'trade diversion' to a higher-cost supplier.[75] Advanced Tariff Reformers argued that this would not happen, since their vision encompassed such an increase in the volume of inter-Empire trade that organizational and technical economies of scale would ensue. At its extreme, this argument amounted to the claim that Britain's trade with the rest of the world would continue to grow in absolute terms in spite of becoming smaller as a proportion of her total trade, since the scale economies effected through an imperial system would give a new vitality to exports for whatever destination—'trade creation' would be the accompaniment of 'trade diversion'.[76]

Obviously, by definition, there was a potential for increasing the proportion of Britain's trade being conducted with the Empire. But how much is difficult to estimate, even in the vaguest of terms. This is because there was an increase in the proportion of British trade going to the Empire in any case. On average, in the early twentieth century, 34.7 per cent of British exports went to the Empire. In the 1920s the figure stood at 42.7 per cent and in the 1930s 46.6 per cent. The rising trend was even more marked for imports. In the years 1904 to 1910, 36.08 per cent of UK wheat and flour imports came from the Empire. UK-Empire trade grew by 0.4 per cent per annum in the period 1904 to 1913 (compared with 3.3 per cent for UK-foreign trade).[77] In both these periods there was Empire preference for British goods, and in the later period there was limited UK preference for a narrow range of Empire goods. But even commodities which were not touched by preference showed the same trend. Before 1904 the proportion of British wheat and flour imports coming from the Empire was rising, though a change in the basis of the official statistics destroys comparison with later years.[78] In the period 1904 to 1910, 36.08 per cent of UK wheat and flour imports came from the Empire. By the period 1922 to 1928, this had risen to 51.95 per cent.[79] This increase had taken place despite the fact that the imperial preferences introduced by Britain after the 1919 budget did not apply to wheat.

Whilst some sought to deny it, anticipating the development of manufacturing in the Dominions in a truly integrated economic system,[80] the Tariff Reformers'

---

[75] The literature on the economic effects of customs unions is complex. For a straightforward exposition of 'trade diversion' and 'trade creation', see H. G. Johnson, *Money, Trade and Economic Growth* (1962), ch. 3.

[76] 'An Economist' [W. A. S. Hewins], 'The Fiscal Policy of the Empire: iv', *The Times*, 29 June 1903, 9 (hereinafter cited as 'FPE'); 'FPE: v', *The Times*, 4 July 1903, 14; 'FPE: vi', *The Times*, 11 July 1903, 6. For Hewins' analysis of the economic effects of an imperial policy, see A. J. Marrison, 'British Businessmen and the "Scientific" Tariff: A Study of Joseph Chamberlain's Tariff Commission, 1903–1921', unpubl. Ph. D. thesis, Univ. of Hull (1980), ch. 2.

[77] F. Capie, *Depression and Protectionism*, 20, and Table 2. 6.

[78] In 1904 the origin of imports was changed from 'port of shipment' to 'port of consignment'.

[79] *Statistical Abstract for the United Kingdom, 1896–1910*, Cd. 5841 (1911), Table 43, 142–3; *Statistical Abstract for the United Kingdom, 1919–1932*, Cmd. 4489 (1934), Table 243, 370–1.

[80] [Hewins], 'FPE: xii', *The Times*, 20 Aug. 1903, 10.

ERRATUM for p. 20: In the second paragraph, line 7, delete the sentence beginning 'In the years 1904 to 1910 . . .' On line 9 of that same paragraph, it should read '4.0' not '0.4' per cent and the following text should be added to the end of that sentence: 'and again 4.0 per cent per annum in the period 1922 to 1929 (compared with 3.6 per cent for UK-foreign trade).

imperial designs did to a considerable extent assume the continuation of a nineteenth-century imperial relationship in which the metropolitan country supplied manufactures and capital and the periphery furnished raw materials and foodstuffs; Leo Amery, half in jest, recollected of the Exchequer's agreement to extend preference to the McKenna duties in 1919, that 'I am not sure that he [Austen Chamberlain] knew that Canada actually produced motor-cars'.[81] Free Traders argued that colonial determination to foster domestic industry would impose limits on those designs. It is true that, in general, colonial pressure to introduce preference was unremitting, and that, when wide-ranging preference was introduced in 1932, it appears to have had a greater effect on Britain's exports to the Empire than Empire exports to Britain.[82] Furthermore, UK–Empire trade grew by 7.9 per cent per annum between 1933 and 1938, compared with a 4.5 per cent annual growth in UK–foreign trade.[83] Nevertheless, in spite of the fact that Empire trade was becoming relatively more important to Britain, British goods were becoming a smaller proportion of the Empire's imports.[84] It has to be assumed that, even before 1914, there were limits to which the colonies would have been prepared to abandon options for the development of manufacturing in the future—an imperial *Zollverein* was never a real possibility, as was finally demonstrated at Ottawa in 1932.[85] Furthermore, a preferential margin on an import duty was obviously less dramatic in scale than the duty itself, and could be cosmetic. Before 1914 Empire countries showed themselves not averse to juggling with the level of unilateral preference accorded to Britain in their periodic tariff revisions.[86]

IV

It has not been the intention of this introduction to prove the benefits or the dangers of Tariff Reform, but rather to raise the main economic issues and argue that assessing them is not simple. In a bewildering debate, both Free Traders and Tariff Reformers made valid contributions, and few of the participants mastered all the complexities or produced coherent, unified cases. This discussion has neglected the interests of shipowners, a group whose rage at the prospect of Tariff Reform should be set alongside its own practice of price-collusion on a global scale, a practice that did not generate one-hundredth of the public

---

[81] L. Amery, *My Political Life*, ii. (1953), 186.

[82] F. Capie, *Depression and Protectionism*, 134.

[83] Ibid. Table 2. 6, 20.

[84] W. R. Garside, *British Unemployment, 1919–1939* (Cambridge, 1990), 144.

[85] I. M. Drummond, *Imperial Economic Policy, 1917–1939* (London, 1974), ch. 6.

[86] As with Canada's introduction of an intermediate tariff in her revision of 1907. See 'Preference and the New Canadian Tariff Arrangements with France, Germany and the United States', Tariff Commission Memorandum No. 41 (7 May 1910), 7.

criticism that the manufacturers' cry for protection could expect.[87] It has also neglected brokers and merchants. Most noticably, it has been dismissive of imperial preference and has omitted consideration of agricultural protection, where there was the clear potential to inflict considerable damage upon the economy.

Furthermore, it should be emphasized that, if there was a period in which selective duties on the products of the newer industries, or tariffs for negotiation imposed more generally, might have served to promote Britain's industrial development and lessen her export-orientation whilst shifting her trade towards higher-income foreign markets, that period probably began considerably before Chamberlain launched his campaign. If the factors we have outlined above carry any weight, then the 1880s, the decade of Fair Trade and the Royal Commission on the Depression of Trade and Industry, would have been more appropriate. Then, the European and American return to high protectionism was less entrenched, the rise of large scale and the corporate economy in the USA less advanced, the German cartel system less developed. In short, 1903 was already rather late in the day.

If this reservation applies to the Edwardian period of Tariff Reform, it also applies to the 1920s. In particular, quasi-infant-industry tariffs, or negotiating tariffs, or perhaps even a general tariff, would have been a doubtful solution to the heavy unemployment that, according to the rhetoric of politicians and academics, employers and trade unionists, Free Traders and protectionists alike, was the dominant policy preoccupation of that decade. Such unemployment was concentrated heavily in the staple export trades. Certain newer industries were now protected—most notably automobiles, dyestuffs and fine chemicals, and certain electrical components—yet their growth had relatively little effect on overall employment levels.[88] It seems unlikely that extending safeguarding to other, often smaller, industries of this kind, whatever its long-term effect on the growth, aggregate productivity, and export-orientation of the British economy,[89] would have contributed substantially to the reduction of unemployment in the short term. And a more widespread introduction of duties through a general

---

[87] F. E. Hyde, *Blue Funnel* (Liverpool, 1956), ch. 4; F. E. Hyde, *et al.*, *Shipping Enterprise and Management, 1830–1939* (Liverpool, 1967), chs. 4–7.

[88] For the difficulty in distinguishing between 'old' and 'new' industries, and the relatively patchy growth and productivity record of the newer industries in the inter-war period, see J. A. Dowie, 'Growth in the Inter-war Period: Some more Arithmetic', *Economic History Review*, 21 (1968), 93–112; B. W. E. Alford, 'New Industries for Old? British Industry between the Wars', in R. Floud and D. N. McCloskey (eds.), *Economic History of Britain since 1700* (Cambridge, 1981), ii. ch. 13. For the failure of employers in the British motor industry to move to American levels of mass production by establishing full control over work practices, see W. Lewchuk, *American Technology and the British Vehicle Industry* (Cambridge, 1987), chs. 8–9.

[89] For the positive case, see J. Foreman-Peck, 'Tariff Protection', and *'British Tariff'*, M. Kitson and S. Solomou, *Protectionism and Economic Revival*.

tariff, with the strong pre-war growth in world trade now given way to stagnation, might have intensified the international spiral into autarky, cold comfort for the staple industries.[90]

To argue that Tariff Reform may have represented a missed historical moment, a moment in which Britain could have turned from a stagnating cosmopolitanism to a development path grounded more securely on the higher per capita incomes of the domestic market and a greater engagement with the economies of the leading industrial nations, would almost certainly be to overstate the case. Tariff Reform, especially on its own, would not have been sufficient. But that Tariff Reform stood as a *symbol* of the changes in mentalities and practices necessary for such a transition is more plausible. Although it doubtless attracted its share of the bruised, the defeated, and the demoralized, it was in essence a forward-looking policy. 'Under a well-directed and continuous policy of Little Englandism we can no doubt sink quite confortably to the rank of a fifth-rate Power', wrote Tariff Reform economist W. A. S. Hewins in 1903.[91]

But enough has been said to show the importance to the issue of British long-run development of the subjects which the Tariff Reform programme raised, and to hope that the arguments by which it was commended will be the subject of more intensive research by scholars in the future. For present purposes, it is perhaps sufficient to remember that '[i]n the end, it is never the plausibility of a policy in the abstract, but the power of those who think they will benefit directly from it, which matters in politics'.[92] On this ground alone, it is appropriate to attempt the first full-scale treatment of the involvement of the protectionist businessman in the politics of the early twentieth century.

The study that follows charts the history of Tariff Reform chiefly through examination of the business associations which advocated it—the Tariff Commission before 1914, and its successor organizations thereafter. It also examines opinion in less committed groups, such as the Chambers of Commerce and the Federation of British Industries. It does not deal in detail with high politics, nor does it attempt a full survey of the relation of sectional business groups with government and the Board of Trade. The reason for this is simple. Until 1929, irrespective of the degree of tacit sympathy for protection felt by successive governments, and with one or two exceptions helped along by war, business

---

[90] The exception is probably the steel industry, where safeguarding might well have reduced unemployment. Politicians were, however, fearful that protection would preserve excess capacity in the industry and delay rationalization (see below, 279–80). For an excellent analysis of contemporary academic economists' opinions on the employment effects of a general tariff, see Barry Eichengreen, 'Sterling and the Tariff, 1919–1932', *Princeton Studies in International Finance*, 48 (1981), repr. in his *Elusive Stability* (Cambridge, 1990), 180–214.

[91] [Hewins] 'FPE: v', *The Times*, 4 July 1903, 14.

[92] S. Pollard, *Britain's Prime*, 243.

pressure was remarkably unsuccessful. But that does not mean that such pressure was not growing. Hazarding that 'Tariff Reform may have appealed to a majority of businessmen', John Turner adds, with commendable caution, that '[n]o reliable estimate of its support could ever be obtained'.[93] No completely reliable estimate, certainly. But, weighed against the quiet and unobtrusive opposition of bankers and financiers, and the implacable opposition of the great bulk of the merchant community, we can, I think, make significant advances in our knowledge of the extent of protectionism within the industrial sector, and its distribution within that sector. Furthermore, we can reveal the curiously subordinate position of the manufacturer in both British politics and British society, a subordination which ensured that protectionism, though widespread and growing strongly, was largely rendered impotent through the cultural, institutional, and political constraints on its expression.

[93] J. Turner, 'The British Commonwealth Union and the General Election of 1918', *English Historical Review*, 93 (1978), 531, 531n.

1

Birmingham to Leeds

When Chamberlain delivered his famous speech at Birmingham on 15 May 1903, he instantly converted Tariff Reform, which had for a quarter of a century been smouldering in a Britain beginning to lose confidence in her economic strength and supremacy, into a fiercely burning political issue. The result was the first major debate on an economic issue since the battle over the Corn Laws, and the first electoral contest on an economic issue in the new age of mass democracy. In this it can be represented as the most significant single step in the transition towards a twentieth-century politics dominated by continual conflict over economic policy.

The economics of the Tariff Reform question were inherently complicated, especially when compounded by the imperial considerations which were integral to the political debate. This worked heavily in favour of the Free Traders, who had the tremendous advantage of defending the status quo. Free Trade had become an institution defended at many levels. At the lowest, which counted most in electoral terms, the Free Traders could invoke the image of a Christian defence of the poor man's loaf, a tactic as old as the Free Trade movement itself.[1] The power of the cry of cheap bread was immense. Also, the Free Traders monopolized the channels by which the work of the classical economists had been popularized—the glib and simple sermons of Harriet Martineau and Mrs Fawcett. Though new editions might appear reflecting the heightened need to restate the case for economic liberalism,[2] these were long-familiar works which pre-dated the debate by decades, and seemed to escape the taint of having been produced for propagandist purposes in immediate response to political controversy.

The Tariff Reformers had no such prepared and familiar propagandas. Even their most populist arguments—imperialism and perhaps retaliation—were remote appeals compared with cheap bread. To do their case full justice, they needed to stretch the debate beyond the limits likely to carry electoral impact. They needed to correct popular misconceptions which drew no distinction between the principles of the classical economists and their more pragmatic approach to economic policy.[3] They needed to expose and question the more tendentious assumptions of orthodox economics, assumptions such as perfect

[1] N. McCord, *The Anti-Corn Law League 1838–1846* (1958), 27.
[2] M. G. Fawcett, *Political Economy for Beginners* (9th edn., 1904), p. viii.
[3] L. Robbins, *The Theory of Economic Policy in English Classical Political Economy* (1952); D. P. O'Brien, *The Classical Economists* (Oxford, 1975), 189–97, 272–92.

competition in factor and product markets, and synonymity between private and social costs and benefits. They needed to invoke economies of scale. Yet of course they had no help from the hostile bulk of the economics profession. Alfred Marshall was reluctant to see his own analytical apparatus of increasing returns used to generalize the 'infant industry' argument for protection to fit any case where scale economies were in operation.[4] And when Tariff Reform economist W. A. S. Hewins taunted the professors to recast the Ricardian theory of comparative costs to account for the new conditions of foreign trade—of trustification and monopoly—he was ignored.[5]

Joseph Chamberlain appreciated the problem: 'working men will not pay attention to many figures or to abstract economics. These must be addressed to the more limited class of educated people and then they filter down into a more popular form'.[6] Even the middle classes were no easy target. In 1908 T. Mendelssohn Horsfall, a Cheltenham JP, complained that '[t]here are millions in this country, *educated and uneducated,* who do not yet know what Tariff Reform is and aims at'.[7] But the working class posed the most ineluctable problem, and the mechanism of filtering down was never solved satisfactorily. After some years' experience, Sir Joseph Lawrence of the Tariff Reform League's literary committee was well aware of the contemptible nature of much propaganda material on both sides of the debate. But he knew also the difficulty of combining sophistication with ease of understanding and brevity.[8]

Tariff Reform was, above all, a press debate. Its lingering image is of the great set speeches, of Chamberlain 'stumping the country', and being trailed by Asquith and Harcourt. But the biggest meetings reached directly only some 5,000 or 7,000 people, and much of this was preaching to the converted. The only contact of most people was through the press. Here the major speeches were reported verbatim, there was widespread coverage of minor speeches, endless columns of editorial comment, and thousands of letters to scores of editors. Yet, even in those jewels of Victorian and Edwardian publishing, the political reviews whose readership lay in the more educated sections of the middle and upper classes, many of the contributions were of very low quality. Politicians, too, even those placed by the opposing movements in the vanguard of their campaigns, were frequently little more impressive. Chamberlain's lack of confidence in his own economic understanding is well-known,[9] yet

[4] A. C. Pigou (ed.), *Memorials of Alfred Marshall* (1925), 449; C. F. Bickerdyke, 'The Theory of Incipient Taxes', *Economic Journal*, 16 (1906), 519–35; N. Jha, *The Age of Marshall: Aspects of British Economic Thought 1890–1914* (2nd edn., 1973), 46, 51.

[5] Hewins to Ed., *The Times*, 20 Aug. 1903, 10.

[6] Chamberlain to Hewins, 24 Sept. 1903; HP.

[7] Horsfall to Sir Joseph Lawrence, 2 Jan. 1908; 6/4/18, TCP (Horsfall's emphasis).

[8] Lawrence to Horsfall, 3 Jan. 1908; ibid.

[9] A. W. Coats, 'Political Economy and the Tariff Reform Campaign of 1903', *Journal of Law and Economics*, 11 (1968), 187.

there seems little to distinguish him from many other public figures on both sides of the controversy. Nor were professional economists effective in crystallizing and elucidating the problem—indeed, their most famous contribution to the debate, the issue of the professorial 'manifesto', aroused considerable antagonism on account of its dogmatic and pontifical nature, did the economists' public image considerable harm, and made them wary of repeating the exercise.[10]

I

Though, by 1903, Chamberlain was well aware that preference was the only form of imperial consolidation likely to be acceptable to the self-governing dominions, he was cautious in specifying his intended policy. In a literal sense, he did not so much advocate preference at Birmingham as urge upon his audience the need to discuss it. In the Commons, on 28 May, he resisted attempts to pin him down on detail, only reluctantly conceding that 'if you are going to give a preference to the colonies—I do not say that you are—you must put a tax on food'.[11]

The Times had hoped for more—that Chamberlain would develop his ideas 'with greater fullness and precision'. Obviously there were potential dangers in doing so, and by August Chamberlain had advanced no further in the direction of concrete proposals. But he did then put on record his opinion that taxation of raw materials would be unnecessary. Asquith counter-attacked with the assertion that if preference were confined to food alone, there would be huge inequalities between and within the colonies, South Africa being particularly hard hit. Harold Cox and the *Free Trader* also asked why raw materials should be exempt if semi-manufactured materials, inputs for finished goods manufacture, were not.[12]

Historians would accept that Chamberlain's primary motive at the outset of his campaign was imperial consolidation, rather than domestic protection,[13] and it is certainly true that during the summer he said little or nothing about duties on semi-manufactures or, indeed, on fully manufactured goods. But, already, revenue considerations were making their inclusion in his scheme inevitable. Harcourt predicted that Chamberlain's desire for old-age pensions would

[10] Ibid. 191–3.

[11] Chamberlain at Birmingham, in *The Times*, 16 May 1903, 8; *Parliamentary Debates*, 4th ser., 123 (28 May 1903), cols. 143–4, 147, 178–9, 185. For background, see S. H. Zebel, 'Joseph Chamberlain and the Genesis of Tariff Reform', *Journal of British Studies*, 7 (1967), 138–41; and J. E. Kendle, *The Colonial and Imperial Conferences, 1887–1911* (1967), chs. 2–3.

[12] *The Times* (editorial), 28 May 1903, 7; Chamberlain to Arthur Griffith-Boscawen, in *The Standard*, 18 Aug. 1903, 3; *The Standard*, 17 Aug. 1903, 3; Asquith at Cinderford, 8 Oct. 1903, in T. L. Gilmour (ed.), *All Sides of the Fiscal Question* (1903), 70; *Free Trader*, 28 Aug. 1903, 34, 37.

[13] R. Jay, *Joseph Chamberlain: A Political Study* (Oxford, 1981), 45.

necessitate duties on manufactures as well as wheat,[14] and his point remained valid even when Chamberlain modified his plan at the Constitutional Club on 26 June, offering the working class the choice between pensions and reductions on the existing revenue duties. Reductions of the tea, sugar, and tobacco duties could, if desired, 'fully, entirely' compensate for any price rises resulting from the new food duties.[15] Without apparent authority from Chamberlain, anonymous Tariff Reformers published two schemes, in the *Daily Telegraph* and *The Times*, to show how bread and meat could be taxed without increasing working-class budgets. But, as the scheme in *The Times* recognized, the reduction of the revenue duties would have to be larger than the amount brought in by the duties on wheat and meat, since the price of home and colonial food would rise alongside that of foreign imports. There would therefore be an exchequer shortfall. To make this up, the scheme in *The Times* recommended a 7 per cent duty on manufactures.[16] 'Already, therefore', remarked the *Free Trader*, 'the controversy gravitates towards the central point of the protectionist ideal'.[17] Opponents also urged that the revenue shortfall was underestimated, and that the government was morally bound to repeal the sugar tax in any case, this being an emergency measure imposed only for the duration of the Boer War.[18]

At Birmingham, Chamberlain had come close to advocating retaliation 'if necessary, . . . whenever our own interests or our relations [with] our Colonies . . . are threatened'. The rest of his speech was even vaguer on this issue. But, whilst not saying anything specific on manufactures meant that he had not *quite* burned his bridges on domestic protection, he had left the question of government revenue very much in the air. In June, C. A. Vince, secretary of the Birmingham Imperial Tariff Committee and a confidant of Chamberlain, interpreted the policy as one of eliminating unfair competition by imposing a countervailing duty to offset foreign bounties, 'direct or indirect'. Beyond this, Chamberlain 'would adhere in every case to Cobden's principle of free interchange at the natural price'.[19] The Tariff Reformers thus refused to recast their policy in terms of any concrete structure, and where they had come closest to presenting specific proposals, those proposals had not been endorsed by Chamberlain himself. The Free Traders interpreted this as testing the water; Cham-

[14] *Free Trader*, 31 July 1903, 4.

[15] Chamberlain at the Constitutional Club, 26 June 1903; *Free Trader*, 4 Sept. 1903, 45.

[16] 'A Revenue Official' to Ed., *The Times*, 28 July 1903, 6; *Daily Telegraph, Imperial Reciprocity: A Study of Fiscal Policy* (1903), 76–83; A. J. Marrison, 'The Development of a Tariff Reform Policy during Joseph Chamberlain's First Campaign', in W. H. Chaloner and B. M. Ratcliffe (eds.), *Trade and Transport: Essays in Economic History in Honour of T. S. Willan* (Manchester, 1978), 219–20.

[17] *Free Trader*, 7 Aug. 1903, 10–11.

[18] Ibid.; 'Questioner' to Ed., *The Times*, 7 Aug. 1903, 5.

[19] Chamberlain at Birmingham, in *The Times*, 16 May 1903, 8; C. A. Vince to Ed., *The Times*, 10 June 1903, 12. Vince's letter had been approved by Chamberlain's private secretary. Furthermore, when Vince later published his book, *Mr Chamberlain's Proposals: What they Mean and What we shall Gain by Them* (1903), its authority was increased by the inclusion of a preface by Chamberlain himself.

berlain 'allows his lieutenants to put forward scheme after scheme and argument after argument, so that he may see which will take with the public, and hastily drop, all without prejudice to himself, those which obviously will not do'.[20]

If the Tariff Reformers' lack of precision in outlining their policy caused confusion in the public mind, so too did the controversy over the likely effect of a duty on wheat on its price. Politically, this was central to the debate, and it dominated the chaotic proliferation of the Tariff Reform question in the editorial and correspondence columns of the press. The result was immensely confusing to the reader. Many Free Traders presented baffling 'historical' exercises purporting to show that price would rise by the full amount of the duty, or even more.[21] On the other hand, Tariff Reformers seemed to disagree amongst themselves. Agriculturalists looked to a rise in wheat prices to restore rural prosperity, whilst imperial enthusiasts argued that the supply of wheat from the colonies would be so increased by preference that in a few years the price of wheat in the British market would fall.[22] In a debate which frequently descended into farce, the official response was unhelpful. Balfour received advice from the Treasury that was diametrically opposed to that submitted by three Board of Trade officials.[23] Academic economists were little more impressive. The famous 'manifesto' of the 'fourteen professors' brutally oversimplified contemporary theory in its attempt to show that price would rise by the full amount of the duty, and expounded the received wisdom in pompous and baffling *ceteris paribus* terms which did not even attempt to meet the Tariff Reformers' claim that their policy would produce radical and dynamic changes in Empire supply to offset the static price-rise. In *The Times*, a little later, A. C. Pigou corrected these distortions, presenting a reasoned estimate that price would probably rise by slightly less than 80 per cent of the duty imposed. To do so, however, he had to construct a tight economic argument which introduced his audience to concepts such as elasticity of supply. It is doubtful that public comprehension was significantly advanced.[24]

II

Finally, at Glasgow on 6 October, Chamberlain gave details of his policy. In brief, the tax on corn was 'not to exceed 2s. a quarter', whilst maize was to be

---

[20] *Free Trader*, 7 Aug. 1903, 11.

[21] Marrison, 'Development of a Tariff Reform Policy', 222. See esp. A. Branscombe Wood to Ed., *The Times*, 28 July 1903, 6; R. Gamman to Ed., *The Times*, 4 Aug. 1903, 2; *Free Trader*, 7 Aug. 1903, 16.

[22] *The Times*, 16 May 1903, 9, 11; H. A. Brassey to the chairman of the Rye (Sussex) Conservative and Unionist Association, *The Times*, 7 Aug. 1903, 6; Sir Gilbert Parker to Ed., *The Times*, 6 Aug. 1903, 9; Sir V. H. P. Caillard, *Imperial Fiscal Reform* (1903).

[23] A. W. Coats, 'Political Economy', 191–3.

[24] C. F. Bastable *et al.* to Ed., *The Times*, 15 Aug. 1903, 4. In fact an expansion of empire supplies was doubted rather than explicitly denied. See also 'Tariff Reformer' [L. S. Amery] to Ed., *The Times*, 18 Aug. 1903; A. Pigou to Ed., *The Times*, quoted in A. W. Coats, 'Political Economy', 216n.

exempted because it was a food of the poor and a raw material for pig farmers. A 'corresponding tax' was to be put on flour. A 'small tax of about 5 per cent on foreign meat and dairy produce' was suggested, though bacon was to be excluded, again because of its importance in the budgets of the poor. There would be a preference on colonial wines and perhaps on colonial fruits. And, in compensation, a remission of 'three-fourths of the duty on tea and half of the whole duty on sugar, with a corresponding reduction on cocoa and coffee'.[25] Using Board of Trade figures of household budgets, Chamberlain estimated the maximum effect of this proposal to be 4*d.* a week to the labourer and 5*d.* a week to the artisan, the extra expenditure being totally remitted by the compensating reductions. This was calculated on the assumption that food prices would rise the full amount of the duty. But, having consulted an unnamed 'official expert', who predicted that the price rise would be directly related to the proportion of the commodity taxed (i.e. imported from foreign countries), Chamberlain now conceded a probable price rise of only 75 per cent for wheat and 22 per cent for meat. In such circumstances the consumer would gain, since goods relieved from the revenue duty would fall by the total amount of the duty remitted, there being no home production of such goods.

Chamberlain's estimate of the Exchequer shortfall was smaller than earlier forecasts of his policy, but was still some £2.8 million per annum. He now proposed an average duty of 10 per cent on manufactures, 'varying according to the amount of labour in these goods', and yielding an estimated £9 to £15 million per annum.[26] Revenue and protectionist objectives appeared explicitly for essentially the first time.

Though corn prices were not forgotten, after Glasgow the Free Traders seem to have changed their emphasis somewhat towards taxation of manufactured goods. The close follow-up of the speech at Glasgow by those at Newcastle and Tynemouth later in October gave them ample ammunition. The base on which Chamberlain hoped to raise between £9 and £15 million included semi-manufactures as well as manufactures.[27] Asquith portrayed this as an attack on the manufacture of finished goods, even though it was Chamberlain's intention that semi-manufactures would be subjected to a lower rate of duty.[28] Besides, this meant that the rate on wholly manufactured goods would have to be higher than 10 per cent, and these would include some capital goods. Hicks Beach forecast dire consequences of a possible 20 per cent duty on agricultural machinery upon the sorely depressed agricultural sector.[29]

[25] Chamberlain at Glasgow, 6 Oct. 1903; repr. in J. M. Robertson, *The Collapse of 'Tariff Reform': Mr Chamberlain's Case Exposed* (1911), 52–8.
[26] Ibid. 61–2.   [27] Ibid. 62.
[28] Asquith at Paisley; in *Morning Post*, 2 Nov. 1903, 4.
[29] Hicks Beach at Manchester; in *Morning Post*, 6 Nov. 1903, 7.

The Free Traders also mobilized the eminent statistician, Sir Robert Giffen, to argue that Chamberlain's use of the official trade statistics was misleading, and they also did not let it go unnoticed that Chamberlain, in asserting that his 10 per cent tariff would raise between £9 and £15 million, was assuming that there would be no reduction in the volume of manufactured goods imported. They also pointed out that if Chamberlain was concerned to prevent dumping—they, themselves, were not—then to stop it would require duties far higher than a maximum of, say, 20 per cent. In this sense it was perhaps unfortunate for the Tariff Reform cause that Ashley's book, *The Tariff Problem*, was published so near in time to the Glasgow speech.[30] For in that volume, commonly regarded as one of the finest statements of the Tariff Reform case, Ashley expressed the opinion that duties of 50 to 75 per cent might well be necessary to prevent a determined campaign of dumping.[31] And, naturally, the Free Traders discerned the thin end of the wedge. Once tariffs were established they would then tend to rise: 'Protection is an inclined plane. Once you put your foot on it there is no logical halting place until you get to the bottom'.[32]

The Free Traders also criticized Chamberlain's statement, in justification of duties on manufactures as a bargaining weapon, that British exports had been stagnant for the previous thirty years. Giffen's argument, that the export figures should be presented after deducting the value of imported raw materials, seems to have been a refinement neglected by Free Trade spokesmen. Rosebery and Asquith were both more in tune with the popular debate when they criticized Chamberlain for comparing 1902 with the abnormal year of 1872, though Chamberlain took pains to point out, at Newcastle on 20 October, that this criticism was oversimplified. But Tariff Reformers affected bemusement at being pilloried for using what were, after all, the official returns, and they could take comfort from Giffen's warning that for many purposes these were exceedingly difficult to use. And Asquith and Harcourt were both as amateur as Chamberlain in the technique of historical comparison, Asquith glibly changing the base year under consideration from 1872 to 1877, and Harcourt contenting himself with a comparison between 1892 and 1902.[33]

[30] Asquith at Paisley, *Morning Post*; Giffen to Ed., *The Times*, 24 Oct. 1904, 12; Chamberlain to Ed., *The Times*, 27 Oct. 1903, 9; Giffen to Ed., *The Times*, 29 Oct. 1903, 6; see also the exchange of letters between Giffen and Chamberlain in J. Amery, *Life of Joseph Chamberlain*, vi. (1969), 479–80; W. J. Ashley, *The Tariff Problem* (1903).
[31] Ibid. 133.
[32] Asquith at Cinderford, 8 Oct. 1903, in T. L. Gilmour (ed.), *Fiscal Question*; Goschen at Passmore Edwards Settlement, in *The Times*, 17 Oct. 1903, 8.
[33] Giffen to Ed., *The Times*, 29 Oct. 1903, 6 (see also his *Essays in Finance*, 1st ser., (1877), 145); Rosebery at Sheffield, 13 Oct. 1903, Asquith at Cinderford, 8 Oct. 1903, in T. L. Gilmour (ed.), *Fiscal Question*, 110; Chamberlain at Newcastle, in *The Times*, 21 Oct. 1903, 10; *Morning Post* (editorial), 2 Nov. 1903, 5–6; Austen Chamberlain at Aberdeen, *Morning Post*, 4 Nov. 1903, 4.

The Free Traders also criticized the Tariff Reformers' tendency to omit coal from the figures, highlighting a difference between the nationalist and the cosmopolitan outlook on the economic situation. And they did introduce, to a greater extent after Glasgow than before, the vexed question of invisible exports, which the *Morning Post* rather unconstructively dismissed as a 'kind of providence for the rescue of distressed Free Traders'.[34] Again, dispute over the desirability of paying for imports with the dividends on overseas capital revealed a basic difference of approach to further confuse the public. 'We should be glad,' the *Morning Post* said, 'if Mr. ASQUITH would go carefully into the question of foreign investments, and explain in detail the advantage of the transference of British manufacturing enterprise to foreign countries'.[35] But it is doubtful whether many of the public could have followed Felix Schuster, in a widely reported paper before the Institute of Bankers in December, where he pointed to the inherent tendency to exaggerate the visible import surplus through the valuation of exports as f.o.b. and of imports as c.i.f., and to the fact that an 'undue' import surplus could not exist because of the strength of the exchanges and the stability of interest rates.[36]

As the complex and convoluted controversy raged after the Glasgow speech, Tariff Reformers saw its excesses and distortions as an indictment of the party system. The fiscal question was one of 'National and Imperial interest, which ought not to be discussed as a matter of party politics'.[37] As Sir Vincent Caillard wrote in exasperation to *The Times*, 'one might as well discuss Euclid on party lines as this'.[38] Partly, this was merely a propagandist device to take the tariff out of politics, but it was also couched to appeal to those adherents of National Efficiency who likewise found difficulty in accepting traditional party distinctions. At Burnley, Rosebery had forecast that Tariff Reform would cut 'diagonally' across party lines, and though his own Liberal Imperialists were less severely divided than he may have feared, there were significant defections. The conscience of the Fabian Society, too, was tested by the illicit attractions of Tariff Reform.[39]

Again, as in the case of the economists' intervention, the appeal to authority satisfied no-one. Balfour's 'inquiry by the Cabinet for the Cabinet' led to the famous Board of Trade 'Fiscal Blue Book', but this was commonly regarded as a mere collection of statistics with no attempt to draw conclusions.[40] Resisting

[34] *Morning Post* (editorial), 2 Nov. 1903, 5–6.
[35] Ibid.
[36] 'Bankers and the Fiscal Question', *Morning Post*, 17 Dec. 1903, 4.
[37] Chamberlain to Sir W. Treloar, in *The Times*, 11 Dec. 1903, 6.
[38] Sir Vincent Caillard to Ed., *The Times*, 28 May 1903, 5.
[39] Rosebery at Burnley, in *The Times*, 20 May 1903, 12; H. C. G. Matthew, *The Liberal Imperialists*, (1973), 101; A. M. McBriar, *Fabian Socialism and English Politics, 1884–1918* (Cambridge, 1962), 131–4.
[40] A. W. Coats, 'Political Economy', 200, 206n. (remarks of the Duke of Devonshire and economist Edwin Cannan); *British and Foreign Trade and Industry. Memoranda, Statistical Tables, and Charts*

pressure from the press and advice from the King downward, Balfour also discerned the uselessness of a Royal Commission in examining 'fundamentals'. The result would be 'a series of widely divergent Reports', as had happened with the Royal Commission on Labour of 1891–1894, notwithstanding the fact that this had 'dealt with, on the whole, far simpler problems'.[41]

III

After Glasgow, the dispute over the effects of Tariff Reform policy, and even, still, over the content of it, raged as fiercely as ever. It raised fundamental questions over the use of statistics in proving causation and serious doubts about even the best of British statistics. It was pushing the public comprehension well beyond all normally accepted limits. The incursion of expert authority had been ineffective: the civil service was divided, academic economists were, after the manifesto, distinctly reluctant to intervene, and the prospect of a Royal Commission seemed remote. Since by late 1903 neither side was obviously winning the propaganda war, things were going less well for the Tariff Reformers than appeared on the surface. In August, Harmsworth's opinion poll of 2,000 people showed a mass of hostility to Chamberlain's scheme.[42] By November similar indications were coming from organized labour, signs which Chamberlain attempted to discount by using the Webbs' argument that the TUC and its parliamentary committee were out of step with the rank and file.[43] The danger in which the Tariff Reformers stood was one of stalemate. If an audience rapidly losing its grip on the debate as it became more complex could not be given an unequivocal demonstration of the superiority of the new policy, it would retreat, at the polls, into an inertia which rested on the habits, practices, and conditioning of the previous half-century. It was as much with hope as with conviction that the *Morning Post* anticipated Chamberlain's forthcoming speech at Leeds: 'We do not agree with the critics on either side who say that as far as the general aspects of the controversy are concerned there is nothing more to be said'.[44]

The new thrust came in combining the need for a 'scientific', impartial enquiry with the belief that 'business principles' and the hard-headed pragmatism of the businessman could succeed where politicians and economists had failed. On 11 November the TRL, in response to enquiries about the place of different industries in Chamberlain's design, asserted that the duties put forward at

Prepared in the Board of Trade, with Reference to Various Matters Bearing on British and Foreign Trade and Industrial Conditions, Cd. 1761 (1903).

[41] Balfour, quoted in A. W. Coats, 'Political Economy', 204.

[42] 'Our Walking Inquirers', *Daily Mail*, 29 Aug. 1903, 4; A. M. Gollin, *Balfour's Burden* (1965), 87–8.

[43] S. and B. Webb, *Industrial Democracy*, (1st edn., 1897), esp. vol. i, chs. 1 and 2. In this connection, see *Morning Post*, 11, 12, 23, 25, 28, and 30 Nov. 1903 (4 or 5 in each case).

[44] *Morning Post* (editorial), 14 Dec. 1903, 6.

Glasgow 'must not be treated as anything but tentative' and that it was 'an essential part' of Chamberlain's policy that an expert committee should be established 'which will take evidence and will carefully consider the conditions of each trade, only fixing a tariff after having heard all that was to be said'.[45] The time had now come to move towards a specific formulation in which everyone could see the bearing of the new proposals on his particular circumstances. Chamberlain made his announcement at Leeds on 16 December:

Let us make a tariff, let us make a scientific tariff . . . Let us make a tariff, if that be possible—and I think it is—which shall not add by one farthing to the burden of any taxpayer, but which by the transference of taxation from one shoulder to another . . . may not only produce the same amount of revenue which will always be necessary for our home expenditure, but may incidentally do something to develop and extend our trade . . . It is true that we are told we cannot make a scientific tariff. We cannot distinguish between the raw material and manufactures, that we cannot be fair all round, that if . . . we prevent the dumping of iron below cost, we shall ruin the tinplate trade, that if we stop the excessive importation of cheap foreign labour we shall ruin the boot and shoe trade, that if we stop the excessive importation of foreign yarn there will be an end of the clothing industry . . .

Why should we suppose that our scientific economists, that our manufacturers cannot do what every other country has been able to do without finding their way into exaggerated difficulties? Now we are going to try to do it . . . We are going to form, nay, have gone a long way in the direction of forming, a Commission, not a political Commission, but a non-political Commission of experts . . . to consider the conditions of our trade and the remedies which are to be found for it.[46]

The new commission would consist of 'leading representatives' of the major British industries and the Empire, who would, after hearing witnesses, 'frame a model tariff', a tariff not designed 'merely in regard to the special interests of any particular trade, but also in regard to the interests of all the other trades which may be in any sense related to it'.[47] It would be headed by Professor W. A. S. Hewins, a historical economist, one of what Tariff Reformers commonly called the 'modern' or 'younger' school of economists as distinct from those 'musty theorists' of orthodox persuasion, 'evangelists of a fossilised doctrine'.[48] Hewins, director of the LSE since its foundation in 1895, had been a supporter of the imperial cause for some time, and in the summer had written sixteen influential articles in *The Times* under the pseudonym 'An Economist'. Now he was out in the open he was applauded in the Tariff Reform press as an economist who had 'always tried to base the study of economics on a study of industry and

---

[45] Chamberlain and the Duke of Sutherland in *Morning Post*, 11 Nov. 1903, 5.
[46] Chamberlain at Leeds; *Sheffield Daily Telegraph*, 17 Dec. 1903, 7–8.
[47] Ibid.
[48] For such remarks by Tariff Reformers, see A. W. Coats, 'Political Economy', 210–11.

commerce' and had been in 'close contact with business all his life'.[49] Having close relations with German scholars such as von Halle of Berlin, he was influenced by the close relationship between industry and the state in Germany, and aware of the close intercourse and elaborate discussion of detail between businessman and bureaucrat which went into the formulation of a tariff. Here, therefore, was the ideal link between the business approach to complex problems and the technical expertise required to draw up a scientific tariff.

The Chamberlainite newspapers now intensified their portrayal of Tariff Reform as a modern, virile movement. A Royal Commission was 'not Mr Chamberlain's way. He has no intention of having the great subject "hung up" indefinitely. The question demands attention'.[50] The Commission's task was 'not to multiply difficulties and stifle action with academic objections, but to arrange a practicable scheme which can be carried into effect with the least possible delay'.[51] This stress on direct and immediate action, far removed from the unhelpful, equivocating realm of theory, played on the distaste of the theoretician in the public eye, emphasizing the 'representative' quality, the common sense, and the stature of the business members of the Commission.

Free Traders retaliated by criticizing the Commission on two main grounds. The first was to criticize the fifty-eight members as a 'ring of vested interests . . . of managing directors who have hundreds of thousands of pounds to gain by the imposition of a skilful tariff',[52] and to claim that they were not representative of the whole sphere of British economic activity. It became almost a hobby to find gaps in the list—in the House of Commons it was asked 'Why it was that not a single banker of repute sat on the Tariff Commission?' Lloyd George asked why no working men were represented. At Halifax, Churchill pointed to the absence of the cotton trade, the professions, and the Free Traders.[53]

The second criticism, more fundamental, was that the enquiry was not to be impartial in the manner of a Royal Commission. It would not concern itself with the issue of Free Trade versus protection, but with how a tariff could be 'best framed in the interests of those who are advocating it'.[54] To *The Standard*, this was 'a tribunal starting with preconceived opinions, and pledged, beforehand, to a particular conclusion'.[55]

The Tariff Reform answer to this was that some kind of modification of policy was required to meet changing conditions of international trade and the rise of industrial rivals. There were, after all, plenty of Liberals who advocated reforms

---

[49] *Morning Post* (editorial), 18 Dec. 1903, 4.
[50] *Sheffield Daily Telegraph* (editorial), 18 Dec. 1903, 4.
[51] *Morning Post* (editorial), 18 Dec. 1903, 4.
[52] *The Echo*, (editorial), 18 Dec. 1903, 2 (unpaginated).
[53] *Parliamentary Debates*, 4th ser., 129 (9 Feb. 1904, col. 822; 10 Feb. 1904, col. 954); Churchill at Halifax, in *Sheffield Daily Telegraph*, 21 Dec. 1903, 9.
[54] *The Echo* (editorial), 18 Dec. 1903, 2 (unpaginated).
[55] *The Standard* (editorial), 17 Dec. 1903, 6.

in technical education or in the Consular Service. A tariff could not be evaluated in abstract, and someone had to draft a plan, 'for obviously, the details of a tariff must be worked out before, not after, the country expresses its final judgement'.[56] If Free Traders could greet such arguments with incredulity, it was because they undoubtedly served to conceal a substantial element of political and propagandist opportunism. But when seen in terms of the inductive approach of the historicist they were more than mere rhetoric. Nothing illustrates this better than an exchange of letters between Hewins, L. T. Hobhouse, and Herbert Gladstone in *The Times* in March 1904, initiated by Hewins' condemnation of the methods of the Free Trade Union as unscientific. Hewins denied that, in setting up the Commission, the Tariff Reformers considered their case proved and that the next step was to draft a tariff. Rather, his opponents were inclined to make dogmatic statements as to the effects of a tariff without justifying them. Such criticism implied that the Free Traders had already constructed a tariff and found that it would not work. If this was so, bantered Hewins, the nation should be told the results. Was this hypothetical Free Traders' tariff drawn up in the most beneficial way? What goods were on the free list? How had the Free Traders decided on the merits of specific and *ad valorem* duties? Had they consulted widely with manufacturers?

Mr Chamberlain has described a practical situation, with regard to which it is desirable to take action. The figures on which that description is based have not, so far as I know, been disputed . . . If we are to deal with the situation . . . you will, I feel sure, agree that we must have a policy. It is open to the free-traders to sketch an economic and commercial policy, which will deal with actual problems, alternative to that suggested by Mr Chamberlain. But they have not done so.[57]

It is doubtful that Hewins considered that such an argument would weigh heavily with committed Free Traders. He knew well that Chamberlain's figures *had* been disputed: indeed, his own role in the controversy had developed partly through the Liberal Unionist leader's wish to be defended from criticism in the press.[58] More importantly, the purist Free Trader could scarcely accept that Free Trade was not itself a policy in the regenerative sense meant by Hewins. But by no means all Free Traders held the view that Britain's economic condition was so sound that no positive action would be required in the forseeable future. Free Traders may have accused Chamberlain of gross exaggeration, but even Asquith had been prepared to admit that the situation was not perfect. As early as May

[56] *Morning Post* (editorial), 23 Dec. 1903, 4; Chamberlain at first meeting of Tariff Commission, in *Sheffield Daily Telegraph*, 16 Jan. 1904, 4.

[57] L. T. Hobhouse to Ed., *The Times*, 14 Mar. 1904, 6; Hewins to Ed., *The Times*, 15 Mar. 1904, 8; Hobhouse to Ed., *The Times*, 16 Mar. 1904, 2. Also H. J. Gladstone to Hewins, 3 letters, 18 Mar., 15 and 19 Apr. 1904, and Hewins to Gladstone, 2 letters, 30 Mar. and 15 Apr. 1904, all printed in *The Times*, 20 Apr. 1904, 4.

[58] See below, Ch. 2.

1903 he had counselled, 'Until some better substitute [than Chamberlain's policy] could be discovered, let us stick to our well-tried policy of free markets and an open door'.[59] There were many who were not complacent, and not all were Tariff Reformers—most common among the others were the advocates of National Efficiency, with their Charlottenburgs, their schemes for administrative reform, meritocracy and businessmen in government, and their vague conceptions of spiritual regeneration on an imperial basis.[60] To them, perhaps, Hewins' reasoning was understandable: certainly it was at them, at the middle ground, that it was directed. The Tariff Commission was to examine how the industrial situation could best be remedied by means of a tariff: it was up to others to suggest alternative remedies with which to compare that tariff.

Even if the Tariff Reformers' premisses were accepted, the Tariff Commission had been given a daunting task. Chamberlain had come close to claiming that everyone would benefit, or at least would not be harmed, by his policy. He had not been able to show how it was to be done. But, by definition, it could be done. That was the function and, more than that, the *meaning*, of a scientific tariff. Indeed, the objectives of the tariff were now clear. On the narrow industrial front the Commission had to ensure that protection was graded and dovetailed so as not to damage user industries, or exports, or the consumer interest. It had to benefit wages and employment. In the broader application of the policy, there had to be a system of agricultural protection and preference which would benefit both British and imperial farmers without raising the price of food. The interests of industry and agriculture had to be harmonized. And in addition to this, preferential terms had to be engineered which were acceptable to every single colony, no matter what its economic base. Put this way, Tariff Reformers would no doubt have disclaimed any ability to achieve success in all these dimensions, but by any account they set the Commission a formidable agenda.

IV

However difficult the task that lay before the Tariff Commission, the new strategy was certainly bold in concept, and in its innovative use of the businessman in politics it gave a fresh, radical, even progressive dimension to Chamberlain's campaign. In view of the importance of the fiscal issue to the business community, it is remarkable what little obvious impact that community had had upon the debate in its opening stages.

In March 1902, during that period of 'phoney war' in the tariff controversy as the economy slid into depression after the Boer War, Harry Marks of the *Financial News* and Ernest E. Williams of 'Made in Germany' fame assembled

---

[59] Asquith at Doncaster, 21 May 1903, in H. H. Asquith, *Speeches by the Rt. Hon. H. H. Asquith*, 149–53.

[60] See G. R. Searle, *The Quest for National Efficiency* (Oxford, 1971), *passim*.

twenty-four prominent industrialists to form a Fiscal Reform Association. According to George Byng of the General Electric Company, a manifesto was issued bearing the signatures of 2,500 manufacturers. Whether this involved some exaggeration is not known, for no copy of that remarkable document has yet come to light. These events led to the formation on 14 May 1903 of the Protection League, short-lived predecessor of the TRL.[61]

But the industrial links of the early TRL were by no means as explicit as its origins seemed to portend, and in any case Chamberlain was initially concerned to maintain a distance from the new organization.[62] The Tariff Reformers remained cautious about linking their cause too openly with the industrial protectionist. Their reasons need to be understood against a background in which their Free Trade opponents assumed unquestioningly that the moral high ground in this area belonged to them. Perhaps the best illustration of this was given in Harold Cox's *British Industries under Free Trade*, published late in 1903. Its nineteen contributors included important industrialists such as Sir Swire Smith, a prominent Keighley worsted spinner; Alfred Mond of Brunner, Mond and Co.; D. A. Thomas MP of the Cambrian Collieries; Albert Spicer, the papermaker; Hugh Bell, the Cleveland ironmaster; and two shipowners, M. W. Davies of Alfred Holt and Co., and Walter Runciman of the Moor Line. There were contributions by less prominent businessmen, and by some who were professional commentators rather than practising businessmen—for instance, Elijah Helm, secretary of Manchester Chamber of Commerce, and the editors of two trade journals, the *Shoe and Leather Record* and *Machinery Market*.

In his introduction, Cox claimed that the contributors were not 'pedants . . . who are content to mutter exploded shibboleths . . . [but] practical business men, writing . . . of their personal knowledge'. They were concerned 'not with the events of 1846, nor even with the prophecies of Cobden, but with the actual business needs of to-day'. If this was so, his authors had a curious way of demonstrating it. Swire Smith, for instance, spent fourteen of his eighteen pages getting from the early fourteenth century to the 1880s. Frederick Callis's essay on 'a century's progress' in cutlery used oral evidence to get back into the conditions of master and men in the 1840s. Hugh Bell spent one and a half pages quoting from Jonathan Swift's *Voyage to Laputa* and followed this with extensive treatment of petitions under mercantilism, ending with a six-and-a-half-page quote from Adam Smith's pamphlet on the importation of bar iron from the North American colonies, written in 1756. In his treatment of engineering, Arthur Wadham ranged liberally over the nineteenth century, with only a brief mention of Edward III. These essays were not untypical. The predominant flavour of the book was of a 'historical' proof of Free Trade based on the

---

[61] F. Coetzee, *For Party or Country* (New York, 1990), 46.
[62] Ibid. 47.

expansion of trade in the early- and mid-nineteenth century. It was the anonymous contribution on banking and those on shipping which had most to say about current conditions.[63]

These essays had a certain pontifical quality, the air of elder statesmen pronouncing upon their trade in its larger cultural environment, which the heavy stress on the historical context only served to reinforce. The *Free Trader* reported businessmen's views similarly, a particularly good example being Sir John Jenkins of the Welsh tinplate trade, whose silver hair positively shone through its pages.[64]

Now, at Leeds, Chamberlain revealed that he was assembling 'the most wonderful representation of British industry that has ever been brought together'.[65] It was time to use the Tariff Reform businessman in a new and more radical way, a way that would use a new methodology to cut through the anaesthetizing confusion of the press debate and avoid a stalemate which could not but work to the advantage of the Free Traders, and, at the same time, to legitimize the support of the businessman for Tariff Reform.

V

Many manufacturers, however, had strong inhibitions about joining the campaign for protective duties. Scholars have sometimes seen the manufacturing interest as central to the finances and objectives of Chamberlain's movement, industrial interests at the heart of the TRL.[66] There is room for doubt. There is a huge, unwritten history of the local activity of county, town, and even village branches of the TRL, where the predominance of industrial interests is to be doubted. So much of this took place in the southern and home counties that, in the correspondence columns of the national and provincial presses, or in the League's *Monthly Notes*, we can glimpse another world of Tariff Reform, the Tariff Reform of minor country society, of the retired major in Sevenoaks, the solicitor of Tunbridge Wells, the Winchester publican, the students of Oxford, and the ladies of Salisbury. Relatively little is known of the Tariff Reform of the spas and the shires, but it is more than plausible that its industrial links were remote. To an extent, our ignorance extends to finance. Though information is sketchy, TRL income was small compared with that of the Anti-Corn-Law League sixty years earlier,[67] and its opponents' claims that it could outspend the

---

[63] H. Cox (ed.), *British Industries under Free Trade* (1903), *passim*.

[64] See interview with Jenkins, in *Free Trader*, 11 Dec. 1903, 157; also *Westminster Gazette*, 20 Nov. 1903, 2.

[65] Chamberlain to Lady Jeune, quoted in J. Amery, *Life of Joseph Chamberlain*, vi. (1969), 532.

[66] B. Semmel, *Imperialism and Social Reform* (1960), 102; S. Pollard, *Britain's Prime and Britain's Decline* (1989), 239.

[67] F. Coetzee, 'Pressure Groups, Tory Businessmen and the Aura of Political Corruption before the First World War', *Historical Journal*, 29 (1986), 839–40; cf. N. McCord, *Anti-Corn Law League*, 137–9, 160–1, 173–5, 200.

Free Trade League by ten to one[68] were certainly exaggerated. However, though Coetzee has demolished the 'myth' of inexhaustible finances from Tariff-Reform 'millionaires', we are little nearer any estimation of the proportion of League income provided by industry.[69] It may be significant that TRL income was much higher between 1908 and 1910, when Liberal taxation policy was emerging as a threat not only to industrial interests but also to the professional and rentier middle classes, than it was from 1903 to 1906 when, as beneficiaries of Chamberlain's policy, industry and agriculture seemed to stand alone.

It is nevertheless with industrialists, especially manufacturers, that this work will mostly be concerned. In the study of Tariff Reform we can reconstruct, albeit imperfectly, not only the hopes and fears of the Tariff-Reform business-man, but also, to an extent, the social and moral ethos in which he worked, the constraints which Free-Trade British society and politics, almost uniquely, imposed upon him, the barriers to political effectiveness that lay in his path. To say that Free Trade, the last bastion of unreconstructed liberal *laissez-faire* ideology, encouraged individualism and held the corporate and co-operative ideal at a discount is scarcely sufficient. It leaves buried the rich complexity of the dissenter's place under the hegemony of that dominant ideology. The element which is missing from almost every existing treatment of Tariff Reform is embarrassment, and it is that with which we will start.

Amongst Britain's major industrial rivals, the social barriers to the entry of businessmen into tariff politics were low. In the USA, the tariff had been a sphere of legitimate interest group-politics ever since the Anglo-American War of 1812–15, and the close identification of local business and community interests could result in absurd excesses in the protection afforded.[70] There was, of course, no complete unanimity; division persisted not only between merchants and manufacturers but also between different industrial groups.[71] But, as could be seen in the conflict over the Dingley Tariff of 1897, differences were relative, between those who wanted the continuance of high tariffs and those who wanted reductions and reciprocity treaties to aid exports. To represent the latter, the National Association of Manufacturers quickly developed sophistication and a talent for working through the administration rather than Congress. By the early twentieth century it had achieved some success in 'weakening protectionist sentiment within the Republican party'.[72]

---

[68] e.g. Herbert Gladstone, cited in A. K. Russell, *Liberal Landslide* (Newton Abbot, 1973), 41.

[69] F. Coetzee, 'Pressure Groups, Tory Businessmen and Political Corruption', 838–46.

[70] R. V. Reimini, 'Martin Van Buren and the Tariff of Abominations', *American Historical Review*, 63 (1957), 903–17.

[71] S. Coben, 'Northeastern Businessmen and Radical Reconstruction: A Re-examination', *Mississippi Valley Historical Review*, 46 (1959–60), 68–78; I. Unger, *The Greenback Era: A Social and Political History of American Finance 1865–1879* (Princeton, 1964).

[72] W. H. Becker, *The Dynamics of Business-Government Relations: Industry and Exports 1893–1921* (Chicago, 1982), ch. 4, 78.

The moderates had formidable opponents, however. In 1924 the secretary of the US Tariff Commission, Thomas Walker Page, outlined the dangers of close interaction between protectionist manufacturers and politicians. The necessary reliance on interested parties could result in congressional hearings being fed with biased and dishonest information, helpless 'against the importunity of predatory interests'. The lobby system compounded this. When a tariff was being prepared in Washington:

some members of congress are accused of being swayed by unworthy motives; others are suspected of lacking decision, and pressure in many forms is brought to bear upon them ... Innumerable delegations and individuals visit Washington to argue, pursuade, threaten, and plead. Many organizations open offices there to watch proceedings, keep their members informed, and mobilize all possible forces that might aid in securing the kind of tariff that would serve their particular needs.[73]

Page was, retrospectively, justifying the establishment of his own Commission. If his analysis was relatively sober, his words temperate, polemicists such as Ida Tarbell and New York lawyer Franklin Pierce were more vigorous. In true muckraker style, Pierce lambasted the 'unholy alliance' between political leaders and captains of industry. A 'considerable proportion' of congressmen received bribes, or benefited from the large contributions made by the trusts to political parties. It was, in Senator McDuffie's phrase of 1828, 'political prostitution'.[74]

In Germany, where there was no anti-business movement equivalent to the anti-trust sentiment of populism and progressivism, there reigned perhaps the classic case of tariff formulation under heavyweight economic interest groups. Each side of the debate found no difficulty in proclaiming its interests to coincide with the national economic interest. Heavy industry was long in the ascendancy, in a pattern established in the accord reached with the Junkers in the famous alliance of iron and rye in 1879:

The instruments for the protection of [heavy industry's] autonomy and the presentation of their wishes and demands were the interest groups, and the weakness of parliamentary institutions in so highly advanced an industrial society as Germany encouraged the development of interest groups and a very exaggerated form of interest group politics in which heavy industry had particularly distinguished itself.[75]

Heavy industry's domination of industrial policy, particularly the use of tariffs to ensure high home prices to subsidize exports, caused bitter lament amongst those businessmen who used the semi-products of the cartels in further manufacture,

[73] T. W. Page, *Making the Tariff in the United States* (New York, 1924), 3–4, 7–8.
[74] F. Pierce, *The Tariff and the Trusts* (New York, 1907), ch. 4, McDuffie quoted 119; Ida Tarbell, *The Tariff in Our Times* (New York, 1912).
[75] G. D. Feldman, *Iron and Steel in the German Inflation 1916–1923* (Princeton, 1977), 40–2; see also Ivo N. Lambi, *Free Trade and Protection in Germany 1868–79* (Wiesbaden, 1963).

much to the satisfaction of gloating British Free Traders.[76] By the new century, the Berlin-based *Centralverband deutscher Industriellen* was being forced into considerable expense to secure the election of Reichstag deputies friendly to heavy industry. This was in response to increasing opposition from the newer and lighter industries represented by the *Bund der Industriellen*, formed in 1895,[77] and agitation from the merchants and smaller industrialists of the *Handelsvertragsverein* of 1897, who sought to maintain the relative economic liberalism of the Caprivi interlude.[78] Von Bulow, faced with the political necessity of raising agricultural tariffs, resorted to the time-honoured expedient of *quid pro quo* in increasing duties on manufactures in the Tariff of 1902. This increased discontent, especially in chemicals and electrical engineering. Though the *CdI* still possessed great strength and influence in 1914, it had been somewhat embarrassed by the more extreme demands of its agrarian allies in the new century. The government was discomforted by increasing complaint from light industry, not only from the *BdI* and *Handelsvertragsverein*, but now also from Chambers of Commerce and trade associations concerned over the effects of foreign retaliation on Germany's trade treaties.[79]

After the Cobden–Chevalier Treaty of 1860, French tariff politics became the province of influential interest-groups of manufacturers and merchants, each camp represented in the Senate and Chamber of Deputies. Free Trade merchants and export manufacturers gathered under the *Association du libre-échange*, formed in 1845 and modelled on the Anti-Corn Law League. But 1846 did not destroy the ability of the protectionist textile, metals, and mining industries to 'mobilize their political interests in their behalf',[80] as was the case in Britain, and in 1878 the *Association de l'industrie Français* was set up largely to lobby on the tariff. Furthermore, Chambers of Commerce were long accustomed to receiving requests from government for their views on tariff policy, or, when necessary, submitting them unsolicited. The Méline Tariff of 1892 has been interpreted as the peak of a protectionist reaction gathering force since 1860, or, alternatively, as a compromise between more and less protectionist interests necessary to the search for industrial and political stability within the Third Republic.[81] Either way, both sides of the struggle were organized into pressure groups and were politically articulate, and both could count on political representation in the legislature. As in Germany and the US, tariff politics were an acceptable and legitimate form of interest, an established forum of business activity.

[76] e.g. *Free Trader*, 23 Oct. 1903, 98, 102.

[77] G. D. Feldman, *Iron and Steel*, 48–9.

[78] K. D. Barkin, *The Controversy over German Industrialization 1890–1902* (Chicago, 1970), 218.

[79] Ibid. 260–5.

[80] M. S. Smith, *Tariff Reform in France 1860–1900* (Ithaca, NY, 1980), 38.

[81] A. L. Dunham, *The Anglo-French Treaty of Commerce of 1860 and the Progress of the Industrial Revolution in France* (Ann Arbor, 1930); E. O. Golob, *The Méline Tariff*, (New York, 1944); M. S. Smith, *Tariff Reform*, esp. ch. 5.

Though differing in detail, Germany, France, and the US present a common picture of the open prevalence of tariff politics, with little social or institutional constraint upon its expression. Both Feldman, and, implicitly, Page related this in some way to imperfections in the system of parliamentary democracy; through such imperfections jobbery (in the US case) or pressure groups (in the German) could thrive. British Free Traders, reflecting the belief that in Britain parliamentary democracy had reached a higher stage of evolution, would have endorsed this, and it is certainly true that in Britain the popular vote was always a great stumbling block to the advancement of Tariff Reform. But that democracy reflected the cultural hegemony of an idea, Free Trade, whose superiority was accepted unquestioningly as axiomatic, when few could have realized all its implications. Under this hegemony, what was a legitimate field of debate abroad was not so in Britain. Abroad, the public were prepared to discern a closer identification between the interests of consumer and producer than was the case in Britain. Not surprisingly, the xperience of the British protectionist in the early twentieth century was very different from that of his counterpart in Germany, France, and the USA.

In Britain, the Free Trade press treated the prospect of the self-interested protectionist gaining access to political power with both contempt and alarm. The public mind was receptive to its charges; 'protectionism was popularly assumed to be a corrupt cause, and by extension, any organization lobbying on behalf of protectionist principles was likely to be corrupt as well'.[82] Such fears were not confined to the public and the sensationalist press. Some of Alfred Marshall's most fundamental objections to Tariff Reform reflected a fear of political corruption.[83] The professorial manifesto, with Marshall as one of the signatories, put the matter even more explicit:

There are also to be apprehended those evils other than material which protection brings in its train, the loss of purity in politics, the unfair advantage given to those who wield the powers of jobbery and corruption, unjust distribution of wealth and the growth of 'sinister interests'.[84]

When, in 1903, the editors of the *Economic Journal* published a modest and moderate letter in support of imperial preference from John Lysaght, manufacturer of galvanized sheet-iron who specialized in supplying the Australian market,[85] they felt it incumbent upon them to 'answer for the ability and good

---

[82] F. Coetzee, 'Pressure Groups, Tory Businessmen and Political Corruption', 839.

[83] Marshall to Lujo Brentano, 20 and 24 July 1903, quoted in H. W. McCready, 'Alfred Marshall and Tariff Reform, 1903: Some Unpublished Letters', *Journal of Political Economy*, 63 (1955), 263–4. See also D. P. O'Brien, 'A. Marshall, 1842–1924', in D. P. O'Brien and J. R. Presley (eds.), *Pioneers of Modern Economics in Britain* (1981), 57.

[84] C. F. Bastable *et al.* to Ed., *The Times*, 15 Aug. 1903, 4.

[85] K. Warren, *The British Iron and Steel Sheet Industry since 1840* (1970), 35, 109–10.

faith of our correspondent'.[86] Apparently, to advocate preference, let alone protection, in the *Economic Journal,* one needed character references. Churchill, though no stranger to polemic, was in serious vein when he cautioned Balfour that protection would inevitably lead to the 'Americanisation' of British politics.[87] Even some prominent ultra-imperialists, supporters of Chamberlain, expressed sentiments which betrayed similar fears. Alfred Milner was highly sensitive to the allegation that he and his friends were 'protectionists seeking guaranteed profits for their industrial connections',[88] whilst Leo Amery hoped to keep protectionist manufacturers, alongside Chamberlainite 'whole-hoggers', parliamentary place hunters, and 'all that clan' out of the newly formed Compatriot's Club.[89]

In retrospect, we can link this deep distrust of protectionist businessmen with another, more positive, image of businessmen common at the time. This was the belief that the businessman, as a practical man of affairs, somehow 'got things done'. He didn't equivocate, he was pragmatic, direct to the point of bluntness, hard-headed, efficient in getting what he wanted. Such an image lay behind the National Efficiency movement—the Webbian 'cult of the expert' and the attraction of the businessman in politics were closely related.[90] Perhaps the best-known statement of this touching belief in the virtues of business qualities in government is Arnold White's panegyric on Chamberlain at the Colonial Office.[91] Chamberlain himself discerned the same qualities in others. When opening the proceedings of the Tariff Commission early in 1904, he spoke of 'these fifty-eight gentlemen, princes of commerce, who have grown grey and bald in the trade fight for success, have ever their feelings under perfect control, and allow only the doorway to reason to remain open'.[92] It is hard to calculate whether this was more likely to reassure or to alarm the public at large.

In 1903 Bernard Holland, biographer of Unionist Free Trader the Duke of Devonshire and himself no out-and-out Tariff Reformer, recorded a valid protest at the language used by Liberal opponents of the emergency corn-registration duty imposed in the Boer War:

Sir William Harcourt, an ex-Chancellor, called the 1*s.* duty an 'infamous' tax, and Sir Henry Campbell-Bannerman said that the conduct of those who imposed it was 'atrocious'. This language would have fairly astonished their Whig predecessors, the Russells and the Greys, once the advocates of a fixed duty of 8*s.* or 5*s.* on wheat.[93]

---

[86] J. Lysaght, 'Preferential Tariffs in the Sheet Iron Business', *Economic Journal,* 13 (1903), 421–3.

[87] Churchill to Balfour, 25 May 1903; quoted in K. Young, *Arthur James Balfour* (1963), 211–12.

[88] A. M. Gollin, *Proconsul in Politics* (1964), 125–6.

[89] Amery to Milner, 26 Feb. 1904; quoted ibid. 105.

[90] G. R. Searle, *Quest for National Efficiency,* 80–92.

[91] A. White, *Efficiency and Empire,* (2nd edn., ed. G. R. Searle, Brighton, 1973), 129.

[92] *Sheffield Daily Telegraph,* 16 Jan. 1904, 9.

[93] B. Holland, *The Fall of Protection 1840–1850* (1913), 324.

Infamy and atrocity? The Tariff Reformer could expect far worse. When, in 1887, the local associations of the Conservative Party passed a protectionist resolution by 1,000 votes to 12, John Bright, acting in the long radical tradition of quoting from the Bible, observed, 'They return, shall I say, like a dog to his vomit.'[94] Such emotive language about what was, after all, only a legitimate dispute about commercial policy reveals much about the social parameters in which the protectionists had to live and work, and explains the early tendency to euphemism in the choice of titles for such organizations as the Reciprocity Free Trade Association, the National Association for the Defence of British Industries, the National Fair Trade League. In 1899 Ernest E. Williams sought to rid the 'proscribed word' of its stigma:

Among certain tribes of African savages particular words are taboo. If the missionary efforts of the late Mr. Cobden had extended to the African hinterland, one of those dread, unnameable words would of a surety have been 'Protection' . . . [Under] the Cobdenite Gospel . . . no politician who would escape the horrified frowns of his caucus, no rising young economist with an eye to a well-endowed professorship, will dare to breathe in public the anathematized word 'Protection' . . .
This complicates my task.[95]

Williams' plea had little effect. When, shortly afterwards, George Byng published a book with the provocative title, *Protection: The Views of a Manufacturer* (1901), Free Traders professed amusement and surprise. Subsequent proto-Chamberlainites were more cautious. A change of name was deemed essential to distance the TRL from the image associated with its predecessor, the Protection League; Sir Joseph Lawrence urged substitution of the euphemism because he 'was not in favour of "protection" in its proper economic sense'.[96]

If the atmosphere was so highly charged that words could hold such significance, then personal situations must have counted for even more. The result, no doubt, was that 'closet protectionism' was common. This may explain why, until the Leeds speech, the Tariff Reformers had allowed the Free Traders the initiative in what limited use of the businessman there had been in the controversy. Practising businessmen figured surprisingly little, even in the pages of the TRL's *Monthly Notes on Tariff Reform*. Had not Lysaght suffered condescension, Byng ridicule? No doubt in consequence, Sir Vincent Caillard's well-reviewed *Imperial Fiscal Policy* bore no trace of his position as a director of Vickers, Sons and Maxim. Even William Ashley, in the preface to *The Tariff Problem*, chose not to stress his close association with British businessmen at the Birmingham Faculty of Commerce. Rather, his views 'were formed long before

---

[94] B. H. Brown, *The Tariff Reform Movement in Great Britain, 1881–1895* (New York, 1943), 67–70; Bright quoted, 70.
[95] E. E. Williams, *The Case for Protection* (1899), 1–2.
[96] W. E. Dowding, *The Tariff Reform Mirage* (1913), 5, 7.

I returned to England, and while I was still a teacher, first in a Canadian and then an American university'.[97]

Of course, during thirty years of Tariff Reform many protectionist manufacturers were willing to make their views public, but it has seldom been appreciated that stepping into the public eye was not always lightly done. This may be because scholars in general have found it easy to accept the contemporary public view. If the manufacturer grasping at protection was corrupt, why should he not also be brazen? There is also the difficulty of assembling the information. But in one quarter evidence has survived which gives some indication of the courage (if that is not too strong a word) needed and the embarrassment felt by manufacturers in coming out into the open on the issue. That evidence, examined below, centred around the problems of recruitment experienced by Chamberlain's Tariff Commission.[98]

Two other peculiarities of the protectionist businessman's position in the Tariff Reform campaign will be recurring concerns of this study. Both are closely related to his embarrassment and his perception of vulnerability. The first is the businessman's curiously subordinate role in relation to politicians. The second concerns the constraints imposed on the legitimacy of discussion within businessmen's organizations. Both will be examined fully below, the first in connection with the relationship between Chamberlain and his body of Tariff Commissioners,[99] and the second in relation to the activities of chambers of commerce.[100] In large part, we will discover hesitancy, indecision, timidity, even subservience, patterns of behaviour which were lessened, but not eradicated, by the mud of Flanders and the broken landscape of the 1920s. The depth of the emasculation of the manufacturing interest, perhaps the most pervasive and least discussed of the effects of Free Trade, will be revealed.

[97] W. J. Ashley, *The Tariff Problem*, pp. v–vi.
[98] See below, Chs. 4, 5, and 6.
[99] See below, Chs. 4, 5, and 6.
[100] See below, Chs. 3 and 9.

2

The Establishment of the Tariff Commission

I

By the autumn of 1903, Chamberlain was in close consultation with three men who were to be central figures in the Commission's operation. Sir Vincent Caillard, the financial director of Vickers, was already known as the author of three articles in the *National Review* advocating imperial unity through preference. Sir Arthur Pearson was chairman of the TRL Executive and, as proprietor of the *Daily Express*, had run an energetic campaign which centred around the higher level of employment to be gained from Tariff Reform. Henry Chaplin, whose extravagance lost him his Lincolnshire estate of Blankney in the 1890s, remained throughout the remainder of his colourful life the leading spokesman of the agricultural interest in Parliament. For him, Tariff Reform was merely a resumption of the Fair Trade agitation of the 1880s after a brief flirtation with bimetallism.[1] Reminiscing on the foundation of the Tariff Commission in 1917, all three spoke of a formative meeting with Hewins at Caillard's rooms in Half Moon Street. Pearson's claim, on that occasion, to have been 'mainly instrumental in, or responsible for, its foundation' was exaggerated, though he did play an important role in early finance.[2] Rather, the surviving evidence supports Hewins' claim, made in his autobiography, that he was the initiator.

There was some speculation in the press about the authorship of the articles in *The Times*, much of it accurate,[3] and Hewins's backstage role in the campaign was probably common knowledge: certainly Beatrice Webb thought that he endangered relations between the LSE and the London County Council by

[1] For Caillard's writings, see V. H. P. Caillard, 'Foreign Trade and Home Markets', *National Review*, 29 (1902), 51–77; 'Some Suggestions Toward an Imperial Tariff', *National Review*, 39 (1902), 209–27; ' "The Dream of a British Zollverein": A Reply to Sir Robert Giffen', *National Review*, 39 (1902), 597–605; *Imperial Fiscal Reform* (1903). Caillard's book was well reviewed by Free Trade economist J. Shield Nicholson in *Economic Journal*, 14 (1904), 57. For Pearson's campaign in the *Daily Express*, see B. Semmel, *Imperialism and Social Reform* (1960), 112; R. D. Blumenfeld, *R. D. B.'s Diary 1887–1914* (1930), 194–6. On Chaplin, see Marchioness of Londonderry, *Henry Chaplin* (1926); J. Hamilton, 'Henry Chaplin and English Agriculture, 1875–1895', unpubl. B. A. Thesis, Univ. of Manchester, 1977.
[2] 'The Tariff Commission—Dinner to Mr. Hewins, MP, Savoy Hotel, Nov. 6th. 1917', 8/7/2, TCP.
[3] e.g. *Western Mercury*, 19 Nov. 1903.

letting out the identity of 'An Economist'.[4] Chamberlain knew Hewins only slightly before the first article appeared. In the letter that marked the beginning of their working relationship, he offered 'any assistance in my power, and [to] discuss with you the general question or details if you desire'.[5] By July, however, it was clear that the flow of information was the other way, with Chamberlain seeking advice on technical aspects of the controversy, such as the desirability of financing imports with the returns on overseas investment.[6] The Liberal Unionist leader's opinion of a leaflet written by Hewins for trade unionists was not favourable, since 'working men will not pay attention to many figures or to abstract economics'. Rather, he saw Hewins's influence as being on 'the more limited class of educated people'.[7] By the Glasgow speech, Chamberlain clearly regarded Hewins as the 'scientist', the 'expert' who could descend to the levels of the correspondence columns and pronounce discursively and definitively on the critics:

What . . . I do ask from you is that, whenever possible, you should take up . . . criticisms and deal with them from an expert point of view . . . Anonymous letters in small print are of little value, but an article or letter from a recognised authority . . . is of the utmost advantage in such a controversy.[8]

Whether Chamberlain had, at this time, any specific plans to use Hewins more directly in the campaign is unknown, but the period from June to September was clearly that of Hewins's probation. Apart from responding to specific requests for information and providing Chamberlain with 'a weekly résumé of the arguments used against him and the replies thereto',[9] Hewins was becoming deeply involved elsewhere in the press controversy, writing for the *Fortnightly Review*, more regularly for the *Saturday Review*, and at the request of Dunn and Borthwick supplying all the relevant leaders for the *Morning Post*.[10]

Hewins did not see Chamberlain between July and December,[11] but he arranged a meeting with Caillard, whom he had known for several years, on 22 October.[12] They both feared that even if Chamberlain were successful at the polls, the technical enquiry necessary to institute a tariff would take so long that '[d]ifferences would develop. The enthusiasm of Chamberlain's supporters would die down and even if he succeeded in getting a suitable scheme worked

[4] Beatrice Webb, *Our Partnership* (1948), 269.

[5] Chamberlain to Hewins, 10 June 1903, HP.

[6] Chamberlain to Hewins, 14 July 1903, HP.

[7] Chamberlain to Hewins, 17 and 21 July 1903, HP.

[8] Chamberlain to Hewins, 12 Oct. 1903, HP; see also J. Wilson (PS to Chamberlain) to Hewins, 26 Oct. 1903, HP.

[9] W. A. S. Hewins, *The Apologia of an Imperialist* (1929), i. 72.

[10] Moberly Bell to Hewins, 5 June 1903, 46/15–16, HP; Hewins, 'My Connection with the Fiscal Controversy', MS, 31 Jan. 1904, unmarked black diary, HP, 23–38.

[11] W. A. S. Hewins, *Apologia*, i. 69.

[12] 'My Connection with the Fiscal Controversy', 27; Caillard to Hewins, 19 Oct. 1903, 46/71–2, HP.

out, it would not at that stage be possible to carry it through the House of Commons'.[13]

On 2 November Caillard introduced Hewins to Pearson, who thereafter acted as go-between with Highbury, and who told Chamberlain of Hewins's view on the need to draw up a detailed tariff after his Bingley Hall speech.[14] They probably decided to make an informal invitation to Hewins to administer the proposed commission on 4 or 5 November, since on the 5th Pearson twice telegraphed Hewins stressing the urgency of a meeting that evening.[15] Chamberlain received an indication of Hewins's willingness almost immediately:

I . . . greatly appreciate your readiness to undertake the heavy task I have suggested. I do not know what is the state of the finances of the Tariff Reform League, but subject to there being sufficient I should think there would be no difficulty in regard to remuneration. But I must confess that I am a little concerned to find that you think it necessary to break your connection with the school which is really your creation and which has done so much good work.[16]

Though Chamberlain considered that the new position 'by the necessity of the case can only be temporary', Hewins had bigger ideas. At meetings with Caillard, Pearson and now Leverton Harris, shipowner and close friend of Austen Chamberlain, he sought to stress the scale of the operation that was being contemplated. The result was a long and detailed *modus operandi* that Pearson carried to Highbury on 12 November and Chamberlain endorsed.[17] Pearson thereupon wrote to Hewins on TRL notepaper personally guaranteeing a salary of £1,200 p.a. for four years.[18]

In a letter to Hewins on 16 November, in which he outlined the purpose of the new 'private commission . . . of practical . . . experts in Agriculture, Commerce, and Manufacture' in very similar terms to those of the Leeds speech a month later, Chamberlain laid claim to having had the original idea,[19] just as Pearson was to do over a decade later. But, as has been shown, he seems to have come late into the matter. Indeed, it certainly seems that it was Hewins's enthusiasm that carried the Commission into being with so few setbacks.

Above we have seen how the Tariff Reformers were to concede the Free Trade point that the Commission, composed of supporters of a Chamberlainite policy, was not impartial in the matter of deciding between Free Trade and protection, and to make a virtue of necessity by arguing that it was perfectly

---

[13] W. A. S. Hewins, *Apologia*, i. 73–4.
[14] 'My Connection with the Fiscal Controversy', 34.
[15] Pearson to Hewins (two telegrams), 5 Nov. 1903, HP.
[16] Chamberlain to Hewins, 7 Nov. 1903, HP.
[17] 'My Connection with the Fiscal Controversy', 34; W. A. S. Hewins, *Apologia*, i. 75–6 gives a shortened version of this document.
[18] Pearson to Hewins, 14 Nov. 1903, HP.
[19] Chamberlain to Hewins, 16 Nov. 1903, HP

proper for the advocates of scientific protection to draft a tariff so that the nation could judge.[20] Free Traders may have considered this argument specious, but Chamberlain's concern over 'the association of [his] name with the Commission' suggests that at the outset it was envisaged that the Commission would have a high degree of independence:

He is willing, and indeed anxious, that [the Commission] should be connected with him as closely as possible, but he forsees difficulties which we did not consider the other day, the main one being that if he really connects himself with the Commission in such a capacity as president, he feels he would be more or less bound by the conclusions arrived at.[21]

II

By 18 December, the date of Hewins's formal resignation from the LSE, Sidney Webb had already known he would be leaving for about a month.[22] In that time, there had been considerable preparatory exploration into possible members. By 19 November the organizers thought they could count on Sir Andrew Noble of Armstrong, Whitworth & Co.; A. W. Maconochie MP of Maconochie Bros.; Sir William Lewis, the famous coal-owner; Sir Alfred Jones of Elder, Dempster & Co.; Sir Charles Tennant of United Alkali; and Sir Alexander Henderson MP, stockbroker. To these were soon added Richard Burbidge of Harrod's Stores; Alfred Mosely, just returned from heading his own unofficial commission into US education; John Corah, the Leicester hosiery manufacturer; and Sir Alfred Hickman MP, the prominent ironmaster. Even with some of these there lay uncertainty, significant since the organizers were reluctant to send invitations to unwilling businessmen lest their opponents made political capital out of any refusal. Indeed, of a list of 'probables' drafted by Pearson, eight out of twelve were not destined to serve—Cosmo Bonsor of Watney, Combe, Reid & Co.; Willie Coats of J. & P. Coats, the sewing-thread amalgamation; Rider Haggard, novelist and active in agricultural politics; Inglis Palgrave, the banker and financial journalist; Sir Charles Cayzer MP, of the Cayzer-Irvine and Clan shipping lines; Sir Ernest Cassel, a banker of German extraction and a close associate of Caillard in Egyptian finance; Lord Duncannon; and William Berry of the Royal Niger Company. With a further list of 'People whose view I wish you [Hewins] would endeavour to discover' Pearson had even less success, only three out of thirteen (S. J. Waring of Waring & Gillow; Charles Parsons, inventor of the steam turbine; and J. J. Keswick, late of Jardine Matheson & Co.) subsequently agreeing to serve. Among others on this list, little or nothing more

[20] See above, Ch. 1.
[21] Pearson to Hewins, 14 Nov. 1903, HP.
[22] W. A. S. Hewins, *Apologia*, i. 77.

was heard of a Mr Callard, 'the big Banking Man'; Sir George Mackenzie, explorer and retired director of the British India Steam Navigation Co. and the Imperial British East Africa Co.; W. J. Pirrie of Harland and Wolff; Lord Iveagh, chairman of Guinness; George Trollope, the London builder and contractor; and Lord Iddesleigh, who had headed the Royal Commission on the Depression of Trade and Industry in the 1880s.[23]

Chamberlain, who took on the task of sending formal invitations, was 'particularly anxious not to write to anyone unless it is quite certain that they are favourable to his policy'.[24] He certainly did not follow blindly the advice of the London organizers, being 'a little doubtful' not only about Palgrave but also about Sheffield steelmaker Charles Allen, who was subsequently to become a stalwart of the Commission.[25] Lord Cawdor's position was doubtful, Lord Strathcona was unwilling to accept because 'he had not heard yet from his folk'.[26] Coats and Noble had still not replied to letters. For someone of Pearson's temperament, the uncertainties on every side were exasperating:

I suppose you have not found out about Lord Iveagh. Mr. Chamberlain is very keen upon him. He is writing to Mr. Burbidge. He says that he has been told that Cosmo Bonsor is doubtful. Didn't you say he was all right? He thinks Ernest Cassel better left out. He is writing to Palgrave, Keswick, Mosely and Sir Walter Peace.[27]

One exception to this uncertainty was Charles Booth. He had probably known Hewins for many years through the connection of Beatrice Webb and the LSE with the London studies, and had already written an article in the *National Review* endorsing Tariff Reform.[28] Booth was probably approached because of his expression of sympathy with Hewins's motives in leaving the LSE, and he took little time to make up his mind to serve. Whereas in most cases the organizers were intent on secrecy, in Booth's case they were only too willing for early publicity, with Pearson making arrangements for Booth to issue a statement to the *Daily Express* and Chamberlain requesting a statement from the social investigator for use in the forthcoming Leeds speech. The latter, however, Chamberlain found 'not suitable for a big popular audience', and the version he used on the platform was diluted, being confined to the assertion that Booth considered the welfare of the poor better served by prosperous trade than by cheap food.[29]

[23] Pearson to Hewins, 19 Nov. 1903, 6/1/26, TCP.

[24] Pearson to Hewins, 2 Dec. 1903, 6/1/26, TCP.

[25] Pearson to Hewins, 19 Nov. 1903, 6/1/26, TCP.

[26] Pearson to Hewins, 28 Nov. 1903, 6/1/26, TCP.

[27] Ibid.

[28] Charles Booth, 'Fiscal Reform', *National Review*, 42 (1903–4), 686–701.

[29] 'My Connection with the Fiscal Controversy', 35; Pearson to Hewins, 28 and 30 Nov. 1903, (two letters) 6/1/26, TCP; Chamberlain at Leeds, 16 Dec. 1903, in *Sheffield Daily Telegraph*, 17 Dec. 1903, 7–8.

Though not unique, Booth's path onto the Commission was unusually smooth. In other cases, however, a welter of detail survives to show how, by the end of November, the process of selection and acceptance had almost degenerated into confusion. Even some of those to whom the organizers of the Commission had considered it safe to make an approach had either not replied or had equivocated.

This uncertainty and confusion testifies less to the opinions of businessmen on the fiscal issue than it does to the initial impact of the campaign on the business community. Very few of the industrialists whose names survive in the records of the Commission as having been considered or approached, but who subsequently did not serve, are known to have been Free Traders—W. J. Pirrie was rather the exception. The explanation lies much more in the fact that businessmen were as unprepared for Chamberlain's 'great inquiry' as was the public in general, in spite of the immediacy of their involvement in it. Given the complexity of the fiscal issue, indeed, some may not have yet made up their minds upon it. But, more than that, the early Edwardian years lie squarely within Cornford's period of transition, wherein the business vote transferred heavily from the Liberal to the Conservative Party.[30] Many businessmen still with Liberal Imperialist leanings, even perhaps some who had made the more distinct transition to Liberal Unionism, must have felt their allegiance torn between Rosebery and Chamberlain.[31] Others, more solidly Conservative in their political leanings, might have been reluctant to spend the time, even though in sympathy with the Commission's aims, firstly because of their commitment to their own firm and secondly because the enquiry was the child of a faction within the Unionist Party rather than of official Unionist policy. Equally important were those who felt that it was inexpedient, even improper, to mix party politics with business; certainly, as we shall see, this was a position commonly adopted in the Chambers of Commerce, while some Tariff Commissioners, notably those from the Free-Trade citadel of Manchester, had initial doubts about joining a quasi-official body whose objects ran counter to the opinions which prevailed in their own local business environments, or even within their own firms.[32] Thus it was that those who did know their own minds were not always prepared to reveal their views to a quick-acting, impulsive newspaperman like Pearson:

In the choice of the right people to serve on the Commission, Pearson was continually annoyed by the difficulty of finding out whether this man or that was really a Protectionist or a Free Trader. He himself always knew what he believed and what he did not believe,

[30] J. Cornford, 'The Transformation of Conservatism in the Late Nineteenth Century', *Victorian Studies*, 7 (1963–4), 35–66.

[31] See the Chamberlainite press's remarks about Commissioner J. J. Candlish, who had '[a]nnounced himself in favour of Tariff Reform, but still holds to his Liberal principles'; *Sheffield Daily Telegraph*, 18 Dec. 1903, 8.

[32] Esp. Ivan Levinstein and Charles Eckersley.

and he never had any patience with the Laodicean. In this connection the following characteristic little outburst occurs in one of his letters to Mr. Chamberlain: 'Really the difficulty of getting accurate information about how people think is appalling.'[33]

Though the Commission attempted to vet candidates and rule out those likely to refuse so that its credibility and authority were not undermined, mistakes were inevitable. Bonsor, Coats, Strathcona, Palgrave, Sir Edward Clarke, and, probably, Sir William Houldsworth, chairman of the Fine Cotton Spinners' and Doublers' Association, were all invited, but declined to serve. Clarke gave as his reason that the Commission was 'too political'.[34] It should be stressed, however, that many of those industrialists mentioned in the exchanges between Hewins, Pearson, and Chamberlain who did not serve were, or were subsequently to be, active supporters of Tariff Reform. Sir Ernest Cassel made heavy contributions to the TRL and the Tariff Commission, while Sir William Houldsworth was chairman of the Manchester branch of the TRL. Rider Haggard was an active proponent of agricultural protection. Furthermore, though nothing more was heard of Bonsor and Trollope, their companies supplied others to sit on the Commission—C. J. Phillips and Howard Colls.

The need for secrecy determined that the organizers used their wide net of political and industrial acquaintances to search for members. After the Leeds speech and into January, by which time most of the best-known industrial appointments had already been made,[35] this need became less, but personal knowledge and contact still counted for much. Overall, there was certainly no shortage of aspirant Commissioners, and a major problem was to thin them down. The organizers estimated that there were some 600 or 800 distinct trades within the UK, and, as Chamberlain observed at the inaugural meeting on 15 January, it was impossible to include them all.[36] Log-rolling met with variable success. Chairman Sir Robert Herbert failed to get a representative of the printing industry included, but the agricultural engineers were more successful. It is worthwhile to quote Hewins at length:

Aveling and Porter of Rochester are keen Radicals, and no good for our purpose. Of the rest on the list, Davey, Paxman & Co., Robey & Co., Henry Gwynne; R. & W. Hawthorne; Thwaites Bros.; are all thoroughly represented by Henry Marshall. Dick, Kerr & Co., with George Flett as their representative, would clear satisfactorily the whole of the electrical department . . . With regard to the agricultural [machinery side] . . . Mr. W. Harrison, the President of the Agricultural Engineers' Association, and head of the firm of Harrison, MacGregor & Co., of Leigh, Lancs., has been down today specially to see me on the situation. I think he has made out a completely satisfactory case for

---

[33] S. Dark, *Life of Sir Arthur Pearson* (n.d.), 108.
[34] Chamberlain to Lord Granby, 27 Dec. 1903, JC/18/18/69, JCP.
[35] See the lists of new members published in the *Sheffield Daily Telegraph* on 18, 19, 20, and 30 Dec. 1903 and 13 Jan. 1904 in turn.
[36] Reported in *Sheffield Daily Telegraph*, 16 Jan. 1904, 9.

representation on the Commission; . . . all the firms [in agricultural engineering] are keenly desiours that somebody should be on the Commission to represent them . . . there is unanimous desire that Henry Marshall or, failing him, Ransome, should be on, and also Harrison himself. There are several reasons why this should be granted. First of all, the Trade is a large trade which is heavily hit by foreign competition; secondly, Harrison, MacGregor & Co. are household words throughout the agricultural districts . . . the inclusion of Mr. Harrison would beyond all question, be regarded as adding to the agricultural representation on the Commission to a very considerable extent. This is of course important from a political point of view. I feel very much inclined to press the claims of Mr. Harrison to be included. I told him that Marshall had already been invited, and I further told him that the points he had put before me this afternoon should be laid before Mr. Chamberlain.

With regard to the textile machinery and other specialised branches, I scarcely think it is necessary to do anything. The makers of textile machinery of course do a considerable export trade with foreign countries. They may have something to gain by the lowering of foreign tariffs, but I gather that they are not likely to make any move at present for representation on the Commission on their own initiative. Agricultural machinery really stands apart and deserves special consideration.[37]

This shows clearly the effort to maximize the representation of trades and industries whilst at the same time keeping the size of the Commission to a minimum. The correct choice of a 'representative man', with wide and varied business interests and experience, could be regarded as representing a whole trade group. Thus Pearson clung to the opinion that Marshall was sufficient for agricultural engineering, and that he and Flett, the electrical engineer, would satisfactorily complete the representation of the engineering industry,[38] given the inclusion of Caillard, Sir Andrew Noble, and Arthur Keen. In the event, however, Hewins, or rather Harrison, got his way. Hewins's advocacy of Harrison was by his own admission partly on the grounds that his inclusion would be looked on favourably in the farming districts, at a time when the Tariff Reformers were far from sure how heavily they could count on the farmer's support because of the element of imperial preference in Chamberlain's scheme.[39] Indeed, if agricultural engineering stood to become over-represented on the Commission, agriculture itself stood in danger of being under-represented. As prominent as Chaplin was in national farming circles, he represented most closely the landowning aristocracy and the eastern grainlords. The difficulty was one of representing the farming regions adequately with one or two extra appointments, since Chamberlain thought it impossible

[37] Hewins to Pearson, 24 Dec. 1903, 6/1/26, TCP.
[38] Pearson to Hewins, 24 Dec. 1903, 6/1/26, TCP.
[39] A. J. Marrison, 'The Tariff Commission, Agricultural Protection and Food Taxes, 1903–1913', *Agricultural History Review*, 34 (1986), 173–5.

to have four agricultural representatives on the Commission.[40] John Dennis, who belonged to an important family firm of farmers, potato growers, and potato merchants which also did a brokerage business in English and foreign fruit and vegetables at Covent Garden, and W. H. Grenfell MP (later Lord Desborough), a member of the prominent family of merchant bankers and owner of 3,200 acres in Buckinghamshire, were subsequently appointed, but the problem was only properly solved by the creation of an agricultural sub-committee.[41]

In one area, however, the founders of the Commission would have been only too pleased to increase the number of members. Correctly anticipating that the movement would be criticized if there were no attempts to secure the support of the representatives of organized labour, Chaplin had arranged as early as August an interview with Thomas Ashton, chairman of the Amalgamated Association of Cotton Operatives, but he had to be content with the rather vague expressions of sympathy and support which the Lancashire workers felt for the architect of workmen's compensation, and the promise that Ashton's members would receive Chamberlain's proposals with an 'open mind'.[42] Ashton was not approached again when the decision to form the Commission was taken. One labour representative, James Macdonald, secretary of the London Trades Council, was invited onto the Commission by Chamberlain himself, an act which appalled Mosely, who had included him on his own industrial commission to the US in 1902 and regretted it.[43] After consulting his executive Macdonald declined the position, a decision which the Commission managed to keep secret.[44] This was fortunate, since, being unable to secure a trade union representative, Chamberlain was subsequently to argue in public that Free Trade criticism on such grounds was misplaced:

another great complaint has been made, that labour as such is not represented on the Commission. I think this is partly due to a misapprehension. On this Commission trades are represented, but not classes, and as I have pointed out, I deny absolutely any distinction between classes in reference to the interests of trade.[45]

[40] Pearson to Hewins, 26 Dec. 1903, 6/1/26, TCP.

[41] A. J. Marrison, 'British Businessmen and the "Scientific" Tariff: A Study of Joseph Chamberlain's Tariff Commission, 1903–1921', unpubl. Ph. D. thesis, Univ. of Hull, 1980, 370–382.

[42] Memo of conversation between Ashton and Chaplin, 30 Aug. [1903], JC/18/18/25, JCP.

[43] Macdonald had neglected to submit his report on the US visit upon his return to the UK; Mosely Industrial Commission to the United States of America, *Reports of the Delegates* (Manchester, 1903), 6.

[44] Hewins confided to his diary that, after deciding not to serve on the Tariff Commission, Macdonald 'went [to the *Daily Express* offices] dead drunk and when Pearson asked him to hand over his correspondence with Chamberlain he did so without a word'. 'My Connection with the Fiscal Controversy', 35.

[45] Chamberlain at the first meeting of the Tariff Commission, in *Sheffield Daily Telegraph*, 16 Jan. 1904, 9.

Whilst this approach was consistent with the Tariff Reformers' stress on the importance of business prosperity to the worker, the primacy of the individual-as-producer over the individual-as-consumer, it concealed the hypocrisy evident in Chamberlain's attempt to recruit Macdonald. Hewins, also, sought to maintain this façade in one of his frequent anonymous contributions to the editorial columns of the *Morning Post*. He remarked contemptuously that 'it might no doubt have been well from the electioneering standpoint to include some prominent "Labour leader" in the Commission', but pointed out that in his desire to formulate a scientific tariff Chamberlain 'does not care in the least where the evidence comes from':

As a matter of fact it would have been perfectly easy to include any number of labour representatives . . . Mr CHAMBERLAIN's commission has not been constructed on the basis of class representation or the idea of currying favour with any group of 'interests'. If any working man has figures at his command which will guide the commission in formulating a fair tariff his evidence will be welcomed. Whatever decisions are reached by the commission must obviously be referred to working men for their approval, and no tariff can ever be adopted which does not win their support . . . The criticisms of the Free Traders are based on the idea that the 'Labour interest' should be represented as such. If that idea is accepted we must have employers' associations, railway interests, middle-class interests, investors' interests, and so on represented. Mr. CHAMBERLAIN will not accept this view of the constitution of his commission. He rightly insists on the solidarity of the British community, and wants the men who can give the data he requires because they are recorded in the accounts of which they have custody.[46]

III

Two of the most widely read writers on the fiscal alignments within British industry during the Edwardian period have seen support for Tariff Reform as being concentrated within a narrow band of industries. Evidently in sympathy with Churchill's fear that if the Tariff Reformers were successful the Conservatives would become 'a party of great vested interests',[47] Bernard Semmel's analysis of the economic interests of the Tariff Commission, in his influential *Imperialism and Social Reform*, postulates what virtually amounts to a 'conspiracy' thesis. He particularly mentions the four representatives of the iron and steel industry on the Commission, and then goes on to list a heterogeneous group of representatives of meat-packing, armaments, glass manufacturing, electrical engineering, building and contracting, and chemicals.[48] These ten, selected from the list of fifty-nine members, lead Semmel to conclude that: 'Iron and steel, tin,

---

[46] *Morning Post* (editorial), 16 Jan. 1904.
[47] Quoted in B. Semmel, *Imperialism and Social Reform*, 100.
[48] Charles Allen of Sir Henry Bessemer & Co., Sir Alfred Hickman, Arthur Keen of GKN, and Sir William T. Lewis. It should be noted that Lewis had larger interests in coal than in iron and steel.

building materials, glass and chemicals, all midlands products hard hit by German and American competition. These interests constituted the heart of the Commission and of the [Tariff Reform] League itself.'[49]

In some senses, Richard Rempel is even more bold than Semmel. Concentrating on the opposition to Tariff Reform rather than the support for it, he slightly confuses the issue by discussing the views of the workforce as well. Nevertheless, his overall message is clear enough:

The major reason for the failure of Chamberlain's campaign was that, apart from iron and steel, the major industries in the country still prospered under free trade . . . Even in the iron industry itself there was no solidarity behind Chamberlain . . . Indeed, the only groups completely supporting Chamberlain were the clearly declining industries such as silk [and linen], badly hit by competition at home and badly desiring simple protection.[50]

Cotton remained 'particularly strong in its commitment to free trade', whilst coal 'remained unshaken in its attachment'. The interests of shipping and shipbuilding 'remained largely bound up with free trade', as did those of their 'kindred' industry, engineering. Rempel thus musters a considerable Free Trade support; it is therefore curious that, citing Semmel approvingly, he should conclude that 'the Tariff Reformers had most of the heavy industry interests'.[51]

Behind these two analyses lies a common and widely accepted approach. There is a long-established tradition amongst historians that businessmen's support for free trade or protectionist policies can be analysed according to determinist considerations. We are used to dividing industries into two camps, a 'free trade interest' and a 'protectionist interest', and to making the assumption that, historically, they have acted according to a 'given' interest, an interest at once real, obvious, and unambiguous. 'Cosmopolitan' business groups, such as bankers, financiers, merchants, and manufacturers with a high degree of export orientation, have traditionally been seen as supporting free trade, whilst 'nationalist' groups, mostly manufacturers without large export markets and perhaps with home markets vulnerable to foreign competition, have been regarded as the typical centres of protectionist sentiment. As Michael S. Smith observes of France after 1860:

one could say that the conflict on the tariff was part of a struggle between two mutually exclusive capitalist communities seeking to project French economic development in opposite directions . . . between cosmopolitan commercial capitalists, striving to integrate

---

[49] *Imperialism and Social Reform*, 102. Semmel further notes (102) that 'Woollen goods and cotton goods had no representation upon the Commission'. In fact there were two cotton men (Frederick Baynes and Charles Eckersley) and one worsted spinner and manufacturer (W. H. Mitchell), in addition to the Commission's later established Textile Committee.
[50] R. A. Rempel, *Unionists Divided* (Newton Abbot, 1972), 97.
[51] Ibid. 97, 98, 101, 104.

France into the world economy, and nationalistic industrial capitalists, striving to make France economically self-sufficient.[52]

Such explanations are widespread and familiar, not only in the literature on France but also in that on Germany and the USA, and other examples need not be documented here. But their application to the British Tariff Reform movement needs to be handled with care. Hilferding and Schumpeter, whose distinction between cosmopolitan and nationalist interests forms the basis of such analyses of differences over tariff policy, knew well that there was less close an alliance between 'high finance and the cartel magnates' in Britain before 1913 than there was elsewhere. Subsequent research has confirmed that the merger movement was relatively limited and did not involve finance capital on the German or American scale.[53] Hence the confusing tendency for finance capital to espouse protectionist causes because of its links with manufacturing industry, acting 'in the actual interest of only a *small* proportion [of capitalists] and, indeed, . . . sometimes not even in the interests of capital as such at all', becomes less important in the British case, and Schumpeter's 'typical and fundamental' conflict between capitalists and entrepreneurs is maintained.[54]

At this level, it would seem that Britain offered the conditions for a more straightforward application of the Schumpeterian divide than did other countries before the First World War. This is largely illusory, however. In the context in which he used it, Schumpeter's 'typical and fundamental' conflict presupposed that all manufacturing industries should be protectionist by interest and instinct.[55] The mid-nineteenth-century tariff history of the countries which Schumpeter principally had in mind usually supports this. Taussig's classic study of the antebellum US tariff found no industrial support for the powerful free trade lobby of merchants and raw cotton exporters, even non-cotton farmers being protectionist, whilst List's *National System* was a broad appeal based on the 'productive powers' of industry. Furthermore, what appear in some of the tariff histories as 'free-trade' manufacturing interests were usually only interested in

---

[52] M. S. Smith, *Tariff Reform in France 1860–1900* (Ithaca, NY, 1980), 148. Export-orientated manufacturers are included with cosmopolitan commercial capitalists in Smith's classification of free trade interests (149).

[53] R. Hilferding, *Finance Capital: A Study of the Latest Phase of Capitalist Development* (1st Austrian edn., Vienna, 1910; Eng. edn., ed. T. Bottomore, Transl. M. Watnick and S. Gordon, 1981), esp. ch. 21; J. A. Schumpeter, *Imperialism and Social Classes* (Oxford, 1951), 106; L. Davis, 'The Capital Markets and Industrial Concentration: The US and UK, a Comparative Study', *Economic History Review*, 19 (1966) 255–72; L. Hannah, *The Rise of the Corporate Economy* (1976), 24–5.

[54] Schumpeter, *Imperialism and Social Classes*, 106–7 (original emphasis).

[55] Schumpeter underlines this. Entrepreneurs 'are benefitted only by the tariff that happens to be levied on their own product. But this advantage is substantially reduced by the countermeasures adopted by other countries . . . and by the effect of the tariff on the prices of other articles, especially those which they require for their own productive process. Why, then, are entrepreneurs so strongly in favour of protective tariffs? The answer is simple. Each industry hopes to score *special* gains in the struggle of political intrigue, thus enabling it to realize a net gain'. Ibid. 103 (original emphasis).

promoting tariff moderacy: in Europe and American free-trade agitation was of a relativist kind.[56] Even in the hegemonic Britain of the 1830s and 1840s, less prey to infant industry sentiment, we must be careful of the textbook view of manufacturers joining the political economists in the vanguard of the free-trade movement. Ship-owning and agriculture may have been entrenched defenders of protection, but it does not appear that their stance was as isolated as is often assumed. McGregor and the Select Committee on the Export of Machinery had to admit that, in certain other industries also, opinion was predominantly hostile to a change of system. Generally, the Committee gave 'a misleading impression of the extent of the support which they actually enjoyed'. Apathy, sometimes hostility, was the order of the day. 'In formulating a general criticism of the tariff it would seem that the Board of Trade was leading a new movement of opinion, rather than expressing one which was already there'.[57]

This is not to suggest that, in the early 1900s, we should expect that general predisposition towards protection among British manufacturers that Schumpeter considered typical elsewhere. The mere occurrence of free trade gave the question a historical dimension. But the fact that other scholars have, essentially, grafted the criterion of export orientation onto the cosmopolitan–nationalist divide results in the Schumpeterian model losing its power of explanation, and raises in a much more empirical way the question of which particular industries were protectionist and which were Free Trade. Furthermore, to recall Schumpeter's original formulation is to remind ourselves that he, at least, considered that the manufacturing community had an inbuilt predisposition to protectionism. If true, this raises the possibility that, even in the untypical British case, attitudinal changes might have been highly sensitive to changes in circumstance.

From the complementary writings of Semmel and Rempel, we can compile a composite view of the 'interests' in the British Tariff Reform controversy. To the objection that this composite is artificial, it can be answered that Rempel's acceptance and endorsement of Semmel's earlier work has been noticed by other scholars.[58] On the Free Trade side Rempel includes cotton, coal, shipping and shipbuilding, and engineering. Semmel would apparently add woollen manufacture to this list. On the protectionist side we have iron and steel, tin, building materials, glass and chemicals, as well as meat-packing, armaments, and electrical engineering. We are told that these industries not only supported Tariff Reform, but also that they lay at the centre of it.[59]

---

[56] F. W. Taussig, *Tariff History of the United States* (1st edn., New York, 1888), esp. 70–6; F. List, *The National System of Political Economy* (1904 edn.), esp. 156 and chs. 26–7; M. S. Smith, *Tariff Reform, passim.*

[57] L. Brown, *The Board of Trade and the Free Trade Movement 1830–42* (Oxford, 1958), 181–3. See also A. E. Musson, 'The "Manchester School" and Exportation of Machinery', *Business History*, 14 (1972), 17–50.

[58] See P. F. Clarke's review of *Unionists Divided* in *English Historical Review*, 89 (1974), 688–9.

[59] See B. Semmel, *Imperialism and Social Reform*, 103 for the inclusion of woollens.

How valid, however, is the claim that industrial interest and business opinion in the Tariff Reform controversy can be classified with such broad and bold strokes? Can industries always be marshalled into huge, cohesive blocs? Already, in the above composite, armaments and electrical engineering have been separated from the rest of the engineering trades and placed in the protectionist camp. It would seem that industries need to be examined for internal divisions along product or market lines.[60] Secondly, even within the more narrowly defined industry-group, how far should we expect unanimity of opinion? When examining smaller groups such as the Unionist Free Traders or the members of the House of Commons, Rempel freely acknowledges many exceptions. Is deviation from economic determinism merely the prerogative of the politically active? In any case, economic determinism cannot simply imply that men act out of their own self-interest: rather, it must mean that they act according to their own *perception* of what their particular economic interest is. Often, no doubt, the two coincide clearly. But the Tariff Reform debate was not simply a controversy over short-term economic interests and objectives: occuring in the context of Britain's industrial retardation, it involved fundamentally different perceptions and interpretations of the desirable and the probable path of Britain's long-term development over the next 50 or even 100 years.[61] Under such conditions even partners in the same firm might have had different conceptions and made different predictions. And thirdly, closely related to this point but analytically separable from it, the existence of an imperial element in Chamberlain's scheme, with its surrounding political motives and objectives, may have tended both to confuse and to modify a simple determinist stance. There are infinite variations, from complete incongruity to perfect complementarity, in which profit and patriotism can be combined, as was shown by that group of contributors to the newspaper debate who argued that it might be worth trading off the economic benefits of Free Trade for the sake of imperial unity.[62]

Any discussion of economic interest in the Tariff Reform campaign needs to distinguish between two issues: the role of economic interest in explaining the allegiance of individuals and parties actively participating in it, and the stance of particular industries on the fiscal question generally. The broader of these issues will be the concern of later parts of this work,[63] but it would seem sensible to

---

[60] See M. S. Smith, *Tariff Reform*, as a model in this respect, and my review of it in *Business History*, 24 (1982), 121–3.

[61] The best analyses of the long term by Tariff Reformers were contained in W. J. Ashley, *The Tariff Problem* (1903); V. H. P. Caillard, 'Foreign Trade'; and in Hewins's 16 articles in *The Times* between June and Sept. 1903, all entitled 'The Fiscal Policy of the Empire'.

[62] A. J. Marrison, 'The Development of a Tariff Reform Policy during Joseph Chamberlain's First Campaign', in W. H. Chaloner and B. M. Ratcliffe (eds.), *Trade and Transport: Essays in Economic History in Honour of T. S. Willan* (Manchester, 1977), 223.

[63] See below, esp. Chs. 3 and 10.

begin with the narrower, by discussing industrial representation on the Tariff Commission in the light of Semmel's analysis of it.

IV

A systematic examination of the business representation on the Tariff Commission illustrates certain difficulties that stand in the way of precise categorization, notably those of sources of income and overlapping interests. Certainly, businessmen were heavily represented. If we classify the members into four groups—agricultural, industrial and commercial, imperial, and miscellaneous—we find the second to be by far the largest, comprising forty-seven out of the fifty-nine original members. It is necessary to point out that some members overlapped even these large categories, as with John Dennis, who combined farming with merchandizing of farm produce, or Sir William Lewis, who had interests in both coal and tinplate. More importantly, six of the eight 'imperial' members had (discovered) interests in industry and commerce, whilst several 'industrial–commercial' members had some kind of interest in colonial enterprise.

Ideally, an analysis of economic interest needs to take account of source(s) of income and proportion of income from each source. Since we are denied access to Inland Revenue information, our data are far from perfect and often impressionistic.[64] Obviously this is unimportant for 'single-interest' Commissioners, those who derived their income from only one source. But only thirteen of the forty-seven industrial–commercial members seem to fit this category clearly: J. M. Harris, bacon curing; C. J. Phillips, brewing; F. Tonsley, baking and confectionery; W. H. Mitchell, worsted spinning and manufacturing; J. A. Corah, hosiery; F. Elgar, shipbuilding; W. Harrison, agricultural engineering; H. Bostock, boots and shoes; L. Evans, paper making; W. Cooper, meat wholesaling; C. A. Pearson, newspapers; A. Mosely, diamond merchant; and I. Levinstein, dyestuffs. It should be stressed that inclusion in this single-interest group necessarily rests on the negative proof that no further interests have been discovered, and that we are obliged to assume that income from the interest specified was not overshadowed by investment or property income from accumulated family wealth.

The remaining thirty-four industrial–commercial members are less clear-cut cases in that they possessed dual or multiple interests (sometimes within the same

---

[64] The main sources for this examination are 'Members of the Commission', in *Report of the Tariff Commission*, i. *The Iron and Steel Trades*, (1904), para. 1; 'Members of the Tariff Commission', 8/2/17, TCP; *Who Was Who*, i–iv; H. H. Bassett (ed.), *Men of Business at Home and Abroad 1912–1913*, (n.d.); T. Skinner, *Directory of Directors* (1904 and 1905 edns). These have been supplemented with other sources. More detailed biographical treatment of the 59 Commissioners than space here allows can be found in A. J. Marrison, 'British Businessmen and the "Scientific" Tariff', App. 1.

Table 1. *Multiple-Interest Commissioners: Straightforward Cases*

	Primary Interest	Secondary Interest
Charles Lyle	sugar-refining	steam-shipping
A. W. Maconochie	meat-packing	tinplate
Joseph Rank	flour-milling	oil-milling
Thomas Gallaher	tobacco	steam-shipping
Charles Allen	steel	iron and coal; banking
Alfred Hickman	iron and steel	coal; property-development
Charles Eckersley	cotton-spinning	coal
R. H. Reade	flax-spinning	railways
H. D. Marshall	agricultural-engineering	coal
Alfred Jones	shipowning	banking; importing; oil-milling; coal; cotton-growing; mining and quarrying; railways
W. Bridges Webb	grain-importing	insurance
Howard Colls	building	interior decorating; cabinet-making
W. H. Goulding	agricultural chemical	railways; docks

firm or group of associated firms), but with thirteen of them it seems fairly clear that those interests can be readily divided into major and minor components, as shown in Table 1. Such interests as railway directorships and involvement in shipping lines can be regarded as subsidiary. Sometimes such minor interests were internal to the firm, as with Gallaher and Lyle,[65] whilst at others they were external, for it was common for businessmen to become involved in local and even national transport concerns by accepting directorships which imparted prestige to both sides of the compact. Two iron and steel representatives, Allen and Keen, held bank directorships, but they were essentially local and it is likely that they saw them as complementary to, and not in conflict with, their industrial interests. Thus, though railways, shipping, and banking might appear on the cosmopolitan, Free Trade side of the fiscal balance, such directorships would have been unlikely to constitute a significant economic interest for industrialists of the stature of most Commission members.[66] Furthermore, it seems clear that in many other cases additional interests were even more directly subordinate to the main one, as with Maconochie's tinning and tinplate concern, Joseph Rank's involvement in oil-milling,[67] Charles Eckersley's very marginal and Henry Marshall's somewhat stronger connection with coal-mining, and Howard Colls's minor interest in interior decorating inherited from the Trollope side of the

---

[65] Though Abraham Lyle & Co. had developed from a shipowning firm; G. Fairrie, *The Sugar Refining Families of Great Britain* (priv. publ., 1951).

[66] For support, see M. Robbins, *The Railway Age* (Harmondsworth, 1965), 76–9.

[67] Rank regarded oil milling as a 'diversion' and 'little more than a challenge to his business abilities'. See H. Janes, *The Master Millers* (priv. publ., 1955), 37.

merger of 1903.[68] Alfred Jones's multifarious activities in West Africa and the Caribbean were virtually all through wholly- or partly-owned subsidiaries of Elder, Dempster.[69]

The remaining twenty-one industrial–commercial Commissioners were interested in two or more distinctly different branches of activity. Even where such distinctions existed within the same firm, we cannot be sure of the proportion of direct personal income which accrued from each branch. In some cases it seems fairly safe to divide such interests into primary and secondary interests. Frederick Baynes's partnership in a cotton merchant business may have developed merely as a device for placing the products of his own mills with export merchants.[70] Sir Samuel Boulton's timber-importing business was presumably subsidiary to his chemicals business, which was largely tar-distilling. Though GKN's general engineering activities were growing in 1904 they were still minor compared with iron and steel,[71] Arthur Keen's main interest. Sir William Lewis's many interests in local South Wales railways, docks, water and electric utilities, insurance, iron and steel, and tinplate all seem to have been consequent on the development of his coal-mining interests, first as agent for the Bute estates and then as an independent colliery proprietor.[72] Directorships held by Sir Andrew Noble in oil, nickel, copper, and silver companies were minor compared with the chairmanship of Armstrong-Whitworth, which employed 22,400 in 1904. Alfred Gilbey's interest in the production of wines and spirits had developed considerably since the 1880s, but our impression is that *dealing* in those same commodities was still the main element in his firm's profits.[73]

But in other cases, even where different activities were carried on within the same firm, we can be less sure about the accuracy of such assessments. Though the late Professor John's study of Alfred Booth & Co. shows clearly the decline of leather-merchant business, it gives no very clear indication of the relative importance of steam shipping and (US) leather manufacturing for Charles Booth's personal income, though the general impression created is that the two were relatively equal in importance.[74] The very extent and variety of the trading,

[68] A. Tough, 'Colls, John Howard (1846–1910): Builder', in D. J. Jeremy (ed.), *Dictionary of Business Biography: A Biographical Directory of Business Leaders Active in Britain in the Period 1860–1980*, i. (1984), 743–6; Anon., *History of Trollope and Colls*, (priv. publ., n.d. but 1978).

[69] P. N. Davies, *Alfred Jones* (1978); and *The Trade Makers* (1973); A. H. Milne, *Sir Alfred Lewis Jones* (Liverpool, 1914).

[70] I am indebted to D. A. Farnie for this suggestion.

[71] D. Burn, *An Economic History of Steel-Making 1867–1939* (Cambridge, 1940), 224; J. C. Carr and W. Taplin, *A History of the British Steel Industry* (Oxford, 1962), 268.

[72] *DNB*; C. Wilkins, *History of the Iron, Steel, Tinplate and Other Trades of Wales* (Merthyr Tydfil, 1903); J. H. Morris and L. J. Williams, *The South Wales Coal Industry 1841–1875* (Cardiff, 1958), 128; W. E. Minchinton, *The British Tinplate Industry* (Oxford, 1957), 96–7.

[73] This is the impression gained from Sir Herbert Maxwell, *Half-A-Century of Successful Trade* (priv. publ., 1907).

[74] A. H. John, *A Liverpool Merchant House* (1959).

mining, and manufacturing interests of merchants and bankers Antony Gibbs & Sons in Latin America and Australia is sufficient to make an assessment of the precise origins of the components of Vicary Gibbs's income bewildering, except to say that they were channelled through one of the great mercantile houses of the nineteenth century.[75]

Those with dual or multiple interests in unconnected firms cause no less problems. Henry Birchenough's family silk firm suffered badly in the late nineteenth century,[76] but even at its peak it would have been a small concern compared with the Imperial Continental Gas Association, capitalized at nearly £6m in 1900, of which he was also a director.[77] Leverton Harris's links with the family firm of shipowners, Harris and Dixon Ltd., seems to have been fairly slight by 1904, on an administrative level at least, but it seems to have been this rather than his other interests in Indian coal-mining, the London discount market, and electricity supply that was the basis of his 'considerable fortune'.[78] Sir Alexander Henderson, in addition to being the head of an important stockbroking firm, had not surprisingly acquired significant investments in railway and canal companies.[79] Even Sir Charles Tennant, head of the huge St Rollox complex and president of United Alkali, may not be as straightforward as he appears. An adept speculator and company promoter, he had large interests in railways, oil companies, and insurance as well as in hugely profitable gold, sulphur, and copper extraction companies (though many of his mining ventures were tied to his chemicals business, they did not exist to supply St Rollox alone). Given Rubinstein's findings, which suggest that great wealth more readily accrued from trade and finance than from manufacturing in the nineteenth century, it may be wondered just how central was the ailing St Rollox to Tennant's personal fortune.[80] In a similar vein, Sir Vincent Caillard's long involvement in international finance and financial diplomacy should make us wary of identifying his personal economic interests too closely with Vickers. It is likely that the period

[75] J. A. Gibbs, *History of Antony and Dorothea Gibbs* (1922); D. C. M. Platt, *Latin America and British Trade 1806–1914* (1972), 138–9; R. Greenhill, 'Merchants and the Latin American Trades' and 'The Nitrate and Iodine Trades 1880–1914', in D. C. M. Platt (ed.), *Business Imperialism 1840–1930* (Oxford, 1977), 159–97, 231–83.

[76] *Report of the Tariff Commission*, ii. 6: *Evidence on the Silk Industry* (1905), paras. 3258–73.

[77] N. K. Hill, 'Accountancy Developments in a Public Utility Company in the Nineteenth Century', *Accounting Research*, 5 (1955), 328–9.

[78] In 1909–1910 Harris's active concern with wider aspects of the maritime trade was shown in his campaign against the Declaration of London. In the Great War he worked in the Trade Division of the Admiralty, the Foreign Office Department of Restriction of Enemy Supplies, and the Ministry of Blockades. See *DNB*.

[79] *Sheffield Daily Telegraph*, 18 Dec. 1903; D. A. Farnie, *The Manchester Ship Canal and the Rise of the Port of Manchester* (Manchester, 1980), 12–14. Around 1890 Henderson had an interest in the Shelton Iron and Steel Co. of North Staffordshire, but he may have shed this by 1906.

[80] N. Crathorne, *Tennant's Stalk* (1973), 131–47; see also W. D. Rubinstein, 'The Victorian Middle Classes: Wealth, Occupation, and Geography', *Economic History Review*, 30 (1977), 602–23.

1903–5 was one of transition in Caillard's economic interests as he rose to prominence within the firm, and no arbitrary division (such as that made in Table 2) can adequately reflect his position.[81]

This catalogue of imprecision is not offered by way of apology. Rather, it demonstrates the difficulty of making accurate assessments of direct personal

TABLE 2. *Tariff Commission Members With Significant Dual Interests: 1904–1905*

	Primary	Secondary
Frederick Baynes	cotton-manufacturing (FT)	cotton-shipping (FT)[a,b]; railways (FT)
J. H. Birchenough	silk-manufacturing (P)	fgn. gas utilities (FT); misc. colonial (IP)
Charles Booth	steam-shipping (FT)	fgn. leather production (FT); leather merchant (FT)
Sir S. B. Boulton	chemicals (P?)	timber-importing (FT)
Richard Burbidge	retail-trading (FT)	colonial-trading (IP)
Sir V. Caillard	international finance (FT) (*or*) arms engineering and shipbuilding (FT)	public utilities (FT); motor cars (P); explosives (?)
J. J. Candlish	glass bottles (P)	newspapers (FT)
John Dennis	wholesale produce (FT)	farming (P)
George Flett	electrical engineering and traction (P)	coachbuilding (?) rolling stock (FT); motor cars (P); electricity supply (FT)
Vicary Gibbs	merchanting and banking (FT)	insurance and finance (FT with some IP); nitrates and other minerals extraction (FT); fgn. land development (FT); misc. fgn. manufacturing (FT)
W. A. Gilbey	wines-and-spirits merchant (qual. FT)[c]	wines-and-spirits producer (qual. FT)
F. Leverton Harris	shipowning (FT)	electric utilities (FT); finance (FT); impl. coalmining (IP)
Sir A. Henderson	stockbroking (FT)	railways (FT); canals (FT); foreign investment (FT)
Arthur Keen	iron and steel (P)	engineering (subsid) (FT); fgn. iron ore (subsid) (FT); banking (FT)
Sir W. T. Lewis	coal-mining (FT)	iron, steel, tinplate (P); railways, docks, public utilities, insurance (FT)
Robert Littlejohn	impl. banking (IP?)	distribution & storage (IP?); tramways & property (IP?); mineral extraction (IP?)
Sir Andrew Noble	arms, engineering, and shipbuilding (FT)	oil, nickel, silver, copper extraction (FT); water utilities (FT)
Charles Parsons	electricity-generating equipment (P); marine engineering (FT)	electric utilities (FT); optical lenses (P?)

[81] Though Caillard became a director of Vickers on leaving the Ottoman Public Debt Council in 1898, his role in the company was probably relatively small until the death of Sigmund Loewe (effectively the company's financial controller) in 1903, but increased thereafter until he was made financial controller in 1906. But he remained a director of the National Bank of Egypt until 1908, and banking and finance may well have been his dominant interest in 1903–5. See *The Times*, 20 and 29 Mar. 1930; *DNB*; C. Trebilcock, *The Vickers Brothers* (1977), 45, 51; J. D. Scott, *Vickers: A History* (1962), 77–8, 92.

TABLE 2. (Continued)

Sir Charles Tennant	chemicals (P?)	oil, gold, sulphur & copper extraction (FT); railways, insurance, company promotion, banking (FT); explosives (?); iron and steel (P)
Sir John Turney	leather production (P)	light engineering (FT)
S. J. Waring	furniture-making (P)	furniture-retailing (FT); interior decorating (FT)

[a] FT = Free Trade, P = Protectionist, IP = Imperial Preference. It should be mentioned that IP is a difficult category: the mere fact that a businessman had, say, banking or mining interests in the Empire would not necessarily have given him a determinist interest in a policy of imperial preference.

[b] The categories FT, P, and IP are not meant to signify that the trade concerned, or even the individual Commission member, necessarily exhibited those sympathies. Rather, they are categories which a narrow determinist approach might lead us to expect.

[c] Qualified FT. (W. A. Gilbey). The liquor trade would, prima facie, have had an interest in cheap grain imports, but the heavy-liquor duty already in force made possible the prospect of a compensating reduction in this in any overall fiscal package.

economic interest. Whilst it is true that, very often, twenty years' experience in a trade must have 'conditioned' belief,[82] there must in 1904 have been many retired or semi-retired businessmen, and perhaps even many fully active ones, who had a *rentier* component in their income sufficient to make their direct present economic interest contrast strongly with their experience of a working lifetime. But inherited and accumulated wealth versus industrial income is not the only problem. Table 2 highlights the more marked examples of Tariff Commissioners with dual or multiple interests. The *expected* affiliation of the trade (according to the determinist considerations discussed above) is given in brackets. Clearly, this table shows a considerable presence of expected Free Trade interests (a feature, it should be emphasized, not peculiar to the dual- or multiple-interest Commissioners). It also shows some members, for instance Birchenough, Boulton, Burbidge, Dennis, Keen, Lewis, Parsons, and Waring, whose business activities were a mixture of expected Free Trade and Tariff Reform interests.

Rubinstein has suggested that 'the vast majority of Britain's wealth-holders earned their fortunes overwhelmingly in one trade or line of business, and held other interests only as a clear sideline to their main field', and that 'for the majority, the family firm was enough'.[83] Indeed, we have tried to sort out above those dual interests of obviously minor importance. However, the examples Rubinstein tabulates are for millionaries and half-millionaires, a complete sample for his purposes but one which numbers only 101 for millionaires in 1900–1919 and 78 for half-millionaires in 1900–1906. Furthermore, the proportion of those

[82] Here we come near to the issue of 'economic determinism' vs. 'economic interpretation'. For the classic discussion, in the context of the debate over the interests behind the American constitution, see Lee Benson, *Turner and Beard* (Glencoe, Ill., 1960), pt. 3.

[83] W. D. Rubinstein, *Men of Property* (1981), 58, 178.

holding multiple directorships is pushed down by the high proportion who held none. If we remove this group from Rubinstein's figures, we find 71.4 per cent of millionaires with directorships who died in 1900–1919 held two or more, and an identical proportion of half-millionaires with directorships who died in 1900–1906.[84] Furthermore, some may have shed directorships before their deaths, and partnerships are not included. Rubinstein's purpose is to separate family-firm interest from outside interests. Mine, in addition, is to point out that, from the point of view of fiscal stance, there may be dual and even contradictory interests within the same firm.

Nevertheless, we must be wary of exaggerating the importance of secondary interests. Table 3 summarizes our information on the primary economic interests

TABLE 3. *Tariff Commission: Industrial-Commercial Members*

Primary	Food-Processing	Secondary	Tertiary
		(*Textiles*)	(*Distribution*)
Sir W. T. Lewis	T. Gallaher	F. Baynes	R. Burbidge
	J. M. Harris	J. H. Birchenough	W. Cooper
	C. Lyle	J. A. Corah	J. W. Dennis
	A. W. Maconochie	C. Eckersley	A. Gilbey
	C. J. Phillips	W. H. Mitchell	A. Mosely
	J. Rank	R. H. Reade	W. B. Webb
	F. Tonsley		
		(*Iron and Steel*)	(*Shipping*)
		C. Allen	C. Booth
		Sir A. Hickman	F. L. Harris
		A. Keen	Sir A. L. Jones
		(*Engineering*)	(*Other*)
		Sir V. Caillard	J. H. Colls
		F. Elgar	V. Gibbs
		G. Flett	Sir A. Henderson
		W. Harrison	R. Littlejohn
		H. Marshall	C. A. Pearson
		Sir A. Noble	
		C. A. Parsons	
		(*Chemicals*)	
		S. B. Boulton	
		Sir W. J. Goulding	
		L. Levinstein	
		Sir C. Tennant	
		(*Other*)	
		H. Bostock	
		J. J. Candlish	
		L. Evans	
		Sir J. Turney	
		S. J. Waring	

[84] W. D. Rubinstein, *Men of Property* (1981), 178–82, esp. Tables 6.1 and 6.2.

of the forty-seven industrial–commercial Commissioners.[85] Representation was quite heavily weighted towards manufacturing, though those representing primary production, food processing (including tobacco) and the tertiary sector did comprise twenty-two out of the forty-seven. The biggest industry blocs were engineering and food processing (seven Commissioners each) and textiles (six Commissioners).[86] Chemicals and distribution could count four members each, iron and steel and shipping three each.[87]

The inaccuracy of Semmel's analysis of the Commission can be seen from Table 4, which shows the number of Commissioners who represented the 'heart'[88] of the Commission. These thirteen separate industry representations were held by eleven individual members. Since no-one had primary interests in tin,[89] and since any (small) interest Colls had in building materials was in producing them for his building firm's own use, there is strong ground for reducing the number of Commissioners representing these trades to ten or even nine. It is to be conceded that the heart is a relatively small part of the body, but if it is Semmel's supposition that this group exercised a functional importance within the Commission greater than its size would indicate, there is no basis for this. Arthur Keen was, if anything, a disruptive force, whilst Sir William Lewis and Sir Charles Tennant were infrequent attenders.[90]

TABLE 4. *Representation of Iron and Steel, Coal, Tin, Building Materials, Glass, and Chemicals on the Tariff Commission: 1904–1905*

	Primary Interest	Secondary Interest	
Iron and Steel Coal	4	–	*Allen,*[a] *Hickman, Keen, Lewis*
Tin or Tinplate	–	2	Lewis, Maconochie
Building Materials	–	2	Colls, Boulton[b]
Glass	1	–	*Candlish*
Chemicals[c]	4	–	*Tennant, Levinstein, Goulding, Boulton*

[a] Those members holding primary interests are emphasized.

[b] Boulton has been included, in building materials, as a timber importer. It is unknown, however, how much of the timber he imported was used in the building trade.

[c] Chemical interests are here defined to exclude explosives.

[85] In Table 3, Caillard's primary interest has been given as engineering, rather arbitrarily in view of the treatment in n. 35 above and the entry in Table 2.

[86] There was also a Textiles Committee on which sat, in addition to Commission members, one flax and jute spinner and manufacturer (J. B. Don, Dundee); one worsted manufacturer (J. H. Kaye, Huddersfield); one woollen manufacturer (J. Peate, Guisely); one tweed, worsted and flannel manufacturer (A. J. Sanderson, Galashiels); and two carpet manufacturers (G. Marchetti of Crossley's, Halifax, and M. Tomkinson, Kidderminster).

[87] Of course, many in related trades would have indirect knowledge of the trade or bloc concerned.

[88] B. Semmel, *Imperialism and Social Reform*, 102.

[89] Ibid. 102n. Semmel points out that Maconochie was chairman of the Solderless Tin Co. Ltd., but misses Lewis's chairmanship of the much more important Mellingriffith Tinplate Works. Of course, the tinplate trade had close relations with the iron and steel industry, and so other Commissioners may have had indirect knowledge (W. E. Minchinton, *British Tinplate Industry*, 95–7).

[90] Semmel's stress on the regional element in support for Tariff Reform and his specific mention of the Midlands are presumably meant to imply that Midlands industrialists fell within Chamberlain's

IV

The wide range of industry representation on the Tariff Commission suggests that a thesis which postulates a conspiracy originating in a narrow and distinct group of trades unique in experiencing the blast of foreign competition is incorrect. Foreign competition was felt more widely than this,[91] and it was felt unevenly, not only between different branches of the same industry, but also between different firms within the same branch. In fact, the objective pursued in selecting members of the Tariff Commission was to secure as wide a range of industry representation as possible, consistent at least with securing men willing to assist in the drafting of a 'scientific' tariff, and with keeping the Commission down to a manageable size.[92]

Although examination of the industrial–commercial representation on the Tariff Commission offers little support to the variant of economic determinism invoked by Semmel to explain it, this does not necessarily negate the importance of economic motivation. Of course it is possible that some Commission members held strong 'political' views which led them to advance a cause against their own economic interest. Most exhibited a considerable personal loyalty to Chamberlain, and several can be identified with the Germanophobia of Maxse and the *National Review* or the militant imperialism of the territorial movement.[93] But most did not support Tariff Reform out of altruism: they expected that their industries would gain from a policy of economic nationalism. Because many of them came from industries which have traditionally been classified as 'Free Trade' interests, this does not mean they were economically irrational. This is for two reasons. First, their prediction of the likely effects of a Tariff-Reform policy may have differed from that of others within their trade (and the impossibility of the counterfactual proposition means that the historian cannot know which proposition was correct). And, secondly, the traditional location of 'Free Trade' interests rests heavily on the presumption that an industry's experience of

sphere of influence, through personal acquaintance and the influence of the Birmingham Liberal Unionist Association which he dominated. Whilst this probably holds some general truth, it scarcely fits the Tariff Commission's membership or several of the industries that he mentions. Only three Commissioners had West Midlands addresses (Sir Alfred Hickman, Arthur Keen, and Henry Bostock, the Stafford boot and shoe manufacturer), though to this group we should probably add Unionist MPs Henry Chaplin, W. H. Grenfell, Leverton Harris, Sir Alexander Henderson, and A. W. Maconochie, two of whom represented agriculture and none of whom represented Midlands industry as such. Likewise, to regard iron and steel as a 'Midlands industry' is to deny the great variety of the 10 or so main UK producing regions, some of which fared better under foreign competition than the admittedly hard-hit South Staffordshire region. Chemicals, too, was scarcely a Birmingham-centred industry. In 1901 the industry employed less than 7,000 in the West Midlands compared with, for example, nearly 23,000 in the North West. See C. H. Lee, *Regional Employment Statistics 1841–1971* (Cambridge, 1979).

[91] This is not to say that it was not frequently exaggerated by those who felt it.
[92] See above, Ch. 4.
[93] For instance, Henry Birchenough and Charles Allen.

export-orientation or import competition was not only homogeneous but also relevant, a presumption which is buttressed by a *belief* (seldom proven) that the great majority of businessmen in that industry were of one mind. To put the issue baldly, since we can never know whether Tariff Reform was right or wrong, we cannot question the rationality of a minority view in an industry without also similarly questioning the majority view, especially when we have assumed rather than proven that the minority was a minority and the majority was a majority.

In consequence, the Tariff-Commission example also exposes weaknesses in a wider use of the conventional model of industry alignment in the fiscal controversy. Many of those interests labelled 'Free Trade' (FT) in Table 2 may only remain so at a very superficial level. Furthermore, under the Semmel-Rempel scheme at least thirty out of the forty-seven industrial–commercial Commissioners would have come from 'Free-Trade' industries (coal, food processing,[94] textiles, engineering, distribution, and shipping).[95] Since the Commission was a specially picked body of businessmen prepared to help in the construction of a tariff scheme, it is perfectly possible that this was so. But it is unlikely that all these industries were in fact so heavily inclined towards Free Trade as has been implied, and important areas of distinction need to be made within them.

As we shall see below,[96] engineering was far from a uniform or unified industry. In 1906 Hewins found the attempt to collate the information received in reply to the Commission's questionnaires 'an entirely disgusting business. I thought cotton was sufficiently complicated. Wool made Cotton seem quite simple, but Engineering seems to me more complicated than all the others put together'.[97] He found some 500 groups of engineering products in which foreign competition was complained of, so that engineering 'is not one industry, but is really a large group of industries'.[98] Much earlier he had noted differences in the willingness of industrialists from the different sectors of the industry to join the Commission. Whilst there was no shortage of electrical or agricultural engineers, he knew that the textile engineers had such a large export trade that 'they are

---

[94] Except for brewing and distilling, historically and with reason anti-Liberal, and sugar refining, hit by export bounties on European beet sugar, this would seem the logical alignment for food processing, even though the industry is not mentioned (except for meat-packing) by Semmel or Rempel. Chamberlain encapsulated the issue nicely: 'Sugar has gone: Let us not weep for it—jam and pickles remain'. See Chamberlain at Greenock, 7 Oct. 1903; in J. M. Robertson, *The Collapse of 'Tariff Reform'* (1911), 100.

[95] This assumes that, in Table 3, both 'other secondary' and 'other tertiary' are not classified as 'Free Trade' interests. If, as seems plausible, 'other tertiary' were included on the Free Trade side, the figure would rise to 35 out of 47. However, the removal of those exceptions admitted by Semmel or Rempel (silk, linen, and electrical engineering) would reduce the figure to 31 out of 47.

[96] See below, Ch. 7.

[97] Hewins to P. Hurd, 6 Sept. 1906, 6/1/14, TCP.

[98] Tariff Commission Minutes (verbatim typescript), 23 May 1907, 28; 2/1/14, TCP.

not likely to make any move at present for representation on the Commission'.[99] Thus, at the very least, it seems necessary to apply a product-market analysis to the main sectors of engineering. Intuitively we might expect those branches in which British firms still retained something of their mid-nineteenth-century glory—textile machinery,[100] shipbuilding,[101] perhaps marine engineering, and so on—to incline towards Free Trade, whilst expecting those branches under threat from the 'American System' or German applied science—light machine tools,[102] some branches of agricultural machinery,[103] electrical engineering,[104] and per- haps motor cars[105]—to exhibit a protectionist posture. Of course, some British firms were remarkably successful even in the teeth of strong American competi- tion,[106] but this would not preclude protectionist sentiment, sometimes along quasi-infant-industry lines.

Chemicals presents further difficulties for the Semmel-Rempel case. Haber has noted that in the late nineteenth century, English industrial chemists 'were often Free Traders and Liberals'.[107] The dominant alkali section of the industry, though its export growth was decelerating through foreign competition and tariffs, was heavily dependent on exports. Furthermore, the firm of Brunner, Mond & Co. the self-styled and rather pompous mouthpiece of the progressive Solvay branch of the alkali trades, was largely dominated by Free Traders and Liberals.[108] Protectionist Ivan Levinstein admitted that cheap raw materials and high transport costs kept the home market relatively immune from foreign

[99] Hewins to Pearson, 24 Dec. 1903, 6/1/26, TCP.

[100] S. B. Saul, 'The Market and the Development of the Mechanical Engineering Industries in Britain, 1860–1914', *Economic History Review*, 20 (1967), 111–30.

[101] S. Pollard, 'British and World Shipbuilding, 1890–1914: A Study in Comparative Costs', *Journal of Economic History*, 17 (1957), 426–44.

[102] S. B. Saul, 'The Market and the Development of the Mechanical Engineering Industries', and 'The Machine Tool Industry in Britain to 1914', *Business History* 10 (1968), 22–43.

[103] For the two branches of the industry, see S. B. Saul, 'The Market and Development of the Mechanical Engineering Industries in Britain, 1860–1914'; R. J. Munting, 'Ransome's in Russia: An English Agricultural Engineering Company's Trade with Russia to 1917', *Economic History Review*, 31 (1978), 257–69.

[104] I. C. R. Byatt, *The British Electrical Industry 1875–1914* (Oxford, 1979), ch. 9; and 'Electrical Products', in D. H. Aldcroft (ed.), *The Development of British Industry and Foreign Competition 1875–1914* (1968), ch. 8.

[105] S. B. Saul, 'The Motor Industry in Britain to 1914', *Business History*, 5 (1962–3), 222–44.

[106] As would be Saul's general presumption for the industry. See also A. E. Harrison, 'The Competitiveness of the British Cycle Industry, 1890–1914', *Economic History Review*, 22 (1969), 287–303. Some branches of light engineering responded well to the transatlantic threat, the more dynamic firms introducing American methods, machinery, and machine tools. Even so, differences in the way machinery was used, differences in the way the 'effort bargain' between management and labour was concluded, could result in British labour productivity remaining lower than American. See e.g. W. Lewchuck, *American Technology and the British Vehicle Industry* (Cambridge, 1987), chs. 3–7.

[107] L. F. Haber, *The Chemical Industry during the Nineteenth Century* (Oxford, 1958), 196.

[108] A partial exception was conservatively minded Ludwig Mond. See J. M. Cohen, *Life of Ludwig Mond* (1956), 168; S. E. Koss, *Sir John Brunner* (Cambridge, 1970), 193–9; A. Mond, 'The Alkali Industry', in H. Cox (ed.), *British Industries under Free Trade* (1903), 214–26. On Brunner, Mond's strong position in Empire markets, almost *de facto* imperial preference secured by market sharing agreements, see W. J. Reader, *Imperial Chemical Industries* (1970), 169–72.

competition.[109] Even the ponderous and technically backward United Alkali Co., of which Tariff Commissioner Sir Charles Tennant was president, would not co-operate with the Commission.[110]

In dyestuffs, however, we might expect a different stance. Here British failure was more obvious, with output twenty to thirty times less than that of Germany, and with 90 per cent of home consumption imported. Furthermore, in this branch the industry spokesman was a protectionist: Ivan Levinstein was a long-time campaigner against foreign tariffs and abuses of the patent system.

It has been suggested that even the dyestuffs firms had nothing to gain from protection,[111] but nevertheless the three manufacturers who essentially comprised the British dyestuffs industry did agree to give evidence before the Tariff Commission, though only two did so.[112] The inorganic sector was, however, much harder to mobilize. The Tariff Commission's investigation into chemicals began in June 1905, when trade recovery was well under way, but even so it found the search for willing witnesses a terrible struggle. As a last resort, Levinstein supplied the Commission with a complete list of members of the Society of Chemical Industry, marking 500 or so who he thought might give information, but he stressed that 'I cannot warrant however that all, or how many are favourable to a tariff reform'.[113] Even though the Commission apparently acted on his advice to invite them all,[114] it appears that only four chemicals witnesses were examined, and two of these were Tariff Commission members.

It is tempting, therefore, to discern a split between Free-Trade alkali producers and protectionist dyestuffs manufacturers. But it is nevertheless hard to understand how so few open supporters of fiscal change could be found amongst the Society of Chemical Industry's 2,400 members, especially given widespread dissatisfaction over the related area of patents legislation, and the bleak position of both the Leblanc and dyestuffs interests. The Tariff Commission's experience certainly refutes the heavy protectionist alignment of the industry postulated by Semmel, but it is hard to imagine these interests so firmly united behind Free Trade. It may be that the alkali interests, more or less immune to foreign competition in the home market because of transport costs, were apathetic or indifferent towards the fiscal controversy. Such a conclusion would gain some

[109] Printed proof copy of Levinstein's evidence before the Tariff Commission, 6/1/21, TCP.

[110] Both John Brock and F. Davidson (chairman and joint managing director) refused to give evidence. According to Levinstein, this reflected division on the Board over the fiscal issue. See Levinstein to Hewins, 29 Oct. 1905, 6/1/21, TCP.

[111] L. F. Haber, *The Chemical Industry 1900–1930* (Oxford, 1971), 148.

[112] Levinstein and L. B. Holliday. If Martin Dreyfus of the Clayton Aniline Co. Ltd. gave evidence, it has not survived.

[113] Levinstein to Hewins, 25 Oct. 1905, 6/1/21, TCP.

[114] P. Hurd to Levinstein, 26 Oct. 1905, 6/1/21, TCP.

support from the examination below of fiscal controversy within the Federation of British Industries in the 1920s.[115]

The woollen industry seems an equally problematic case. Bradford has a good claim to be regarded as the 'cradle' of the Fair Trade movement of the 1880s, and included among its leading citizens several influential manufacturers who paved the way for Chamberlain's later campaign.[116] In pre-war Leeds, Huddersfield, and Dewsbury, manufacturers were also questioning economic liberalism.[117] Whilst admitting variations between the different sections of the industry, Jenkins and Ponting conclude that on the whole it was 'more adversely affected by tariffs than almost any other British industry'.[118] B. H. Brown, working impressionistically, counted the industry's enthusiasm for Fair Trade as second only to that of iron and steel, hardware, cutlery, implements, and tools.[119] By 1904, protectionist feeling in Bradford at least had been maintained, as can be seen from Sigsworth's analysis of the unusually detailed record of a vote on the fiscal issue in the Bradford Chamber of Commerce in 1904, which is examined below.[120] Certainly, the Bradford Chamber had 'departed a long way' from its Free-Trade posture of the early 1880s.[121]

The armaments industry, held to be heavily protectionist in the Semmel-Rempel scheme, presents difficulties of a different kind. Certainly the iron and steel industry was heavily in favour of Tariff Reform,[122] and the bigger, integrated armaments firms had interests in this field. But they were by their nature more closely related to Free Trade shipbuilding and to engineering, which was at least less committed than iron and steel. Furthermore, in a market situation where arms producers sought a special relationship with the British government and where a large export business depended on delicate negotiations with foreign governments,[123] Tariff Reform may simply have been irrelevant. This was certainly the view of Douglas Vickers when invited to give evidence before the Tariff Commission.[124] Even Commissioner Sir Andrew Noble, of Armstrong Whitworth, admitted being in a 'special position', having 'neither the

---

[115] FBI leaders in the 1920s spoke of the opposition of cotton and chemicals to Tariff Reform. However, only evidence of opposition from the cotton industry survives in the FBI's records. See below, Ch. 10.

[116] *The Economist*, 19 Nov. 1881, quoted in B. H. Brown, *The Tariff Reform Movement in Great Britain 1881–1895* (New York, 1943), 11–12. Wollen and worsted manufacturers involved in the early campaign in Bradford included Farrer Eckroyd and J. H. Mitchell.

[117] B. H. Brown, *Tariff Reform Movement*, 10, 130, 141.

[118] D. T. Jenkins and K. G. Ponting, *The British Wool Textile Industry 1770–1914* (1982), 293.

[119] *Tariff Reform Movement*, 139–40.

[120] See below, 112.

[121] E. Sigsworth, *Black Dyke Mills* (Liverpool, 1958), 107.

[122] See below, Ch. 5.

[123] C. Trebilcock, *The Vickers Brothers* (1977), 11, 22.

[124] Albert Vickers, on the other hand, was a Tariff Reformer. See Hewins to D. Vickers, 2 Mar. 1904, D. Vickers to Charles Allen, 15 Mar. 1904, 6/1/1, TCP; J. D. Scott, *Vickers*, 76.

competition nor the same difficulties...that other manufactures have'.[125] Producers of smaller weapons systems or certain components may have been more vulnerable to foreign competition abroad or even at home, but there was little emphasis on these trades in the Commission's report on engineering.[126] Of course, considerations of small-group sociology may have meant that most of the industry's leaders, with strong determinist reasons for being Unionist in politics, supported Tariff Reform, but their interest in a tariff in itself was probably small and even negative.[127]

Similar considerations apply to the later period, *c*.1909–1918, when many of the leaders of the industry are known to have advocated Tariff Reform.[128] Even if it is shown that a substantial majority in this concentrated industry supported the movement during the War, it is hard to explain this on the determinist basis of self-interest in a tariff *per se*, given the industry's insulated and favoured market position. More important would be the appendicular elements of Tariff Reform (for example, patents legislation, tied loans, and proposals for a Ministry of Commerce), and the broader political implications that underlay the movement (business-government relations, state assistance, post-war economic relations with Germany). It is feasible that the leaders of a highly concentrated industry might well have a more homogeneous view of the future, based on commonly perceived political and 'extra-tariff' determinist considerations, than businessmen in less concentrated industries. Whether the armaments manufacturers were united in support of Tariff Reform or not, their case offers little support for a narrow view of market-led tariff determinism.

V

The analysis above shows the dangers inherent in any simple approach to the determination of individual economic interest posed by dual or multiple interests, rentier income, differences in perception of the future, and prior political

---

[125] Evidence of Sir Andrew Noble, *Report of the Tariff Commission*, iv.: *The Engineering Industries* (1909), para. 509. Noble claimed to speak on behalf of engineering generally, as president of the Engineering Employers' Federation (1898–1915). Francis Elgar of Fairfields endorsed his remarks on naval shipbuilding: 'The battleship industry is really a protected industry as far as the Admiralty is concerned'; ibid. para. 501.

[126] John Thorneycroft recorded that foreign competition in torpedo boats had led his firm to diversify over the previous 25 years; ibid. paras. 528–38.

[127] For support, see P. M. Kennedy, *The Rise of Anglo-German Antagonism 1860–1914* (1980), 299–300. An industry with little or no import competition in the home market is unlikely to be aided by a policy which raises its input costs. In this case, a negative rate of effective protection on the final product would, given the semi-monopolistic position at home and the large element of non-tariff protection, be less important than the effect on the competitiveness of the industry's exports.

[128] Arms makers such as Caillard, Francis Barker, Sir Trevor Dawson, and F. Orr-Lewis of Vickers were prominent in the establishment of the British Commonwealth Union in 1916. See below, 345–55.

allegiance. Furthermore, the example of the Tariff Commission in itself and the record of its experience when securing the participation of different trades suggests that any concept that simple and unilinear economic pressures acted upon whole industries to result in a largely homogeneous 'industry view' on the fiscal issue needs close scrutiny.

This is not to deny the strengths of a determinist scheme based on Schumpeterian principles. There is no doubt that the financial sector retained its loyalty to Free Trade with the exception of some firms closely associated with colonial finance. The Tariff Commission met with a wall of silence when it tried to extend its enquiries into banking,[129] in spite of the strong Conservative sympathies of many in the City. There is no evidence, either, of substantial merchant support for Tariff Reform.[130] Levinstein, who resigned the presidency of the Manchester Chamber of Commerce to join the Tariff Commission, even blamed the cotton merchants alone for Manchester's hostility to the cause. It was 'the game of many of our merchants to set the foreign producer against the British in order to squeeze down prices', he commented. 'They don't care whether the working classes are employed.'[131] Whilst he exaggerated the conflict between merchant and manufacturer in the cotton trade, it is at least clear that the merchants were Free Traders.[132]

We can also agree with other elements in the Semmel-Rempel composite. Iron and steel, coal, shipbuilding, and electrical engineering seem to require no modification. Furthermore, criticisms of Semmel and Rempel do not necessarily imply criticisms of the underlying principles on which their analyses are based. The chemical industry, for instance, could simply be moved into the Free-Trade camp on the basis of acceptable economic considerations, though it would probably be unwise to do so.

But further difficulties arise when trades were heavily divided. Of course, no trade was 100 per cent solid. Even in banking, Sir Ernest Cassel donated an incredible £5,000 to the TRL and later made heavy contributions to the Commission:[133] Cassis and Mock have recently documented other examples of bankers sympathetic to the cause.[134] Where division was more marked, we are

[129] See below, Ch. 7.
[130] See below, Chs. 6 and 7.
[131] Levinstein to Hewins, 8 Feb. 1904, 6/1/21, TCP.
[132] P. F. Clarke, who otherwise discovers considerable division within the cotton industry, endorses this point. See 'The End of Laissez-Faire and the Politics of Cotton', *Historical Journal*, 15 (1972), esp. 510.
[133] 'Tariff Commission Account, 1915–1922', 9/1/2, TCP; J. Amery, *Life of Joseph Chamberlain*, v. (1969), 288, 301.
[134] Referring to the period c.1903–8, Youssef Cassis counts all of the Hambros's and all of the Gibbs's partners as Tariff Reformers, but otherwise discovers only a handful of open supporters of Chamberlain. By 1913, he is able to record eighteen City figures as having been vice-presidents of the Tariff Reform League, though he is still doubtful about the depth of their commitment to the cause; see *City Bankers, 1890–1914*, (Cambridge, 1994), 304–6, and W. Mock, *Imperiale Herrschaft und Nationales Interesse: 'Constructive Imperialism' oder Freihandel in Großbritainien vor dem Ersten Weltkrieg*,

still left with the question of whether it simply reflected the different market experience of different products and branches, or whether there were more random and personal divisions reflecting differences in politics and perceptions. Nevertheless, such difficulties apart, the recognition that intra-industry division was more common than is suggested by those who stress inter-industry differences carries with it the implication that, even in the early days of Tariff Reform, protectionist sympathies had permeated British manufacturing industry widely.

Detailed study of trade associations, which might be thought to offer a convenient overview of industry-wide opinion, gives little hope of clarifying even the simple issue of business alignment, let alone the more complex one of its motivation. But the very difficulties involved carry with them a lesson. Such organizations frequently left poor records of their members' views precisely because fiscal reform was so contentious, and the organizations' leaders were reluctant even to find out themselves what the balance of opinion was. Often, perhaps, the somewhat 'closed' nature of trade associations was more due to fear of publicizing differences among members than to any reluctance to attract wider public attention to businessmen's supposed 'hawkishness'. On labour relations, employer consensus was relatively easy,[135] but those associations dealing with trade matters were on less certain ground.[136]

Thus it was that the Commission, which warmly encouraged trade associations to give evidence before it, met with little success, with only a handful of minor associations replying to its invitations.[137] James Hamilton, secretary of the Scottish Iron Manufacturers' Association, spoke for the majority: 'I had the matter brought before a meeting of this Association and it was agreed not to ask any member to give evidence before the Commission, but to leave individual firms to act on their own account, as they thought best.'[138] Even in the rare case of the secretary of an association being delegated to give evidence, his position was still not necessarily straightforward. As J. S. Jeans of the British Iron Trade Association explained, he was 'not instructed [*sic*] to put forward any views or to express any leanings . . . on the fiscal question'. Even when he had, in 1903, been authorized to elicit views on the tariff question, only just over 70 out of 225

(Stuttgart, 1982), app. IV, 393–7, reproducing H. A. Gwynne's memorandum to Joseph Chamberlain in Dec. 1903.

[135] E. Wigham, *The Power to Manage* (1973), 1.

[136] For support, see J. Turner, 'Servants of Two Masters: British Trade Associations in the First Half of the Twentieth Century', in Hiroaki Yamazaki and Matao Miyamoto (eds.), *Trade Associations in Business History*, International Conference on Business History, 14, Proceedings of the Fuji Conference (Tokyo, 1988), 173–98, esp. 186–7.

[137] Including the British Tube Trade Association; the Paper Makers' Association; The India Rubber Manufacturers' Association; the Institute of British Carriage Manufacturers; the Timber Trades Federation; the Musical Instrument Traders' Protection Association; the Warwickshire Felt Hat Manufacturers' Association; and the National Glass Bottle Manufacturers' Association.

[138] Hamilton to Hewins, 27 Feb. 1904, 6/5/25, TCP.

member firms had replied, though of these 95 per cent had favoured 'some reform of the existing situation . . . although hardly any suggestions were made as to . . . the precise character of that reform'.[139]

This cautious approach is understandable. Even to businessmen, Tariff Reform was, in all its complexity, a political as much as an economic question. Political alignments in the previous generation had been largely decided upon very different issues: in any real sense, the politics of Home Rule were remote from factory floor and counting house. Many businessmen now found it uncomfortable that their own position had become a primary issue of party conflict. Though many were, defensively and half-ashamedly, to claim the mantle of 'true free trader', others kept their own counsel, inhibited by the fact that the very word 'protection' invoked contempt.

Nevertheless, this situation could scarcely be static. There was also a temporal aspect to business opinion, a dimension which further limits the usefulness of the traditional analysis of 'cosmopolitan' versus 'nationalist' economic interest. In a study which has profound implications for industries less cosmopolitan than cotton (and how many were not?), Peter Clarke has presented a strong case for arguing that even the cotton industry was heavily divided, and that after 1906, as the Liberals departed from *laissez-faire* in their welfare reforms, the cotton bosses were forced to re-order their priorities, so that by the 1910 elections they were even less united behind Free Trade than they had been in 1903.[140] Such a change cannot be put down to tariff-orientated determinism because of the rapid growth of exports between 1900 and 1913.[141] Rather, defence of Free Trade was not worth the price of continued support of the Liberal Party. Similar examples can be found amongst Tariff Reform businessmen. There were those who, after the election defeats of 1906 and 1910, thought that the wider aspects of Tariff Reform, especially food taxes, were preventing realization of their more immediate objective of industrial protection.[142] Some, too, joined with other Unionists in fearing that food taxes delayed the return of a Unionist government needed to counter Home Rule and the Liberal attack on the House of Lords.[143]

Thus, the period 1906 to 1914 was one in which prosperous trade probably lessened the tariff-based determinist support for Tariff Reform in most industries, whilst at the same time being a period in which businessmen's fear of socialism

---

[139] *Report of the Tariff Commission*, i.: *The Iron and Steel Trades* (1904), para. 929.

[140] Clarke argues convincingly that, even in 1903–6, cotton bosses may have had only a 2:1 majority in favour of Free Trade, compared with the 9:1 that Free Traders often claimed. See 'The End of Laissez-Faire', esp. 499, 511.

[141] By volume, yarn exports grew 34.1% and piece-goods exports 22.3% between 1900–1904 and 1909–1913. Figures derived from *Annual Statement of Trade of the United Kingdom*.

[142] For instance, Tariff Commissioner and ex-Unionist MP Sir Alfred Hickman. See Hickman to Hewins, 26 Apr. 1906, HP.

[143] On this reaction, see A. Sykes, *Tariff Reform in British Politics 1903–1913* (Oxford, 1979), chs. 10–12; and below, 215–16.

and liberal collectivism led to a wider reassessment of political priorities which, though not being 'non-economic', were much less immediately related to the specific issue of tariffs. At least until the immediate pre-war period, therefore (when a growth of nationalist and anti-German feeling may have influenced the picture), we might expect an almost paradoxical pattern where the determinist support for a tariff subsided but non-tariff determinist support for the Unionists was increasing amongst businessmen in general. The evidence we have presented so far throws little light on this issue. Given the nature of surviving evidence, it is best pursued through an examination of the fiscal issue within the Chambers of Commerce.

3

The Chambers of Commerce and Tariff Reform, 1903–1913

This chapter surveys the trend of opinion on the fiscal issue in the chambers of commerce before the First World War, and gives a clearer picture of the factors which influenced the formation of Tariff-Reform sentiment over time than has been possible so far. Detailed treatment is necessarily restricted to a narrow range of sources covering nine Chambers, but references to other Chambers in those sources, and the piecing together of the story of Tariff Reform in the twice-yearly meetings of the Associated Chambers of Commerce of the United Kingdom (ACCUK), enables a wider perspective. The surviving evidence has its limits, particularly due to the fact that Chambers were not one-trade. Since votes were almost never ascribed to individuals, it is usually impossible to discern interest- or industry-alignments within each Chamber: the examples of Macclesfield and Bradford below are very much the exceptions.[1] Chambers generally had a mixed membership, in which merchants and accountants could count alongside the representatives of large, nationally known firms. This weakness of the evidence would not be overcome by a wider survey of Chambers than has been attempted here. On the other hand, study of Chambers of Commerce does allow an insight into fiscal attitudes in those small- and medium-sized firms which, though so characteristic of British industrial structure, are prone to be overlooked.

I

The London *Chamber of Commerce Journal*, in a regular monthly column devoted to news from the provinces, gives useful information on a wide range of Chambers, which can at least partly be used to refute the charge that most of the in-depth studies presented below are of reasonably large manufacturing centres in the north-central and south-central areas of England. This column's reporting of the fiscal issue was, however, largely confined to 1903–1904.

After the Birmingham speech a few Chambers acted quickly and decisively. The Birmingham Chamber passed Chamberlainite resolutions on 27 May and 22 July, with only one or two dissenters. In the Kidderminster Chamber, on 8

[1] See below, 110–12.

June, the Free-Trade vote was also negligible. The Leeds Chamber, at about the same time, confined itself to a preferentialist resolution. On 2 July the Burnley Chamber endorsed Free Trade by fifty votes to twenty-eight, on 6 July the Manchester Chamber proclaimed its faith, and on 8 July the Newcastle Chamber followed suit by thirty-two votes to eighteen.[2]

But much more common was a mood of caution. The Cheltenham Chamber found itself so divided that it avoided a vote. Dundee limited itself to a discussion. The directors of the Edinburgh Chamber were directed to keep a watching brief. The businessmen of Bradford, Sheffield, Glasgow, Greenock, Aberdeen, Blackburn, Plymouth, Swansea, Macclesfield, Huddersfield, Limerick, and Hull passed resolutions urging an impartial government enquiry. On the reporting of the *Chamber of Commerce Journal*, therefore, Chambers were running about two-to-one in favour of avoiding a decision.[3]

Clearly there were different motives for advocating a Royal Commission. The Macclesfield Chamber's 'overwhelming' vote for one was soon to be overtaken by an almost certainly more overwhelming vote for protection. The Limerick Chamber's call for an enquiry was carried at a meeting where there was reported to be strong support for Chamberlain's policy. At Dublin, on 23 November, on the other hand, the call for an enquiry was endorsed only after a Chamberlainite resolution had been lost by a large majority.[4]

Chamberlain's Glasgow speech in October marked a turning point. Between then and April 1904 only three Chambers are recorded in the *Chamber of Commerce Journal* as advocating an impartial inquiry—Wakefield, York, and Londonderry. A poll of the Bristol Chamber was generally in favour of retaliation and preference. Leeds narrowly favoured a modification of fiscal policy by seventy-six to sixty-five. A motion advocating preference and retaliation in the North Staffordshire Chamber attracted only twenty opponents at a meeting of around 200 members. Wolverhampton voted for retaliation and preference by thirty-one to seven. At Edinburgh, perhaps surprisingly, a vaguely worded and conditional retaliationist resolution scraped through by two votes. The Belfast Chamber endorsed Chamberlain's policy by sixty-five to twenty-five. Only two voted against a Chamberlainite motion in the Stroud Chamber, at a meeting attended largely by woollen manufacturers. Nottingham opted for retaliation by twenty-six votes to nine, whilst Walsall endorsed Chamberlain's policy by thirty-nine votes to twelve. Even those centres in which port and trading interests bulked large showed favour to Chamberlain's policy. Dundee supported retaliation and preference by ninety-two votes to forty-five. Grimsby passed a Chamberlainite resolution unanimously, Leith by forty-three to seventeen, and Dover by thirty

    [2] *CCJ*, July 1903, 172, 174; Aug. 1903, 198–200.
    [3] *CCJ*, Aug. 1903, 198–200; Sept. 1903, 228; Oct. 1903, 256.
    [4] On Macclesfield, see *CCJ*, Aug. 1903, 200, cf. below, 110–12; on Limerick and Dublin, see *CCJ*, Sept. 1903, 228, Dec. 1903, 299.

to seven. Southampton declared for retaliation by the narrower margin of thirty-five to thirty-two, Barrow with only one dissenter. At the same time it became known that in their poll Sheffield members favoured retaliation by a margin of three to one. A similar questionnaire issued by the Halifax Chamber was plagued by a poor response rate (sixty-three out of 300) and ambiguous replies, but the independent firm of Price, Waterhouse and Co., called in to interpret the findings, judged that there was a general sentiment in favour of import duties and preference.[5] During this period the *Chamber of Commerce Journal* reported only two decisions in favour of Free Trade, and these were both repeat performances by the Manchester and Newcastle Chambers.[6]

Even though protectionist sympathy in most Chambers was large from an early date in Chamberlain's campaign, the rift over Tariff Reform within the Unionist party seriously damaged the possibility of the protectionist business interests developing any very active or politically effective consensus, especially before the Valentine compact and the reconciliation with Balfour in 1906–8. Even after then, the situation was not easy. As Stiebel of Nottingham observed testily of ACCUK in the relatively favourable conditions of 1909, if the 'Parliament of Commerce' could not discuss what was 'purely a matter of economics', it had better abdicate its functions.[7] Before 1906, though differences within the Unionist Party were even less discussed in most Chambers than was inter-party conflict, the very often meticulous distinctions in the wording of resolutions reveal this clearly. Particularly significant were those resolutions which confined themselves to Balfourite retaliation, resolutions which could be supported by businessmen opposed to the taxation of food. Behind such motions lay the long-frustrated plea for justice, for equity of treatment, that historians have for long underestimated in the analysis of Tariff Reform. Often such motions had a conditional form of wording—retaliation should be resorted to only after negotiation on genuine reciprocity—and an almost apologetic ring, as if the proposer was expressing regret at entering the forbidden territory of inter- or intra-party conflict. Whether this reflected the true sentiments of the proposers or whether it was just a device to secure wider support matters little; it still testifies to the widespread feeling of tariff injustice and retaliationist feeling in Britain's Chambers of Commerce.

The call for a Royal Commission, the cautious response of the business community to Tariff Reform in the summer and early autumn of 1903, was even seen in Chambers such as Bradford, Sheffield, Greenock, and Macclesfield, which were subsequently to demonstrate protectionist majorities; it may be that

[5] *CCJ*, Dec. 1903, 299–300; Jan. 1904, 21–2, 24; Feb. 1904, 49–50; Mar. 1904, 76–7; Apr. 1904, 99–100; June 1904, 149–50.

[6] *CCJ*, Mar. 1904, 76; June 1904, 149–50.

[7] Stiebel at Nottingham Chamber of Commerce Council Meeting, in *Nottingham Daily Guardian*, 3 Feb. 1909.

some who favoured protection hoped initially that the recommendation of fiscal change by an official enquiry would save manufacturers the public opprobrium of having to ask for it. But, as we have seen, after October some kind of declaration for preference or retaliation became much more common. Of twenty-five decisions reported in the *Journal* between 28 October 1903 and 22 November 1904, only two went in favour of Free Trade and five urged an enquiry. Eighteen supported some change in fiscal policy.[8]

However, voting in the Associated Chambers suggests that the *Journal* may have under-reported the Free Trade Chambers. Maybe they were small or felt no need for a vote. Furthermore, if most of the Chambers reported exhibited some kind of protectionist majority, it was often not a heavy one, and could be sensitive to the particular form of recommendation. In such a situation, it was frequently the case that Chamber officials considered it unwise to treat Tariff Reform as agreed policy. The Leeds Chamber, for instance, had demonstrated a small protectionist majority in November 1903, but it maintained a stance of 'neutrality' in the Associated Chambers until 1908.[9] This is significant, since ACCUK's ruling on neutral votes was to dominate its proceedings on the fiscal question down to 1914, as the constituent Chambers first became restive and then lost interest.

II

The record of ACCUK's dealings with the fiscal question before 1914 is one of a Free Trade presidency determined to maintain its dominance, ostensibly and perhaps genuinely to prevent the Association being split. In his presidential address for 1903 Lord Avebury correctly divined that no other issue would 'engender so much heat because views were so strongly held on each side'.[10] At the Annual Meeting of March 1903 there were five fiscal resolutions on the agenda. The Nottingham and South of Scotland (Hawick) Chambers (soon to become almost ritualistic movers of protectionist resolutions in ACCUK, like Charles Villiers of Free Trade motions in the pre-1846 Parliament)[11] were joined by the London Chamber, which urged retaliation only if all other courses had been tried, if it had a reasonable chance of success, and if related branches of British industry and commerce were not harmed. The London resolution was conceived by Avebury, himself a Free Trader, though more pragmatic and flexible than some. An amendment proposing the removal of its conditions to produce a straightforward retaliationist resolution was defeated by sixty-nine to

[8] Count made from relevant issues of *CCJ*.

[9] See below, 97–101.

[10] A. R. Ilersic and P. F. B. Liddle, *Parliament of Commerce* (1960), 154.

[11] W. O. Henderson, 'Charles Pelham Villiers and the Repeal of the Corn Laws', unpubl. typescript (1975), 1.

twenty-seven, and Dublin's motion for a Royal Commission was accepted. Some observers interpreted this as supporting negotiation without the sanction of retaliation, and were quick to report back to their Chambers that such a policy would be unlikely to be successful.[12] The London Chamber tried again in March 1904, after polling its members on Avebury's policy of 'conditional Retaliation' in February,[13] but Newcastle's resolution for a Royal Commission was successful and other fiscal resolutions were withdrawn. This time, however, the majority was much more slender, fifty-eight to forty-five.

Under the new presidency of Sir William Holland, Liberal MP for Rotherham, fiscal policy was the 'great debate' of the 1905 meeting. A full-blooded protectionist resolution from the Nottingham Chamber was subjected to an amendment for a Royal Commission from the Swansea Chamber, which was lost by forty-one votes to forty (or forty to thirty-nine), with twenty Chambers classified as 'neutral'.[14] In the debate, the protectionists were led by C. J. Wilson of Hawick, and Howard Vincent and A. J. Hobson (himself a Free Trader) of Sheffield. The Free Traders fielded heavier guns: Avebury, Felix Schuster, and Winston Churchill. According to the Leeds delegates, the resolution provoked 'possibly the greatest division of opinion at the whole meeting'. Birmingham and Liverpool sat on the fence. The voting of the four London delegates caused a minor sensation when one of them, Tariff Commissioner Sir Samuel Boulton, correctly questioned the votes cast by the other three, led by Schuster, resulting in the London Chamber being disqualified and turning what would have been a narrow victory for Swansea into defeat.[15] The Nottingham resolution was then carried by forty-two votes to twenty-one with thirty-nine neutral.

The victory of the Nottingham resolution has been regarded as of great significance by Redford but, as he recognized, it was of no short-term consequence because it was ruled not to have obtained the necessary two-thirds majority.[16] This followed from Holland's decision to depart from precedent and record the neutral votes not as 'abstentions', Redford's word for them,[17] but as votes against the resolution, which in its turn had followed from the insistence of a Mr Jobson, a delegate of the Derby Chamber, that neutral votes should be recorded. Rotherham admitted that this was 'quite unusual, if not unprecedented . . . but the occasion was a special one'.[18]

According to the historians of the Associated Chambers, 'During the next few years the Council did its best to unify the members' views so as to make effective

[12] ACCUK Official Programme for Mar. 1904 Meeting, (copy in Leeds CC Minute Book no. 4); Leeds CC, *Annual Report* 1904.

[13] LCC, Council Minutes, Dec. 1903–Mar. 1904; see also below, 94.

[14] Hull CC, *Annual Report*, 22 Nov. 1905, 40.

[15] LCC, Council Minutes, 9 Mar. 1905; see also below, 94–5.

[16] A. Redford, *Manchester Merchants and Foreign Trade*, ii. *1850–1939* (Manchester, 1956), 104–5.

[17] Ibid.

[18] *CCJ*, Supplement, Mar. 1906, 24.

representations to the Government, but without success'.[19] In fact, it attempted to head off the growing support for Tariff Reform with ambiguous and potentially anodyne compromise resolutions, and adopted a determined defence of the policy of counting neutrality as abstention. A retaliationist resolution failed to get a two-thirds majority in March 1906,[20] whilst in September a preferential-ist resolution moved by the South of Scotland and seconded by Bristol was subject to an amendment introduced by Colonel Harding of Leeds, professing sympathy with the desire to foster imperial trade, but declining to recommend a departure from Free Trade 'in the absence of practical proposals'.[21] The amendment was carried by a show of hands, and then the floor called for a chamber vote. To the astonishment of the delegates from the London Chamber, Holland simply put this demand to the meeting, with the predictable result that the same voters put up their hands again, knowing the demand would be denied. Again there had been a complete break with precedent.[22]

Lord Brassey, assuming the presidency in 1907, soon demonstrated his determination to continue its Free-Trade tradition. In September, a resolution from Hawick that ACCUK, 'while approving of Free Trade in principle, recognises the grave danger to which our industrial population is exposed by the action of scientifically imposed Foreign Tariffs, and is of the opinion that steps

TABLE 5. Main Resolutions on Tariff Reform in the Associated Chambers: 1904–1913

		Resolution	For TR	Against TR	Neutral
1904		Royal Commission	45	58	
1905	(1)	Royal Commission	41	40	20
	(2)	Tariff Reform	41	21	39
1906	(1)	Retaliation	[failed to get 2/3 majority]		
	(2)	Preference	[chamber vote refused by Holland]		
1907		Tariff Reform	[withdrawn under pressure from Brassey]		
1908	(1)	Tariff Reform	40	30	31
	(2)	Sugar Duty	[tied]		
1909		Tariff Reform	46	31	32
1910		Retaliation & Preference	51	12	41
1911	(1)	Tariff Reform	[withdrawn]		
	(2)	Royal Commission	[compromise agreed by both sides]		
1912		Royal Commission	[adopted without debate]		
1913		Royal Commission	[adopted without debate]		
1914		Royal Commission	[adopted without debate]		

Sources: London Chamber of Commerce, Council Minutes, 10 Mar. 1904, 209; 11 Oct. 1906, 446–7; Leeds Chamber of Commerce, *Annual Report*, 1906; Hull Chamber of Commerce, *Annual Report*, 22 Nov. 1905, 40; 18 Nov. 1907, 53; 18 Nov. 1908, 29–30; 17 Nov. 1909, 33; 16 Nov. 1910, 53; 15 Nov. 1911, 22–3; A. R. Ilersic and P. F. B. Liddle, *Parliament of Commerce* (London, 1960), 156.

[19] A. R. Ilersic and P. F. B. Liddle, *Parliament of Commerce*, 155.
[20] Leeds CC, *Annual Report*, 1906.
[21] Hull CC, *Annual Report*, 14 Nov. 1906, 37.
[22] LCC, Council Minutes, 11 Oct. 1906.

should be taken to mitigate the evil by the reform of our tariff', aroused fierce opposition from the Manchester Chamber and Austin Taylor MP of Liverpool. Brassey prevailed in getting the resolution withdrawn: 'the great fiscal question had become political . . . [and] he strongly deprecated any attempt to capture the Association as a party organisation.'[23]

Brassey knew, however, that growing Tariff-Reform strength was threatening his powers of guillotine. 'It will be my endeavour', he announced in the presidential address in March 1908, 'to steer clear of the controversy in which, to my regret, we are about to engage.' The protectionist victory which he anticipated would cause 'secessions, and they will be regretted'.[24] Hawick's resolution was seconded by Edward Parkes MP of Birmingham, and supported by Bonar Law, who made what was acknowledged to be the most effective contribution to 'a lengthy and lively debate'. The Tariff Reformers won the day by forty to thirty, with thirty-one neutral.[25]

By now the fine distinctions between retaliation, preference, and Tariff Reform had become largely redundant in the eyes of protectionist businessmen, just as they always had been in the eyes of Free Traders. This can be seen clearly in C. J. Wilson's advocacy of Hawick's preferentialist resolution in September 1906, in which he dwelt more on protection of the home market and retaliation than on Empire trade.[26] In March 1908, John Roberts accepted the suggestion that Hawick's resolution on Tariff Reform should be merged with Belfast's on preference. Now he added fear of the Liberal's plans for social reform to the growing business impatience. Advocating a shift towards indirect taxation, he proclaimed that the 'present direct taxation of the country was beyond all reason'.[27]

In September 1908, the delegates unanimously accepted a resolution lamenting the injury done to British trade by foreign tariffs and urging the Government to consider steps to remedy it, in spite of its protectionist overtones. More significant, however, was the reaction to the Manchester Chamber's resolution urging that the *entente cordiale* presented a new opportunity for a 'special treaty of commerce with France, involving much lower duties in France and the French Colonies than those which at present exist'. The Leeds Chamber, for long neutral, led the opposition to this, demanding not simply the reduction of French tariff levels but parity of treatment: 'no treaty will be satisfactory which does not leave this country at liberty to accord the same treatment to French manufactures

[23] Hull CC, *Annual Report*, 18 Nov. 1907, 53–4. Brassey was, himself, the author of a Free Trade polemic, *Sixty Years of Progress and the New Fiscal Policy* (1904; 2nd edn. 1906).
[24] A. R. Ilersic and P. F. B. Liddle, *Parliament of Commerce*, 155.
[25] ACCUK Official Programme for Mar. 1908 Meeting (copy in Leeds CC Minute Book no. 4); Hull CC, *Annual Report*, 18 Nov. 1908, 29; A. R. Ilersic and P. F. B. Liddle, *Parliament of Commerce*, 155.
[26] *BCCJ*, Sept. 1906, 137–8.
[27] A. R. Ilersic and P. F. B. Liddle, *Parliament of Commerce*, 155.

imported into this country as is given to manufactured goods exported from here to France.' The Leeds amendment lost by sixty votes to eighty, but the Leeds delegates considered the matter badly handled:

had there been time prior to the Meeting to have taken the opinion of Chambers upon its terms, there is little doubt that the amendment would have carried. Delegates of many Chambers stated that they would have voted for the resolution as amended, had not their instructions, which were confined to the resolution as it appeared on the programme, precluded them from so doing.[28]

Independent sources, too, complained that many Chambers had not had prior notice of the amendment, and considered this the only explanation for its failure.[29] As the Nottingham delegates reported, 'It was astonishing to see how many men who were formerly most strongly in favour of free imports had changed their minds. And there was strong reason for it.'[30] Manchester's resolution, which must have seemed to its architects unexceptionable, had misfired.

These concerns resurfaced at the meeting of March 1909. Belfast's resolution demanded a 'release . . . from the rigid system of so-called Free Trade', stronger words than were usual, but in spite of this, Tariff Reform prevailed by forty-six votes to thirty-one, with thirty-two remaining neutral. The Bury Chamber's resolution was less expected: the 'time has arrived' for Tariff Reform:

so as to enable the Government to carry out the great and costly social reforms in hand or projected without detriment to other branches of the public service, and in order that all classes of HM subjects may contribute their fair share in bringing about the social amelioration of the people; and that this revision of Tariffs should aim at fostering those industries likely to mitigate the great and growing evil of unemployment.[31]

For its part, the Leeds Chamber reintroduced its defeated amendment of the previous meeting as a resolution. Seconded by Bristol, it was now carried by a large majority. For the London delegates, now instructed to remain neutral in spite of the vote in favour of Tariff Reform in the Chamber's poll of members in 1907,[32] this was the high spot of the meeting; otherwise the standard of debate was poor, 'and more than once degenerated to the level of a third-rate debating society'.[33]

The Belfast resolution suffered the same fate as its predecessors on account of the inclusion of neutral votes, but now there was more open unrest.[34] The executive council attempted to exclude Nottingham's resolution on the association's by-laws from the agenda of the March 1910 meeting, but was forced

---

[28] Leeds CC, *Annual Report*, 1908.   [29] *The Trader*, 8 Oct. 1908.
[30] *Nottingham Daily Guardian*, 7 Oct. 1908.
[31] ACCUK Official Programme for Mar. 1909 Meeting (copy in Leeds CC Minute Book No. 5).
[32] See below, 96–7.   [33] *BCCJ*, 31 Mar. 1909, 46.
[34] Leeds CC, *Annual Report*, 1909.

into an examination of them itself.[35] By a masterly piece of inactivity, however, after beginning to consider the matter in leisurely fashion in January, it did not set up a sub-committee until May, and in its turn the sub-committee did not report back until November,[36] so that any impact that a protectionist stance from ACCUK might have had upon the turbulent politics of 1910 was lost. This was in spite of the fact that a Tariff Reform resolution was passed by fifty-one votes to twelve at the March meeting, with forty-one neutral. Again, much importance was placed on the outcome by both sides. The Tariff Reformers fielded Sir Joseph Lawrence of the TRL, Sir Thomas Wrightson, the well-known Tariff Reform ironmaster, Edward Parkes MP, and Samuel Storey MP; their opponents Sir Swire Smith and Alfred Mond. The Tariff Reformers had come within an ace of outnumbering both Free Traders and neutrals, but again the necessary two-thirds majority was denied them by the system of counting votes.

The subcommittee on the articles of association recommended continuing the existing practice. A neutral vote was not to be likened to abstention. Rather, it:

more nearly approaches a vote for the previous question, i.e. a desire on the part of the Chamber not to commit itself or the Association for or against the resolution. Obviously this is tantamount to a declaration that such Chambers do not wish the Association to be committed to any action in its corporate capacity . . . The point is not of importance so long as it is made quite clear to the Chambers what action the Council will take in regard to these matters. We therefore strongly advise that the Chambers should bear in mind, in giving their delegates instructions as to voting, this suggested distinction between neutrality and abstention.[37]

This recommendation was the result of the deliberations of three men—Brassey, Holland (now Lord Rotherham), and Tariff Commissioner W. H. Mitchell. Ex-president and president, the one having made the original ruling in 1905 and the other having used it so determinedly since 1907, had a built-in majority on the subcommittee. Their recommendation was moved at the November meeting of the executive council by Free Traders A. J. Hobson of Sheffield and J. S. Taylor of Liverpool, but was rejected in favour of a reversing amendment by J. H. Howell.[38] Evidently, the meeting did not share the view that the matter was 'not of importance', and thought November 1910 rather late in the day to be 'suggest[ing] distinction[s]' between abstention and neutrality.

As can be seen from Table 5, the decline in the number of Free Trade chambers in the Association was paralleled by an increase in those opting for neutrality as well as those supporting Tariff Reform. Whether Free Trade Chambers frequently made the conversion all at once, or whether it was more typical for them to move to neutrality at the same time as formerly neutral Chambers espoused Tariff Reform is unclear, but it is evident that the process

[35] ACCUK Executive Council Minutes, 11 Jan. and 5 Feb. 1910.
[36] Ibid. 10 May and 8 Nov. 1910.　　[37] Ibid. 8 Nov. 1910.　　[38] Ibid.

as a whole involved a distinct and considerable increase in the popularity of a Chamberlainite programme. Furthermore, it is to be remembered that probably the most common reason for neutrality was division within the membership: the Leeds Chamber spent four years as a neutral even though its poll of members had revealed a protectionist majority amongst those who had voted.[39] It is highly probable, therefore, that protectionist businessmen were in a majority amongst the chambers represented by ACCUK from as early as 1904 or 1905, and almost certain that this was so by 1908. Nevertheless, the Liberal Governments after 1906 seem to have been somewhat more successful in causing a visible shift in business support than had been the Tariff Reformers before 1906: an important element in the gathering momentum for Tariff Reform was the repulsive force of alternative policies.

Brassey's strategy had been successful, however. After 1910 any hope of influencing national opinion was lost. By the meeting of March 1911 even the Dublin Chamber was prepared to sponsor a protectionist resolution, but the assembled delegates agreed to confine their attention to Hull's resolution for a Royal Commission. In this even the Free Traders sounded more militant. Edward Bolton pleaded for the issue to be 'lift[ed] . . . above politics', arguing that the Association was at least agreed on the problem of foreign tariffs, if not the remedy: 'It seemed little use for British manufacturers . . . to sit idle and bewail their loss'. The resolution passed unanimously, and also passed into ritual, being repeated at the Annual Meeting for each of the next three years, a clear indication that the Tariff Reformers had conceded that there was no purpose in pressing more radical proposals upon the Government.[40]

III

Manchester Chamber of Commerce was, of course, dominated by an industry which was highly export-orientated, some 80 per cent of Britain's cotton goods being sent abroad in the late nineteenth century.[41] Cotton could accommodate a loss of position in advanced, protected markets in Europe and North America by a heavy and increasing dependence on the Indian market,[42] where tariff policy was dictated by British interests.[43] Furthermore, imperial preference remained

---

[39] See below, 97–101.

[40] Hull CC, *Annual Report*, 15 Nov. 1911, 22–4; A. R. Ilersic and P. F. B. Liddle, *Parliament of Commerce*, 156.

[41] P. Deane and W. A. Cole, *British Economic Growth 1688–1959* (Cambridge, 2nd edn., 1967), 188.

[42] The proportion of Britain's yarn exports going to India fluctuated between 15 and 20% in 1870–1911; India's share of Britain's piece-goods exports rose from 28% in 1870 to around 40% in 1900–11. See R. E. Tyson, 'The Cotton Industry', in D. H. Aldcroft (ed.), *The Development of British Industry and Foreign Competition 1875–1914* (1968), 105–10.

[43] P. Harnetty, 'The Indian Cotton Duties Controversy, 1894–1896', *English Historical Review*, 77 (1962), 684–702.

unattractive to Manchester merchants and manufacturers because of the relatively small market for cotton goods afforded by the Dominions.[44]

This heavy and increasing dependence on India held, buried deep within it, worrying signs for the future. As Sandberg notes in his exhaustive statistical study, the rate of growth of the Indian market for Lancashire's goods was 'almost certainly on a long-term downward trend'.[45] When this was compounded by the natural protection of Indian producers in the First World War and the actual implementation of tariffs against British goods in 1917 and their raising in 1921 and (twice) in 1931,[46] the effect on Lancashire was little short of disastrous. But few in Manchester yet foresaw such trends, and in the decades before 1914 a certain comfortable complacency pervaded the Manchester Chamber.

Until the end of the 1870s the dominance of Free Traders was more or less complete, only a few lingering silk manufacturers, papermakers, and sugar-refiners proclaiming their heresy in the Chamber. But during the Fair Trade agitation of the 1880s, especially in several meetings in 1886 and 1887, the Fair Traders had done increasingly well, culminating in the celebrated meeting of December 1887, when H. F. Hibbert's Fair Trade resolution won by 'a large majority' of the seventy-three members who stayed to vote.[47]

The directors were confident enough of members' opinion to authorize a poll, which elicited responses from 621 of the 1,004 members entitled to vote. There were 397 members (with 556 votes) who supported Free Trade, whilst 187 (with 221 votes) dissented. Though the result bore out the allegation that the December meeting had been 'packed' by Fair Traders, it scarcely confirmed the directors' opinion, a year earlier, that in a poll less than one-tenth of the members would support Fair Trade. The implication of the result was not lost at the time, the president admitting that Cobden 'would have been disappointed'.[48]

According to Redford, most Fair Traders effectively abstained from Chamber debates on the fiscal question after the poll. Indeed, after the heavy defeat of a protectionist motion in 1892, no vote was taken until 6 June 1903, when in response to the new challenge from Birmingham a special meeting passed a Free Trade resolution by 300 to 120. Further debates in 1904, 1909, and 1910 saw Free Traders in a majority of three or four to one.

The significance of such voting figures is much less obvious than some have assumed. In particular, Redford's conclusion, that 'protectionist feeling in Manchester was no stronger in 1913 than it had been a generation before; it may even have been a little weaker',[49] is a classic example of academic

[44] A. Redford, *Manchester Merchants*, ii. 107–8.

[45] L. G. Sandberg, *Lancashire in Decline* (Columbus, Ohio, 1974), 143.

[46] Ibid. 185–9.

[47] *Manchester Guardian*, 20 Dec. 1888, quoted in Redford, *Manchester Merchants*, ii. 106.

[48] Quoted ibid. 107.   [49] Ibid. 108.

doublespeak with a rhetorical purpose. It begs the question of whether 25 or 30 per cent was a historically significant level of dissent, and creates the impression of a heavily united Chamber. Contained within Redford's own work we can find signs that the directors of the Manchester Chamber were far from certain that their members would exhibit the public face that they desired. They 'did not wait to be attacked, but took the initiative' in calling the meeting of June 1903. Furthermore, they did not repeat the mistake of 1888, and a poll on the fiscal issue was not attempted again until the very different conditions of 1916.[50]

Indeed, it is Peter Clarke's opinion that 'by 1910 the Tariff Reformers in the cotton industry were both numerous and vocal'.[51] The chamber was dominated by merchants, a feature which would not only understate protectionist sentiment in the industry as a whole, but would also tend to inflate the Free-Trade vote within the Chamber, because meetings at the Manchester offices 'were altogether more accessible to a merchant with offices next door than to a mill owner from, say, Eccles'. Furthermore, the loss of a Tariff-Reform motion in February 1909 took place in a 'tumultuous meeting', after which the directors' tactics were vilified by the Tariff Reformers, who claimed that two or three hundred members considered the result unrepresentative and the vote unconstitutional.[52]

Certainly Roland Smith's assertion that the Manchester Chamber was a 'cross-section of the Lancashire cotton community' is untenable.[53] In a brief examination of the cotton trade organizations, Clarke uncovers further evidence of support for Tariff Reform, and especially an increase in that support between the elections of 1906 and 1910. Clarke's excellent analysis demonstrates that even the example of Lancashire can be used to support much of the thesis being advanced in the present work. Free Traders were to claim, unwarrantably, the support of 90 per cent of cotton bosses. Leading figures such as Charles Macara were prone to 'pontificate', to pretend disingenuously to the position of industry spokesmen.[54] In an executive meeting of a local (North and North-Eastern Lancashire) branch of Macara's Cotton Employers' Parliamentary Association in 1903, twenty-two cotton bosses were reluctant to come to a vote because it was feared that 'so much difference of opinion existed amongst the members on the question that friction might arise'.[55] This very reluctance played into the hands of the Free Traders: 'Probably the Free Traders did not ask for a poll because without one they had a better change of exaggerating their

---

[50] *Manchester Guardian*, 20 Dec. 1888, quoted in Redford, *Manchester Merchants*, ii.107–8.

[51] P. F. Clarke, 'The End of Laissez-Faire and the Politics of Cotton', *Historical Journal*, 15 (1972), 498.

[52] Ibid. 499–502.

[53] R. Smith, 'The Manchester Chamber of Commerce and the Increasing Foreign Competition to Lancashire Cotton Textiles, 1873–1896', *Bulletin of the John Rylands Library*, 38 (1955–6), 508.

[54] As can be gauged from the tenor of Macara's speeches and published articles. See e.g. his *Trade Stability and How to Obtain It* (Manchester, 1925) and his *Modern Industrial Tendencies* (Manchester, 1926).

[55] Recollection of Albert Simpson, quoted in Clarke, 'The End of Laissez-Faire', 497.

predominance.'[56] After Clarke's revision, cotton might still return a majority of businessmen for Free Trade, but the reduction of that majority from 90 per cent to, say, 60 or 65 per cent has profound implications for the other industries encountered in the present study, and supports its thesis that, well before 1914, protectionist sentiment had already widely permeated British industry.

IV

In 1903 Hull Chamber of Commerce represented the trade and industry of the UK's third largest port, with a trade the size of Glasgow and Leith combined, and had over 300 members. Sensing a divided membership, its council was cautious, and parried the ACCUK circular of July 1903, attempting to elicit Chambers' views on the fiscal question, by protesting that Chamberlain's intentions were still uncertain, his policy as yet unformed. Subsequently, the Chamber twice invited Chamberlain to explain his policy before them, but Chamberlain declined owing to pressure of engagements. Thereupon, with the ACCUK circular still to be answered, a general meeting was held and a proposal for a Royal Commission passed by a large majority.[57]

Justifying its position, the council argued that it had 'exercised a wise reticence' in not polling the membership: 'The question is a National one and ought not to be made one of party politics . . . The wellbeing and prosperity of the whole community is to be considered before the personal gain of any particular class'.[58]

Free Traders were critical of the council's decision for neutrality. At the AGM of 1903, C. H. Wilson, Liberal MP for Hull West and head of the port's largest shipping company,[59] warned of the danger of taxing food, 'the bulk of our [incoming] cargoes', and of any policy which by encouraging Canadian trade would disadvantage Hull to the benefit of the west-coast ports. Mindful also of Hull's heavy dependence on coal exports, he feared that 'the feeling that the export of coal ought to be . . . put a stop to . . . influences the actions of our present Prime Minister to some extent'. But he did discern some division of opinion within the Chamber, regretting 'that the views I entertain . . . are not more supported by the Chamber'. More strongly voiced sentiments came from Free Trader H. F. Smith: 'the council had taken upon themselves a responsibility and a duty that they had no business to do, because it must be looked upon as an implied approval of the policy' of imperial preference. He was then cut off for 'exceeding the scope of the resolution': his protest that he was not the first to do so was surely correct. T. H. Sissons defended the Chamber's council. Admitting that the new policy would damage his own import trade from

---

[56] Ibid.   [57] Hull CC, *Annual Report*, 18 Nov. 1903, 10–12.

[58] Ibid. 13.   [59] H. Pelling, *Social Geography of British Elections 1885–1910* (1967), 294–5.

Germany, and probably shipping overall, he urged that this must be set alongside the benefits to seed-crushers, millers, and other industrial interests of the port, and only a Royal Commission could balance the interests.[60]

In Hull, therefore, unusually, the vote for a Royal Commission may have been a Tariff-Reform tactic by some of the council. If so, it effectively failed. Whatever the precise numbers, supporters of Free Trade in the Hull Chamber were too important an element of the membership to allow them any leeway. Though its *Annual Reports* gave full accounts of the fiscal debates in the Associated Chambers, down to 1914 the Hull Chamber was largely inactive in fiscal politics of any kind. At the meeting of ACCUK in March 1908, for instance, the Hull representatives did not vote on the issue, 'knowing that the members of the Chamber held divided opinions', and that the commercial community, to 'maintain its legitimate influence', was 'wise to avoid questions on which they differed'.[61]

The Chamber's fear of destroying its credibility by exposing its division to the public view was itself not uncommon. That it was the Free Traders who were critical of the resolution calling for a Royal Commission in September 1903 is more surprising. Not until 1911 did attitudes become more relaxed. Following a unanimous vote at a special meeting, the Hull Chamber tabled a resolution urging a Royal Commission at the spring meeting of the Associated Chambers, in view of the 'conflicting opinions of commercial men' on Tariff Reform.[62] As has been seen above, it is not without significance that this resolution attracted unqualified support from both Sir Algernon Firth, the Halifax protectionist, and Sir Felix Schuster, the City banker and Free Trader.[63]

The surviving evidence of the debate in the Hull Chamber presents the most intractable problem, and perhaps also the most intriguing, of all the detailed studies undertaken here. The *Annual Reports*, taken literally, point to very deep division, and more than once give the impression that it was between shipowners and merchants on the one hand and industrial interests on the other. But no protectionist is ever named in the record; only Sissons is quoted as having had some sympathy with the Tariff Reformers, and it would be quite tenable to regard his remarks as no more than a plea to let their case be heard. It would seem most prudent, therefore, to regard the Hull Chamber as one in which the Free-Trade interest was heavily predominant, but one in which there was some Tariff-Reform support, probably from those engaged in manufacturing or food-processing industries, and in which there was sympathy for their case by at least some of those on the other side of the fiscal divide. Generally merchants (particularly coal and grain dealers) and shipping interests were predominant in the Hull Chamber, and it would appear that in consequence the port's industries

[60] Hull CC, *Annual Report*, 18 Nov. 1903, 57–63.
[61] Hull CC, *Annual Report*, 18 Nov. 1908, 85.
[62] Hull CC, *Annual Report*, 15 Nov. 1911, 22–3.
[63] See above, 88.

were under-represented. In the 1880s it had been asserted that the Chamber's interest in shipping had discouraged the expansion of the Chamber. According to Bellamy, this bias lessened after 1880, with the continued expansion of local industry, but it still persisted.[64] Since the Chamber did not completely reflect local economic interests, division within it revolved more upon whether a call for a Royal Commission was legitimate, rather than where the balance of opinion within the Chamber lay.

V

The council of the London Chamber of Commerce was heavily divided from the very beginning of Chamberlain's campaign. As early as April 1903, discussions of the arrangements for the Fifth Congress of Chambers of Commerce of the Empire at Montreal in October exposed intractable differences, with the predictable result that it was decided to limit the London Chamber's initiative at Montreal to a motion for a Royal Commission.[65]

Council chairman J. Innes Rogers interpreted the Chamber's articles of association as precluding discussion of Tariff Reform due to its political nature. Initially, the council agreed, refusing to join the Central Chamber of Agriculture's deputation to Balfour and Austen Chamberlain on the abolition of the Corn Registration Duty, a decision made easier by the opposition of the London Flour Trade Association to the deputation.[66] But by July there was growing support within the council for a plebiscite of members' opinions, following the lead taken by Birmingham and Glasgow. Some wanted this done through a questionnaire; others preferred that opinion should be solicited through the Chamber's trade sections, as had been done in the 1880s for the Royal Commission on the Depression of Trade and Industry.[67] Opposition to a poll came mainly from Felix Schuster and Sir Albert Rollit, on the grounds that it was premature to issue a questionnaire when the details of the policy were still unspecified. Their determination increased with the return of the London delegates from Montreal. J. C. Pillman urged that the Chamber should 'confine its good offices to submitting the Montreal Resolution to the Government', and select representative witnesses in anticipation of a Royal Commission being appointed. The adoption of his resolution 'without discussion' at a council

---

[64] J. Bellamy, *The Trade and Shipping of Nineteenth-Century Hull* (East Yorkshire Local History Society, Publication No. 27, 1971), 56.

[65] LCC Council Minutes, 30 Apr. 1903.

[66] LCC Council Minutes, 14 May 1903. For Henry Chaplin's deputation to Balfour, see J. Amery, *Life of Joseph Chamberlain*, v. (1969), 181–3.

[67] Members of the council supporting a plebiscite included W. C. Anderson, Stanley Machin, Albert Spicer, F. Faithful Begg, and Charles Charleton.

meeting in November had the consequence of shelving any plans for a poll 'for the time being'.[68]

There was always the threat, however, that the Chamber's trade sections might take matters into their own hands. The Manufacturers' Section pressed for permission to issue a questionnaire to its own members, whilst the Cement Trade Section passed a resolution critical of the free import of cement and simultaneously announced its intention to give evidence before the Tariff Commission. To Pillman, the council's acceptance of this resolution would be tantamount to the Chamber itself advocating protection. But an LCC 'by-law' held that no resolution from a trade section bound the Chamber unless confirmed by the council, and the council therefore agreed, with some reluctance, that trade sections should be free to appear before the Tariff Commission provided it was made clear that they did not speak for the Chamber as a whole.[69]

Implicitly, however, this gave the trade sections permission to ascertain opinion within their own ranks. Soon the Manufacturers' Association, the Timber Trades Section, and the Perfumery Trade Sub-section had issued questionnaires. The Electrical Trades Section dispensed with formalities, and urged its members to reply to the Tariff Commission individually. Fearing an avalanche of autonomous action, the council authorized the issue of a questionnaire to the entire membership.[70]

The questionnaire tested Lord Avebury's resolution, carried by thirteen votes to twelve in council in December 1903, that the LCC would support retaliation on a product if every effort in negotiation had failed and if it should not seriously hurt other branches of industry and commerce. About 10 per cent of the members responded, 207 in support (with an additional thirty-eight wanting a stronger, Chamberlainite, stance) and 126 dissenting. Avebury's resolution was therefore put onto the agenda of the March 1904 meeting of ACCUK, where it was pressed by Tariff Commissioner Sir Samuel Boulton on account of Avebury's illness, and was finally defeated by an amendment of fifty-eight to forty-five in favour of a Royal Commission.[71]

The 90 per cent abstention rate in the LCC poll daunted a council not far off equally balanced in its fiscal inclinations; and in July 1904 it decided by a narrow margin that it would be inappropriate to invite Chamberlain to address the Chamber.[72] Delegates to the spring meeting of ACCUK in 1905 were given the explicit instruction to 'be neutral—not vote as Chamber' on a protectionist motion from Nottingham. However, neutrality bore different interpretations. Schuster interpreted an amendment by the Swansea Chamber to the Nottingham

[68] LCC Council Minutes, 12 Nov. 1903.   [69] Ibid. 28 Jan. 1904.
[70] Ibid. 18 and 25 Feb. 1904.   [71] Ibid. 25 Feb. 1904; see also above, 82–3.
[72] Ibid. 14 July 1904.

resolution as in accordance with the LCC's earlier resolution at Montreal. With the assent of two other delegates, he cast the Chamber's votes in favour of the amendment, hence against the Nottingham motion on which the delegates had been instructed to take a neutral stance. As we have noted above, the fourth delegate, Boulton, objected and the LCC's four votes were disallowed, the amendment thus failing by one vote instead of being carried by three.[73]

Schuster's annoyance at being frustrated in supporting an amendment which he maintained reflected LCC policy was equalled by the vehemence of Boulton's contention that the Montreal resolution differed from the Swansea amendment, which was in fact no different from the amendment which had been moved at the 1904 meeting of ACCUK to wreck Avebury's motion of 'conditional' retaliation. Even Free Traders such as Sir Albert Rollit on the LCC council were forced to concede the right to Boulton: 'the London Chamber was not entitled to vote for the amendment directed against the resolution in favour of Fiscalism . . . the Tariff Commissioner was right on a point of order.'[74]

Now public humiliation had been added to uncertainty and division, and the council sought delay. But it was still reluctant that LCC neutrality should have the effect of reinforcing the Free Trade status quo. Faced with hosting the Sixth Congress of Chambers of Commerce of the Empire, the LCC's general-purposes committee recommended that the Chamber should submit an amendment to all resolutions on imperial commercial relations, that the Congress should reserve its position until after the forthcoming Imperial Conference of 1907. The council initially endorsed this by thirteen votes to eleven. But vigorous protest by Boulton and Evans Jackson on grounds that this stance could not be represented as one of neutrality was successful, and the decision was reversed by twenty-two votes to one.[75] The London council was also infuriated by Holland's refusal, in the Associated Chambers in Autumn 1906, to allow a vote by Chamber after the South of Scotland's preferentialist resolution had been lost to a neutral amendment by a show of hands.[76]

This being said, however, the London council remained more or less evenly divided, attendance at individual meetings being critical. In January 1907 Sir Thomas Brooke-Hitching and Stanley Machin pressed for a poll of members, whilst the council chairman, Charles Charleton, admitted that the time for neutrality was coming to an end. The council obviously felt itself prompted by protectionist motions put by the Belfast and South of Scotland Chambers on the agenda of the forthcoming meeting of the Associated Chambers in March. In order to forestall a poll of members, Frederick Coysh quickly introduced a Free Trade motion before the council. This failed, by twenty-one votes to fourteen, but then so did Charleton's subsequent preferentialist motion, by twenty to

---

[73] See above, 83.   [74] LCC Council Minutes, 9 Mar. 1905.
[75] Ibid. 5 July 1906.   [76] Ibid. 11 Oct. 1906; see also above, 84.

twelve. The council could by now see no recourse but to allow a poll of the membership, carried out at a general meeting.[77]

The general meeting, held at the Great Hall, Cannon Street Hotel, on 21 March 1907, took the form of speeches on a Free Trade resolution moved by Coysh and seconded by B. Rosenfeld, and a protectionist–preferentialist amendment moved by Faithful Begg and seconded by Bonar Law. The amendment was passed by 'a large majority' and was then put as the substantive motion. J. Innes Rogers and Sir Joseph Lawrence then pressed for a poll of the entire membership.[78] This was duly carried out, the result being announced at the AGM on 10 April. Out of a total membership of 3,200, 1,077 voted in favour of Begg's Tariff Reform resolution and 472 against. In Charleton's words, the poll was 'a record one in the Chamber's history', and would enable the council 'to give their delegates more precise instructions at future Congresses and meetings'.[79]

There was little formal dissent from the poll in the trade sections. In May, the Leather Trade Section expressed regret, but as only five members had attended the meeting, the council attached no importance to their decision. In Autumn the LCC supported the South of Scotland's preferentialist motion at the Liverpool meeting of ACCUK, which was, however, withdrawn.

But by February 1908 the oppostion was regrouping. Coysh and Pillman argued against accepting the GPC's recommendation to support the South of Scotland's preferentialist motion at the forthcoming ACCUK meeting, Coysh objecting to the words 'approving of Free Trade in principle' on the grounds that the London Chamber obviously did not! Optimistically, Rollit argued that the poll of 1907 could not be held to bind the Chamber 'for all time'. Though now heavily outnumbered, Coysh and Pillman could still muster nine votes on council.[80]

They came nearer to realizing their objective early in 1909. The Tariff Reformers on the LCC council were divided over the form of words on Belfast's proposed resolution for the pending March meeting of ACCUK. Coysh urged that Belfast be supported in accordance with the poll of 1907, obviously seeking to foment a dispute between the Tariff Reformers. Pillman, not up to such Machiavellian tactics, urged neutrality, and in a deciding vote the council was evenly divided, fourteen votes to fourteen, and therefore determined upon neutrality. This led to a special council meeting in March, demanded by the Tariff Reformers, who argued that the decision flew in the face of the 1907 poll. A long debate ensued between high-powered participants—Avebury, Faithful Begg, Sir Albert Spicer, Brassey, Sir John Cockburn, Rollit, Innes Rogers, Frank Debenham, Charleton, Coysh, L. A. Martin, Brooke-Hitching, and others.[81]

---

[77] LCC Council Minutes. 28 Feb. 1907.   [78] *CCJ*, Apr. 1907, 93–7.
[79] Ibid. May 1907, 126, 130.   [80] LCC Council Minutes, 13 Feb. 1908.
[81] Ibid. 11 Feb. 1909; 1 Mar. 1909.

The council was now gravitating back towards stalemate. The meeting was adjourned, its decision inconclusive. When, in March, the council received the reports of the London delegates to the ACCUK meeting, there was no mention of the Chamber's indecisive discussion, or whether London had supported the Belfast and Bury resolutions, or even whether they had been carried. Rather, there was total silence.[82]

Preparations for the Seventh Congress of Chambers of Commerce of the Empire found the London council once again at sixes and sevens, with Free Traders led by Avebury, Brassey, and Felix Schuster objecting to a preferentialist motion to be put by the London Chamber. The motion survived by seventeen votes to sixteen, and went unaltered to Sydney where, in September, it was carried by an individual vote of eighty-one to thirty-one, and a Chamber vote of sixty to eight, with eleven neutral.[83] The proposed motions by Belfast and the South of Scotland for the March 1910 meeting of ACCUK survived the London council by a slightly larger margin, twenty-two votes to eighteen.[84]

Thereafter, interest in Tariff Reform in the London Chamber petered out until the First World War. This inactivity should not be allowed to conceal the fact, however, that it was an oscillating stalemate on the LCC council which effectively defused the potential impact of a distinct Tariff-Reform majority amongst the ordinary membership of the Chamber. Sir Keith Hancock described the pre-1914 controversy as 'a three-cornered struggle, with the old individualist-cosmopolitan City of London joining forces with Manchester to keep Birmingham in check'.[85] Though true of the banking and financial interests of the City, classically defined, this was much less accurate an assessment of the leanings of the manufacturing and even to an extent the merchant interests of inner London.

VI

Deep division in the Leeds Chamber, both on the council and amongst the membership, ensured neutrality of the fiscal question until 1908. In June 1903 a motion urging a Royal Commission to examine trade relations with the Empire was carried *nem con* after a wrecking amendment proposed by Free Traders had been defeated by seven votes to four. This small protectionist victory, coupled with the frenzied debate in the press during the second half of 1903, led to a poll of members' views at a Special General Meeting in November, when Free-Trade banker and local Liberal MP, E. W. Beckett, moved that Chamberlain's policy

[82] Ibid. 11 Mar. 1909.
[83] LCC, Minutes of Special Council Meeting, 7 June 1909; Council Minutes, 14 Oct. 1909.
[84] LCC Council Minutes, 10 Feb. 1910.
[85] W. K. Hancock, *Survey of British Commonwealth Affairs 1918–1939*, ii. *Problems of Economic Policy 1918–1939*, 1 (1942), 92.

was 'injurious' to British trade and commerce. The motion was opposed by F. W. Tannett-Walker, of a local engineering and boilermaking firm, and Jonathan Peate, soon to be a member of the Tariff Commission's Textile Committee. The protectionists won by seventy-six votes to sixty-five, but of an initial attendance of 300 half abstained or left before the two-and-a-half hour meeting came to a vote.[86] Regarding this to be unsatisfactory as an endorsement of Chamberlain's policy, the council decided privately not to entertain him to lunch on his forthcoming visit to Leeds, in view of the 'great differences of opinion within the Chamber on the Fiscal Question'.[87]

The council were open in admitting the deep rift within the Chamber. Maybe in an attempt to resolve the issue or restore amicability by having the issue taken out of the Chamber's hands, the Free Traders dropped their opposition to a Royal Commission. Indeed, the Leeds delegates to the Fifth Congress of the Chambers of Commerce of the Empire at Montreal late in 1903, Peate and Ewing Matheson, joined in supporting a successful resolution for a Royal Commission. Thereafter the Leeds Chamber was effectively unanimous on this aspect of the issue.[88] This attempt at reconciliation was evident at the annual dinner in January 1904. Sentiments towards the newly-established Tariff Commission, now in the process of formation after Chamberlain's announcement at Leeds on 16 December, were quietly favourable. Guest speaker J. H. Clapham, soon to publish his authoritative work on the woollen and worsted industries,[89] reflected the mood of the occasion:

For his own part, he did not resent in the least Mr. Chamberlain's Commission, though he was among those who [it had been said] were supposed to denounce it. He welcomed that Commission because when it had obtained information they would have something to criticise, but he would have preferred a Royal Commission.[90]

This set the pattern for instructions to the Leeds delegates at the Associated Chambers of Commerce meetings in the next few years. In March 1904 Leeds delegates supported the Dublin Chamber's motion calling for a Royal Commission, but abstained from motions from the London, Nottingham, South of Scotland, and Paris Chambers advocating retaliation.[91] The London Chamber's resolution was hedged about by conditions, and an amendment proposing retaliation more unequivocally was defeated by sixty-nine votes to twenty-seven,

[86] Council Meeting, 30 June 1903; General Meeting, 3 Nov. 1903; Leeds CC, Minute Book No. 4.
[87] Ibid. Special Private Council Meeting, 1 Dec. 1903.
[88] Leeds CC, *Annual Report*, 1903.
[89] J. H. Clapham, *The Woollen and Worsted Industries* (1907).
[90] Leeds CC, Annual General Meeting, 26 Jan. 1904.
[91] The Leeds Council's instructions to delegates can be obtained from marginal notes (in the secretary's hand) to the motions listed in the official programmes issued before each annual or autumn meeting of ACCUK. These official programmes, contained in the Leeds Chamber's minute books, are not footnoted separately.

but a further, blander motion calling for negotiation and a Royal Commission was passed. This result was observed with smug satisfaction, and some judicious fence-sitting, by the Leeds Council:

It will be seen, therefore, that the meeting supported negotiation rather than retaliation—although it is open to question whether the former would be effective without the power to retaliate in case of need—and approved of the appointment of a Royal Commission of Enquiry, which your Chamber had . . . already . . . recommended.[92]

At the autumn 1906 meeting it was the amendment of Leeds delegate Colonel Harding, neutralizing the South of Scotland's preferentialist motion, which led to Holland's unprecedented refusal to allow a chamber vote.[93] When Harding retired from the Associated Chambers' council, he was replaced by another Free Trader, Rowland Barran. Commenting on the passing of a preferentialist resolution at the Sixth Congress of Chambers of Commerce of the Empire, Leeds president Henry Barran observed that the Canadian delegates did not 'fully appreciate England's peculiar economic position', whilst the Australians seemed to favour preference 'in the abstract, but they did not seem to understand what it would mean when reduced to actual facts'.[94]

This stance, with Free Trade council members maintaining the status quo over the heads of a deeply divided chamber, continued throughout 1907. At the instigation of Barran and C. S. Sykes, Mr Zossenheim was prevented from putting a preferentialist motion onto the agenda of ACCUK's September meeting.[95] In March 1908, Leeds remained neutral at the Associated Chambers in the face of a protectionist motion from the South of Scotland Chamber and a preferentialist motion from Belfast, but gave 'leave to the delegates to vote for [a] Royal Commission'.

But in the second half of 1908 came a sea change. Faced with advance notice that the Manchester Chamber was to table a motion favouring a commercial treaty with France at the September meeting of the Associated Chambers, a special meeting of the Leeds council agreed that Manchester's demands were insufficient.[96] As we have seen, the failure of Leeds's amendment was blamed by several Chambers on inadequacies in ACCUK's circularizing of members and the inflexibility of the delegate system.[97] In Leeds this was regarded as an insult, and it strengthened the Chamber's resolve in its new course of action. Shortly afterwards, the French dimension served to accelerate Leeds's drift towards protection even more. In response to a French government announcement of an increase in duties, the Chamber expressed concern over the new schedules on woollens, engineering and heavy machine tools, leather, and boots and shoes.

[92] Leeds CC, *Annual Report*, 1904.   [93] See above, 84.
[94] Leeds CC, *Annual Report*, 1906.   [95] Leeds CC, Council Meeting, 25 June 1907.
[96] Leeds CC, Special Council Meeting, 8 Sept. 1908.
[97] Leeds CC, *Annual Report*, 1908. See also above, 86.

Receiving advance notice of the March 1909 meeting of ACCUK, the Leeds council conducted a poll of members on the Belfast Chamber's resolution that 'by broadening the basis of taxation and reforming the Fiscal System [the UK] should place itself in a position to meet Foreign Competition on equal terms'. Of 320 members, 164 voted for the Belfast resolution, seventy-one against, and nineteen abstained, whilst sixty-six didn't reply. For the first time, Leeds was demonstrated to have an actual majority of the membership in favour of Tariff Reform.[98]

Leeds delegates went to the March 1909 meeting of the Associated Chambers with their own resolution on trade with France, identically worded to the amendment to the Manchester resolution that had failed in September 1908. The Leeds members were also prompted by fears over the Liberals' financial policy as presaged in the 1907 budget. This was implied by their support for the Belfast Chamber's resolution, and made even clearer by their support for the resolution of the Bury Chamber that tariffs should be used to increase revenue to pay for social reform.[99] In 1910 the Chamber supported Tariff-Reform resolutions from Belfast and the South of Scotland at the March meeting of ACCUK. The Belfast resolution, in similar vein to that from Bury in 1909, juxtaposed the 'continuing and alarming' increase in unemployment with the need to widen the basis of taxation 'to meet increasing national necessities'.[100] The Liberal welfare reforms exercised a pincer effect on businessmen's attitudes to Tariff Reform. Not only was there a demand that the balance between direct and indirect taxes be altered to ensure that the main burden did not fall on higher incomes and property, but there was also the realization that at best this would only be partly achieved, and hence some recognition of the desirability of keeping unemployment down in the interests of those who would have to finance the larger share of unemployment benefits when introduced.[101] Lloyd George had already, in his 1909 budget speech, announced that the government favoured a tripartite system of contribution to future health and unemployment schemes, so that it was clear that even employers in uninsured trades would be vulnerable via the state contribution.[102]

---

[98] M. W. Beresford, *The Leeds Chamber of Commerce* (Leeds, 1951), 119, contains the important typographical error of reporting the abstentions as numbering 91, not 19, though it is added that 'the Leeds Chamber had shown where the majority of its members now stood'. I reproduced Beresford's error in 'Businessmen, Industries and Tariff Reform in Great Britain, 1903–1930', *Business History*, 25 (1983), 163.

[99] See above, 86; Leeds CC, *Annual Report*, 1909.

[100] Annual Meeting of ACCUK, 15–17 Mar. 1910, *Official Programme*.

[101] Such a business reaction is not discussed in J. R. Hay, 'Employers and Social Policy in Britain: The Evolution of Welfare Legislation, 1905–14', *Social History*, 4 (1977); or in his 'Employers' Attitudes to Social Policy and the Concept of "Social Control", 1900–1920', in P. Thane (ed.), *The Origins of British Social Policy* (1978).

[102] Lloyd George in the House of Commons, 29 Apr. 1909; repr. in *The People's Budget* (1909), 13.

Feelings of injustice in the scope of most-favoured-nation treatment contained in the new Japanese tariff of summer 1910 ensured that the Leeds membership made no retreat. The council, too, now had a distinct protectionist majority, only three preferring the establishment of a Royal Commission to immediate fiscal change.[103] Yet the *Annual Report* for 1911 exhibited a shift in the attention of Leeds businessmen. Commenting on the March 1911 meeting of ACCUK, the Leeds council neglected the four protectionist and preferentialist resolutions in their concern over picketing and the Trades Disputes Act of 1906. The *Annual Report* also devoted much space to the National Insurance Bill and the fear that its cost would 'gravely imperil' productive industry, but without explicitly linking the issue to the fiscal question.

By early 1912 this diversion of attention had become quite clear. Leeds's instructions to its delegates to the March meeting of the Associated Chambers on fiscal resolutions were contained in the word 'open', this replacing the directive, 'support', which had been the instruction since 1908.[104] A similar shift in emphasis away from the more controversial aspects of Tariff Reform is also seen in the proceedings of the Associated Chambers in that year.[105] Under threat from industrial unrest and a profligate government, it made sense not to sow again the seeds of division within business circles.

Tariff Reform and imperial preference were becoming overshadowed by other matters, especially labour unrest. This was ironic given that the presidents of ACCUK and the Leeds chambers were now both Tariff Reformers with Tariff Commission connections, Lord Desborough and Sir Algernon Firth. And it is doubly ironic that it was the loss of a case in the House of Lords against the London Society of Compositors which prompted many chambers to agitate for repeal of the Trades Disputes Act on the grounds that trade-union immunity from liability for tort was unjust. That case was brought by Vacher and Sons, one-time printers to the Tariff Commission.

VII

The Nottingham Chamber's council was sufficiently sure of its members' fiscal views to submit protectionist resolutions to the meetings of the Associated Chambers from March 1903 onwards. At its first discussion of the fiscal question, in response to the ACCUK circular of July 1903, Chamberlain's scheme was scarcely made welcome, some supporting the call for a government inquiry, others seeking a positive expression of Free Trade by the Chamber. But this lukewarm reaction was partly because the doubters included those who took the

---

[103] Leeds CC, Council Meeting, 3 Jan. 1911.
[104] Marginal notes to ACCUK Official Programme for Mar. 1912 in Leeds CC Minute Book no. 5.
[105] See, generally, the entries for 1912 in Leeds CC Minute Book no. 5.

restiveness of Canadian manufacturers under unilateral preference to demonstrate that it would be impossible to gain protection for manufactures under the scheme, and it is evident that, doubts though there were, the council was generally in support of an interventionist policy if it could be tailored to local needs. When M. G. Goodall sought to commit the council to a Free Trade resolution, he lost by fifteen votes to four.[106]

Like most Chambers, Nottingham let the matter rest over the summer, and by November the protectionists, led by B. F. Stiebel and a Mr Homberger, were becoming restive. They used the occasion of a more routine event in the Chamber's business, a special meeting to discuss pending tariff changes in Austria-Hungary, Germany, and Russia, to force a retaliationist motion. Only three out of the twenty-six present, Goodall, W. Bridgett, and J. M. Perry, opposed it.[107] Exchanges with twelve other Chambers and correspondence with the Board of Trade which, if anything, promoted the view within the Nottingham Chamber that the new European tariffs were even worse than had been anticipated,[108] led to a further special meeting at which Stiebel's retaliationist motion was passed by twenty-five to ten, a Free-Trade amendment being defeated by a slightly larger margin. Given an attendance of forty, the level of abstention was remarkably low,[109] and in the course of the debate Free Trader W. B. Baggaley was excited to remark with exasperation that the leaders of the Chamber 'were getting very grey hair, and were getting very antiquated'.[110]

Yet events must have been some comfort to Baggaley. At the annual meeting in January, Edward Bond, Conservative MP for Nottingham East, sat on the fence by raising again the call for an inquiry,[111] and thereafter little mention was made of the fiscal controversy until December, when Stiebel manoeuvred to put a full-blown Chamberlainite motion on the agenda of the March meeting of ACCUK in the Nottingham Chamber's name. Several thought this had been sprung upon the Chamber without due notice, whilst even Tariff Reformer A. Durose thought the motion too strongly worded, and it passed by only a small majority.[112] Liberal opinion gloated. 'Several members of the Council and a great number of members of the Chamber, who were not present when the resolution was introduced, had not subscribed to the Birmingham fiscal confession of faith,' concluded the *Nottingham Daily Guardian*.[113]

To an extent this was wishful thinking. The inactivity of the previous year had not lessened Tariff Reform sentiments: even Bridgett, at the annual general meeting of 25 January 1905, admitted that Stiebel's motion represented the views

---

[106] *Nottingham Daily Express*, 29 July 1903.   [107] Ibid. 11 Nov. 1903.
[108] Ibid. 2 Dec. 1903.   [109] Ibid. 16 Dec. 1903.
[110] *Nottingham Daily Guardian*, 16 Dec. 1903.   [111] *Nottingham Daily Express*, 30 Jan. 1904.
[112] Ibid. 7 Dec. 1904.   [113] *Nottingham Daily Guardian*, 26 Jan. 1905.

of the majority of both Chamber and council.[114] Yet during this period the minority of Free Traders in the Nottingham Chamber lost little ground, and their opposition, continued even after Bridgett's death in September 1906 deprived them of one of their most effective advocates.[115] The Liberal election victory strengthened their position and encouraged inactivity on the part of their opponents. At the same time, Lloyd George's Patents and Designs Bill, touching as it did on the many grievances of the Nottingham lace trade, may have thawed the hearts of some Nottingham protectionists to a government which had effectively blocked progress towards Tariff Reform.[116]

When protectionist activity revived in the Nottingham Chamber, during the depression of 1908, it was due to the stimulus of events at the autumn meeting of the Associated Chambers. New French tariff proposals, which dominated the discussion at Cardiff, included increases on leather, boots and shoes, and the whole range of 'Nottingham goods'. The Nottingham council was gratified by Stiebel's report that Cardiff had witnessed a strong reaction against Free Trade by Chamber delegates.[117] Indeed, Stiebel's account of the mishandling of the Leeds Chamber's amendment urging retaliation against France was essentially similar to that given by the Leeds delegates.[118] 'It was all very well to talk about the *entente cordiale*, but there was no such thing in business.' To Stiebel, the support of formerly Free Trade Chambers for retaliationist motions by Cardiff and the South of Scotland were clear signs that businessmen were waking up. Even the *Nottingham Daily Guardian*, in its headline, discerned a 'Movement Growing'.[119] Though there were no special meetings held or resolutions passed on Tariff Reform during this period, it is evident that the Free Traders had become increasingly beleaguered.

Stiebel was a colourful character whose extreme views on such issues as the extravagance of the poor law, the 'spinelessness' of the middle class in the face of industrial unrest and socialism, and the impropriety of hobble and harem skirts varied from the bizarre to the over-harsh.[120] But his chairmanship of the Chamber's Foreign Trade Committee gave him a wide and receptive constituency. His ability to keep the fiscal issue before the Chamber was aided by Nottingham's continuing annoyance over the French tariff, which was still evident in the run-up to the election of January 1910,[121] whilst by late 1912 attention was being focused on the American and Russian tariffs.[122]

---

[114] *Nottingham Daily Express*, 26 Jan. 1905.   [115] Ibid. 5 Sept. 1906.

[116] *Nottingham Daily Guardian*, 8 May 1907.

[117] Ibid. 7 Oct. 1908.

[118] See above, 85–6, 99; *The Trader*, 8 Oct. 1908.

[119] *Nottingham Daily Guardian*, 7 Oct. 1908.

[120] *Nottingham Daily Express*, 22 Jan. 1908; *The Trader*, 11 Mar., 8 Apr. and 23 Sept. 1911.

[121] *The Trader*, 8 Jan. 1910.

[122] NCC Council Minutes, 5 Nov. 1912 and 7 Jan. 1913.

VIII

The Birmingham Chamber was initially less receptive to the Fair Trade movement of the 1880s than might be expected. In the 1870s it assumed the common stance of a Free Trade body injured but not daunted by foreign tariffs. In 1881 it defeated an impishly ambiguous motion urging a policy to encourage closer imperial trade, introduced by Sampson S. Lloyd, translator into English of List's *National System*. In October 1885 the council was censured by sixty-two votes to forty-six for drafting a response to the Royal Commission on the Depression of Trade and Industry recommending selective protective duties. But even this vote represented a significant increase in Fair Trade sympathy, and in the depression of 1887, after hearing a deputation from the National Fair Trade League, a special meeting of the Chamber adopted a Fair Trade resolution by a large majority. By 1889 the council was advocating an Empire customs union, according to the US treaty pattern in which there would be no extension of tariff reductions to third parties via the MFN clause.[123]

It is evident, however, that given the large number of members who did not attend meetings, voting could be very erratic. In 1893 the Chamber 'decline[d] to . . . recommend . . . a policy [an Empire customs union] which . . . would involve a departure from the principle of Free Trade' by seventy-six votes to sixty-one. And, in spite of increasing protests as to the impotence of the British government in the face of tariff changes on Birmingham goods by France, Germany, and the US in the 1890s, the council still had not got a very sound knowledge of members' opinion to work with. Commenting on the unsatisfactory response to a questionnaire issued in 1901, the Secretary later remarked:

In explanation of the apparent indifference of local manufacturers to the proposed increases of duty in Germany it might be said that this was probably due to a want of knowledge as to the trend of events, and to the effect of the erstwhile supremacy of the British manufacturer . . . the overthrow of which [*sic*] was pending.[124]

In spite of this chequered history, when Chamberlain's crusade erupted the Birmingham council acted as if it were sure of the way opinion would move. Shortly after Chamberlain's speech, it drafted an additional twenty-one members onto the Chamber's Tariff Committee to discuss the new proposals. Furthermore, bypassing a general meeting 'in order to save time', the council circulated a list of questions soliciting members' views directly.[125]

Eighty-nine members replied to the questionnaire (probably no more than a fifth of the total),[126] fifty-eight of whom thought that preference would materially

---

[123] G. H. Wright, *Chronicles of the Birmingham Chamber of Commerce* (Birmingham, 1913), 242–3, 258–9, 271–2, 284–5, 308–10, 328, 342.

[124] Ibid. 342, 369, 400–1, 407, 422–3.   [125] *BCCJ*, 30 June 1903.

[126] Membership in 1903 is unknown, but in July 1905 it was approximately 650; *BCCJ*, 31 July 1905, 97.

aid their exports to the colonies. About fifteen dissented and the same number expressed no opinion. Whilst some held the view that imperial preference would provoke foreign retaliation, most seemed to believe that foreigners would lower their tariffs in response, or that the gain from colonial trade would 'amply' compensate any loss of foreign sales. Seventy members replied to a question on the value of domestic protection, but the Tariff Committee, in its report, did not quantify the response, merely stating that 'many' were in favour but 'others' thought it ineffective or harmful. There was concern that production costs might be increased by duties on food or raw materials.

Sixty or seventy members discussed the Tariff Committee's report at a special meeting on 23 September. A preferentialist resolution was passed by forty-eight votes to nine.[127] In spite of the fact that only about one in ten of the membership voted, it seems unlikely that the outcome seriously misrepresented general opinion. Vehement opponents of Tariff Reform would only have been discouraged from having their opinions counted if they had realized their position to be hopeless. Apathy may have been of some account in explaining the small attendance, but then so too may have been the knowledge that the protectionist victory was safe and assured. The council's actions all along are best explained as those of a leadership which believed that rank-and-file opinion would not object if it cut corners.

The preferentialist vote in the Chamber would probably have been bigger but for the inhibitions that some felt were imposed by the Chamber's articles of association. Yet formally inconvenient articles of association were not likely to present a serious obstacle to an effectively unanimous Chamber, since endless fine distinctions could be drawn as to what were political and what were business questions—distinctions which were essentially meaningless when trade policy itself was a political issue. Hence they alone would not explain why, in spite of the convincing expression of opinion in September 1903, the Chamber articulated its views precious little in the subsequent decade. It was the real reluctance of members to be drawn into politically controversial areas, rather than any formal limitation of their scope for action, which bound them. According to the Chamber's *Journal*, the unfortunate fact that fiscal policy had been 'drawn into the whirlpool of party politics' made it 'practically impossible' for the Associated Chambers to discuss it.[128] The secretary of the Birmingham Chamber, G. H. Wright, provided convincing additional reasons for torpor when, in an impressive speech on the status of Chambers of Commerce at the Liège meeting of ACCUK in September 1905, he encapsulated the problems posed for Chambers of Commerce by the Tariff Reform campaign:

[127] *BCCJ*, 30 Sept. 1903, 110–111, 114.
[128] *BCCJ*, 31 Jan. 1905, 13–14.

The duty of a Chamber of Commerce was to give its opinion as to what was desirable or necessary in the interests of trade and commerce. It was a strange thing, with their voluntary status, that an expression of opinion by the Chambers of Commerce on not a few occasions was . . . very dangerous to them in consequence of the vast extent of party politics. England's commercial men unfortunately appeared to be brought up in party grooves, and if a Chamber ventured to express an opinion, from a purely commercial point of view, on any question which might happen to have been discussed on a party platform, then a few resignations were bound to follow. How many Chambers of Commerce, for instance, had been able to express a definite opinion on the question of Tariff Reform? . . . It was said that under an official status Chambers of Commerce would lose their independence. He ventured to assert that they would *gain* their independence. At present they were not independent. On the contrary, they were dependent on an uncertain constituency; their income was slender and precarious, and was subject to diminution at any moment if any section of members became dissatisfied with any opinion expressed by the Council.[129]

As if to reflect Wright's comments, the *Birmingham Chamber of Commerce Journal* had a curiously schizophrenic appearance. Its pages contained endless articles on preference, the possibilities of Empire trade, and the effects of duties on prices, which at times came close to the style of Tariff Reform League pamphlets, yet in reporting conferences and events it displayed a sensitivity towards the delicate political situation which is in retrospect surprising, given Birmingham's reputation as a hotbed of protectionism. The Chamber's discomfort over the restrictions on debate on economic issues imposed by politics was undoubtedly a main factor in its support for a Minister of Commerce and Industry. Following the recommendations of the Jersey Committee of 1904, such a bill was introduced in 1905, but still had not become law when the Balfour government fell in 1906.[130]

Hence the delicacy of the Chamber's position continued. Its delegates to the 1906 Congress of Chambers of Commerce of the Empire intended to support a resolution urging preference, but declined to support a rider to the resolution that Chambers should press their respective governments to implement preference at the Imperial Conference of 1907, arguing instead that the Conference should be 'free and open'.[131] Reporting the fiscal discussions at the autumn 1906 meeting of ACCUK in Bristol, the *Journal* recorded its 'appreciation of the ability and temper of the speeches. We were particularly happy to observe the rigid exclusion of references to party politics.'[132]

This situation persisted until 1914. The Birmingham Council, and no doubt the membership, remained committed to support of imperial preference, and the

[129] Reported in *BCCJ*, 30 Sept. 1905. 134–5 (my emphasis).
[130] See *BCCJ*, 30 Apr. 1904, 47–9; 31 Jan. 1905, 9; 28 Feb. 1905, 26; 31 May 1905, 79; 31 Jan. 1906, 20. Also *Report of the Committee on the Board of Trade and the Local Government Board*, Cd. 2121, 1904.
[131] *BCCJ*, 31[?] Aug. 1906, 116–7.
[132] Ibid. 29 Sept. 1906, 137–8.

tenor of the *Journal*'s comments made it clear that it did not shrink from the implication for food taxes that its position contained.[133] The debate over a Minister of Commerce rumbled on into 1907 and 1908. Birmingham continued to fulminate against foreign tariffs, and pressed for improved legislation on merchandise marks. It registered concern over the increasing burden of direct taxation, and gave a full account of the inaugural meeting of the Income Tax Reduction League in 1908, a body comprised of both Free Traders and Tariff Reformers.[134] It echoed the sentiments expressed in other Chambers on the debate on fiscal policy at the ACCUK meeting of March 1909 in London: 'the less said about the debate the better. It never reached a high level, and more than once degenerated to the level of a third-rate debating society.'[135]

All these issues held implications for the fiscal controversy. Yet on Tariff Reform the Birmingham Chamber's opinions, though lurking constantly in the background of the comments in the *Journal*, were increasingly seldom openly stated. Reporting of the Sixth Congress of Chambers of Commerce of the Empire in September 1909 was limited to a listing of the contributions of over thirty speakers in the debate on imperial commercial relations, with no editorial comment.[136] At the AGM in March 1911, president J. S. Taylor found common agreement between the political parties that the 'policy of *laissez-faire* has gone never to return', but lamented that fiscal reform had become a party question, since this 'prevents our Chamber of Commerce from dealing with it as it ought to be dealt with, viz., on its business merits'.[137] His words differed little from the sentiments expressed by Wright and others in 1905. Perhaps a mood of resignation had come to dominate a mood of frustration. But, in any event, after a bright start and after being the earliest Chamber in the UK to poll its members on the fiscal question, the Birmingham Chamber had scarcely wielded its potential for exerting pressure in the direction of any sustained protectionist propaganda.

IX

Though 'on the whole a nonconformist town with a certain Catholic element', Sheffield remained before 1914 predominantly a Unionist stronghold, with only one of its five divisions returning a Liberal in the 1900 election.[138] Howard Vincent's unexpected victory over Samuel Plimsoll in the largely working-class

---

[133] In this, the position of Jesse Collings as president of the Chamber may have been influential. The new edition of his *Land Reform* (1906) had a chapter on fiscal policy and agriculture.

[134] *BCCJ*, 31 July 1908, 111.

[135] Ibid. 31 Mar. 1909, 46.

[136] Ibid. 30 Sept. 1909, 41–2.

[137] Ibid. 29 Apr. 1911, 51.

[138] H. Pelling, *Social Geography*, 232.

Central Division in 1885 was partly explained by his enthusiastic support for Fair Trade.[139] Trading conditions, particularly dumping and merchandise marks abuses, experienced similarly by the large steel works of the east end and the small masters of the central and western valley districts, gave rise to an unusual homogeneity of opinion throughout the size range of manufacturing industry. It might therefore be thought that Sheffield Chamber of Commerce would be less than usually discomforted by the rebirth of the tariff debate in 1903, but it was not until shortly after Chamberlain's Glasgow speech in October that the Chamber's Tariff and Treaties Committee was directed to draft a questionnaire to discover members' view on Tariff Reform.[140]

No clear analysis of the responses has survived, nor does it appear that any detailed results were released at the time. What information was circulated suggests that the majority of replies favoured imperial preference and retaliation, but that the council felt less than happy with the exercise as a test of opinion:

a good many members did not respond, many probably because they came more under the heads of dealers and retailers than manufacturers, yet the answers may be taken by the members to be adequately representative of the large and small manufacturing firms in Sheffield.[141]

The Sheffield Daily Independent commented that the responses had revealed 'divided opinions' on Tariff Reform,[142] which might suggest a stronger Free Trade presence than Sheffield's previous history would lead us to expect. However, the Chamber's own view, of the over-representation of manufacturing, might be taken to suggest the reverse. Three-quarters of the replies believed that retaliation would help; whilst if respondents were less hopeful of preference it was because they considered it could never be large enough to have any 'sensible effect'.[143] Nevertheless, the SCC council felt it unwise to use the poll as a mandate for the Sheffield delegates to the March 1904 meeting of ACCUK, and in consequence a special general meeting was held to determine the Chamber's stance.

Only fifty or sixty of around 266 members attended the meeting of 4 March 1904.[144] Discussion centred around a retaliationist motion, though its supporters frequently strayed into the Tariff Reform borderlands of agriculture and preference. Parenthetic indications of audience reaction in the press suggest that the main Free Trade spokesman, Albert Hobson, commanded a surprising amount of support in regarding shipping as 'the most important British interest ... placing it even before agriculture'.[145] The vote of twenty-seven to nineteen in

---

[139] S. H. Jeyes and F. D. How, *Life of Sir Howard Vincent* (1912), ch. 9.
[140] Sheffield Chamber of Commerce, Council Minutes, 23 Oct. 1903.
[141] Sheffield Chamber of Commerce, Annual Report, 27 Jan. 1905.
[142] *Sheffield Daily Independent*, 5 Mar. 1904.
[143] Sheffield Chamber of Commerce, Annual Report, 27 Jan. 1905.
[144] Alderman Clegg at meeting of 4 Mar., quoted in *Sheffield Daily Independent*, 5 Mar. 1904.
[145] Quoted ibid.

favour of retaliation did not in itself suggest such a heavy bias towards protection as might have been expected in Vincent's Sheffield.[146] Curiously, it was the Free Traders who lamented the 'unrepresentative character' of the meeting, with an estimated one-fifth of those present being from the professions.[147]

But if the Tariff Reform cause in the Sheffield Chamber was strengthened by the support of the free professions, its adherents showed little interest in consolidating their position during the next few years. As always, foreign tariffs and tariff changes excited much comment, but Tariff Reform as such was scarcely on the agenda, even when politicians visited the city to speak on the fiscal question.

Thus the questionnaire, the meeting of March 1904, and the flavour of Chamber proceedings between 1904 and 1908 all illustrate the difficulty of gauging the strength of protectionist feeling from the Chamber's record. We might almost conclude that the city's businessmen were seriously divided, but for the fact that Lord Robert Cecil, guest at the annual dinner in February 1909, admitted his apprehension at speaking to an audience so opposed to his own Free Trade views. Cecil was preceded by W. F. Beardshaw, managing director of a firm which converted, refined, and rolled steel as well as manufacturing it into files, saws, and edge-tools,[148] who gave a cautious retaliationist speech, disavowing protection but arguing for genuine free trade in the long run, and voicing Sheffield businessmen's alarm at threatened French tariff changes. Cecil had never 'approached a task of addressing any audience with greater diffidence':

The speech to which we have listened is certainly to me a revelation of how moderate I gather a large section of Sheffield Tariff Reformers are, and if that spirit prevails, I don't know that agreement is out of the question. [Applause][149]

That Cecil and Sheffield might ever find their fiscal views compatible was of course doubtful, and Cecil took a rather impish delight in avoiding the issue in his speech that night. But if, in the conditions of 1908–1910, the Tariff Reformers' arguments seemed less radical than they had done in 1904, there was also to be seen a greater tolerance of them on the part of some Free Traders. After a visit to France on which he had gathered that the Senate was unlikely to moderate its new tariff proposals, even Hobson was prepared to concede that 'there was no country on which a threat of retaliation would have had as much effect as upon France'.[150] He even advocated that all British firms trading with France should join the British Chamber of Commerce in Paris to strengthen its

---

[146] B. H. Brown, *The Tariff Reform Movement in Great Britain 1881–1895* (New York, 1943), 139–40.
[147] Alderman Clegg, quoted in *Sheffield Daily Independent*, 5 Mar. 1904.
[148] *White's Directory of Sheffield and Rotherham*, 31st edn., 1909.
[149] *Sheffield Daily Independent*, 13 Feb. 1909.
[150] *Sheffield Daily Telegraph*, 26 Feb. 1910.

arm; as he doubtless knew, that Chamber had endorsed retaliation as long before as 1904.

In the *Sheffield Daily Telegraph*, the city possessed one of the most stalwart of Chamberlainite newspapers. But the Chamber, surprisingly, expressed more muted sentiments on Tariff Reform, and it seems likely that retaliation was its greater concern. More like Birmingham than like Nottingham, the Sheffield Chamber made little impact on the proceeding of the Associated Chambers. The reasons were much the same. In April 1911 Cammell, Laird & Co. forwarded a letter advertising Dudley Docker's newly-formed Business League.[151] The council was 'in cordial sympathy with the objects of this League, but felt that the matter involved party politics to an extent which made it impossible for the Chamber to take any corporate action with regard thereto'.[152]

X

Macclesfield Chamber of Commerce provides an interesting and unusually precise illustration of the links between a dominant industry and the local business community. Hard hit by commercial policy ever since the Cobden Treaty of 1860, silk had survived better in Macclesfield than in Spitalfields, Derby, or Coventry, but nevertheless in 1907 UK imports were about five times larger than home production.[153] The *Macclesfield Courier* had long shown a protectionist stance in its editorial policy, combined with a strong antipathy towards France.[154]

Though the archives of the Macclesfield Chamber have not survived, it is clear that it was strongly protectionist. Deputizing as president for Tariff Commissioner Henry Birchenough during his visit to South Africa as a Special Commissioner of the Board of Trade, W. H. L. Cameron interpreted the Duke of Devonshire's plea that Chambers of Commerce should conduct a preliminary enquiry on Tariff Reform[155] to mean that Chambers should be used 'to find out by what means we might hit our opponents . . . hardest'.[156] The Chamber was also used to holding joint meetings with the Silk Trade Protection Association, thus demonstrating a cavalier disregard for political neutrality that might well have been envied by Tariff Reformers in other Chambers.

---

[151] For the Business League, see R. P. T. Davenport-Hines, *Dudley Docker* (Cambridge, 1984), ch. 4.

[152] Sheffield Chamber of Commerce, [Council?] Minutes, 4 Apr. 1911.

[153] A. E. Musson, *The Growth of British Industry* (1978), 211.

[154] *Macclesfield Courier*, 6 June 1903, 5.

[155] This in itself seems to have been a distortion of the Duke's position. See Devonshire to Sir Edward Hamilton (Treasury), 9 June 1903, quoted in B. Holland, *Life of Spencer Compton, Eighth Duke of Devonshire* (1911), ii. 310–311.

[156] *Macclesfield Courier*, 20 June 1903, 6.

In July 1903, during the Chamber's first full-scale debate of the fiscal question, Birchenough's rather tame motion in favour of an inquiry was, fortunately for the historian, too 'colourless' for J. O. Nicholson, a Free Trade silk manufacturer, who insisted on putting an amendment that 'this Chamber believes that the system of Free Trade is the foundation of the present prosperous condition of the nation'. His obvious intent was to split the Chamber. In spite of several attempts to adjourn the meeting or get the amendment withdrawn, Birchenough was unable to avoid a vote. The original motion was passed 'overwhelmingly', however, only four votes being cast for the amendment.[157]

We cannot know what proportion of the total membership of the Chamber the forty who attended this meeting represented. Furthermore, abstentions were not recorded, but use of the word 'overwhelmingly' suggests they were very few. Against these difficulties, however, is the unusual advantage that we know from the *Courier*'s reporting of the discussion who at least three, and possibly all four, of the dissenters were. These were Nicholson; A. J. King, owner of a bleaching and finishing firm in neighbouring Bollington; H. Rowson, a silk throwster and merchant;[158] and possibly Bradley Smale. Smale's own precise occupation is unknown, but several of his family were silk manufacturers and one was a solicitor.[159]

Of those who supported Birchenough (remembering, however, that a handful may have abstained) a large minority were connected with the silk industry. Including Birchenough and Cameron,[160] and one listed merely as a 'trimming manufacturer', there were seventeen of these, including two or possibly three silk merchants or brokers. Of the remaining supporters, one was a cork manufacturer; the rest can be classified as small-town tradesmen. There were three bootmakers; two who combined repair engineering with dealerships in cycles, agricultural and electrical machinery, and so on; one saddler and carriage proprietor; one printer, stationer, bookbinder, and local newspaper proprietor; four or possibly six merchants (two hardware dealers; one corn merchant; one who might have been a shopkeeper or a builder or a builders' merchant; one who was either a coach builder or a coal merchant; and one who was either a draper or a wheelwright or a salter). In addition, there were a bank manager (or publican) and an estate agent and accountant. The occupations of two are unknown.

The Macclesfield Chamber demonstrates clearly the importance of local community in small manufacturing centres. Silk, the only industry of national

---

[157] Ibid. 18 July 1903, 5.

[158] In 1907 *c.* 70% of UK silk output was exported. See Musson, *Growth of British Industry*, 211.

[159] Information on occupations from *Kelly's Directory of Cheshire* for 1902.

[160] Cameron was a 'shirt manufacturer'; Birchenough probably, by 1903, had larger economic interests outside the silk industry than within it, though to him local ties remained important.

consequence in the immediate area, had been under increasing threat for many decades. Small tradesmen obviously had an immediate economic interest in the health of the local economy. More than this, it is likely that there was genuine sympathy with the local silk manufacturers, with the 'justness' of their case, and with the way they had been 'sacrificed' on the remote altar of Free Trade. In small market or county towns, it cannot be assumed that the small merchant or the banker would display the same adherence to Free Trade which seems to have been largely typical of the factors, brokers, and merchants of the large manufacturing centres and ports, or the financiers of the City of London.

XI

Study of the Macclesfield meeting has allowed us to attribute votes to the various trades because those who attended were named, abstentions were negligible, and all but one of the Free Traders are known because they spoke in the debate. Using more direct evidence, Sigsworth is able to give an excellent and perhaps unique breakdown of support for retaliation in the Bradford Chamber early in 1904. As shown in Table 6, 115 (including fourteen solicitors and bankers) were in favour, 120 (including thirteen solicitors and bankers) against. Sigsworth observes that it was those concerned with piece goods, the Bradford goods experiencing most severe foreign competition, who were most in favour of Tariff Reform, and registers surprise only at the orientation of the dyers, wool merchants, and top makers.[161] It might also be observed, however, that Sigsworth's data also suggest a surprising degree of unanimity between manufacturers and piece-merchants. Such a finding conforms with fragmentary evidence from Leeds and the East Midlands in the 1920s that local merchants and manufacturers' agents showed a greater tendency to side with domestic manufacturers than did the export and import merchants of London and Manchester.[162]

TABLE 6. *Bradford Chamber of Commerce: Poll of Members in 1904*

	For Tariff Reform	Against Tariff Reform
Piece-Merchants	28	15
Spinner-Manufacturers	19	16
Manufacturers	19	14
Wool-Merchants and Top-Makers	18	10
Spinners	9	21
Yarn-Merchants	5	13
Piece- and Yarn-Merchants	0	4
Dyers	3	9
Combers	0	5
Solicitors and Bankers	14	13

Source: E. Sigsworth, *Black Dyke Mills: A History* (Liverpool, 1958), 106.

[161] E. Sigsworth, *Black Dyke Mills: A History* (Liverpool, 1958), 105–7.   [162] See below, 282, 293.

XII

This survey of opinion within chambers of commerce has been based on a fairly small sample, albeit one which, at least for the purposes of charting industry-wide opinion on fiscal reform, would not improve with size. Regrettably, also, the surviving records of ACCUK do not even allow us to reconstruct how whole chambers voted at its meetings. This study must remain a qualitative assessment of a quantitative matter, and for that purpose at least the tendency of patterns to recur, of common sentiments and tactics to repeat themselves in different chambers, gives confidence in the belief that the results bear weight.

It is clear that, with the exception of Macclesfield and perhaps Hull, all the Chambers studied in detail had substantial groups of both Tariff Reformers and Free Traders. Rempel might be literally correct in arguing that the 'only groups completely supporting Chamberlain . . . [were] clearly declining industries, such as silk, hit badly by competition at home', but his additional comment that 'apart from iron and steel, the major industries in the country still prospered under free trade' creates the impression that Tariff Reform was very much a minority cause.[163] Events in the chambers of commerce suggest otherwise.

Surprisingly, even Arthur Redford, whose own analysis of the Manchester Chamber tended to exaggerate its Free Trade inclination, would have agreed on this point. To him, it was left to Manchester businessmen to conduct the 'defence of free trade' against the 'slow return to protectionist sentiments' within the wider community of British businessmen, a process in which the passing of a protectionist resolution in the Associated Chambers was 'a most significant turning point'.[164]

Though there were always Tariff Reformers to mount a significant attack on Free Trade in the Chambers, what was their relative strength? How far had Redford's 'slow return' progressed by 1903–1906, or by 1910–1914? The Chambers examined suggest considerable progress, even by 1906. And even in Manchester, over one-quarter opposed the Free Trade resolution in June 1903.[165] Nottingham passed resolutions on retaliation, both in council and in special meetings, by heavy margins, and if attendances were fairly small in comparison to total membership, even Free Traders were willing to concede that Stiebel's full-blown Chamberlainite resolution represented the views of the majority of members. Running the London Chamber was a nightmare. The council was so evenly divided that results depended on the vagaries of attendance, or on the precise wording of a resolution. But a poll returned by 10 per cent of members early in 1904 ran about two to one in favour of retaliation, whilst another returned by 48.4 per cent of members in 1907 ran nearly 2.3 to

[163] R. A. Rempel, *Unionists Divided* (Newton Abbot, 1974), 97.
[164] A. Redford, *Manchester Merchants*, ii. 104.
[165] P. F. Clarke, 'The End of Laissez-Faire', 500.

one in favour of protection and preference. The Birmingham council, in contrast, acted as if it was certain of the protectionist inclination of the membership; and the poll of July 1903, though only exciting about one-fifth of the members, was nearly four to one in favour of Tariff Reform, excluding abstentions. The margin at a subsequent special meeting in September was more than five to one. A similar poll in Sheffield revealed three to one in favour of retaliation, though all sides were, for different reasons, dissatisfied with its representativeness, and the attendance at meetings never showed such a degree of protectionist sentiment. Indeed, if there was substantial support for Free Trade in Howard Vincent's city of steel and cutlery, why should there not be more protectionist feeling in cottonopolis than is normally recognized? In Leeds, the council was ready to admit deep division, but of the 141 who voted at a large meeting of 300 late in 1903, over half supported a Chamberlainite policy, and it is open to conjecture how much higher that vote would have been if the resolution had been confined to retaliation. Macclesfield was so heavily protectionist that it requires no extended comment, except to say that unusually precise evidence on individual voting shows clearly how, in a small manufacturing town, community interest and sentiment could mobilize unlikely occupations, such as small merchants, shopkeepers, and bank managers, in defence of beleaguered local industry. More tenuously, the same conclusion might be drawn from Bradford, where merchants and manufacturers showed a surprising degree of unanimity.[166] Only in Hull, of the chambers studied here in detail, does it seem that the protectionist camp was overwhelmingly outnumbered, and even this conclusion is dependent on setting aside contemporary evidence that there was a substantial division of opinion within the chamber.

Therefore, apart from the Hull and Manchester Chambers, the latter's large membership, of course, giving it considerable importance, the Chambers considered were, neglecting abstentions, actually producing some measure of majority opinion in favour of Tariff Reform. The London *Chamber of Commerce Journal*'s reporting in 1903 and 1904 supports the view that Hull and Manchester were in a minority. The immediate response of many businessmen to the Birmingham speech was cautious and uncertain, and initially some of the support for Tariff Reform in the chambers was limited to the advocacy of retaliation. But after 1906, and very markedly by 1908 to 1910, the distinction between retaliation, protection, and preference became less prominent.

Examination of the record of the Associated Chambers on the fiscal question supports this view. The vote of February to March 1905 is easier to interpret than that of March 1904, but clearly the support for protection was considerable in 1904 and grew thereafter. Whilst the abstention rate in 1905 was nearly 40 per cent, Tariff Reform attracted nearly twice as many votes as Free Trade.

---

[166] E. Sigsworth, *Black Dyke Mills*, 105–7.

Indeed, in ACCUK, abstention had its own special relevance, given the highly unusual voting category of 'neutrality', contrived by the Free Trade clique around Holland and Brassey, who manipulated the Associated Chambers' meetings. Since chamber representatives at ACCUK meetings were delegates, usually under precise instruction, neutrality almost certainly betokened deep division, often perhaps an almost even balance, of opinion back home. That the Tariff Reform vote could make such visible progress from 1905 onwards in such difficult institutional circumstances testifies to its growing popularity. The available evidence suggests that Redford was correct to impart particular significance to the ACCUK meeting of 1905.

The increasing popularity of Tariff Reform in the chambers of commerce after 1907, and in particular the record of voting in ACCUK, offers some support to those historians, notably Emy and Clarke, who discern a significant loss of business support for the Liberals due to trends in social reform and taxation policy.[167] However, though in the chambers the tide of business opinion was running in favour of the supporters of Tariff Reform, they showed little ability to capitalize on it. The ideological hegemony of Free Trade not only made it difficult to transmit support for protectionism from the business community into the political arena, but also muted expression of that support within the business community itself. Such considerations reinforced what was probably already a naturally high abstention rate that stemmed from the nature of chambers of commerce as institutions, and high abstentions then interacted back upon the chambers' willingness to act. There was something in Tariff Reform of the illegitimate child: loved and wanted, but difficult to proclaim to the world.

Compounding the moral overtones of the intellectual and cultural hegemony of Free Trade were the structural constraints associated with it. For a long time business had been able to operate largely outside the orbit of political structures. As the parties crafted new alignments in the late nineteenth and early twentieth centuries, the conventions of business institutions remained. Again, Tariff Reform was the casualty. Perhaps the most eloquent testimony of all was that of G. H. Wright, one of the most professional of all pre-war secretaries of Britain's chambers of commerce. The chambers lacked status, were under-recognized by government. Nevertheless, they were expected to abide by rules highly advant-

---

[167] Of course, a vote for Tariff Reform in the Chambers of Commerce did not necessarily translate into a vote for the Unionists in the elections of 1910. Indeed, Searle is more circumspect, arguing that the positive attractions of Free Trade, or at least traditional party loyalties, may have resulted in a maintenance of the Liberal business vote, especially in Northern constituencies, in spite of concern over the New Liberal predilection for social reform. See H. V. Emy, *Liberals, Radicals and Social Politics, 1892–1914* (Cambridge, 1973), 285; P. F. Clarke, 'End of Laissez-Faire' loc. cit. G. R. Searle, 'The Edwardian Liberal Party and Business', *English Historical Review*, 98, 1983, esp. 47–50. For an excellent summary, see G. R. Searle, *The Liberal Party: Triumph and Disintegration, 1886–1929* (1992), 102–7.

ageous to government, before Balfour's defeat almost as much as afterwards. Tariff Reform was political. Having lived for years under regimes where the difference between Unionist and Liberal governments was of little practical consequence to business, Britain's chambers had perhaps too readily accepted this. In the Tariff Reform campaign it was a bias the Free Traders could exploit heavily.

To the aid of bias came circumstance. With the Unionist defeats of 1910 rendering Tariff Reform a lost cause, at least temporarily, businessmen recognized its displacement by more immediate issues—social reform, labour unrest, and the political maelstroms of Home Rule and the Lords. Within the business community, as in the Unionist Party, Tariff Reform had to follow the agenda of politics, rather than set it.

4

The Tariff Commission at Work

An examination of some of the day-to-day aspects of the administration and operation of the Tariff Commission between 1904 and the general elections of 1910 tells us much about the methods, biases, and attitudes of its organizers which does not readily emerge from its published writings. Recent research has increased our knowledge of the ideological baggage of the Tariff Reform League, particularly in the context of Edwardian right-wing nationalism, and of the TRL's relationship with the Conservative Party.[1] The paucity of records, however, has meant that less is known of its internal operation and decision-making, and of the interaction between League headquarters and the 250 provincial branches and forty women's association branches.[2] Of the Birmingham Liberal Unionist Association's Imperial Tariff Committee, or of the Free Trade League, Free Food League, and Free Trade Union, even less is known.

The Tariff Commission is unique amongst these institutions in that its records have survived, but it was scarcely typical. It was not at the centre of the propaganda campaign, though it moved towards it after 1906. Nor would its supporters have considered it simply a propagandist body: indeed, its curious blend of 'scientific' enquiry and propagandist activity makes it the most interesting and incongruous of all the partisan bodies operating in the campaign.

I

At the outset few Tariff Reformers had any realistic concept of the length of the Commission's task. Chamberlain initially thought Hewins might run it on a part-time basis, and even Hewins thought the industrial inquiry would only take three years. As the inquiry dragged on, the organizers were made very aware that successful businessmen had pressing commitments which took precedence over a long drawn-out fiscal enquiry. At least up to 1905–1906, it appeared that

---

[1] B. Semmel, *Imperialism and Social Reform* (1960), ch. 5; K. D. Brown, 'The Trade Union Tariff Reform Association, 1904–1913', *Journal of British Studies*, 9 (1970), 141–53; R. J. Scally, *The Origins of the Lloyd George Coalition* (Princeton, 1975), esp. 98–107; and A. Summers, 'The Character of Edwardian Nationalism: Three Popular Leagues', in P. Kennedy and A. Nicholls, (eds.), *Nationalist and Racialist Movements in Britain and Germany before 1914* (1981), 70–2, 81–6.

[2] Important exceptions are F. Coetzee, 'Pressure Groups, Tory Businessmen and the Aura of Political Corruption before the First World War', *Historical Journal*, 29 (1986), 839–40, 843; and *For Party or Nation* (New York, 1990), esp. ch. 2. Coetzee uses the Weardale [Ridley] Papers.

the original plan of a self-terminating Commission would be realized: in April 1905 Percy Hurd, most senior of the full-time staff, was advised to seek another post since the work was 'nearly finished'.[3]

Commission activity did increase in the second half of 1905, as Hewins and Pearson sought to complete the industrial reports, in part because of the impending election. By late 1905, however, the original deadline had become obviously unrealistic: several major industrial reports, including those on agriculture and engineering, were still unfinished. Furthermore, Chamberlain now pressed the Commission to 'accept an addition to the original [terms of] reference' by enquiring into the type of concessions desired by British manufacturers under a scheme of imperial preference. This, together with the need for a 'Final Report' linking the industrial series together, ensured that proposals for amalgamating the League and the Commission got no further. Yet 1906 was a watershed for the Commission. Though there was much to do in completing the industrial series, there was now a new and less 'scientific' task. Chamberlain felt it 'open to further consideration' whether his suggested report on preference 'should be immediately published, or . . . privately communicated to the Governments of the respective Colonies'.[4]

The period around the 1906 election roughly separates the 'scientific' commission of inquiry from the more politicized and propagandist Commission of later years. But political propaganda was never far from Hewins's mind even in the early days, and his view that his own commitment to an imperial policy could be compatible with an inquiry of 'the greatest impartiality' suggests deliberate naïveté.[5] On the other hand, neither is it true that serious 'scientific' and empirical study was forsaken for the production of propagandist copy after 1906. Down to 1910 the industrial series and related projects were the main work of the Commission.

II

Working within a framework of sub-committees, initially resisted by Hewins and Pearson but pressed on them by Chamberlain,[6] the Commission's approach to each of the industrial inquiries involved four preliminary elements. The first was the construction of a product classification of the industry, to give a clearer view of industrial structure and to provide a framework on which to hang a tariff

[3] Chamberlain to Hewins, 7 Nov. 1903, HP; 'The Tariff Commission–Dinner to Mr. Hewins, MP, Savoy Hotel, Nov. 6th 1917', 8/7/2, TCP; Charles Eckersley to Caillard, 11 Nov. 1906, 6/1/5, TCP; Joseph Rank to Hewins, 23 Jan. 1904; 6/1/28, TCP; Pearson to Hurd, Pearson to Hewins, both 8 Apr. 1905, HP.
[4] Chamberlain to Hewins, 29 July 1905, 48/10–12, HP.
[5] Lecture delivered by Hewins to the Women's Branch of the TRL, St. Peter's Institute, London, 22 Feb. 1904, 32, copy in 19/112–47, HP.
[6] Pearson to Hewins, 28 Nov. and 2 Dec. 1903, 6/1/26, TCP.

should it be found necessary. The other three elements involved collection of information: firstly from existing printed sources, secondly by circularizing British firms, and thirdly by cross-examining witnesses.

The drafting of industrial classifications soon ran into difficulties. Even the relatively simple product structure of iron and steel caused disagreement between Commission experts. Many of the Commission's businessmen had a surprisingly undeveloped comprehension of the product structure of their own industries. The initial classification of the building and furnishing trades confused a bewildering variety of their final products with a considerable number of their inputs, such as lathes and tools, which were more properly the province of other Commission studies. Henry Mitchell, the worsted manufacturer, at first resisted the logic of a product classification for his trade, preferring to concentrate on processes. When sent copies of the cotton classification and of a classification of worsteds, alternative to his own, drawn up by a member of the Textile Committee, he wrote:

It appears to me that the cotton classification is all wrong in its divisions. Again, if I were to attempt to divide the [worsted] weaving industry into the different kinds of goods made, as is done I see in cotton, the list would be far too long, and you can't divide manufacturers, or spinners either, in that way. The same firm of either spinners or manufacturers will, in Bradford, produce an immense variety of yarns, or of pieces, changing from year to year, as the fashion calls for one or other description of fabrics.[7]

The *Woollen Report* of 1905 contained no classification except for a long list of products in which British firms experienced foreign competition and a product-orientated discussion of the prosperity of the 'several branches' of the industry. There was no discussion of the significance of these divisions or of their ranking in a formal 'scientific' classification. It was, in fact, typical of the later industrial studies.[8]

Simple amateurism is not sufficient to explain this. It was a facet of a deeper problem—the fragmentations and, paradoxically, the insularities in British industry. Ironically, these were in part caused by Free Trade itself. If the Free Trade movement of the 1830s and 1840s had led to an explosion of statistics,[9] that growth had wasted by 1900; partly because of the needs of their tariff designers, protectionist America and Germany had much better economic statistics than liberal Britain. In iron and steel, Alfred Hickman used the Board of Trade returns to adapt Hewins's original construction into a reasonably

---

[7] 'Waring and Gillow Ltd: Questions as to the Classification of Industries Affecting the Building and Furnishing Trades', 6/1/33, TCP; Mitchell to Hewins, 18 Nov. 1904, 6/1/24, TCP. Also Mitchell to Hewins, 18 Jan. and 28 Mar. 1904, and Hewins to Mitchell, 17 Nov. 1904, 6/1/24, TCP.

[8] *Report of the Tariff Commission*, ii. *The Textile Trades, 2: Evidence on the Woollen Industry*, (1905), (hereinafter cited as *Woollen Report*), paras. 1316–70 and 1870–77.

[9] L. Brown, *The Board of Trade and the Free-Trade Movement 1830–42* (Oxford, 1958), esp. ch. 5; M. J. Cullen, *The Statistical Movement in Early Victorian Britain* (Hassocks, 1975), esp. ch. 1.

successful classification, and the classification used in the *Cotton Report* was similarly loosely based on them.[10] In more complex industries, however, the trade returns were usually less adequate. But classification was essential to 'scientific' tariff-making, whereby duties were graded according to labour content, as Chamberlain had promised at Glasgow. In modern terms, the Commission needed some concept of 'value-added' by the British industry. When Ivan Levinstein urged, 'We want a scientific tariff and we need to have as a starting point a scientific classification', he was correct.[11] The Commission's inability to find or construct an adequate substitute for the Board of Trade classifications was undoubtedly a large factor behind the decision, in the later reports, to omit publication of a provisional tariff schedule.[12]

Difficulties were more successfully overcome in the collection of information on industrial conditions. Though Hewins spoke contemptuously of British official data, and Rosenbaum, the Commission statistician, constantly plied the Board of Trade with suggestions for improving it, there was at least plenty of material to collate and index, especially in areas such as agriculture.[13] Foreign government publications and academic works were voraciously assimilated too, some even being republished in extract in the various reports. In 1905 the Commission was receiving seventy newspapers, periodicals and trade journals.

The main effort of data collection, however, was a series of questionnaires in which the Commission sought to obtain information from every industrial and commercial undertaking in the UK. The preliminary questionnaire, 'Form No. 1 (Issued to All Manufacturers)',[14] contained eleven questions. Commissioners originally suggested over forty, but fearing that manufacturers would never answer such a list, Hewins, Chamberlain, and the General Purposes Committee pruned it radically, and subsequently the full Commission only managed to persuade them to add one question, on the effects of international patents legislation on British firms. Hewins received 'no end of suggestions' for additional questions, 'but I had given orders to the printer and would not budge'.[15]

[10] See below, Chs. 5 and 6. With both these industries, the classification used by the Commission is quite compatible with that adopted by subsequent economic historians. I have attempted to show elsewhere that the classification of cotton goods adopted by the Board of Trade in 1888 did reflect 'value added' in the industry. See A. J. Marrison, 'Great Britain and her Rivals in the Latin American Cotton Piece Goods Market', in B. M. Ratcliffe (ed.), *Great Britain and Her World 1750–1914* (Manchester, 1975), 315–16.

[11] Levinstein to Hewins, 16 Jan. 1904, 6/1/21, TCP. He and Boulton could not agree, however, on a classification of chemical products. See Levinstein to Hewins, 24 Jan. 1904, 6/1/21, TCP.

[12] Except in the report on agriculture. There were also political reasons for ceasing to publish provisional tariff schedules. See below, Ch. 7.

[13] Henry Chaplin was initially convinced that so much information existed in the public domain that the Commission had no need to gather any for itself. See Chaplin to Hewins, 31 Jan. 1904, 6/1/2 (file I), TCP.

[14] Reproduced in *Iron and Steel Report*, para. 90.

[15] W. A. S. Hewins, 'My Connection with the Fiscal Controversy', ms, 31 Jan. 1904, unmarked black diary, HP, 36–7.

It was obviously desirable to limit the size of the questionnaire, and in any case its weaknesses went beyond inadequate coverage. Questions on the range and extent of foreign competition at home and in colonial markets, the effects of foreign tariffs on British exports, and the extent to which imports undercut British products in the home market, could be answered by firms with reasonably objective information. But it was unlikely that British firms could provide realistic information on the production costs of foreign firms suspected of dumping in Britain, on the significance of foreign labour costs, or on the size of tariff reductions necessary to allow British exporters to compete successfully overseas.[16] Furthermore, the Commission was reluctant to question firms on their own production costs, even though this was necessary both to ascertain the reduction of foreign tariffs desirable in tariff bargaining and to construct a tariff schedule graded on labour content. The more specialized forms designed for individual industries sought better information on costs, but the response from firms on such questions was in any case poor.[17]

The questionnaires had other shortcomings. Hewins's claim that the case for a tariff rested on a process of reduction or 'isolation'[18] meant that if Britain's relative decline could be shown to be unrelated to factors such as foreign wages and labour conditions, patent laws, technical education, and railway rate policies, then, by elimination, it must be related to commercial policy. In spite of the importance of this methodology to the Commission's procedures, only two questions on Form No. 1 related to other causal factors in the reduction process,[19] and it is likely that many of the questions vetoed by Hewins concerned areas in which British producers were felt to be disadvantaged compared with foreign rivals.

Contacting 'every manufacturer in the Kingdom who could be discovered' entailed considerable difficulty. When trade directories failed, the Commission was forced to adopt a personal approach, asking trade associations and Chambers of Commerce for lists of members. They met with varying degrees of success: whilst the Boot and Shoe Manufacturers' Association and the Scottish Iron Manufacturers' Association were helpful, Hewins found it 'extremely difficult to get a really good authentic list of textile manufacturers'. Manchester Chamber of Commerce being unhelpful, it was left to Frederick Baynes and Charles Eckersley to bear the brunt of the search for cotton firms, an instance of the common tendency for Commissioners to search through their personal connections, casting an ever-widening net in aid of the Commission's activities.

---

[16] Qus. III, IV, IX, V, VI, and X respectively on Form No. 1.

[17] See, for instance, 'Form No. 4 (Issued to Iron and Steel Manufacturers)', reproduced in *Iron and Steel Report*, para. 92, Qu. V. See also below, Ch. 5.

[18] Tariff Commission Minutes (verbatim typescript), hereinafter cited as TCM(VT), 17 Mar. 1904, 7; 2/1/6, TCP.

[19] Form No. 1, Qus. VI and X.

As early as mid-February 1904, by which time the exercise was by no means finished, some 77,200 firms had been contacted.[20]

The third element in the collection of information was the search for witnesses. Most industrial Commissioners gave evidence, but they were a minority among the 400 industrialists and 147 agriculturalists who by 1910 had appeared before the Commission. Whereas the questionnaires were sent indiscriminately to firms whatever their opinion on the fiscal question, we need to examine more closely the procedure of selecting witnesses, especially given the widespread suspicion among Free Traders that the Commission took evidence from only one side.[21]

The majority of witnesses were selected through informal channels, and here undoubtedly occurred a considerable degree of discrimination, some intentional and some less so. In a series of visits to manufacturing districts Hewins sought both to acquaint businessmen with the objects of the enquiry and to secure witnesses. Ivan Levinstein was asked to arrange a meeting with 'representative Manchester men including merchants', and Hewins sought to involve Percy Glass, a Stockport manufacturer with whom he had earlier corresponded with a view to securing the 'best possible expert evidence' from the cotton industry.[22] There followed visits to Middlesborough and Sheffield, arranged by Charles Allen of Henry Bessemer and Co., and Bolckow, Vaughan and Co., and to Bradford, Halifax, Leeds, Dewsbury, and Huddersfield, arranged by Henry Mitchell and A. F. Firth, a Brighouse carpet manufacturer and member of the Textile Committee. A subsequent visit to Leeds concentrated on the engineers rather than the textile manufacturers, as did a rather unsuccessful visit to Glasgow and the meetings with Birmingham businessmen held during Hewins's stay with Chamberlain at Highbury in December 1904.[23]

Such meetings inevitably developed a protectionist bias. Levinstein arranged the Manchester meeting under TRL auspices, and Hewins, conscious of the importance of being seen to conduct a scientific inquiry, felt it important to stress that subsequent meetings should be impartial and unconnected with the TRL.

---

[20] Hewins to Womens' Branch of TRL, St. Peter's Institute, London, 22 Feb. 1904; TCM(VT), 17 Mar. 1904, 4, 2/1/6, TCP. See also Tariff Commission Minutes (printed) (hereinafter cited as TCM(P)), 21 Jan. 1904, 2/1/4, TCP; Hewins to Eckersley, 6 May 1904; Eckersley to Hewins, 9 May 1904, 6/1/5, TCP; George S. Smith and Co. Ltd. to Hurd, 28 Jan. 1904, Hurd to Smith and Co., 30 Jan. 1904, Smith and Co. to Hurd, 16 Feb. 1904, 6/7/6, TCP.

[21] e.g. in S. J. Chapman, 'The Report of the Tariff Commission on the Iron and Steel Trades', *Economic Journal*, 14 (1904), 617. See also 'The Introduction of Tariff Reform: Statement by the Secretary of the Tariff Commission', released to the Press Association, 10 Jan. 1910, copy in 6/1/26, TCP.

[22] Levinstein to Hewins, 5 Feb. 1904, 6/1/21, TCP; Hewins to Glass, 30 Dec. 1903, 6/3/10, TCP.

[23] Ponsonby to Keen, 25 Feb. and 1 Mar. 1904, 6/1/19, TCP; Douglas Vickers to Charles Allen, 15 Mar. 1904, 6/1/1, TCP; Mitchell to Hewins, 8 and 29 Aug. 1904, Hewins to Mitchell, 9 Aug. 1904, 6/1/24, TCP; A. F. Firth to Hewins, [?] Sept. 1904, 6/2/13, TCP; Tariff Commission memo to Hewins, 22 Oct. 1904, 6/1/14, TCP.

But both Mitchell and Firth were active Tariff Reformers in their districts, and there was an ominous ring in Mitchell's intention that Hewins should 'meet a few of the men who can give us the most help, at my house, quietly' during the first visit to Leeds.[24] Thus it was likely that the meetings held would have consisted predominantly of protectionists, not least because Free Traders would have been likely to avoid them.

A similar bias occurred when the Commission received suggestions for possible witnesses from outsiders, or when the Commission invited a businessman to give evidence on the basis of the 'quality' of his replies to the questionnaires. Quality was a subjective concept, and in any case Tariff Reformers were more likely to return the forms carefully and completely answered. Indeed, occasionally such methods misfired. When Hewins drew up a list of Irish agricultural witnesses on the basis of the 'best' replies to the agricultural questionnaire, Sir William Goulding found that the Irish nationalists were completely unrepresented.[25]

The belief that the Commission deliberately sought out protectionist witnesses should be strongly tempered by the fact that it often tended to approach the nationally known leaders of an industry as a matter of course, because their participation would increase the authority and respectability of the enquiry. It was often the Free Traders and the unaligned who refused. In reluctant industries this could lead to an undiscriminating blanket-search for witnesses. When Sir Thomas Dewar, whose grain-distilled whisky was 'hardly affected by foreign competition', refused to give evidence, Commissioner Alfred Gilbey bombarded an almost despairing Hewins with lists of names which almost certainly included Free Traders.[26] Levinstein was so convinced that the response from bleachers and dyers would be low that he submitted huge lists of possible witnesses and suggested that all be invited. Later, for the chemical industry proper, he supplied the complete list of members of the Society of Chemical Industry, marking the 500 or so whom he thought might give information and putting 'two crosses against those whom it is desirable to get to give evidence'. He stressed that 'I cannot warrant . . . that all, or how many are favourable to a tariff reform'. By now desperate for chemical witnesses, the Commission followed his instructions.[27]

[24] Ponsonby to Keen, 1 Mar. 1904, 6/1/19, TCP; Mitchell to Hewins, 29 Aug. 1904, 6/1/24, TCP; Firth to Hewins, 4 Oct. 1904, 6/2/13, TCP. Mitchell was active in the Bradford Branch of the TRL and Firth president of the Halifax Branch.

[25] Firth to Mitchell, 11 Feb. 1904, 6/1/24, TCP; Goulding to Hewins, 11 July 1905, Hewins to Goulding, 12 July 1905, Goulding to Hewins, 25 Jan. and 10 Feb. 1904, Hewins to Goulding, 13 July 1905, Goulding to Hewins, 20 Sept. 1904, 6/1/11, TCP.

[26] Dewar to Hewins, 12 Oct. 1905, Hewins to Gilbey, 19 Oct. 1905, Gilbey to Hewins, 20 Oct. 1905, 6/1/10, TCP.

[27] Levinstein to Ponsonby, 4 Oct. 1904, Ponsonby to Levinstein, 13 Oct. 1904, Levinstein to Hewins, 25 Oct. 1905, Hurd to Levinstein, 26 Oct. 1905, 6/1/21, TCP.

Furthermore, the Commission could not exercise control over selection when trade associations nominated their own delegates as witnesses. It must be stressed that this was encouraged by the Commission. Sometimes, as with the Birmingham-centred British Tube Trade Association, the delegates were sympathetic to Tariff Reform. A position of neutrality was, however, more common. The Paper Makers' Association appointed six witnesses, three known by Lewis Evans to be hostile.[28] The evidence of the British Iron Trade Association, given by its secretary, J. S. Jeans, was a model of caution in avoiding antagonizing different beliefs among its members. But most common of all was a decision not to co-operate, associations preferring their members to act as individuals. Mitchell feared that the Bradford Dyers' Association 'would decline to act as an Association. You might try them.' But the same was true of the Scottish Iron Manufacturers' Association, a body almost certainly heavily protectionist. Not surprisingly, the greater protectionist consensus in agriculture led to a much higher proportion of farming witnesses being nominated by chambers of agriculture than manufacturers being nominated by trade associations.[29]

Examples survive of Hewins actually seeking Free Trade witnesses on an individual basis. One such was Walter Cliff, mentioned to him as a Free Trade ironmaster willing to give evidence. Another was Sir Christopher Furness, the prominent shipowner.[30] When the Commission heard that William Pirrie, chairman of Harland and Wolff, had spoken of offering to give evidence but being refused because he was a Free Trader, an obviously hurt Hewins explained that an invitation had been sent to the firm but no reply had been received. Leverton Harris wrote to Pirrie enclosing Hewins's explanation and expressing the Commission's delight at his intention to give evidence: 'We want to get the views of Free Traders as well as the Tariff Reformers'.[31] Though Pirrie declined, he did substantiate Hewins's version of events:

as Mr Hewins says in his letter, an invitation was actually given to my firm, but I did not feel disposed to supply the information desired and therefore thought the simplest way was to leave the communication unanswered, especially as I myself have not had at any time the smallest desire to give evidence before the Commission on such a subject, upon

---

[28] Evans thought six of the eight major firms in the UK to be hostile to Tariff Reform. See Evans to Hewins, 1 July 1904, 6/1/6, TCP.

[29] James Hamilton to Hewins, 27 Feb. 1904, 6/5/25, TCP; Mitchell to Hewins, 27 Apr. 1904, 6/1/24, TCP; 'The Introduction of Tariff Reform: Statement by the Secretary of the Tariff Commission'.

[30] On Cliffe, see Hewins to Evans, 5 May 1904, 6/1/6, TCP. On Furness, see Jones to Hewins, 25 May 1904, Hewins to Jones, 26 May 1904, 6/1/17, TCP. Furness was Liberal MP for Hartlepool, and had numerous interests in coal and iron and steel as well as in shipping: H. H. Bassett (ed.), *Men of Business at Home and Abroad* (n.d. but 1913), p. 150.

[31] Hewins to Leverton Harris and Leverton Harris to Hewins, both 9 Nov. 1905, Leverton Harris to Pirrie, 11 Nov. 1905, 6/1/13, TCP.

which I take a very strong side. I am, however, none the less obliged to you for kindly interesting yourself in the matter to the extent you have done.[32]

Thus, though the method of recruiting witnesses through the thoroughness of their replies to the forms of enquiry tended towards a protectionist bias, as doubtless did many cases where individual Commissioners made informal suggestions as to whom to invite, there was a second type of bias which reflected less discreditably on the Commission. Many Free Traders, when approached, simply refused to co-operate. Yet often the Commission would have been glad of their participation, for its desire to be seen to conduct an objective enquiry which commanded public credibility was strong and heartfelt.

This is the less surprising since, in one sense at least, the Commission's leaders saw little danger in the participation of Free Traders. Though there was an element designed for public consumption in Hewins's statement that 'the Commission are alone interested in obtaining the facts with respect to each industry without regard in any way to the views which firms or witnesses may happen to hold on fiscal or other questions',[33] it did also reflect the historist belief that facts were facts, that facts revealed causation and of themselves suggested remedies, and that in consequence it was unimportant where those facts came from.

More Free-Trade participation might have produced more reports such as that on cotton, where the weaknesses showed. But Free Trade involvement in the enquiry was unthinkable. Tariff Reform was a 'debate' only in the political sense of that word—each side asserted its position, poured sarcasm and abuse on the foe, and turned to its friends to receive applause for its antics. When, in such a climate, the Commission was criticized as the usurper and grotesque mimic of the proper function of a Royal Commission, the die was cast. There was no real possibility of Free Trade participation, even to thwart the inquiry's objects.

III

Following the collection of information, the Commission had two tasks: to examine it to determine a given industry's condition and the strength of its need for protection, and, if necessary, to design the best-structured tariff to meet that object. Discussion of the tariff-construction process is best left for the moment,[34] but an examination of the Commission's demonstration of the need for a tariff is important to an understanding of its whole fabric and operation, and therefore deserves mention at the outset.

[32] Pirrie to Leverton Harris, 13 Nov. 1905, 6/1/13, TCP.
[33] Hewins to Leverton Harris, ibid. (This letter was forwarded to Pirrie).
[34] See below, Chs. 5 and 6.

The large amount of information gathered was split up, indexed, and cross-indexed on cards. In charge of this work was Julius Kaiser, who had developed his system in previous appointments with British Westinghouse and the Philadelphia Commerical Museum, where he had had a staff of twenty-eight under him.[35] Information from the questionnaires was combined with material from published sources into special memoranda. Initially confidential, these were discussed in committee and amended versions usually incorporated in the reports. But in the meantime this process uncovered the 'points on which it is desirable to obtain more information', usually accomplished by the examination of witnesses.[36]

Hewins admitted that 'the whole scheme of the inquiry would break down unless it were conducted in a strictly impartial and scientific manner'.[37] His use of the word 'scientific' rested on the assumption, never clearly spelled out but implied in his correspondence with Pirrie, that description revealed causation. Faith in this assumption allowed him to formulate a mechanical and sequential analytical procedure:

The result of this inquiry, so exhaustively conducted, and so completely tested by expert evidence, should be to show clearly;-

Whether, in fact, any given industry is declining or progressing;

What are the causes of the decline, where such a decline has taken place;

To what extent the fiscal policy of this and other countries has been a factor in bringing about this state of affairs;

And to indicate whether it is likely that these conditions can be altered by a change of policy on the part of Great Britain.[38]

Only the first of these four steps could be proved adequately by largely objective criteria. On the second, Hewins's method relied on accepting manufacturing opinion on what were often complex comparisons between industrial conditions and performance at home and abroad, with the likelihood that the discovered 'causes' would consist of a traditional and predictable catalogue of manufacturers' complaints—labour practices and trade unions, taxation, patents legislation, and sharp practices by foreigners and merchants, in addition to foreign tariffs. The third step involved manufacturers not only in listing the causes of Britain's decline, but also in quantifying them. Such information was hardly likely to emerge from the questionnaires, and the difficulties presented by this were only overcome by the introduction of a theory, undoubtedly originating with Hewins, that all the causes of decline could be linked, in the 'reduction'

---

[35] Hewins to Pearson, 1 Jan. 1904 [mis-dated 1903], 6/1/26, TCP; Hewins to Kaiser, 7 Jan. 1904, 47/155, HP.

[36] Tariff Commission, 'Memorandum on the Work of the Tariff Commission', Memorandum no. 21, 11 Feb. 1905, 1–2 (copy in 1/8/1, TCP).

[37] Ibid.   [38] Ibid. 2–3.

process, into a monocausally related package in which overseas trustification was the proximate cause of decline and tariff policy was the determinant of trustification.[39] Indeed, it was only in the fourth step, when dealing with the future, that Hewins admitted that there was any element of speculation in his method at all.

In a pure sense, manufacturers were being asked for information they could not possibly give. They supplied instead opinion, reason, and prejudice, which the Commission, by its nature, chose to regard as fact. Of course, the Commission had discovered no new scientific methodology for analyzing British industrial retardation,[40] and to an extent all enquiries into human and economic affairs must evaluate opinion in the absence of laboratory-determined proof. But the Commission had, after all, promoted the view that its 'scientific' method made its own Tariff-Reform sympathies irrelevant. What was portrayed, and I think at first genuinely conceived, as a 'scientific' and objective study of industrial conditions, developed into a contentious thesis: not an indefensible one, but pursued, by academic standards, with overriding determination. What is curious about the industrial series is the paradoxical juxtaposition of immense detail with incautious use, of technical vocabulary with partial argument. Here was academic appearance without academic detachment, the spirit of enquiry without the discipline to control preconception.

That the Commission was indifferent towards, perhaps even unconscious of, the flaws in its own approach does not detract from its interest. No combatant in the Tariff-Reform controversy publicly retracted his contributions, and few regarded them as less than axiomatic truth. The Commission was, after all, one of the few participants which recognized there were points to be made on both sides.[41] And it was not surprising if businessmen had little working knowledge of the philosophies of history and of science, and hardly less surprising that Hewins did not seek continually to remind them. For it is important to recognize that the grounds on which we have criticized the inquiry's methodology are in themselves too metaphysical to have found favour with the Commission. If practical men, listening to the evidence of hundreds of other practical men, could not describe industrial decline, and thereby understand and explain it, who could? And, if the mechanism of tariff-induced combination as a prime reason for Britain's beleaguered position was theory, was it not realistic theory derived from inductive study?

[39] The way in which this was done is best left for consideration in the case study of the enquiry into iron and steel. See below, Ch. 5.

[40] It is interesting to note that the Commission's process of 'reduction' was methodologically not dissimilar to A. L. Levine's academic study, *Industrial Retardation in Britain 1880–1914* (1967).

[41] In private, Marshall recognized the shortcomings of the professorial manifesto. See Marshall to Lujo Brentano, 26 Aug. 1903, in H. W. McCready, 'Alfred Marshall and Tariff Reform, 1903: Some Unpublished Letters', *Journal of Political Economy*, 63 (1955), 266.

IV

The Commission established its offices at 7 Victoria Street, close to parliament, in the same building as the TRL and across the road from the Free Trade Union. No doubt there was informal contact with League headquarters: that there was little correspondence between them may merely suggest that written communication was unnecessary. Nevertheless, the two bodies were separate and distinct, having different functions within the Tariff Reform movement, despite some confusion on this issue by politicians and public alike.

In July 1904 the Commission employed between fourteen and sixteen weekly staff and three quarterly staff (Hewins, Kaiser, and Percy Hurd, the assistant secretary).[42] This had probably been its size since January, and there remained between thirteen and seventeen weekly staff until the late summer of 1905. Most were employed as clerks, typists, indexers, and collaters.

With such an establishment, Hewins was able to produce three of the industrial reports and twenty-six memoranda, some of which were published. Pressure on the printers was at times extreme, a constant flow of last-minute alterations made necessary by the changing whim of the Commission on frequently trivial points. Relations with the printers were strained when Hewins and Hurd questioned some of their charges, and provoked a rather tearful rebuke which eloquently testifies to the tightness of the Commission's schedule:

As regards the item of £66. 12/– it must be apparent that this is not excessive. Mr Hurd knows that our premises and staff were entirely given over to your work from Saturday 1 o'clock until Monday 8 a.m. and he is also cognisant of the fact that the effort we made to carry out your instructions that the work '*must* be done' was an achievement of which we have every reason to feel proud, and which at the time you expressed your satisfaction with. It may not have come to your knowledge that our Mr Smith hardly had any sleep during that time, as at all hours of the night he had to go on his bicycle to Mr Rosenbaum's house at Acton and get proofs passed for the machines which were waiting to print off. We have not charged you a penny for his services, and we do not believe that another man in London could be found who, at the risk of his health, would have done what he did, nor is there any Firm who would not have charged for such exceptional attention.[43]

In August 1905 staff shortages and printing problems intensified, as work began on the preparatory stages of the report on agriculture at the same time as Hewins was pressing for completion of the textiles series. Hurd hired additional staff 'as the work requires it', but a shortage of typists was still holding up the processing of the agricultural questionnaires.[44] By the autumn, staffing levels had reached a

---

[42] Statistician Stanley Rosenbaum was appointed later.

[43] Vacher and Sons to Hewins, 22 Mar. 1905; cf. Hewins to Vacher and Sons, 22 July 1904, 6/7/10, TCP.

[44] Hurd to Hewins, 15 Aug. 1905, Kaiser to Hewins, 15 Aug. 1905, 6/1/14, TCP.

plateau of nearly thirty, sufficient to allow work to begin on processing the engineering evidence, though this was only possible because key workers like Kaiser postponed their holidays until Christmas.[45] Peak employment of thirty-two was reached in December, with the election very much in the air. But this peak was not significantly higher than the plateau of September to October, well before Balfour resigned. Whether connected to the election or not, however, Hewins's plan to finish the industrial series by early 1906 was not accomplished: by the election the *Iron and Steel Report* and most of the textile volumes had been published, but important reports on agriculture and engineering were far from complete.[46]

Early memoranda were posted free to all Chambers of Commerce and trade associations, to MPs, 'effective' peers, and colonial ministers and 'other Colonial authorities'. In line with its policy of seeking wide press-coverage of its activities, the Commission supplied the press with ready-written advance notices of its publications. This could cause difficulties, as when the *Evening Standard* pre-empted a publication date, or when the *Standard* distorted the release and ascribed it to the 'Tariff League Commission', but given the predominant bias of the press towards Tariff Reform the procedure ensured wide publicity. Sixty-nine newspapers printed the advance notice of an early memorandum on the iron and steel industry, many also mentioning it in their editorials.[47]

Furthermore, though Hewins was anxious to establish the Commission's reputation for scientific impartiality, he encouraged members to act 'outside the Grange' in promoting its findings. When, doubtless partially because of Alfred Jones's presidency, the Liverpool Chamber of Commerce sent large orders for the early memoranda, Hewins pressed Jones to arrange discussions in the Chamber to 'thoroughly ventilate' the problems of British industry. W. H. Grenfell was deputed to keep Balfour aware of progress in the inquiry into iron and steel. But perhaps the largest such programme of advertisement was carried out by the Agricultural Committee. When Henry Chaplin spoke to the Lincoln-shire Chamber of Agriculture on the *Agricultural Report* late in 1906, Agricultural Committee member William Frankish, acting as if from the Chamber itself, had arranged national press coverage, while A. H. H. Matthews had distributed 1,000 copies of the report from the Central Chamber of Agriculture, encouraging local Chambers to discuss it.[48] Hewins would doubtless have claimed he was merely ensuring the wide circulation of the results of his objective enquiries, for

---

[45] Hurd to Hewins, 11 Aug. 1905, 6/1/14, TCP.

[46] The report on engineering did not appear until 1909. See below, Ch. 7.

[47] Hewins to Alfred Jones, 12 Mar. 1904, 6/1/17, TCP; Hewins to Ed. *Evening Standard*, 20 Dec. 1905, and Hurd to Ed. *Standard*, 12 Feb. 1904, 6/1/26, TCP; Tariff Commission memo to Pearson, 9 Mar. 1904, 6/1/26, TCP.

[48] Jones to Hewins, 4 Mar. 1904, Hewins to Jones, 7 Mar. 1904, 6/1/17, TCP; Hewins to Grenfell, 20 May 1904, Grenfell to Hewins, 21 May 1904, 6/1/4, TCP; Hewins to William Frankish (telegram), Frankish to Hewins, both 27 Nov. 1906, 6/1/9, TCP; Hewins to A. H. H. Matthews, 26 Nov. 1906, 6/1/23, TCP.

discussion in the non-partisan spirit suggested by Chamberlain. But it is easy in retrospect to see the hand of the Tariff Reform propagandist.

Much Commission literature was inevitably destined for partisan hands, with the TRL purchasing large quantities and supplying them to local branches as a matter of course, and with Commission members such as Baynes and Charles Follett ensuring that their own branches kept complete files of Commission works. But intended circulation was wider than this. Firms which supplied information, and anyone who contributed to Commission finance, could expect to receive copies, as could many public and university libraries at home and abroad. If the Board of Trade was embarrassed by the Commission's complimentary copies it never actually said so, and in the calmer post-election period it actually requested memoranda on the structure of colonial tariffs. Requests from the Colonial Office were, however, much more frequent.[49]

The output of Commission literature is not precisely known, but it was certainly small compared with more blatant propaganda. A thousand copies of the *Iron and Steel Report* sold in the first six weeks certainly compared poorly with the much larger output of TRL pamphlets.[50] But the *Report*'s price of 2s. 6d. was equivalent to a low-priced academic publication like those in Methuen's well-known 'Books on Business' series,[51] and its purpose was less to reach the public directly than to influence those who themselves influenced the masses. The best information we have relates to the distribution of the *Iron and Steel Report* as at 5 May 1905. Of an initial print of 6,000, 2,651 copies had been circulated by Commission and League to the press, peers, MPs, and witnesses, 1,067 sold through the publisher P. S. King and Son, 100 were on sale with a large bookseller, and 2,182 copies remained in hand. As the *Report* remained on sale for several years after this, we cannot gauge total distribution precisely, though it does seem that the heaviest sales occurred amidst the publicity accompanying the launch of a report, and that subsequent circulation was probably more due to the gratuity of the Commission and the League than to continued purchase by the public. Fragmentary evidence suggests that the *Cotton Report* had the smallest circulation, perhaps as low as 2,400 copies, of which 500 went to Harold Tremayne, literary secretary of the TRL, whilst it is almost certain that the *Agricultural Report* had the largest, being widely distributed among the farming community.[52]

---

[49] Hewins to N. Grattan Doyle (Northern Tariff Reform Federation), 28 July 1908, 6/5/21, TCP; Follett to Hewins, 6 Feb. 1909, 6/1/8, TCP; H. Heydeman (secretary of Manchester TRL) to Anderson, 15 Oct. 1907, 6/5/28, TCP; C. J. Bickerdike (Board of Trade) to Hewins, 9 Jan. 1908, G. C. L. Maunder (Board of Trade) to Hewins, 31 Mar. 1909, 6/5/3, TCP; for requests from Colonial Office, see 6/5/11, TCP.

[50] Hurd to Hewins, 1 Sept. 1904, 6/1/14, TCP.

[51] Including Sidney Chapman's *Cotton Industry and Trade* (1904) and J. S. Jeans's *Iron Trade of Great Britain* (1906).

[52] Hewins to Pearson, 5 May 1905, 6/1/26, TCP; Smith to Hewins, 15 June 1905, 6/7/10, TCP.

Many Commissioners were far from satisfied with the extent to which their work was being read in the country at large. The *Iron and Steel Report* had been out less than a month when Alfred Jones told Hewins that too few people were getting hold of it: 'if we could see our way to distributing say 10,000 copies to the different Workingmen's institutions and such like places it would be a very good thing'. His feeling was shared by the GPC. Following Chamberlain's strategy that complex and statistical material should 'filter down' to working men in 'a more popular form', a threepenny abridged version of the *Iron and Steel Report* was issued in the hope of a 'substantial sale'.[53]

Pearson was originally an advocate of 1*d.* popular editions of all the reports, but by June 1905 his TRL experience inclined him to pessimism; abridgements would not sell on a large scale unless manufacturers 'could be induced to buy at a rate to cover cost of production, and distribute them among workmen'.[54] His letter suggests, surprisingly, that six months before the election the TRL was deliberately reducing its literature rather than increasing it. By early summer 1905, 10,000 copies of the popular edition of the *Iron and Steel Report* had been printed, over half being distributed by the Commission and the League and nearly a quarter being sold direct. The initial print of the abridgement of the *Woollen and Worsted Report* was 20,000, its currency undoubtedly being increased by the proximity of the election. Copies were sent to all Unionist candidates, and the TRL took 5,000.[55] To popularize the Cotton Report, Chamberlain suggested another tactic:

Would not the best way be for some correspondent, who should himself be in the Cotton trade, to send me . . . his interpretation and summary of the Report of the Commission, and enquiring whether it correctly expresses my views?

Then I could reply in the affirmative in 2 or 3 lines expressing my sense of its importance and my entire agreement.[56]

Thus a contrived exchange, between Baynes and Chamberlain, was forwarded to the press and also printed by the Commission in leaflet form in large numbers: Jones alone ordered 10,000 copies of this 'Cotton Summary' for his proselytizing in Liverpool.[57]

In a time when much of the electorate must have been heartily sick of the Tariff-Reform debate, such expedients had only limited success. Few firms responded to the publisher's circular quoting low wholesale prices for bulk orders: the Staffordshire tile manufacturer who gave all his employees a copy of

[53] Jones to Hewins, 14 Aug. 1904, 6/1/17, TCP; Hewins to Pearson, 18 Jan. 1905, 6/1/26, TCP.
[54] Pearson to Hewins, 7 June 1905; 6/1/26, TCP.
[55] Hewins to Pearson, 5 May 1905, 6/1/26, TCP; Hurd to Hewins, 30 Dec. 1905 and (two letters) 1 Jan. 1906 [both mis-dated 1905], 6/1/14, TCP.
[56] Chamberlain to Hewins, 10 June 1905, HP.
[57] Baynes to Chamberlain, 17 June 1905, 47/177, HP; Hewins to Jones (telegram), 1 July 1905, 6/1/17, TCP.

the *Pottery Report* was a rarity.[58] In 1909 a Mr Turner, a chief partner in the great Leeds firm of Fowlers, had not even heard of the *Engineering Report*. Hewins put part of the blame on a 'conspiracy of silence' in the Free Trade press: the *Daily Chronicle, Daily News, Morning Leader, Star,* and *Manchester Guardian* all ignored the publication of the *Agricultural Report*. But the problem touched even Tariff Reform ranks. In 1911 Sir John Jackson, Unionist MP for Devonport and a sizeable contributor to the TRL, did 'not quite understand whether the Tariff Commission is the same [as the League] or no', a statement which Caillard found 'quite astonishing'.[59]

In the disappointment after the 1906 election, Hewins blamed the TRL's literary department for not disseminating the Commission's findings more effectively. Though the predominantly protectionist press had done its share, it had been 'anticipated' that the League would make a 'systematic attempt' to popularize Commission reports in leaflets and pamphlets.[60] But he admitted this was difficult for anyone not closely familiar with the Commission's work: experience showed the Commission's own popular reports to be the more promising vehicle. After the election, he joined the League's Literary Committee, and in 1911 was elected its chairman, but on the evidence available it cannot be said that the League's efforts became conspicuously more successful. Though they continued to enjoy popularity with Tariff-Reform MPs and supporters, the direct impact of the 'Red Books' on the electorate probably reached its peak with the *Agricultural Report* of November 1906.

Some of the failure perhaps lay with the heavy and solid argument of the reports, a quality that the Commission would have defended as serious and objective study. More sensational and obvious fiscal propaganda was, after all, criticized for the opposite reason. Arnold Forster thought much of it 'perfectly contemptible' and 'good businessmen here and in the North' said much the same to Sir Joseph Lawrence of the TRL's Literary Committee.[61] But criticism was easy; the perfect blend of accuracy, authority, brevity, and simplicity was unattainable. Lawrence knew well that no Tariff-Reform literature pleased everybody. His own policy was to overcome the 'dense ignorance' of the mass of voters and 'reach their intellect by simplistic means', appealing to the 'sectional' interests of workers in different industries, even though this might do injustice to Chamberlain's vision of harmonious and integrated scientific

[58] Hurd to Hewins, 27 Mar. 1907, 6/1/14, TCP. Some Tariff Commissioners, such as Baynes, Firth, and Jones, responded favourably to the circular. The 100 copies of the popular edition of the *Iron and Steel Report* ordered by the papermakers John Dickinson & Co. may have been for Lewis Evans' own workforce. See John Dickinson & Co. to Hewins, 1 Mar. 1905, 6/1/6, TCP.

[59] Sir Joseph Lawrence to Hewins, 2 Feb. 1909, 6/4/18, TCP; Hewins to Pearson, 23 Nov. 1906, 6/1/26, TCP; Jackson to Caillard, 18 July 1911, 6/1/1, TCP; Caillard to Hurd, 20 July 1911, 6/1/1, TCP.

[60] Hewins to Pearson, 19 Feb. 1906; 6/1/26, TCP.

[61] Lawrence to Hewins, 3 Jan. 1908; 6/4/18, TCP.

protection.[62] If Lawrence's bleak view had any basis in fact, then the Commission indeed faced a difficult task.

A last reason for narrow circulation may simply have been price. As the TRL expanded its publishing between the two elections of 1910, Lawrence attempted to persuade authors and publishers to reduce book prices 'down to the capacity of persons in working-class circumstances'.[63] But in spite of conspicuous success with Sir Guilford Molesworth's *Economic and Fiscal Facts and Fallacies*,[64] publishers and authors were unconvinced that an elastic demand existed, and few followed the example. That the Commission did not reduce its own prices is nevertheless surprising, in view of the tiny extent to which it relied on sales as a source of finance. Between 1904 and 1909 the sale of reports represented only 2.1 per cent of Commission income, with the unusually high proportion of 8.1 per cent being achieved in 1907. By May 1905 sales of the *Iron and Steel Report* had realized only a fifth of the cost of printing it, whilst the proportion for the popular edition was less than half, largely because so many copies had been given away free. Given a total Commission expenditure of £9,000 in 1904, it would have cost only some £700 to have doubled the amount printed and given them all away.[65]

V

The Commission was in its early years financed entirely by donations and subscriptions from firms and individuals, with no support from outside propaganda or political institutions.[66] The proportion of funds provided by the members themselves was high. Very early, at the second meeting, the new Commissioners were confronted with financial reality by vice-chairman Pearson, who 'rather tactlessly told . . . [them] they had to contribute. Many of them did not like this, but perhaps it is just as well they should "know the worst". I [Hewins] said afterwards that if the Commission would stand that, it would stand anything.'[67]

Perhaps as many as twenty were able to withstand this pressure, and have left no record of having made any financial contribution. Amongst this group the 'imperial' members were prominent. These apart, the amounts contributed varied widely, from the £10 p.a. of Leverton Harris and the £25 p.a. of Ivan Levinstein to the much larger sums donated by Booth, Chamberlain, Flett, Maconochie, and Mosely.

[62] T. Mendelssohn Horsfall to Lawrence, 2 Jan. 1908, Lawrence to Horsfall, 3 Jan. 1908, 6/4/18, TCP.

[63] Lawrence to Ellis Wynter, 17 Mar. 1910, 6/4/18, TCP.

[64] Published in 1909. A threepenny limp-cloth edition showed no sign of TRL involvement in its publication.

[65] A. J. Marrison, 'British Businessmen and the "Scientific Tariff": A Study of Joseph Chamberlain's Tariff Commission, 1903–21', unpubl. Ph. D. thesis, Univ. of Hull, 1980, Table 8, 169.

[66] Though Hewins's salary may have been guaranteed by the TRL.

[67] W. A. S. Hewins, 'My Connection with the Fiscal Controversy', HP, 36–7.

TABLE 7. *Discovered Financial Contributions of Members: 1904–c.1907*

£50	F. L. Harris; J. M. Harris; Henderson; Levinstein; Littlejohn; Webb.
£100	Boulton; Corah; Eckersley; Goulding; Jones; Keen; Pearson.
£150	Bostock; Evans.
£200	Dennis; Gilbey; Keswick; Lyle; Parsons; Peace; Rank.
£250	Elgar; Marshall.
£400	Colls.
£500	Baynes; Hickman; Waring.
£600	Lewis; Phillips.
£700	Noble.
£1000	Booth; Maconochie; Noble.
£1150	Flett.

[a] This table excludes Burbidge and Pearson, who are known to have made substantial contributions, and also Chamberlain's £1,000 in 1906.
[b] Certain Commissioners, especially Flett, Gallaher, Goulding and F. L. Harris, are known to have collected substantial donations from business associates and acquaintances. These have not been included. Where, however, a discovered contribution originated from a Commission member's own firm, it has been included, except in the case of Vickers, Sons and Maxim (Caillard).
[c] The table should not be taken as indicating that the 21 Commissioners not mentioned made no contributions during this period.
[d] The figures are rounded in only three cases (to the nearest £10).
Sources: Pearson to Burbidge, 30 June 1908; 6/1/26, TCP, supplemented where possible by miscellaneous information from correspondence files.

Surviving evidence on pre-1910 finance is incomplete. In 1908 Pearson handed the treasurer's control to Burbidge, supplying with it a list of contributors in the 'early days'.[68] Apart from the list being incomplete, the time period covered is uncertain and may differ for different people mentioned on it.[69] Table 7 is based on Pearson's list, with any omissions discovered in the correspondence files added. Where an entry is made, it probably gives a correct indication of the amount furnished by an individual, but there may be some members not included as contributors because their correspondence files have not survived. In one case this is known to have happened: Pearson purposely left Burbidge's 'own generous amounts' out of the list sent to the new treasurer.[70]

Furthermore, there is difficulty in determining a Commissioner's precise contribution if his influence on his own firm's generosity is included. In Table 7 the amounts for George Flett and Sir William Goulding include contributions from their firms. Lewis Evans's personal contribution, however, stands alone: though his firm sent substantial sums the precise total is unknown. Sir Vincent Caillard is not included even though he persuaded Vickers to contribute

[68] Pearson to Burbidge, 30 June 1908, 6/1/26, TCP.
[69] In Table 7, Leverton Harris's £50 is known to have been spread equally over the years 1904–8. But Dennis's contributions, as revealed in his correspondence file, gell imperfectly with Pearson's letter no matter what time period we assume that letter to have covered.
[70] This was more than mere courtesy: Pearson commented to Hewins that Burbidge's contributions were 'exceedingly generous'. Pearson to Hewins, 23 Mar. 1906, HP.

generously, and in 1911 was trying to 'get the consent of the Chairman to subscribing more than [the] £250' which had become the firm's standard annual contribution.[71]

Despite these difficulties, we may attempt a crude estimate. Total donations were £25,012 from 1904 to 1906, £29,318 from 1904 to 1907, and £37,012 from 1904 to 1908. The discovered contributions of members (Table 7) represent 44.6 per cent of donations made in the period 1904–1906, or 38 per cent of those made in 1904–1907, or 30.1 per cent of those made in 1904–1908. Since Pearson's list neglects the five-year guarantee fund of 1906, and since it is known that the record of Commissioners and, more important, the firms in which they had influence is incomplete, it seems safe to reject the lowest estimate and conclude that Commissioners themselves provided about 40 per cent of Commission income.[72] The inclusion of funds known to have been collected by members from friends and industrial acquaintances would increase the percentage to 52.9 in the years 1904–1906 or 45.2 in the period 1904–1907. But this still almost certainly underestimates the real proportion, since it is doubtful that the donations of all firms in which members had influence have been identified.

Relatively few of the larger contributors appearing in Table 7 represent those industries commonly thought to have had the strongest pecuniary interest in backing the Tariff Reform campaign. Of those contributing £250 or over, only Hickman (iron and steel) and Flett (electrical engineering) came from industries commonly acknowledged to be heavily protectionist, though to these we should add Marshall (agricultural engineering). Elgar, Noble, and Caillard represented what was in effect already a protected industry, with a substantial shipbuilding component. Colls and Waring came from building and furniture manufacture and retailing, Baynes from cotton, Lewis from papermaking, Phillips from brewing, Booth from shipping, and Maconochie from food processing. Mosely was a diamond merchant. Of course, all believed that they personally, as well as the economy generally, would benefit from Tariff Reform. Nevertheless it is well to remember that, in the economist's terms, the protection sought was a public good. If it had been obtained, it would have been available to all, and thus it was not economically rational for a manufacturer to participate in, still less to finance, a movement in which his individual contribution was unlikely to be critical.[73] This is obviously of limited use in explaining the great upsurge of pressure-group activity in twentieth-century Britain, but it does serve to remind

[71] Caillard to Hewins, 7 July 1911, 6/1/1, TCP. Vickers' contributions were generally made indirectly through Caillard.

[72] Small amounts of bank interest and income from sales of reports have been excluded from this calculation.

[73] Mancur Olson, *The Logic of Collective Action* (Cambridge, Mass., 1965, repr. 1971), 11–12, 15–16, 21.

us of the extent to which political and economic, personal and public, motives interacted on the Commission.

VI

Descriptions of the Commission as the 'Tariff League Commission' or the 'Tariff Reform Commission' were common in many quarters: in the press, in Whitehall, even among Commissioners themselves.[74] Though Hewins sought to dispel the implication of partisanship in the press, his claim was a weak one. It is true that he regretted the involvement of the League in organizing the Manchester meeting in February 1904, but his habit of making speeches in pairs, and following a cautious statement of the Commission's procedures and objectives with a strong and direct address on fiscal and imperial policy, was not likely to reassure the sceptic.[75]

Thus it is tempting to assert that the Commission was a mere propaganda device, a façade of methodological caution and sane business pragmatism serving to hide a baser and more emotional core of crude protectionism and Tory xenophobia. Then, Hewins's apparent ability to reconcile his running of a sober, moderate Commission of Enquiry with his other activities in the Tariff-Reform cause can be interpreted simply as that brazen hypocrisy that comes so much more easily to politicians than to those who must tolerate them.

There was of course a large propagandist element in the Commission's conception and in its subsequent history. Nevertheless, Hewins and his associates had another view of their own motives, a view held at times strongly and obsessively, and at others less strongly and somewhat tongue-in-cheek. In Hewins's explanation that '[w]e acted on the principle that if the industries and the problems they suggested could be accurately *described* the solution of those problems would almost suggest itself',[76] we can see clearly the influence of historism. Undoubtedly in the early years of the Commission there was a belief that it alone in the controversy was laying bare the skeleton of the fiscal issue, and that of all the participating groups it came the nearest to truth by virtue of its inductive method. This legitimized extra-curricular activities in dissemination, by allowing a distinction to be drawn between education, the dissemination of established truths and facts, and outright propaganda. When Commissioners— whether MPs such as Chaplin and Leverton Harris, or those active in local politics such as Jones, Evans, and Mitchell—made speeches, the Commission

[74] Earl of Elgin (Colonial Secretary, 1905–8) to Hewins, 25 Apr. 1907, HP; Eckersley to Hewins (n.d. but early 1904), 6/1/5, TCP; Jones to Hewins, 20 Jan. 1904, 6/1/17, TCP.

[75] *Morning Post* (editorial), 17 Dec. 1903; *Manchester Guardian*, 27 Feb. 1904.

[76] W. A. S. Hewins, *Apologia of an Imperialist* (1929), i. 86 (my emphasis).

willingly supplied information and argument. Of course, it was not feasible to stop them, but nor would the Commission have wished to, save when Pearson launched his own unauthorized and unrealistic schemes for Empire Free Trade in the *Standard* and *Daily Express*, which ran counter to Chamberlain's policy in an uncanny parallel to Beaverbrook's 'Empire Crusade', launched from the same offices some two decades later.[77]

Early in the inquiry Hewins, torn between loyalty to an imperial policy and the attractive idea of an omniscient scientific bureaucracy, could be seen attempting to keep these opposing tendencies in check. When asked for help in the campaign in Manchester he wrote that 'it does not fall within my province to make any suggestion, or to interfere in any way with that Department—the work of Tariff Reform'.[78] When he heard that the Bradford TRL was to send a deputation of 'tariff trippers' to study the standard of living of German textile workers, he urged scientific caution:

I do not think the opinion of people who have not been specifically trained . . . is of the least value. If your deputation goes to Germany, and comes back and issues a report which is in conflict, as it may very easily be, with the conclusions of important scientific experts, I do not think that any very useful purpose will be served.[79]

Though Hewins was evidently concerned with preventing the League from looking foolish and perhaps damaging Chamberlain's campaign, there was an equally evident desire to keep separate the work of methodical enquiry from more sensational schemes. The LSE had led the country in precisely this sort of study. Its first director could scarcely condone the trivialization of the very branches of study that it had done so much to develop.

Hewins was not alone on the Commission in his mild schizophrenia between propaganda and scientific enquiry.[80] But as time went by the Commission's distinction between moderacy and immoderacy became weaker, and by the election of 1906 the thin divide between propaganda and popularization of material laid before the Commission had become harder to discern. The Commission willingly placed its resources at the disposal of Unionist MPs and candidates, whilst Chamberlain deliberately sought Tariff Reform candidates from the Commission's ranks.[81]

---

[77] Early in 1905, Pearson's proposals of a change in Tariff Reform policy in The *Standard* provoked Chamberlain, who considered it would be 'fatal to swap horses while crossing a stream', into urging the Commission to 'pass a resolution strongly disapproving of them', a course Hewins successfully resisted on the grounds that the incident would pass over. See Chamberlain to Hewins, 3 and 9 Feb. 1905, HP. On Beaverbrook's 'Empire Crusade', see A. J. P. Taylor, *Beaverbrook* (1972), chs. 11–13.

[78] Hewins to Glass, 30 Dec. 1903, 6/3/10, TCP.

[79] Hewins to Mitchell, 15 Apr. 1904, 6/1/24, TCP.

[80] For instance, as will be shown in ch. 5, Alfred Hickman was a cautious spirit in the derivation of the tariff on iron and steel, yet both he and his son contested the 1906 election as Tariff Reformers.

[81] Chamberlain to Hewins, 21 Feb. 1905, HP.

VII

Chamberlain's place in the hearts of most Commissioners is not to be doubted.[82] When he attended meetings the turnout was good and his speeches enthusiastically received. But in some ways he was careful about how he used the Commission. His opening speech, though containing a fair measure of polemic and rhetoric, had as its main thrust the emphasis on the scientific function, the need to meet objections to his policy by demonstration of a scientific tariff which would stimulate industry and commerce without making income distribution less equal and without affecting industrial efficiency.[83] Thereafter, he tended to leave the Commission alone, except when seeking material for his speeches or when attending meetings to discuss the final proofs of the Reports.

When using Commission material Chamberlain's requests were fairly objective, as when he sought information on the cotton trade for his speech at Preston in January 1905. The help he requested was mainly statistical, and it was clear that he intended to interpret the Commission's information in his own way. 'I was much obliged to you for your prompt compliance . . . and for the figures which enabled me to complete my argument', he wrote afterwards. More questionable, perhaps, was his hope that Hewins would defend his statistics, and by implication his analysis, in the press afterwards, though it was expected that the League rather than the Commission would be the vehicle for this defence.[84]

Chamberlain was by no means alone in using the Commission as an information bureau, and his use of Commission material for his own ends cannot be counted as interference in any significant sense, even when Hewins sprang to his support in the press. More significant, perhaps, was his request that the enquiry's terms of reference be widened to include a study of imperial preference.[85] The statesman's most blatant interference came not in influencing the conduct of the enquiry as such, but in influencing the Commission's decision to publish preliminary results, and, perhaps more important, in establishing a proposed tariff structure within which the Commission was forced to operate. This influence is best seen in the inquiry into iron and steel, and it is to this that we now turn.

---

[82] On Chamberlain's birthday the Commissioners presented him with a handsome piece of Georgian silver. On the regard and affection in which Chamberlain was held, see Eckersley to Hewins, 2 July 1906, 6/1/5, TCP.

[83] *Sheffield Daily Telegraph*, 16 Jan. 1904, 9.

[84] Chamberlain to Hewins, 13 Jan. 1905, HP.

[85] See above, 118.

5

The Tariff on Iron and Steel

It is understandable that iron and steel was one of the industries at the forefront of the argument for Tariff Reform. To economic nationalists, it was central amongst the producer goods which formed the backbone of the economy, its strength fundamental to that ascendancy of heavy engineering which carried Britain into the late nineteenth century. It was of great importance for national defence—even Liberal governments allowed the Admiralty to specify British steel in contracts for naval vessels—and it had been particularly subject to American and German import penetration in the 'invasions' of the 1890s. Furthermore, the Tariff Commission's enquiry into the industry began in propitious circumstances for the Tariff Reformers, since in the aftermath of the Boer War German and American steel producers once more turned their attention to the British market.

I

Unlike recruiting the Tariff Commissioners themselves, recruiting witnesses from iron and steel was easy. Within a month, fifteen out of the seventeen who were to give evidence had accepted the invitation.[1] There was some difficulty in finding witnesses from the North-East, the steel-producing district least sympathetic to Tariff Reform. Hewins wanted to hold a meeting with Middlesborough businessmen, but Arthur Keen feared that an unsuccessful meeting would damage the Commission, because 'so far as my knowledge goes the Boards of the largest Companies in that district are very divided'.[2] In the event the Commissioners contented themselves with taking evidence from ardent Chamberlainite Sir Thomas Wrightson and from Keen himself, as a director of Bolckow-Vaughan.[3] Outside the North-East however, there is no evidence that the Commission had difficulty in securing witnesses, the only major disappointment being the persistent refusal of Douglas Vickers of the great armaments firm to appear, despite several entreaties.

The Commission made attempts to secure evidence from known Free Traders. Alfred Jones and Hewins both attempted to persuade Sir Christopher Furness,

---

[1] TCM(P), 21 Jan., 4 Feb., 16–17 Mar. 1904, 2/1/4, TCP; Hewins to Keen, 12 May 1904, 6/1/19, TCP.
[2] Keen to Ponsonby, 1 Mar. 1904, 6/1/19, TCP.
[3] Typescript of Wrightson's evidence, May 1904, qu. 2260, TCP.

Liberal MP for Hartlepool, who had numerous interests in iron and steel as well as in shipping. A Walter Cliff, supposedly a Free Trade ironmaster willing to give evidence, was the subject of a fruitless search. In spite of this, all of the eventual seventeen witnesses supported Tariff Reform. The most important were Commissioners Hickman and Allen; F. W. Gilbertson, of Pontardawe and Glynbendy, important steel and tinplate companies; Wrightson of the Northeastern Steel Co.; and A. K. McCosh of the Scottish giant, William Baird and Co.[4] The others included John Strain, forthright chairman of the Lanarkshire Steel Co.; William Rylands of the well-known Warrington wire manufacturing firm and president of the Iron and Steel Wire Manufacturers' Association; and three members of the British Tube Trade Association, Harris Spencer, Rowland Lewis, and A. W. Hutton. There were several distinctly minor figures in the industry, such as A. E. Barton of the Carnforth Hematite Ironworks; Thomas Davie of the Waverley Iron and Steel Co. of Coatbridge; and W. H. Davies of the Skelton Iron, Steel and Coal Co. of Stoke on Trent.

Within three weeks 295 firms, employing 148,875 in total, had replied to the initial questionnaire. Early respondents seem to have been biased towards the lower branches of production, especially pig iron, and towards Yorkshire, Staffordshire, and Scotland. Declining Staffordshire was heavily over-represented, whilst the reverse appears to have been true of the Cleveland district. By the completion of the enquiry into iron and steel, information had been received from 458 firms, employing 230,986 or 87.2 per cent of the workforce, so presumably such imbalances had largely been redressed. But the sample remained biased towards larger firms, and consequently towards firms with an export business. This may have been due to the design of the questionnaire, which smaller firms with a home trade only seem to have regarded as inapplicable to them, even though they might be 'fully in sympathy with the objects of the Commission'.[5]

II

The Commission soon discovered the difficulty of following a purely inductive method without introducing interpretation and analysis. When Hewins compiled the early responses to Form No. 1 into a working memorandum of preliminary results, Memorandum 5, he was criticized for reading too much into the evidence. Some Commissioners were even critical of his treatment of the relatively simple first stage of the procedure, assessing the extent of foreign

---

[4] This is the evaluation in J. C. Carr and W. Taplin, *A History of the British Steel Industry* (Oxford, 1962), 198.

[5] 'Summary of Evidence Contained in Answers to Form of Inquiry (No. 1) issued to Manufacturers', Tariff Commission Memorandum 5, 14 Mar. 1904, copy in 1/8/1, TCP (hereinafter cited as TC Memorandum 5); *Iron and Steel Report*, paras. 10–12.

competition.[6] The more complex second stage, the analysis of the causes of decline through the process of 'reduction' or 'isolation', brought greater problems. In this, it was necessary to rule out the possibility that Britain suffered natural disadvantages which no foreign tariffs could have caused and which a British tariff was unlikely to remedy. Hewins was forced to admit that Form No. 1 had been poorly designed for such a purpose, but was reluctant to circularize firms with a supplementary list of questions. Instead he suggested that, since the prevalent view amongst the respondents was that it would only take reductions in foreign tariffs, rather than their total abolition, to enable them to compete successfully overseas despite transport costs, 'there appears some presumption that British goods can still be produced at least as cheap as in any other country'.[7]

The Commissioners, however, doubting the ability of respondents to comment accurately on such a matter, were nervous of proceeding on this assumption. If additional questions could not be submitted to respondents, they could at least be put to the witnesses.[8] There was friction when chairman Sir Robert Herbert sought to take advantage of the absence of Keen, Perceval, and Grenfell, the most vehement critics of the memorandum, to push ahead. Whilst the Commission was 'indebted to [Keen] for having put strongly before us the necessity of knowing what we are doing and where we are going', this was 'a very short story indeed . . . we are here to ascertain whether, on a scientific basis, a tariff suitable for the iron and steel trades can be devised'. But he underestimated the widespread dissatisfaction. Hickman reminded him that 'the first thing we want to do is to prove that a Tariff is required',[9] whilst Maconochie stressed that Keen's objections had commanded general support:

Mr. Keen was not in any doubt about what we are trying to obtain, but . . . about . . . whether the questions [sent out in the Forms of Inquiry] were of such a nature that would elicit the information that the Commission desired to obtain to get the necessary results. It was understood yesterday, I think, that questions over and above those that have already been arranged might be obtained from the Experts on the Commission.[10]

Hewins was quick to retreat. The examination of witnesses was the ideal opportunity to remedy deficiences in information from the questionnaires. Keen's fear that, given its disorganization, the Commission would not be ready to begin examining witnesses in March could thus be turned on its head. Arthur Pearson supported him: in case the questions asked of witnesses were not 'absolutely perfect in the first instance', the Commission's own experts on the

---

[6] Critics were A. W. Maconochie, Sir Westby Perceval, and Leverton Harris.

[7] TC Memorandum 5, 7; qu. VIII on Form No. 1, in *Iron and Steel Report*, para. 90; TCM(VT), 16 Mar. 1904, 15, 2/1/6, TCP.

[8] TCM(VT), 17 Mar. 1904, 2, 2/1/6, TCP.

[9] To which Herbert replied, 'Yes, I intended to say that'.

[10] TCM(VT), 17 Mar. 1904, 2–5, 2/1/6, TCP.

industry could be examined first in a trial run. Allen agreed: the problems being encountered were largely for the very reason that no verbal evidence had been taken. Keen was excessively 'nervous because he is thinking about his one particular Trade'.[11] There can be no doubt, however, that Keen was reflecting a general anxiety on the Commission that public reaction to unsupported and apparently self-interested assertion would be harsh. In the prevailing climate the Commissioners were highly sensitive to criticism.

III

As Hewins processed further questionnaires, however, he was able to recapture lost ground and assert a dominance over the Commission that he never lost thereafter. In this, his treatment of the 'reduction' process was critical. In a slightly later working memorandum, Memorandum 9, he simplified the 'reduction' process into three groups of causes 'usually alleged' to explain it: 'natural disadvantages', technical education, and the organization and policy of foreign countries.[12] It is clear in retrospect that these stood as proxy for the three main contemporary explanations of the challenge to Britain's industrial supremacy—the Free Trade (comparative-costs) explanation, the Rosebery–Haldane explanation, and the Tariff Reform explanation.

Hewins now sought to give primacy to the third of these areas of alleged causes, the organization and policy of foreign countries, at the centre of which he discerned 'the economic causes of dumping and the export policy of foreign trusts'. He was now aided by having processed more questionnaires from manufacturers. It is central to an understanding of the working of the Commission to quote at length:

The evidence shows, on the whole, that the advantages enjoyed by the United States and Germany turn upon—

(A) The development of combination;
(B) Continuous running of the works;
(C) Unity in administration;
(D) Organisation of transport;
(E) Inducements to industry and invention;
(F) Fiscal Policy as a condition precedent to most of the advantages under (A), (B), (C), (D), and (E).

A great deal of extremely valuable information is given in the memoranda on the United States Iron and Steel industry . . . It is . . . clear that the possibility of organisation such as

---

[11] TCM(VT), 17 Mar. 1904, 5–9. 2/1/6, TCP

[12] 'Memorandum on the Evidence Respecting the Iron and Steel Trades', 1, Tariff Commission Memorandum 9, unrevised proof copy, 16 Mar. 1904, copy in 1/8/1, TCP (hereinafter cited as TC Memorandum 9).

we find it in the United States is largely the outcome of the operation of the tariff. These conditions make dumping possible, and really afford the explanation of the state of affairs which is described in the evidence derived from the forms. On . . . inducements to industry and invention . . . much information, from the point of view of investment and security, is given in the summary of evidence; but the question of Trade Union action has so far been scarcely touched. This must be carefully kept in view. The conclusions indicated by the evidence, so far as it has been examined, are (1) That the British Iron and Steel trade is seriously threatened under existing conditions; (2) That those conditions are not the result of natural disadvantages; (3) That they arise from the policy and methods of foreign countries, coupled with special conditions at present prevailing with regard to British trade (The evidence on wages is not conclusive, but points to the existence of a disadvantage so far as this country is concerned in respect of the proportion labour bears to total costs); (4) That unless those conditions are altered to our advantage, it is useless to expect that British manufacturers will run the risk of laying down expensive plant and bringing their works up to date; (5) That a condition precedent to further action is the alteration of the fiscal policy of the country; (6) That such alteration must provide adequate defence of the home market and provision for finding new markets for British wares, both in foreign countries and the colonies.[13]

Hewins's agenda comforted the Commission: the greater volume of information from firms, coupled with the earlier concession that close attention would be given to the evidence from witnesses, would 'meet Mr. Keen's view a good deal'. But perhaps more important than this was the way in which Hewins had first simplified the bewildering complexity of the tariff debate into the three main strands of natural resources, technical education, and organization and policy, and then, in effect, subordinated the first two to the third and tied the third to the tariff. Putting the emphasis on the changes in business organization and, especially, the growth of scale abroad, could be calculated to act straight upon the central nervous system of the Edwardian businessman! Many British steelmakers, in particular, were well-travelled, and the industry was served by an active trade association and a respected trade press. They were acutely aware of the rise of the German cartel system, of the large increase in US plant size in the last two decades of the nineteenth century, and in particular of the recent formation of the United States Steel Corporation, the first 'billion dollar trust'. And Commissioners were probably also aware of the considerable body of populist and progressive polemic in the US which denounced that diabolic yet awesome maternity, the tariff as 'mother of the trust'. Earlier resistance to Hewins's rather peremptory handling of the 'reduction' process had rapidly melted away almost to nothing.

Commissioners still harboured some doubts. The most important element of the first alleged cause, 'natural disadvantages', was raw-material costs. Whilst none of the members thought iron ore or coal costs themselves to be at the heart

---

[13] Ibid. 2–3.

of Britain's problems, several of them still considered transport costs to be a significant factor. A. W. Maconochie had been a long-time campaigner for reform of railway rates both in and out of Parliament, and he was joined by Levinstein and Alfred Mosely, who both put canal rates and shipping charges alongside railway rates. On the second alleged cause, technical education, Hewins did not deny German superiority, but argued that the 'evidence available' could not support the assertion that better educational provision 'would have sufficed to maintain the lead of Great Britain'.[14] Facing opposition from Alfred Mosely, however, he admitted that this was 'only an expression of opinion'.[15]

Hewins was careful to allow such Commissioners their pet enthusiasms, even if those enthusiasms might lead them into areas used by Free Traders to deny the validity of the Tariff Reformers' case. To a certain extent, he could relate some of these apparently autonomous factors to the Tariff Reform analysis—for instance, by relating transport costs to the policy of foreign cartels. Furthermore, he was aided by the fact that committed Tariff Reformers were unlikely to put such causes above the tariff.

More important were the Commission's difficulties in applying the 'reduction' process to wages and trade unions, though here there were political reasons rather than substantive differences between members. Criticism of trade unions was likely to be interpreted as smacking of reaction and self-interest. Though Boulton favoured examination of the scope for 'removing obstacles [such as the] limitation of production' imposed by the unions, Hickman urged against antagonizing them, whilst Sir John Cockburn feared that 'If we appear to . . . show a desire to diminish the efficiency of Trade Unions, we may gain a lot of information, but our hope of success has gone.' Initially, few agreed with Hewins, that 'If the Commission can say that the question of Wages is not an important factor in foreign competition, you will win all the Trades Unions over.'[16]

The main question was whether union responsibility for the erosion of British supremacy, if it emerged from the enquiry, should be minimized to gain working-class support or faced squarely in the interest of 'scientific' objectivity.[17] To Caillard the issue had to be faced, whilst Allen prophesied, 'We shall have to face the music with the Trade Unions one of these days'. But the majority favoured the softer approach of Candlish, who thought it best to stress the beneficial effect of a tariff on wages and neglect the effect of trade unionism on

---

[14] TC Memorandum 9, 1–2.　　　[15] TCM(VT), 17 Mar. 1904, 14, 2/1/6, TCP.

[16] Ibid. 19–20.

[17] The issue of unions restricting industrial efficiency had wide currency due to E. A. Pratt's influential articles in *The Times*, reprinted as *Trade Unionism and British Industry* (1904). See also Chamberlain's exhortation to workers in May 1905: 'Be Free Traders if you like; but you cannot be Free Traders in goods and not be Free Traders in labour', in C. W. Boyd (ed.), *Mr. Chamberlain's Speeches* (1914), ii. 318.

industrial performance.[18] Furthermore, Caillard's view that wages in Britain were higher than those abroad carried with it the implication that they were a 'given' disadvantage, like poor natural resources, and would therefore have strengthened the Free Traders' case that the tariff was not at the root of Britain's problems.

The wage data available to the Commission from the replies to the first questionnaire was in fact extremely limited. Only about twenty firms supplied any, a third of them considering that lower wages and longer hours in Europe were insufficient to explain the difference in price of British and imported steel in the British market. Only one firm mentioned the high wages in the US industry, and only three mentioned productivity differentials, even in the crudest terms.[19] But data was not the centre of the Commission's dilemma. Even on an intuitive level, the role of the unions in influencing Britain's relative wage level was clouded by the fact that wages were themselves affected by tariff policy. The confusion this injected into the debate was well illustrated by Hickman: 'They are paying much higher wages in America, and they are able to . . . because of their tariff. It is true they are lower in Germany'.[20] The Commission's reluctance to use a pluralistic analysis made for difficulties in analysing the two different object-lessons of Germany and the US. The reductionist thesis that Britain's competitive decline was due to foreign tariffs and no other significant factor was vulnerable where German wages were so much lower than British. At the same time, it was embarrassing for the Tariff Reform case that low wages should exist in the country that was the leading exponent of 'scientific protection'. This would alienate workers by leading them to believe that businessmen expected a British tariff to lower real wages, and would conflict with the propaganda of Chamberlain and the *Daily Express* that a tariff would protect labour.

Few members grasped all the intricacies of the wages dilemma, and there was a certain instinctive pragmatism in the opinion of Harrison, Maconochie, Mosely, and Keen that concentration should be focused on the American situation.[21] But the Commission was now losing confidence. Against their claim that some Pittsburgh steelworkers earned as much as £16–£20 per week, Charles Allen argued that the British and German wages cited in Memorandum 5 were themselves too low. Far from earning the 20 to 30 shillings per day stated, English forgemen were at present receiving £3, whilst certain 'special' men on thirty-to-forty-ton crankshafts earned £4.[22] German forgemen, too, were typically earning double the 10 to 15 shillings mentioned. Strategically, Hewins

[18] TCM(VT), 17 Mar. 1904, 20–4, 2/1/6, TCP.
[19] TC Memorandum 5, 7–8 and App. V, 19–20 (esp. replies of F.312, F.1349, F.1516).
[20] Upon which Pearson added, 'But higher in Germany compared to what they were before there was a tariff'.
[21] TCM(VT), 16 Mar. 1904, 16, 2/1/6, TCP.
[22] Such figures probably related to the heads of teams on piecework contract. See S. Pollard, *A History of Labour in Sheffield* (Liverpool, 1959), 231.

added that all the publicly available information, even that in the 'Fiscal Blue Book', was inadequate to the Commission's purposes, and that 'better comparisons with French and American wages' were needed. The Commissioners were playing into his hands, and the thought of having to include France in the tangle probably appalled them. Grenfell voiced their uncertainty, proposing that 'we omit this wages question, as it is very incomplete and misleading . . . what there is of it tells against us'. The chairman and secretary were able to promise 'a separate memorandum on wages', and the subject was dropped.[23] Hewins had prevailed on the wages issue. More important, perhaps, he had also obtained implicit acceptance of the validity of the controversial 'reduction' approach in spite of the Commission members' high sensitivity to public criticism.

The primacy of the tariff in Hewins's model, the assertion that tariff-induced large scale in the US and Germany, and the lack of it in Britain, explained virtually all the steelmaker's ills, is obviously too narrow in retrospect. Today we would recognize that capital markets, business attitudes and heritage, factor prices, and the structure of market demand all contributed to the low degree of concentration in British industry, though obviously lack of tariff protection was an important contributory factor.[24] We would also need to introduce the possibility that technological backwardness had autonomous causes, one candidate favoured by many historians being the quality of entrepreneurship,[25] with its implications for over-commitment to old methods such as acid Bessemer and old products such as wrought iron, for lack of science-based expansion, and for relatively slow adoption of labour- and fuel-saving processes.[26] Nevertheless, whilst many of these wider elements were not unfamiliar to informed contemporaries,[27] the Commission's analysis is to be seen in a context where both Free Traders and Tariff Reformers put far more emphasis on the filial relationship between 'monopoly' and the tariff than is the case today, when post-1945 experience has shown that huge corporations do not necessarily depend for their growth upon high-tariff regimes.

[23] TCM(VT), 16 Mar. 1904, 17, 2/1/6, TCP.

[24] P. L. Payne, 'The Emergence of the Large-Scale Company in Great Britain, 1870–1914', *Economic History Review*, 20 (1967); L. Davis, 'The Capital Markets and Industrial Concentration: the US and the UK, a Comparative Study', *Economic History Review*, 19 (1966); L. Hannah, *The Rise of the Corporate Economy* (1976), ch. 2.

[25] In sum, the whole pessimistic indictment of D. L. Burn, *An Economic History of Steelmaking 1867–1939* (Cambridge, 1940), and T. H. Burnham and G. O. Hoskins, *Iron and Steel in Britain 1870–1930* (1943). Tariff Reformers, stressing the lack of market security caused by Free Trade, would have denied any autonomous deficiency in British entrepreneurship. As Hickman put it, the iron trade was 'quite prepared to compete in the markets of the World . . . with any country, providing that country has not artificial profits' arising from tariff protection. See TCM(VT), 16 Mar. 1904, 15, 2/1/6, TCP.

[26] The omission of this last-mentioned factor was noticed in 'The Report of the Tariff Commission on the Iron and Steel Trades', *The Economist*, 30 July 1904, 126, 128–9.

[27] A. Marshall, *Industry and Trade* (1919), esp. iii.

Furthermore, Hewins's contention that 'reduction' showed little inferiority in Britain's potential position was broadly confirmed by the witnesses. Most supported 'reduction' with regard to ore supplies. Hickman, Barton, Strain, Allen, and, essentially, Davies all gave support to the lengthy and judicious assessment presented by J. S. Jeans, secretary of the British Iron Trade Association and with a wide knowledge of foreign industry:[28]

The present conditions do not allow any one country . . . an overmastering advantage over others . . . on striking a balance of the whole. Germany has in one district dear ore and cheap fuel, and in another dear fuel and cheap ore. The United States have cheap ore at the mines, but a transport of a thousand miles, more or less, and two breakages of bulk neutralises (*sic*) much of the gain from this source . . . Great Britain is in most districts favourably situated for sea transport, but both her ores and her fuel are getting dearer.[29]

Most witnesses also supported Hewins's line on technical education, five out of eight, including Hickman in spite of his long association with improvements in Wolverhampton,[30] considering its importance insufficient to account for prevailing differences.[31] On railway rates, it is true, the witnesses endorsed the dissent that had been expressed by Commission members, but their opinion was divided over whether wage differences in Germany, Britain, and the US were offset by differences in productivity. It is clear, however, that overall the witnesses thought that conditions in the three countries were approaching a rough parity. Strain considered that 'we can produce [pig iron and steel] quite as cheaply as the German or American'. Allen concurred. Jeans estimated that there was scarcely 2 per cent difference in pig-iron costs between Pittsburgh, Cleveland, and Westphalia, though he admitted that some less efficient districts had higher costs.[32]

The Commission's findings were thus in accord with recent work which argues that there was an approximate equalization of resource costs and pig-iron-production costs in the three main producing countries in this period.[33] With

---

[28] See BITA, *Report of the Delegation . . . on the Iron and Steel Industries of Belgium and Germany* (1896); BITA, *American Industrial Conditions and Competition* (1902).

[29] *Iron and Steel Report*, para. 998. Also paras. 554–7, 597, 617, 659. Those mentioning coal specifically were unanimous that America held the advantage, though they concentrated on the exceptional Connelsville mines. Germany and Belgium were felt to have no such advantage. Jeans agreed more or less completely. See paras. 495, 780, 984–5.

[30] W. O. Henderson, 'Origins of Technical Education in Wolverhampton', Wolverhampton and Staffordshire Technical College, *Studies in Local History* 1 (Apr. 1948), 4.

[31] *Iron and Steel Report*, paras. 601–2, 629, 773, 902. Allen, Davie, and Davies valued technical education most highly (paras. 509, 694, 737).

[32] Ibid., paras. 519, 523–9, 617, 671–4, 769, 780, 819, 916, 1055–77 on transport costs; 514, 581, 625, 685, 1046, 1049 on wage rates; 611, 616, 640–1, 966 on production costs. Much of the evidence on transport costs concerned rates per mile, ambiguous in view of the fact that higher rates could still be compatible with lower overall transport costs due to smaller distances.

[33] P. Temin, 'The Relative Decline of the British Steel Industry, 1880–1914', in H. Rosovsky (ed.), *Industrialization in Two Systems* (New York, 1966), 141, 146; also D. Burn, *Economic History of Steelmaking*, ch. 9.

steel production, though Jeans described US labour costs as 'phenomenally low', there was rough consensus that production costs in Britain and America were little different when British industry was working at full capacity, but that undercapacity forced British costs up. The Commission would have thus been unlikely to support McCloskey's conclusion that the *'average* superiority' of the American steel industry in the years before the Great War was only about 2 to 3 per cent.[34] Indeed, McCloskey's findings are still subject to controversy,[35] and we should not be surprised that the Commission felt it had some difference to explain away. Hewins's own explanation, that the export policy of foreign trusts prevented full-capacity working in Britain and so increased costs, was thus enhanced. The witnesses having largely vindicated his position on 'reduction' in the eyes of the members, he could now extend his intellectual dominance over the Commission.

IV

Hewins's handling of the complex issue of dumping, another area central to the Commission's inquiry, further consolidated his position with the members. Dumping had received much exposure in the press campaign. Orthodox Free Traders argued that any cheapening of imports acted to Britain's advantage, though the fact that they were not above taunting Tariff Reformers with the discovery that Canadian pig iron was being exported to Britain with the aid of production bounties betrayed a certain ambivalence in their position.[36] Whilst Chiozza Money regarded the Canadian policy as a direct advantage for higher branches of British industry, Sir Michael Hicks Beach indicated tentatively that he was prepared to consider counter-subsidy legislation along the lines of the Sugar Convention Act.[37] Though few other Free Traders went even this far, many realized the awkwardness of their position. Thus, at Paisley, Asquith felt it necessary to reassure his industrial audience that the present wave of dumping 'cannot possibly last long'.[38]

[34] D. N. McCloskey, *Economic Maturity and Entrepreneurial Decline* (Cambridge, Mass., 1973), 124.

[35] P. Berck, 'Hard Driving and Efficiency: Iron Production in 1890', *Journal of Economic History*, 38 (1978), 879–90; R. C. Allen, 'International Competition in Iron and Steel, 1850–1950', *Journal of Economic History*, 39 (1979), 911–37; and 'Entrepreneurship and Technical Progress in the Northeast Coast Pig Iron Industry, 1850–1913', *Research in Economic History*, 6 (1981), 35–71; S. B. Webb, 'Tariffs, Cartels, Technology and Growth in the German Steel Industry, 1879–1914', *Journal of Economic History*, 40 (1980), 309–39. But see also the recent and far-reaching criticism of Burn, McCloskey, Allen, and Webb in U. Wengenroth, *Enterprise and Technology* (Cambridge, 1994), esp. ch. 6.

[36] It was naturally a source of delight to Free Traders that, of all countries, Canada should be guilty of this perfidy.

[37] L.G.C.M., [Leo G. Chiozza Money], 'Preferential Tariffs and British Trade: II', *Free Trader*, 7 Aug. 1903, 15; Hicks Beach at Bristol, *The Times*, 14 Nov. 1903, 12. See also *Free Trader*, 13 July 1903, 2, 7 Aug. 1903, 13; W. S. B. McLaren to Ed., *The Times*, 24 Nov. 1903, 10.

[38] Asquith at Paisley, 31 Oct. 1903; in H. H. Asquith, *Trade and the Empire* (1903), 62.

Many examples were used to show how Britain gained by foreign dumping. Sir Charles McLaren, chairman of the Palmer Shipbuilding and Iron Co., told of imports of German forgings and castings at 30 per cent below English quoted prices which had materially helped his firm's exports. James Cox, secretary of the Iron and Steel Workers' Union, considered that the competitive edge which dumped steel gave British exporters in foreign markets safeguarded employment.[39] Sir Christopher Furness told his Hartlepool constituents that he regretted the need to use imported billets, but there was an over-riding necessity to 'supply the shipbuilder at such a low price'. In any case, the import of 10,000 tons of German steel billets at 75s. per ton by a firm with which Furness was associated had stimulated the Cleveland industry 'to new efforts', and now some North-Eastern producers were quoting 60s. per ton.[40]

Free Traders went on to stress the effects of the double-pricing policy of German combines on German home industry. When Chamberlain chose the wire-drawing industry of Manchester and Warrington as a prime example of an industry in decay, the Free Trade retort was that those 'pure' German concerns which did not roll their own wire but merely purchased it for further processing were so 'threatened with extinction' by a syndicate which charged 250s. per ton at home and 140s. abroad that they were discussing the formation of their own syndicate as a countervailing force.[41] Sir John Jenkins, whose experience in the tinplate trade went back to the 1850s, recalled how South Wales had been assisted by German dumping of steel bars when searching for new markets in Latin American and Australia after the McKinley tariff. He even maintained that tinplate firms with no facilities for producing their own bars depended on dumping for their existence. The other side of the coin was that the German tinplate trade was relatively undeveloped, supplying only 40 per cent of home consumption, whilst the US's 320 mills could do little more than supply domestic needs. In other steel-using trades, such as US shipbuilding and Hamburg fine-plate rolling, the same situation was diagnosed.[42]

[39] *Free Trader*, 2 Oct. 1903, 80; *Ironworkers' Journal*, Dec. 1903, 4.

[40] Furness's speech was widely reported in the Northern press and cited indirectly in *Free Trader*, 1 Jan. 1903, 3. His opinions were put in a somewhat different light in 1908, when he was quoted as urging German Steel producers to 'Dump as long as you can!' See Cobden Club, *Report of the Proceedings of the International Free Trade Congress* (1908), 105.

[41] Chamberlain at Liverpool, 28 Oct. 1903, in his *Imperial Union and Tariff Reform* (1903), 58; *Free Trader*, 20 Nov. 1903, 134, 23 Oct. 1903, 98, 102. The Free Traders seemed oblivious of their own evidence, appearing elsewhere, that even in such a position the German wire drawers were still apparently able to undercut home producers in the British market. See *Free Trader*, 14 Aug. 1903, 20, 15 Jan. 1904, 17.

[42] *Westminster Gazette*, 20 Nov. 1903, 2; *Free Trader*, 11 Dec. 1903, 157, 15 Jan. 1904, 19, 11 Dec. 1903, 157; *The Nation* [New York], cited in *Free Trader*, 6 May 1904, 138; *Kölnische Zeitung*, cited in *Free Trader*, 22 Jan. 1904, 25. See also *Free Trader*, 1 Jan. 1904, 2–3, 22 Oct. 1903, 102, for further examples.

In widening the impact of tariff, monopoly, and dual-pricing beyond the effect on user industries, the Free Trade case became a sermon on economic morality. Individual concerns abroad which disclosed losses in their annual reports, or even did less well than expected from previous experience, were held up as examples of a general law. Closures and wage reductions reported by the US trade journals *Iron Age* and New York *Journal of Commerce* were cited in the British press with the gleeful assurance of a Job's comforter. There was even an inference that the 'clubbing of men away from work by policemen' at a Pennsylvania steelworks was caused by US fiscal policy.[43]

For all this, Free Traders were less than totally consistent when they perceived that dumping might be coming to an end. From their own argument that dumping could not be profitable they were bound to conclude that it could not carry on indefinitely, and that 'sooner or later it would disappear'. By February and March 1904 they discerned signs of strain in the protectionist yoke, but they showed little sadness at the passing of a practice so beneficial to the British iron and steel industry. Indeed, one notes a sense of relief when Free Traders held an advance in Pittsburgh pig and bar prices to signify that Tariff Reformers' fears were 'unfounded'. The German Steel Works Association was formed in March, according to Free Traders for the purpose of preventing 'reckless cutting of quotations abroad'. '[D]umping was to cease', this being 'a moral on the unwisdom of premature predictions'. Indeed, in one admittedly uncharacteristic statement, the *Free Trader* came close to giving a reason for its apparent satisfaction at the ending of dumping. 'Dumping *might be* so worked as to be an injury to the importing country, but it is unavoidably an injury to the country which practices it'. A grudging admission, but clearly there was an element of 'doublethink' in the propagandist Free Trade attitude towards dumping.[44]

V

Whilst recognizing the wider definition of dumping which prevails today of differential pricing between home and export markets, the Commission chose to put its main emphasis on the tighter definition of dumping below cost of production.[45] The reason for doing this was probably political—Free Traders

---

[43] *Free Trader*, 4 Sept. 1903, 43, 8 Jan. 1904, 16, 11 Dec. 1903, 157, 18 Dec. 1903, 164, 8 Jan. 1904, 12, 29 Jan. 1904, 36, 11 Mar. 1904, 87.

[44] *Free Trader*, 18 Mar. 1904, 90, 4 Mar. 1904, 78, 15 Jan. 1904, 17, 22 Jan. 1904, 25, 5 Feb. 1904, 42, 18 Mar. 1904, 90, 8 Apr. 1904, 106, 11 Dec. 1903, 153 (my emphasis). See also S. J. Chapman, 'The Report of the Tariff Commission on the Iron and Steel Trades', *Economic Journal*, 14 (1904), esp. 620–1.

[45] W. M. Corden, *Trade Policy and Economic Welfare* (Oxford, 1974), 235. Differential pricing seems to have became the accepted definition in the 1920s and early 1930s. See G. von Haberler, *Theory of International Trade* (Eng. edn. 1936), 296. The Commission seems to have been concerned with average cost of production only. There is no evidence that it considered dumping below marginal cost.

could argue that to sell at different margins *above* cost in different markets was perfectly legitimate practice. But it made it extremely difficult to find empirical evidence. Even the most likely example furnished by a British firm, and given in Memorandum 5, was not conclusive. Since the Commission had no information on the internal production costs of the integrated German firm accused of the practice, it had to use the German domestic market price of pig and estimate the prime cost of conversion to steel. As the Commission's steel experts knew, this made no allowance for the saving in transaction costs achieved through vertical integration. Most Commissioners appreciated that to seek further information from British firms would be fruitless. Furthermore, Allen thought dumping had become so 'perpetual and continuous' that respondents would by now be unable to distinguish it from more legitimate practice.[46]

During its labours the Commission collected many examples of alleged dumping, a proportion of them no doubt valid, but few, if any, beyond question. But the Commission's main contribution to the controversy over dumping was in fact more abstract—the *Iron and Steel Report*'s demonstration that '[long-term] dumping was profitable to the producer'.[47] It is significant that Hewins had made out a similar case in *The Times* as early as August 1903,[48] and, though the *Iron and Steel Report* marshalled much circumstantial evidence in support, the argument was still essentially analytical and deductive rather than empirical.

If we put together the statements made in Memorandum 5 and the *Iron and Steel Report*, we find the following assertions: first, that long-term dumping was profitable; secondly, that it was profitable only if the home market was protected; and thirdly, that it did not necessarily raise the dumper's home-market price above what it would have been in its absence, since '[t]he smaller output limited to supplying the demands of the home market might and generally does mean a lesser economy of production; and the selling price might again be the same as before'.[49] This clearly had two implications. First, the Free Traders' assertion that German dumpers of semi-finished steel were destroying the higher branches of their own industry and aiding those in Britain did not necessarily follow. Secondly, without being the victim of dumping, British intermediate producers might well be able to increase output and reduce cost. This argument for 'continuous running' or full-capacity working was to become of central importance to the fiscal beliefs of most Commission members, and will be considered below.[50]

There is strong evidence that Hewins did not require the profit-maximizing condition of orthodox economics—the Historical Economist and the pre-1914

---

[46] TC Memorandum 5, 5; TCM(VT), 16 Mar. 1904, 10–12, 2/1/6, TCP.

[47] W. A. S. Hewins, *The Apologia of an Imperialist* (1929), i. 91.

[48] 'The Fiscal Policy of the Empire: IX', *The Times*, 3 Aug. 1903, 12.

[49] TC Memo. 5, 6; *Iron and Steel Report*, paras. 62–75.

[50] See below, 156–62.

businessman would probably have considered that condition absurd.[51] In spite of this, his three assertions can be shown to be compatible with the conventional theory prevailing amongst academics at the time of the fiscal controversy, though a full appreciation of this probably required the fuller development of the theory of monopolistic competition in the inter-war period. Marginalist theory easily supports the first assertion, that long-term dumping is profitable as long as the firm operates under monopoly or monopolistic competition and can separate two markets. If elasticity of demand (at the export-market price) in the foreign country is higher than it is (at the home-market price) in the home country, profits can even be maximized. For profits to be maximized, however, export price will be greater than (or in the limiting case equal to)[52] marginal cost of production. Thus, dumping in the modern sense of price differentiation, or in the tighter sense of selling abroad below average cost but above marginal cost, may maximize profits. Dumping below average cost is only able to maximize profits if the average cost curve is falling, but given the tendency of capital-intensive industries to work at under-capacity this is a far from unrealistic condition.[53]

The second assertion, that protection is a necessary precondition for long-term dumping, is hardly less acceptable to modern theory. The only fundamental condition is that elasticity of demand abroad is higher than at home, and transport costs might also operate to separate markets; but, as Corden observes, today 'tariffs are probably more important causes of market separation'. Of course, transport costs were higher in 1900 than they are today, but then, as Corden points out, so too were tariffs.[54]

The third assertion, that dumping might reduce home price below that obtaining in the absence of dumping, or, as Hewins had it, at least leave it unchanged, is theoretically valid given economies of scale, or more strictly falling marginal cost, especially if the argument is confined to the long run.[55] The dumper's condition of equilibrium is that his marginal revenue is equal in both markets. Cessation of dumping would reduce total equilibrium output, so that the marginal cost pertaining to that output would rise, and would now lie above marginal revenue. Thus domestic (which now equals total) output must be reduced and price raised, to restore equilibrium. This is seen in the standard analysis reproduced in Fig. 1. In the dumping situation aggregate marginal revenue is MRaMRa and discriminatory home market price is OPh. Without

---

[51] *Iron and Steel Report*, para. 65; also the example of F.312 in TC Memorandum 5, 6.
[52] Where foreign demand is infinitely elastic.
[53] W. M. Corden, *Trade Policy*, 239; G. von Haberler, *Theory of International Trade*, 312.
[54] W. M. Corden, *Trade Policy*, 238. Little work has been done on the historical importance of transport costs. McCloskey (*Economic Maturity*, 29–34) finds that, between the British producing regions, transport costs allowed a significant degree of local monopoly only in the rail trade.
[55] Falling marginal cost is unlikely in the short run. But it is warrantable to switch our attention to the long run at this point, given Hewins's evident concern with long-run dynamics and his tendency to see dumping as a well-thought-out weapon of strategic policy.

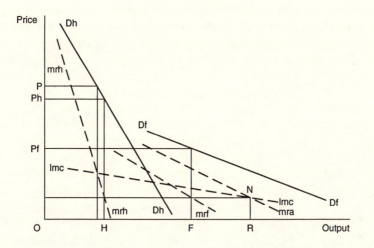

Fig. 1 Monopolistic price discrimination in home and foreign markets

dumping, aggregate marginal revenue reduces to MRhMRh, and the single home-market price appropriate to this is OP, a price higher than OPh.[56]

Of course, this analysis demonstrates only that dumping can result in home market price lying below the post-tariff price, the tariff being necessary to dumping in the first place. It does not in itself show that home-market price, even if lowered by dumping abroad, will necessarily be lower than it would be under a Free Trade regime—indeed, it seems likely that it will not be. Yet several Commissioners were discomfited by Hewins's third assertion, and it may be because they thought it would be interpreted by the public and the opposition as a sign that the industry saw tariff protection as a prelude to a systematic programme of dumping. Hickman did not 'wish to emulate the example . . . [of] maintaining a high price in the home market in order to be able to dump', and such statements were ubiquitous in the evidence laid before the Commission.[57] The only witness for whom such a possibility had attraction was Allen:

If we could prevent the Germans from dumping their surplus output into this country it would reduce their production, and would soon close many of their works. We should

---

[56] For a dynamic exposition of the attainment of equilibrium, see Haberler, *Theory of International Trade*, 307–9. We have examined this assertion only in relation to the modern definition of discrimination between home and export prices. Use of Hewins's definition of dumping below average cost does not change the analysis except to make it less likely that the assertion will hold in the short run. Authorities are agreed, however, that concern over the relationship between export price and average cost is not analytically significant. See *Theory of International Trade*, 312 and W. M. Corden, *Trade Policy*, 239.

[57] *Iron and Steel Report*, para. 544 (Witness No. 2); see also evidence of W. H. Davies (Witness No. 8) and Earnest Gearing (Witness No. 10), paras. 727, 781.

then be able to treat them as we are now being treated, because, by keeping our works fully employed, we should produce at a minimum price, as against their maximum.[58]

Most Commissioners, however, clearly did not wish to be associated, at least publicly, with a practice which discriminated against home consumers and in favour of foreigners. After appearing in Memorandum 5, this part of the analysis was quietly omitted from the *Iron and Steel Report*.

If the Commission's treatment of the profitability of long-term dumping was reasonable or, in Burn's words, 'sound and important',[59] it still rested heavily on a largely abstract and deductive proof. To a Commission which believed in the virtue of studying 'real events' and the 'actual state' of the business community,[60] it was important that the factual basis of the argument was confirmed.

As Sir Robert Herbert appreciated, there was need for empirical support from witnesses, and a substantial part of each cross-examination concerned dumping. The evidence gave mixed support to the Commission's belief that dumping was continuous rather than being, as Free Traders maintained, a cyclical phenomenon depending on the state of the home market of the dumper. One witness, Albert Barton, had even arranged for a quantity of US pig to be dumped in the European market in 1896 and 1897. Though the policy had been prompted by depression in the US,[61] the effect was to 'induce other American manufacturers to adopt dumping as a steady policy'.[62] Allen was also of this opinion, whilst W. H. Davies thought that Germany's dumping of the previous 'several years' would soon become permanent because of her rapidly increasing productive capacity.[63]

Others were less certain. Gilbertson, who purchased steel plates for tinplating, had experienced dumping only since 1900, and was uncertain of its permanence. Jeans's cautious statement was even more doubtful that the practice would endure, though it is significant that he confined his remarks to the US and neglected Germany. US steel exports had begun to fall in autumn 1903 and, according to the Pittsburgh correspondent of the *Iron and Coal Trades Review*, the US Steel Corporation was dissatisfied with the attempts of its predecessors to dump semi-manufactures in Britain. But even Jeans admitted that the formation of US Steel did not necessarily presage the end of US dumping: he merely remarked that in future it 'must be justified to shareholders'.[64]

---

[58] *Iron and Steel Report* (Witness No. 4), para. 702.

[59] D. Burn, *Economic History of Steelmaking*, 96.

[60] W. A. S. Hewins, *Apologia*, i. 15, 86.

[61] It is a common interpretation that business fluctuations lay behind the differing appeal, over time, that export markets held for US manufacturers. See W. H. Becker, 'American Manufacturers and Foreign Markets 1870–1900', *Business History Review*, 47 (1973), 466–81.

[62] *Iron and Steel Report*, paras. 606–7 (Witness No. 5).

[63] Ibid. para. 654 (Witness No. 8).

[64] Ibid. para. 1116 (Witness No. 16).

In retrospect, Jeans' careful words were an accurate prediction. There was to be no recurrence of dumping on the 1900–3 scale before 1914. But even Jeans knew that dumping had been a 'serious handicap', and might 'easily break the British market and entirely disorganise British conditions'.[65] Though the evidence taken by the enquiry was as inconclusive as any on this subject is likely to be, it reflected a concern widespread amongst contemporary ironmasters that modern observers, acquainted with inter-war conditions and the spread of anti-dumping legislation since 1918, can understand more easily than could the pre-1914 Free Trader.[66]

Replies to the questionnaires were as divided as the witnesses on whether long-term dumping was being practised. Though some firms independently made close approximations to Hewins's analysis,[67] only two stated explicitly and unambiguously that dumping was 'carefully planned, and lasting, and not merely temporary', and they were both wire drawers.[68]

Yet even Free Trade economist Sidney Chapman, in admitting in a review of the *Iron and Steel Report* that 'the policy in its recent form has not been sufficiently well tested to enable an unhesitating judgement' of its permanence,[69] clearly conceded the theoretical point. Whilst this had the chill air of an academic economist discussing the destruction of his country's industrial base as he would a laboratory experiment, it is probably true that US and German dumping was concentrated in the period 1900–1904, and that it then declined until late 1907.[70]

This was certainly not true in all sectors of the industry, however. Burn has shown that the German steel-rail makers operated a two-price policy continuously throughout the period 1881–1913, save for the boom of 1898–1900, though surprisingly the price difference decreased after 1896, more because German home prices fell than because export prices rose.[71] Burn's task, without the self-imposed concentration on dumping below cost, was easier than the Commission's, but it is nevertheless curious that Hewins, as a historicist, made no attempt at a historical demonstration of price discrimination. Partly, this may

---

[65] Ibid. paras. 1128, 1098.

[66] Early examples of anti-dumping provisions appeared in the Canadian tariff of 1904 and the Australian tariff of 1906. See A. Shortt, 'The Anti-dumping Feature of the Canadian Tariff, *Quarterly Journal of Economics*, 20 (1906), 250–8; J. Viner, *Dumping: A Problem in International Trade* (New York, 1966 edn.), ch. 1.

[67] Firms Nos. 275, 844, 862, 886, 984, 1408, 1508, 1512.

[68] Firms Nos. 768 and 808 (paras. 257, 260).

[69] S. J. Chapman, 'Report of the Tariff Commission on the Iron and Steel Trades', 621.

[70] J. C. Carr and W. Taplin, *British Steel Industry*, 232. A similar time period has been discerned in electrical engineering. See I. C. R. Byatt, *The British Electrical Industry 1875–1914* (Oxford, 1979), 4 n. 5.

[71] Burn finds similarly for bars, girders, etc. In some lines, e.g. plates, he cannot prove discrimination before 1900. He adds that price discrimination 'establishes a strong presumption' that dumping below total cost occurred; *Economic History of Steelmaking*, 104–12. For the depression of the 1870s, see U. Wengenroth, *Enterprise and Technology*, 129–34, which has the singular advantage of being based on German archives.

have been because dumping was thought to be a relatively new phenomenon. In the case of rails, German dumping may have gone unnoticed in Britain as long as German efficiency was lower than British—until 1895 or 1900 according to Burn. Indeed, it might be that it was not long-term dumping that was new in 1904, but an achievement of parity in productivity, so that now Britain was being dumped on by her equal, and not her inferior. Partly, also, Hewins had to reckon with a Free Trade stance which considered price discrimination in itself as totally legitimate.[72] This issue cannot be pursued here, but it is a small irony that the Commission, the apostle in Britain of the inductive method, should base its case so heavily on arguments with greater deductive strength than evidential backing, and that the empirical-historical proof of that case should be provided thirty years later by a scholar from the Cambridge of Marshall and Pigou.

VI

The inquiry into iron and steel was also important in producing the most developed argument in favour of 'continuous running' that appeared in the fiscal controversy. The foundation of the argument lay in the empirical demonstration of excess capacity in the British industry. Witnesses were consistent in estimating over-capacity at between 18 and 25 per cent.[73] At the same time, total iron and steel imports stood at about 8 to 9 per cent of home production.[74] Largely but not entirely because of its analysis of dumping, the Tariff Commission held that a tariff was necessary 'to remove the present causes of irregular working and insecurity, or, at any rate, greatly diminish their force'.[75] The figures suggest that even the complete displacement of imports by a prohibitive tariff, never contemplated by the Tariff Reformers, would, in a *ceteris paribus* situation,[76] have reduced under-capacity working only by about half. In some branches, however, the effect would have been greater—in bars, blooms, and billets, and in the Wolverhampton tube trade, the imports-to-home-production ratio appears to have been higher than average, yielding a potential for a larger reduction in excess capacity.[77]

Free Traders might have conceded that a reduction in under-capacity working was a likely effect of a tariff in the short run, but would have argued that the increase in domestic output was dependent upon the tariff raising prices. Thus, the Commission sought to demonstrate that improvements in producers' welfare

---

[72] For the survival of this stance into the post-1918 world, see below, Ch. 9.

[73] *Iron and Steel Report*, paras. 490, 594, 615, 652, 746.

[74] See Appendix II.

[75] *Iron and Steel Report*, para. 79.

[76] i.e. assuming that a tariff would not reduce UK consumption. This aids the Tariff Reform case and for present purposes can be regarded as a *reductio ad absurdum*.

[77] *Iron and Steel Report*, paras. 809, 826; P. L. Payne, 'Iron and Steel Manufactures', in D. H. Aldcroft (ed.), *The Development of British Industry and Foreign Competition 1875–1914* (1968), 87–8.

would not be offset by a decline in that of the rest of the community. The crux of the argument was that if the home market was secured from dumping, 'greater continuity of working, and, therefore, reduced costs would result. The domestic competition of manufacturers would then bring prices down, probably below their present level'.[78] If we analyse this proposition in terms of marginalist theory, as we did with the Commission's treatment of dumping, the result is less impressive.

The treatment presented in the *Iron and Steel Report* is slightly ambiguous in terms of the theoretical model. Did the 'domestic competition' that was expected to follow the imposition of a tariff occur in the short run, between existing manufacturers, or in the long run, allowing for changes in plant size and new entrants? The Commission's emphasis on under-capacity and the benefits of 'continuous running' struck an almost emotional chord with members, witnesses, and respondents alike, in a lament at existing plant lying idle. Several examples exist in the *Report* to show the effect of fluctuating output in a given plant, and much trouble was taken in difficult circumstances to collect them.[79] Clearly, therefore, we must not ignore the short run. But, less prominently perhaps, the Commission also referred to greater security and the laying-down of new plant, the implication being that a tariff might enable the industry to capture latent economies of scale.[80] The Commission would probably not have regarded this distinction as important, but it does in fact have considerable practical significance in a historical evaluation of the protectionist campaign.

Whether a profit-maximizing firm, if under monopolistic competition at home and experiencing import competition, will charge a lower price when faced with an increase in demand due to a tariff, will depend on the interaction between, firstly, the effect of the tariff on the price-elasticity of demand and, secondly, the shape of the marginal cost curve. Figures 2 and 3 isolate these conditions in turn.

Figure 2 shows that, with constant marginal costs, the post-tariff price will be the same as the pre-tariff price if the elasticity of the old and new average-revenue curves are the same at the original, pre-tariff price, that is, if AR and ARt are 'iso-elastic'.[81] Pre-tariff price NE and post-tariff price NtG both equal OP. But if ARt is less elastic (at price NtG = NE) than AR, as illustrated by ARt_1 and mrt_1, then post-tariff price $(Nt_1 \, F)$ will be higher than pre-tariff price (NE). And if ARt is more elastic (at price NtG = NE) than AR, as with ARt_2 and mrt_2, then post-tariff price $(Nt_2 \, H)$ will be lower than pre-tariff price (NE).

[78] *Iron and Steel Report*, para. 80.
[79] Ibid. paras. 55–7, where one firm put estimated savings at 6*s*. per ton on steel (compared with 75% capacity), and another firm gave much higher figures on billets, bars, and ship plates (compared with 50% capacity). In discussion, Commissioners Allen and Hickman made more conservative estimates of 'at least 2*s*. 6*d*. a ton'; TCM(VT), 16 Mar. 1904, 14, 2/1/6, TCP.
[80] *Iron and Steel Report*, para. 79.
[81] i.e. if they meet on the *y*-axis. See J. Robinson, *The Economics of Imperfect Competition* (1933), 43, 61.

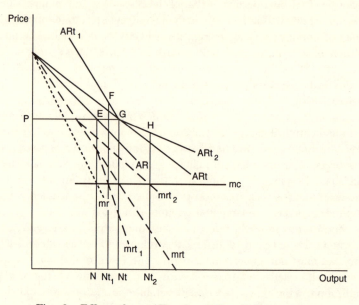

Fig. 2   Effect of a tariff under different demand shifts

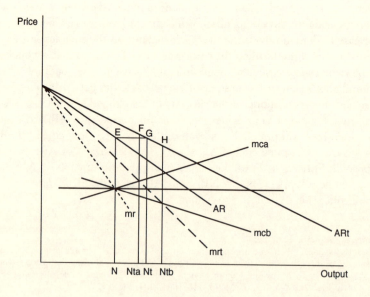

Fig. 3   Effect of a tariff under different cost conditions

In Figure 3 instances are given of constant, rising, and falling marginal costs, but now in all three cases the upward demand shift is kept 'iso-elastic'. If marginal cost is constant (mc), post-tariff price (NtG) will equal pre-tariff price (NE). If marginal cost is rising (mca), post-tariff price (NtaF) will lie above pre-tariff price (NE). But if marginal cost is falling (mcb), then post-tariff price (NtbH) will lie below pre-tariff price (NE).

In reality, both variables would tend to move in attainment of a new equilibrium. If marginal costs are rising, price will still fall if post-tariff demand is more elastic than pre-tariff demand to an extent more than sufficient to compensate for the rise in marginal cost. Equally, if post-tariff demand is less elastic than pre-tariff demand, price will still fall if the marginal cost reduction is sufficient to outweigh its influence.[82]

It should be stressed, however, that satisfaction of the conditions necessary to produce a reduction in price in the short run is unlikely—little more, perhaps, than a theoretical curiosity. Though iron and steel typically operates below capacity, and average costs may therefore fall as capacity is approached, it is less likely that *marginal* costs, dependent as they are on variable elements of cost, will continue to fall over a sufficient range of output. Equally, price-elasticity of demand is unlikely to increase. Demand for home-produced goods rises because of the now-higher price of imports. This will tend to reduce rather than increase elasticity of demand for the home product.[83]

This pessimistic verdict should perhaps prompt the question of whether it is legitimate to subject the ideas of a Historical Economist and his pragmatic business associates to the ideological constructs of an orthodoxy from which they would have dissented. It is perhaps relevant to observe that the framework we have used, that of monopolistic or imperfect competition, was developed with the purpose of bringing the assumptions of economics 'nearer . . . to the complicated conditions of the real world'.[84] This fits closely with Hewins' view that the theories of orthodox economics were 'probably approximately true under certain defined conditions, but they did not explain the complicated activities of the modern industrial world'.[85] But this does not really exhaust the issue. Perhaps

[82] Ibid. 61.

[83] Ibid. 71, point (4). Mrs Robinson's analysis, which I have adapted for this purpose, concerns itself only with an increase in demand, not a tariff-induced increase.

[84] J. Robinson, *Imperfect Competition*, 2; also E. Chamberlin, *The Theory of Monopolistic Competition* (Cambridge, Mass., 1933). Wengenroth's stress on different steel qualities suggests scope for product differentiation: *Enterprise and Technology, passim*.

[85] W. A. S. Hewins, *Apologia*, i. 18. A handful of other contributors to the fiscal debate raised questions about the implications of imperfections in competition and factor pricing. See e.g. L. L. Price, 'Economic Theory and Fiscal Policy', *Economic Journal*, 14 (1904), 382–6; J. A. Hobson, *International Trade* (1904), 113, 121–45. As late as 1974, however, Corden could report that the literature relating monopolistic competition to international trade theory was 'relatively sparse'; *Trade Policy*, 201n.

more important is that, in profit-maximization, we have a heavier burden of proof than Hewins and the Commission would have required. Above we have seen the Commission using arguments which suggest that it considered some kind of full-cost pricing as more realistic and characteristic of prevailing practice. This would allow the above conditions to be relaxed. As long as marginal costs, whether rising or not, are below average costs, such a pricing policy would allow prices to be reduced. Obviously, if pricing is dependent on cost, rather than on the interaction between cost and demand, anything which reduces average cost will allow a reduction in price.[86]

If we return once more to the orthodox analysis, the long run is a much wider issue. The extent to which the demand curve would rise (and, as is likely, become less elastic) would depend on the extent to which the tariff drives foreign firms out of the domestic market, which in turn would depend in part on the closeness of substitutability of the domestic and foreign products. If domestic firms were in equilibrium before the tariff, its imposition would cause abnormal profits and encourage new entrants.[87] Each firm's demand curve would then move back towards AR. But whether original price is returned to depends on whether original demand elasticity is reproduced and the original cost curve remains unchanged as the firm retraces its steps.[88] Recent theoretical work in this area suggests a range of possible outcomes.[89]

The lessons that can be learned from such theoretical analysis are thus limited. But this examination does suggest that any lowering of price consequent upon a tariff would have been due to firms operating upon lower cost curves, rather than adjusting their position optimally along given cost curves, and to the nature of the new entrants. This suggests the need for improved technology, organization, and company structure. If these were the proximate changes necessary, it seems unlikely that the tariff would have been sufficient.

Of course, a tariff might promote combination and vertical integration; in the US and Germany it probably did. It also might promote 'X-efficiency', through the effect of increased optimism on managerial effort and strategic thinking within firms.[90] But it also might postpone the need for change, and in the British steel industry there is considerable evidence to suggest complacency and reluctance to change, especially if change involved loss of family control. The

[86] Virtually no research has been done on how the pre-war steel firm priced its products. In addition, there is the thorny question of whether manufacturers who practise 'cost-plus' are really acting to maximize profits without realizing it. Certainly, British, German, and US firms altered price according to market fluctuations. These fluctuations affected cost, but they also reflected demand.

[87] Of course, many ironmasters in 1904 would have claimed they were not making normal profits.

[88] Interestingly, long-term equilibrium would have still involved producing at a point above the minimum on the short-run average-cost curve.

[89] For an excellent survey, see N. Vousden, *The Economics of Trade Protection* (Cambridge, 1990), ch. 7, esp. 161-7.

[90] See W. M. Corden, *Trade Policy*, 224-31.

pre-war steel industry's problem was that, by comparison with international best practice, it was showing signs of backwardness in technology, structure, and organization. Such a situation, analytically distinct from the infant-industry case, seldom attracts the attention of the theoreticians, and it may therefore be the case that formal analysis under-estimates the potential of a tariff. It could be argued that the industry was not seriously backward before 1914, and that increased market security might have initiated a dynamic managerial response. If so, it is conceivable that long-term domestic price might have fallen, and even if the response was not large enough to effect price reduction, the industry's long-term prospects might have been improved. But, in historical terms, the absence of protection was not the sole cause of the British industry's deficiencies, and it is unlikely that its introduction would have been sufficient on its own to remedy them. In the inter-war period government policy-makers were concerned to promote concentration, vertical integration, and 'rationalization'; the prospect of greater competition from new entrants would probably have appalled them. At the same time, the steelmakers were reluctant.[91] In the easier conditions before the First World War, it seems quite possible that steel producers would have accepted the windfall gains from protection, but would then have been reluctant to embark upon the technological or organizational changes necessary to bring the industry's structure into line with that in the USA and Germany. Owners would have been even more reluctant to lose family control through merger and vertical integration than they were after 1921, because the industry's problems were still in a relatively early stage. To expect them to have embarked upon an extensive programme of modernization without state intervention is unrealistic, and to imagine that state intervention was a possibility is unhistorical.

It is worth repeating that Hewins was careful to argue that price reductions were the probable, rather than inevitable, result of the effects of a tariff on costs.[92] Though to the impartial observer even this was perhaps overstating his case, it was a modest claim for a zealot. But the Commissioners were not inclined to be reined back. They were firmly converted to the benefits of continuous running, most seeing the concept as the cardinal discovery of the iron and steel enquiry. When, in a proof version of the *Report*, it was stated that a tariff would allow continuous running, more up-to-date technology, greater security, investment, and employment, and would not 'materially or permanently raise prices', sober members like Mosely joined stronger spirits like Birchenough in considering this too weak. Surely, the 'one point that the whole of this evidence has strongly brought out' was the likelihood of an actual reduction in price. Only when Allen sought to tie the benefits of continuous running to the promise of a 10 per cent

[91] S. Tolliday, 'Tariffs and Steel, 1916–1934: the Politics of Industrial Decline', in J. Turner, *Businessmen and Politics* (1984), 50–75. See also below, Ch. 9, and, more generally, S. Tolliday, *Business, Banking, and Politics* (Cambridge, Mass., 1987).

[92] *Iron and Steel Report*, para. 80.

increase in wages did members dissent. Harrison, voicing the widespread fear that this would destroy the Commission's credibility as a neutral, scientific body, urged that 'anything in the Report that might be taken by our Opponents as merely electioneering' should be avoided. But on the effects of continuous running on prices no-one disagreed, and this was to lead to the stronger statement incorporated in the final version of the *Report*.[93]

VII

Though Hewins had said much about the complex business of deriving a scientific tariff through empirical study, the last critical step had not been taken when the Commission met to discuss the draft report on 28 June 1904. Chamberlain, in the chair, wanted the report to contain precise recommendations:

if this Report is to attract the attention we desire, and if its publication by itself is to give us great advantages in the preparation of subsequent Reports by allowing us to see what criticisms are forthcoming, it should, I think, end with a definite conclusion. In other words we should suggest a Tariff for the Iron and Steel Trades.[94]

Commission members were strongly opposed. Sir Westby Perceval preferred 'a pure presentation of the facts . . . without . . . any suggestions as to the remedy'. No doubt the majority of the Commission believed that a tariff remedy was 'the logical outcome of the enquiry', but political expediency dictated caution, and the Commission would be accused of 'hav[ing] axes to grind' if a tariff was recommended. R. H. Reade agreed, whilst Caillard felt the drafting of a tariff would take too long when most of the Commission seemed to want early publication. The report had to be able to withstand criticism with 'the utmost ease', since it was 'to be a model for all Reports that are to follow it, and . . . is to be unique in its construction, far better than anything any Royal Commission has ever drawn up'.[95]

Others feared the danger of publishing a tariff schedule for iron and steel without due consideration of related trades. As Vicary Gibbs noted, the schedule could only be provisional and would have to be altered as new reports appeared. Even Hickman, though an ironmaster and Chamberlainite MP, agreed. Though Chaplin saw criticism as inevitable and felt able to bear it 'with considerable complacency', he saw a published tariff as likely to alienate groups to whom the movement looked for support. In agriculture, 'unnecessary anxiety, perhaps alarm' might be created. William Harrison forecast a similar reaction from the agricultural engineers. J. J. Candlish, convinced that the main thrust of the

[93] TCM(VT), 28 June 1904, 38–42, 2/1/8, TCP.
[94] Ibid. 1–2, 2/1/8, TCP.
[95] Ibid. 6–21, 2/1/8, TCP.

report should be to counter the optimistic propaganda of Hugh Bell and other progressive Cleveland ironmasters by proving that dumping harmed even the most efficient producers, argued that it would be stronger to delay publication of a tariff until 'at the finish, having regard to all the trades generally, we suggest a certain Tariff with the full knowledge of how it will help every body'. Twelve of the Commission having spoken, only two, W. H. Mitchell and Henry Birchenough, in favour of Chamberlain's proposal, Chamberlain accepted the mood of the meeting and withdrew it.[96]

When the meeting reconvened a fortnight later on 11 July, Chamberlain again took the chair, and almost immediately there came a dramatic reversal of the decision at the previous meeting. Resurrecting his desire to publish a provisional tariff schedule, he now suggested 'a sort of compromise' in which a final paragraph would be added to the report as follows:

Subjoined to this Report is a provisional scheme of Tariffs which at the request of the Commission, the Secretary Mr. Hewins has prepared on the lines laid down in the Report as an indication of the nature of the practical reforms which may be hereafter recommended. The Commission have not yet accepted these particulars; but will consider them further as soon as they have completed their enquiry into the trades which are closely connected with the Iron and Steel manufacture, and meanwhile they will be glad to receive suggestions and criticisms ... [which] will be tabulated for the information of the Commission before they proceed to the work of final revision.[97]

Most Commissioners were Chamberlainites in a personal as well as a political sense. Chamberlain commanded their respect and admiration, often their affection and friendship. Even so, he might have been surprised by the speed with which the Commission reversed its earlier decision. Hickman threw the offer of compromise aside:

I venture to urge on you to go back to your own proposals, if you still think they are better. I submit that ... it is your scheme, and that you ought to have the guidance of it, and that though we are here to assist you we ought by no means to attempt to dictate to you. We recognise that you have an unrivalled power and opportunity of acquainting yourself with the trend of public opinion.[98]

Rather less deferentially, and without endorsing Hickman's view of the subordinate position of the Commission, other members supported the reversal. Maconochie agreed that Chamberlain was 'a past master of feeling the pulse of the public', and added more constructively that 'it may be if we do not create criticism and discussion at the present time we may not have the assistance which is required'. Henderson thought Chamberlain's original proposal better than the 'rather roundabout' compromise offered in its place. Caillard, exhibiting a sanguinity which must have made him squirm, even attributed the events of

---

[96] Ibid.   [97] TCM(VT), 11 July 1904, 3–6, 2/1/9, TCP.   [98] Ibid. 7.

28 June to a misunderstanding. Then he had thought the proposed provisional tariff to have been 'a tariff on everything from a girder to a needle; but if it is only a heading of tariffs I never meant to raise any opposition whatever'.[99]

Though Chamberlain was still unwilling to tie the Commission to a definite tariff which might affect allied or subsidiary industries and therefore require 'further consideration', he thought that his original proposal was 'straighter and more lucid' than the compromise and put less of the onus of responsibility for the tariff on the secretary's shoulders. No voice of opposition was raised. Chamberlain had now divined the opinion of the Commission sufficiently to risk a resolution, that they 'consider and . . . propound a provisional Tariff', which was carried *nem con* without further discussion.[100]

The remarks of Sir Robert Herbert and R. H. Reade show that the events of 28 June had been much discussed in the intervening fortnight. But no real evidence survives to allow a reconstruction of the offstage manœuvring which led to the volte-face. Hewins said nothing in either meeting that revealed him as anything but the model servant of the Commission, and on previous occasions he had often stressed the interrelated nature of a final tariff and the need to postpone a final judgement until all enquiries were complete. Nevertheless it is hard to imagine that he was not involved in weaning the Commission away from the very ideas and strategies he had once propounded. Chamberlain, too, had presumably been active behind the scenes, and it is probably significant that Hickman, Maconochie, Henderson, and Vicary Gibbs, all of whom had immediately stepped in to support the reversal on 11 July, were Tariff Reform MPs.

Indeed, it had been anticipated that there would be a change of heart. On 8 July the GPC had discussed a provisional General Tariff drawn up by Hewins. Though no copy survives, it was on the table on 11 July. Since at one point Hewins read from it we have a clear idea of some of the rates suggested: pig iron, 5 per cent *ad valorem*; ingots, $6\frac{1}{4}$ per cent; blooms, billets and rails, $7\frac{1}{2}$ per cent; and plates, 10 per cent. But there were higher rates than 10 per cent, and these caused surprise to some who had attended the GPC discussions. After the GPC meeting Hewins and Allen inserted a further category of more highly finished goods into the schedule above plates, and consulted Sir William Lewis about it on the evening before the meeting of 11 July. As Lewis reported the next day, '[at] that time I had a good deal of hesitation about going up to 15 per cent'.[101]

Just how high the maximum rate of the General Tariff should be was one problem. Another was that of correctly gearing 'scientific protectionism' within a limited range of duties given imperfect information on production costs. The grading of duties was critical to Hewins's 'scientific method', and Allen stressed

---

[99] TCM(VT), 11 July 1904, 8, 2/1/9, TCP   [100] Ibid. 9–12.   [101] Ibid. 17–19.

that in Germany the construction of industrial classifications for this purpose had been the subject of 'scientific study for many years past'.[102] Several present at the meeting of 11 July repeated the call for a tariff structure based on labour content, as hazarded by Chamberlain at Glasgow. 'The working man is certainly quite ready to protect labour', observed Mitchell in an opaque reference to trade unionism, 'and if they [*sic*] are quite sure it is a mere question of labour they would not be afraid of the word "Protection" at all.' To Bolton this 'should go forth to the world'. Booth considered it important to stress in publication that 'the labour consideration will rule the intermediate [General Tariff] scale'.[103]

Ironically, it was now Chamberlain who needed convincing that it would be possible to structure the tariff according to labour content, given the difficulties involved in obtaining information. Hewins defended the amended version of the schedule he had put before the GPC on 8 July, which had been drafted according to:

careful calculations based on the labour involved in these different grades. We took the cost sheets which many firms had been good enough to place at our disposal . . . and we then got the proportion of labour from pig iron up to plates, and starting with pig iron at 5 per cent we worked out a series of duties.[104]

This was perhaps a trifle disingenuous. The GPC had expressed doubts over the accuracy of Hewins's information on domestic labour costs, and there is little doubt that he was exaggerating the number of firms which had furnished such information in reply to the questionnaires; elsewhere, he virtually admitted as much.[105] But the GPC's own recommendation was even less satisfactory. It advised a cautious, skeletal plan in which 5 per cent on pig and 10 per cent on plates were published as concrete figures, but with no rates attached to the intermediate items.

In spite of their shortcomings, Hewins's tabulations of labour costs were sufficient to convince Chamberlain, who accepted them as 'a very defensible basis' for the specification of the intermediate rates. Hickman, though having his own reservations about Hewins's schedule, joined with Maconochie in the view

---

[102] Ibid. 16.

[103] TCM(VT), 28 June 1904, 36, 2/1/8, TCP; TCM(VT), 11 July 1904, 22, 2/1/9, TCP; J. M. Robertson, *The Collapse of 'Tariff Reform': Mr. Chamberlain's Case Exposed* (1911), 62.

[104] Henderson's account of the deliberations of the GPC is worthy of note: 'I do not know that the Commission generally have had before them that statement that has been prepared with regard to the amount of labour on these various items; but it is a fact that taking the amount of labour on pig iron at 100 per cent, the amount of labour on plates would be fully 200 per cent, and therefore there is a reason for the figures of 5 per cent and 10 per cent, and the intermediate items are also classified in the same way according to the amount of labour that is in them. I do not think this has been calculated, but it does show that taking pig iron at 100 per cent, when you get to ingots labour represents 141; castings 136 and blooms 166, so that it does not seem to me to be quite wise to propose that the duty upon pig iron, ingots, iron castings etc. should be all 5 per cent.' See TCM(VT), 11 July 1904, 18–19, 2/1/9, TCP.

[105] See below, Ch. 7.

that the public would see the GPC's plan as a rather lame result after six months' deliberations. Few members supported the GPC in its desire to excise all the details.[106]

This still left the top rate of the General Tariff schedule unspecified. With plates agreed at 10 per cent, the decision made after the GPC meeting to introduce a higher classification of 'forgings, steel castings and special steels'[107] naturally meant that the top range of duties in the Tariff Commission schedule would rise above 10 per cent. This went beyond a casual but not a strict interpretation of the Glasgow speech.[108] Most of the members present on 11 July were prepared to move above 10 per cent as a top rate, but many preferred that this should not be published. Henderson felt that the Commission should simply state that, with these 'special items . . . a higher duty would be applied', whilst Lewis considered it better not to exceed 10 per cent 'as a definite sum'. Keen thought it 'unwise to go to this 15 per cent; not but what we shall have to do it at a later stage, but if we invite criticism we had better invite it on the lower scale'. Chamberlain endorsed this as the general 'desire of the Commission'.[109]

Only two members objected to a top rate of above 10 per cent. Lewis Evans, the papermaker, argued that a country with a long Free Trade tradition would regard 'any industry that wants a greater protection than 10 per cent [as] one for which the country is not fitted'. Booth, mindful of the fact that there would be a higher Maximum Tariff to be applied to countries who refused to treat, felt 'very strongly that 15 per cent is too high for the highest figure of the General Tariff'. But they did not push their objections. When Chamberlain moved that the GPC, in preparing the final draft for publication, should work with a maximum published rate of 10 per cent, but should stipulate 'that all highly manufactured articles may be hereafter subjected to a higher duty', the resolution was carried unanimously.[110]

Whether Booth was persuaded, or whether he subsequently carried on the fight in the GPC, is unknown, since the GPC meeting which finally drafted the tariff has passed undocumented. But significant alterations were made. Duties that had been agreed within a range of 5 to 15 per cent were now compressed into the range 5 to 10 per cent, with higher quality goods at 10 per cent, and plates reduced to $7\frac{1}{2}$ per cent. Blooms, billets, and rails were moved from $7\frac{1}{2}$ per cent to $6\frac{1}{4}$ per cent. No corresponding reduction was made at the lower end.

---

[106] TCM(VT), 11 July 1904, 20–2, 2/1/9, TCP.

[107] Hickman's neglect of this category may well have reflected his own firm's concentration on less finished goods (see Witness No. 2, *Iron and Steel Report*, paras. 520–64), whilst Allen's interest in it is explained by the fact that his firm had been a world pioneer in the casting of steel ingots. See Sir Henry Bessemer, *An Autobiography* (1905), *passim*.

[108] Chamberlain had suggested an *average* level of 10% on manufactures. There was, of course, nothing in the Commission's terms of reference to bind it formally to the Glasgow proposals.

[109] TCM(VT), 11 July 1904, 18–22, 2/1/9, TCP.

[110] Ibid. 23.

Ingots still attracted $6\frac{1}{4}$ per cent, pig iron 5 per cent. Other categories of goods, which had not figured strongly in the discussion of 11 July, had been added at $6\frac{1}{4}$ per cent. Thus the lower intermediate rate of $6\frac{1}{4}$ per cent had become very compressed. On 11 July, Hickman had criticized Hewins's schedule, even with the later addition of the higher rates of duty, as being over-simple and compressing products into too few categories, and had urged closer con-formity to the classification used in the Board of Trade returns. But the tariff as published in the *Iron and Steel Report* was even more compressed than Hewins's original version, even though it contained more named items in the manner of the official returns. That compression was due to the need to limit the top rate. To do this, the Commission was prepared to distort the ranking of products, and hence the relative protection afforded. This was not the act of an impartial tariff-making body, not quite what was meant by taking the tariff out of politics.[111]

In discussion, the Commission had agreed to a General Tariff averaging 10 per cent in line with the Glasgow proposals, and rising to a maximum of 15 per cent. But the published version recommended less; duties were 'in no case to exceed 10 per cent'.[112] Given the hostile political environment, it would have been personally difficult for a member to have rejected the conclusions, which in any case were only provisional, as too moderate. Many members probably welcomed the reduction of duties which took place so mysteriously after 11 July, because it lessened somewhat the danger of adverse publicity and preserved the Commission's reputation as being the more acceptable face of Tariff Reform. But this did not alter the fact that the tariff as finally published was decided not collectively in open meeting, but by a hidden group of Commission leaders acting on the political need for moderacy. Was this Charles Booth's gift to the shipbuilders and shipowners—an act of Five Per Cent Philanthropy?

VIII

Even without the reduction from 15 to 10 per cent, the top rate was modest indeed by international standards, so modest that in later years Hewins could portray the Commission's General Tariff proposal as a 'revenue' tariff.[113] But this was not true of the whole package that was being developed in Victoria Street. On 28 June, the same meeting which rejected Chamberlain's proposal to publish a schedule for iron and steel was much more friendly to his desire that there

---

[111] *Iron and Steel Report*, para. 88. The schedule as published was: iron ores, free; pig iron, 5%; bars, ingots, blooms, billets, rails, girders, joists, bars, rods, etc., 6.25%; plates, 7.5%; sheets, 10%; with duties on miscellaneous manufactures such as nails, screws, nuts and bolts, wheels, and axles, 'in no case to exceed 10 per cent'.

[112] Ibid.

[113] See below, Ch. 7.

should be a statement of policy on the tariff structure necessary for effective negotiation and retaliation.

Chamberlain advocated a three-tier tariff structure. An 'extremely moderate' General Tariff should be implemented immediately and generally, 'with possibly, I think advisedly, the exception of the Colonies'. Colonial manufactures should come in free 'in the event of our negotiations with the Colonies being generally satisfactory'. Manufacturers in the Empire were not sufficiently developed to offer a serious threat to the British market, but if in future colonial producers developed the capacity to 'dump . . . on these shores . . . at prices below the home cost', then 'we should take the necessary steps to defend ourselves'.[114]

Other countries would be faced with either the moderate General Tariff or a much higher Maximum Tariff. Perhaps thinking on his feet, Chamberlain then mentioned two criteria for countries seeking access to the General Tariff which differed. The first was that such countries 'must make us a proportionate reduction' in their own. But then Chamberlain continued:

probably we might say as a general thing that whenever they would reduce their Tariff to the level of our normal Tariff, we should be quite ready to give them that normal tariff; but if on the contrary they continue their present high duties, then they would come under that higher Tariff.[115]

In suggesting that colonial manufactures be admitted free, Chamberlain had made an advance on the Glasgow proposals, where such goods had not been mentioned.[116] But the recognition that future industrial development in the Empire might necessitate a change in British commercial policy, and the requirement that the colonial tariff was not to be granted automatically but earned by reciprocal agreement, opened the possibility that Chamberlain's colonial policy might become progressively less liberal in the longer term. The possibility of an industrially developed colony continuing to enjoy free access to the British market had been reduced considerably. Even in the short term, colonists might encounter Britain's anti-dumping measures.

The implications of Chamberlain's statement for the treatment of foreign countries were even more profound. The conditions that they would have to meet in order to gain access to Britain's 5–10 per cent General Tariff were both unlikely to be achievable. The first, a 'proportionate reduction' in the foreign tariff, might have been easy or not for foreigners to meet, depending on the proportionate difference between Britain's General and Maximum Tariffs. But few would or probably could have met the stricter condition of a reduction of

---

[114] Significantly, the Canadian iron industry was given as an example of this potential threat.

[115] TCM(VT), 28 June 1904, 3–4, 2/1/8, TCP.

[116] At one point, Chamberlain had proposed 'a moderate duty on *all* manufactured goods, not exceeding 10 per cent on the average'. See J. M. Robertson, *Collapse of 'Tariff Reform'*, 61–2 (my emphasis).

their duties on British goods to the level of a British tariff set at 5–10 per cent, and they would therefore have been forced onto Britain's 'fighting' tariff, as yet unspecified. If Chamberlain hoped for a multinational reordering of tariffs to the British 'normal' level, he neglected nationalistic aims overseas. As W. H. Mitchell observed:

I am afraid that no retaliatory tariff we might adopt will at this stage do very much to improve our conditions of entering into the markets of the great protectionist Nations . . . do what you will, you are certainly not going to persuade them to break down the industries they have built up.[117]

It should be emphasized that tariff bargaining is a pragmatic and contingent process requiring adjustment and modification. Doubtless a Chamberlainite Board of Trade would have adapted, relaxing such criteria in the search for the best deal. Nevertheless, Chamberlain's words represented a distinct step beyond the Glasgow programme towards high protection, certainly with regard to foreign countries and possibly also with regard to the Empire. But members were not hostile to it. Mitchell's remarks did not disguise his support of Chamberlain's scheme, which would benefit the home manufacturer in any event. If a moderate tariff had little effect on imports, it would at least provide revenue to 'lighten the taxation which already exists on various industries, and especially on the great agricultural industry', and he had no objections to a 'fighting tariff . . . considerably higher' than the General Tariff. Hickman considered Chamberlain's three-tier tariff 'altogether admirable'. A small handful of members shrank from broadcasting the Commission's thinking, but they were in a minority. Sir Walter Peace and Henry Chaplin were prepared to accept immediate publication of the three-tier principle if no figures were mentioned. Charles Booth went further, arguing that figures might be used as actual illustrations of the principle.[118]

By the meeting of 11 July, however, doubts had grown. Speaking before the offstage reduction of the General Tariff, Hickman considered the 15-per-cent limit:

high enough for all purposes, and I think it would be . . . undesirable . . . even to mention any high, and extravagant rates, which would be absolutely, practically, inoperative . . . I do not think they are rates which any Ironmaster, or steelmaker, would desire; and I think they would prejudice our case in the eyes of the Country.[119]

---

[117] TCM(VT), 28 June 1904, 8, 2/1/8, TCP.

[118] Booth heartily endorsed the 3-tier principle, with 'very moderate minimum Tariffs for those who may be called our commercial friends and much higher Tariffs for those who cannot be so counted'. Characteristically, he also urged that the report should not be rushed, as it 'contains material of the utmost value, and it is important that it should be put together in as finished a shape as possible. Its use is not for the next two or three months, but for certainly the next two or three years, and I think it ought to be information which will stand good for two or three Centuries, if we can make it. At any rate it must be as good as we can possibly make it, and we must not count the days that are necessary for that Report'. TCM(VT), 28 June 1904, 24–5, 2/1/8, TCP.

[119] TCM(VT), 11 July 1903, 23, 2/1/9, TCP.

If Hickman had changed his stance, the new one was naïve. The majority agreed with Birchenough that Chamberlain's scheme demanded a Maximum Tariff; without it there would be no power of negotiation. But, that said, there was a familiar reluctance to advocate any specific rates for the Maximum Tariff. This reluctance was shared by the GPC, whose recommendation, Sir Robert Herbert confirmed, was that there should 'on no account . . . [be] any figures referring to a maximum Tariff'.[120]

In deciding not to consider the Maximum Tariff in any detail, the Commission was leaving a major part of its work undone. Nominal tariff levels had been rising since 1865 or 1870,[121] and a British General Tariff maximum of 15 per cent would have seemed mild in a world where German duties of 20 to 30 per cent were already seen as moderate compared with those of the USA and Russia.[122] Few foreign countries would have entertained reducing their tariffs to an average of 10 per cent, still less a maximum of 10 per cent, as was finally published.[123] Leverton Harris put the matter pungently; the public reaction to the Commission's scheme would be to say:

You can always find an excuse. It is all very fine, your General Tariff; it is only to put us off the scent; your maximum tariff is the one you are going to enforce. You can always say to any Country 'You have not met us, and we are going to enforce our maximum Tariff.[124]

By July 1904 the Chamberlainite policy was thus heading in a direction of higher protectionism than had been outlined in the Glasgow speech, a development apparently unappreciated by historians of Tariff Reform. The plan only maintained its moderacy if foreign countries agreed to sweeping and unrealistic tariff reductions. Yet in no sense was Chamberlain pressured by the Commission, enticed by wily capitalists down Asquith's inclined plane. Rather, it was the other way round. Chamberlain, perhaps primed by Hewins, had introduced the concept of the Maximum Tariff, had suggested the criteria for invoking it, and had suggested that it would 'be high enough in all probability' to keep the goods of offending nations out of the British market.[125] Though he never made this the

---

[120] TCM(VT), 11 July 1903, 24, 2/1/9, TCP

[121] Effective protection, i.e. taking account of changes in relative rates on raw materials, semi-products and finished goods, did not necessarily increase correspondingly. See G. R. Hawke, 'The United States Tariff and Industrial Protection in the Late Nineteenth Century', *Economic History Review*, 28 (1975), 84–99, and, more generally, W. M. Corden, *The Theory of Protection* (Oxford, 1971).

[122] As a crude illustration we may take the Commission's own figures on rails. The *ad valorem* equivalents of specific duties (based on Hickman's estimated selling price of £4 per ton) were Russia, 123%; Austria, 63.5%; France, Spain and Italy, 61%; USA, 40.75%; Germany, 31.75%; Belgium, 10%. See *Iron and Steel Report*, para. 153.

[123] Many Americans, particularly, were disillusioned with the reciprocity treaties they had negotiated in the previous 20 years. In 1903 the stardard authorities considered reciprocity 'a failure so far as tariff reform through that means is concerned'. See J. L. Laughlin and H. P. Willis, *Reciprocity* (New York, 1903), 421.

[124] TCM(VT), 11 July 1904, 24, 2/1/9, TCP.   [125] Ibid. 13.

focal point of his public pronouncements on policy, it did take its place in his speeches. In his major speech on the cotton trade at Preston in 1905, he stated his aim of securing a revision of foreign tariffs by threatening retaliation: 'If you continue your exclusive and prohibitive tariffs we will pay you in your own coin'.[126] The element of retaliation, on which the appeal to the cotton trade was to be largely based, had become a central element in Tariff Reform policy. It was a development which, in all probability, carried with it a far higher degree of risk than did the low General Tariff that was the descendant of the Glasgow policy.[127]

IX

The businessmen, for their part, had initially approached the enquiry with a caution, sensitivity to criticism, and hesitancy almost bordering on reluctance. Almost paradoxically, such feelings only increased their vulnerability to a manipulation against which they were incapable of defence. Hewins's assessment of their malleability when finance had been mentioned at the first meeting had proved correct.[128] Firstly, they had been persuaded—in spite of their reluctance—to accept the validity of the contentious 'reduction' process. Then they had been wooed into supporting a hypothetico-deductive analysis of the effects of dumping and of a tariff on prices and output, an analysis at variance with the very philosophy behind the establishment of the Commission in the first place. And, finally, they had been induced to throw away their caution over publishing an incomplete and premature tariff proposal in the interests of explicitly political considerations. Committed Tariff Reformers they may have been, but their recommended tariff on iron and steel was born less out of avarice than out of loyalty and subservience.

---

[126] 11 Jan. 1905. In C. W. Boyd (ed.), *Mr. Chamberlain's Speeches*, ii. 293.

[127] Chamberlain realized this was a gamble, that his threat of retaliation might meet with less response than he argued would be the case at Preston. See Chamberlain to Organised Labour Branch of the Tariff Reform League, London, 17 May 1905, in C. W. Boyd (ed.), *Mr. Chamberlain's Speeches*, ii. 324.

[128] See above, 133

6

The Cotton Industry and Retaliation

There was probably no manufacturing industry where Free Trade sentiment was so concentrated as it was amongst Lancashire's cotton masters. And perhaps nowhere but Manchester was the merchant's voice so synonymous with the city's own image of its culture and its interest. With around 80 per cent of its output sent abroad, and with a long tradition stretching back well before the Anti-Corn Law League, the industry's attachment to Free Trade was an indefinable mixture of immediate practical utility and religious faith. Over generations, pragmatic self-interest had rationalized itself indistinguishably into economic and political principle.

I

Aware of the difficulties of pursuing their enquiries within earshot of the Free Trade Hall, the Commission attempted a unique arrangement with a respected editor of the Manchester trade press. Though, through Pearson, the Commission had many allies in the Unionist press who were willing to devote large space to its opinions, and to summarize its opinions at length, this is the only case known where an attempt was made to hide Commission propaganda behind the façade of independent press comment. In March 1904 Pearson wrote to the publishers of the *Textile Mercury*:

I am now able to tell you that the General Purposes Committee of the Tariff Commission have decided to extend to the 'Textile Mercury' the same subsidy as has been hitherto paid by the Federation of Master Cotton Spinners Associations. This subsidy is, I gather, £250 per annum, and we propose that it should extend from your issue of Saturday the 16th of April for one year. In return it is understood that two pages of every issue of the 'Textile Mercury' are placed at the disposal of the Tariff Commission, which will make itself responsible for the matter with which these pages are filled. These pages will be in no way distinguishable from the ordinary matter pages of your journal.[1]

The editor's reply shows clearly the constraints within which a Lancashire Tariff Reformer who wished to avoid losing circulation had to work. Stressing the secrecy of negotiations, he remained unwilling to advocate the full Chamberlainite programme:

---

[1] Pearson to Marsden and Co., 23 Mar. 1904, HP.

I can see my way . . . to meet you on the lines you now suggest . . . that is, that the matter supplied should not be distinguishable from the other contents of the journal. This also I prefer, and it would be certainly more desirable from your committee's point of view . . . I am prepared to advocate systematically in the editorial columns of 'The Textile Mercury' the policy of retaliation. Beyond this . . . (as I explained to you in my interview) it would not at present be advisable to go . . . at any rate in Lancashire.

Any articles, therefore, going beyond retaliation . . . would need to be dissociated with [*sic*] editorial matter. This might of course be done by their bearing the names of the authors; or being lectures, or papers, delivered or written under the auspices of the Commission or otherwise.[2]

This was perhaps less than the Commission desired, and Pearson suggested that the arrangement should be made monthly instead of for the year, so that either party could end it 'should they not find it adaptable to their purposes'. This was acceptable to Marsden. Shortly afterwards he wrote requesting material in good time for publication, and advising that 'the readers of the "Textile Mercury" appreciate short articles and notes . . . more than lengthy articles'.[3]

Living amongst Tariff Reform's most concentrated, entrenched, and self-confident opposition, Levinstein was aware of the personal hostility likely to be encountered in Manchester. At the outset he preferred not to join the Commission 'publicly and officially at the present time', for what he termed 'purely local' reasons, and it took several entreaties from Chamberlain before he agreed to change his mind. Even then he was far from happy. 'I beg you', he wrote, 'to publish my name as past president of the Soc[iety] of Chem[ical] Ind[ustry] and Vice President of the Soc[iety] of Dyers and Colourists, but not in connection with the Manchstr. Chamber of Commerce.' Shortly afterwards, doubtless to the severe disappointment of the Commission's organizers, he resigned the presidency of the Manchester Chamber, since 'I cannot hold both positions at the same time with entire comfort'.[4]

Eckersley too has left testimony to the awkwardness in which Lancashire members felt that their new position put them at home:

When I agreed to become a Member [of the Commission], I had no idea that I should be the only representative of the Cotton Spinning interest and I feel the responsibility very much . . . It does seem a little ridiculous that I should speak for the [entire] Cotton Spinning Trade of Lancashire.[5]

Though Hewins sought to allay his fears by explaining that the large and complex structure of the industry necessitated a large effort to secure expert

[2] E. E. Marsden to Pearson, 26 Mar. 1904, HP.
[3] Pearson to Marsden, 28 Mar. 1904; Marsden to Hewins, 7 Apr. 1904, HP.
[4] Levinstein to Chamberlain, 14 Dec. 1904; Levinstein to Hewins, 3 Feb. [in fact, Jan.] 1904; Levinstein to Hewins, 8 Jan. 1904, 6/1/21, TCP.
[5] Eckersley to Harrison, 1 Jan. 1904, 6/1/5, TCP.

evidence from many different quarters, and that it was Eckersley's role 'to advise the Commission as to the manner in which it should set about consultation of expert opinion representing all branches . . . and . . . as to the manner in which the Commission might select its witnesses', Eckersley still feared his participation 'liable to be misconstrued'. Throughout the enquiry he insisted that his knowledge was limited to the cotton spinning branch, even to the extent that he underlined the phrase in correspondence as if in formal limitation of his own terms of reference.[6]

The Commission was faced with a new problem in its study of the cotton industry. With iron and steel, the merchanting function was concentrated amongst a limited number of firms, whilst many manufacturers practised direct selling. Direct selling by cotton manufacturers was exceptional, export business especially having been long handled by an anonymous multiplicity of shippers.[7] Though one of the two cotton representatives on the Commission, Frederick Baynes, carried on some merchanting business, it was most probably limited to acting as an agent between manufacturers and exporters: in the words of his partner, 'In many cases we do not know where our goods go'.[8] Nor did the remaining six members of the Commission's Textile Committee remedy this absence of the export merchant on the Commission.[9]

Eckersley perceived early the need to secure evidence from export merchants. The questionnaire designed for the iron and steel trade demanded a knowledge of foreign market and production conditions that few cotton producers would possess. But it was also recognized that the shippers made up the most cosmopolitan sector of a cosmopolitan industry, and after making soundings Eckersley feared that '[t]here would be a difficulty getting the Experts to appear be[fore] the Commission'. Nevertheless, he supplied Hewins with the names of seventy or eighty of the most important exporters of yarn, whilst it was left to Baynes to do the same for the shippers of manufactured cottons.[10]

Levinstein had a particularly harsh view of the merchant: 'it is the game of many of our merchants to set the foreign producer against the British in order to squeeze down prices. They don't care whether the working classes are

---

[6] Hewins to Eckersley, 4 Jan. 1904; Eckersley to Hewins, 7 Jan. 1904; Eckersley to Hewins, 11 Jan. 1904, 6/1/5, TCP.

[7] S. J. Chapman, *The Lancashire Cotton Industry* (Manchester, 1904), 138; E. Helm, 'The Middleman in Commerce', *Transactions of the Manchester Statistical Society* (1900–1), 55–65.

[8] *Cotton Report*, para. 513.

[9] In addition to the 15 Commission members on the Textile Committee, there were also 2 carpet manufacturers (G. Marchetti of John Crossley and Sons Ltd., Halifax; M. Tomkinson of Kidderminster): 3 manufacturers of woollens and/or worsteds, tweeds, flannels, etc. (J. H. Kaye of Huddersfield; J. Peate of Guiseley; and A. J. Sanderson of Galashiels): and 1 flax and jute producer (J. B. Don of Dundee).

[10] Eckersley to Hewins, 18 and 23 Jan. 1904; Eckersley to Harrison, 1 Jan. 1904; Eckersley to Hewins, n. d. but late Jan. or early Feb. 1904; Eckersley to Hewins, 18 Jan. 1904; Eckersley to Hewins, 1 Mar. 1904, 6/1/5, TCP.

employed.' Since Manchester was 'a far larger distributing centre than manufacturing', it was 'the most difficult city in England'.[11] But even he recognized the central importance of securing merchant evidence, and he was the principal architect of Hewins's meeting with Manchester businessmen early in 1904. This was only thinly attended,[12] and in the weeks that followed Levinstein was busy attempting to remedy its lack of success. In March he informed Hewins that he had persuaded S. M. Bles, of a highly respected shipping firm, to join the Committee. Bles, who had initially been unreceptive, was apparently annoyed by Dutch proposals to increase duties both at home and in their colonies, but for some reason his anger cooled and he withdrew his support. Levinstein was equally certain that he could recruit H. E. Wollmer, a former partner of Sir Jacob Behrens, but was again frustrated. The home-trade houses could be equally difficult. Levinstein was also led into believing that a Mr Kendall, of the substantial Messrs. George Peake and Co., would accept an invitation to join the Committee. But Kendall replied with a string of unconvincing excuses. That Levinstein was so similarly misled suggests that each of these may have initially expressed some sympathy with the Commission, but were subsequently daunted by the Manchester business community's hostility to Tariff Reform. Kendall certainly didn't hesitate to suggest a replacement. Walter Sparrow of Messrs. Sparrow, Hardwicke and Co. was 'I know . . . in *active* sympathy with the objects of the Commission. Shall I ask him?' Again, Sparrow appears to have accepted a position on the Committee, and then changed his mind.[13]

The difficulty in obtaining merchant representation extended to the witnesses. Only two, excluding Baynes and his partner Dixon, had merchant interests. One, F. B. Ross, was a Free Trader.[14] The other, de F. Pennefather, was a Liverpool merchant who was already involved in Unionist politics, and subsequently to become MP for Kirkdale (1925–1929). As master of the North Hereford foxhounds (1901–1903) he was in any case scarcely a typical Lancashire shipper.[15]

It should, however, be stressed that Levinstein's view of a cleavage of interests between cotton merchants and manufacturers, whilst it may have been valid in other respects, certainly did not extend to fiscal policy. When Eckersley sent a list of some of the most prominent spinning concerns for Hewins's use, he excluded some because he knew they would not respond. 'I think all my Cotton

[11] Levinstein to Hewins, 8 Feb. 1904; 6/1/21, TCP.

[12] *Manchester Guardian*, 27 Feb. 1904.

[13] Levinstein to Hewins, 11 Mar. 1904; Hewins to Levinstein, 12 Mar. 1904; Levinstein to Hewins, 19 June 1904; Hewins to Levinstein, 20 June 1904; Kendall to Levinstein, 27 June 1904; Levinstein to Hewins, 23 June 1904; Hewins to Levinstein, 24 June 1904; Levinstein to Hewins, 29 June 1904, 6/1/21, TCP.

[14] *Cotton Report*, paras. 392, 406–7.

[15] M. Stenton and S. Lees (ed.), *Who's Who of British Members of Parliament* (Brighton, 1979), iii.

Spinning friends are free traders . . . and I think it is possible you will have no reply fm. many of the names I have given you.'[16]

II

To chart the relative decline of the British industry, the starting point of all the Commission's industrial inquiries, proved less easy for cotton than for iron and steel. Hewins initially put weight on the long-term decline of UK raw-cotton consumption as a proportion of the world total: the UK's share of total US and European cotton consumption had fallen from 42 per cent in 1876–1880 to 25.7 per cent in 1903.[17] But, as the nervous Eckersley was at pains to stress, any tendency to produce finer counts would make this an unreliable indicator of decline. Study of the Factory Returns supported Eckersley's contention that there had been an 'appreciable increase' in labour and capital employed in the industry.[18] International comparisons of cotton consumption per spindle were recognized to be of limited value without knowing the degree of short-time working and changes in the speed at which machinery was run in each country.

Eckersley put his finger on the problem: the trend towards finer counts in Britain was 'generally known . . . but . . . there has been no record kept of what has actually been done'.[19] Most contemporaries, indeed, shared his belief that there was a long-term and general move to finer counts.[20] But few had an accurate oversight of the industry in aggregate, and not all experts were convinced of the existence of the trend.[21] Though Britain spun finer yarns than her rivals,[22] it was the *relative* trend, and its magnitude, that mattered. In this, the Commission was doubtful that the change was substantial. Eckersley's calculation that a decrease of 0.8 lbs (2.6 per cent) in consumption per spindle between 1890 and 1903 was equivalent to an increase in average count from 31*s*. to 32*s*. seemed to show a very limited movement when the industry regarded counts of fifty to eighty as medium and above eighty as fine.[23]

As Hewins observed, the paucity of information made it impossible 'to be very dogmatic on the subject'. Essentially, Eckersley, in spite of his own figures, held to the view that the fine-counts tendency was of substantial importance, whilst

[16] Eckersley to Hewins, 9 May 1904, 6/1/5, TCP.

[17] *Cotton Report*, paras. 9–12, Tables I and II, Figs. I and II. Estimates given for British cotton consumption differ slightly but not significantly from those in B. R. Mitchell, *British Historical Statistics* (Cambridge, 1988), 332–3.

[18] Hewins to Eckersley, 8 Apr. 1904, 6/1/5, TCP.

[19] Eckersley to Hewins, 1 and 11 Apr. 1904, 6/1/5, TCP.

[20] *Textile Mercury*, Aug. 1890, 104, Sept. 1892, 195; *Textile Recorder*, Jan. 1893, 239; May 1896, 3; July 1896, 188; E. E. Todd in *Manchester Guardian*, repr. in *Textile Recorder*, Sept. 1911, 143.

[21] H. B. Heylin, *Buyers and Sellers in the Cotton Trade* (1913), 104.

[22] S. L. Besso, *The Cotton Industry in Switzerland, Vorarlberg and Italy* (Manchester, 1910), 10–11, 19.

[23] *Cotton Report*, paras. 20, 22, 27–8, 28n; Textile Committee Minutes, 30 May 1905, 19, 2/3/3, TCP. (All Textile Committee minutes are verbatim transcripts).

Baynes thought it unimportant except as a short-term, cyclical occurrence, and Hewins occupied a middle position. Therefore it became necessary to use 'a variety of [additional] tests' of the industry's prosperity and progress.[24]

The obvious second choice was spindleage. The sources of the Commission's estimates were not specified, but the estimates themselves showed a sustained though moderate increase from 44.3 m spinning and doubling spindles in 1885 to 47.8m in 1903. These figures compare closely with the standard index in use today, though the Commission's estimates did conceal significant short-term declines. The Commission did, however, exaggerate the increase between 1903 and 1904, probably because it was forced to rely too heavily on impressionistic contemporary comment about the strength of trade revival.[25]

Members of the Textile Committee were reluctant to interpret the increase in spindleage as signifying prosperity. Baynes considered that most of the mill building of the previous decade had been undertaken by speculative mill builders and textile engineers. To Mosely's objection that there must be some final sale to mill operators which signified optimism as to the state of trade, he replied, 'You can always make a good return for the first few years: you do not depreciate sufficiently, and so on'. Though several members saw some truth in his assertion, most thought it exaggerated and difficult to use as evidence. As Birchenough observed, 'not one person in five thousand' would be familiar with the role of the speculative mill-builder in the recent extension of capacity.[26]

Most found more convincing the Commission's finding that there had been a climacteric in the growth of UK cotton consumption in 1890. Furthermore, UK power looms had increased by 19.6 per cent between 1878 and 1890, but by only 11 per cent since then. The corresponding figures for yarn consumption were even more dramatic; 30 per cent and 6 per cent. Comparison of the censuses of 1891 and 1901 also suggested that employment in the industry had started to decline around the early 1890s.[27] Calculations of net value of output by Commission statistician Rosenbaum reinforced this perception of a virtually stagnant industry, though the basis of Rosenbaum's figures was not explained. 'It is a very technical Table', observed Textile Committee chairman Leverton

---

[24] Textile Committee Minutes, 30 May 1905, 20, 2/3/3, TCP; Textile Committee Minutes, 18 May 1905, 11–13, 2/3/2, TCP; Textile Committee Minutes, 15 Dec. 1904, 26, 30, 2/3/1, TCP.

[25] The Commission put the increase of spinning spindles at 3.1m between 1903 and 1904, whereas Worrall's index gives an increase of only 0.6m for spinning and doubling spindles. See *Cotton Report*, Table VII, para. 26; Textile Committee Minutes, 30 May 1905, 17, 2/3/3, TCP. Worrall's index is reproduced in B. R. Mitchell, *British Historical Statistics*, 372.

[26] Textile Committee Minutes, 18 May 1905, 16–17, 2/3/2, TCP. North-East Lancashire was indeed the centre of speculative mill building, though it appears to have lessened in spinning (whilst increasing in weaving) after 1875. See D. A. Farnie, *The English Cotton Industry and the World Market, 1815–1896* (Oxford, 1979), 291–5.

[27] *Cotton Report*, paras. 9–13, 27–8, 34–6. The Factory Returns put the decline in employment from c. 1895. See B. R. Mitchell, *British Historical Statistics*, 377.

Harris. 'I have no doubt our staff can defend it if it is challenged.'[28] With exports, too, the Commission found something of a climacteric in the late 1880s; with the US market stagnant and the long-term decline of export volumes to Europe, piece-goods exports were increasingly dependent on the state of demand in British India. Since 1892–1896 yarn exports had contracted sharply whilst piece-goods exports had risen only 4.5 per cent by volume. In value terms, expansion was more marked, but nevertheless progress had been slower than in Germany, Holland, Belgium, France, Italy, Austria, and the USA, not to mention India and Japan. It was the claim of the Commission that the evidence of the witnesses and the 942 responding firms (employing 272, 073) supported their statistical analysis. The revival of trade after 1903 was 'regarded by witnesses as exceptional and transient... Looking at normal conditions, the general view... is that trade as a whole is stationary, but not necessarily going backwards'.[29]

That the Commission exercised care in its statistical analysis was grudgingly admitted by contemporary Free Traders, who were forced to admit that, by and large, 'the statistical review seems to be accurate',[30] though containing 'some noticeable gaps'.[31] Though at times the Commission would have been more accurate in talking of slower growth rather than stagnation, subsequent historians have corroborated much of the specific detail in the *Cotton Report* relating to a climacteric around 1890. Cotton consumption per spindle fell by 2.6 per cent between 1890 and 1903.[32] The number of power looms in the industry rose from 485,264 in 1882 to 606,585 in 1890, but to only 647,372 in 1903.[33] Exports of yarn peaked in 1884, whilst the rate of growth of piece-goods exports slackened after 1888, with grey cloth reaching a plateau in 1890 and thereafter being displaced relatively by bleached, printed, and dyed cloth.[34] If the industry was not stagnant, its growth in the quarter-century prior to 1905 gives some credence to the pessimistic tenor of the *Cotton Report*. The annual rate of growth of production was about 1.4 per cent between 1873 and 1896, only about a quarter of that achieved between 1780 and 1872.[35]

[28] *Cotton Report*, para. 39; Textile Committee Minutes, 30 May 1905, 25–7, 2/3/3, TCP.
[29] *Cotton Report*, paras. 44–5, 50–61, 63. The response rate (para. 5), an apparently respectable one from a markedly Free Trade industry, cannot be verified because of the incomplete survival of cotton questionnaires in the Tariff Commission's papers.
[30] S. J. Chapman, in *Manchester Guardian*, 6 June 1905, 7–8.
[31] S. J. Chapman, 'The Report of the Tariff Commission', *Economic Journal*, 15 (1905), 420.
[32] R. E. Tyson, 'The Cotton Industry', in D. H. Aldcroft (ed.), *The Development of British Industry and Foreign Competition 1875–1914* (1968), 108.
[33] *The Lancashire Textile Industry* (J. Worrall Ltd., Oldham, 1956 edn.), 147.
[34] D. A. Farnie, *English Cotton Industry*, 185; A. J. Marrison, 'Great Britain and her Rivals in the Latin American Cotton Piece-Goods Market, 1880–1914', in B. M. Ratcliffe (ed.), *Great Britain and her World 1750–1914* (Manchester 1975), 312.
[35] D. A. Farnie, *English Cotton Industry*, 187.

If, therefore, with hindsight, we can agree with Sidney Chapman that the *Report* was 'unduly alarmist', it is perhaps due to our knowledge that Lancashire was on the eve of one of her biggest-ever cyclical booms. Furthermore, it is almost certainly the case that the Commission underestimated changes in quality not reflected in volume indicies. Sandberg has demonstrated that, if the decline in the rate of growth of British piece-goods exports is adjusted by his own index of average quality, the real slump in performance was concentrated in the decade from 1885 to 1894.[36] Indeed, in concentrating fruitlessly on the fine-counts question, the Commission neglected other improvements in quality, notably the development of cheap dyed goods by British manufacturers which, as has been argued elsewhere, were more important than count, especially in low-income markets.[37]

It is clear, however, that the Commission was not unaware of quality changes of this type. Rather, the avoidance of competition from indigenous producers or rival exporters in overseas markets by moving to higher qualities was, with some justice, seen as an impermanent solution. Witnesses laid much stress on the rise of foreign competition, itself the result of overseas development of the industry behind tariff walls. Britain's trade with the more advanced producers such as Germany and the US had already become one in 'highly expensive goods, fancies and novelties', high in value but low in volume.[38] The Commission regarded this trade as somehow less wholesome, and certainly less stable, than the older staple lines that were being displaced:

In general, manufacturers have been forced into novelties, fancies and specialities instead of their old trade in staple lines. But these cannot so readily be made to stock; and it is impossible to look far ahead. In such circumstances, costs tend to increase and the competing power of British manufacturers is diminished.[39]

This trade 'depends ultimately in the view of witnesses on the rapidity and skill with which British manufacturers can invent new designs, and stimulate the tastes and demand of other countries for such designs', so that '[t]he trade tends to become merely a trade in patterns'.[40] It would also be impermanent, as foreigners eroded Lancashire's superiority in finer cloth, displacing even higher-quality imports, and then emerged as export rivals in the same sequential process.[41] The China market was already threatened by the US, India, and

---

[36] S. J. Chapman, 'Report of Tariff Commission', 420; L. G. Sandberg, *Lancashire in Decline* (Columbus, Oh., 1974), Table 21, 40, and App. C for the derivation of the quality index on which this is based.

[37] A. J. Marrison, 'Great Britain and her Rivals', *passim*.

[38] *Cotton Report*, para. 69.

[39] Ibid. para. 73.

[40] Ibid. para. 69.

[41] This is shown well for the USA in M. T. Copeland, *The Cotton Manufacturing Industry of the United States* (Cambridge, Mass., 1912), 240.

Japan, whilst Italy and Germany stood poised to conquer the Levant. Only in South America was the UK 'still on the whole more than holding her own'.[42] Relative displacement was even characteristic of colonial markets, whether by indigenous producers of coarse goods as in India, or by foreign exporters as in Canada.

III

In cotton, the Commission placed little emphasis on the 'reduction' process that had been so important to the iron-and-steel inquiry. It might be 'impossible to reduce the [international] comparisons of costs to a statistical basis', but witnesses and committee members were agreed on the technical and economic efficiency of the British industry. The cost of building and equipping mills was lower than in Europe and the USA. There were admitted to be some shortcomings in mill operation, such as the slow speed of machinery compared with American best practice, and the coarse spinner Baynes questioned the British reluctance to adopt ring-spinning and the Northrop loom; but generally the deficiencies were held to be minor.[43]

But there was a strong feeling that the industry would be put in jeopardy in future by low wages overseas. Responding firms recognized the high efficiency of British labour: pieceworkers had 'maintained their weekly wages through improved machinery and extra exertion', and it was claimed that low wages and long hours abroad were 'practically indistinguishable from the sweating system'. India and Japan excited most comment. When, in discussion, Hewins cited information on Japanese wages for a ten-hour shift in 1890, Kaye and Corah were incredulous. Corah wondered 'how many pounds of beef' such wages would buy, only to be informed by Leverton Harris that the Japanese ate rice and fish. Still bemused, Corah observed, 'It shews you we ought to have protection. We shall have Japanese stuff here very shortly.'[44]

Importantly, in contrast to the iron-and-steel inquiry, there had been no significant dumping of cottons in the British market. Levinstein persisted in his belief in the systematic dumping of velveteens, whilst Baynes produced isolated examples of dumping by Austria and Russia, but they were recognized to be

---

[42] *Cotton Report*, para. 71; see A. J. Marrison, 'Great Britain and her Rivals', for confirmation.

[43] *Cotton Report*, para. 81. The extensive recent debate on technology and organization in the pre-war British industry cannot be fully cited here. For important contributions, see L. G. Sandberg, 'American Rings and English Mules', *Quarterly Journal of Economics*, 83 (1969), 25–43; and *Lancashire in Decline*, esp. chs. 2–4, 7; W. Lazonick, 'Factor Costs and the Diffusion of Ring Spinning in Britain prior to World War I', *Quarterly Journal of Economics*, 96 (1981), 89–109; G. Saxonhouse and G. Wright, 'Stubborn Mules and Vertical Integration: The Disappearing Constraint?', *Economic History Review*, 40 (1987), 87–94.

[44] *Cotton Report*, paras. 74, 89, 95; Textile Committee Minutes, 30 May 1905, 39–40, 2/3/3, TCP; TCM(VT), 31 May 1905, 22–3, 2/1/10, TCP.

trivial. Mosely, annoyed that this absence weakened the Tariff Reform case, emphasized that foreign dumping in neutral markets would 'indirectly affect us' through our export trade. Hewins replied that this 'does not establish the case for a tariff', whilst Birchenough added that, 'No power on earth can prevent dumping in neutral markets'. To Mosely and Caillard, this was to deny the dynamic implications of the *Iron and Steel Report*. Mosely argued that dumping overseas might prevent attainment of 'maximum production' in the British industry by reducing exports, whilst Caillard stressed the model of discriminatory pricing: 'By their tariff they [foreign producers] keep up their prices and get more profits on the home trade, and so can afford to export very cheaply.'[45] The Commission had discovered few cases of dumping even in neutral markets, however—a rather vague reference to US dumping in Australia and a consular accusation of Italian dumping of prints in Constantinople.[46] Hewins interpreted the witnesses as 'distinctly' denying that dumping was responsible for the state of the cotton industry.[47]

The weakness of the Mosely–Caillard argument was that even abroad the cotton industry was not as concentrated nor as monopolistically organized as was iron and steel. The corollary was that Lancashire's capacity to dump would remain negligible even under a tariff: 'You cannot have it: you cannot get it.' To Hewins, the very export-orientation of the cotton industry made necessary 'a different line to the argument' that had been pursued for iron and steel. Mosely and Caillard nevertheless persisted in their belief that a British tariff would aid continuous running, and they were supported by Charles Allen, J. J. Candlish, J. H. Kaye, and Alfred Gilbey, all of whom considered that the cotton industry's tendency to work below capacity was insufficiently stressed in the draft report and that a tariff would reduce costs by allowing higher capacity working. To Grenfell, this was 'the cardinal point of our whole enquiry . . . the foundation of our whole policy'.[48]

But even Gilbey admitted that cotton manufacturers had dwelt less on the increase in unit costs consequent upon short-time working than had other textile witnesses, whilst Chamberlain was reluctant to stress the importance of continuous running in reducing costs because '[i]t has not been proved in the case of the cotton trade by the evidence'. In this he was supported by Hewins, Pearson, and Baynes, but he was well aware that the majority of the Commission desired some reference to continuous running in the report. Clearly reluctant to introduce an argument he felt was not backed by the evidence given before the Commission, he urged that the Commission should stress that the 'element of

---

[45] Textile Committee Minutes, 15 Dec. 1904, 7, 42–7, 2/3/1, TCP; Textile Committee Minutes, 18 May 1905, 26–7, 34, 2/3/2, TCP.

[46] *Cotton Report*, para. 180. See also *Diplomatic and Consular Reports*, Annual Series, no. 3140, 1904.

[47] Textile Committee Minutes, 18 May 1905, 26, 2/3/2, TCP.

[48] Ibid.; TCM(VT), 31 May 1905, 31–2, 2/1/10, TCP.

quantity is of enormous importance' to the textile industries as a whole, without singling out cotton as an example. Having led the business members down the seductive path of continuous running in the iron-and-steel inquiry, Chamberlain and Hewins now led them away from it in that of cotton. The objective arguments for doing so were strong in each case, but once again we can see that the Commission's true power-base lay with the men of affairs rather than the men of business.[49]

IV

The Tariff Commission's recommended tariff schedule allowed free entry of raw cotton, yarns and twists (i.e. doubled thread), and grey tissues (i.e. grey cloth), but proposed duties of a maximum of 10 per cent on 'Other Cotton Tissues and Manufacturers'.[50] It was clear early in the inquiry that the cotton trade was not clamouring for protection: as Hewins observed, 'I . . . do not think there is much case for a tariff on cotton yarns. There is not much case for a tariff on [plain] cotton [goods] at all.' Though Eckersley, the fine spinner, could not agree 'that there is no case for any tariff on plain cotton yarn', Hewins did not encounter serious opposition on the Commission or even on its Textile Committee. Indeed, the exclusion of less-finished cottons from the Commission's final schedule was seen as politically advantageous. 'The sooner you can make this known the sooner you will kill Mr. Asquith,' beamed Levinstein, 'and the more satisfactory it will be for Lancashire.'[51] Such arguments easily secured the positive endorsement of the sensitive Eckersley.

Thus, a draft recommendation that 'No duties are at present required on yarns, or on grey cloths'[52] passed easily through both the Committee and the Commission. Curiously, the only member who questioned the recommended schedule was Kaye, the Huddersfield woollen manufacturer:

Assuming we are seeking the employment of our own people why should we suggest that cotton tissues grey should come in free, if yarns and twists even are free[?] It is a question of employment. This is the key of all our efforts and desires. Raw cotton of course should be free, but why these things [yarns, twists and grey tissues] free[?][53]

Kaye was presumably fearful lest this moderacy set a precedent for the other textile industries. But Chamberlain was determined to support 'The Textile Committee [who had come] . . . to the conclusion that there was no evidence to justify a Tariff in those cases.' 'It is a good thing,' he maintained, 'to show how

---

[49] TCM(VT), 31 May 1905, 31–2, 2/1/10, TCP.
[50] *Cotton Report*, para. 113.
[51] Textile Committee Minutes, 15 Dec. 1904, 52–4, 2/3/1, TCP.
[52] Textile Committee Minutes, 30 May 1905, 2, 45, 2/3/3, TCP.
[53] TCM(VT), 31 May 1905, 34, 2/1/10, TCP.

moderate we are, and that we are not asking for anything to raise prices, or make a profit, but only where it is absolutely necessary to defend our trade.' He turned to Baynes for confirmation that 'the overwhelming majority of the people engaged in these trades do not want a tariff'. Though he concurred, Baynes's reply was double-edged. Opinion in Lancashire was divided, but only a minority stressed the state of the market: 'the bulk of Lancashire look for cheapness of cost', considering that 'we have had markets in the past and might have them again'. A tariff was at present inappropriate because 'we shall [not] be attacked in our home trade until we have been attacked in our neutral markets—our export trade. It is in the 80 per cent, the export trade, that we are particularly liable to be hurt by foreign tariffs'.[54]

As sensible as this may have sounded, the Commission had sidestepped an important part of its own brief. Yarns, twists, and grey cloth had for many years been undergoing a relative decline in British cotton production. Yarns and unbleached grey piece-goods, comprising 41.99 per cent of the value of British cotton exports in 1890–1894, had shrunk steadily to 33.88 per cent by 1900–1904, a proportion they were to hold until 1913. Bleached, printed and dyed piece-goods, and miscellaneous cotton manufactures had risen from 58.00 per cent of exports by value in 1890–1894 to 66.11 per cent by 1900–1904, again stabilizing in the great pre-war boom.[55] The more highly finished cottons, which the Commission had no doubt should be subjected to duties, now constituted the majority of the industry's product. Whilst the Commission had agreed to recommend denying protection to one-third of Lancashire's output, it had not come to a concrete decision on the grading of the other two-thirds.

This grading was, as has been shown, at the heart of the 'scientific' tariff envisaged at Glasgow. Chamberlain dismissed the Commission's failure lightly: 'We have not gone into so much detail [as in the iron-and-steel tariff] here, but I understand that is because of the number of specialised products'.[56] Early in the cotton inquiry Hewins had found that the breakdown of the industry into 'innumerable branches of a most complicated character' had required radical changes in the Commission's system of card-indexing that had been developed to process the information collected in the iron-and-steel inquiry.[57] But it is evident that these changes had not been completedly successful, and that the Commission had not gained a clear insight into the cost-components of the bewildering variety of Lancashire goods. In November 1904 Hewins had claimed

[54] Ibid. 35–6.
[55] *Annual Statement of Trade of the United Kingdom*, 1890–1913. For detailed quinquennial averages by product type, see A. J. Marrison, 'British Businessmen and the "Scientific" Tariff: A Study of Joseph Chamberlain's Tariff Commission, 1903–1921', unpubl. Ph. D. Thesis, Univ. of Hull, 1980, Table 17, 326.
[56] TCM(VT), 31 May 1905, 35, 2/1/10, TCP.
[57] Textile Committee Minutes, 18 May 1905, 4, 2/3/2, TCP; Hewins, *Apologia of an Imperialist* (1929), i. 96.

to have produced a product-classification of the industry,[58] but a year later he was reluctant to subject it to public scrutiny when asked by Levinstein whether it would appear in the *Cotton Report*:

> As I explained . . . what we wanted the classification for was initially the logical and practical arrangement of all the evidence so that the argument, whatever it is, may be developed in the right order. We do not want necessarily to publish a classification. It is of very great value if we can, but the classification of an industry is a subject on which, as Mr. Levinstein knows, scarcely two experts would agree.[59]

Thus the cotton inquiry had not succeeded in drafting a scientifically graduated tariff, according to labour content or any other criterion; its achievements in this direction had been limited to distinguishing between goods in which there was virtually no competition in the home market (these to be allowed in free) and goods in which the degree of competition was somewhat higher. The second group remained undifferentiated, the relative position of each in the allotted range of tariff rates, from 0 to 10 per cent, still to be decided. By contrast the relatively simple iron-and-steel tariff represented a considerably greater achievement.[60] But to the Commission this was perhaps of small importance: its appeal to the cotton trade was to rely on retaliation and reciprocity rather than the promise of protection.

The Commission recognized the threat to future prosperity in the British industry as indigenous producers became rival exporters. The public needed 'a very strong word of warning' that in time a tariff would be necessary to prevent European manufacturers 'having two free markets—their own and ours'. More ominous for the export trade was the situation in the Far East, which the Commission saw as quantitatively and potentially more important than that in Europe. American competition in China could be discounted; as Mosely remarked tersely, 'Japan will have it'. Under threat from the rise of the Japanese and Indian industries, the British presence in the Far East would be 'fairly well wiped out'. Chamberlain feared the appearance of Japanese cotton in European markets, whilst Kaye and Leverton Harris thought Australia and India would be next to come under pressure, but all agreed with Kaye that 'It would gradually come West.' Hewins might forsee the day when 'Lancashire is going to be the head quarters of protection', but opinion was not yet ready. In view of the political expediency of recommending a moderate tariff, the threat could be met

---

[58] Hewins to Mitchell, 8 Nov. 1904; Mitchell to Hewins, 21 Nov. 1904, 6/1/24, TCP.

[59] Textile Committee Minutes, 15 Dec. 1904, 10, 2/3/1, TCP.

[60] This is not meant to imply that the Commission was in any real way failing to emulate the 'scientific' tariff formulation of other countries, though Hewins may have imagined this was the case. It was easy for a protectionist administration to produce a very elaborate schedule whose arbitrary nature was concealed by its scientifically detailed appearance. W. W. Rich's *Handbook of the United States Tariff* (F. B. Vandegrift and Co., New York, 1913), printed a schedule 557 pages long. There is little doubt that Hewins underestimated the crudity of the ways in which foreign tariffs were drafted. See F. W. Taussig, *Free Trade, The Tariff and Reciprocity* (New York, 1920), 180.

when it came. The British tariff, noted Chamberlain, could be 'altered from time to time, and when the pressure comes I suppose the people will wake up in the cotton trade'.[61]

Thus the Commission was forced into emphasizing Tariff Reform as a vehicle for retaliation and reciprocity. For the cotton industry, it was 'far more important for us to use our fiscal system for reducing the tariffs of foreign countries than for actually imposing a tariff on goods coming into this country', observed Leverton Harris. As Hewins discerned, a tariff for such purposes might well be 'on other things than cotton'; that was 'the difference between the intermediate and the final Report'. But he was forced to admit that business opinion painted a bleak picture of the chances of success. Witnesses were unanimous that 'there is not the remotest chance of getting down the tariffs of anybody', those with factories in France, such as Kersley and Ross, being particularly insistent on the point. Some on the Committee were unwilling to accept this. Birchenough, the silk spinner, clearly having in mind the difficulties encountered in trying to renew the Cobden-Chevalier treaty in the early 1880s, considered that a British tariff might pressure the French into negotiating a new treaty, in which Britain could 'sacrifice' silk, fancy woollens, and wines. Hewins' approach was fatalistic: 'You never know until you try. If you cannot do it, there is a rather poor look out for cotton.' This was indeed the logic behind the plea for retaliation.[62]

Preference also presented huge unknowns. Statistically, the *Cotton Report* tended to hide the fact that exports to the Empire were doing less well than those to neutral markets by including the neutral markets with the 'principal protected countries', which of course depressed the figures. According to Hewins, witnesses and questionnaires were 'practically unanimous' in judging existing colonial preferences to be beneficial, though only forty-four replies from firms on this matter were printed in an appendix to the *Cotton Report*, thirty-three in favour.[63] However, given that there is some evidence that in the early years the Commission printed all the replies received, this was a low response-rate by the 942 firms returning the questionnaires. Whilst Corah might stress in December 1904 that his hosiery firm, normally on short time before Christmas, was 'working now till nine o'clock at night . . . and it is all for the Colonies', the Commission disagreed on how successful existing preferences had been. Chamberlain considered that 'we have had very little experience. The preference given in some cases, as for instance in South Africa, is so small that I believe it has no effect at all at present.' Conceding to Sir John Cockburn that trade with New

---

[61] Textile Committee Minutes, 18 May 1905, 40–1, 2/3/2, TCP; Textile Committee Minutes, 15 Dec. 1904, 54, 2/3/1, TCP; TCM(VT), 31 May 1905, 14–15, 2/1/10, TCP.
[62] Textile Committee Minutes, 15 Dec. 1904, 54, 2/3/1, TCP; Textile Committee Minutes, 18 May 1905, 39, 2/3/2, TCP.
[63] *Cotton Report*, paras. 46–7, 109, 111, 1063–1107. The 'Principal Protected Countries' were defined as Germany, Holland, Belgium, France, Italy, Austria, and the USA.

Zealand did show 'some increases', he persisted that the only impressive experience was in the Canadian trade, which 'we *know* has increased'. When Corah was provoked into suggesting that Britain, 'having had all the expense of the War', should force an upward revision of the South African tariff to allow a greater margin for preference, Chamberlain chided, 'Whom did we conquer? The majority of the people are British now ... My own expectation is that we shall get better, but this is a free gift from the Colonies and we can not force it.'[64]

V

Though in several exchanges with Harold Cox of the Free Trade League the editor of the *Textile Mercury* vehemently rejected the label of protectionist,[65] he ensured that retaliation had a platform in the Manchester trade press. Urging the cotton trade to return the Commission's questionnaires, and so contribute to a 'public benefit of the greatest importance', the *Mercury* also reported regularly on the activities of the Commission and the appearance of witnesses before its Textile Committee. When the *Cotton Report* appeared, it was heralded as 'a splendid record of thorough investigation', and four lengthy articles were devoted to it.[66] The Free Trade press was less charitable. In a few brief lines the *Manchester City News* contented itself with the ambivalent remark that a body which had attracted 'a good deal of ridicule' had produced an 'elaborate and carefully compiled' document. The *Textile Recorder*, in a dismissive treatment, remarked that spinners and manufacturers had 'received the report in a very easy spirit, and have not given very serious thought to the remedies suggested'. Only the *Manchester Guardian* gave the *Report* the emphasis the Tariff Reformers considered it deserved, describing it as 'a monument ... to the ability, ingenuity and indefatigable energy of Mr. Hewins. What it would have been without him we tremble to think ... [The Tariff Commission] have had a very hard nut to crack in the cotton industry, and they have made a very courageous attempt upon it.'[67]

But even the *Manchester Guardian* could not accept the Commission's pessimistic analysis of the condition of such a 'robust' industry. In a review, Professor Chapman congratulated Hewins on 'an impressive piece of work' and an

[64] Textile Committee Minutes, 15 Dec. 1904, 54, 2/3/1, TCP; TCM(VT), 31 May 1905, 29–30, 2/1/10, TCP.

[65] 'For the past fifteen years we have advocated the resumption of fiscal powers wherewith to persuade Protectionist nations to be free traders, but we have never gone beyond that limit, to favour either a protective or a preferential tariff'; *Textile Mercury*, 6 Feb. 1904, 102.

[66] *Textile Mercury*, 23 Jan. 1904, 60–1, 7 May 1904, 360, 14 May 1904, 378, 10 June 1905, 401. In the summer of 1904 the *Textile Mercury* was teetering on the brink of openly espousing Chamberlain's programme. In July there was full and favourable reporting of the Commission's report on iron and steel, and the fiscal poems and cartoons that first appeared in April often had the moral of imperial preference.

[67] *Manchester City News*, 10 June 1905, 4; *Textile Recorder*, June 1905, 33; *Manchester Guardian*, 6 June 1905, 6.

'accurate' statistical treatment. But the *Report* was 'unduly alarmist', and needed to be corrected for the shift towards finer counts and the fall in prices before 1896. Chapman admitted, however, that his own index 'of exported real values [at constant prices] makes our trade seem too favourable', an admission that led one irate Free Trader to complain that he had 'concede[d] a point to the enemy unnecessarily', and led to a controversy between the two.[68] Whilst the Free Traders thus fell to arguing amongst themselves, J. Roy Campbell of the Manchester TRL pressed the argument that the rate of growth of the British industry had fallen below that of its rivals. Free Traders countered that Lancashire's smaller rate of growth represented a larger absolute increase. 'Mr. Campbell and his tariff friends may prefer the percentage increase,' concluded H. Smalley sarcastically. 'I prefer the actual increase.'[69]

Chapman's review of the *Cotton Report* in the *Economic Journal* in September covered much of the same ground, though putting more stress on quality-improvements other than fineness. His stress on the expansion of dyed goods, the most expensive piece-goods exports, was sound,[70] and he did not share the Commission's regret that trade in mixed goods, fancies, and novelties was replacing the old trade in plain goods, since the new lines were 'more remunerative to all concerned'. Overall, he viewed competition in world markets with equanimity: 'Our trade grows and we still hold the lion's share of the trade of the world'.[71] These arguments were restated in a book-length criticism of the *Cotton Report* published by the FTL in October, regarded by Hurd as a 'most elaborate document and in its way a compliment to the T.C. though it seems to have fallen very flat in the press'.[72] Chapman's *Reply* effectively conceded that employment in the industry was not keeping pace with population, and that cotton's role within the British economy might be declining; as long as this brought no hardship it was in the interests of the country, and 'ought not ... to be checked'.[73] If the Commission's prognosis was unduly pessimistic on the grounds of the historical experience available to the Edwardians, there is no doubt that the Free Traders, even the undogmatic Chapman, exhibited that Lancashire complacency so effectively lampooned by Benjamin Bowker a quarter of a century later.[74] Indeed, with the unwelcome hindsight of the 1920s, it can well be argued that the Commission foresaw the future of the cotton

[68] *Manchester Guardian*, 6 June 1905, 6–8; J. W. Hartley to Ed., *Manchester Guardian*, 8 June 1905, 5, and 16 June 1905, 4.

[69] J. R. Campbell to Ed., *Manchester Guardian*, 10 June 1905, 7; H. Smalley to Ed., *Manchester Guardian*, 13 June 1905, 3.

[70] S. J. Chapman, 'Report of Tariff Commission', 420–1; A. J. Marrison, 'Great Britain and her Rivals', 312, 316.

[71] S. J. Chapman, 'Report of Tariff Commission', 421–5.

[72] S. J. Chapman, *A Reply to the Report of the Tariff Commission on the Cotton Industry* (Manchester, 1905); Hurd to Hewins, 18 Oct. 1905, 48/89–91, HP.

[73] S. J. Chapman, *Reply*, 53.

[74] B. Bowker, *Lancashire under the Hammer* (1928).

industry more clearly than did its opponents. For the moment, however, in the early stages of Lancashire's greatest-ever boom, the Free Traders could well heed Chapman's advice to reject the 'percentage fallacy'.[75]

In criticizing the Commission's tariff recommendations, rather than its historical analysis, Chapman was correct to highlight the effect of a general tariff on the industry's input costs, a matter 'apt to be overlooked when each industry is reported upon in isolation'.[76] But of more general concern was Lancashire's fear that Tariff Reform would reduce exports by reducing imports, and would sting foreign countries into retaliation; and the greatest fear of all was that the policy would presage a modification of the Indian tariff.

Chapman's fear that India stood in greater danger from retaliation than other parts of the Empire because of the 'large balance of exports [necessary] to meet her financial obligations to England', though a common one, was weak in view of the fact that virtually all Indian exports to Europe and the US were raw materials.[77] In reality the cotton industry's concern for Indian welfare was less wholesome. In 1909 Sir Roper Lethbridge, a long-standing advocate of India's inclusion in a preferential system, wrote to the *Manchester Guardian* arguing that India would welcome and gain from such an arrangement. Mancunian William Barton could only agree, but Lancashire wanted Free Trade in the Indian market, not mere preference. William Tattersall, well known for his writings on the industry in the Manchester press, put the matter bluntly: 'There cannot be any protection of the cotton industry in our dependency' was the real demand of Lancashire.[78] It is significant that when Hewins gave a speech to 300 spinners and manufacturers in Manchester in July 1909 (an audience he would have been unlikely to attract before 1906), mentioning Indian fiscal autonomy only briefly to state that the Tariff Reformers had no definite policy upon it, question-time was dominated by cotton men afraid of losing the jewel in the Free Trade crown.[79]

In fact, the Tariff Reformers were having great difficulty with India, an issue which has largely escaped the attention of modern scholars. They were aided by the fact that, in the national debate at least, Free Traders also wished to avoid the issue, being reluctant to expose the extent to which a free trade system was forced upon an unwilling Indian people. Few had the conviction to follow Lord

[75] S. J. Chapman, *Reply*, 3.
[76] S. J. Chapman, in *Manchester Guardian*, 6 June 1905, 7–8.
[77] S. J. Chapman, *Reply*, 133; see also *Manchester Guardian*, 11 Jan. 1905, 6 for a similar argument; 'The Trade Relations of India with the United Kingdom, British Possessions and Foreign Countries—Part I', Tariff Commission Memorandum 38, 9 Nov. 1908, 17.
[78] Sir Roper Lethbridge to Ed., *Manchester Guardian*, 4 Aug. 1909, 4; W. Barton to Ed., *Manchester Guardian*, 5 Aug. 1909, 4; W. Tattersall to Ed., *Manchester Guardian*, 9 Aug. 1909, 4. See also Lethbridge, *The Indian Offer of Imperial Preference* (1913). Lethbridge had been in the Indian Civil Service in the 1860s and 1870s. As chairman of the Devon Branch of the TRL, he provided most of the few propaganda contributions of the Tariff Reformers on the Indian question.
[79] *Manchester Guardian*, 21 July 1909, 10.

Brassey, that since the Indians were protectionist 'almost to a unit', Britain only had the 'moral right' to impose free trade on India as long as she clung to the policy herself.[80] But the Tariff Reformers were also noticeably silent. Viscount Ridley's observation of 1904, that India 'still stands outside' the focus of Tariff attention, was still true in 1908, when Milner opined that the advocates of preference had devoted 'insufficient attention' to how India would fit in.[81] As late as 1909, Austen Chamberlain thought it necessary to submit a proposed statement of policy to Hewins:

A British Government cannot be expected to acquiesce in the imposition by India of differential duties against British products; but under Tariff Reform India would regain the freedom to deal as she liked with her foreign trade of which she is now deprived in deference to the prejudices of our insular Free Trade . . . Low duties within the Empire, and a free hand for every part of the Empire in dealing with its foreign trade are the ideal of Tariff Reformers . . . The essential feature of our policy is to . . . promote the development of every portion of [the Empire] by the grant of a preference to British goods in British markets everywhere throughout the world.[82]

Hewins was fearful of the public reaction to this implication of Indian fiscal autonomy, the constitutional issues it would raise, and the 'disquiet' in Lancashire. A Commission memorandum on India had already been released, but it had deferred any statement of policy on the inclusion of India in preference until a later report. He doubted 'the expediency of making a declaration on this subject without careful consultation with representatives of the Indian Council'. After reflection, Austen agreed.[83]

Three years later Hewins had shifted noticeably towards Austen's position. The Morley-Minto reforms had unintentionally afforded the Indians 'new means of giving expression to their desire for protection', and the protectionist movement in India had become so strong that it was likely to become unstoppable. The choice now lay between an autarkic Indian protectionism which would be 'fatal to Lancashire' and the incorporation of India into a policy of Tariff Reform and preference.[84] He considered the latter to be politically possible: it was only the reduction of India to the 'industrial annexe of Lancashire' that explained the nationalism of Mehta's 'Young India' party. India should be given 'adequate opportunities of developing its nascent manufacturing industries and obtaining a larger share in its vast home market' on a 'similar'

[80] Lord Brassey, *Sixty Years of Progress and the New Fiscal Policy* (1906), 111; also L. G. Chiozza Money, *Money's Fiscal Dictionary* (1910), 142.

[81] Ridley to Hewins, 10 Apr. [1904], HP; Milner in House of Lords, 20 May 1908, repr. in *The Nation and the Empire* (1913), 268.

[82] A. Chamberlain to Lethbridge (draft), 26 June 1909; Lethbridge to Chamberlain, 17 Dec. 1909, 6/4/5, TCP.

[83] Hewins to A. Chamberlain, 5 July 1909, 6/4/5, TCP; Chamberlain to Hewins, 6 July 1909, 6/4/5, TCP.

[84] Hewins to A. Chamberlain, 10 Dec. 1912, 6/4/5, TCP.

basis to the rest of the Empire, whereby '[e]ach State in the first instance organises its tariff and its policy under the system of complete autonomy to suit its own financial and economic needs, and . . . [then grants] to other parts of the Empire as large a measure of trade advantage over foreign countries as is consistent with its own economic development'.[85]

This conception was not, however, shared by Bonar Law. In 1912, when undisputed leader of the Tariff Reformers in Parliament, Law advocated tariff autonomy to India in her relations with foreign countries, but the maintainance of free trade with the UK (and perhaps the Empire). In spite of detailed arguments by Lethbridge, by now desperate to prove that even this would leave room for India to apply duties to a wide range of imports and protect a substantial part of her economy, this would have been hardly less 'hateful to Indian opinion' than the existing system.[86] But ironically, Bonar Law was now suggesting the tariff to protect Lancashire that the Tariff Commission had been unable to provide before 1906. Lancashire would have had her largest market protected from foreign competition. In the short run, this would have had little effect—in 1913 Britain provided over 90 per cent of India's total cotton imports—but the 1920s would have put a different perspective on the policy, as Japanese cotton exports to India rose inexorably, to the point where, in 1935, they exceeded those from the UK.[87]

Bonar Law's plan, of course, did not get that far. Free Traders criticized it roundly, effectively, and indeed with some hypocrisy. To George Peel, who assumed unfairly that Law intended to remove the existing Indian duty on cottons to achieve complete freedom of trade irrespective of revenue considerations, the policy was 'fraught with evil', cutting 'at the very root of that principle of mutual goodwill which is the true essence of the British Empire'.[88] But it is important to notice that the earlier Tariff Commission solution, a more orthodox preference along the lines being pressed by the white Dominions at the Colonial Conferences, was similarly unacceptable to Indian nationalist opinion. After the Fiscal Autonomy Convention and the Indian Fiscal Commission of the early post-war years, Indian tariffs and excises became the arena for a complex struggle between nationalist sentiments, the revenue needs of the Government of India, the financial interests of the City, and the interests of Lancashire. In that

[85] Hewins to A. Chamberlain, 10 Dec. 1912, 6/4/5, TCP. App. 3–5. British concessions to India would presumably have included preference on wheat. Hewins also favoured a preference on the tea duty. Since tea was price-inelastic and India dominated the market because of a shift in taste away from green to black tea, it is doubtful that such concessions would have been valuable to India.

[86] Cited in Sir R. Lethbridge, *Indian Offer*, p. iii. Bonar Law delivered an earlier and more guarded statement at the Free Trade Hall, Manchester, on 8 Nov. 1910. See his 'Tariff Reform and the Cotton Trade', *National Review*, 56 (1910–11), 588.

[87] Sir R. Lethbridge, *Indian offer*, 92–6; D. A. Farnie, *English Cotton Industry*, 127; L.G. Sandberg, *Lancashire in Decline*, 167, 182–91.

[88] G. Peel, *The Tariff Reformers* (1913), 135.

struggle Lancashire, now converted to preference as the most favourable option available, was reduced almost to a mute, conscious that if Indian policy were seen to be framed in the interests of Lancashire there would be an outcry. Whitehall might strive for a measure of preference to limit damage to Lancashire, but its refusal to put this above all else was a recognition of the inevitable.[89]

VI

By the late nineteenth century the British cotton industry had evolved to a stage where capital costs were not so significant that under-capacity working pushed up costs significantly. This is not entirely because the industry was labour- rather than capital-intensive. Rather, it reflected a situation where, both in large and small firms, labour and capital costs were both low in relation to final product-price, which was governed largely by raw-materials cost—hence the cotton master's obsession with 'margin', the difference between raw cotton and cloth prices. The Tariff Commission's analysis of the steel industry, which members hoped could become a core element in the economic case for Tariff Reform, was not universally applicable.

The disappointment which this engendered may have contributed to what was a curious shortcoming in the Commission's later industrial research. The *Engineering Report*, which appeared in 1909, was an unfocused and in many ways toothless contribution to the Tariff Reformers' arsenal. Partly this was to be explained by Hewins's failure to draft a product classification for the industry and partly by his diversion into political activity.[90] But the *Report* also failed to make sufficient of recent advances in production engineering, particularly the rise of systematic and scientific management and the emergence of mass production in US mechanical engineering.[91] Here was an obvious area where a high and stable home demand, perhaps tariff-protected, could result not only in economies through full capacity utilization, but also in radical changes in the whole basis and philosophy of production. Correct or not, the Tariff Commission's analysis of 'continuous running' was superficially just as plausible for mechanical engineering as it was for iron and steel.[92] The same was true of electrical engineering. With Commissioners of the intellectual quality and stature of Caillard, Charles Parsons, and George Flett, the omission becomes more than surprising.

---

[89] B. Chatterji, *Trade, Tariffs, and Empire* (Delhi, 1992), chs. 4–6.

[90] See Ch. 7.

[91] For the American background, see D. A. Hounshell, *From American System to Mass Production, 1800–1932* (Baltimore, 1984); D. Nelson, *Managers and Workers* (Madison, Wis., 1975).

[92] For an application of the 'continuous running' thesis to agricultural machinery (by Tariff Commissioner William Harrison), see *Monthly Notes on Tariff Reform*, Jan. 1910, 72.

It is in a way ironic that a Commission which in many ways had such an accurate vision of the future of British industrial prosperity, especially when compared with the complacent views of so many Free Traders, was curiously locked in to a traditional perspective of Britain's industrial structure. This was perhaps due, ultimately, to the fact that businessmen are seldom their own best critics. The Commission seldom dwelt on deficiencies in British production methods and capital equipment. When it did acknowledge them, it took refuge, almost automatically and reflexively, in the belief that 'scale' was the solution, and market stability the precondition. The Tariff Commission might see larger production units as the answer, but there was no recognition of wider and perhaps ultimately more fundamental changes—of the managerial structure of firms and organizational change within them, of the linking of production and distribution, and of what was later to become known as 'rationalization'. To expect appreciation of such issues is ahistorical. In the largely good years between 1905 and 1914, almost literally Britain's 'Indian summer', Britain's protectionist businessmen faced both ways. They looked to the future with apprehension, but in doing so they still carried the baggage of the past.

7

The Failure of the Scientific Tariff

The period 1906 to 1910 saw Hewins becoming more and more embroiled in Unionist Party affairs, the Commission machine becoming used more directly in support of Tariff Reform propaganda, and Commission strategy being bent to the dictates of Unionist Party unity. At a time when, as our survey of Chambers of Commerce has shown, there was a marked shift in the balance of business opinion towards Tariff Reform, it became increasingly evident to insiders that the construction of a scientific tariff, the primary purpose of the Commission, was not being achieved. There were three proximate reasons for this: the failure in later surveys to emulate the tariff schedules of the early single-industry reports, the failure to deal satisfactorily with banking and foreign investment, and the failure to produce an integrated tariff in a 'Final Report'. Behind such factors lay the political dangers in exposing concrete Tariff Reform proposals to public scrutiny, and an increasing diversion of Hewins's own attentions into political activity.

I

To the Commission, Unionist success in the 1906 election would have heralded the first step towards a mandate for preference and protection. Amongst its members, as elsewhere in the movement, hopes had run high. Leverton Harris, defending Tynemouth, had thought Tariff Reform to be 'making very rapid progress in all manufacturing centres': his Liberal opponent's canvasser had advised him to avoid the issue.[1]

But these were days when polling 43 per cent of the votes cast[2] did not form a government. Chamberlain was deeply shocked. By May 1905 he could admit to the Commission that 'We anticipated a defeat, although . . . not . . . so complete a defeat'. But the 'exceptional prosperity' of 1905 to 1906 could not long mask Britain's relative economic decline, and the election had not been 'a proper or a sufficient test of the opinion of the people'. His wish that the election should not dismay or divert the Commission reflects a lingering belief in its unique, 'non-party' character:

---

[1] Leverton Harris to Hewins, 26 Jan. 1906, 6/1/13, TCP.
[2] A. K. Russell, *Liberal Landslide* (Newton Abbot, 1973), 166.

We must all admit for the moment it would be useless to continue the agitation upon anything like a sensational scale; but it is more than ever necessary that the work of education should go on, and above all, that we should be prepared to complete the task which we have undertaken, and that when the inevitable reaction comes about we shall be fairly ready to put forward our definite and detailed proposals.[3]

Thus the Commission determined to complete the outstanding reports, or as many as possible, by the end of the parliamentary session, and to draft a 'Final Report', an overall tariff scheme which allowed for the interactions of one trade or industry upon another. Hewins thought a complete set of reports 'might powerfully affect public opinion in the autumn and next winter [1906–1907]'.[4] Chamberlain, Hewins, and Pearson all discerned an informal consensus among members that the Commission should not be turned into the 'statistical department' of the TRL:

The Commission has been supported both financially and more extensively from the evidence of important political people who are not among your [Chamberlain's] political supporters. It is doubtful whether the Commission could hand over its materials to any body which is merely propagandist in character without causing widespread discontent and distrust.[5]

Thus the Commission survived the threat of amalgamation with the League, and a guarantee fund was established to place its finances on a longer-term basis.[6]

This plan for rapid completion of the industrial reports was frustrated. What at first was regarded as the Commission's strength, its determination to explore industries in all their detail and complexity, was to be its undoing. The Commission enquired first into the simplest industries. Yet, as we have seen, even in iron and steel and cotton, designing a product classification was not without difficulties, whilst the problems posed by woollens and worsteds were even more intractable.[7] Engineering proved even worse. Whilst the replies to the questionnaires were '[e]xtraordinarily good . . . almost the strongest case we have for the application of Mr. Chamberlain's policy', Hewins was almost engulfed by the sheer amount of information. 'I thought cotton was sufficiently complicated, Wool made Cotton seem quite simple, but Engineering seems to me more complicated than all the others put together.'[8] In May 1907, the Engineering Report was still unfinished. The questionnaires had revealed 'something like 500 groups of Engineering products in regard to which Foreign importation, and dumping, is [*sic*] complained of . . . and [discovered] that most of these groups

[3] TCM (P), 3 May 1906, 2/1/5, TCP.

[4] Hewins to Chamberlain, 20 Apr. 1906, HP.

[5] Hewins to Chamberlain, 12 May 1906, HP. Needless to say, the claim of financial support from non-Tariff Reformers seems disingenuous.

[6] See below, 217.

[7] See above, Chs. 5 and 6; Mitchell to Hewins, 18 Nov. 1904, 6/1/24, TCP.

[8] Hewins to Hurd, 6 Sept. 1906, 6/1/14, TCP.

impinge on different industries, and that the Engineering industry is not one industry, but is really a large group of industries'.[9]

In trying to impose order on the data, Hewins found, as have many economic historians since, that the classification of engineering products adopted in the official returns was 'hopelessly defective', both for drafting a tariff and for ascertaining the state of trade and the extent of foreign competition. Thus there was nothing to test the accuracy of the statements of witnesses; 'the classification adopted by the Board of Trade does not correspond in the slightest degree to the Engineering industries that are carried on'.[10] Tariff Commission statistician Stanley Rosenbaum frequently plied the Board with detailed changes in the presentation of the returns and, in the continual but slow revisions in the classifications, these were usually complied with.[11]

But such changes could not be in time for the Commission's purposes. As Caillard predicted, an attempt to use the trade returns of Britain's trading partners proved relatively unsuccessful, and Hewins was far from satisfied that his attempts were doing justice to such an important industry. Late in 1908, he still found it 'extremely difficult, indeed almost impossible . . . [to draw] precise and accurate deductions as to what the state of the industry really is', and was still attempting to collect supplementary information from co-operative firms.[12] For all its length and detail, the *Engineering Report* was to contain no tariff schedule.

The reliance on official returns and industry experts in drafting an industry classification was forced on the Commission by its own inability to discover the manufacturing costs of different products, which would have allowed a more direct way of grading the tariff along lines approximating to a 'value-added' criterion in order to protect labour.[13] Nowhere, except perhaps roughly in iron and steel, had it been able to do this. In 1908, S. J. Waring, appointed a member of the Furniture Committee for the Census of Production, sent Hewins a questionnaire in which the Board of Trade sought information on net selling-value of product; fuel, raw-material, and semi-manufactured input costs; value of work given out and done for the trade, and so on. Hewins's experience was

[9] TCM (VT) 23 May 1907, 28, 2/1/14, TCP.

[10] Ibid.

[11] See e.g., Rosenbaum to Permanent Secretary of the Board of Trade [Sir Hubert Llewellyn Smith], 17 Jan. 1911; George Stanley to Rosenbaum, 30 Jan. 1911; Rosenbaum to Stanley, 5 Oct. 1911; Stanley to Rosenbaum, 24 Nov. 1911; 6/5/3, TCP. It might be noted that, even in the Liberal ministries of 1906–14, the Commission's relations with the permanent officials of the Board of Trade were always amicable, perhaps partly in view of Hewins's long-standing friendship with Hubert Llewellyn Smith. Relations with the Dominions Office were similarly cordial, though our impression is that those with the Foreign Office and Treasury were somewhat cooler! On the improvement in overseas trade statistics, see R. G. D. Allen and J. E. Ely, *International Trade Statistics* (New York, 1953), 292–3.

[12] Hewins to Watson, Laidlaw & Co. Ltd. (Glasgow), 25 Nov. 1908, 6/2/44, TCP.

[13] See above, 164–6.

that firms would be unable to answer the questions without 'due notice which would enable them to recast their accounts in such a manner as to bring out the points in question'.[14]

The keenness with which Hewins felt failure in this area and the importance he ascribed to it were shown in 1908, when Henry Angst, British Consul General in Switzerland,[15] wrote to Austen Chamberlain offering his assistance in the 'difficult and laborious task' of drafting the tariff which would be necessary when the Unionists came into power:

I should like to help your party in this, but being a Government Official find myself in a somewhat difficult position . . . On the other hand it would be of considerable use for you to know how the Swiss went to work about their tariffs . . . I might have . . . [an exposé of the tariff movement in Switzerland and the methods used to bring it about] . . . written by a thoroughly versed man *under my personal supervision*; thus my name need not appear on the face of it.[16]

Hewins, however, wanted information in only two areas, one of which need not detain us.[17] Of eleven questions he enclosed to Chamberlain for dispatch to Angst, the first six exclusively concerned the matter of costs:

(1) Does Switzerland graduate her Tariff according to the labour involved?
(2) If not merely in accordance with labour cost, what additional factors are taken into account?
(3) Is any other principle adopted in the graduation of the tariff rates?
(4) Is it possible to obtain specimens of the cost sheets submitted to the Customs officials which form the basis of the Tariff calculations?
(5) If the labour cost is taken as a guide, is the Tariff adjusted to protect the whole of the labour involved or only a percentage of that labour, and if so, what percentage?
(6) Is it possible to obtain some actual illustrations of the calculations that are made showing the method in detail?[18]

Angst could not assist, but the incident shows clearly how Hewins had been defeated in perhaps the critical part of drafting the 'scientific' tariff. This is scarcely surprising. Firms were less likely to impart information on costs to an unofficial body such as the Commission than they would have been to an official bureaucracy actually in the process of implementing a tariff. More than this, however, Hewins almost certainly had an exaggerated conception of the scientific precision with which foreign tariffs were constructed.[19]

---

[14] Waring to Hewins, 10 Feb. 1908, Hewins to Waring, 12 Feb. 1908, 6/1/33, TCP.
[15] From 1896 to 1916. See *Who Was Who*, ii. 1916–1928 (London, 1929).
[16] H. Angst to A. Chamberlain, 28 Nov. 1908, copy in 6/4/5, TCP.
[17] This concerned the technical operation of a system of drawbacks.
[18] Enclosure in Hewins to A. Chamberlain, 7 Dec. 1908, 6/4/5, TCP.
[19] F. W. Taussig, *Free Trade, the Tariff and Reciprocity* (New York, 1927), ch. 10.

The hardware industry was so immensely complicated that the report never appeared at all, even without a tariff schedule.[20] Of the glass industry, Hewins warned, 'trades . . . small in volume are frequently trades of greater complexity than the big trades on which we have reported'; though providing a mass of data, the questionnaires were still insufficient for 'detailed and precise . . . calculation of a tariff'.[21] The Commission began work on the paper classification in the summer of 1908, when Lewis Evans sent one of his clerks to sea for a week with a pile of index cards. But the results were 'of little use', inferior to the latest revision of the Board of Trade classification as used in the Census of Production. Hewins remained unhappy, and the paper classification was still undecided in 1911. When Rosenbaum sent a seven-page classification to Evans, the paper-maker thought it too complicated and recommended it be 'condensed onto the classical half sheet of notepaper'.[22]

II

Agriculture was the single exception. When the report of the Commission's Agricultural Committee appeared, shortly after the election defeat, it contained a tariff schedule which made significant modifications to the skeleton plan of food duties that Chamberlain had given at Glasgow nearly three years earlier.[23]

This schedule, however, was not based on any close hierarchy of costs according to a considered product classification. Nor did it embody the proclaimed methodology of the Commission, the 'reduction' process, which, as we have shown elsewhere, sought to ensure that British industry was protected against unfair commercial practices and superior forms of economic organization in foreign countries, not against classic 'comparative advantage'.[24] For agriculture, such niceties were discarded. The Agricultural Committee started from the assumption that there was a social benefit in protecting agriculture from New World competition. But, in pursuing this objective, they were soon to find how severely their actions were prescribed by political necessities.

The Committee recognized immediately that a duty of 2s. per quarter on foreign wheat, as hazarded by Chamberlain in his Glasgow speech, would do little to restore wheat acreage to the golden levels of the 1870s. Some members,

---

[20] TCM(VT), 3 May 1906, 7, 2/1/11, TCP. Given the severity of German competition in hardware this was doubtless a matter for regret on the Commission. See E. E. Williams, '*Made in Germany*' (1896), 53–60, for the sensationalist view; also R. J. S. Hoffman, *Great Britain and the German Trade Rivalry 1875–1914* (Philadelphia, 1933), 246, 325.

[21] TCM(VT), 31 May 1906, 17, 2/1/13, TCP.

[22] Evans to Hewins, 28 Aug. 1908; Evans to Rosenbaum, 12 Dec. 1911, 6/1/6, TCP.

[23] For a more detailed treatment of the subject of this section, see A. J. Marrison, 'The Tariff Commission, Agricultural Protection and Food Taxes, 1903–13', *Agricultural History Review*, 34 (1986), 171–87.

[24] See above, Chs. 4 and 5.

including Wiltshire bacon curer J. M. Harris, were willing to abandon the wheat duty altogether, a course resisted by Chamberlain, who saw the duty as having a symbolic importance in the Tariff Reform movement. So the 2*s.* duty was retained, though the Committee did secure Chamberlain's agreement to a 1*s.* duty on colonial wheat—as Chamberlain conceded, the Glasgow speech's exemption of colonial wheat from duty might stimulate scale economies in Canada and Australia and 'leave the [British] farmers worse off than ever'.[25]

Bolder spirits on the Committee sought a bounty on wheat production, either by a direct subsidy or by the 'earmarking' of some proportion of the revenue raised from food duties for the assistance of agriculture. But, in Britain, bounties were frowned upon in the age of the Brussels Sugar Convention, and earmarking was a practice alien to the British fiscal tradition. The Commission establishment firmly resisted such proposals. A. H. H. Matthews, secretary of the Central Chambers of Agriculture, summed up the widespread mood of resignation; bounties were 'beyond the scope of practical politics'.[26]

Chaplin and Hewins attempted to draft a scheme in which the farmer would be compensated for the inadequacy of the wheat duty by a disproportionately heavy duty on barley. This would have requried a compensating reduction of the liquor duties to prevent working-class budgets from being adversely affected. Acceptable to the brewers, the plan caused friction between malt- and grain-whiskey distillers. A heavy barley duty was also inimical to the interests of feeders, particularly producers of quality bacon such as Harris, who mounted a persistent opposition to the scheme in the Committee. In the end, barley, along with other white grains, was subject to a duty 'equivalent to that on wheat' in the Agricultural Committee's provisional tariff.[27]

Easy agreement on meat (recommended duties of 5 per cent)[28] and market-garden produce (5 to 10 per cent) could not offset a feeling of disappointment among Agricultural Committee members. It was recognized that the main hurdle was getting food duties accepted by the electorate: if these moderate proposals helped, Chaplin ventured that 'a little bit more' might be possible later on.[29] Nevertheless, there was little here to attract the farming vote, and the Committee attempted to supplement the tariff proposals with 'non-fiscal' measures of assistance. These, however, were small and cautious. The *Agricultural Report* recommended implementation of the full reduction in rural rates that Chaplin had intended when, as president of the Board of Agriculture, he had secured the

[25] TCM(VT), 11 July 1906, 11–17, 2/2/7, TCP.

[26] Ibid. ACM (VT), 22 Oct. 1906, 20, 2/2/10, TCP; 9 Nov. 1906, 4, 2/2/11, TCP.

[27] *Agricultural Report*, para. 394. The Committee also entertained the idea of a high duty on flour, but then retreated from it.

[28] The tenacious Harris also secured the inclusion of bacon in the schedule, originally excluded by Chamberlain because he thought it a main component of the diet of agricultural labourers.

[29] ACM(VT), 9 Oct. 1906, 35, 2/2/9, TCP.

passage of the Agricultural Rates Act in 1896.[30] The estimated cost to the Exchequer was only £0.75m p.a. The Committee also endorsed the latest of Jesse Collings's land-reform schemes, the Land Purchase Bill (England and Wales), a measure to provide low-interest loans to tenants wishing to purchase their holdings. The Committee's motives were avowedly electoral, and subsequently land reform was to become a more central part of Tariff Reform policy on agriculture, many Unionists hoping that such measures would 'cut at the very root of Socialism' and provide a counter to the Liberals' Land Tenure Bill.[31] But, again, there was no large public expenditure involved in the Committee's proposal. After an initial outlay of some £12m, the loan fund would have revolved, and the recurrent cost would probably have been less than £0.33m p.a.

One of the biggest ironies of Tariff Reform was that whereas, in the public mind, the agricultural community stood as one of its main beneficiaries through the iniquitous 'stomach taxes', its real position was essentially appendicular. Farmers and landowners, deeply suspicious of what they perceived as an urban–industrial movement, appreciated this. As Rider Haggard perceived, Chamberlain's policy 'was not made with any special reference to agriculture, and if agriculture did come in it would only be by a side wind'.[32] The support of the farming community was given only grudgingly, and largely on the ground that it could expect no better elsewhere. To farmers, probably the biggest of the Agricultural Committee's modifications of Chamberlain's original scheme was the non-exemption of colonial produce. But, as a gain, even this was far from secure. Even the TRL was divided over it, and in 1907 T. A. Brassey's motion supporting it was lost to Sir Joseph Lawrence's defence of the original Glasgow policy. In 1908 Lawrence was to claim that taxation of colonial wheat had 'never been adopted by the League'.[33] Though prominent Unionists such as Austen Chamberlain, Bonar Law, Ridley, and Milner endorsed the 1 shilling duty, Tariff Reformers and Unionists were divided over it in the January 1910 election campaign,[34] and it was subsequently abandoned as policy by Balfour in April 1910, nearly three years before the Unionists, under Bonar Law, officially abandoned food duties altogether.[35]

[30] *Agricultural Report*, para. 368–9. The Royal Commission on Agriculture of 1894–7 had recommended the removal of three-quarters of the rates on agricultural land, but the Exchequer had subsequently pressed for the reduction to be limited to half. See J. F. Rees, *A Short Fiscal and Financial History of England 1815–1918* (1921), 178.

[31] J. L. Green (secretary of Collings's Rural Labourer's League) to Chaplin, 9 Oct. 1906, 6/1/2 (file II), TCP; A. Sykes, *Tariff Reform in British Politics, 1903–1913* (Oxford, 1979), 199–201, 214, 263–4, 274–5.

[32] *Sheffield Daily Telegraph*, 4 Nov. 1903. See also R. Haggard, *Rural England* (1906 edn.), i. p. xiv.

[33] Lawrence to Caillard, 15 May 1909; Lawrence to Hewins, 21 Feb. 1908, 6/4/18, TCP.

[34] W. E. Dowding, *The Tariff Reform Mirage* (1913), 108.

[35] N. Blewett, *The Peers, The Parties and The People* (1972), 160; A. Sykes *Tariff Reform*, 216–17; A. M. Gollin, *The Observer and J. L. Garvin 1908–1914* (1960), chs. 4–11.

The Agricultural Committee's recognition of the political limits on aiding agriculture by a tariff, and of the consequent need to step outside fiscal policy narrowly defined, was important in the development of Conservative Party policy. As Ewen Green has argued, the Committee's work was central to the developing ideas of the 'Radical Conservatives', a group around Milner who 'stressed an organic conception of economic and social life in which all interests had to be catered for'.[36] Thus the Committee took a pioneer step in the direction that Unionist policy was to take after Bonar Law's retreat in 1913.[37]

This should not be taken to imply, however, that the collectivist vision of the Milnerites was widely shared amongst the Tariff Commissioners. Increasing competition in export markets may have led the Radical Conservatives to view British agriculture as 'the best and readiest market for [the] nation's manufac-tures',[38] but this was not a perspective discussed by the Agricultural Committee. Still less did it represent the views of the industrial and commercial members on the main body of the Tariff Commission.

Of the twenty-three members of the Agricultural Committee, seven were members of the full Commission. Only Sir William Goulding, manufacturer of agricultural feeds and fertilizers, stood to benefit precisely in this way from the market effects of a revival of rural prosperity. Of the other six, two, Chaplin and Desborough, were representatives of the landowning class; and four, Cooper, Dennis, Harris, and Phillips, were food processors or produce merchants, who bought from farmers rather than sold to them. Surprisingly, and perhaps significantly, even the two Commission members who manufactured agricultural machinery, William Harrison and Henry Marshall, did not elect to sit on the Agricultural Committee. There is no evidence here of any developed feeling on the part of manufacturers as to the critical importance of the rural market.

Such a conclusion is reinforced by examination of the joint meeting at which the Agricultural Committee and the full Commission discussed the Committee's recommendations.[39] There was some small friction over farmers' criticisms of the railway companies, but generally the industrial and commercial members of the Commission made little contribution to the proceedings. Two Commissioners, Sir Walter Peace and Sir Charles Follet, supported bounties on wheat—indeed, it was they who had actually introduced them onto the agenda some time earlier, and they were actually more enthusiastic in pressing for them than many Agricultural-Committee members. But neither was an industrialist, Peace being an imperial Commissioner and Follet Solicitor to the Board of Customs and Excise, now retired and living in the country. On the Committee's proposals to

[36] E. H. H. Green, 'Radical Conservatism in Britain, 1900–1914', unpubl. Ph. D. Thesis, Univ. of Cambridge, 1985, 224–5, 39.

[37] For Conservative agricultural policy after 1913, see A. F. Cooper, *British Agricultural Policy 1912–36* (Manchester, 1989), passim.

[38] E. H. H. Green, 'Radical Conservatism', 236–7; also 199, citing *The Tariff Dictionary* (1904).

[39] See, generally, TCM(VT), 11 July 1906, 2/2/7, TCP.

extend the protection Chamberlain had outlined at Glasgow, the industrial-commercial Commissioners were silent. Loyal Chamberlainites, they accepted the justice of an even treatment which gave some material gain to farmers and hence the inclusion of agriculture in a General Tariff. They also appreciated the need to improve the electoral popularity of Tariff Reform amongst the farming community. But there can be no doubt that they did not positively welcome food duties, and became little involved with a positive agricultural policy beyond Tariff Reform. Michael Tracy has asserted, more generally, that manufacturers wished to exclude food duties from Tariff Reform because they wished to preserve 'cheap food and cheap raw materials'.[40] But it was not the desire for cheap wages and raw materials which counted with the manufacturer—it was his fear that food taxes would destroy the chances of a Tariff Reform victory and the introduction of an industrial tariff.

III

The Tariff Commission's failure to produce an all-round, integrated tariff in which different interests were harmonized and reconciled was not due merely to the failure to produce industry classifications for more complex industries. Of equal concern was the lack of information and evidence from bankers, financiers, and merchants, who co-operated little with the Commission.

After the 1906 election the Commission was trying to reduce the size of the minor industrial reports on grounds of economy and public appeal. In such circumstances, most members, with the producer-orientated sympathies of the Tariff Reformer, were happy to postpone consideration of the views of bankers, merchants, and shipping companies until the promised Final Report. But behind this willingness lay the difficulty in mobilizing the participation of those groups. A questionnaire to merchants was drafted as early as February 1904, but response was poor. It is unclear whether a proposed replacement was actually sent out, but even if it was it would appear there were only some forty replies to both.[41] The matter of examining witnesses from the mercantile sector was also in hand in 1906, but nothing came of it.[42]

The Commission's discussion of a draft questionnaire to bankers in May 1906 revealed a belief that Britain's large visible import surplus was eating into her overseas-capital stock, a belief which had rumbled through the late-Victorian reviews and which had concerned Chamberlain since the very beginning of his

---

[40] M. Tracy, *Agriculture in Western Europe* (1st edn, 1964), 59.

[41] Form no. 2, reprinted in *Report of the Tariff Commission*, i. *The Iron and Steel Trades* (1904), para. 91, and *Report of the Tariff Commission*, ii. *The Textile Trades*, 1, *The Cotton Industry* (1905), para. 237. In addition, 45 'general merchants' returned Form no. 1, and 24 cotton merchants responded to the Textile Committee's enquiry. See TCM(P), 10–11 Feb. 1904, 2/1/4, TCP; TCM(VT), 17 May 1906, 4, 2/1/12, TCP.

[42] TCM(VT), 17 May 1906, 7–8, 2/1/12, TCP.

campaign.[43] In spite of refutations by economists such as Sir Robert Giffen,[44] the Tariff Reformers persisted in the belief. More sophisticated, Hewins sought to prove a lesser charge; if Britain was not actually disinvesting, at least she might be using earnings from foreign investment to finance her merchandise-import surplus. Giffen's work, he asserted, could not show this. In trying to assess how payment for Britain's trade deficit was divided between investment earnings and shipping earnings, Giffen, with no 'actual evidence or actual figures', had merely divided the import surplus into two, ascribing half to each; 'there was no calculation about it'. Hewins believed that if Britain could be shown to be living on her capital, or even merely using investment earnings to finance consumption, this would then prompt the question of how long Britain could continue as a pre-eminent industrial power.[45]

Those, like Caillard, with financial experience, doubted that bankers would be able to provide the information required to answer this. And Hewins conceded that, though a City man might have 'excellent information' on the 'particular branch of the business in which he is engaged', he would be unable to give aggregate figures. Rather than seeking the information from questionnaires, a more sensible approach would be to draft statistical memoranda on the principal issues and then submit them to the scrutiny of practical experts on international trade and investment, thus 'reversing the [usual] order of the investigation'.[46]

Accordingly, Rosenbaum made an ingenious attempt to split up the merchandise import surplus, around £180m p.a. in 1900–5, between earnings on overseas investments and freight earnings, and then to make estimates of the existing overseas capital stock, probably by capitalizing investment earnings according to an appropriate rate of interest. Surviving details are sketchy, but it appears that freight earnings were calculated by totalling world merchandise exports (commonly valued f.o.b.) and deducting them from world merchandise imports (c.i.f.), and then dividing the world total between countries according to their shipping returns. He also seems to have attempted a 'direct' estimate of British overseas investment and net accretions to it by investigating the Stock Exchange Register 'in great detail'. But in May 1906 the study was far from complete; Leverton Harris thought Rosenbaum's task 'Herculean'. Furthermore, the secretary was aware of the novelty of Rosenbaum's method, and perhaps therefore of its vulnerability to criticism.[47]

That Rosenbaum's scheme got little further is hardly surprising; many of the issues he faced, even such bedrock ones as the total stock of British overseas

[43] Chamberlain to Hewins, 14 July 1903, HP.

[44] A. Offer, 'Empire and Social Reform: British Overseas Investment and Domestic Politics, 1908–1914', *Historical Journal*, 26 (1983), 119–20. For Giffen, see his famous 'Are We Living on Capital?', repr. in *Economic Inquiries and Studies* (1904), ii. 283–90.

[45] TCM(VT), 17 May 1906, 17–19.

[46] TCM(VT), 31 May 1906, 2–3, 2/1/13, TCP.

[47] Ibid. 8–10.

investment, were, more or less contemporaneously, the subject of major academic studies by George Paish and C. K. Hobson, and dispute over them has continued to bedevil economic history to this day.[48] In May 1907 Caillard, chairing a meeting, reminded the Commission members that 'there still remain Shipping, the Import and Export figures and the Relation of Banking Interests to . . . Tariff Reform'.[49]

The poor response-rate from bankers and shippers demanded that the enquiry into the tertiary sector be successively postponed. Though Hewins made a virtue out of necessity by arguing that the Final Report was the logical place for examination of the service industries, there was genuine disappointment on the Commission. Mosely thought that relegation to the Final Report was undervaluing the carrying trade, 'so large a proportion' of the nation's business, whilst the Commission was informed that Chamberlain was 'most anxious to have this question [of banking] cleared up'.[50]

Indeed, the Commissioners remained confused about why the financial sector should be so entrenched in its opposition to Tariff Reform. How long could Britain remain the financial centre of the world if her manufacturing supremacy were inexorably stripped away? Phillips found it hard to understand why 'almost every banker [was] . . . opposed to Tariff Reform'.[51] Mosely argued that the centre of hostility lay with the brokers and bankers on the Stock Exchange, as opposed to 'those . . . doing a general business . . . who would benefit by the increased prosperity to the country [and who] more or less favour [Tariff Reform]'. Hewins, too, thought that 'a great many people in the City . . . are not strong opponents', a view endorsed by Vicary Gibbs.[52] However, such optimism, which may to an extent have confused the City's conservatism and imperialism with a belief in its nationalism, was never consistently held: on another occasion Hewins remarked, 'The position of the bankers is I gather that any change in our fiscal system would be disastrous to London as a banking centre.'[53] He persisted in the view that the problem lay in the bankers' inability to perceive the seriousness of the overall situation; 'the number of people in the City who

---

[48] For recent contributions to this long-running debate, see D. C. M. Platt, *Britain's Investment Overseas on the Eve of the First World War* (1986), and S. Pollard, *Britain's Prime and Britain's Decline* (1989), ch. 2. Offer, 'Empire and Social Reform', 124–9, shows that Paish's contribution to this debate was in fact heavily partisan.

[49] TCM(VT), 23 May 1907, 12, 2/1/14, TCP.

[50] TCM(VT), 17 May 1906, 7–8, 31, 2/1/12, TCP.

[51] TCM(VT), 31 May 1906, 14, 2/1/13, TCP.

[52] Ibid. 14–15; TCM(VT), 17 May 1906, 31, 2/1/12, TCP.

[53] TCM(VT), 17 May 1906, 31, 2/1/12, TCP. In Dec. 1903 H. A. Gwynne had reported similarly to Joseph Chamberlain. In spite of some support from stockbrokers and colonial bankers, most representatives of the banks and finance houses were opposed to Tariff Reform. Gwynne's memorandum is reproduced in W. Mock, *Imperiale Herrschaft und Nationales Interesse* (Stuttgart, 1982), App. IV, 393–7. Recent scholars, however, regard the *depth* of the City's opposition as somewhat uncertain. See Y. Cassis, *City Bankers, 1890–1914* (French edn., 1984; Eng. edn., Cambridge, 1994), 301–7; P. J. Cain and A. G. Hopkins, *British Imperialism: Innovation and Expansion, 1688–1914* (1993), 214–18.

can give you an accurate account of a big movement is extremely small'.[54] In May 1907, he reported that the search for prominent bankers who could see the whole sphere of international finance in overview had continued, but without success. It was still the intention to produce memoranda and take evidence, but the 'special sitting' now contemplated was scarcely comparable with the extensive examining of witnesses that had taken place in the industrial inquiries.[55]

By the Liberal budget of 1909, the Commission's attempts at enquiry into the financial sector had largely withered away. It is doubtful, however, that they would have been more successful at that time. The City was incensed by Lloyd George's predatory taxation, and it swung back to the Unionists in the elections of 1910.[56] Did this represent the same choice between 'tariff or budget' that could be discerned in the Chambers of Commerce?[57] Probably not; informed minds in the City could judge better than provincial businessmen that the Party consensus on Tariff Reform was not yet stable or secure, and they would have been more confident of their own ability to influence it. Thus, a return to their historic loyalties was simply the lesser risk. In addition, rentier and banking capital had another dimension to its choice—that of flight. Thus, the 'drain of capital' became an 'expulsion of capital', as funds flowed abroad, allegedly to escape the Goat.[58] There was little dissipation of the City's great reserves of cosmopolitanism. It may be that there was a weakness in the Tariff Reformers' strategy, that they were 'not sufficiently intent upon altering the values and priorities of the elite'.[59] Certainly, the Tariff Commission had conspicuously little success in this regard.

IV

The production of a Final Report was also made more difficult by division and uncertainty within the Unionist Party on Tariff Reform. After 1906 Hewins was prepared to admit in private, as he did to Hugo Hirst of GEC, the extent to which the Commission was involved in Tariff-Reform propaganda. It was always the Commission's claim that its work was objective, educative and scientific 'groundwork' rather than outright propaganda,[60] but there had always been a direct propaganda element. After 1906 this escalated. The Commission provided Unionist leaders like Austen Chamberlain, Balfour, and Bonar Law with information for speeches and debate, and Unionist MPs with a deluge of parliamentary questions with which to harrass the Government. Hewins's outside

[54] TCM(VT), 31 May 1906, 14, 2/1/13, TCP.
[55] TCM(VT), 23 May 1907, 23–4, 2/1/14, TCP.
[56] H. Pelling, *Social Geography of British Elections 1885–1910* (1967), Table I, 30.
[57] The phrase is from J. L. Garvin, *Tariff or Budget?* (n. d. but 1909).
[58] A. Offer, 'Empire and Social Reform' 120, quoting E. A. Sassoon.
[59] Ibid. 137.
[60] Hewins to Hirst, 9 Nov. 1911, 6/1/1, TCP.

work in TRL affairs and his own speeches in the country also became more frequent; hence he became more reluctant to forge ahead with any independent Commission strategy which might increase friction within the Party.

This was most marked in agricultural policy. The TRL clung to the exemption of colonial corn as mooted in Chamberlain's original Glasgow policy, and was similarly unwilling to accept the taxation of bacon.[61] The division within Tariff Reform ranks persisted even after the election of January 1910, and Free Trade publicists made capital out of it.[62] Hewins urged Austen Chamberlain to avoid details when answering queries, and 'merely say that the points . . . raise[d] . . . will be carefully considered before a detailed and complete scheme is drawn up'.[63] Even where there was less disagreement between Tariff Reformers, however, there was a growing reluctance to commit the Commission to detailed proposals. This was true of a system of drawback of duty on goods subsequently re-exported, and on the thornier question of duties on semi-products. Thus Hewins and assistant-secretary Hurd fended off enquiries from the Scottish agricultural districts about whether the Commission recommended duties on feedstuffs and fertilizers to protect the chemical industry.[64]

By 1907 it had not gone unnoticed by the Free Traders that the scientific tariff had still not appeared. 'I think that we shall do well to choose *our moment* for issuing our Final Report,' commented Caillard drily in a Commission meeting.[65] He explained the delay by stressing the tremendous amount of other business in which the Commission was now involved—the production of memoranda, the preparation of statistical material for the 1907 Imperial Conference, the supply of information to Tariff-Reform politicians. But his statement that the Final Report should be timed with the next general election in view stirred the conscience of the Commission. Sir John Cockburn was fearful that if the the Final Report had 'the imprimatur of party upon it . . . even a suspicion of party, its value is largely discounted'. The Commission must maintain 'its devotion to facts, and association with neither political party—an independent body pursuing the question in the interests of national welfare and enlightenment'. All were agreed: to Caillard it was not the Commission's doing that 'the Tariff Reform movement had taken a party colour', whilst Hewins argued that the Commission's relations with the Board of Trade showed it to be 'accepted as being

[61] 'A Policy for Agriculture: Tariff Reform and Imperial Preference', TRL Leaflet no. 116, [n. d.], 4 pp.; A. J. Marrison, 'The Tariff Commission', 183; on Chamberlain's agreement to the inclusion of a duty on bacon in the scheme, see Neville Chamberlain to Hewins, 25 Nov. 1906, HP.

[62] W. E. Dowding, *Tariff Reform Mirage*, 108.

[63] Hewins to Austen Chamberlain, 19 July 1907, R. E. S. Tanner (a Chippenham barley miller) to A. Chamberlain, 16 July 1907, 6/4/5, TCP.

[64] Hewins to Bonar Law, 30 Sept. 1907, 6/4/3, TCP; Hewins to Hurd, 5 Jan. 1910, 6/1/14, TCP.

[65] TCM(VT), 23 May 1907, 10, 2/1/14, TCP.

practically non-partisan, and purely official. Of course the whole effort of the Commission has been to establish that reputation, and . . . we shall not destroy it'.[66]

Many Commissioners, doubtless many other Tariff Reformers too, felt that their objectives were not subject to narrow party aims. But whether such sentiments were as sincerely held as in the heady days of 1903 to 1904 is open to doubt. The budget of 1907 broadcast the Liberal Government's adoption of the principle of graduated direct taxation, an important element in the 'fundamental difference in party philosophies' that crystallized in the years before 1914.[67] This was a time of flux; in 1919, Sir Josiah Stamp reflected that progressive taxation, though 'now wellnigh universal . . . [was] only two decades ago . . . still looked upon askance by all but advanced thinkers in this country'.[68] The need to choose between Tariff Reform and 'socialism' had become less remote, more pressing.

In autumn 1908 Hewins spoke of completion of the Final Report by the following spring. His proposal 'that the volume should not include a scheme of tariffs' was accepted by the Commission on condition that the drafting of an integrated tariff should proceed, even though it would not be expedient to publish it. Even this objective was not achieved, and by December 1909 it had been quietly changed. Now it was indicated that 'the Commission would be ready to present a draft tariff within 3 or 4 months of the accession of a Unionist ministry to power'.[69] Though not presented as such, this was a large retreat from the original purpose of the Commission, which had been to present the voters with a prepared scheme for consideration prior to an election.[70] This became clear in a statement to the Press Association in the run-up to the January election of 1910:

Assuming that a Tariff Reform Government were in office as a result of the general election, then, so far as the technical difficulties of tariff construction are concerned, there is no reason why it should not in its first Budget give a definite fulfilment of its pledges to the country . . . Provisional schemes published by the Tariff Commission show that there are practical methods of carrying out a Tariff Reform policy, that those methods would not disturb existing interests, . . . and that they would meet with the approval of the vast majority of the business firms of the country.[71]

Thus, from late 1908 onwards, the original intention to publish a draft overall tariff before a Tariff Reform government came into power had gradually been

---

[66] TCM(VT), 23 May 1907, 14–16, 2/1/14, TCP.

[67] H. V. Emy, 'The Impact of Financial Policy on English Party Politics before 1914', *Historical Journal*, 15 (1972), 126–7, 131.

[68] Sir Josiah Stamp, *The Fundamental Principles of Taxation in the Light of Modern Developments* (1921), 38.

[69] TCM(P), 28 Oct. 1908, 20 Dec. 1909, 2/1/5, TCP.

[70] See above, 34–6

[71] 'The Introduction of Tariff Reform. Statement by the Secretary of the Tariff Commission'; copy in Hewins to Blumenfeld, 10 Jan. 1910, 6/1/26, TCP.

dropped. There were occasional expressions of dissatisfaction. In 1911, sugar refiner Charles Lyle refused to contribute further to the funds. After nearly ten years' work the Commission 'has not yet done what it was originally formed to do, viz. to frame a tariff; and it has developed into a statistical bureau doing, no doubt, good work but work I am not inclined to participate in'.[72] But Lyle had other grounds for discontent, and most appear to have accepted the retreat in silence.

In fact, even the Commission's new, reduced objective was probably optimistic given the technical difficulties still to be overcome. In February 1910, ex-Chancellor Austen Chamberlain doubted that the planning stage of a Unionist tariff had been reduced to three or four months: 'a Tariff Reform Budget cannot, in spite of all Hewins may say, be produced at a moment's notice'.[73] Alfred Mond put the matter more pungently: 'There is not one single item of the elementary machinery of a tariff which this great and almighty Commission, with this learned professor of economics as its secretary, has yet endeavoured to handle'.[74] Mond surely knew that the Commission's difficulties lay as much in publicizing its recommendations as in formulating them. But, whilst many of his criticisms were unjustified, his verdict on the precise issue of tariff formulation was substantially correct.

V

The sensitivity of the Commission's position was further heightened by the emergence of a special relationship between Hewins and Balfour in the aftermath of the 1906 election defeat. Whilst contemporary estimates that two-thirds of the Unionists returned in the 1906 election were Tariff Reformers overestimated the strength of the fully committed whole-hoggers, Balfour clearly had to reach some accomodation with the Chamberlainites. At Austen Chamberlain's instigation, Hewins was deliberately used as the vehicle to effect the conversion of the formerly reluctant and equivocal leader. Most scholars accept that Hewins had a significant influence, not necessarily in turning Balfour around, but in facilitating his move to a new position that circumstance dictated.[75]

Indeed, it has been argued that Balfour's conversion to Tariff Reform was not a one-way affair. In the process, Tariff Reform became narrower than the Chamberlainite vision of constructive imperialism. In a major work of revisionism, Alan Sykes established the new orthodoxy. 'In all probability, the tariff

---

[72] Lyle to Richard Burbidge, 23 June 1911, 6/2/26, TCP.

[73] A. Chamberlain, *Politics from Inside* (1936), 209.

[74] Alfred Mond at the Memorial Hall, Manchester; reported in *Manchester Guardian*, 24 July 1909, 10.

[75] A. Sykes, *Tariff Reform*, 100, 129–30; F. Coetzee, *For Party or Country* (New York, 1990), 72, 88.

reformers, the whole-hoggers, had always been a small minority within the party.' After the 1906 election, in Balfour's hands and with the tacit approval of the moderate bulk of the parliamentary Party, the policy became one used in the defence of traditional Conservative concerns, particularly the domestic fight against progressive taxation and income redistribution, rather than one in which a genuinely imperial and collectivist policy was seen as a tool for uniting the classes in an organic conception of society.[76]

Even this, however, was a long process, in view of Balfour's reluctance to commit a party in opposition to a specific policy. The Valentine letters of February 1906 recognized fiscal reform as 'the first constructive work of the Unionist Party' and declared that a moderate general tariff on manufactures and a small duty on foreign corn were 'not in principle objectionable',[77] but were so steeped in qualifications that there was no real advance in Balfour's position. By late 1906 frustration was mounting in the TRL and amongst the more advanced Tariff Reformers within the Unionist Party.

It was during the course of 1907 that Balfour's conversion became apparent, his speeches to the National Union at the Savoy Hotel in February and at Birmingham in November being the best outward manifestations of the beginning and the end of the process.[78] During these months Balfour and Hewins were in close contact. Austen Chamberlain contrived to bring the two together late in 1906. Hewins's account of his first meetings with Balfour shows him to have come at least partially under the influence of the ex-premier. Balfour convinced Hewins that, but for electoral hostility to food taxes, he was in favour of Tariff Reform. Though Balfour was 'unduly sensitive to inaccuracies of expression', and particularly distrustful of the TRL, Hewins nevertheless discerned no 'substantial difference as to aims or methods between what [Joseph] Chamberlain wants and what Balfour wants'.[79]

Hewins may have fallen under Balfour's guileful charms and known talent for flattery, but Balfour was equally taken by Hewins's intellectual approach and detailed grasp of the vast subject. He confided to his private secretary that it was 'very agreeable talking to a fiscal reformer who really knows something about his case'.[80] The relationship that developed between the two, though at its most significant in 1907, was to last to 1910 and beyond. Long after the responsibilities of leadership had been removed from his shoulders Balfour was a close ally of Hewins on the Balfour of Burleigh Committee in the Great War.[81]

---

[76] A. Sykes, *Tariff Reform*, chs. 5–6, 9–10, quot. 286. The following paragraphs lean heavily on Sykes's analysis as a framework.

[77] Balfour to Joseph Chamberlain, 14 Feb. 1906, in J. Amery, *Life of Joseph Chamberlain*, vi. (1969), 846–7.

[78] A. Sykes, *Tariff Reform*, 131–2, 140–44.

[79] W. A. S. Hewins, *The Apologia of an Imperialist* (1929), i. 187.

[80] Quoted in F. Coetzee, *For Party or Country*, 88.

[81] See below, 253.

The first meetings took place when Balfour was under pressure from Austen to put a fiscal amendment to the Address on preference, which would in effect commit the Party to food taxes. Balfour resisted, but at an early stage his exchanges with Hewins provided an avenue for accommodation.[82] Hewins suggested that weight should be put upon the danger of imperial disintegration if the dominions were forced into negotiation with foreign powers by Britain's refusal to consider preference. Early in 1907 he sketched an outline that he was to develop in correspondence over the next four years. Canada was the centrepiece, at a watershed where her future economic relations could develop either in the direction of imperial preference or trade treaties with the major powers. The prospect of Canada negotiating new arrangements with Germany to end more than a decade of trade war, and simultaneously entering into reciprocity with the USA, was particularly disturbing to Balfour. Hewins's line of attack also fitted with Balfour's conviction that the business of the opposition was to oppose. 'To make the British public understand the fiscal perils which are ahead is certainly much more our duty while we are in Opposition than to make ourselves responsible for any special scheme for meeting them when they arise'.[83]

Balfour was impressed both by Hewins's knowledge of the intricate pattern of world trade treaties and by his sources of intelligence on events within the dominion legislatures. Demonstrations of the colonial support for preference at the Colonial Conference in April 1907 confirmed the authority of Hewins's arguments, and Balfour became quite active in criticizing the government for the jeopardy in which inaction on preference was placing Empire relations. After the Conference had ended, however, attention became diverted towards domestic issues.[84]

The immediate cause was Asquith's budget of 1907, but this was in a wider context of rising government expenditure, the emergence of Labour, and social reform, all closely related. After the 1906 election defeat, Joseph Chamberlain had quickly sensed the need for the Tariff Reformers to develop a constructive social reform policy, to prevent the Liberals from establishing a monopoly in this area and to help regain working-class votes.[85] Other Chamberlainites soon went further, analysing the future in terms of an inevitable conflict between radical imperialism and insular socialism. At Wolverhampton, Alfred Milner did not shrink from labelling his own combination of imperialism and social reform 'a nobler Socialism', the alternative to an 'odious form' which thrived upon confiscation and class hatred.[86]

---

[82] A. Sykes, *Tariff Reform*, 127.

[83] Hewins to Balfour, 25 Jan. 1907 (two letters), 3 and 12 Feb. 1907, 23 Mar. 1907, 13 and 23 Apr. 1907, 11 Oct. 1907, 26 Nov. 1907, 30 Dec. 1907, 10 Jan. 1908, 10 and 13 June 1908, 22 July 1908, 26 May 1909, 12 Apr. 1910, Add. Mss. 49779, xcvii, Balfour Papers.

[84] e.g. Hewins to Balfour, 25 Jan., 23 Apr. and 30 Dec. 1907, enclosing Deakin to Hewins, 27 Nov. 1907; Add. Mss. 49779, xcvii, Balfour Papers.

[85] A. Sykes, *Tariff Reform*, 107.

[86] Milner at Wolverhampton, 17 Dec. 1906, in A. Milner, *The Nation and the Empire* (1913), 152–63.

Balfour doubtless found the full dosage of Milnerite collectivism distasteful, but disagreement with the remedy implied no disagreement with the diagnosis. Balfour had been shaken by the emergence of Labour, and recognized the inexorable pressure on the public purse that was likely to follow. If this was inevitable, then it must be met by means other than confiscatory taxation. At the Savoy Hotel, before he became fired by Hewins's imperial enthusiasms, he effectively ranked the priorities of a Tariff Reform policy—firstly, a broader tax-base; secondly, safeguarding of industry from unfair competition; thirdly, retaliation and reciprocity; and fourthly, preference.[87]

This shift in emphasis, towards revenue and away from preference, had, paradoxically, been facilitated by the arguments Hewins had used to catch Balfour's interest in the imperial dimension. Aware of Balfour's cautious nature, he had emphasized the 'moderacy' of the scheme necessary to unite the Empire. Though reduced, there remained a wide margin for negotiation in the new Canadian tariff, and even Britain's adoption of a 'system of low revenue duties' would still allow the conclusion of a preferential scheme welcome to all Canadian interests. The semantics of the way Hewins used the words 'low' and 'revenue' in relation to import duties are interesting. The word 'low' was clearly justified when comparing Tariff Commission recommendations with the tariffs prevailing abroad, but was then used to imply a moderacy of approach within the British political context. At the same time, Hewins almost made a definitional equation of a 'low' tariff with a 'revenue' tariff. In this way, a revenue tariff could achieve a protective effect.[88]

Neither the need for revenue nor the concept of tariff moderacy were novel features in the persuasive techniques of the Tariff Reformers, but Hewins used them systematically when dealing with Balfour. On one level, this simply reflected the need to bring Balfour on. It is significant that the 'four-fold Birmingham resolution' in November, which harked back to the Savoy Hotel speech and endorsed Balfour's priority on revenue, was proposed by Tariff Commissioner Henry Chaplin.[89] But, on another level, there was a link with Commission claims before the election that modest duties would have a significant effect. Thus, for Hewins, emphasis on revenue and on moderacy held no implication that protection had been forgotten. Even a moderate scheme of duties would 'have the desired effect of safeguarding our great industries' from instability and unfair competition. But it was downgraded: 'our tariff... would be a revenue tariff, not protective as in the United States'.[90] In 1908 Hewins reminded Balfour, slightly inaccurately, that the maximum duty

[87] A. Sykes, *Tariff Reform*, 131.

[88] Hewins to Balfour, 25 Jan. 1907, 11 Feb. 1907, 26 July 1909, Add. Mss. 49779, xcvii, Balfour Papers.

[89] A. Sykes, *Tariff Reform*, 141.

[90] Hewins to Balfour, 16 Jan. 1908, Add. Mss. 49779, xcvii, Balfour Papers.

advocated by the Tariff Commission was 10 per cent, and the average duty considerably less.[91]

This should not be taken to imply that Hewins was only concerned with the tactics of Balfour's conversion and was unconcerned about revenue. Here he fully shared the anxieties of other Unionists, radical imperialists and moderates alike. Tariff Reformers knew that the 1907 budget presented them with a clear opportunity for gain; if wealthier Free Traders were confronted with the inevitability of increased public expenditure and the choice of rises in direct or indirect taxation to pay for it, their priorities might well change. Austen Chamberlain posed the choice in the *Outlook* in January 1907, a choice between Tariff Reform and 'robbery or jobbery'.[92] The question was no longer whether to have social reform or not, but rather who should pay.

In his advice to Balfour, Hewins implicitly recognized that, whilst middle- and higher-income earners might vote against 'robbery', the mass of the electorate might demonstrate a cheerful lack of concern. The Tariff Reformers had to rest their case on more than a debatable concept of 'justice'. The Milnerite solution was to offer a positive programme of social reform to recapture the Tory Democracy. Hewins's emphasis was different. If Milner saw social reform as good business, Hewins mounted a businessman's opposition to Liberal methods of public finance. Asquith's budget suffered from two defects. The first was that it brought direct taxes, and existing indirect taxes, nearer to their elastic limit. The high level of income tax was in itself a problem, but also the lowering of the tax threshold to £160 would cause resentment from large numbers of foremen, clerical workers, and 'superior' workmen. Along with this went immense problems of administration:

The proposed extension of income tax to working-class incomes by extracting a compulsory return from employers could not be administered without very great friction, because in many industries where working men nominally earn above the income tax limit the amounts with wh[ich] they are credited are not the net amounts received. It w[oul]d be necessary to devise machinery to deal with a whole new class of deductions wh[ich] are extraordinarily difficult to estimate.[93]

In retrospect, this was unduly alarmist. Austen Chamberlain thought the 1907 budget 'sound' and 'not an easy budget to fight', and ironically Asquith was aided by inheriting a budget surplus from Austen himself.[94] Even applied to Lloyd George's later budgets, Hewins's argument would have had its weaknesses.

---

[91] Ibid.

[92] Quoted in B. K. Murray, *The People's Budget, 1909/10* (Oxford, 1980), 88; for an earlier statement, Austen Chamberlain in House of Commons, 16 May 1906, *Parliamentary Debates* (4th Series, clvii), 520–9.

[93] 'Inelasticity of the Present Revenues', Hewins to Balfour, 15 July 1907, Add. Mss. 49779, xcvii, Balfour Papers.

[94] A. Chamberlain, *Politics from Inside*, 70–1; T. Balderston, 'War Finance and Inflation in Britain and Germany, 1914–1918', *Economic History Review*, 42 (1989), 231–3.

Lloyd George's success in 1909 lay in providing a financial basis for social reform which bore heavily neither on the working classes nor on the less-affluent income-tax payers.[95] But, accurate or not, Hewins's argument gave a sort of academic justification to those whose real opposition was based on 'robbery'. Tariff Reform, broad or narrow, became the alternative not only to the budget but to an unworkable budget.

The second defect posed an even darker threat, and here Hewins's criticism was less vulnerable to falsification. Income tax 'becomes a fixed charge upon the industry of the country which must be taken into account in all calculations as to costs', whilst the new distinction between earned and unearned incomes would discriminate against public companies and in favour of partnerships, thus acting 'as a premium against what has proved to be the most economic form of business organisation'.[96] In other words, Asquith's approach would raise wages, act as a tax on employment, and discourage the development of the large company at a time when Britain was struggling to maintain her competitiveness and her place in world markets.

Clearly this was a 'business' argument, a producer-orientated argument that the hard-pressed, hard-faced businessman of the 1920s would have recognized. It does suggest that Hewins was not attracted to any radical coupling of Tariff Reform with social reform in a Milnerite package. This is further confirmed by Hewins's reaction to Henderson's Sweated Industries Bill, a measure close to Milnerite sympathies and not beyond the interest of Austen Chamberlain.[97] Advising Balfour to lend the Bill no support, Hewins declared himself against any attempt 'to enforce by law the theory of the Legal Minimum Wage'. Discerning the influence of the Webbs, he interpreted the bill 'not [as] the outcome of a ... demand on the part of the employers and workers concerned, but [as] the result of vicarious philanthropic zeal'.[98]

This is significant because Hewins has been closely identified with Amery, Garvin, and Mackinder as one of a small but dynamic group of Milnerites which led the League into its 'most aggressive period' with policies which closely identified Tariff Reform with social reform.[99] Furthermore, Hewins might well be thought to have had the credentials for membership of such a club. As a prominent Historical Economist, he was likely to bring the ethical concerns of

[95] B. K. Murray, *People's Budget, passim.*

[96] Hewins to Balfour, 15 July 1907, Add. Mss. 49779, xcvii, Balfour Papers.

[97] A. Sykes, *Tariff Reform*, 195–7.

[98] Hewins to Balfour, 19 Feb. 1908, Add. Mss. 49779, xcvii, Balfour Papers. Hewins was, however, aware of the likely opposition of Ramsay MacDonald to Henderson's scheme. For background, see J. A. Schmeichen, *Sweated Industries and Sweated Labour* (1984), ch. 7.

[99] R. J. Scally, *The Origins of the Lloyd George Coalition* (Princeton, 1975), 95. For Garvin's excellence as a propagandist, see A. M. Gollin, *Observer and J. L. Garvin, passim.* For Amery, see *My Political Life*, i (1953), 242–56, esp. 247.

that group into politics.[100] In May 1903 he had told fellow Co-efficient Sidney Webb that Tariff Reform would necessarily involve a 'social and labour policy'. He was also a member of the Compatriots' Club, and in places his sixteen articles in *The Times* in 1903 anticipated Garvin's 'doctrine of development' and Mackinder's geopolitics, propounding a neo-mercantilist, stage theory of economic development in which the future lay with great empires, each of which went through defined stages of development. As late as the eve of the First World War he was a member of the Unionist Social Reform Committee, whilst twenty years later he was to reflect that 'Conservatism divorced from its historic policy of social reform had no chance whatever in the country'.[101] For their part, the Milnerite group of Tariff Reformers were certainly prone to citing the Tariff Commission as authority for the economic aspects of their vision.[102]

Hewins's direction of the Tariff Commission squared with his advice to Balfour. With Chamberlain's illness, and with most of the Tariff Commission MPs defeated in the 1906 election, he was now more than ever the person who dictated the Commission's role in the Tariff Reform movement and its relationship with the TRL and the Unionist Party. He was clearly in a position to introduce into Commission business the matter of recharging Tariff Reform policy with socially orientated measures. He did not do so. Just as his lack of emphasis on defence and the naval question distinguished his position from that of Garvin and the other members of Milner's radical circle,[103] so, too, his direction of the Commission put little emphasis on social reform. In stressing what he claimed was the impracticability of Liberal taxation policy, he recognized the inevitability of increased expenditure on social programmes, but outwardly the Commission stayed neutral on social reform.

Even in 1903 to 1906, the heyday of Chamberlainite radical imperialism, the Commission acted as a group of businessmen who saw Tariff Reform as a tool of commercial policy and industrial regeneration, with social betterment a consequence—it would be unfair to say a by-product. Hewins had an exposure to business opinion unparalleled in the movement, and believed in business solutions. Whilst he shared with the Milnerites a belief in the dynamic welfare benefits of growth, he put less weight on the social-reform or distributional elements, believing that the working class would benefit naturally from the correct economic organization of society. Without being unduly cynical, it might

---

[100] G. M. Koot, *English Historical Economics, 1870–1926* (Cambridge, 1987), esp. 1–2, 118–19.

[101] Hewins to Sidney Webb, 31 May 1903, quoted in R. J. Scally, *The Lloyd George Coalition*, 90; A. J. Marrison, 'British Businessmen and the "Scientific" Tariff: A Study of Joseph Chamberlain's Tariff Commission, 1903–1921', unpubl. Ph. D. thesis, Univ. of Hull, 1980, ch. 2; J. Ridley, 'The Unionist Social Reform Committee, 1911–1914: Wets before the Deluge', *Historical Journal*, 30 (1987), 391–413; W. A. S. Hewins, *Apologia*, i. 251.

[102] Milner at Rugby, 19 Nov. 1907, in A. Milner, *Nation and Empire*, 245–6. Interestingly, Milner also emphasized the moderacy of the Tariff Reformers' schemes.

[103] P. Yule, 'The Tariff Reform Movement and Germany, 1900–14', *Moirae*, 7 (1982), 1–8.

also be observed that he was alone amongst the advanced Tariff Reformers in being dependent on business support for his personal income.

In addition, management of the Commission had changed Hewins, given him the taste for high politics. Originally an academic like Milner and Amery, and a theorist like all the TRL clique, he had now developed a love of bureaucratic process, with its political manœuvring and its technical complexity. Beatrice Webb captured his reaction to the defeat of 1906:

From his private point of view it is a catastrophe: he thought, I am convinced, that in a few years, if not immediately, he would be arranging tariffs, and tariff wars, and tariff treaties, at the Board of Trade—hurrying from continent to continent, in close and confidential intercourse with ministers and great financial personages—one long, delightful intrigue with a World Empire as a result.[104]

As a partial exception to Hewins's and the Commission's indifference to social reform, we should mention again the Agricultural Committee's measures to assist agriculture, significant because they took a direction compatible with the main thrust of the Milnerites' collectivism.[105] These, however, were small and limited, and had received direct endorsement from Chamberlain. They also harked back to a long-standing Conservative interest in land reform, and had a powerful advocate on the Committee in Chaplin. The businessmen on the main Commission accepted this; they were willing to follow Joseph and Austen Chamberlain in seeing in the revenue from Tariff Reform some scope for agricultural assistance.[106] That they had any broader ideal of economic and social regeneration of the countryside is unsubstantiated and improbable.

The Commission's potential for collectivist policies in more conventional areas was even more limited. More radical Tariff Reformers might support social legislation on old-age pensions, sickness insurance, regulation of sweated industries and working hours, statutory holidays for certain trades, and a minimum wage,[107] but none of these were concerns of the Commissioners, who would certainly have seen legislative controls as vexatious. The radicals also put considerable emphasis on reducing unemployment. This was an issue on which the business Tariff Reformer could agree—the tariff itself would be the curative and no public expenditure would be involved. Even here, however, the Commission expended little effort. Of twenty-five memoranda issued between January 1906 and October 1913, only one touched upon unemployment—four out of a total of 548 published pages—and even that was confined to discussing the difficulties of international comparison, without any statement on policy at all.[108]

[104] B. Webb, *Our Partnership* (1948), 328–9.
[105] E. H. H. Green, 'Radical Conservatism', 236–7; A. F. Cooper, *British Agricultural Policy, passim*.
[106] For Joseph Chamberlain's reaction to the *Report*, see Mary Chamberlain to Hewins, 24 Nov. 1906, Neville Chamberlain to Hewins, 25 Nov. 1906, HP.
[107] A. Sykes, *Tariff Reform*, 195–7.
[108] Tariff Commission, 'Unemployment', Memorandum no. 37, 23 Mar. 1908.

The Commission's earlier discussion of the effect of Tariff Reform on wages during the iron-and-steel inquiry had also shown a distinct reluctance to promise an advance in wages consequent upon the policy.[109] As it was proselytized by the Commission, the Tariff-Reform appeal to labour was that 'continuous running' would allow high wages and employment levels. It was essentially a business approach—indeed, one is reminded of Henry Ford and the 'five-dollar day'.[110] It was an approach which was to emerge intensified after the Great War, little changed save for the increased urgency of warnings against labour militancy and restrictionism, in business groups which were clearly conservative rather than radical.[111] For the Commission, the welfare benefits of Tariff Reform were to be achieved through growth rather than social reform, and through labour passivity rather than labour participation.

Though he could stay aloof from the social concerns of the Milnerites, Hewins's tactics in his contacts with Balfour signified no fundamental retreat from the imperial or the protectionist objectives of Tariff Reform. His creed had always been that Empire and domestic economy would be intertwined. The position of Hewins and the Commission in the spectrum of Tariff Reform politics after 1906 was one in which, by silence, conflict with the radical social-imperialist and reformist accent of the Milnerites was avoided, and the claims of radical economic imperialism were pressed upon Balfour by an appeal to essentially conservative principles of moderacy, and to what was becoming the essentially conservative principle of non-progressive taxation. To this extent, the Commission conspired in the conversion of a radical policy to conservative ends.

Hewins did, however, stay loyal to the Commission's agricultural policy. That Balfour's conversion to Tariff Reform was based primarily on expediency was perhaps shown when he bowed to the pressure of the moderates and abandoned the Commission's proposed 1*s.* duty on colonial corn in 1911. In effect, this increased the weight of preference in the Tariff Reformers' policy, but Hewins chose to support the British farmer in his protests to Balfour.[112] The same was true when Bonar Law abandoned food taxes altogether in 1913. There were some Commission members, such as Leverton Harris, who responded with what could earlier have been regarded as Balfourite pragmatism. Unless food taxes

---

[109] See above, Ch. 5.

[110] D. A. Hounshell, *From the American System to Mass Production, 1800–1932: The Development of Manufacturing Technology in the United States* (Baltimore, 1984), 256–9. It should be noted that Green's insistence ('Radical Conservatism', 324) that the Tariff Reformers' constant emphasis on improving employment was a radical component of their policy causes particular difficulty for the study of business Tariff Reformers. Businessmen could, and indeed did, endorse such a strategy. But the motive was more questionable. The protectionist manufacturer would find it easy to embrace the employment objectives, but he would gain directly whether or not these were achieved.

[111] See below, Ch. 11.

[112] A. Sykes, *Tariff Reform*, 216–17.

were abandoned for the moment, the Unionists would 'imperil the defeat of Home Rule, Welsh Disestablishment, Land Robbery, etc.—in fact the defeat of everything our supporters want defeated'. To Goulding, in Ireland, the priority was even more straightforward: 'here we are full up with the Home Rule defence which is a far more important matter to us, as a case of existance [*sic*]'. But effectively condoning Chaplin's agitation against Bonar Law's retreat in the rural districts, Hewins remonstrated with Unionist Central Office. Agriculture would be harmed by 'a purely urban policy of industrial protection'.[113] He left unsaid that preference was similarly vulnerable to an abandonment of food duties.

Hewins may on occasion have spoken in a more radical voice when making speeches for the League, but in general any potential for social radicalism which he may have possessed at the outset of the Tariff Reform campaign did not develop. What emerged instead was a desire to work within the orthodox structures of the Unionist Party. In December 1907 his name was canvassed as Unionist candidate for West Wolverhampton, apparently with the support of the two Chamberlains and Sir Alfred Hickman. By October 1908 he claimed to have been approached in regard to eight more constituencies.[114] At the time he was adopted as the Unionist candidate for the Shipley division in the last week of 1909 his parliamentary ambitions had, according to his memoirs, 'dated back for many years'.[115] Unsuccessful at Shipley, Hewins fought the Middleton division of Lancashire twice, in December 1910 and at a by-election in 1911, before being elected unopposed for Hereford in 1912.

VI

After the 1906 election Hewins wrote an informal policy document which seemed for the first time to accept a conscious and deliberate political role for the Commission. The Commission should increase its output of memoranda on specific problems related to trade policy, 'in view of the fact that the Unionist Party is now committed to a Fiscal Campaign, but has no official body of experts to present the case in regard to concrete questions that arise'.[116] Even more explicit was the desire to 'develop the machinery which is already in embryo for instructing Members [of Parliament]'. Though Hewins might still bluster about the neutral role of the Commission as a body of experts on the construction of tariffs and their effects in public, this was a distinct move towards acceptance of a direct political function. That the majority of members acquiesced with at least

---

[113] Leverton Harris to Austen Chamberlain, 4 Jan. 1913, AC 9/5/33, ACP; W. Goulding to Hewins, 1 Dec. 1911, 6/1/11, TCP; Hewins to A. D. Steel-Maitland, 17 Nov. 1913, HP.
[114] Hewins to Sandars, 2 Mar. 1910, Add. Mss. 49779, xcvii, BP.
[115] W. A. S. Hewins, *Apologia*, i. 248.
[116] Hewins to Pearson, 19 Feb. 1906, 6/1/26, TCP.

some degree of enthusiasm is shown by the fact that no less than 38 of the 48 surviving original members either attended or contributed to finance after the December election of 1910.

Also in 1906, a guarantee fund was established to 'maintain the Commission in a state of efficiency' for five years. Some £2,500 to 3,000 p.a. was pledged, in addition to a timely donation of £1,000 from Chamberlain. But annual expenditure averaged nearly £7,200 in 1906 to 1907, and Hewins calculated that an extra £2,500 p.a. was needed to maintain current levels of operation and ensure completion of the reports. The fund was not intended as sufficient in itself for Commission needs, but as a stable base to be topped up by less predictable contributions. As its partial failure was realized, other fund-raising was stepped up. With Chamberlain's support members 'unanimously agreed' to arrange meetings between Hewins and local businessmen in their localities, and a postal appeal was mounted as well. By September 1907, £1,860 had been raised by these methods. This was regarded as insufficient by Hurd and Rosenbaum, who wanted to institute a massive postal appeal, but Hewins, who thought the response 'not too bad' in post-election circumstances, was less convinced that their suggestion would prove profitable.[117]

These were years of financial stringency. The worst was 1907, and 1909 was the only other year when donations totalled less than £6,000; but even in the relatively good year of 1908, when trade was bad, the position was difficult. Hewins pointed to the obligation to 'supply information throughout the movement', in addition to expenses incurred in continuing the original project.[118] In seeking funds, Burbidge took the typically optimistic Tariff-Reform view that there would be an election early in 1909 and this would 'probably' be the last call he would have to make on members, but reminded them that the £2,070 received in the second half of 1908 was very low. By July 1909 Rank was meeting with Burbidge 'with regard to the liquidating of the debt on the working of the Tariff Commission'. Even the imminence of the first election of 1910 did little to attract funds. In November 1909 Burbidge wrote to S. J. Waring that 'the interest of our old supporters now seems to be flagging . . . financially, presumably because they think now we are nearing our goal, little money will be needed, and not a few, no doubt, feel that having done their share, others must come forward'. In fact, the position had improved slightly in 1909; during the first six months expenditure exceeded income by £914, in the second there was a surplus of £404. But at the end of November, despite office economies, reserves were running low, and in December 1909, with a January

---

[117] Hurd to Levinstein, 29 June 1907, 6/1/21, TCP; Caillard to Rank, 13 Nov. 1906, 6/1/28, TCP; Hewins to Chamberlain, undated copy, *c.* June 1907, HP; Chamberlain to Hewins, 24 June 1907, HP; Hewins to Eckersley (circular), 29 June 1907, 6/1/5, TCP; Hurd to Hewins, 5 and 14 Sept. 1907, Hewins to Hurd, 17 Sept 1907, 6/1/14, TCP.
[118] Hewins to Keswick, 8 May 1908; 6/1/20, TCP.

election now inevitable, Burbidge urged the raising of £5,000 for 'immediate contingencies'.[119]

Thus, for the Commission at least, the period after the 1906 election was difficult for sustaining Tariff Reform agitation. In particular, as is shown in Table 8, the Commission was much less well endowed than the League for the campaigns of 1909 and 1910. The Commission undoubtedly obtained a higher proportion of its funds from businessmen than did the League. That it experienced financial difficulties in spite of our finding that, in the Chambers of Commerce, these years saw a pronounced increase in business sentiment in favour of Tariff Reform suggests that businessmen took a pragmatic view of the realism of influencing the Liberal Governments, as well as raising the possibility that the healthiness of League provision during this period was due to an increasing level of support from the non-industrial middle classes of the South, resentful of financing social reforms by progressive taxation. Of course, the two groups were not exclusive, and it may simply be that the League was seen as more likely to influence the political outcome, so that new donors increasingly

TABLE 8. *Finances of TRL and Tariff Commission: 1903–1915* [All TRL figures are approximate or estimates]

	TRL		Tariff, Commission
1903	13,000[a]	(approx. income)	—
1904	14,000[b]	(approx. income)	10,364
1905	20,819	(estimated expenditure)	7,673
1906	14,000	(expenditure)	7,410
	12,400	(Jan–June income × 2)	
1907	17,000	(Jan–June income × 2)	4,687
1908	24,200	(Jan–June income × 2)	7,743
1909	42,000+	(income)	5,945
1910	33,000	(income)	n.a.
1911	16,600	(income)	5,125
1912	n.a.		3,474
1913	n.a.		4,994[e]
1914	n.a.		3,527[d]
1915	n.a.		5,220[e]

[a] Excludes donations and subscriptions under £50.
[b] May exclude donations and subscriptions under £50.
[c] Includes £2,500 from the Imperial Fund.
[d] Includes £1,635 from the Imperial Fund.
[e] Includes £2,050 from the Imperial Fund and £2,000 from Sir Vincent Caillard.
Sources: (TRL) F. Coetzee, 'Pressure Groups, Tory Businessmen and the Aura of Political Corruption before the First World War', *Historical Journal*, 29 (1986), 839–40; A. Chamberlain, *Politics from Inside* (London, 1936), 131.
(TC) 'Summary of Income and Expenditure for the Five Years 1904–1908', and Income and Expenditure Accounts, 1909–1915; TCP.

[119] Burbidge to Rank, 4 Dec. 1908, Rank to Burbidge, 7 Dec. 1908, Burbidge to Rank, 12 Dec. 1908, Rank to Burbidge, 6 July 1909, 6/1/28, TCP; Burbidge to Waring, 25 Nov. 1909, 6/1/33, TCP; TCM(P), 112th sitting, 20 Dec. 1909, 2/1/5, TCP.

left the finances of the Commission in the hands of long-time subscribers whose enthusiasm was beginning to pall.

Charles Allen, who had borne election expenses of £350 as well as other financial losses, needed time to decide whether to respond to the 1906 appeal, though he was 'more than ever one of Mr. Chamberlain's strongest supporters', and Henry Bessemer and Co. cancelled their subscription at the same time.[120] Not only was the fevered activity of 1904 to 1906 difficult to sustain: it had also created a plethora of different organizations, each pressing their claim on individual Tariff Reformers. Arthur Keen refused a guarantee because he still had £500 of a £1,000 guarantee to the ITC outstanding for 1907 and 1908. A. F. Firth was needed by Burbidge's appeals. 'I am probably better posted about what Mr. Burbidge has done for Tariff Reform than he is about what I have done,' he wrote. His activities for the Halifax branch of the League and the West Riding Tariff Reform Association showed 'that I am doing my share'. Percy Glass, founder of the Cotton Trade Tariff Reform Association, complained that he was 'directly assisting your League because I am frequently called on by provincial Branches . . . and it costs me money every time'.[121]

Furthermore, some were unenthusiastic about local and industrial fund-raising. Alfred Gilbey, unhappy about the Unionists' half-heartedness on Tariff Reform in the election, thought that both in Buckinghamshire and in the liquor trade prospects were poor. Rank thought any appeal to his friends in the grain trade, mostly Liberals, would be doomed to failure.[122] Eckersley thought the prosperity of trade would ensure a good response in Lancashire, but Levinstein was probably more correct in suspecting that good times would lessen the incentive to support Tariff Reform:

business is yet too good. It is true that there are a number of men . . . [in the Manchester business community] who sympathise with our movement, but most of these have not the courage to publicly acknowledge their sympathy. I should therefore advise to postpone your contemplated visit to the town until the boom has simmered down.[123]

The aftermath of the January 1910 election was also bad for the Commission. Donations were only £2,751 in the first half of 1910, and a reduced expenditure still slightly exceeded income. Hickman, who had contributed £1,930 to the movement since 1904, was annoyed by the TRL's refusal to aid him in fighting his unwell son's constituency, and Pearson also declined a Commission appeal because of his heavy expenses in the Tariff-Reform cause, not least in his own

[120] Allen to Hewins, 20 Mar. 1906, Henry Bessemer and Co. Ltd. to Hewins, 20 Mar. 1906, HP.
[121] Keen to Caillard, 6 Nov. 1906, 6/1/19, TCP; Firth to S. Summerscale, 20 Nov. 1908, 6/2/13, TCP; Glass to Hewins, 15 Dec. 1907, 6/3/10, TCP.
[122] Gilbey to Hewins, 29 Mar., 19 July, [?] Nov. 1906, 6/1/10, TCP; Rank to Hewins, 2 July 1907, 6/1/28, TCP.
[123] Levinstein to Hurd, 30 June 1907, 6/1/21, TCP; Eckersley to Hewins, 2 July 1907, 6/1/5, TCP.

newspapers. 'An Election is popularly supposed to be a good thing for the newspapers,' he wrote. 'It is nothing of the kind. Adverts are dull, and expenses are enormously increased.'[124] The League, which had prospered much more than the Commission between the elections of 1906 and 1910, now joined it in a financial downturn that had scarcely lifted by the outbreak of war.[125]

Added to this, after six years the Commission was beginning to try the patience of some members. Members noted that the much-vaunted scientific tariff was still incomplete. Even before the January election Charles Lyle found it difficult to make potential contributors 'believe that the Commission is doing anything'.[126] Clearly, the Commission's hand-to-mouth existence during 1910 could not carry on indefinitely, and subsequently, around 1911 or 1912, Burbidge was to launch a second guarantee fund.

Disaffection was, however, for the minority. The 1906 election did not have any dramatic effect on the loyalty of most members. Attendance figures did tail off, but the significance of this should not be exaggerated. Even in the early days, few members assiduously attended meetings to hear evidence unless they were immediately concerned in the industry involved—indeed, they were not expected to—and after his stroke there was no longer Chamberlain's presence to ensure well-attended meetings.

Fourteen of the original fifty-eight members of the Commission did not attend after the 1906 election, though death accounted for one, and at least five continued to send financial contributions. A further fifteen did not attend after the election of December 1910, though at least six of these had died and seven continued to make donations, for an average of seven and a half years after the date of their last attendance. The number who were still alive yet had entirely severed their connection with the Commission by 1910 was thus remarkably small—only around ten.[127] Furthermore, only a handful of these had resigned through disagreement or disaffection. Sir George Ryder resigned in 1904 because the Commission was unwilling to confine itself to examining the Balfourite position on retaliation on manufactures,[128] Sir Alfred Hickman resigned after the election, angry that the Tariff Reformers' insistence on food taxes was preventing voters from accepting retaliation on manufactures,[129] and Sir Charles Elliott resigned after the election for unknown reasons.

---

[124] Hickman to Hewins, 5 Jan. 1910, 6/1/14, TCP; Pearson to Burbidge, 11 Jan. 1910, 6/1/26, TCP.

[125] F. Coetzee, *For Party or Country*, 144–9.

[126] Lyle to Burbidge, 15 Dec. 1909 and 23 June 1911, 6/2/26, TCP.

[127] For a full analysis, see Marrison, 'British Businessmen and the "Scientific" Tariff', 189–95, 503–4.

[128] G. L. Ryder, 'Mr. Chamberlain's Tariff Commission of 1904: Its Objects, and Methods of Procedure', 1, typescript in 6/1/30, TCP. See also Ryder to Hewins, 17 Jan., 27 Feb., 19 Mar., and 15 July 1904, 6/1/30, TCP.

[129] Hickman to Hewins, 26 Apr. 1906; 46/109–110, HP.

There was thus no large-scale disaffection with the Commission, either because of its failure to produce a tariff schedule or because of its assumption of a more directly political role. Lapsed attendance was far more common than outright resignation, and indeed some of the heaviest contributors never felt strongly the obligation to attend. The Commission's staff never easily regarded lapsed attendance as resignation, and this attitude was frequently vindicated. Arthur Keen clashed with Hewins over methodology and procedure and ceased attending in 1904, but he continued to contribute.[130] Agricultural engineer William Marshall attended last in July 1904, but he continued to supply a hefty £250 p.a. until his death, after which the family firm made the same contribution until the Commission was disbanded. Sir John Turney of Nottingham only attended the early meetings, but maintained financial support to the end of the Commission's life.[131]

After 1910 the slow process of attrition continued. What is perhaps surprising in view of Bonar Law's abandonment of food duties in 1913 and the torpor which crept over the Tariff Reform movement from 1911 to 1914 is that it was not more rapid. No less than thirty-eight of the surviving forty-nine original members either attended or contributed to finance after December 1910, though the fall-off in attendance was more marked than that in providing funds. Four new members were appointed in March 1911—Hugo Hirst of GEC; John Hunter, the Clydeside shipbuilder and engineer; R. B. Thomas, the Mellin-griffith tinplate manufacturer; and Christopher Turnor, landowner and well-known writer on agriculture. But generally there was no attempt to maintain Commission numbers through new appointments. Hewins's parliamentary career, his statistical work, and his production of memoranda on imperial affairs and the treaty position had come to dominate the work of the Tariff Commission, and in this there was little active role for the industrial members.

[130] See above, Ch. 5, also Keen to Caillard, 6 Nov. 1906, 6/1/19, TCP.
[131] O'Farrell to Hurd, 7 July 1905; 6/1/26, TCP.

8

Swinging at Anchor

Until its final downfall in December 1916, Asquith's cabinet moved towards mobilization for a war economy at a pace which left its critics increasingly dissatisfied. Recent research has shown that this apparent complacency was due less to an ideological aversion to intervention than to an initial belief that, as in Napoleonic times, Britain could confine her role to the maintenance of naval supremacy and the finance of her allies, and that it was compounded by administrative difficulties and poor information networks from which to judge the seriousness of the situation.[1] Nevertheless, it would be unwise to dismiss totally the personal inclinations and instincts of cabinet members, or regard them as having been immune from the pacifist sentiments traditional within the Liberal Party. Furthermore, whilst Liberals always recognized that war required some temporary departure from strict Liberal principles and freedoms,[2] it was only prudent to avoid any unnecessarily large interventions that might be harder to roll back in the peace.

War seemed to confirm the Tariff Reformers' perception that trade rivalry, military antagonism, nationalism, and expansionism were indissolubly linked. It graphically illustrated their contention that the real economic rivalries were between nations, not classes. Their prescriptions enjoyed unprecedented popularity with the public. Their task was therefore simple—to take advantage of the tide and push hard for their policies. Assessing progress, on the other hand, was less easy. Could interventionism be contained in areas acceptable to the Tariff Reformers? Could it be pushed so far that it would be technically impossible to abandon all controls afterwards? How far would war permanently alter the Liberal vision? Would the growing interventionist strand within Liberalism, exemplified by Lloyd George but before the War confined largely to social issues,[3] now spread to areas of economic and industrial policy? War seemed to provide easy terrain for a Tariff-Reform advance, but the features of that terrain could be amorphous and misleading, distances hard to measure.[4]

---

[1] S. E. Koss, *Asquith* (1976), chs. 7–8; D. French, *British Economic and Strategic Planning* (1982), *passim*.

[2] O. Anderson, *A Liberal State at War* (1967), 228, 275–83.

[3] M. Freeden, *The New Liberalism* (Oxford, 1978), *passim*; H. V. Emy, *Liberals, Radicals and Social Politics 1892–1914* (Cambridge, 1973), passim.

[4] War also seemed to open the prospect of participation by business groups in the determination of economic policy, but those whose hopes lay in this direction were to be similarly disappointed. Whilst organized interests were given a new hearing, the locus of power within the political process

I

By the opening of 1915, the Unionists were smarting under the wartime party truce. There was an annoyance that the Liberals 'appear[ed] to be still pursuing many of their most partisan measures [Irish Home Rule and disestablishment of the Welsh Church] under the cloak of national necessity',[5] and a mounting discontent over the conduct of the War. Organized backbench activity first emerged in the Unionist Business Committee, 'an important milestone in the evolution of the modern party',[6] instigated by Ernest Pollock and Basil Peto. Walter Long was made the Committee's first chairman at the suggestion of Bonar Law,[7] who may have intended that it should provide a channel for constructive criticism without disrupting the front-bench truce. When Long was appointed to the Local Government Board in the First Coalition, he was succeeded as chairman by Pollock.

Not until after the Nigeria debate of November 1916, when he determined to represent Unionist backbench opinion more closely within the Asquith Coalition, was Bonar Law entirely safe from challenge from within his own party. The UBC probably never represented the same level of threat that Carson's later and much larger Unionist War Committee did. Membership was modest, in the region of between twenty-five and forty. More important, it has been suggested that, unlike the UWC, the UBC lay to an extent within the influence of the Unionist leadership,[8] and it is certainly true that it reserved its most pungent criticisms for the Liberal rather than the Conservative members of the two coalitions.[9] Nevertheless, the UBC did have a fierce view of its own independence, and the potential for independent action. It continued in being when the UWC was created, and it is not always easy to separate their activities or their effectiveness.[10]

Establishing a structure of an executive committee and five sub-committees, on contraband, industries, supplies, aliens, and employment,[11] the UBC met forty-five times in its first six months, during which time Peto, Stanley Baldwin, Almeric Paget, Joynson Hicks, Hewins, Sir Philip Magnus, Roland Prothero, and Evelyn Cecil led it in debates in the House, and it mounted four deputations to

remained essentially unchanged. Interpreted in this wider context, the present treatment endorses that in J. Turner, *British Politics and the Great War* (New Haven, 1992), 334–89.

[5] R. Blake, *The Unknown Prime Minister* (1955), 237.

[6] J. Stubbs, 'The Impact of the Great War on the Conservative Party', in C. P. Cook and G. R. Peele (eds.), *The Politics of Reappraisal* (1975), 24.

[7] J. Ramsden, *The Age of Balfour and Baldwin, 1902–1940* (1978), 112, 114; UBC Minutes, 27 Jan. 1915, 26/19–21, HP.

[8] J. Ramsden, *The Age of Balfour*, 112–14.

[9] Long to Bonar Law, 20 May 1915, 4/11, Bull Papers; Edward Talbot to Bull, 22 Apr. 1916, 4/13, Bull Papers.

[10] Hewins, quoted in J. Stubbs, 'Impact of the Great War', 26.

[11] UBC Minutes, 27 Jan. 1915, 22 Feb. 1915, 26/19–21, 26/27–9, HP.

ministers.[12] During the second half of the year there were four further deputations, including one to McKenna on the foreign exchanges, and frequent
informal contacts with ministers.

The UBC's concerns were many and various, but all related to the mobilization of a war economy—concerns such as the army estimates, finance, and
taxation; the production of aniline dyes, munitions, optical glass, and food;
exports and export licences; the supply of imported raw materials (especially
where these were perceived to be threatened by German control over the sources
of supply); contraband and purchases by neutrals; labour relations in the docks,
the shipping companies, and in engineering; and national registration and
compulsory service.[13] In such matters, Hewins was well-placed to take a
prominent part. At the outbreak of the War he had sought to establish the Tariff
Commission as an unofficial bureau to put UK firms in contact with others who
could supply inputs that they had previously purchased abroad. Aware of many
of the difficulties being experienced by British firms in importing raw materials
or semi-manufactured inputs, he had good intelligence of German efforts to
obtain overseas supplies and to divert the trade of neutral countries. He assisted
other members by providing statistical information, was commonly in the small
group who drafted questions for the House or went on deputations, and was
singled out for praise for his part in the successful deputation to McKenna on
the budget of September 1915. In November he was elected chairman when
Pollock resigned to head the Foreign Office Contraband Committee, an
appointment in itself a sign of the effectiveness of the UBC.[14]

The UBC's early concerns reflected a dissatisfaction with a war being
conducted on unplanned, unco-ordinated, unbusinesslike lines. At times it
appeared as an ultra-patriotic group rushing headlong into a militarist-inspired
collectivism. But, representing most closely the non-landed section of an 'increasingly urbanised, commercialised and industrialised' Unionist Party at a time
when so many young landed MPs were away at the front,[15] it saw itself as the
defender of business interests, resisting unnecessary encroachments by the state.
It joined with the brewing interest in trenchant opposition to Lloyd George's
plans to take over the liquor industry during the first half of 1915.[16] Its intense
interest in export permits reflected a desire to prevent needless restrictions on

[12] 'Report of Work of Business Committee: January to June 1915', copy in 4/11, Bull Papers.
[13] Ibid. Also 'Unionist Business Committee: Annual Report, 1915–16', copy in 4/13, Bull Papers.
[14] The other members of the Executive Committee were Walter Long (chairman), Ernest Pollock
(vice-chairman), Basil Peto, George Cave, J. F. Hope and Samuel Samuel. See UBC Minutes, 4 Feb.
1915, 26/24–6, HP; UBC Executive Committee Minutes, 30 Mar. and 5 May 1915, 26/31 and
26/37–8, HP; UBC Minutes, 15 June 1915, 26/48, HP; UBC Executive Committee Minutes, 22
Sept. 1915, 26/65, HP; UBC Minutes, 30 Nov. 1915, 26/73–4, HP.
[15] J. Stubbs, 'Impact of the Great War', 24; J. Ramsden, *The Age of Balfour*, 112.
[16] J. Turner, 'State Purchase of the Liquor Trade in the First World War', *Historical Journal*, 23
(1980), 589–615.

exporters, and it frequently consulted firms and trade associations on matters of wartime policy. Demands for a full war economy were not seen as incompatible with the support for the 'business interest', and where the Committee could not discern a fairly united business opinion it was hesitant to act. This was the case with Excess Profits Duty. First reactions were that any tax extending the control of profits beyond the existing legislation on controlled firms should be 'moderate' and contain generous capital depreciation allowances.[17] Subsequently a small committee found opinion so divided that it was decided to adopt no policy on the duty.[18]

The UBC achieved some prominence in the well-known 'shell scandal' of the spring of 1915.[19] Whilst sharing the widespread concern over the supply of munitions, it rejected Lloyd George's claim that drink was a major cause, and was dismissive of his attempts to reach accord with the trade unions. The solution lay rather in increasing the number of firms involved in munitions production.[20] Getting little official response, the UBC decided to force the issue in Parliament, and mobilized Bonar Law's support.[21] On 21 April Hewins moved that 'all firms capable of producing or of co-operating in producing munitions of war should be enlisted under a unified administration'. On the surface, the debate was not a hard-edged affair, with the UBC's opponents frequently expressing their support for its general objectives, and the motion was in any case defeated. But it has been interpreted as a 'blistering attack'.[22] Furthermore, Bonar Law's participation provided an early indication of the limits to which the Unionist leadership could afford to lose touch with its rank and file. As the drink issue persisted into May, Law's willingness to accommodate with Lloyd George on a scheme of state purchase provoked concerted opposition from the UBC and the liquor lobby. Admiral Fisher's resignation over the Dardanelles and Colonel Repington's revelations in *The Times* heightened the vulnerability of both front benches to backbench Unionist pressure. Asquith decided for the coalition that had been in his mind for some time, and Bonar Law accepted: '[n]ot to have done so would have destroyed his credibility as leader'.[23] Afterwards, the UBC may have been prone to exaggerating its own role in the 'shell scandal', and the importance of that episode in the sequence of events leading to coalition,[24] but

[17] UBC Executive Committee Minutes, 10 Aug. 1915, 26/59–60, HP.
[18] Consisting of Basil Peto, Evelyn Cecil, de F. Pennefather and William Joynson Hicks.
[19] For detailed discussion of the 'munitions crisis', see D. French, *British Economic and Strategic Planning*, chs. 9–10; R. J. Q. Adams, *Arms and the Wizard* (1978), chs. 2–3.
[20] W. A. S. Hewins, *Apologia of an Imperialist* (1929), ii. 4–5, 10, 16–17, 20, 22–5.
[21] Ibid. 25–6.
[22] *Parliamentary Debates*, 5th ser., lxxi, 21 Apr. 1915, cols. 277–374; J. Stubbs, 'Impact of the Great War', 25.
[23] Ibid. 26. On leadership motives for coalition, see C. Hazlehurst, *Politicians at War* (1971), 227–305; M. D. Pugh, 'Asquith, Bonar Law and the First Coalition', *Historical Journal*, 17 (1974), esp. 813–24. See also J. Turner, 'State Purchase of the Liquor Trade'.
[24] Ernest Pollock to Hewins, 15 Apr. 1916, 59/153–4, HP; Walter Long to Hewins, 18 Apr. 1916, 59/164, HP.

it did deliver the most focused expression of backbench criticism at the time, and it is highly probable that UBC action in mid-May would have carried the rest of the Unionist backbenches into open revolt.

II

After the munitions crisis, the next milestone in the UBC's history was McKenna's budget of September 1915. Given the historical importance which many writers have ascribed to the McKenna duties, it is remarkable that their passage has attracted so little attention from historians and political biographers, who typically skip lightly from the downfall of Asquith's first wartime ministry in May 1915 to the fundamentally important controversy over conscription.[25]

Late in August the UBC drafted a letter to Asquith on the foreign exchanges, and Asquith arranged a meeting with McKenna at the Treasury.[26] Already apprehensive,[27] Hewins, Pollock, and Shirley Benn felt that the meeting demonstrated the lack of any positive policy on the balance-of-payments problem, though McKenna did intimate that a tariff was not out of the question if it could be shown to be practicable. Hewins and Caillard lunched with Lloyd George, who 'would support strong action though he is not the man to take the initiative', and with Balfour, who 'pitched questions at me, inventing difficulties and waiting for me to meet them'. Balfour gave no assurance that he would support fiscal change, indeed feeling it 'unfair that people shd. expect me to act', but Hewins was nevertheless pleased with the meeting. According to his autobiography, he threatened independent UBC action if the cabinet remained inert.[28]

On 3 September McKenna sketched out his budget in the cabinet. Of the £90 to £100m sought from increased taxation (mostly income, profits, and revenue taxes), he anticipated that a 'tax on imported motor cars should bring in £1m', one-third of the amount expected from increased postal charges.[29] On 10 September the cabinet deputed Lloyd George, Runciman, Bonar Law, and Austen Chamberlain to examine the proposals.[30] Lunching with Caillard and Hewins afterwards, Curzon thought the cabinet reluctant to implement any bold policy and likely to delay by arguing the impossibility of preparing large schemes at short notice.[31] By now Balfour, Long, and Curzon had all suggested that Hewins outline his proposals in a memorandum which they would lay before the

[25] See e.g. S. E. Koss, *Asquith*, ch. 8.

[26] W. A. S. Hewins, *Apologia*, ii. 48–9.

[27] Hewins to Margaret Hewins, 2 Sept. 1915, 58/82–3, HP.

[28] Hewins to Margaret Hewins, 8 Sept. 1915, 58/90–2, HP (Balfour quoted); W. A. S. Hewins, *Apologia*, ii. 50–1.

[29] Asquith to the King, 3 Sept. 1915, Ms. Asquith, 8/87–8.

[30] Asquith to the King, 10 Sept. 1915, Ms. Asquith, 8/90–1.

[31] Hewins to Margaret Hewins, 10 Sept. 1915, 58/102, HP.

cabinet. But Hewins, who had 'been writing memoranda for 20 years',[32] threatened instead an open revolt in the Commons. To his wife he wrote, 'there can be no drawing back now, and I am certainly in for the fight of my life. I shall not give way'.[33]

But the cabinet meeting of 16 September proved a tranquil affair. The cabinet committee recommended additional duties on clocks, watches, musical instruments, and hats, yielding an additional £500,000 p.a.[34] After talking to Long, Hewins wrote, 'This morning the scene has changed. Import duties on selected articles are to be included, and McKenna is to make a statement that there is to be a supplementary budget carrying things further . . . Lloyd George threw a note across to Walter Long: "So the old fiscal system *goes*, destroyed by its own advocates" '.[35]

Lloyd George's dramatic flourish was echoed in later years by the impeccable Free Trader, Francis Hirst, who considered the implementation of the McKenna duties to have been a 'definite and really sensational sacrifice of principle'. In his view, 'most of the Unionist leaders were also Tariff Reformers, and by some intellectual process Mr. Asquith and his colleagues arrived at the conclusion that gratitude to their opponents for joining them in office required something more positive than abstention from Liberal measures'.[36] It is unlikely, however, that any of the coalition leaders regarded the duties as representing a permanent policy shift—rather as a temporary expedient requiring compromise on both sides. The Unionists were only weakly represented in Asquith's cabinet, and Asquith had, in effect, already demonstrated his intentions on commercial policy by ensuring that Bonar Law was denied the Exchequer on the formation of the coalition.[37]

The Tariff Reformers were delighted by McKenna's innovation, and UBC members immediately pressed for further duties in the budget debate itself. Even Labour's Tim Healy was able to rejoice 'that the Free Trade fetish is dead'.[38] Led by Sir Alfred Mond, Josiah Wedgewood, and Philip Snowden, the Free Traders concentrated on exposing the protectionist intent that underlay the introduction of the duties.

McKenna's strength was that he could admit this; the duties were necessarily protective to safeguard the exchanges and restrict imports of luxuries. No fiscal principle of any kind was compromised, he promised, and Parliament would have the opportunity of refusing to renew the duties on 31 July 1916. Bonar Law and Asquith both supported him, formally denying that the Conservatives in the

[32] W. A. S. Hewins, *Apologia*, ii. 52.
[33] Hewins to Margaret Hewins, 8 and 10 Sept. 1915, 58/102, HP.
[34] Asquith to the King, 16 Sept. 1915, Ms. Asquith, 8/93–4.
[35] Hewins to Margaret Hewins, 16 Sept. 1915, 58/116–7, HP.
[36] F. W. Hirst and J. E. Allen, *British War Budgets* (1926), 73.
[37] R. Blake, *The Unknown Prime Minister*, 249–52, 256–7.
[38] T. M. Healy, quoted in F. W. Hirst and J. E. Allen, *British War Budgets*, 89.

cabinet had exerted pressure: 'let these controversies which are in a state of suspended animation continue during the war in a state of suspense'.[39] Their position was strengthened by the fact that many participants in the debate, not least those Free Traders who considered that increased borrowing was a direct contravention of Gladstonian principles of war finance, still considered war taxation too light. No one could doubt the need for extra tax revenues.[40] Furthermore, McKenna showed his willingness to act empirically by abandoning the duties on hats (as undefinable), plate glass, commercial vehicles, and motor tyres.[41] The coalition leaders prevailed, albeit in somewhat ragged order.

The Ministry of Munitions, direct result of a 'shell scandal' which had caused outrage on both sides of the House,[42] might be a victory for interventionism, but it was one which few, not least the Tariff Reformers of the UBC, would have wished to survive into the peace. To the Tariff Reformers, the McKenna duties represented a more welcome and a more hopeful threat to Liberal principles. Yet the duties were not in themselves evidence that such principles had already been abandoned, and the UBC remained unsatisfied. John Gretton's increasing fury with Asquith was matched by a growing contempt for the Unionist leadership: 'A whole evil tradition has been evolved in which the present Cabinet is enmeshed—we must have fresh men and fresh minds quite apart from the honesty of the present lot. Our own leaders are hopeless'.[43] Hewins, elected UBC chairman late in November on a secret ballot, commented tartly to Bull that 'you may as well ask the Government to drink a bottle of cholera germs as come to a definite decision'.[44]

Dissatisfaction erupted early in the new year. In Hewins's important speech in the Commons on 10 January 1916, the Tariff Reformers of the UBC went beyond measures which others could accept as extraordinary measures *during the War itself*, and for the first time propounded policies that had clear implications for the postwar period. The UBC emerged as the champion of trade warfare in the House of Commons. It is probably fair to regard it as the effective vanguard of such ideas in wartime Britain, for it had doubtless prepared its ground carefully. An important article in the *Morning Post* the previous October, on 'The Coming Trade War', which sparked off demands from some Chambers of Commerce for a central body of representative business interests to determine post-war policy, was almost certainly the work of Hewins. Equally, he must have been well aware of the impending and spectacular report of a sub-committee of

[39] B. Mallet and C. O. George, *British Budgets*, 2nd ser., *1913–14 to 1920–21* (1929), 74–85, quoting Bonar Law 83.

[40] S. McKenna, *Reginald McKenna 1863–1943* (1948), 224, 229; E. V. Morgan, *Studies in British Financial Policy 1914–1925* (1952), 92.

[41] B. Mallet and C. O. George, *British Budgets*, 2nd ser., 84–5.

[42] R. J. Scally, *Origins of the Lloyd George Coalition* (Princeton, 1975), 255.

[43] Gretton to Hewins, 25 July and 12 Dec. 1915, 6/2/18, TCP.

[44] Hewins to Bull, 2 Dec. 1915, 6/4/4, TCP.

the advisory committee of the Board of Trade, appointed in July 1915 to examine post-war policy on certain branches of industry where Britain had been heavily dependent on German and Austrian imports.[45]

Putting a motion that the Government consult with the Dominions in order 'to bring the whole economic strength of the Empire into co-operation with our Allies in a policy directed against the enemy', Hewins warned of discussions among the Central Powers aimed at creating a 'central European system', a network of bilateral commercial treaties in which tariff classifications would be drafted so as 'to exclude as far as possible British trade'.[46] Quoting from the official report of the Secret Congress of the Central European Economic Associations at Vienna, published in December 1915, he voiced his fear that, *before* they entered any peace negotiations, Germany, Austria and Hungary would embark upon a 'comprehensive economic rapprochement', through long-term reciprocal trade preferences which would not be accorded to other countries through the most-favoured-nation clause, whilst negotiations with foreign countries would be carried out by the three governments 'in agreement with one another, and with mutual support and simultaneously'.[47]

Germany's economic war had started before 1914 and would continue after hostilities had ceased:

It is a matter of small importance to Germany whether or not these countries and territories which she now occupies are politically subjected to her, if she is able to extend the powers of her various financial syndicates and general economic powers, and if she can dictate in these matters Germany will be satisfied. That is what she desires.[48]

The same design could be seen in German activity beyond Europe. How often, in the decade before the First World War, had German businessmen and financiers been encountered in different parts of the British Empire, seeking to weaken it through a 'network of diplomacy'? Had not German syndicates virtually controlled supplies and transport of Australian zinc and Canadian nickel for many years, to the discomfort of both Dominion governments? Did not the continuity of penetration, both in peace and war, mean that Britain and her allies should expect little respite after the peace?

Hewins couched his words carefully, claiming that his motion had 'only an indirect and inferential relation to the policy that may or may not be pursued when the War is over'; its main intention was to shorten the War. And if the speech is interpreted literally, that was true. A fairly equal peace treaty would allow a Vienna scheme which, even if impossible to implement fully, would still

---

[45] 'The Coming Trade War', *Morning Post*, 18 Oct. 1915. On the Board of Trade committee, see below, 232. On the 'trade warriors', see P. B. Johnson, *Land Fit for Heroes* (Chicago, 1968), 242–5; R. P. T. Davenport-Hines, *Dudley Docker* (Cambridge, 1984), esp. 4–5.

[46] *Parliamentary Debates*, 5th ser. lxxvii, 10 Jan. 1916.

[47] Resolutions 1, 2, 4, 5, and 7 of the Vienna report, quoted by Hewins.

[48] *Parliamentary Debates*, 5th ser., lxxvii, 10 Jan. 1916.

'give Germany a self-sufficient area within which she can reconstruct her own system', and consolidate economic gains made during the War. This would become a necessity in the post-war period, since Germany would be forced to export in view of her paper currency,[49] and would probably embark upon a state-directed and -controlled export policy. The allies should head off this strategy by negotiating a 'Western system of which England and the Empire shall be the centre' to increase the post-war bargaining power of the entente. If that were made known to Germany during the war period itself, 'I venture to say that the anticipation of dangers of that kind will act upon the German mind in a way which would make them reconsider where they are and what they are going to achieve by this War'.[50] The claim to be interested only in the war period itself was, of course, transparent—Hewins might literally argue that the threat of an allied-imperial commercial agreement would be sufficient to curb German ambitions, but his speech seemed to speak of the necessity of one.

III

It has recently been doubted that 'Germany was making elaborate plans to launch an "economic offensive" as soon as the war ceased to achieve complete ascendancy in markets where she had long been challenging British trade'.[51] But there can be no doubt of the strong presence in Germany's pre-war search for colonies of an economic element, whether expressed as a need for raw materials, or a need for markets, or indeed as a use of financial influence in achieving political influence. Furthermore, even if there were no elaborate plans for a trade war, there were certainly discussions of a possible *Mitteleuropa* customs union. In fact, such discussions were not new in 1914 and were given a new impetus with the outbreak of hostilities, culminating late in 1915 with the publication of Friedrich Naumann's influential *Mitteleuropa*, and the Dresden Conference of November, which was widely interpreted in France as the first step towards a customs union of the Central Powers.[52]

In the debate of 10 January, Alfred Mond argued that only the ultra-right in Germany favoured economic warfare and advocated *Mitteleuropa*. This is in retrospect untenable. Many groups did so, including more liberal business groups as well as right-wing agrarians and the representatives of heavy industry. Indeed, to some, *Mitteleuropa* represented the less extreme policy—the 'policy of the

[49] Presumably the argument was that Germany would seek to return to the gold standard, making an import surplus necessary to reduce the gold premium caused by inflation and bring the external and internal values of the mark back to parity.

[50] *Parliamentary Debates*, 5th ser., lxxvii, 10 Jan. 1916.

[51] V. H. Rothwell, *British War Aims and Peace Diplomacy 1914–1918* (Oxford, 1971), 267.

[52] D. Stevenson, *French War Aims against Germany 1914–1919* (Oxford, 1982), 33; G. W. Shanafelt, *The Secret Enemy: Austria-Hungary and the German Alliance 1914–1918* (New York, 1985), 72–80. An English edition of Neumann's book, *Middle Europe*, was published by P. S. King and Son.

diagonal', in Hardach's phrase.[53] Nevertheless, Mond was on stronger ground in stressing the difficulty of achieving *Mitteleuropa*. Austrian and Hungarian politicians were resistant to Germanification and Prussian political domination, whilst Hungarian industrialists, especially, were fearful of the lowering of tariff barriers against more efficient German competitors. In addition, many German businessmen saw their best markets to be in the West.[54]

Beyond such difficulties, any arrangement for a central European customs union depended on Germany securing an equal peace, or else it stood in danger of being torn up by the allies.[55] But an equal peace is precisely what informed opinion in Britain expected, in 1916 and beyond.[56] Hence, realistic or not, *Mitteleuropa* caused mild hysteria. Congratulations flooded in after Hewins's speech. Joseph Lawrence predicted that it would galvanize the nation's morale, adding gleefully that Lord Farrer, the eminent Free Trader, was 'rather depressed about it'. William Cunningham applauded 'the triumphant success of your motion', and, like Lawrence, stressed the significance of the 'abandonment of Cobden by Mond and Runciman' in the subsequent debate.[57] Charles Booth thought the speech 'an example of "how to do it" invaluable at the present time'.[58] With public opinion so excited, the Unionist Business Committee's belligerence was a difficult thorn in the flesh of the Government. As Oxford historian C. H. Firth later observed, Hewins 'seem[ed] to have taken advantage of the tide in the affairs of tariff reformers. "In the light of experience gained during the war" is the decisive argument'.[59]

Hewins's initiative was well-timed. Whilst there had been talk of 'trade war' amongst businessmen almost from the beginning of hostilities,[60] much of it had concerned efforts to continue trading during wartime conditions. In the closing months of 1915, attention switched markedly to the post-war situation, probably in response to the *Morning Post* article in October. In November, acting upon intelligence from the Sheffield Chamber that German merchants and manufacturers were planning a co-ordinated export drive after the War, the ABCC made representations to Asquith, McKenna, and Runciman on the need to design a government-led strategy to meet the threat. But the member Chambers were unwilling to leave the matter in government hands. By mid-December fifty Chambers had notified the ABCC of their support for the Norwich Chamber's

[53] G. W. Hardach, *The First World War* (1973; Eng. edn. 1977), 230.

[54] G. W. Shanafelt, *The Secret Enemy*; G. W. Hardach, *The First World War*, 236.

[55] See e.g. J. A. Hobson, *The New Protectionism* (1916), 54, 58.

[56] P. Cline, 'Winding Down the War Economy: British Plans for Peacetime Recovery, 1916–19', in K. Burk (ed.), *War and the State* (1982), 160–72.

[57] Lawrence to Hewins, 11 Jan. 1916, 59/30–1, HP; Cunningham to Hewins, 12 Jan. 1916, 59/32–3, HP.

[58] Charles Booth to Hewins, 19 Jan. 1916, 59/44, HP.

[59] C. H. Firth to Hewins, 6 Feb. 1917, 64/139–40, HP.

[60] 'Britain's Trade War against Germany', *BCCJ*, 31 Aug. 1914, 134–5; *BCCJ*, 31 Dec. 1914, 205; M. W. Beresford, *The Leeds Chamber of Commerce* (Leeds, 1951), 124.

proposal that the ABCC should itself convene a special meeting to discuss post-war trade policy. The Leicester Chamber already spoke of 'a scheme of commercial union' with the allies and dominions.[61]

The impact of Hewins's speech on the business community was heightened further by the almost simultaneous appearance of a report by a subcommittee of the Advisory Committee of the Board of Trade on Commercial Intelligence, a coincidence that he may have engineered. Appointed in July 1915, the subcommittee had five members—Sir Algernon Firth, Heckmondwike carpet manufacturer and former president of the ABCC; Stanley Machin, manufacturing confectioner and a former chairman of the London Chamber; Ebenezer Parkes, MP for Birmingham Central and an ironmaster; A. J. Hobson, the Sheffield cutlery manufacturer; and Sir Albert Spicer, Liberal MP for Central Hackney, a former president of the London Chamber and a wholesale stationer and papermaker. Before the War, Firth, Machin, and Parkes had been Tariff Reformers, Hobson and Spicer Free Traders. On the subcommittee, they found a new unanimity.

The subcommittee was instructed to examine a narrow range of trades—paper, printing and stationery; jewellery; cutlery; fancy leather-goods; glassware, china and earthenware; toys; brushes; hardware; electrical apparatus and magnetos—where over half of pre-war consumption had been obtained from Germany or Austria. Some of its recommendations were for that fairly standard set of 'institutional' improvements that the chambers of commerce had long considered it legitimate to press—more generous financing of the new Committee on Industrial Research, better enforcement of patents, the prevention of preferential freight rates for imports, and better credit for manufacturers from joint stock banks. But in recognizing that these were of secondary importance to the tariff protection which virtually all the firms and trade associations giving evidence demanded, the subcommittee went much further. Anticipating post-war German dumping, it advocated protection for the goods included in its brief. For other products, where Britain had been less dependent on German supplies, there should be a system of allied and Empire preference. Spicer even urged a planned general tariff rather than the *ad hoc* approach that this implied. In this report lay the seed of the key industry duties and more.[62]

Discomforted, Walter Runciman had authorized publication of the Report 'without of course taking responsibility for any of its conclusions', and the chambers of commerce were by now well aware of it. In January 1916 an extraordinary general meeting of the Birmingham Chamber heard an address from Wilfrid Hill, an 'unrepentant Free Trader', who advocated post-war

---

[61] ABCC, Executive Council Minutes, 9 Nov. and 14 Dec. 1915, 11 Jan. 1916.

[62] *Report of the Sub-Committee of the Advisory Committee of the Board of Trade on Commercial Intelligence with Respect to Measures for Securing the Position, after the War, of Certain Branches of British Industry*, XVI, Cd. 8181, 1916. Summaries of evidence appeared in XVI, Cd. 8275, 1916.

prohibitions. Germany, 'having grossly abused our hospitality, must be kept at home'. But more typical was a wider view of post-war arrangements. 'For many years the policy of *laissez-faire* has been abandoned to an extent,' proclaimed a *Birmingham Chamber of Commerce Journal* editorial. 'Now it must be abandoned *in toto*.'[63] Also in January, the resolutions tabled for the meeting of the ABCC in February or March were circulated. The constituent Chambers had submitted no less than seventy-three resolutions on trade policy after the War, and these had been boiled down by the ABCC's officers to two which incorporated their 'aim and sense'.[64] They included demands for closer trading relationships with the allies and the Empire after the War, and prohibitions on trade with the enemy. These were passed, with significant additions—the 'fostering and safe-guarding' of industries in areas where Britain had been dependent on German supplies before the War or where there had been strong German competition, and the prevention of post-war German dumping.[65] The use of the phrase 'by tariffs or otherwise' perhaps allowed the faint-hearted to imagine that they had not crossed the Rubicon, but in reality all the proposals were protectionist in intent. Indeed, the proposal for allied and imperial preference could scarcely have been implemented without the prior introduction of a British general tariff. The chambers of commerce had unequivocally lined up behind Hewins and the Board of Trade subcommittee. And they spoke with an assertiveness and self-assurance unknown before the War. They could march proudly behind their new mistress, Patriotism, and gladly too, for she held what seemed to be their self-interest in her hands.

The same policy prescriptions were endorsed at the AGM of the Birmingham Chamber on 30 March, after a Free Trade amendment had been defeated by 165 votes to three. Reviewing the Chamber's catalogue of demands upon the Government, president H. W. Sambidge opined that '[t]he whole business community was ... unanimous in these suggestions ... To attempt to win the war with the intention of resuming things ... as they were before the war would be to plunge headlong to national suicide'. To this Neville Chamberlain, then Birmingham's mayor, added that Britain must make commercial treaties with her Empire and allies to counter the post-war threat from the USA, which had 'been growing fat' upon the War and 'evolving vast and ambitious schemes for the capture of our trade in South America'.[66]

In seeking to conflate the seventy-three resolutions submitted for its spring meeting, the ABCC followed closely those submitted by the London Chamber, which in turn originated in the first report of an LCC Special Committee on Trade during and after the War. Before November 1915 the council of the London Chamber, unwilling to endanger the party truce, had avoided public

---

[63] *Parliamentary Debates*, 19 Jan. 1916; *BCCJ*, 31 Jan. 1916, 1, 5–7.
[64] Hull CC, *Annual Report*, 1916, 50.
[65] *BCCJ*, 31 Mar. 1916, 38–40.   [66] Ibid. 40–44.

embroilment in the wartime fiscal controversy, though it was obviously sympathetic to the views of Stanley Machin and E. B. Tredwen that there should be post-war protection of aniline dyes, chemicals, metal smelting, sugar beet, and other trades whose dependence on overseas supplies had proved vulnerable in war.[67] When the *Mitteleuropa* threat raised the question of a preferential customs union between Britain, the allies, and the Empire, the council reserved its position, though this was largely a formality, since all but the pre-war Free Traders, Pillman and Coysh, supported the idea. Faithful Begg proposed a prize essay competition to formulate a 'working plan', but guarantees for the £1,000 prize money came in slowly, Messrs. Rothschilds and the Chartered Bank of India being amongst those who declined to subscribe. More importantly, the Special Committee on Trade during and after the War was established.[68] At this point, doubtless emboldened by the presence of two of its leading members on the five-strong Board of Trade subcommittee, the London Chamber really mobilized for war.

The first report of the special committee recommended preference with the Empire and allies, favourable terms for neutrals, restriction 'by tariffs or otherwise' of trade with enemy countries, and the prevention of enemy dumping. Endorsed by a meeting at the Guildhall, the report was taken to the ABCC's spring meeting. Here Lionel Martin of the Chamber, seconded by the Liverpool Chamber, secured approval of its recommendations by a 'very large majority', and the ABCC organized deputations to Runciman at the Board of Trade and Bonar Law at the Colonial Office.[69]

The special committee's second report was much more detailed. Prohibitions were rejected—there was 'general recognition' that, though workable in war, they would do nothing to help preference or reciprocal trade with the allies in peace. But the committee had received '[p]ractically no objections' to a post-war tariff. A 'tentative tariff' should be erected on an *ad valorem* basis, then refined by a Royal Commission into a specific tariff. Britain would have to terminate her MFN treaties, and difficult negotiations would be involved, but there would be plenty of scope for reciprocity and preferential treatment. An anti-dumping surtax should be levied to offset completely any difference between a dumper's home and export prices.

The committee even went so far as to publish figures for its 'tentative tariff', the more remarkable since they contained recommendations for duties on food. Raw materials would be admitted free. A maximum tariff (enforced against enemy countries) would subject raw food to 5 per cent *ad valorem*, manufactured foodstuffs to 7.5 per cent, semi-manufactures to 15 per cent, and wholly manufactured goods to 30 per cent. The corresponding figures for the general

[67] LCC Council Minutes, 14 Jan. 1915.
[68] LCC Council Minutes, 11 and 17 Nov. 1915, 9 Dec. 1915.
[69] LCC Council Minutes, 9 Mar. and 13 Apr. 1916.

tariff (applied to neutrals) lay between 2.5 per cent and 20 per cent. Under the minimum tariff raw food would enter free from allied countries, but duties on other products would range between 2.5 and 15 per cent. Empire countries could avoid even the minimum tariff by maintaining reciprocal arrangements as before the War. Interestingly, the report's use of the phrase 'present allies', and its evident distaste of the US's habit of concluding reciprocity arrangements without generalizing them under her MFN treaties, pointed to a reluctance to accord the US minimum-tariff status should she enter the War.[70]

The appendices to the report showed huge support from the Chamber's trade sections. In stark contrast to its post-war stance,[71] the Fancy Goods Section wanted duties of 33 to 50 per cent on German goods. The Textile Trades Section wanted 25 to 30 per cent, the Fur Trade Section 40 per cent. The Silk Trade and Trimming Sections wanted virtually prohibitive duties. The Chemicals, Watch, Metals, Electrical, and Paint and Varnishes Sections endorsed the report. The Institute of British Carriage Manufacturers, the British Electrical and Allied Manufacturers' Association, and the Music Publishers' Association all concurred. Even groups largely associated with the import of raw materials—the Home and Foreign Produce Exchange, the London Master Builders' Association, the London Copra Association, the London Oil and Tallow Trades Association, the Seed Crushers' Association, the London Cattle Food Association, and the Oil Trade Section of the Chamber—identified themselves with the report. Only rarely was a voice of protest heard.[72]

In May, it was reported to the council that the special committee and its subcommittees had been 'practically unanimous'. In the council itself, even Free Trader J. C. Pillman was reduced to arguing that the 15-per-cent minimum tariff was too high to apply to Empire manufactures, given Empire support of the mother country in the War. There was some sympathy with this, and the rate was reduced to 10 per cent. A further attempt by Pillman to secure a reduction of the 2.5-per-cent duty on Empire manufactured foodstuffs was, however, defeated.[73]

Whilst the LCC special committee was explicit in advocating a general tariff, even Chambers formerly aligned to Free Trade now seemed to accept the need for some departure from it in post-war policy. The Hull Chamber tentatively endorsed key industry duties and supported the UK Chamber of Shipping's demand that 'enemy ships should not be left free after the war to extend their

---

[70] LCC *Second Report of the Special Committee on Trade during and after the War* (1916), 4–8. US practice was to make concessions in commercial treaties which were not then generalized to third parties with whom she had an MFN treaty. See P. B. Whale, *International Trade* (Oxford, 1932), 210–11.

[71] See Ch. 9.

[72] London Chamber of Commerce, *Second Report of the Special Committee on Trade during and after the War* (1916), Apps. E–I, 13–19.

[73] LCC Council Minutes, 25 May 1916.

share of the world's carrying trade and so profit by the losses which their Government by means mainly piratical have inflicted upon the ships of the Allies'.[74] Even the Manchester Chamber was not immune. In February 1916, a memorandum submitted by the directors of the Chamber, 'a very full restatement of Manchester's continued devotion to economic liberalism', was rejected by 988 to 527 votes, with 975 abstaining. All but three of the directors resigned. The new Board of Directors quickly produced a plan advocating penal trade sanctions against Germany and preferential trade with the Empire, which was approved by 932 votes to 234, though now over half the members abstained.[75]

IV

Mitteleuropa erupted onto the British political stage at a time when there were mounting tensions in the Asquith coalition over universal male conscription, the 'symbolic divide between a whole-hearted commitment to all-out war . . . and respect for the historic faith of individual liberty'. Asquith was forced to introduce the compromise Military Service Bill in January. Home Secretary Sir John Simon resigned. Runciman, at the Board of Trade, and McKenna, at the Exchequer, almost joined him. A newly formed Liberal War Committee, with Alfred Mond prominent among its forty members, pressed for 'more effective direction of the war effort, unencumbered by Liberal principles'. Asquith's government 'now hung in the balance'.[76]

This increasing vulnerability gave the unusually militant clamour coming from the Chambers of Commerce an unparalleled significance. Furthermore, Britain's major ally could not be left out of consideration. The French government was pushing for concerted economic measures against Germany. Apparently with official backing, Phillipe Millet, a senior civil servant in the *cabinet* of the *Ministère des Affaires Étrangers*, sought to follow up Hewins's speech. How the liaison began is unclear, but in March Millet claimed that 'I have made sure that my government approves of all our schemes. I have been given a free hand in the whole matter. I may tell you confidentially that our minister of commerce himself [Étienne Clementel] is in favour of informal conferences between businessmen, as devised by you'.[77]

At this time, the allies had already agreed on the principle of holding a conference on wartime economic policy. The French had been deliberating the possibility of post-war economic co-operation before the end of 1915, and news

---

[74] Hull CC, *Annual Report*, 1915, 82; *Annual Report*, 1916, 81.
[75] A. Redford, *Manchester Merchants and Foreign Trade*, ii (Manchester, 1956), 203–5.
[76] K. and J. Morgan, *Portrait of a Progressive* (Oxford, 1980), 48–9.
[77] Millet to Hewins, 7 Mar. 1916, 59/96–7, HP. On Clementel, see J. F. Godfrey, *Capitalism at War* (Leamington Spa, 1987); M. Trachtenberg, ' "A New Economic Order": Étienne Clementel and French Economic Diplomacy during the First World War', *French Historical Studies*, 10 (1977–8), 315–41.

of the Dresden Conference gave added impetus to their internal discussions, Fearing acute post-war shortages and German dumping of goods stockpiled during the war when France's own export potential would be low, the Ministry of Commerce sought inter-allied trade preferences and agreement on a policy of reparations. The 'main obstacle' to such plans was Britain.[78]

Asquith knew that the claims of Hewins and the French could not be dismissed out of hand. An unsigned Board of Trade memorandum recognized that there was circumstantial evidence that Germany was intent on trade war after the War—confiscation and destruction of industrial machinery, deliberate targeting of industrial areas in artillery bombardments, plans to strengthen the export cartels and to acquire concessions on overseas mineral supplies, and continuing discussions on an Austro-German commercial agreement.[79] He was also planning a committee on post-war industrial and trade policy, eventually to be the Balfour of Burleigh Committee, as early as February.[80] Yet at the same time he shared Runciman's fear of becoming enmeshed in a system of allied trade-preferences. This was reinforced when he received a memorandum from Llewellyn Smith at the Board of Trade on Britain's treaty position. Most importantly, an allied system might invite retaliation from the USA, expose British interests in Central and South America even more to US competition, and drive the small and neutral countries of Europe into the arms of Germany.[81]

To reach his 'private understanding' with Runciman in February, Clementel had to concede that tariffs would be excluded from discussions.[82] Nevertheless, it is clear that Hewis and Millet were indeed working along the lines of reciprocal trade treaties, a limited customs union between the allies, as envisaged in Hewins's speech. Millet counselled caution, since 'it is not quite certain whether *all* the allies will at once share our views on the subject'; he had already spoken to representatives of the British press in Paris in an attempt to curb rash speculations and 'sanguine expectations'. But he was determined to push ahead in testing the opinions of French business pressure-groups, and had directed a Captain Savy of the French Embassy in London, a man 'who knows both business worlds perfectly well', to assist Hewins in 'organising our business conferences'. Savy would be aided by economic historian Paul Mantoux,[83] who during the War was professor of French history in the University of London.

Millet and the French Ministry may have been playing a double game to keep the pressure on Runciman, or they may have misinterpreted his apparent

---

[78] D. Stevenson, *French War Aims*, 32–4.

[79] Ms. Asquith, 133/71–3.

[80] Asquith to the King, 24 Feb. 1915, Ms. Asquith, 8/142–3.

[81] Llewellyn Smith to Asquith, 10 Mar. 1916; 'Post-Bellum Tariff Policy and British Commercial Treaties', Ms. Asquith, 29/219–20, 29/221–36.

[82] D. Stevenson, *French War Aims*, 32–4.

[83] Author of the famous *Industrial Revolution in the Eighteenth Century* (Paris, 1906; Eng. edn., 1928). See *Who's Who in France*, 1953–4 edn.

willingness to consider pragmatic modifications of policy in wartime circumstances. But, either way, their choice of Hewins underlined the influence of his Commons speech and his potential to embarrass the Asquith coalition. At the same time, Hewins's own position was far from comfortable. Unofficial negotiation with a foreign government in time of war was a dubious activity for a patriot. With the Paris Chamber of Commerce and the *Association Nationale d'Expansion Économique* in favour of the proposal for business conferences, things were happening in what was for him a rather embarrassing hurry. The *Association Nationale* was pressing to know which British and French industrialists should be the first to meet, and had apparently got two French trade associations, the *Syndicat professionel des industries électriques* and the *Syndicat des Mécaniques*, lined up and waiting:

My suggestion is that we should organise a meeting of one or two sections as soon as possible. For instance, if you could get 4 or 5 men representing your electrical industries to come to Paris next week and meet an equal number of the French corresponding industry, I believe this first experience would throw more light on the way we ought to proceed than if we exchanged a number of academic propositions.[84]

Less than a week later Millet had embarked upon the organization of another two groups of manufacturers, representing the cotton and woollen industries. The French Ministry of Commerce was by now fully involved.[85] Hewins delayed.[86] More time would be necessary to collect facts and figures on the French situation, an objection Millet brushed aside by explaining that the Ministry was currently preparing such information. Hewins objected that it would be difficult to find businessmen willing to travel to France given their heavy wartime commitments, to which Millet replied that he preferred Paris as the venue since 'our government is backing us up very strongly'.[87]

But Hewins's hesitancy was not entirely procrastination. Soon, Millet was finding it difficult to persuade French businessmen to travel to London, and suggested instead separate meetings of British and French industrialists, with 'some *liaison* agent such as myself' to 'carry the proposals backwards and forwards'.[88] And Hewins did attempt to arrange a conference of British electrical engineers, whilst Clementel himself had an 'exchange of views' with British chemicals manufacturers.[89]

Hewins's speech of 10 January presented difficulties for the Government. Though the UBC was largely composed of Tariff Reformers, their appeal was

[84] Millet to Hewins, 14 Mar. 1916, 59/117, HP.
[85] Millet to Hewins, 24 Mar. 1916, 59/136, HP.
[86] Millet to Hewins, 18 Mar. 1916, 59/124, HP.
[87] Millet to Hewins, 24 Mar. 1916, 59/124, HP.
[88] Millet to Hewins, 27 Mar. 1916, 59/139, HP.
[89] Hewins to Hugo Hirst, 29 Apr. 1916, TC 6/1/15, TCP; Millet to Hewins, 25 Apr. 1916, 59/171, HP.

reaching a wider constituency, and the speech acted as a focus for all who believed that trade strategy had a place in a more active prosecution of the war. To regard the fevered interest of the Chambers of Commerce in post-war trade policy as 'an exodus of Free Trade businessmen from the old fiscal policy'[90] would be premature. Spontaneous expressions of anti-German feeling did not necessarily imply changing attitudes on wider trade policy. Furthermore, the cry for post-war prohibitions was widespread. As the more astute Tariff Reformers recognized, the calculating Free Trader could support them, perceiving them to be unworkable and determined that they should be short-term.[91] Nevertheless, in the prevailing state of opinion, public awareness of such apparent changes in faith increased the imperative that the Government respond, and also the expectation that it would do so, since many felt that both Runciman and Mond had made significant retreats from *laissez-faire* on 10 January.[92] It was against this threatening background that Hewins's unofficial contacts with the *Quai d'Orsay* took place. It is not known when the Cabinet first became aware of them, but they certainly knew by 22 or 23 March, when Hewins decided it was time to inform Asquith personally.[93]

By this time, and doubtless influenced by such considerations, Runciman had begun to respond more positively to the overtures of the French Ministry of Commerce on the allied economic conference. But the new relationship between Clementel and Runciman threw Hewins's unofficial status into sharp relief:

Mr Runciman is now in complete accord with M. Clementel, not only as the economic conference of Paris is concerned, but also as regards the necessity of promoting all sorts of practical and industrial understandings, such as you have already contemplated yourself.

M. Clementel feels therefore that Mr. Runciman must have a hand in the business conferences which are going to take place. On my part, I have insisted upon the necessity for leaving the direction of these conferences in your hands, and I have pointed out to M. Clementel, that although you have been connected with the Tariff Reform mouvement (*sic*), you are approaching these new problems with quite a broad mind.[94]

Millet's suggestion was unrealistic, and he may have known it to be so. His contacts with Hewins were already causing Runciman considerable annoyance. Acting on information from Millet, Hewins and Hugh Law, Nationalist MP for West Donegal and a member of Lloyd George's secretariat at the Ministry of Munitions, sought to raise the fear that the new import restrictions on luxuries were seen by French husinessmen as directed particularly against themselves. To

---

[90] P. Cline, 'Winding Down the War Economy', 162.
[91] See below, 243, 251.
[92] Lawrence to Hewins, 11 Jan. 1916, 59/30–1, HP; Cunningham to Hewins, 12 Jan. 1916, 59/32–3, HP.
[93] W. A. S. Hewins, *Apologia*, ii. 66–7.
[94] Millet to Hewins, 27 Apr. 1916, 59/178–9, HP.

Hewins, Runciman explained that he had already relaxed the issue of licences for French goods, since the voyage was short and the shipping space involved small,[95] but he could not publicize this since it would 'render it more difficult to resist demands for similar treatment from our other Allies'.[96] But in private he was needled by Hewins's pretension to superior knowledge of French opinion, and angered by his claim that there was more to the McKenna duties than the saving of shipping space.[97] Almost immediately after this incident, Millet informed Hewins cryptically that 'you are presonally much feared by some members of your government and they apparently object to me seeing you'.[98] Though he claimed he would ignore such pressure, his correspondence ceased.

The Tariff Reformers of the UBC, and even the more cautious Arthur Balfour, may have believed that Hewins had 'outwitted the Government'.[99] But Hewins knew that UBC pressure would be insufficient to force Asquith to allow him to participate in the Paris Economic Conference.[100] He resisted requests from the Director of the *Association Nationale d'Expansion Économique*, backbenchers like Wickham Steed, and even the ultra-patriotic Australian Premier W. M. Hughes,[101] to attend the conference unofficially. Gretton regarded Asquith's decision to send Runciman, 'a secondary minister without authority', as 'letting [Hewins] down as he does everyone except his own familiars in the Cabinet'. It 'treat[ed] the whole business with contumely'.[102] But Hewins, though aware of Runciman's intrigues, remained confident: 'The situation is not as described in the papers. Bonar Law is to be one of our representatives and no doubt there will be others. I have no doubt we shall have difficulties but I think the business will go very well.'[103] To his diary, he confided that the Government 'will do what I want on the whole'.[104]

As far as the Conference itself was concerned, this was justified, for in spite of Runciman's attempt to impose limitations on the agenda the conference produced a series of recommendations highly acceptable to British Tariff Reformers.[105] Partly this was due to the fact that French Ministry of Commerce and *Quai d'Orsay* officials introduced new measures onto the agenda beyond those

[95] Private motor cars and parts were an exception.

[96] Runciman to Hewins, 15 May 1916, 59/207, HP.

[97] R. W. Matthew to Bonham Carter, 20 Apr. 1916; Millet to Hugh Law, 6 Apr. 1916; Runciman to Law, 12 Apr. 1916; Hewins to Asquith, 27 Apr. 1916; Matthew to Bonham Carter, 8 May 1916; Ms. Asquith, 29/258–64.

[98] Millet to Hewins, 16 May 1916, 59/211–12, HP.

[99] W. A. S. Hewins, *Apologia*, ii. 66–7.

[100] Ibid. 72.

[101] W. K. Hancock, *Survey of British Commonwealth Affairs 1918–1939*, ii. *Problems of Economic Policy 1918–1939*, Pt. 1 (1942), 95.

[102] Gretton to Hewins, 25 or 26 Mar. 1916, 6/2/18, TCP.

[103] Hewins to Gretton, 28 Mar. 1916, 6/2/18, TCP.

[104] W. A. S. Hewins, *Apologia*, ii. 73.

[105] For the 'ingenious and safe' resolutions drafted for the British delegates by Runciman and Llewellyn Smith, see L. Harcourt to Asquith, 5 June 1916, Ms. Asquith, 30/116–7.

anticipated in Clementel's agreement with Runciman in February, amongst which were measures designed to deny Germany the capacity to embark upon a trade war after the peace. Perhaps on the suggestion of Hewins,[106] these were divided into measures to be applied for a 'transitional period', a device introduced largely to 'mollify liberal opinion in Britain', and measures intended to be permanent.[107] Even the first group, in Clementel's private opinion, would operate for twenty to twenty-five years. The Conference sustained the Tariff Reformers' optimism that the tide was turning. Most of the French agenda was adopted, and in addition there was a form of agreement on raw-materials supplies and anti-dumping provisions in the post-war period.

The recommendations of the Paris Conference were never to be fully implemented. Russia and Italy, both concerned that there was nothing in an inter-allied agreement to compensate for the probable loss of Central Europe as a market for their food exports, refused to ratify, and for different reasons Belgium followed. The hostility of President Wilson and American public opinion also inhibited acceptance.[108] Asquith's government took comfort from the fact that the Paris Resolutions were '*ad referendum*', mere recommendations to the participating governments.[109] Yet for the British Tariff Reformers the outcome appeared, and in many ways was, eminently satisfactory. Although, as Hewins recognized,[110] there was no political consensus within Britain on the protectionist implications of the Paris Resolutions, the Government ratified them along with France, when the refusal of the other participants gave it opportunity to back away. Furthermore, even before the Paris Conference met, it was decided to appoint a committee to consider post-war trade policy in the light of its recommendations. Not only to the Tariff Reformers, but also to trenchant critics of the Paris Resolutions like J. A. Hobson, the Asquith coalition seemed to be boxing itself into a corner.[111]

V

Hewins clearly believed that his Commons speech, and UBC activity more broadly, pressured the Government not only into attending the Paris Conference but also into establishing the new Committee. No doubt he exaggerated, but the coalition did deem it prudent to give some weight to his opinion. He was consulted by Austen Chamberlain and Bonar Law on whether the Tariff Reformers would object to Balfour of Burleigh as chairman and Alfred Mond as a member. Hewins raised no objection, as long as the members had 'brains and

---

[106] W. A. S. Hewins, *Apologia*, ii. 74.   [107] D. Stevenson, *French War Aims*, 34.
[108] Ibid. 34–5.
[109] Board of Trade, Memorandum on the Paris Economic Conference; Ms. Asquith, 30.
[110] W. A. S. Hewins, *Apologia*, ii. 74.
[111] J. A. Hobson, *The New Protectionism*, pp. x–xii.

practical intelligence'. In co-ordinating the work of the committees on various industries already set up by the Board of Trade during the War, the new Committee would 'virtually supersede Runciman and become the germ of the Ministry of Economic Policy I asked for'. When his attempt to include ex-Tariff Commissioner Richard Burbidge was rebuffed, he was sanguine: 'the progress of this great design . . . is so wonderful that I am prepared to work with any committee'.[112]

The protection of key industries caused virtually no controversy on the Balfour of Burleigh Committee; an interim report included synthetic dyes, spelter, tungsten, magnetos, optical and chemical glass, hosiery needles, thorium nitrate, barytes, limit and screw gauges, and a long list of pharmaceutical drugs.[113] The same was true of anti-dumping measures, though there were one or two who were doubtful of whether regulations of the type becoming common abroad were enforceable. In other areas of policy three clear groups can be discerned, and their proportions did not change markedly as members resigned and were replaced.[114] In the later stages there was only one unmodified Free Trader, Sir Archibald Williamson, though four others thought some of the fiscal recommendations too extreme. There were five who desired a full Tariff Reform policy. The largest group, however, sought a middle path. Indeed, their beliefs appear to have been in a genuine state of flux. Sometimes confessing to be former Free Traders, they now professed a new willingness to adopt a pragmatic and empirical approach, almost showing signs of embarrassment at their former beliefs, and highly sensitive to how the public would greet their proposals. Roxburgh, not formerly a Tariff Reformer, had 'come to the conclusion that things will have to be altered in some way'. Pearce had formerly been a Free Trader, 'but never a theoretical Free Trader'. Priestley admitted to having been

---

[112] W. A. S. Hewins, *Apologia*, ii. ch. 15, esp. 70–2, and ch. 16, esp. 85.

[113] Committee on Commercial and Industrial Policy, *Interim Report on Certain Essential Industries*, Cd. 9032 (1918). The Board of Trade had in fact reached a departmental view on the desirability of key industry protection before the BBC first met. See Board of Trade, Memorandum on the Paris Economic Conference, Ms. Asquith, 30.

[114] In its final stages, the Committee had 20 members besides the chairman. There were five Liberal MPs—Sir C. S. Henry (London merchant); Sir W. Priestley (Bradford worsted manufacturer); Sir Clarendon Hyde (former MP, overseas railway contractor); Sir W. Pearce (chemical manufacturer); and Sir A. Williamson (Merchant with interests in South American railways and oil). There was one Labour MP, Harry Gosling, and one Unionist MP, Arthur Balfour. Twelve were not MPs: Tariff Commissioners Birchenough, Faringdon, and Parsons; Sir F. H. Smith (india-rubber and cotton manufacturer); G. A. Muntz (non-ferrous metal refiner); G. Scoby Smith (steelmaker); Adam Nimmo (coal-owner); Arthur Pease (family coal and iron interests); Sir Alfred Booth and J. A. Roxburgh (shipowners); A. McDowell and J. O'Neill (both unknown); and W. S. McCormick (representative of Department of Scientific and Industrial Research). During the course of the inquiry there had been seven resignations, all to take up government office: Lord Rhondda (coal-owner); A. H. Illingworth (Liberal MP, worsteds); Sir J. P. Maclay (Liberal MP, shipowner); Sir Alfred Mond (Liberal MP, chemicals); R. E. Prothero (Unionist MP, later Lord Ernle, agriculturalist); C. J. Wardle (Labour MP); and Hewins (Unionist MP). The first five of these resigned in December 1916, probably too early to play much role in shaping the Committee's *Final Report*.

an 'old-fashioned Free Trader'. War had taught McDowell that he had 'got to abandon all those theoretical ideas'.[115] This was the group most closely represented by the chairman; 'Abstract principles . . . are excellent servants but very bad masters', he announced at the opening meeting.[116]

With the public mood intensely against Germany, no-one was willing to oppose post-war discrimination against German imports. In early meetings former Free Traders favoured three-or five-year prohibitions, relaxed by special licence when it was in the British interest.[117] The Tariff Reformers were unenthusiastic; such measures would be impermanent and difficult to maintain. A more covert consideration was that the Tariff Reformers were not satisfied with protection against the Central Powers alone. In focusing attention on Germany, the War diverted attention from the United States, yet at the same time it provided an ideal opportunity for the US economy to become even stronger. In the conditions of 1916, Tariff Reformers could scarcely say this openly—American public sympathies were still uncertain, American munitions supply a precarious and clandestine operation dependent on executive goodwill.[118] But they did so in private. As Hugo Hirst of GEC commented, 'Whilst the country talks of German penetration, America is piercing us'.[119]

Arguing that prohibitions would be impracticable and easily evaded by Germany trading with third countries, Hewins first resurrected the Tariff Commission's three-tier general tariff, modified so that enemy countries replaced countries refusing to treat in being subject to the maximum tariff, but with the moderate general tariff and imperial preference being retained. He was supported by Balfour, Faringdon, and Parsons. This was soon modified into a four-tier scheme, the middle (i.e. general tariff) tier being divided to distinguish between allies and neutrals in order to conform more closely to the intentions of the Paris Resolutions.

With six inclined towards a general tariff, and nine reluctant to commit themselves, confusion abounded over how to make progress.[120] The agnosticism of the majority was strengthened by a Customs and Excise memorandum on the implementation of prohibitions and tariffs, which in Hewins's opinion exaggerated the difficulties of introducing a tariff.[121] Moreover, the ambiguous terms of reference of the Committee hampered attempts to make progress. Was the Committee required to recommend a post-war policy *consistent* with the Paris Resolutions, or merely requested to *bear in mind* the Resolutions when drafting its

---

[115] BBC Minutes, 7 June 1917, BT 55/13/3–54, PRO.
[116] BBC Minutes, 25 July 1916, BT 55/8/2, PRO.
[117] BBC Minutes, 12 and 26 Oct. 1916, BT 55/8/41–4, 47–50, PRO.
[118] M. I. Urofsky, *Big Steel and the Wilson Administration* (Columbus, Ohio, 1969), ch. 3; D. French, *British Economic and Strategic Planning*, 116–8.
[119] Hirst to Hewins, 6 Apr. 1916, TC 6/1/15, TCP.
[120] BBC Minutes, 17 Aug. 1916, BT 55/8/27–9, PRO.
[121] BBC Minutes, 12 Oct. 1916, BT 55/8/41–4, PRO.

proposals? Was the Committee to formulate a general trade policy, or an *anti-German* policy? Was national interest or allied co-operation to be given priority? When Alfred Mond asked whether the Committee was at liberty to disagree with any of the Paris Resolutions, the chairman replied that the Government had formally approved the Resolutions, but that the Committee should report if it considered 'the complete application of any one of the Resolutions would be impracticable'. But senior Board of Trade officials Llewellyn Smith and Vaughan Nash explained that the terms of reference 'are not meant to be exclusive and that Commercial Policy generally . . . is not excluded from consideration in relation to the Paris recommendations'.[122]

These comments were of little help. In its attempts to discuss general policy and anti-German measures simultaneously, the Committee displayed an ambivalence of purpose which was never eradicated, and which at least one astute contemporary observer recognized.[123] There was a predictable division over whether a decision on long-term, permanent policy was necessary before any recommendation could be made on measures for the transition period. In Faringdon's opinion, what the country wanted to know was 'whether the Committee will recommend a general tariff or not'. But Balfour of Burleigh, joined by Mond, Sir Frederick Smith, and Rowland Prothero, thought consideration of 'the difficult questions of permanent policy' would delay the Committee in making recommendations for the transition period.[124]

The first interim report of the Committee, signed on 9 November 1916, represented a victory for the chairman's strategy. Prohibitions were recommended for at least one year after the peace. A licensing system would 'make it possible to mitigate the regime gradually, and thereby prepare the way for the substitution of tariff treatment for prohibition, should that course be thought advisable'. Rhondda, Maclay, Pease, and Booth declared reservations from a Free Trade point of view. But, of the Tariff Reformers, only Hewins formally dissented, on the grounds that prohibitions would be 'impractical' if pursued independent of a clearly formulated policy with regard to the allies, dominions, and neutrals.[125]

In November, Hewins introduced a resolution that the Committee recommend the preparation of a general tariff to ensure industrial security, greater Empire self-sufficiency, closer economic links with the allies, and discrimination against enemy powers. Balfour of Burleigh attempted delay,[126] but he could not forever postpone discussion of permanent policy, and at the next meeting he

[122] BBC Minutes, 25 July 1916, BT 55/8/8–22, PRO.
[123] J. M. Robertson, *The New Tariffism* (1918), 5–7.
[124] BBC Minutes, 12 and 26 Oct., 9 Nov. 1916, BT 55/8/41–4, 47–50, 57–62, PRO.
[125] Committee on Commercial and Industrial Policy, *Interim Report on the Importation of Goods from the Present Enemy Countries after the War*, Cd. 9033 (1918), 2–4.
[126] BBC Minutes, 9 Nov. 1916, BT 55/8/57–62, PRO.

conceded that the Committee was obliged to 'consider not only the expediency of a general tariff but also the many subsidiary questions connected therewith', and should now request the Board of Trade to collect the relevant information.[127] Even so, the Tariff Reformers were becoming frustrated, and Hewins shed no tears at the possibility that the BBC might die with the Asquith coalition: 'I wrote and told B. of B. he was extinct. I have not heard from him in reply'. Annoyed that, whilst the Germans were forging ahead with *Mitteleuropa*, 'we have been fooling around with the B. of B. Committee and other obstructions', he looked forward to Lloyd George's new administration with guarded optimism.[128]

Superficially, Hewins was more successful on imperial preference, discussed at four meetings in January and February 1917. His strategy was to push for the acceptance of the principle of preference by confining it to duties 'now or hereafter existing'. This was at variance with the pre-war programme of the Tariff Commission, but his aim was to make progress along the line of least resistance during the favourable conditions provided by the War. Judging the Committee more likely to favour duties on manufactures than on food, he argued that wartime industrial development in Canada and Australia raised the new prospect of a preference based on non-agricultural goods being acceptable to the colonies. This approach would also be compatible with feeling on the Committee that policy should be settled first according to Britain's own needs.

Birchenough and McDowell apart, all the rest were sceptical—food duties would still loom large in colonial expectations of preference. But Hewins's opponents themselves were split into two camps. Tariff Commissioner Lord Faringdon, supported by Arthur Balfour, pressed for a general tariff including food duties, urging the Tariff Reform commonplace that preference was impossible without the prior imposition of a tariff on foreign food. The former Free Traders, however, were reluctant to adopt food duties. If it demonstrated anything, a confused second meeting seemed to suggest a consensus on industrial protection but a reluctance to advocate food duties.[129] This led naturally to acceptance of Hewins's proposal, but left undecided the critical issue of whether the Committee supported additional duties to give effect to preference. Balfour of Burleigh discerned a general agreement that the 'principle of preference' should be conceded to the colonies. But when he proposed submitting a covering letter to the Prime Minister along with the text of the resolution, stating the Committee's view that, to implement preference, additional duties would probably be necessary in the long run, he opened up a rift on the Committee. Whilst the majority supported him, several agreed with Wardle that the resolution and

[127] BBC Minutes, 23 Nov. 1916, BT 55/8/63–4, PRO.
[128] W. A. S. Hewins, *Apologia*, ii. 99–100.
[129] BBC Minutes, 18 and 19 Jan. 1917, BT 55/8/77–86, 87–92, PRO.

the letter taken together 'clearly recommended wider duties', a matter on which they could not commit themselves.[130]

Nimmo's criticism of Balfour of Burleigh's approach discerned the nub of the issue. If wider duties were going to be mentioned, the Committee should make positive proposals, rather than simply avoiding the issue. The chairman was unconvinced. The Committee had accepted the principle of preference: the details should be left to the Government. Whilst Hewins's gradualist strategy had succeeded, its success was the result of a poor kind of compromise. The Committee's final report recommended preference on duties 'now, or hereafter to be, imposed', and separately alluded to the need for food duties if this was to be of material benefit to the Empire. But it took refuge in the fact that the Corn Production Act would dictate government policy 'for some years to come', and therefore maintained that 'no useful purpose would be served by our considering proposals for the establishment of a wider range of duties on essential food-stuffs'.[131] All were agreed on symbolic imperial preference, but little more than a form of words underlay the Committee's cohesion on any substantial move beyond that.

VI

Satellite to the BBC were a number of trade committees composed almost entirely of active industrialists. Some had been established prior to the BBC, and brought under its wing, others appointed alongside the main Committee. The difficulty of discussing permanent policy before their reports were received had frustrated the Tariff Reformers and strengthened the chairman in his caution.[132] From May to July 1917 the reports were received.

The most extreme was that of the Electrical Trades Committee, chaired by Tariff Commissioner Charles Parsons. Its strongly technocratic report, almost Wellsian in its vision of the future, stressed the domination of a scientifically organized Germany industry, with protected home markets and close assistance from the state and the banks. The British financial market, on the other hand, had contributed to German control of 'ostensibly British' companies and German penetration in imperial markets. It was necessary for British producers to combine to increase scale and co-ordinate effort, a policy the British government had hitherto 'always discouraged', and to remedy the inadequacies of British financial institutions for the development of capital-intensive industries. German penetration would 'certainly continue to progress everywhere after the

---

[130] BBC Minutes, 1 Feb. 1917, BT 55/8/96–102, PRO.

[131] Committee on Commercial and Industrial Policy, *Final Report*, Cd. 9035 (1918), para. 254(4); cf. para. 237.

[132] BBC Minutes, 15 Feb. 1917, BT 55/8/109, PRO.

war'.[133] The committee recommended a three-year prohibition of imports from Germany, and stringent controls on enemy capital in the electrical trades of the Empire. Germany apart, it demanded an anti-dumping measure together with an industry tariff 'sufficiently high to protect effectively the electrical industry', together with government assistance in effecting combinations and the establishment of industrial banks.[134]

The Engineering Trades Committee's report was temperate and judicious. It endorsed key industry duties. It also emphasized the need for an anti-dumping measure, recommending imitation of the US tariff of 1916, which dictated that price in the US should not be less than market value or wholesale price in the country of origin, plus freight and other additional charges.[135] Its discussion of dumping centred upon the practices made possible by the German cartel system. Whilst recognizing in pre-war German penetration 'reprehensible sharp practices and lack of honest dealing', the committee stopped short of outright condemnation; in general German methods were nothing more 'than those which we can and ought to practice'.[136] A plea was made for a post-war surtax on German goods in allied and Empire countries. But really punitive measures, including prohibitions, were discounted by omission.

Such moderacy was dictated by some division within the industry. The committee discerned four main groupings—constructional steelwork, and the boiler and wagon trades (where value-added was low and there was little repetition work); machine tools and locomotives (where value-added, repetition work, and standardization were higher); small auxiliary trades making tools and measuring instruments (similar to machine tools); and the general trade supplying products such as automobiles, agricultural machinery, sewing machines, pianos, and watches to the non-engineering customer (where large-scale production and standardization were vital). It was clearly the constructional steelworkers, doing essentially one-off jobbing or contracting work, who still inclined to Free Trade. The other branches were more fearful of foreign competition, and more aware that average British firm size was too small to achieve the production economies increasingly evident abroad. In these branches, which constituted the majority of the industry, protectionism was much stronger.

Enthusiasm for anti-German measures was also muted by a recognition that the USA was the greater threat. In 1913, Britain's bilateral import-to-export ratio in engineering products was 1.57 to 1 with Germany and 5.53 to 1 with the USA. Furthermore, German trade was to a considerable extent a reciprocal

---

[133] *Report of the Departmental Committee appointed by the Board of Trade to consider the position of the Electrical Trades after the War*, Cd. 9072 (1918), esp. 6, 8, 10–11.
[134] Ibid. 11–12.
[135] Quoted in *Report of the Departmental Committee appointed by the Board of Trade to consider the position of the Engineering Trades after the War*, Cd. 9073 (1918), 28.
[136] Ibid. 39.

trade in similar products. US trade in standardized products, especially cars and machine tools, was of a different order: 'A [Ford] car which can be sold at £80 in the States can hardly be kept out of this country except by direct prohibition'.[137] Germany might be second to the USA as a threat to British engineering,[138] but she was a poor second, and trade measures against her would have the minor impact. Thus, a protectionist majority in the trade and on the committee was effectively muzzled by the belief that protection against Germany would be insufficient:

Whilst the majority of the Committee consider that punitive enactments against Germany and her Allies alone will not meet the case and that import duties are necessary to secure the end desired we have not been able as a Committee to arrive at unanimity. In order to avoid weakening the recommendations on which we are all unified we have decided not to make recommendations as to tariffs. The majority of us believe that the financial needs of the country after the war will compel the imposition of customs duties for revenue purposes and will thus automatically bring about *the system of trade protection which the majority of the Committee believe to be necessary.*[139]

The message was coded. Given the original terms of reference of the BBC, and with the USA now an ally, it was difficult to articulate. Nevertheless, the inference was clear.

The ten-strong Iron and Steel Committee, which had taken evidence widely from manufacturers' and merchants' associations, trade unions, and technical experts, favoured the prohibition of imports from Germany for a 'period of reconstruction' after the War. Though it was considered 'no longer safe to entrust the very life of the iron and steel industry entirely to the efforts of private enterprise', the role of government should be confined to the 'creation of conditions favourable to the industry' rather than 'internal regulation of the industry itself'. Combination and co-operation were advocated in raw material supplies, overseas selling, and production. But the main thrust of the committee's report was the need to increase average firm output by investment in new, large-capacity plant. To guarantee the rate of return on this investment, the industry was 'practically unanimous' that the home market should be protected in German and American fashion. 'Whether this strict preservation of the home market is merely a passing phase, or a necessity of industrial development, it is not possible to judge.' The committee also recommended an anti-dumping measure along Canadian lines. Dumping of semi-finished steel 'seriously . . . imperilled' the industry, and even the finishing trades acknowledged that the advantage it gave them was only temporary. The trade union leaders on the

---

[137] Quoted in *Report of the Departmental Committee appointed by the Board of Trade to consider the position of the Engineering Trades after the War*, Cd. 9073 (1918), 23–4.
[138] French and Belgian competition was explicitly stated to be minor, and the rest of no account. See *ibid.* 21.
[139] Ibid. 37.

committee, William Gavin and John Hodge, agreed with the report. Only Hugh Bell and John Davison dissented, both on orthodox Free-Trade lines.[140]

Amongst the textile trades cotton was closest to the pre-war orthodoxy. Enquiries in the trade had yielded a 'large preponderance of evidence' that a tariff on cottons would be unhelpful.[141] Nevertheless, there was a distinct departure from the straightforward stance of the Edwardian years. Cotton supported the other textile industries in advocating key-industry duties on dyestuffs and hosiery latch needles—a plea which was given considerable emphasis in the report. Furthermore, most witnesses supported restrictions on the import of German goods after the War. Before the War, large and increasing quantities of cotton yarn had been exported to Germany and used in the production there of cotton hosiery, gloves, Plauen laces, Barmen trimmings, and embroideries. Many of these were then exported back to Britain. If this had been eminently satisfactory to Lancashire before the War, it was less so now. There was support for a tariff on hosiery and lace, which would promote large-scale production in the East Midlands trades, aiding exports. This in turn would secure the market for Lancashire's yarns. Even so, spinners feared the loss of the German market, and it was unclear how widely support for restrictions had permeated the cotton trade: 'Considerable diffidence has been shown by trade associations and some large firms in the cotton trade in giving evidence on [future tariff policy], owing to the fact that members and directors were not in agreement on the future national policy with regard to Customs duties'.[142]

Lancashire's new concern for the East Midlands trades coincided for the first time with their own long-standing protectionism. The lace trade required 'drastic' restriction of imports from Germany to safeguard the new producers who had risen to substitute for Barmen and Plauen goods during the War. There was 'practical unanimity' among hosiery and fabric glove manufacturers that 'drastic measures' were needed to counter the German threat. Germany apart, a graded tariff would secure the home market, allow standardization of output, and so promote exports.[143]

Witnesses from the woollen and worsted industry were likewise unanimous on penalizing Germany by duties or prohibitions. Beyond this, they were divided over the need for a duty on men's dress-goods, but agreed that in yarns and women's dress-goods, where foreign competition was more serious, a three-tier tariff was required.

Opinion within the silk trade was collected for the committee by the Silk Association, which received 138 replies to a questionnaire sent to its 238

---

[140] *Report of the Departmental Committee appointed by the Board of Trade to consider the position of the Iron and Steel Trades after the War*, Cd. 9071 (1918), esp. 16, 20–2, 31–4.
[141] *Report of the Departmental Committee appointed by the Board of Trade to consider the position of the Textile Trades after the War*, Cd. 9070 (1918), 58.
[142] Ibid.   [143] Ibid. 99, 104.

members. These wanted duties on piece-goods and made-up goods which distinguished between the Empire (free), allies (15 per cent *ad valorem*), neutrals (20 to 25 per cent), and enemy countries (40 per cent), with lower duties on thrown silk and spun-silk yarns. A meeting of three-quarters of UK carpet manufacturers recommended a similar tariff.

Even the linen and jute trades, which faced little foreign competition in the home market, showed little attachment to fiscal orthodoxy. Linen manufacturers recommended a four-tier tariff which on certain lines could be 'very moderate'. Jute manufacturers, though needing no import duty, nevertheless desired an export duty on Indian jute goods to benefit British-produced goods in export markets.[144]

The hard core of support for a return to nineteenth-century liberalism came from the committees chaired by Nimmo and Booth. The main concern of the Coal Committee was to avoid any prospect of prohibitions on coal exports to Germany after the War.[145] The twelve-strong committee on shipping and shipbuilding considered that restoration of wartime losses in Britain's merchant marine should be the 'first charge on the national resources', but demanded the removal of government controls which would otherwise paralyse the 'British genius' for individual effort. Nevertheless, rebuilding the British merchant fleet should be encouraged by immediate (wartime) increases in government-controlled freight rates to allow the shipping companies to build up reserves, by a liberal tax regime, by confiscations from the German merchant fleet, by improvements in railway services to the ports, and by state assistance to the port authorities for improving dock facilities and transport. The committee's prescriptions for other industries were harsh. Though lamenting Britain's recent poor progress in the 'newer branches of production', the committee appeared to be prepared to leave them to their fate. Indeed, it should be stressed that the shipping industry's concept of *laissez-faire* was a distinctly slanted one. Much space was devoted in the Report to the need to re-institute the 'conference system' of price collusion, and to prevent German lines from undermining it.[146]

Balfour of Burleigh's summary of the reports of the trade committees was broadly accurate:

[The Electrical Committee had] gone out-and-out I think for a very drastic form of what I should describe, without offence, as Protection . . . The other Committees . . ., especially the Textiles Committee, are all of them, I think, unanimous on the two points—against

---

[144] *Report of the Departmental Committee appointed by the Board of Trade to consider the position of the Textile Trades after the War*, Cd. 9070 (1918), 82–7, 88, 93.

[145] *Interim Report on the Treatment of Exports from the United Kingdom and British Overseas Possessions and the Conservation of the Resources of the Empire during the Transitional Period after the War*, Cd. 9034 (1918), paras. 13–14; *Report of the Departmental Committee appointed by the Board of Trade to consider the position of the Coal Trade after the War*, Cd. 9093 (1918); BBC Minutes, 15 Feb. 1917, BT 55/8/109, PRO.

[146] *Final Report of the Departmental Committee appointed by the Board of Trade to consider the position of the Shipping and Shipbuilding Industries after the War*, Cd. 9092 (1918), 18–24, 27, 55, 61–76.

anything in the nature of dumping or of unfair competition; but they are not all, apparently, sure how far a [General] Tariff will be for our advantage or disadvantage.[147]

Coal and shipping were unusual amongst the satellite committees in that their reports put little or no weight on discrimination against German imports, or on anti-dumping duties, or even on key-industry protection. The chairmen of both were signatories to the interim and final reports of the main Committee, where just these measures were recommended; clearly, they felt the obligation to take a wider view than that represented by their own trades. Nevertheless, in themselves, the reports of their committees provided the most tangible evidence put before the BBC of any continued industrial commitment to Free Trade. The other committees, even cotton, appeared to present a rough consensus on what would today be called selective import controls, embracing key industries, anti-dumping measures, and the safeguarding of important industries experiencing severe foreign competition. Though opinion on an all-embracing general tariff might vary, with the electrical engineers unanimously in favour and the cotton producers largely reluctant, war had undoubtedly modified opinion substantially. At the very least, discussion of the fiscal issue had become distinctly more acceptable, and former Free Traders now seemed much more willing to consider it pragmatically rather than maintaining an ideological position.

As the Tariff Reformers discerned in what was, in effect, the minority report of the BBC, the reports of the industry committees did not fully reflect industry opinion as it had been elicited by their inquiries. Predominant opinion in iron and steel, engineering, the electrical trades, woollens and worsteds, the carpet, silk, and linen industries, the lace and embroidery trades, cotton hosiery and fabric gloves, and non-ferrous metals, had favoured a general tariff. The only industries 'reporting against a tariff' were cotton, jute (as long as India was penalized by an export duty), and shipbuilding.[148]

VII

On the main Committee discussion of general post-war policy began in earnest in June 1917. It was clear by then that earlier support for prohibitions had cooled, and the Tariff Reformers' pessimism on their practicability or importance was widely shared. On long-term policy there was unanimity on the need for key-industry duties, anti-dumping legislation, and the granting of preference on duties when imposed. But the Committee recoiled from the idea of an allied customs union. There were several reasons. Firstly, such a scheme would require the repudiation of existing commercial treaties, bringing the threat of retaliation. Secondly, the Committee had no official indication of whether the US would

---

[147] BBC Minutes, 7 June 1917, BT 55/8/176–81, PRO.
[148] Committee on Commercial and Industrial Policy, *Final Report*, Cd. 9035 (1918), 67.

accept the plan. Thirdly, the entry of the US into the War meant that five-sixths of British imports (based on 1913) now came from the Empire, the allies, or countries which had broken off diplomatic relations with Germany.[149] The Committee did not want to be that generous.

This left the question of permanent policy beyond key industries and dumping. In an important memorandum, Balfour of Burleigh outlined the three main proposals entertained by the Committee. He found little to commend the first, a low flat-rate tariff of 10 per cent *ad valorem* on 'wholly or mainly manufactured' goods, with preference for the Empire and a lesser preference for the allies. Of £193.5m of such imports in 1913, around half had been goods subsequently used in further manufacture, or came from the Empire, France, or Belgium. The duty would only yield £10 to 12m p.a., the equivalent of 3*d*. in the pound on income tax, and the uniform rate would be 'excessive in some cases and inadequate in others'. The second proposal, Faringdon's graduated tariff of 5 to 15 per cent depending on labour content, was equally unsatisfactory. Though more defensible in principle, it would bring forth demands for agricultural protection— indeed, without food duties it would 'hardly yield more revenue than a uniform rate of 10 per cent'. This left the third approach:

If then it is desired to meet industrial claims to some tariff assistance beyond that afforded by anti-dumping measures, and by special duties on German products, without however going to the length of an all-round tariff, we must consider the suggestion put forward by various members of the Committee which in effect takes the view that there are certain industries which *while not 'key' or 'pivot' industries,* are industries which must be safeguarded on grounds of national safety and defence. This line of thought proceeds on the principle that, as a matter of national policy, no important branch of industry should be dominated by a foreign country. It is urged that there are certain staple industries necessary for national defence *or commercial well-being* which are not at present strong enough to organise and maintain themselves on an adequate scale without some form of State assistance. Under this principle each industry would be impartially examined on its merits, and, if it made out its case, such tariff protection, or, alternatively, financial assistance would be recommended as appeared necessary in the circumstances.[150]

Under this rationale, commercial criteria for protection became synonymous with strategic ones, and the mere existence of substantial import competition became a justification for an official inquiry. If the Committee recommended such a course, it should 'indicate typical industries which would . . . deserve detailed examination . . . The report of the Textiles Committee is an example of the way in which the principle might be applied.' Whilst an advisory body investigated industries, it would be necessary to maintain wartime import controls. The chairman recognized that political opposition would be stiff, but

[149] BBC Minutes, 12 July 1917, 55/8/204–9, PRO; also *Final Report*, paras. 240–4.

[150] 'Committee on Commercial and Industrial Policy. Chairman's Memorandum on Fiscal Policy', 25 June 1917, 1–5, BT 55/8/646–51, PRO.

he was 'most anxious not to . . . overrate or magnify [difficulties and objections] in respect of abstract principles'.[151]

At a meeting in July, seven members supported Faringdon's graduated tariff—Faringdon himself, Muntz, Hewins, Scoby Smith, Henry, Balfour, and Pease (to whom should be added Parsons, who did not speak). Five of them—Birchenough, Pearce, McDowell, Wardle, and Nimmo—favoured Balfour of Burleigh's selective tariff. Booth and McCormick remained uncommitted, whilst Williamson's position was ambiguous. Only Hyde and Priestley were against all three proposals. At least thirteen out of eighteen required something more than key industry protection and anti-dumping duties.[152]

By early August (by which time Hewins had left the Committee to join the Colonial Office) only three dissented from the Faringdon or Balfour of Burleigh proposals: O'Neil, Hyde, and Booth. Faringdon, Parsons, and Henry continued to press for a graduated general tariff. But Arthur Balfour was prepared to abandon Faringdon's scheme if Balfour of Burleigh's was far-reaching enough, and eight others agreed to the policy of selective protection. As the chairman put it, 'the selection of special industries for assistance was a lesser evil than an all-round tariff. Though there was risk of lobbying and political corruption, . . . [the] policy would be easier to work and control . . . If we take industries separately, there would be less danger of the erection of vested interests'.[153]

This was the recommendation of the Committee's *Final Report*. Protection, 'for reasons of national safety or on the general ground that it is undesirable that any industry of real importance to our economic strength and well-being should be allowed to be weakened by foreign competition', should only be granted after a 'searching examination . . . by a competent and independent authority'. The Committee even directed attention to 'the important industries which will require consideration in the light of these principles':

the heavy iron and steel trades, and numerous branches of the manufacture of iron and steel goods; the engineering trades, including electrical and motor engineering; the production of a considerable number of non-ferrous metals and ferro-alloys; shipbuilding; many branches of the chemical trades; the textile trades almost as a whole; the manufacture of various classes of rubber goods, especially tyres; and the leather industries.[154]

VIII

In reservations to the *Final Report*, Booth, Hyde, O'Neil, and Williamson repeated their earlier objections. As a representative of the Department of Scientific and

---

[151] Ibid. 5–6, BT 55/8/651–2, PRO.
[152] BBC Minutes, 12 July 1917; *Final Report*, paras. 240–4.
[153] BBC Minutes, 2 Aug. 1917, BT 55/8/215–20, PRO.
[154] *Final Report*, paras. 215, 227. See also para. 254(3).

Industrial Research, McCormick properly dissociated himself from the fiscal proposals. Ten members, including both labour representatives and former Free-Trader Priestley, signed without qualification. Faringdon, Henry, Muntz, Parsons, Pease, and Scoby Smith reiterated their preference for a graduated tariff.[155]

Addison thought the Balfour of Burleigh Committee's report 'a nasty blow for any Tariff Reform agitation'.[156] Certainly, the Committee shunned recommending a general tariff or any substantial imperial preference. In that sense, it turned its back on the Chamberlainite vision of the Edwardian years. Even without losing Hewins to the attractions of government office late in the Committee's work, the Faringdon group and the Tariff Commission approach they represented would have been in a minority, if only because theirs was the policy most clearly leading to food duties.

The real significance of the Committee's work, however, was different. In effect, it truncated Tariff Reform, completing the process begun by Bonar Law when he abandoned food duties in 1913. Preference, with its corollary food duties, was clearly separated from protection. Of course, there continued to be industrial protectionists who also genuinely believed in imperial integration. And there were still imperialists who felt the need to mobilize industrial support at home. But, essentially, Balfour of Burleigh established two parallel agendas of Tariff Reform, the industrial and the imperial. When Austen Chamberlain introduced preference on existing duties in the budget of 1919, the process was complete. Industrial protectionists need now have no qualms about their lack of enthusiasm for food duties—preference could be left to grow by itself.

The industrial protectionist agenda of the Committee became the aim of the majority of manufacturers in the 1920s. Here, Balfour of Burleigh was far from discouraging. His Committee were all agreed on key-industry protection for small, specialist trades and effective anti-dumping measures across the whole range of industry. Beyond this, Balfour of Burleigh's policy of selective protection was an empirical one, with the emphasis on some kind of independent tariff board or commission, recommending policy on the basis of inductive study. But, most of all, the list of industries which Balfour of Burleigh considered as legitimate candidates for selective protection was a long one, covering all the major industries with the exception of cotton. Of course there were to be conditions—a requirement to improve efficiency, perhaps[157]—but the Committee did not intend that there should be impossible obstacles for industries in need. In all this, the Committee was reflecting the industry opinion to which it had been exposed. All these provisions, taken together, went a considerable way to giving manufacturing industry the protection that the majority sought.

[155] *Final Report*, 67–73.   [156] Quoted in P. B. Johnson, *Land Fit for Heroes*, 86.
[157] *Final Report*, para. 255(e).

The fate of the Balfour of Burleigh Committee's main recommendations could perhaps have been foretold by the unexplained delay in their publication.[158] In the hands of the governments of the 1920s—Conservative hardly less than Coalition—those recommendations, and the manufacturing aspirations they represented, were to be frustrated. The McKenna duties survived, except temporarily during the Labour Government of 1924, and key industries were protected under the Safeguarding of Industries Act of 1921. But, in spite of superficial appearances to the contrary, the SIA never provided the measures against dumping or the selective protection envisaged by the Committee. Nor was the Act administered by government in such a way as to make its provisions a reality. These were the two complaints on which manufacturers were to reach a rough consensus in the 1920s. The bulk of the manufacturing community found common cause in the policy outlined by the Committee on Commercial and Industrial Policy.

---

[158] P. B. Johnson, *Land Fit for Heroes*, 27 n., 148. Sir Edward Carson, who, in the later stages of the war, used his Economic Offensive Committee to press the recommendations of the BBC upon the Government, protested to no effect.

9

The Laboratory of Safeguarding

By 1921 the McKenna duties had been supplemented by a Safeguarding of Industries Act and a separate measure for protecting the dyestuffs industry. The proportion of British imports covered by the safeguarding legislation was small,[1] and the labour and capital employed in producing many of the items included insignificant—there was indeed a conscious hypocrisy in the criterion, written into the legislation, that the applying industry should be of 'substantial importance'.[2] Nevertheless, there is a tendency to regard safeguarding as a step on the road to protection, following the inexorable march to 1932 that had been set in train by McKenna. To Forrest Capie, the importance of the measures of the 1920s lay in 'their inroads on free trade ideology',[3] and there can be no doubt that, if safeguarding was not always a vehicle of conversion, it did provide a sort of attitudinal preparation for the erosion of economic liberalism.

Yet there was another side to safeguarding. It gave the politicians the opportunity to delay, whilst appearing to be open to pragmatism. This had undoubted benefits in blunting the effectiveness of propaganda in favour of more far-reaching Tariff Reform. As Hewins noted perceptively, it was difficult to sustain Tariff-Reform agitation at a time when the public perceived safeguarding as a legislative reality.[4] Safeguarding also had the potential to damage the emergence of a protectionist consensus in British industry, since, unlike a general tariff, it offered no certainty of a *quid pro quo* to user industries. Despite this, relatively little of the opposition to safeguarding arose from within industry. Much more significant was the hostility from the merchant community, but in the murky complexities of the controversy this was far from clear to outside observers.

I

After the coupon election, demands for a clarification of government intentions on trade policy escalated. As a stop-gap, the Government attempted to remove import controls selectively, leaving in force those on products which had become

---

[1] J. H. Richardson, *British Economic Foreign Policy* (1936), 90.
[2] Board of Trade, *Safeguarding of Industries: Procedures and Enquiries*, Cmd. 2327 (1925).
[3] F. Capie, *Depression and Protectionism* (1983), 41.
[4] See below, 372.

recognized during the War as belonging to the key industries. In February 1919 Sir Albert Stanley's extension of prohibitions to include aniline dyes and organic chemicals used for dyes, pharmaceuticals, and photochemicals brought protests from Lancashire, the *Manchester Guardian* insisting he was intent on implementing the long-term proposals of the Paris Economic Conference.[5] At the same time he disappointed the manufacturers of the NUM in announcing that the economic situation was so unstable that a declaration of permanent policy would be premature.[6] Lloyd George also equivocated before an NUM deputation in July.[7]

Announcing the ending of import restrictions in August, Lloyd George sought to calm fears of import penetration by stressing the appreciation of the dollar and the crippling effect of Versailles on German exports; but he confirmed the widespread expectation that key industries would be protected, and also gave notice of an anti-dumping measure. The issue of the Board of Trade list of exceptions to de-restriction four days later caused predictable protests from industries such as hosiery, toys, and even automobiles, at their omission from it.[8] In retrospect, it was inevitable that many of the early applications for an anti-dumping duty would come from industries denied key-industry status.

Sir Auckland Geddes, Stanley's successor, first attempted to introduce this dual system of key industry and anti-dumping duties in the Imports and Exports Regulation Bill of November 1919. It met intense parliamentary opposition from some seventy-five Coalition Liberals. Its definition of dumping was criticized, as we shall see below.[9] Its proposal for a trade regulation committee of ministers, civil servants, and MPs encountered opposition from Free Traders on the grounds that such a non-parliamentary body would have too much power. Some Tariff Reformers, on the other hand, regarded the committee as too political, and wished the administration of regulation to be in the hands of the Customs and Excise. The Birmingham Chamber of Commerce, voicing its 'profound discontent with . . . an objectionable system of bureaucratic control and interference', even suggested the bill had been drafted purposely to fail, and demanded its replacement with a 'simpler and more direct' measure. It is significant that the Association of British Chambers of Commerce (formerly ACCUK) supported the bill by a large majority, but even here there was a desire to see the politicians on the trade-regulation committee replaced by

[5] R. K. Snyder, *The Tariff Problem in Great Britain 1918–1923* (Stanford, Calif., 1944), 21, 23.
[6] Ibid. 26–7. [7] Ibid. 27.
[8] Sir Auckland Geddes of the Board of Trade was particularly trenchant in his rejection of the claims of the Association of British Motor and Allied Manufacturers for a 33% duty on cars, commercial vehicles and tractors. Cars already had a similar duty under McKenna, which combined with freight, insurance and exchange costs of importing from the US was already equivalent to a duty of 88%. Even commercial vehicles, exempted under McKenna, had the equivalent of a 45% duty. See ibid. 28, 31–2.
[9] See below, 259–61.

businessmen nominated by the ABCC and the FBI.[10] The London Chamber, too, generally supported the bill, though finding it 'complicated and cumbersome'.[11] Reviled by its enemies, the bill was scarcely received with open arms by its friends.

The Coalition leaders' difficulties were increased by the courts. The unpopularity of the dyestuffs restrictions with import merchants was compounded by 'exaggerated' complaints from the textile dyers. Merchants Brown and Forth of Manchester, being denied a licence to import pyrogallic acid from Canada, secured Justice Sankey's ruling that it had not been legitimate to use the Customs Consolidation Act of 1876 for the purpose. Immediately, the British Dyestuffs Corporation was nearly swamped by imports from Germany and Switzerland: the Government was 'under increasingly heavy pressure from users [led by the Manchester Chamber of Commerce and Lancashire MPs] who had forgotten what they endorsed a few years earlier'.[12] Whilst, at Board of Trade suggestion, the Dyestuffs (Import Regulation) Act was subsequently forced through Parliament late in 1920 to close the loophole, Sankey's ruling had wider significance, since it essentially brought to an end the period when executive control of trade policy could be legitimized by the Customs Consolidation Act.[13] In the meantime the controversy further unsettled the prospects for the Imports and Exports Regulation Bill, and Geddes had little choice but to withdraw it.

The Safeguarding of Industries Act 1921, conceived under the Presidency of Sir Robert Horne and enacted under that of Baldwin, established three different types of duty. The parameters of the key-industry schedule had been shaped during the War. The BBC had specified a list of goods which 'should be maintained in this country at all hazards and at any expense. No economic rules apply to these minor but important industries'.[14] The list had much in common with that used by the UBC and the Tariff Commission to embarrass the government during the War, with a somewhat wider range of items displayed at a TRL exhibition at Central Hall, Westminster, in 1918,[15] and with the list of exceptions to de-restriction issued by the Board of Trade in August 1919.[16] The schedule to Part I of the SIA now imposed duties of $33 \frac{1}{3}$ per cent (50 per cent

[10] *BCCJ*, 15 Dec. 1919, 1011–12; 16 Feb. 1920, 118–20; 15 Sept. 1920, 725; LCC, *Council Minutes*, 12 Feb. 1920, 275; ABCC, *Reports*, 1919–20, 22–23.

[11] LCC, *Council Minutes*, 11 Dec. 1919, 231.

[12] L. F. Haber, *The Chemical Industry, 1900–1930* (Oxford, 1971), 242–3.

[13] In fact, wartime import controls were better legitimized by the Defence of the Realm Act than by the Customs Consolidation Act, but this did not alter the implications of Sankey's judgement.

[14] BBC, *Interim Report*, Cd. 9034 (1918), 4.

[15] TRL, *Keys of Industry*, 4. Articles on display included nickel, manganese, lead, antimony, monazite sand, rubber, electric light carbons, and hot metal (brass) pressings.

[16] The list comprised dyes and dyestuffs, synthetic drugs and perfumes, optical and scientific glass, illuminating glassware, laboratory porcelain, scientific and optical instruments, potassium compounds, tungsten powder, ferro-tungsten, zinc oxide, lithapone, thorium nitrate, gas mantles, magnetos, hosiery latch needles, and gauges. See R. K. Snyder, *The Tariff Problem*, 30.

on optical glass) for five years.[17] It was ultimately to comprise some 6,500 items, generally under the headings of synthetic organic chemicals, scientific and optical instruments, optical glass, laboratory glass and porcelain, magnetos, wireless valves, permanent magnets, and hosiery latch needles.[18]

Part II of the Act appeared to afford a twofold protection against dumping— dumping facilitated by the exchange depreciation common to many European countries in the aftermath of the War, and dumping as a deliberate business practice. In fact the limits to its application were crippling. Much of Part II was inoperable, whilst the remainder served a very different purpose from that which appeared on the statute book. The story of this perversion of the anti-dumping duty goes back to 1919 or even 1917.

II

At first sight, the withdrawal of the Imports and Exports Regulation Bill in December 1919 represented a merely temporary setback for the Tariff Reformers on their road to the Safeguarding of Industries Act, a second and more successful attempt at the same objectives. In fact, it revealed the fragile nature of the apparent convergence of opinion in the War, and had more enduring consequences than have been generally appreciated.

Publication of the key-industry schedule of the Bill created the same alarms and disappointments within excluded industries as had the Board of Trade list of exceptions to de-restriction in August 1919.[19] The Nottingham Chamber of Commerce, for instance, lamented the denial of key-industry status to embroideries, Barmen laces, cotton hosiery, glove fabrics, fabric gloves, and press-studs, and joined with the relevant trade associations in pressing their demand for tariffs on the Board of Trade.[20] In effect an overspill category for those industries seeking protection, the anti-dumping provision in the Bill was thus the ancestor of Part II of the Safeguarding of Industries Act.

But the later measure was more restricted in scope, and hence the cause of considerable dissatisfaction among the protectionists within the business community. The Balfour of Burleigh Committee had envisaged an anti-dumping measure based on a dual-pricing criterion. So too had a Ministry of Reconstruction Committee in 1919.[21] This definition had widespread acceptance in the Chambers of Commerce; it was used in the reports of the Special Committee of

---

[17] This was renewed for a similar period in 1926. See below, 270–4.

[18] Dyestuffs were not covered by the Act in view of their prohibition except under licence in the Dyestuffs (Import Regulation) Act. Licences were granted if there was no home production or if UK price was more than three times that of imports, (reduced to 1.75 times by 1930). See Haber, *The Chemical Industry*, 243.

[19] See above, 257.

[20] NCC, *Annual Report*, 1919, and Appendix to same.

[21] Cmd. 455 (1919).

the London Chamber of Commerce on Trade after the War, whilst several Chambers advocated legislation 'along Canadian lines'.[22] The failure of the Imports and Exports Regulation Bill, which had been framed according to this dual-pricing criterion, demonstrated that though wartime conditions might have persuaded some Liberals of the need to protect against dumping below cost of production, they still did not accept the need to protect against price discrimination. A minority of unreconstructed Free Traders (the delegates from the Hull, Preston, and Bolton Chambers)[23] opposed all forms of anti-dumping legislation in the ABCC in January 1920. They were joined by R. K. Calvert of Leeds, who used *The Manchester Guardian*'s argument that since prices in protectionist countries were normally higher than in free-trade Britain, it was scarcely surprising that 'foreigners, if they were to sell in Great Britain at all, could only do so at a lower price, though still including a profit, than they charged their own countrymen'.[24]

This twisted logic, almost casting the foreign dumper in the role of the injured party, completely distorted the fact that he was already enjoying the benefit of higher, tariff-determined domestic prices, and that these materially assisted his dumping strategy in the first place. By a curious act of doublethink the very arguments pioneered by the Tariff Commission were now being used to deny the policy prescriptions which followed from them. To concede that dumping was undesirable was in line with twentieth-century world trends from the Canadian tariff of 1904 to GATT and the Kennedy round, but to adopt cost of production and not price as the criterion was not.[25] Nevertheless, doubtless because of the opposition encountered during discussion of the Imports and Exports Regulation Bill, the Safeguarding Bill of March 1921 did not attempt explicitly to protect British manufacturers against dual pricing. Dumping (other than 'currency' dumping, which will be considered below) was defined as selling at below cost of production.

There was perhaps a concealed attempt to overcome this limitation, in that the Bill took as the measure of cost of production 'the current sterling equivalent of 95 per cent of the wholesale price at the works charged for goods of the class or description for consumption in the country of manufacture'.[26] As some Coalition Liberals recognized, this did allow penalties against price-discrimination as long as export price was below home wholesale-price by a margin.[27] In practice, however, the question of whether the price discrimination which was

---

[22] LCC, *Council Minutes*, 12 Dec. 1918, 87.

[23] ABCC, *Reports*, 1919–20, 13–16.

[24] *Manchester Guardian*, 22 Nov. 1919, paraphrased in R. K. Snyder, *The Tariff Problem*, 35; ABCC, *Reports*, 1919–20, 21.

[25] W. M. Corden, *Trade Policy and Economic Welfare* (Oxford, 1974), 244; O. J. McDiarmid, *Commercial Policy in the Canadian Economy* (Cambridge, Mass., 1946), 217–8.

[26] SIA, Pt. II, cl. 8.

[27] *Parliamentary Debates*, 5th ser. cxlii, cols. 1778–92.

almost certainly a common feature of world trade in the 1920s reached such dimensions is of limited value,[28] dwarfed by the attitudinal significance of a retreat which implicitly recognized that contemporary British opinion accepted cost of production as the central principle.[29] Furthermore, and perhaps even more critical, the specification of wholesale price in the legislation was correctly considered by *The Times* to be vague, unverifiable, and unworkable.[30] As Willie Graham, President of the Board of Trade in the Labour Government of 1929 to 1931 later admitted, those countries which implemented anti-dumping duties, most notably the USA, Canada, Australia, New Zealand, and South Africa, levied duties on the *market* value of the goods in the country of origin, and under their existing general tariffs already possessed 'machinery for ascertaining and checking such market values'. Not only was the British attempt to base an anti-dumping measure on wholesale price in the country of origin 'rendered entirely nugatory owing mainly to the extreme difficulty which complainant industries in this country found in establishing what was the wholesale price in the country of origin', but also the establishment of a successful anti-dumping duty depended on the prior existence of a general tariff.[31]

Nine applications for an anti-dumping duty were received by the Board of Trade. Two of the earliest, relating to glass bottles from Holland and vulcanized fibre from the USA (August and October 1922) got as far as committees, but both failed to prove that imports were below cost of production in the countries of origin. The remaining seven were 'either rejected by the Board of Trade on the ground that a *prima-facie* case had not been established, or not proceeded with': those relating to thrown silk from Italy, microscopes from the USA, and tyres from the USA (all before December 1922); split-wood pulleys from Germany (August 1926); chrome upper-leather from France (April 1927); gallic acid from Germany (May 1927); and vegetable parchment from Germany, Belgium, France, and Italy (March 1928).[32]

Protection against 'currency' dumping—the other form of dumping recognized by the Act—was envisaged if British producers could not meet the home price of the exporter converted into sterling at the prevailing rate of exchange on account of the depreciated foreign currency. It is ironic that this was the only provision of Part II to be implemented before 1925, since, as from their different

[28] Jacob Viner, *Dumping: A Problem in International Trade* (New York, 1966 edn.), 351 (memorandum for League of Nations, written in 1926).

[29] This principle was confirmed in P. Ashley, 'Memorandum on the Operation of Existing Protective Measures in the United Kingdom', 12, Tariff Advisory Committee, Mm. 8, [n.d. but c. Nov. 1923], copy in 1/2/4, Conservative Research Department Papers.

[30] *The Times*, 2 Apr. 1921, cited in R. K. Snyder, *The Tariff Problem*, 79.

[31] 'Anti-Dumping Legislation: Note by the President of the Board of Trade', June 1931, BT 55/58/9, PRO.

[32] Ibid. (appendicular memorandum). Part II of the Act continued to operate in the late 1920s, alongside the Safeguarding of Industries (Customs Duties) Act of 1925, and was repealed by Labour in August 1930. See A. S. Harvey, *The General Tariff of the United Kingdom* (1933), 52.

perspectives *The Economist* and *The Times* both recognized,[33] it more directly controverted that principle of comparative advantage through international trade which welded economic liberalism and Free Trade so indissolubly together. If a country's trade balance and economy were so shattered that its exchanges were heavily adverse, how else could exports revive? The whole theory of the balance of payments, the very essence of the classical gold standard, depended on such equilibriating changes taking place.

The criterion for protection against currency dumping was that the exporter's currency should have depreciated by one-third.[34] At a time when the British monetary authorities were pursuing deflationary policies in their determination to return to gold, even the USA came close, and on this basis the Act might have been invoked widely. But Part II of the Act was limited by the condition that no duty should be imposed which was 'at variance with treaty obligations'. Duties imposed under the Act were not general duties but were aimed at specific countries, named by Order of the House of Commons. Whilst the Board of Trade's law officers advised that a duty on goods dumped below cost or wholesale price was not discimination against the named country but against an avoidable practice, a duty on goods benefiting from a depreciated currency was clearly discriminatory against the country, and was therefore considered likely to be in breach of treaty provisions.[35]

Thus only Germany and Czechoslovakia were ever to experience Britain's measures against currency dumping. With Germany there was no treaty, and she was unable to retaliate because under Versailles and the allied administration she did not possess tariff autonomy, or even the ability to impose duties without corresponding excises on domestic production.[36] According to D. Loebl of the London importers Schindler and Co., the application of the British flint-glass manufacturers for safeguarding of domestic and illuminating glassware had originally encompassed Belgium, but the treaty consideration led the Board of Trade to confine the duty imposed to German and Czechoslovak goods.[37] Treaty considerations also explain the subsequent official inaction when the French franc depreciated. As early as 1922 the Nottingham Chamber of Commerce observed that 'the attitude of the Board of Trade in consistently refusing to recognise [the depreciation of the franc] is

[33] *The Economist*, 29 Nov. 1919, cited in R. K. Snyder, *The Tariff Problem*, 36–7; *The Times*, 2 Apr. 1921, cited in R. K. Snyder, *The Tariff Problem*, 79.
[34] Safeguarding of Industries Act, 1921, 9 & 10 Geo. 5, ch. 47; P. Ashley, 'Memorandum on . . . Existing Protective Measures'.
[35] 'Anti-Dumping Legislation', appendicular memorandum.
[36] T. E. Gregory, *Tariffs: A Study in Method* (1921), 32–3; J. M. Keynes, *Economic Consequences of the Peace* (1919), 93; P. Ashley, *Modern Tariff History* (3rd edn., 1920), 126–7; H. Liepmann, *Tariff Levels and the Economic Unity of Europe* (1938), 59, 116, 231–2.
[37] LCC, Minutes of China and Glassware Vigilance Committee, 29 Nov. 1921; 'Safeguarding of Industries Act, 1921: Minute Book No. 1', (hereinafter cited as SMB(1)), 31–6.

incomprehensible'.[38] Whether Nottingham was simply inciting protest is unclear, but its outburst does raise the question of how widely known to businessmen was the treaty limitation of the SIA.

The economist A. C. Pigou later considered the currency measure 'thoroughly confused'. Depreciation of the mark did not guarantee the German exporter's ability to sell at abnormally low sterling prices if Germany's internal price level had risen concomitantly. 'This elementary truth was not apparently appreciated' by the architects of the Act.[39] But his strictures were largely misplaced. True, from April 1920 to April 1921 the demand for money in Germany was rising because of greater confidence in the German political system both at home and abroad, and its effect was felt more rapidly in the foreign-exchange market than in the domestic price-level, lessening relative undervaluation. Indeed, German businessmen during this period felt the mark was overvalued on the world market. But after the demand for 132 billion gold marks (£6.6 billion sterling) in the London Ultimatum on reparations, the year between April 1921 and June 1922 was one of rapid depreciation and increasing undervaluation. External confidence in Germany was hit by the recommendation of a committee of foreign bankers under J. P. Morgan that foreign loans to Germany should be suspended without a moratorium on reparations, and by the murder of Rathenau, the symbol of Germany's willingness to co-operate with reparations. The subsequent hyperinflation saw increasing undervaluation, though it is noticeable that, based on 1913 unit values, exports actually fell in 1923. This was probably because of a reduction in supply, partly consequent upon the occupation of the Ruhr. Generally, therefore, Pigou's qualification was only approximated for a short period, April 1920 to April 1921, one which actually predated safeguarding.[40]

The Nottingham lace and embroidery manufacturers were preparing an application under Part II even before the Act's passage, and there soon developed a rush of applications. Twenty-four were received in the first five months of the Act, of which sixteen were either rejected or withdrawn and eight referred to committees.[41] By March 1922 seven committee reports had appeared, three adverse and four favourable.[42] The first, and in many ways the test case, was on fabric gloves and glove fabrics. It is difficult to know whether to take seriously Lancashire's extraordinary paranoia that the imposition of a duty on gloves from Germany would result in massive retaliation against the entire cotton

---

[38] NCC, *Annual Report*, 1922.

[39] A. C. Pigou, *Aspects of British Economic History, 1918–1925* (1947), 142.

[40] C.-L. Holtfrerich, *The German Inflation 1914–1923* (1980; Eng. edn., transl. T. Balderston, Berlin, 1986), 18–25, 211.

[41] R. K. Snyder, *The Tariff Problem*, 98; *The Times*, 6 Sept. 1921, 25 Nov. 1921, 28 Dec. 1921, 19 Jan. 1922; *Parliamentary Debates*, 5th Series, cli, col. 827. F. Capie, *Depression and Protectionism* 47, is mistaken in stating that only nine applications for anti-dumping duties were ever made.

[42] K. Middlemas and J. Barnes, *Baldwin: A Biography* (1969), 88.

industry,[43] if for no other reason than that Germany lacked tariff autonomy; but nevertheless Coalition Liberals argued against making a safeguarding order in the hope that Part II of the Act could be kept a dead letter. Baldwin, however, President of the Board of Trade, divided the cabinet on party lines and, at some cost to the cohesion of the Coalition, prevailed by a narrow margin. Duties were imposed on fabric gloves and glove fabric from Germany, domestic and illuminating glassware from Germany and Czechoslovakia, aluminium and wrought enamelled holloware from Germany, and gas mantles.[44] By the end of 1922, the Board of Trade had issued thirteen reports by eleven investigating committees. The gold-leaf trade was denied protection because of the inferiority of its product; that some toymakers could not compete against German competition was held to be for reasons other than currency depreciation; the glass-bottle manufacturers failed to prove the severity of German and Dutch competition; and the allegation of British vulcanized-fibre manufacturers that a price agreement on US exports to the UK was being broken was found to be substantially untrue. Three reports contained some ambiguity, those on optical and scientific instruments (whose makers were seeking protection additional to that granted under the key-industry provisions), on snap fasteners and hooks and eyes, and on wire nails.[45] All these applications were rejected, the four orders approved on 31 July 1922 thus constituting the full extent of safeguarding under Part II before 1925.

Indeed, the handling of the Board of Trade ensured that only a small minority of the 160 enquiries received under Part II by November 1923 were translated into actual applications. Applications received from larger industries, such as machine tools, silk, cotton laces, and worsted dress-goods, were turned down without an enquiry. The application from the silk industry was ruled out because it was held that there were more factors in French competition than the simple depreciation of the franc, but Percy Ashley of the Board of Trade admitted that an important factor had been fear of French retaliation. The machine-tools application was directed against German imports due to currency depreciation, but severe depression in the industry was more due to US imports and the release of stocks by the War Disposals Board. At the time, German imports were small, and the application was made on the likelihood that they would increase. Ashley admitted that the Board of Trade had been unduly secretive about the operation of Part II, and had actively discouraged applications which made out sound *prima facie* cases.[46] There was apparently a safeguarding enquiry

---

[43] An uproar recounted approvingly and uncritically by R. K. Snyder, *The Tariff Problem*, 102–3.

[44] A. Ramsay, *The Economics of Safeguarding* (1930), 52.

[45] Details of Board of Trade Non-Parliamentary Papers from P. and G. Ford, *Breviate of Parliamentary Papers, 1917–1939* (2nd edn., Shannon, 1969), 187–9.

[46] P. Ashley, 'Memorandum on . . . Existing Protective Measures in the United Kingdom', 12, copy in 1/2/4, Conservative Research Department Papers.

into the lace and embroidery trades in 1923, which examined fifty-three witnesses in twenty-two meetings over five months, but this was not conducted under the auspices of the Safeguarding of Industries Act,[47] perhaps being a trial run by a Board of Trade anxious to set up a procedure for investigating and, if necessary, protecting an industry without recourse to an Act which it found troublesome.[48]

III

The Safeguarding Act provoked surprisingly little opposition in the journals of the country's Chambers of Commerce, and most of that was from merchants and importers. One early historian claimed that 'Manufacturers found that they needed in further production activities many of the articles included in the [key industries] list ... and that their operating costs were being increased by the amount of the duty', but the only example he cited was in fact a committee of import merchants.[49] He might have instanced the Edge Tool Trade Section of the Birmingham Chamber, whose opposition to the Act seems to have been grounded on the fear that iron and steel might be included, or the Hull Chamber, which similarly feared inclusion of shipbuilding materials. Significantly, however, the rest of the Birmingham Chamber supported the Act, even though a high proportion of its membership were steel-users in a similar position to the Edge Tool Section. In the Hull Chamber, furthermore, which had in 1916 endorsed a post-war fiscal policy to 'prevent unfair competition arising from dumping and subsidies', and in 1918 supported a protectionist policy drafted by the National Paint Federation which accepted, perhaps as a *quid pro quo*, safeguarding of dyestuffs, a raw material used by Hull paint manufacturers, manufacturers were in a minority compared with shipowners and merchants.[50]

Though Manchester Chamber of Commerce may have lost its wartime enthusiasm for protection of dyestuffs, its reaction to safeguarding was in some ways milder than might have been expected. Indeed, it suggested subsidies rather than duties during discussion of the Imports and Exports Regulation Bill. When this was rejected in the Dyestuffs (Import Regulation) Act, the Chamber simply 'acquiesced'.[51] The Board of Directors condemned the Safeguarding Bill of 1921 by only twelve votes to eleven, again recommending subsidies, and 'did not

---

[47] BT 13/120/E44584, PRO.

[48] See below, 274–6.

[49] R. K. Snyder, *The Tariff Problem*, 97. Whilst acceptable as a narrative of the events in Parliament, Snyder's work accepts at face value the polemical bias of contemporary Free Traders whilst dismissing out of hand those of the Tariff Reformers.

[50] *BCCJ*, 15 Aug. 1921, 589; Hull CC *Annual Report*, 15 Nov. 1916, 41; 11 Nov. 1918, 86–8; 23 Nov. 1921, 14, 80.

[51] A. Redford, *Manchester Merchants and Foreign Trade* ii (Manchester, 1956), 215.

persist in its opposition to the Bill'.[52] The Engineering Section of the Chamber actually supported Part II of the Act.

The Chamber's strongest opposition was aimed at the duty on fabric gloves from Germany, and this led to a poll in which 42 per cent responded, and those favouring repeal won by 1,300 to 300. Again, the Chamber's alternative was subsidies. In spite of this poll, *The Economist*'s claim that 'Lancashire is stronger on the Free Trade issue today than ever before'[53] was 'sadly exaggerated':

the Chamber contented itself with a formal denunciation of the Dyestuffs and Safeguarding Acts, and took no steps to agitate for their repeal. It did not wax enthusiastic over the lapsing of the McKenna duties in ... 1924, and declined to take part in the 'political' discussion on the subject at the meeting of the Association of British Chambers of Commerce ... Even the taxation of rayon in the Budget of 1925, which touched the cotton trade more nearly, evoked only mild protests ... and from the first the Directors of the Manchester Chamber concerned themselves with the administrative details rather than with opposition to the principle.[54]

Acquiescence in protection as it existed was not, of course, the same as support for its extension. Nevertheless, the Chamber's advocacy of subsidies shows a remarkable retreat from the strict tenets of *laissez-faire* (and, curiously for Lancashire, a surprising lack of concern for the foreign retaliation which would the more probably have been provoked by subsidies than by tariffs), and the mildness of its opposition to safeguarding accords with our impression of attitudes in the broader business community.

Most active in opposing the Act were the 'vigilance committees' of the London Chamber. These were set up to monitor the interests of merchants and importers under the Act. Ostensibly their purpose was to co-operate with government in its administration and operation, but their chief business was complaint; the Fancy Goods Vigilance Committee, as its organizer James D. Kiley MP admitted, 'reserved to itself the liberty of criticism'.[55] Indeed, the membership of this committee would have made the blood of pre-war Tariff Reformers or wartime 'trade warriors' boil. Of thirty firms, seventeen had foreign names, mostly German, whilst two of the English-styled firms were represented at meetings by men with foreign names.[56]

The mere holding of a meeting to consider application under Part II, by the manufacturers of dress and garment shields, gold and aluminium bronze powders, picture frame mouldings, toys, or wire nails, prompted the formation of such a committee, or caught the interest of an existing one. The wholesale houses of the Manchester Home Trade Association led the Manchester Chamber

[52] A. Redford, *Manchester Merchants and Foreign Trade* ii (Manchester, 1956), 216.
[53] *The Economist*, 13 Jan. 1923, quoted ibid. 217.   [54] Ibid. 217.
[55] LCC, Minutes of Fancy Goods Vigilance Committee, 29 Sept. 1921, SMB(1)), 5–7.
[56] LCC, Minutes of Fancy Goods Section, 20 Sept. 1921, Fancy Goods Section Minute Book, i. (1921–39), 27.

and a committee of London import merchants in opposing a duty on fabric gloves.[57] Importers of aluminium and enamelled hollow-ware joined with retailers such as Marks and Spencer in opposing the manufacturers' application. Even where using industries were involved, as in the opposition of the Federation of Master Printers and the Master Bookbinders' Association to the application of the Master Gold and Silver Beaters' Association, or in that of the Perfumery Manufacturers' Section of the London Chamber, the National Union of Mineral Water Manufacturers' Associations Ltd. and the Export Beer Bottlers' Association to that of the Association of Glass Bottle Manufacturers, it was the merchants of the vigilance committees who led the agitation.[58]

Kiley, chairman of merchants Whyte, Ridsdale and Co. Ltd. and Liberal MP for Whitechapel and St. George's until December 1922[59] soon came to dominate the activities of these committees. He had to tread carefully with the London Chamber itself, in view of its scrupulous neutrality on safeguarding. In the case of the opposition of the China and Glassware Vigilance Committee to the application of the manufacturers of domestic and illuminating glassware this had revealing consequences. The cost of opposition was estimated at £1,000, and with only £500 raised by the importers the Committee was warned bluntly by the Chamber that it could not be held liable, and that opposition must cease. The importers thereupon persuaded the Illuminating Glassware Group, whose members included London wholesalers and three of the best-known Czechoslovakian manufacturers, to increase their guarantees; they even considered calling the commercial attaché of the Czechoslovak Legation to give evidence before the Board of Trade enquiry.[60] The enquiry into glass bottles cost the opponents £972, of which £600 still needed to be found afterwards:

Mr. B. Jonzen [of B. Jonzen and Co. Ltd.] undertook to get in touch with his suppliers in Holland. Mr. S. C. Mitchell [of the Waterloo Bottling Co. Ltd.] also promised to arrange for a contribution of £100 from the German Manufacturers' Combine and kindly intimated that he would forward a cheque for £50 on account from his firm during the next few days.[61]

Foreign firms, it appears, could not only contest safeguarding applications, but also obtain credit from British importers to do so. Indeed, the Glass Bottle Committee ended up with surplus funds of £169, £25 of which was donated to a 'Special Propaganda Fund' organized by Kiley against the Act and 'recognised

---

[57] LCC, Minutes of Meetings of Importers of Fabric Gloves, 7 and 21 Nov. 1921, SMB(1), 21–2, 25.

[58] LCC, Minutes of Meetings of Firms interested in the Import of Aluminium and Enamelled Hollow-ware Goods, 2 and 5 Jan. 1922, SMB(1), 37–8, 39–40; LCC, *Council Minutes*, 12 Jan. 1922, 259; 9 Feb. 1922, 274; 9 Mar. 1922, 289, 291; 11 May 1922, 18; 8 June 1922, 34, 37; 13 Dec. 1923, 236; 12 Feb. 1925, 97.

[59] M. Stenton and S. Lees (ed.), *Who's Who of British Members of Parliament* (Brighton, 1979), iii.

[60] China and Glassware Vigilance Committee Minutes, 22 Dec. 1921, SMB(1), 48–50.

[61] Minutes of Glass Bottle Committee, 6 July 1922, SMB(1), 89–90.

by the Committee to have been of considerable service to the Glass trade'.[62] The surplus from one opposition to an application could be transferred to fight another.

The large majority of the London Chamber's sixty-five trade sections, even the large Merchants' Section, acquiesced in the policy of safeguarding, but the minority could be an irritant within a chamber which recognized their right to object to the operation of the Act, but which deprecated their taking a public position on the principles underlying it. It was not uncommon that the opponents to an application claimed the full support of the London Chamber: in the opening months President Stanley Machin had twice to correct counsel appearing before Board of Trade inquiries 'as to the interests they actually represented'.[63]

Many of the complaints of the vigilance committees were directed at the key-industries schedule rather than Part II. The Chemical Merchants' Committee considered the schedule 'wider and more far-reaching than was intended', whilst the Joint Vigilance Committee of the Fancy Goods and China and Glassware Sections questioned 'the very wide interpretations' of the items listed in it by the Board of Trade. Indeed, Kiley even affected to suspect the existence of 'private lists' beyond the 6,000 items listed in the official schedule, and demanded their publication.[64] The most common complaint, however, was that certain fine chemicals in the schedule were not produced in the UK. The Perfumery Manufacturers' Section of the London Chamber made such a complaint to an unsympathetic Board of Trade in 1921, whilst in 1923 the Merchants' Sub-Section of the Chemical Trades Section of the Chamber lobbied for removal of sodium phosphate, oxalic acid, acetic acid, formaldehyde, milk of magnesia, and Rochelle Salts from the schedule.[65] By 1925 importers' complaints had escalated to the accusation that British manufacturers were importing scheduled chemicals themselves rather than manufacturing them.[66]

Key-industry products could certainly end up in the most unlikely places and cause problems of definition—dolls' eyes, only 5 per cent of imported dolls by value, were taxed at $33\frac{1}{3}$ per cent, even though not all were the 'lampblown ware' specified in the schedule. The Board of Trade required confirmation from the protectionist Electrical Group of the London Chamber that the carbon rods in pocket batteries were not (dutiable) arc-lamp carbons.[67] The importers'

[62] LCC, Minutes of Glass Bottle Committee, 10 Oct. 1922, SMB(1), 91–2.

[63] LCC, *Council Minutes*, 9 Feb. 1922, 274.

[64] LCC, Joint Meeting of Fancy Goods and China and Glassware Vigilance Committees, 17 Oct. 1921, SMB(1), 11–15.

[65] See LCC, *Council Minutes*, 14 Apr. 1921, 159; 10 Oct. 1921, 233; 11 Jan. 1923, 115; 8 Mar. 1923, 140.

[66] See below, 271–2; also LCC, *Council Minutes*, 10 Oct. 1921, 234; 8 Dec. 1921, 242.

[67] LCC, Joint Meeting of the Fancy Goods and China and Glassware Vigilance Committees, 17 Oct. 1921, SMB(1), 11–15. Such problems were overcome by waiving the duty on goods where only

annoyance was, moreover, increased by the trouble and expense of getting drawbacks on goods re-exported,[68] by 'serious congestion' and delay at ports of entry, especially Hull, Leith, and Folkestone, during the early months of the Act, and by Kiley's claim that the customs authorities at different ports were not consistent, some goods being stopped at Portsmouth but being admitted freely into London.[69]

Complaints of delay from London carriers Gerhard and Hey Ltd., the British Commercial Transport Co. Ltd., and Rosenberg, Lowe and Co.—there were only three examining officers to cover the Swan Lane, Fishmongers' Hall, Old Swan, Monument, Sperlings, Pooles, and Victoria Wharves in London—were raised by Kiley in Parliament, but a Board of Trade inquiry found the Customs Department up to date. As one carriers' representative admitted, rather than using a shipping agent traders themselves were wasting time by attempting to pass incorrect papers through customs, a source of annoyance to a carrier who might have as many as 100 correct papers per day to be processed by officials submerged under the deluge of incorrect forms from independents. In all 'it seemed as if a Continental tariff were being built up without establishing a Continental system to ensure rapid clearance'.[70]

As was shown by Kiley's 'Special Propaganda Fund', merchant opposition, even when dressed up as concern over the administration of the Act, had wider foundations. H. H. Grylls, Secretary of the Board of Customs, pointed out to a deputation from the London Chamber's Fancy Goods Section in May 1922 that many of its complaints were matters of policy, and should properly be addressed to the Board of Trade. Such was the claim that the porcelain case which comprised 80 per cent of the value of a sample imported clock should be regarded as 'furniture', and therefore exempt.[71] Furthermore, if the Fancy Goods Section had initially been set up to monitor the administration of the Act, it had within eighteen months become so exasperated that it was urging repeal of both the safeguarding legislation and the German Reparation (Recovery) Act.[72] Clearly, the vigilance committees combined their ostensible function with an organized and thinly veiled political resistance and opposition to the legislation.

one component was liable to duty, in the Treasury Order of 1922 and the Finance Acts of 1922 and 1923; see P. Ashley, 'Memorandum on the Operation of Existing Protective Measures in the UK', 7, TAC Mm. No. 8, copy in 1/2/4, CRD.

[68] LCC, Report of Deputation to Secretary of HM Customs, 9 May 1922, Fancy Goods Section Minute Book, i. 48–53.

[69] Ibid. Also LCC, *Council Minutes*, 10 Oct. 1921, 233–4, 236; *Council Minutes*, 8 Dec. 1921, 242, 251.

[70] LCC, Joint Meeting of Fancy Goods and China and Glassware Vigilance Committees, 4 Nov. 1921, SMB(1), 16–17; Conference between Fancy Goods and China and Glassware Vigilance Committees and representatives of London Carriers, 4 Nov. 1921, SMB(1), 18–20.

[71] LCC, Report of Deputation to Secretary of HM Customs, 9 May 1922; Fancy Goods Section Minute Book, i. 48–53.

[72] LCC, *Council Minutes*, 10 May 1923.

IV

Chemicals apart, the relatively untroubled history of the key-industry duties in the 1920s, as opposed to duties under Part II and McKenna, suggests a surprisingly high degree of public acceptance. There were criticisms—ridicule over the affair of the dolls' eyes, the contempt of a *Manchester Guardian* which observed that the combined extinction of the key industries would matter less than a week's stoppage of the coal trade, the annoyance of a group of forty-six university scientists at the taxation of German scientific instruments, the best available.[73] But it is noteworthy that the Labour Government left the 6,500-item schedule untouched when it allowed the McKenna duties to lapse, and Baldwin was able to extend its duration for a further ten years in 1926 with little difficulty.

Significantly, the committee which recommended extension, chaired by Sir Burton Chadwick, parliamentary secretary to the Board of Trade, was composed of scientists and civil servants: Sir Arthur Colefax, barrister and Ph.D. chemist, an authority on patent and trademark law; Sir William Pope, holder of the Cambridge chair of Chemistry since 1908 and closely involved with industrial chemistry; Sir Richard Glazebrook, previously director of the National Physical Laboratory and still chairman of the Aeronautical Research Committee; H. T. Tizard of the Department of Scientific and Industrial Research; A. J. Dyke and Charles Grylls of Customs and Excise; and Percy Ashley of the Board of Trade.[74]

Within both the Board of Trade and the Department of Scientific and Industrial Research, there was already a 'departmental view' in favour of extending the key-industry duties, which had been 'of considerable value' in increasing the 'quality, variety and supply' of 'an important range of articles' in otherwise difficult economic conditions. From its outset, Chadwick's committee demonstrated less concern with its brief, which was whether to extend the life of the schedule, than with how exactly to extend it. It was as much in conscience as in conviction that Tizard was prompted to ask whether, since the committee's 'duty is to review the object and effect of the Act, should that not come before any question of details in the Schedule?'[75]

This favourable predisposition existed in spite of some lack of consensus on the definition of a key industry. Ashley's belief that the original meaning of the term had embraced 'an industry on the prosperity of which a very much larger industry depended, although neither industry might have any direct war application' prevailed over Dyke's narrower criterion of 'national safety'. It was in the wider sense that dyestuffs had originally been considered a key industry

---

[73] *Manchester Guardian*, 12 May 1921, 25 June 1921, 11 July 1921, all cited in R. K. Snyder, *The Tariff Problem* 83–4, 87.

[74] *Who Was Who*, ii, *1916–1928* (1929); iii, *1929–1940* (1941); iv, *1941–1950 (1952)*.

[75] Board of Trade (Committee Papers) Safeguarding of Industries Act, 1921. Informal Committee of 1925–1926. 1st Meeting, 13 Nov. 1925; BT 55/57/7, PRO (hereinafter Chadwick Committee).

for the textile trades. Only later were defence considerations added.[76] Though, of course, the cotton industry's opposition to the Dyestuffs Act of 1921 demonstrated that the industry's sympathy with its supplier had quickly evaporated, Ashley was essentially correct. In spite of some connection between dyestuffs and explosives, particularly in the production of TNT, it had undoubtedly been the threat of a dearth of dyestuffs in the textile industries which had made intervention in this field acceptable to so many.

The committee displayed a particular sympathy towards the chemical industry. W. J. U. Woolcock of the Association of British Chemical Manufacturers was encouraged to rewrite his report on the progress of fine chemicals production to greater advantage, giving less emphasis to the War years and more to developments in research and output during the safeguarding period. Indeed, Woolcock almost appeared happier with the treatment of his industry than did the inquisitorial committee he faced, as was shown by his indifference to Ashley's proposal that the chemicals schedule should be defined by exclusion rather than inclusion.[77] Thereafter, using a list provided by Ashley 'on the assumption that the Committee agreed generally to the necessity of further protection . . . not only for organic, but also for inorganic fine chemicals', the committee proceeded to discuss revisions to the schedule. It was only after this had gone on for some time that 'The Chairman added that the Committee have already decided that the Act has been beneficial in its operation, and were now trying to arrive at . . . the correct list for future safeguarding.' Indeed, Ashley could report the 'Departmental view' of the Board of Trade that tartaric and citric acid should be added to the schedule.[78]

In March 1926 the committee examined four representatives of the British Chemical and Dyestuffs Traders' Association, who argued that the schedule was far too wide, and that only explosives and pharmaceuticals should be safeguarded in the interests of national security. Their contention that some scheduled items, most importantly oxalic acid and potassium permanganate, were not produced in the UK was acknowledged by the committee, but it attracted no sympathy. In contesting the importers' claim that they were only trying to make the Act more workable, Colefax did not mince words: 'the Association were merely representing the import trade and it was on that account they were objecting . . . [it was] not clear from the[ir] memorandum that the Association *were* in sympathy with the principle of the Act'.[79] Relations worsened when the merchants accused certain British manufacturers of importing chemicals they did not produce and marketing them as British. Ashley demanded proof of 'such a serious statement':

[76] Chadwick Committee, 2nd Meeting, 27 Nov. 1925; BT 55/57/7, PRO.   [77] Ibid.
[78] Chadwick Committee, 3rd Meeting, 11 Dec. 1925, BT 55/57/7, PRO.
[79] Chadwick Committee, 9th Meeting, 10 Mar. 1925, BT 55/57/7, PRO (my emphasis).

Mr [V.] Blagden, illustrating from the list of the Association of British Chemical Manufacturers, stated that in the case of Prussiate of Potash none of the firms stated to be making this article are in fact now doing so, and that the British Drug Houses Ltd. have never made an ounce.[80]

Many of BDH's 3,000 fine chemicals were simply recrystallizations of imported constituents, he maintained, though under pressure from Ashley he was forced to concede that many German firms did just the same. After the deputation, departed, Ashley explained that BDH had been aware of such accusations for some time, and were anxious to collect evidence in order to institute libel actions. Colefax, certain that in spite of their protestations the merchants were simply opposed to the spirit of the Act, advocated the removal of a small number of chemicals from the schedule to sweeten them.[81]

It became evident in the committee's discussion of specific key industries that, whilst individual members were sometimes opposed to the continuance of safeguarding, they were not inclined to press their cases strongly. Glazebrook argued half-heartedly against Chadwick and Ashley's proposal that in view of endemic foreign dumping and the recent bankruptcy of three firms, the duty on optical glass and optical instruments should be increased to the US level of 45 per cent. But even he conceded that, though the industry's peacetime products— mostly photographic apparatus, microscopes, and binoculars—might not be essential to the services, they preserved a reserve of plant, equipment, and skilled labour for time of war.[82] Pope wished to give Oertling's, manufacturers of chemical balances, 'some kind of warning . . . that in default of improvement protection should cease', but only Tizard agreed. Ashley was particularly nervous of the Board of Trade having the power to remove an item from the schedule if quality improvement did not occur: this was 'not an easy thing to do'.[83] Laboratory porcelain was another industry where, in spite of some improvements at Doulton and Royal Worcester, progress as a whole had been poor, and the British product had a bad name, but again the committee had little doubt that safeguarding should be continued.[84]

If lack of success under safeguarding was no criterion for removal, nor, it appears, was considerable expansion. Rapid progress in the use of thermionic emission valves during the War had resulted in the UK pioneers Marconi, Edison Swan, and A. C. Cossor Ltd. being joined by lightbulb manufacturers GEC, British Westinghouse, and British Thompson-Houston, because of the similar production technologies involved. But up to 1920 service needs were paramount and it was in the USA that commercial development of radio

[80] Chadwick Committee, 9th Meeting, 10 Mar. 1925, BT 55/57/7, PRO.
[81] Ibid.　　[82] Chadwick Committee, 5th Meeting, 15 Jan. 1926, BT 55/57/7, PRO.
[83] Chadwick Committee, 6th Meeting, 29 Jan. 1926, BT 55/57/7, PRO.
[84] Chadwick Committee, 6th Meeting, 29 Jan. 1926, 7th Meeting, 12 Feb. 1926, BT 55/57/7, PRO.

valves had progressed furthest.[85] Hence, in spite of substantial growth and research activity in the UK industry since 1921, the Valve Manufacturers' Association wanted increased protection. Colefax was unconvinced, whilst Ashley considered that, since the industry had now reached 'the field of general production', it was 'no longer a key industry in the sense in which the term was originally used, and indeed in the sense employed in the Schedule to the Act'.[86] But the committee was reluctant to end a practice originally urged by the Air Ministry and Admiralty, concerned that research might cease, and conscious that British prices had fallen by 35 to 60 per cent since 1921, even though continental valves still undercut British by 30 to 70 per cent.[87] Colefax changed his mind: it was 'evident' that the committee required continued protection.

Ashley's views on magnetos were even stronger. Expansion had been so strong, from UK sales of £491,000 in 1921 to £1,158,000 in 1925, and price reductions so marked, that he advocated removal of the duty. Furthermore, the industry might still benefit from protection if proposals to extend the McKenna duties on motor cars to all motor vehicles and parts was successful. As with valves, it is evident that Ashley saw the key-industry duties as somewhat akin to infant-industry duties, but only Tizard supported him. Colefax and Glazebrook reminded the committee of the threat of combination from the German and American Bosch concerns if their present legal dispute was amicably settled. Pope feared the demoralization of safeguarded industries 'if it were seen that as soon as an Industry arrives at a given stage of progress the duty is taken off'. Colefax agreed: since 'the price had been cut by 50 per cent, employment had gone up by 100 per cent and manufacturing had increased, he found very great difficulty in saying that the industry should be interfered with'. Ashley gave in.[88]

Whilst each member may have expressed doubts on the renewal of key-industry status for one or two products, only Tizard and Grylls had more general reservations. Though each supported the maintainance of safeguarding duties in specific cases, they were reluctant, as career civil servants, to express an opinion on 'the desirability of protection or free trade' when the committee's terms of reference did not define what government policy actually was. If it were policy to safeguard all industries requiring 'scientific skill and personnel', maintained Tizard, his difficulties would disappear.[89] The difficulty lay in extending the concept of safeguarding to industries of key importance 'for peace-time

[85] S. G. Sturmey, *The Economic Development of Radio* (1958), 34–5.

[86] Chadwick Committee, 7th Meeting, 12 Feb. 1926, BT 55/57/7, PRO.

[87] Under the Marconi patent valves were sold mostly to radio-assembly firms virtually at cost, whilst the declining proportion of replacements and valves supplied for home assembly were priced very highly. See Sturmey, *Economic Development of Radio*, 44–7.

[88] Chadwick Committee, 7th Meeting, 12 Feb. 1926, BT 55/57/7, PRO.

[89] Chadwick Committee, 10th Meeting, 19 Mar. 1926, BT/55/57/7, PRO.

reasons'.[90] Though Ashley had no such scruples, favouring an extension of ten years and widening the schedule considerably, their qualms may have been the reason that none of the career civil servants signed the report. But this should not disguise the general, often patent, enthusiasm for safeguarding shared by all members of the committee, scientists and civil servants alike. Extensions were to be recommended for industries which had made progress under safeguarding, almost because they had done well, and industries which had not, essentially because they needed to do better. Essentially accepting Ashley's broader 'infant-industry' definition of the rationale behind the key-industries schedule, the committee was unwilling to contemplate criteria for removal of mature industries. Its report showed Ashley's skill in putting the different cases each in their best light.[91]

The anti-dumping provisions of the SIA were much more sensitive, and planning required political decision-making at ministerial level. In May 1924 there was outcry in the Associated Chambers, led by Leicester, Birmingham, and Wolverhampton, over the Labour Government's intention to abolish Part II of the SIA along with the McKenna duties.[92] The Board of Trade, however, found little to say in favour of Part II. It had only been in operation for a year when Cunliffe-Lister argued in cabinet that the exchange provisions should be allowed to expire given the difficulty of imposing a country-specific tariff against any country except Germany. As long as Germany had been the only country with an 'exchange bounty' this had been unimportant, but now the French, Belgian, and Italian currencies had depreciated, and he was particularly concerned at the likely French response to a duty under Part II. Unemployment and the need to finance unemployment relief required a mechanism by which Britain could impose 'a general duty . . . on any particular article . . . [which would be] no breach of any Treaty'. In future the Board of Trade enquiry should be retained, but duties should be implemented by the Chancellor of the Exchequer rather than by Order of the Commons.[93]

On 2 August 1923 the new proposal was considered in cabinet but deferred: no-one supported it strongly whilst Cecil and Salisbury were hostile.[94] It was subsequently overwhelmed by Baldwin's decision to go to the country on a Tariff Reform ticket and the election of the first Labour Government. But with Baldwin back in power Cunliffe-Lister reintroduced it. These two considered the safeguarding of some half-dozen industries a 'reasonable objective' during the course

---

[90] Board of Trade, *Report of a Committee on the Safeguarding of Industries Act, 1921, Part I*, Cmd. 2631 (1926), para. 6.
[91] Ibid. esp. para. 57 on laboratory porcelain.
[92] *BCCJ*, 16 June 1924, 389–400.
[93] 'Safeguarding of Industries Act. Memo by President of Board of Trade'. C. P. 355(23), 27 July 1923, PRO.
[94] J. A. Cross, *Lord Swinton* (Oxford, 1982), 54–5.

of the Parliament. Even Churchill considered this a reasonable interpretation of 'our mandate and pledges'.[95]

Cunliffe-Lister 'believe[d] there is no precedent for imposing a general duty otherwise than through the recognised medium of a Finance Act', and that this method yielded political advantages which would be decisive. The old SIA had been 'difficult to frame and difficult to pilot', and had led to difficult debates in the Commons on phrases such as 'substantial importance' and 'unfair competition'—indeed, 'on every word of doubtful meaning':

> By refraining from a preliminary Bill we should avoid all genuine fear or wilful misrepresentation that the Safeguarding of Industries Act was to be used as a cloak for a general protective tariff of unknown dimensions. The House of Commons would not be invited to commit itself in advance. It would only be invited to impose specific duties in proved cases, supported by the full report of a committee [of the Board of Trade]; and to impose those duties by the regular recognised machinery of a Finance Bill. If we attempt to pass a preliminary Bill, we shall almost certainly have to commit ourselves in advance to a number of definitions and formulæ, which would not work in practice . . . Once a committee has reported, public attention [would be] focused on the facts of the particular industry in question; whereas in a preliminary Bill attention is skilfully diverted to a hundred and one difficulties and dangers, which will not arise in practice.[96]

The President of the Board of Trade's desire to restrict debate to the specific circumstances of each individual case, coupled with his own long-standing protectionist inclinations,[97] reminds us of the appeal to pragmatism of the pre-war Tariff Reformers, especially Hewins in his exchanges with Herbert Gladstone and his management of the Tariff Commission.[98] Before the introduction of the Bill of 1921, Cunliffe-Lister had expressed the hope that its anti-dumping provisions would tackle dual-pricing practices.[99] What he now aimed at was an effective anti-dumping measure, one not limited by having to take the line of least resistance provided by the convenient fact that anti-German feeling could be dressed up as a measure against currency dumping. Yet his new plan represented only a limited escalation of protection: 'If there is a great and general trade revival, we shall have no need to impose duties and we should not have wasted time in passing an unnecessary Bill'. Furthermore, the Board of Trade would have the power to rule a *prima facie* case unproven without an enquiry and without right of appeal.

Cunliffe-Lister considered that 'abnormal imports' should be measured relative to the pre-war period, and that the criterion should be a rise in the ratio of

---

[95] Ibid. 69.

[96] 'Cabinet Memorandum on Safeguarding by President of Board of Trade', C. P. 18(25), 14 Jan. 1925, PRO.

[97] J. A. Cross, *Lord Swinton*, 4–5, 15.

[98] See above, Ch. 1.

[99] Speech to Birmingham Chamber of Commerce, 19 Feb. 1921, in *BCCJ*, 15 Mar. 1921, 208.

retained imports to exports, in view of the difficulty of demonstrating a rise in the retained-imports to home-production ratio because of the lack of a recent census of production. 'Abnormal imports' should also come largely from countries where production conditions were unfair; he appeared to rule out the USA, which had neither depreciated currency nor low wages and long hours, but he did concede that low rates and taxes should be a legitimate criterion if they were 'a substantial factor in the comparative costs of production'.[100] This last was the only proposal which troubled the cabinet committee set up to discuss the new scheme. After 'prolonged consideration', the committee, chaired by Churchill and comprising Cunliffe-Lister, Neville Chamberlain, and Arthur Steel-Maitland, together with Sidney Chapman and Percy Ashley from the Board of Trade and Sir Henry Hamilton from Customs and Excise, substituted a 'catch-all', that the enquiring committee could 'call attention to any special circumstances' which in its opinion placed UK producers 'at a serious relative disadvantage'.[101]

Cunliffe-Lister's memorandum of 1923 demonstrates that Middlemas and Barnes are incorrect in attributing the innovation of using the Finance Bill as the medium for the new safeguarding procedures to Churchill, but their work clearly shows that the Chancellor was temporarily amenable to an extension of safeguarding.[102] Cunliffe-Lister's White Paper appeared in February 1925. Upon the Board of Trade agreeing that there was a *prima facie* case for an application, a committee should report on whether the industry was of 'national importance'; whether imports were in abnormal quantities; whether, by virtue of low wages or other unfair conditions, they were sold at prices which did not allow reasonable profit to British manufacturers; whether imports were likely to cause unemployment; and whether the imposition of a duty would be likely to cause unemployment in any other UK industry.[103] Behind these apparently objective criteria lurked two hurdles: the executive power of decision of the Board of Trade and, even more hidden, the political reluctance of the cabinet.

V

The biggest defeat sustained by the protectionists under the revised procedure for safeguarding was the rejection of the application from the iron and steel industry. Though well known, this merits consideration in some detail.

---

[100] App. to C. P. 18(25).

[101] Cabinet minutes, 21 January 1925; cabinet committee minutes, 26 and 28 Jan. 1925; BT 55/58/9, PRO.

[102] K. Middlemas and J. Barnes, *Baldwin*, 289–90. This gives the date of Churchill's suggestion as 24 Dec., which from the context surrounding the passage is probably 1924 but could be 1925. The ambiguity is compounded by the fact that their footnote references typically omit dates and by what appears to be a misdating of the cabinet meting of 21 Jan. 1925 by a full year.

[103] Board of Trade, *Safeguarding of Industries: Procedures and Enquiries*, Cmd. 2327 (1925).

The Edwardian steel industry's protectionism was undiluted by the favourable conditions of War. During 1915–18, iron and steel imports as a proportion of domestic production fell to an average of 3.65 per cent, less than half the 1906–1914 average and even further below that of 1911–1914.[104] Nevertheless, when Sir Clarendon Hyde was appointed chairman of the Board of Trade Committee on the Iron and Steel Trades after the War in March 1916 there was an outcry, and he was quickly replaced by Scoby-Smith of Bolckow, Vaughan. The *Iron and Coal Trades' Review* also attempted to veto another Free Trader, Sir Hugh Bell, whose views on commercial policy were 'diametrically opposed to the vast majority of his fellow manufacturers'.[105] Though it was unsuccessful, Bell had only one supporter on the ten-strong Committee.

The Scoby-Smith committee's fear of post-war dumping did not immediately materialize. Imports as a proportion of home production were lower in 1919 than the wartime average, and, though rising, were still in 1920 lower than the 1906–1914 average.[106] The industry also had hopes of large export orders during European reconstruction.

It has been argued that there was a 'sudden swing back against protectionism at the end of the War with Free Trade as an acceptable corollary to speedy decontrol of the industry'.[107] Whilst there was no necessary contradiction in supporting protection whilst pressing for the removal of internal controls, the brief and fragile boom from mid-1919 to mid-1920 probably muted protectionist feeling, whilst the National Federation of Iron and Steel Manufacturers' decision not to press hard for protection reflected a fear that to do so might lead to an investigation of costs and profits.[108] But there was little foundation for any real resurgence of Free-Trade sentiment; indeed, some at least of the optimism within the industry was based on the belief that it would shortly be protected against dumping.[109] In 1920 the annual meeting of the NFISM was all but unanimous in favour of an anti-dumping measure.[110]

Nevertheless, the conclusion that the industry 'was working diligently for a tariff'[111] before the 1923 election may be exaggerated. Predictably, an inability to achieve complete industry-consensus had its effect in diffusing any political impact that the industry's political lobby might have had. The NFISM took little

[104] See App. II.
[105] *Iron and Coal Trades' Review*, 24 Mar. 1916, quoted in J. C. Carr and W. Taplin, *A History of the British Steel Industry* (Oxford, 1962), 340.
[106] See App. II.
[107] S. Tolliday, 'Tariffs and Steel, 1916–1934: The Politics of Industrial Decline', in J. Turner (ed.), *Businessmen and Politics* (1984), 53.
[108] J. C. Carr and W. Taplin, *The British Steel Industry*, 350–3.
[109] D. Burn, *Economic History of Steelmaking, 1867–1939* (Cambridge, 1940), 388; also *Iron and Coal Trades' Review*, 17 May 1921.
[110] J. C. Carr and W. Taplin, *The British Steel Industry*, 375.
[111] F. Capie, 'The Pressure for Tariff Protection in Britain, 1917–31', *Journal of European Economic History*, 9 (1980), 434.

interest in the SIA in April 1921 (though it did lobby Lloyd George on unfair European competition immediately afterwards), was 'silent' in the 1923 election, and adopted a position of 'formal neutrality' when the industry applied for safeguarding under the new procedure in 1925.[112] The desire to avoid internal conflict led to the Federation following the precedent of BITA and SIMA before the War.[113]

Clearly, however, the split was uneven. In 1921 imports as a percentage of home production rocketed to over 25 per cent.[114] Yet, in the same year, '[s]ome steel and engineering firms with strong Free Trade interests and views' threatened that committing the Federation to protection might lead to its disintegration.[115] It seems likely that such desperate, almost petulant last-ditch threats betokened their minority position. By 1924 the Federation's leaders were reviewing its position of neutrality, unhappy about the Labour Government's assaults on the McKenna and safeguarding duties. By 1925 Federation members, chafing at the bit under formal neutrality, were acting 'outside the Grange' in lobbying for protection.[116] In June an application for safeguarding was made by the heavy-steel, pig-iron, wrought-iron, and wire makers.

There can be little doubt, therefore, that, even before 1924, Free Traders within the industry were in a small minority, though their very presence had the effect of emasculating the steel lobby's political effectiveness. Effective unanimity among the North-East-coast steelmakers was not achieved until 1924 or 1925, whilst GKN, the largest importer of foreign semi-finished steel in the UK, was internally divided until about 1928. The Board of Colvilles, reliant on imported pig-iron, was not unanimous until 1930, though several leading managers favoured protection much earlier.[117] In some cases fragmentation was a result of shipbuilding firms acquiring important, and sometimes controlling, interests in steel companies in the early 1920s; Colville's, James Dunlop and Sons, and the Steel Company of Scotland are all examples.[118]

By the mid-1920s, the situation had clarified:

Protracted opposition came only from a few small firms such as the Steel Company of Scotland and Dunlops in Scotland who feared that removal of cheap imported steel would increase their dependence on bigger firms, and from the re-rollers who had carved themselves a niche by using cheap imported semi-finished steel to undercut their big rivals. The latter formed an active lobby who were able to exploit the broad political problems raised by the tariff issue to exercise an influence in the debate *out of all proportion to their economic weight*, particularly through the columns of the trade press and their evidence at the major government enquiries.[119]

---

[112] J. C. Carr and W. Taplin, *The British Steel Industry*, 375; S. Tolliday, 'Tariffs and Steel', 53.
[113] See above, 124.   [114] See App. II.
[115] J. C. Carr and W. Taplin, *The British Steel Industry*, 375.   [116] Ibid. 378–9.
[117] S. Tolliday, 'Tariffs and Steel', 53–4.
[118] J. C. Carr and W. Taplin, *The British Steel Industry*, 359.
[119] S. Tolliday, 'Tariffs and Steel', 54 (my emphasis).

By now support for Free Trade seems to have been concentrated in the British Steel Re-Rollers' Association. Even here there was support for general protection, most heroically by L. D. Whitehead, whose own concern was entirely dependent on imported semis, largely from France. Other re-rollers were more cynical in their own self-interest—the sheet trade opposed protection of steel bars, its own raw material, but favoured an export subsidy on its own product. Significantly, objections were raised by a steel firm controlled by shipbuilding interests who feared that an export bounty would subsidize foreign shipbuilders. More important, perhaps, was intelligence that the Government would be unlikely to accept a scheme benefiting only one section of the industry, and the proposal was abandoned.[120] In any case, the dissenting groups were relatively small components of the whole industry. The NFISM's stance had never signified a Free Trade majority, but neturality had almost certainly become redundant by the time Labour was ousted from office.

Churchill's reaction to the industry's application, that to safeguard steel would be tantamount to violating Baldwin's election pledge not to introduce a general tariff, because of the wide effect on user industries and the difficulty of resisting copycat applications, is well known, as is his veiled threat of resignation.[121] His proposal for a Royal Commission led instead, at Cunliffe-Lister's suggestion, to an examination by the newly formed Committee of Civil Research. Most steelmakers appearing before the CCR argued that a defensive tariff would stimulate investment and lower prices. They were supported by corporatist Sir Hugo Hirst and even by Sir Alfred Mond. The Treasury, however, was hostile, as was Sir Maurice Hankey, the Cabinet Secretary. By November Churchill, playing on the fear that 'rush[ing] the Conservative Party onto the slippery slope of Protection' would defeat its longer-term objectives, had the support of Steel-Maitland, and Neville Chamberlain was lukewarm. Though still supported by Cunliffe-Lister, Baldwin was becoming isolated. It was decided that the CCR should abandon an enquiry whose report the cabinet could not undertake to accept, and on 12 December Baldwin announced that the industry's application would not be approved.[122]

The White Paper required that an applying industry should already operate with 'reasonable efficiency'.[123] But the British industry was, by the 1920s, fragmented in structure, with small firm and plant sizes, and often with obsolescent processes, especially the lack of hot- or direct-metal facilities.[124] Such concerns figured prominently in the discussions of the CCR, as well as in those

---

[120] J. C. Carr and W. Taplin, *The British Steel Industry*, 378–80.

[121] J. A. Cross, *Lord Swinton*, 71–2.

[122] K. Middlemas and J. Barnes, *Baldwin*, 310–15; Churchill quoted, 315.

[123] Cmd. 2327.

[124] For a good short summary, see K. Warren, 'Iron and steel', in N. K. Buxton and D. H. Aldcroft (eds.), *British Industry between the Wars* (London, 1979), esp. 103–116.

of the Balfour Committee on Industry and Trade at about the same time. Witnesses were pressed on why inefficiency might not result from protection— might not rationalization be a better alternative, or at least a desirable prelude, to a tariff? The steelmakers argued that a tariff was necessary before rationaliza- tion. Without it, amalgamation would be insufficient; in Sir William Larke's words, 'the small orders which are economically transferable to the big plants are not nearly enough . . . it is the orders for imported steel that can alone give the big plants what they need'.[125] Whilst this had substance, it gave no guarantee of increased efficiency, and both Conservative and Labour governments before 1931 therefore sought to promote mergers to increase efficiency.

This policy, 'more an article of faith than a precise, informed strategy',[126] was pursued with little success, and was scarcely aided by an industry reluctant to provide government with details on production costs. Government could offer few inducements to rationalization. Steel-Maitland thought a tariff might awaken 'the old reactionary individualism of the industry',[127] and in any case the Government could scarcely promise a tariff subsequent to successful rationaliza- tion if it was unsure that it could deliver it. Increasingly, government hopes came to rest upon the efforts of the banks, particularly the Bank of England, to promote mergers among the steel companies with which they were involved.[128]

VI

After Baldwin's return to office fifty applications for safeguarding were received. Sixteen of these were referred to committees, but duties were imposed in only eight cases.[129] In fact, the duty on lace appears to have been imposed under the original Act of 1921, whilst three, the duties on cutlery, leather and fabric gloves, and gas mantles, were incorporated into the new Safeguarding of Industries (Customs Duties) Act itself.[130] Only the last four to be introduced followed Cunliffe-Lister's new procedure, the duty on packing and wrapping paper appearing in the Finance Bill of 1926, that on translucent and vitrified pottery in the budget of 1927, and those on buttons and enamelled hollow-ware in the budget of 1928.

Since the steel industry's application was not allowed, we cannot determine precisely the level of opposition that it would have provoked amongst user industries. Certainly there would have been objection from the shipbuilding and

---

[125] Quoted in S. Tolliday, 'Tariffs and Steel', 56. This and the following paragraph are based heavily on Tolliday's work.
[126] S. Tolliday, 'Tariffs and Steel', 57.
[127] Quoted ibid. 58.
[128] Ibid. 59–63; also below, Ch. 13.
[129] Sir Herbert Hutchinson, *Tariff-Making and Industrial Reconstruction* (1965), 16.
[130] D. Abel, *History of British Tariffs 1923–1942* (1945), 32–6, 41–5.

shipping industries; it was not until 1928 that politicians were able to discern a weakening of the shipbuilders' opposition.[131] But elsewhere among the important user industries, especially automobiles and mechanical and electrical engineering, protectionist sentiment was strong. In FBI opinion it was 'quite on the cards that the Engineering trade might agree not to oppose the iron and steel application with the view to securing safeguarding later'.[132] Furthermore, these industries were the bastions of corporate attitudes in British manufacturing. In spite of initial opposition to a duty on steel by the élitist British Engineers' Association,[133] it may well be that those trades would have shown some degree of the tolerance and sympathy indicated by Sir Hugo Hirst and Sir Alfred Mond,[134] especially because of the precedent that protection of a major industry would have set. Certainly, there were circumstances in which such considerations could weigh with the business community. As the Nottingham Chamber of Commerce reported, Churchill's duties on silk and artificial silk had initially:

> caused consternation amongst local manufacturers, as such duties were regarded as a tax upon raw materials; but after full discussion the council of the Chamber felt that there would not be any seriously detrimental effect on local industries if certain modifications [a drawback of duty on exported goods] were secured. Negotiations with the Chancellor resulted in material modifications and the duties have proved, in some respects, an advantage rather than a hindrance to our trade.[135]

With the less important trades which were granted a Board of Trade inquiry, however, we can gain a clear idea of the opposing forces. Sir Herbert Hutchinson, one of the secretaries of the cabinet committee meetings of January 1925, recollected that those opposing an application were usually importers and distributors, 'with *from time to time* the intervention of a using industry'.[136] This is confirmed by the published reports, in which the two opposing camps are usually clearly delineated.

None of the industries granted a safeguarding enquiry produced intermediate goods of anything like the importance of iron and steel, of course, and some of them, like monumental granite, were finished products in the most literal sense. Nevertheless, as is shown in Appendix III, import merchants, distributors, and wholesalers were overwhelmingly predominant in the opposition to safeguarding applications. Once more we can see the central importance of some trade sections of the London Chamber of Commerce in mobilizing and orchestrating opposition, these appearing unhidden in nine of the nineteen entries in

[131] R. W. D. Boyce, *British Capitalism at the Crossroads 1919–1932* (Cambridge, 1987), 123–4.
[132] Glenday to Roberts (FBI Sheffield District Secretary), 6 Sept. 1925; FBI 200/F/3/D2/3/10.
[133] Ibid.   [134] See above, 279
[135] NCC, *Annual Report*, 1925. That these were more than empty words is shown by the Nottingham Chamber's defence of the silk and artificial silk duties when they came under threat in 1929. See *Annual Report*, 1929.
[136] Sir H. Hutchinson, *Tariff-Making*, 16–17 (my emphasis).

Appendix III. Even where the London Chamber's groups were less obviously involved, the preponderance of London addresses suggests the influence of those groups. Of seven witnesses appearing to oppose in the second enquiry into enamelled hollow-ware, five came from EC1 and one from EC4, heartlands of the import house, wholesaler, and warehouseman.[137] Sometimes there were also merchants from Manchester, and a few from Leeds, but it was the London houses which predominated.

This merchant preponderance was explicitly recognized by several of the committees, and must have been tacitly understood by all. The merchants, importers, wholesalers, and distributors of the Textile Trades Section of the London Chamber were unambiguously opposed to the application for safeguarding of worsteds in 1925.[138] The Worsted Committee received several indignant letters from merchants, including one from Robert Frost, a wholesale and export merchant of Regent Street, who argued that a duty would result in 'great disaster' for Britain's exports since 'our exports are [necessarily] as great as the imports'. The woollen industry's difficulties, he asserted, were 'only because of the vagaries of the [French] exchanges which have depreciated suddenly', and would disappear in due course as French production-costs rose as a consequence of the depreciation.[139]

Refusing to give evidence in public before the same committee, Beaumont Brothers, a manufacturers' agent, gave eloquent testimony, in spite of their punctuation, to the power that merchant groups could possess:

What we have to say is strictly private and confidential, it very much concerns the group of Merchant Importers and Distributors who are objecting through the Chamber of Commerce, (of which we are also members) these Gentlemen are mostly our clientele, and it would not improve our relations with them, for them to know we were taking sides against their interests. Then again we should have to be very careful, that the Foreign Manufacturers we represent, did not know, we were giving evidence against their interests.

Unfortunately the Manufacturer's Agent, who gives evidence, may get into hot water, unless . . . his evidence is kept secret . . . we respectfully submit, that the evidence of Manufacturers' Agents like ourselves, is of the utmost importance, especially those who have represented Foreign makers and British makers, they are unbiased.[140]

Opposition to the second application of the lace and embroidery trades, too, was dominated by the merchant interest. The application was made by some 450 or 550 firms in the Federation of Lace and Embroidery Employers' Associations (amongst which, it is true, were several East-Midlands associations of merchants, dyers, and finishers) and the British Plain Net Manufacturers' Association, supported by two unions, the British Lace Operatives' Federation and the Lace

---

[137] Board of Trade, *Second Report of the Committee on Enamelled Hollow-Ware*, Cmd. 3115 (1928), 10.
[138] LCC, *Council Minutes*, 12 Nov. 1925, 187.
[139] Frost to Brady, 15 Oct. 1925, BT 55/89/117, PRO.
[140] Beaumont Bros. to Worsted Committee, 16 Nov. 1925, ibid.

Workers' Branch of the Workers' Union. Against them stood the Lace and Embroidery Group of the London Chamber: 'As far as I know, I *am* the opposition', asserted C. F. Entwistle, their representative at the enquiry.[141] The Nottingham Chamber reported the 'uncompromising opposition' of importers and distributors to safeguarding applications, mounted 'regardless of cost'.[142]

The re-imposition of the McKenna duties and the publication of the White Paper saw no change in the feuding between some trade sections of the London Chamber. Ex-Tariff Commissioner Sir John Cockburn kept a sharp eye for that minority of the Trade Sections who used the Chamber's name in any agitation against the White Paper.[143] The Fancy Goods and Watch and Clock Sections found themselves at loggerheads over McKenna, the situation deteriorating when Kiley and others attended the Treasury and put views purporting to come from the watch and clock trade.[144] Exasperated by the claims of both to represent the views of importers of clocks and watches, the General Purposes Committee recommended that the watch and clock importers in the Fancy Goods Section should join the Watch and Clock Section, which in future should be the sole voice representing the interest. Kiley, aware that this would swamp the opponents of the White Paper, protested, explaining that 'the Watch and Clock Section consisted of Dealers [manufacturer-retailers] and the Fancy Goods Section mainly of Distributors'.[145] His plea for independence of action went unheeded, however.

In December 1925 Kiley's Fancy Goods Section caused further friction, this time on brushes, and provoked a similar recommendation from the GPC. President Sir James Martin emphasized that the Chamber:

was greatly embarrassed by the fact that Sections had split into groups and were using the name of the Chamber in urging their respective cases. Certain members of the Chamber had called themselves the Import Brush Group, and had used the name of the Chamber in opposing the application for a duty under the Safeguarding of Industries Act. The Brush Manufacturers' Association had in consequence issued a circular asking all their members to withdraw from the Chamber of Commerce . . . if Sections could not agree on a course of action, they should not be allowed to split themselves up in the way they had been doing.[146]

The Fancy Goods, China and Glassware, and Textile Trade Sections were a minority in the London Chamber. Groups opposing safeguarding were, however, *ad hoc* in origin, and a greater number of safeguarding enquiries would doubtless

[141] Lace Enquiry Committee, Minutes of Evidence, 30 Mar. 1925, BT 55/78/80, PRO (my emphasis).
[142] NCC, *Annual Report*, 1925.
[143] LCC, *Council Minutes*, 12 Mar. 1925, 106.
[144] LCC, *Council Minutes*, 11 June 1925, 142–3.
[145] LCC, *Council Minutes*, 9 July 1925, 153.
[146] LCC, *Council Minutes*, 10 Dec. 1925, 149.

have led to some proliferation. Almost as certainly, these would have displayed the same merchant character, and also led to additional splinter groups where the original trade section had a substantial membership in favour of the application or neutral. Furthermore, it may be of significance that the large Import and Export Merchant Section of the Chamber was apparently not involved in any agitation,[147] whilst on occasion opponents of safeguarding within a mixed-trade section could be reluctant to engineer a split. When the GPC agreed to the Chancellor of the Exchequer's request to hear representatives of the Textile and Silk Sections on the silk duty, its insistence that there should be no publicity in order to avoid public confusion on the position of the Chamber annoyed the Free Traders.[148] In the Silk Section there was evidently division between two factions, the merchants and the manufacturers' agents, but in this case the main body persuaded the merchants to form a sub-section rather than break away.[149]

The case of superphosphates, the clearest example of an intermediate that was granted an enquiry, is revealing. Opposition came from the National Farmers' Union in several of its regional organizations.[150] Opposition from a body so strongly supportive of protection for its own members[151] shows how safeguarding could set protectionist against protectionist, fragmenting alliances and preventing the build-up of a protectionist consensus amongst British producers. Indeed, this was in the very nature of safeguarding. In a different way, this is also borne out by the support of the London Employers' Association and the Wholesale Mantle and Costume Manufacturers' Federation for the application of the worsted manufacturers, support that was conditional upon there being a duty imposed on manufactured garments as well.[152] Clearly, the London garment trade supported safeguarding of its input if it received a *quid pro quo* on the final product.

An interesting, though in this sample unique, case was the defence of Free Trade on principle, in the Board of Trade's words 'on general economic grounds', by Tootal, Broadhurst, Lee and Co. Ltd., and the Calico Printers' Association Ltd. in the enquiry into handkerchiefs and household linens.[153] Opposing the Irish and Scottish producers, Tootals maintained that new machinery enabled progressive British makers to meet foreign competition, and that protection would exert upward pressure on the wages of stitchers which

[147] LCC, *Council Minutes*, 10 Dec. 1925, 197.   [148] LCC, *Council Minutes*, 9 Apr. 1925, 129.
[149] LCC, *Council Minutes*, 11 Mar. 1926, 228.
[150] Board of Trade, *Report of the Superphosphate Committee*, Cmd. 2475 (1925), 5–6.
[151] In lobbying the government, the NFU opposed safeguarding of superphosphates, agricultural implements, and iron and steel, unless agriculture was granted the *quid pro quo* of food duties. NFU Committee Report, 16 Feb. 1926, cited in A. F. Cooper, *British Agricultural Policy 1912–36* (Manchester, 1989), 119. This is not to deny that the NFU was cautious in pressing for food duties because of the 'government's electoral predicament'. See Boyce, *British Capitalism*, 123.
[152] Board of Trade, *Report of the Worsted Committee*, Cmd. 2635 (1926), 4.
[153] Board of Trade, *Report of the Committee on Handkerchiefs and Household Linen Goods*, Cmd. 3096 (1928), 6.

might put unprotected trades into difficulty, and might damage the export trade. The CPA feared that safeguarding would prevent foreigners from selling in Britain and hence increase competition in Britain's export markets, and that it would raise the general level of prices, damping down demand.

Though not particularly sophisticated, this was the Free-Trade case in its purest, most universalist form, applicable not just to handkerchiefs but to all industries. If industries in the 1920s were as seriously divided on trade policy as some historians maintain, such arguments would have been much more common. It is thus important to recognize that, whilst the publicists and propagandists of Free Trade were as prone to using such arguments in the 1920s as they had been in the Edwardian period, *manufacturing* opinion was almost always expressed at a less lofty level. This was even true, to an extent, of manufacturer and merchant in the Manchester Chamber of Commerce. The Chamber refused to join the Blackburn Chamber in pressing for repeal of the Dyestuffs Act in 1926, and made no comment on the safeguarding duties appearing in the 1927 budget; 'the commodities affected do not include any upon which Manchester can speak with special authority'.[154] This had become the Chamber's 'usual' response to safeguarding in the 1920s. Why was there no celebration when the Labour Government removed the McKenna duties in 1924? As Arthur Redford knew well, this was scarcely how nineteenth-century Manchester would have behaved.[155] Outside Lancashire, this narrower approach had probably always been more common. But now, for the large majority of manufacturers, conflict over safeguarding had become little more than a squabble between those likely to secure a duty and those likely to be denied it and, moreover, a squabble which was dwarfed by conflict between manufacturer and merchant. It was as if the battlefield for Free Trade had come down from the mountaintops to the back gardens.

VII

The demise of the McKenna duties in May 1924 led the Birmingham Chamber to review its self-imposed restriction on discussion of the 'political' issue of safeguarding. President Gilbert Vyle, an advocate of subsidies for basic industries and sympathetic to food duties,[156] chaired a meeting at which there was heavy support for lobbying Birmingham MPs in support of continuing McKenna; according to one of those present, 'the time had come when they must refuse to be muzzled'.[157]

---

[154] Manchester Chamber of Commerce, *Monthly Record*, Apr. 1927, quoted in Redford, *Manchester Merchants*, 217–8.
[155] Ibid. See also above, Ch. 6.
[156] *Birmingham Post*, 7 Sept. 1923.
[157] *BCCJ*, 15 May 1924, 332.

The Chamber soon found fault with Cunliffe-Lister's new procedure. At the request of its Manufacturers' section, J. B. Burman, MP, sought clarification of the criterion that an industry should be of 'substantial importance', but Cunliffe-Lister insisted on leaving it vague.[158] Still, the Chamber continued to harbour expectations that the new government really would deliver on safeguarding. In November 1924 a meeting was held with Birmingham MPs, in which the Chamber pressed for the safeguarding of hollow-ware.[159] Otherwise, its *Journal* confined itself to the uncritical reporting of safeguarding procedures as periodically released by the Board of Trade. Even Baldwin's refusal of safeguarding to iron and steel provoked little comment. Only in September 1926, after the failure of the applications of the aluminium and enamelled hollow-ware trades, did the Chamber act.

The GPC's report on the difficulties which the safeguarding criteria posed for applying industries was a catalogue of disaffection. It included the delay involved in conducting a *prima facie* investigation to establish whether a case should be sent to committee and the unnecessary duplication involved if the case were taken further; the question of the 'substantial importance' of an industry (at last the committee admitted that it considered Baldwin's treatment of iron and steel 'notorious'); the 'serious difficulty' of defining whether imports were in 'abnormal quantities'; the impossibility of providing documentary evidence to prove that imports were being sold in Britain at prices below home cost of production; and the difficulty of proving that unemployment was caused directly by 'unfair' foreign competition, especially where a depreciated foreign currency had been stabilized, but at a low level. The GPC sent a deputation to meet the Birmingham MPs at the Commons on 28 July, drafted an 'alternative White Paper' for submission to the Board of Trade, and put the motion that the White Paper needed 'considerable amendment' before the Associated Chambers at Hull in September.[160]

Under the Chamber's alternative, the Board of Trade's task of establishing whether there was a *prima facie* case should, in order to avoid unnecessary duplication with the committee enquiry, rest on only two criteria: that the industry employed at least 1,000 people or was important 'in the nature of the goods produced', and that the Board was satisfied that import competition threatened UK employment.[161] Compared with the White Paper, the omissions to the Birmingham version implied that the Board should no longer have to regard imports as 'exceptional', and should lose the discretion to refuse an enquiry to an industry which was 'not carried on in this country with reasonable efficiency and economy', or to an industry whose protection would exert 'a seriously adverse effect' on user industries.[162] The appointed committee's brief

[158] *Parliamentary Debates*, 28 Apr. 1925.   [159] *BCCJ*, 15 Dec. 1925, 803–4.
[160] *BCCJ*, 15 Oct. 1926, 739, 741–3.   [161] Ibid. 746–7.
[162] Board of Trade, *Safeguarding of Industries: Procedures and Enquiries*, Cmd. 2327 (1925), 2–3.

would be similar to that under the White Paper, except that foreign advantages in national and local taxation (as Cunliffe-Lister had originally intended) and preferential transport conditions should be deemed relevant in defining 'unfair' competition alongside currency depreciation, subsidies and bounties, and low wages, long hours, or inferior conditions of work. In addition, the Birmingham version explicitly precluded interested importers from sitting on the relevant committee, and foreign manufacturers being heard in evidence.

Whilst many of the changes reflected the difficulties experienced by applicants in obtaining equitable and consistent treatment when attempting to prove that they experienced 'abnormal' levels of imports or manufactured with 'reasonable efficiency', the main intention of the proposal was obviously to remove the Board of Trade's discretion to refuse an enquiry by committee, to make the *prima facie* examination a formal and fairly mechanical affair. Cunliffe-Lister reacted strongly, but in doing so revealed the Government's essentially hollow position. He made it clear that the *prima facie* enquiry was in the hands of ministers and not of the permanent officials of the Board of Trade, but in doing so he tacitly admitted that, in economic terms, the process could be arbitrary. Furthermore, his accusation that the Chamber was 'in effect, making a claim for general protection . . . precluded . . . by the Prime Minister's pledges', was countered effectively by Henry Wright's observation that the Government 'was equally pledged to a policy of safeguarding British industries which are suffering unduly owing to unfair foreign competition'.[163]

Birmingham's motion was passed at the Hull meeting of the ABCC in September 1926, but by such a narrow margin, thirty-four Chambers to thirty-two, that no representation could be made to the Government.[164] Given the circumstances, this was a disappointment for the Tariff Reformers. There were still, in the later 1920s, signs that the self-imposed embargo on discussion of Tariff Reform continued to operate, or at least that Chambers sympathetic to safeguarding considered extended discussion as a waste of effort. Though it supported Birmingham's motion, even the council of the strongly protectionist Sheffield Chamber had, only a year earlier, refused to take a stance on the inclusion of commercial vehicles under the McKenna duties, and was subsequently, in May 1928, to decline to put a resolution on safeguarding before the membership.[165] The Nottingham Chamber, which had never hidden its views, and which had in 1924 considered the commercial community 'almost unanimous' in its opposition to the Labour Government's threat to the protectionist devices of its predecessor,[166] nevertheless contented itself with a fairly mild

[163] J. G. Henderson to G. H. Wright, 18 Oct. 1926, Wright to Henderson, 9 Nov. 1926, in *BCCJ*, 15 Dec. 1926, 901–2.
[164] ABCC, Executive Council Minutes, 6 Oct. 1926.
[165] Sheffield Chamber of Commerce, *Council Minutes*, 24 Nov. 1925; 27 Mar. 1928.
[166] NCC, *Annual Report*, 1924.

reporting of the reverses experienced by the Nottingham trades before the Board of Trade enquiries. Other chambers were even more reluctant to break their embargoes on discussion of the issue. In November 1927 the London Chamber's GPC recommended continued neutrality on the fiscal question. Machin, afraid of injuring the reputation of the chamber and dividing the Council, invoked the decision of 1911, by now almost a thing of legend. As late as May 1928 the chamber acted in accordance with its 'policy of neutrality on the question of tariffs' at the annual meeting of the ABCC.[167]

In November 1927, the ABCC prohibited discussion of safeguarding; according to a Mr Ledingham of the Sheffield Chamber, the 'general opinion' in Chambers of Commerce was that questions 'irrevocably associated with politics ... should [not] be discussed at meetings'.[168] But it was becoming harder to contain the pressure for redefining protection as an economic rather than a political question, and in January 1928 a resolution was secured that it should 'be open for free discussion by Chambers of Commerce'.[169] In April the Associated Chambers went further, accepting Birmingham's resolution that extension and simplification of safeguarding was 'vitally necessary'.[170]

By May 1928, the Birmingham Chamber's tongue had sharpened even more. The Board of Trade's aim appeared to be 'to reduce the possibility of successful safeguarding applications'.[171] The test under the White Paper was, in fact, 'much more restrictive' than it had been under the Safeguarding Act of 1921: 'We are reminded of the English Poor Laws. To obtain the advantage of them the unfortunate citizens must first become practically destitute, while in some other countries the Poor Laws are defined to prevent destitution'.[172] Contemptuous of Baldwin's advocacy of the transfer of workers from depressed to more prosperous areas, in the Commons in July, the chamber made a further plea for a real public enquiry by an independent committee: safeguarding was 'a method which would be, and indeed is, employed by every other industrial country in the world'.[173]

The council of the Sheffield Chamber was more cautious. Responding to the lifting of the ABCC's embargo on discussion in January 1928, it indicated that it would now allow the motion on safeguarding of iron and steel that it had been blocking for some time. Almost immediately, it changed its mind, whereupon the Membership Committee complained that the chamber was losing members because of its neutrality, whilst the Junior Chamber went ahead and discussed the safeguarding of iron and steel anyway.[174]

---

[167] LCC, *Council Minutes*, 8 Nov. 1927, 123–4; 8 May 1928, 190.
[168] Sheffield Chamber of Commerce, General Purposes Committee Minutes, 23 Feb. 1928.
[169] Ibid.   [170] ABCC General Meeting, 4–5 Oct. 1928; in *Proceedings* 1928–9, 36–53.
[171] *BCCJ*, 15 May 1928, 400.   [172] Ibid. 412.   [173] *BCCJ*, 15 Aug. 1928, 642.
[174] Sheffield Chamber of Commerce, Annual Meeting, 29 Mar. 1928; *Council Minutes*, 22 May 1928, 24 July 1928.

TABLE 9. *Sheffield Chamber of Commerce: Ballot on Safeguarding of Iron and Steel, Jan. 1929*

	In Favour	Against
Iron and Steel trade	208	15
Cutlery, Tools, Silver, etc.	115	10
Engineering	22	1
Other trades	100	9
Professional	70	11
TOTAL	515	46

Note: Response rate was 62 per cent of the membership.
Source: Sheffield Chamber of Commerce, Council Minutes, 29 Jan. 1929.

It is clear that the Sheffield council was in danger of being outflanked by the membership. Into this lurching mêlée came a communication from the Birmingham Chamber, inviting Sheffield to send two representatives to a meeting to discuss the latest version of its alternative to the White Paper. Sheffield president Arthur Neal argued against attending: the chamber, '*it was reasonable to believe, held divergent views*', and if a simplified safeguarding procedure aided applicants it would put opponents at a disadvantage.[175] As he was revealed in the subsequent discussion to be in a minority of two, this was scarcely credible, and less than five months later his words were to be put to the test across the entire membership. The results, shown in Table 9, scarcely need comment.

Birmingham's aggressive forward position was unique. But the example of the similarly protectionist Sheffield Chamber shows the danger in interpreting an absence of a positive and cohesive stance on safeguarding as evidence of deep division within a chamber's membership. Just as before 1914, the effect of embargo was to conceal the support for protection amongst the membership. It seems that in many cases, both before and after 1914, the councils of Britain's chambers were more reluctant to sail into controversy than their members. This may have been because, as the more successful of a community's business leaders, they had less objection to Free Trade. It may have been because of a greater propriety and sense of obligation to their chambers' articles of association. It may even have been because presidency or council status induced a feeling of industrial statesmanship. It was certainly portrayed as a reluctance to split their chambers, not only in circumstances when that was a real prospect but also in those when it was little more than a device for postponing action.

In one way, however, the situation had changed radically from that before 1914. Before 1914 business support for the Liberals may have been declining, but it was still significant and there had been a genuine reluctance to open rifts within chambers, a reluctance that was tested increasingly after 1907 by Liberal taxation policy, but which just about held until the outbreak of the War. After

---

[175] Sheffield Chamber of Commerce, Minutes of Special Council Meeting, 22 Aug. 1928 (my emphasis).

Baldwin's 'tariff election', the leaders of the nation's chambers could still speak of the illegitimacy of discussion on the (uniquely) political tariff question, but, though the words were the same, the meaning was not. If protectionists concurred with an embargo, it was because they feared the political reaction to an openly protectionist business interest and the return of a second Labour Government. As Baldwin no doubt calculated, the business community had little choice but to accept his empty promises on safeguarding. In the heavily protectionist chambers at least, it is surely this consideration which ensured compliance with embargo until as late as 1928.

In October Birmingham's motion that an alternative to the White Paper should be submitted to the Government was finally accepted 'by a large majority' of the ABCC at Plymouth. Only the Manchester, Liverpool, Bury, and Blackburn Chambers, and an individual member from Plymouth, voiced any opposition.[176] But the procrastinations and circumlocutions that followed provide further clear evidence that the embargo policy had been used by Free Traders to slow up public expression of the pent-up dam of protectionist sentiment. A meeting of chamber delegates was held in February 1929, but in the council meeting that discussed their report Sir Ernest Thompson of the Manchester Chamber fought to delay action until after the forthcoming General Election. He had consulted Churchill, who 'deprecated any public agitation on the question of free trade or protection'.[177] Thompson was supported by J. H. C. Hodgson of Bradford and, with reluctance, by Sir Stanley Machin of London. Sir Gilbert Vyle suggested the compromise that the report should be submitted privately to the Prime Minister and President of the Board of Trade. He was supported by Sir Walter Raine and Sir John Allen of Liverpool, F. Anderson of Belfast, John Hutcheson of the South of Scotland Chamber, and A. R. Atkey of Nottingham. Only Harry Parsons of Southampton spoke in favour of a public submission to the Board of Trade following the resolution at the Plymouth conference.

The Vyle-Raine compromise attracted seventeen votes. Seven council members were opposed, apparently prepared to disregard the Plymouth resolution altogether. Even then, Thompson would not lie down, demanding the right to put amendments to the report on safeguarding. This so exasperated Atkey that he threatened, obliquely, to go public, but Thompson got his way. It was not until 1 May 1929, over three months after Baldwin's 'first shot in the election' and less than a month before the Labour Government was returned, that an amended ABCC report was ready to be sent to the Government as a 'confidential document'.[178]

[176] ABCC General Meeting, 4–5 Oct. 1928, in *Proceedings*, 1928–9, 36–53.

[177] ABCC, Executive Council Minutes, 6 Mar. 1929.

[178] ABCC, Executive Council Minutes, ibid. and 1 May 1929. See also K. Middlemas and J. Barnes, *Baldwin*, 512.

In retrospect there was much to commend Thompson's view that action before the election was unwise. With two of the three parties implacably opposed to protection, even the Tariff Reformers within the ABCC might have recognized that the purpose in embarrassing the Conservatives was small, the electoral consequences potentially dangerous. In this light, it is surprising that seventeen of the Council remained determined to carry through the Plymouth resolution, testimony, perhaps, to a new feeling of liberation. Viewed through the internal record of the Associated Chambers, however, the handling of safeguarding was quite predictable. Indeed, it bore no small resemblance to the way in which Rotherham and Brassey had drawn the teeth of the protectionist majority in the period from 1905 to 1914.[179]

VIII

Support for Tariff Reform in Britain's Chambers of Commerce had grown rapidly between 1905 and 1910, and was consolidated at a high level in the War. It appears to have receded somewhat thereafter, but there is little evidence that this represented a large or fundamental shift in business attitudes away from the economic nationalism of the War years.

There are certainly cogent economic reasons to support the argument that Tariff Reform and safeguarding were inappropriate remedies for the trading situation of the 1920s. It was widely recognized that the cause of unemployment, now a perennial business concern if only because of its implications for taxation, was principally centred upon the export trades, and that these depended upon the recovery of Europe. Tariff-Reform businessmen were at one with Free Traders in highlighting the inequity of treatment of labour between the 'sheltered' and the 'unsheltered' trades.[180] In some quarters much faith was pinned on the hopes of tariff reductions and tariff truces, especially after 1924.[181]

It is unlikely, however, that the virtues of such arguments were rediscovered by many among those businessmen who had been supporters of Tariff Reform before 1914, or who had become converts during the War. Many of the traditional nineteenth-century arguments for Free Trade were indirect, 'second-order' arguments, with an almost academic quality which did not come naturally to the pragmatic business mind, and it is no surprise that, in Britain as elsewhere, they were disseminated more easily in times of trade expansion than of

[179] See above, Ch. 3.
[180] See e.g. *BCCJ*, 15 Aug. 1925, 607. Much of this was a barely concealed attack on manual employees in the public sector.
[181] See e.g. the views of Sir Arthur Balfour on the forthcoming World Economic Conference at Geneva, in LCC, *Council Minutes*, 8 Nov. 1927, 123–4. Generally, however, opinion in Britain's chambers of commerce was sceptical of the chances of success. For international negotiations on tariff truces and the removal of prohibitions, see R. W. D. Boyce, *British Capitalism*, 219–26.

stagnancy. The limits to the spread of protectionist ideas were conditioned by more prosaic factors.

One such was the continuing reluctance of businessmen, especially those who favoured Tariff Reform, to enter into political controversy, and the use made of that reluctance by their Free Trade opponents. We have seen that this was not new, being the product of a long-established intellectual and political hegemony of Free Trade,[182] but it is somewhat surprising to see it having resurfaced after the War. This allowed a policy of embargo within the Chambers that seems to have been almost universal, a policy which even circumscribed agitation within some of the most strongly protectionist Chambers and which, with rare exceptions, played into the Free Traders' hands.[183]

Since the Safeguarding Act existed on the statute book, trade associations were in effect exempt from such restrictions, but from the point of view of the advance of the protectionist cause this was of limited value. It quickly became appreciated that large trades stood no chance of applying successfully, so that most of the associations whose dealings with the Board of Trade were reported in the press had titles rendered almost comical by the image of insignificance they conjured up. In any case, the trade association was clearly more vulnerable to the charge of naked self-interest than was the Chamber of Commerce, whose multi-interest consensus had more claim to represent a view on a broader, if local, community welfare.

With more prescience than it perhaps realized, the council of the Leeds Chamber observed as early as 1920 that 'a general tariff may be preferable to the official and probably uncertain control which would be consequent upon "anti-dumping" provisions'.[184] Indeed, the precise form of commercial policy in the 1920s was to test the protectionist manufacturer. In Europe and America, the institution of a general tariff typically offered something to everyone except the producer of raw materials, and there was usually a mechanism to provide hope of adjustment for those who had had a poor deal in the initial grading of duties. Safeguarding gave no such assurances: under the legislation it became rational for the most rabidly protectionist manufacturer to oppose an application from a related industry or trade. In spite of this, manufacturing opposition to safeguarding was remarkably slight, even though many of the products in the key-industries schedule were intermediate goods, and most of it emanated from the Lancashire textile trades.

---

[182] See above, Chs. 1 and 6.

[183] A. Redford, *Manchester Merchants*, ii. 216–18, contains the fleeting implication that the reverse could be the case, that embargo on discussion by the Manchester Chamber left Manchester's opposition to safeguarding understated. From his remarks on the erosion of Free Trade's dominance in the Manchester Chamber, this would appear to be an implication of his work which Redford would not have accepted. Even if so, however, we would argue that the case was untypical, and that embargo generally had the opposite effect.

[184] Leeds Chamber of Commerce, *Annual Report*, 1919.

The re-emergence of the merchant interest in Free Trade after the War only needed the threat of a trade war after the War to recede, and this was evident even before the armistice. Indeed, the main opposition to safeguarding came from merchants. Where specified, they seem to have been mostly import merchants, with some export merchants. Manufacturers' agents were in a more ambiguous position. Furthermore, the merchant opposition to safeguarding seems to have been concentrated in and organized from London, with Manchester playing a strong supporting role. There is some evidence that local merchants in Nottingham and Bradford tended to side with the manufacturers, though this does not seem to have applied in Manchester.

Within the British business community, the headlong slide to protectionism only happened after 1928. But, for the heavy majority of those in the manufacturing sector, this did not represent a sudden or recent conversion. Rather, it represented a new willingness to step out into the open, to disregard the institutional shackles on expression. It is correct to stress the growth of support for protection in the 1920s as a whole, especially amongst manufacturers, but we should not exaggerate by discerning a commensurate growth of protectionist 'pressure'.[185] To the long-standing political weakness of the British manufacturing interest were added the peculiar strategic difficulties of advance in the hostile framework of safeguarding. Baldwin's policy may have been directed towards giving industry what aid he could in the face of an intractable electorate, but its result was confusion, frustration, and some fragmentation. It seems probable that, at least until 1926 or 1927, the pressure for protection would have built up more rapidly without the chimera of safeguarding. Thereafter, however, in the increasing support for the Birmingham Chamber's 'alternative White Paper' and elsewhere, there were signs that the policy's capacity for containment was becoming exhausted. After the bruising experience of steel, we can only conjecture on what the response of the business community would have been if Baldwin had been returned to power in 1929 and had then immediately rejected the recommendations in favour of safeguarding made by the second enquiry into woollens and worsteds.

[185] F. Capie, 'Pressure for Tariff Protection', *passim.*

10

The Federation of British Industries and Protection

To the confusion of Tariff Reformers, who saw the advances they had made in 1916 and 1917 as permanent, the popularity of post-war retaliation against Germany receded in the late wartime and immediate post-war period as it was realized that the German economy had been far more damaged by the War than that of the allies, and in the longer term as it was perceived that European recovery was a condition for the restoration of prosperity in the international economy. Merchants and shippers soon lost their enthusiasm for trade restrictions, mirroring, in their desire to resurrect the pre-war liberal international economy, the deep public yearning to return to normalcy. Many manufacturers, however, found the choice less easy. On the one hand, they looked to a rapid dismantling of internal controls and restrictions, and to a restoration of export markets. On the other, they were less certain than politicians and the public at large that currently prostrate Germany would continue to represent no threat, and were in any case unconvinced that Germany represented the only threat. They continued to hope for a government which would adopt a substantive Tariff Reform policy on the basis of the interventionist lessons of the War.

Unfortunately, we cannot count and classify business opinion on Tariff Reform with great precision. But, in the immediate post-war years, the Federation of British Industries made an attempt to poll its members to ascertain their fiscal views. This was done to give the FBI staff guidance as to the direction of overall policy, and was largely prompted by the desire to effect agreements with two openly protectionist bodies, the National Union of Manufacturers and the British Empire Producers' Organization. Though the 'plebiscite' on fiscal opinion was never completed nor its results broadcast, enough survives in the FBI archives to enable us to construct a qualitative picture of members' views, and to explain the formative influences behind the direction of FBI policy on the tariff in the 1920s. It will be argued that rank-and-file opinion within the FBI was tilted more heavily towards protectionism than other historians have allowed. This is of particular importance, since deep division within the FBI has often been taken as an indication of division within the British manufacturing sector as a whole.

I

Recent historians have taken the view that the FBI was heavily divided in its attitude towards tariffs. Stephen Blank has written of the inability of FBI leaders 'to take any stand in favour of Protection because of the opposition of many groups within it'.[1] R. F. Holland has argued that 'considerable differences existed as to the extent of [FBI members'] dependence on overseas markets. There was consequently no obvious consensus on the desirability of a tariff.'[2] To Robert Boyce, trade protection was one of those issues 'which divided members into opposing camps'.[3] Richard Davenport-Hines takes the view that such fragmentation was the natural result of Britain's early industrialization, which led to her industries being 'so fissiparous as to be almost incompatible'.[4]

There is no doubt that a division of opinion among members prevented the adoption of Tariff Reform as an object of FBI policy right down to the end of the 1920s. Existing treatments, however, in concentrating on the sterilizing effects of division in the membership, have created the impression that, in quantitative terms, the rift was very deep, so that there was something of an even balance between the forces of Free Trade and those of Tariff Reform within the Federation. In the second half of the 1920s, as Boyce has argued, the Federation was 'increasingly by-passed by employers' as protectionism received 'growing support' from the business community.[5] It will be argued here that the Free-Trade forces within the FBI, whilst important enough in functional terms to have a determining effect on policy, were almost certainly a distinct minority, and that, especially in the early years when Docker and the Birmingham 'productioneers' dominated the FBI, they were a source of some irritation to the leadership. Indeed, the increasing business support mentioned by Boyce should not be confined to the period 1925 to 1930, and much earlier it was the FBI leaders' knowledge of this, not least their knowledge of the leanings of their own members, which led them to fear just the sort of bypassing which Boyce discerns in the later period.

The FBI was formed after a meeting of the heavily protectionist British Electrical and Allied Manufacturers' Association early in 1916.[6] The Tariff-Reform objectives of its founder, Dudley Docker of the Metropolitan Carriage, Wagon, and Finance Co., were almost certainly widely shared amongst the 124 initial member firms and trade associations, and among the thirty-strong Executive Council, which was dominated by large-scale heavy industry, especially

---

[1] S. Blank, *Industry and Government in Britain* (Farnborough, 1973), 27.

[2] R. F. Holland, 'The Federation of British Industries and the International Economy, 1929–1939', *Economic History Review*, 34 (1981), 228.

[3] R. W. D. Boyce, *British Capitalism at the Crossroads, 1919–1932* (Cambridge, 1987), 10.

[4] R. P. T. Davenport-Hines, *Dudley Docker* (Cambridge, 1984), 109.

[5] R. W. D. Boyce, *British Capitalism*, 119.

[6] R. P. T. Davenport-Hines, *Dudley Docker*, 105–8.

heavy engineering and armaments.[7] But Tariff Reform, and indeed Docker's wider vision of a new industrial order to meet a 'new industrial age',[8] were difficult to square with his other objective of establishing the FBI as the undisputed mouthpiece of British industry, representing its entire range in a way similar to Marcus Wallenberg's Swedish Industrial Union.[9]

In Stephen Blank's view the FBI sacrificed a radical line on industrial policy for membership size and growth: 'as its membership increased and the range of interests it represented expanded, the leaders of the Federation found it more and more difficult to reach a consensus of opinion on any issue except at the lowest level of agreement'.[10] Such constraints came into effect almost immediately, through a merger with the Employers' Parliamentary Association. Born out of Charles Macara's 'profound discontent' with the National Insurance Act of 1911, the EPA comprised by late 1916 some forty trade associations and 'a great number of important firms'.[11] Though it had members in Liverpool, Leeds, Huddersfield, Leicester, and Nottingham, the location of its headquarters in Cross St., Manchester, near the Cotton Exchange, gave an accurate indication of the centre of its influence.[12] Indeed, Docker welcomed a merger with a businessmen's association which attracted Liberals as members,[13] whilst the prospect of recruiting some 200 new member firms was irresistible to the FBI's first Director-General, Roland Nugent.

'Docker's dream of Tariff Reform was the first casualty of the expansion . . . each interest within the membership was able to wield a veto over its activities.'[14] Should a protectionist-inclined FBI leadership have foreseen the anaesthetizing effects that absorption of the EPA would have? Was it perhaps the case that they were ready and willing to sacrifice Tariff Reform for the achievement of sole representation of the business community?

In fact, the FBI's avid quest for members and inclusiveness should not be taken to imply that its leaders willingly threw over Tariff Reform in a scramble for anodyne policies, nor should the persistence of the effective veto into the late 1920s be taken to suggest that the FBI was anything like equally divided in opinion on fiscal policy. FBI leaders almost certainly underestimated the Free-Trade threat from the new EPA members. Firstly, Nugent was confident

---

[7] R. P. T. Davenport-Hines, *Dudley Docker*, 110.

[8] Blank encapsulates Docker's vision as 'a completely integrated society and economy, in which each industry would have its own organization of workers and managers, the two sets of organizations united by peak federations, and all finally capped by a great national forum of workers and managers and employers, embraced by the protection of an Imperial Tariff'. *Industry and Government*, 14.

[9] R. P. T. Davenport-Hines, *Dudley Docker*, 108–9.

[10] S. Blank, *Industry and Government*, 15.

[11] W. H. Mills, *Sir Charles Macara* (Manchester, 1917), 157–9.

[12] Nugent to Docker, 9 Nov. 1916, John Haworth to Nugent, 17 Jan. 1917, FBI 200/F/3/D1/3/7, Nugent Papers.

[13] R. P. T. Davenport-Hines, *Dudley Docker*, 106.

[14] S. Blank, *Industry and Government*, 15.

that he could wean away the EPA members from the awkward influence of Sir Charles Macara. Macara might be offered an FBI vice-presidency to 'help gild the pill', but Nugent expected him to decline it, clear evidence that Macara would lose control in the process of merger.[15] Secondly, the merger took place at a time when FBI policy-makers could be forgiven for underestimating the Free Trade forces involved. Before the War, Nottingham, Leicester, and Leeds had certainly not been Free Trade bastions, and even Liverpool had always had a strong Tory political tradition.[16] Nor were Lancashire manufacturers, nor even Manchester merchants, immune from the fashion for post-war retaliation against Germany, as had been shown by the spectacular resignations from the board of directors of Manchester Chamber of Commerce in February 1916, and the subsequent approval of a plan for post-war sanctions against Germany and preference with the Empire. In March 1916 the Chamber was urging upon the government key-industry protection of chemicals 'for an adequate period after the War'.[17]

It is not here argued that Manchester's conversion to protection was solid or permanent. Even if we interpret the high level of abstention as signifying indifference, only 191 out of 700 who voted supported the minority report of the Balfour of Burleigh Committee in its call for a 10-per-cent duty on manufactures in the autumn of 1918. But, as late as the Armistice, 494 out of 700 supported either the majority or the minority report, thereby approving at least of protection of key industries and anti-dumping duties.[18]

These events in Manchester were widely reported in the press, and could not have failed to be well known to anyone taking a particular current interest in the Manchester business community. Furthermore, in the context of the intense Germanophobia of 1916 and 1917 they were perfectly normal, and few would have sensed their ephemerality. Thus it would seem more than plausible that Nugent and others leading the FBI may have underestimated the future difficulties that amalgamation with the EPA might pose. This would best explain why, in January 1917, the same month as the EPA merger was negotiated, yet impressed by Hewins's arguments over the *Mitteleuropa* threat, Nugent was considering setting up an FBI committee to work out a detailed policy towards building on the Paris Resolutions. '[W]e are coming to the time when we shall have to ask our Free Traders to make up their minds', he informed Docker. Whilst he realised the need to 'introduce the subject tactfully as an item in the general preparation for meeting conditions after the War and not as a political

---

[15] Nugent to Docker, 9 Nov. 1916.

[16] P. J. Waller, *Democracy and Sectarianism: A Political and Social History of Liverpool 1868–1939* (Liverpool, 1981), chs. 10–16; S. Salvidge, *Salvidge of Liverpool* (1934).

[17] A. Redford, *Manchester Merchants and Foreign Trade*, ii (Manchester, 1956), 203–5; Manchester Chamber of Commerce, *Monthly Record*, Apr. 1916.

[18] A. Redford, *Manchester Merchants*, 206–7.

question', his remarks clearly denote a belief that the War had brought much nearer the possibility of the large-scale acquiescence of the manufacturing community in a protectionist policy.[19] Evidently, he thought the FBI could have its cake and eat it.

His attitude was vindicated in a General Meeting two months later, when A. H. Dixon of Manchester put four resolutions urging the Government to pronounce on economic policy after the War. Free Trade steelmaker Sir Hugh Bell protested that this was 'inextricably bound up with . . . fiscal policy', but amongst the 115 present, including twenty-eight council members, he found not a single supporter.[20] As late as the AGM of October 1918, president R. V. Vassar-Smith's proposal that a joint committee of the main industrial groups should formulate a 'National Policy' on duties, free imports, subsidies, and preference, and should urge on the Government a 'practical test' to apply to 'the practical problems which are bound to arise in connection with the claims which may be advanced by the specific industries to protection from unfair competition', was passed unanimously.[21]

Furthermore, it is not clear that the FBI leaders *consistently* saw the declaration of a protectionist policy as incompatible with future growth. A protectionist FBI might have caused existing members to desert and frightened off new members. But it also might have attracted more new members than it frightened away. In this case, a neutral, rather than an active, fiscal policy might have been a limit on membership growth. And this seems to have been the possibility uppermost in the minds of FBI leaders on frequent occasions: they perceived their difficulty less as frightening away timid Free-Trade suitors than as keeping their existing Free-Trade members in an exercise which would otherwise allow them to recruit more actively under a positive protectionist banner. Indeed, in September 1918, A. E. Hills of the Perfecta Seamless Steel Tube and Conduit Co. Ltd., 'a firm which we certainly do not want to lose', threatened resignation because of FBI inactivity on Tariff Reform. His estimate that 90 per cent of FBI members favoured the policy was not repudiated by the leadership.[22]

Thus it was that, in spite of any lessons learned from amalgamating with the EPA, the FBI leaders were willing to negotiate mergers with two of the protectionist bodies which will be studied in greater depth below,[23] the British Manufacturers' Association (later the National Union of Manufacturers) and the British Empire Producers' Association. Especially in the case of the former, there was an evident jealousy that the NUM was able to recruit

19 Nugent to Docker, 3 Jan. 1917, FBI 200/F/3/D1/3/14.
20 General Meeting, 2 Mar. 1917, FBI 200/F/1/1/211.
21 Annual General Meeting, 30–31 Oct. 1918, FBI 200/F/1/1/211.
22 E. L. Hiley to Docker, 6 Sept. 1918, FBI 200/F/3/D2/3/9.
23 See below, Ch. 11.

without the restriction of a fettered approach to Tariff Reform, and a manifest annoyance that the NUM should describe the FBI in its propaganda as a Free Trade body.

The BMA was founded in 1915 and centred in Birmingham, with Dudley Docker as a founder member and George Terrell MP as its first president. It was unashamedly protectionist and claimed 634 members in 1917. Discussions were held on amalgamation early in 1917, but foundered on the BMA's unwillingness to stop its campaign for Tariff Reform, apparently a condition of the FBI negotiators. But this did not still the desire of the FBI staff for an accord. Nugent, fearing that the BMA would 'steal our thunder' in recruiting new members, and conscious of the BMA's much lower membership subscription in a situation where in all other respects their objectives were precisely similar, considered offering an FBI undertaking that FBI members who supported Tariff Reform should become members of both associations, the FBI paying their BMA subscriptions on their behalf.[24]

The Armistice saw the difficulty unresolved. Probably betraying his own latent protectionism, Nugent anticipated that, when 'Tariff Reform has been passed by Parliament, or the Federation itself shall have declared a Tariff policy', the problem would be solved.[25] By November, he considered that Lloyd George's apparent acceptance of key-industry duties, anti-dumping legislation and imperial preference meant that the essential policy difference between the NUM and the FBI had 'largely disappeared'. As he wrote to Terrell, in language which mirrored precisely the empirical-inductive approach of the historist-inspired pre-war Chamberlainites:

Such a policy opens the door to any modification in Fiscal policy which may be warranted by circumstances, and it will be for the groups of industry to approach the problem each from their own point of view, and seek by direct representation such modification in the duties proposed as in their judgement the interests of their individual industries require. The functions therefore of the National Union in the future will be identical with those of the Federation in this respect . . . [both] being concerned only with constructive criticism and suggestion.[26]

Discussions between the two bodies on a 'definite working arrangement' were held in November 1918, but postponed until after the election. The NUM, anxious that the Board of Trade would soon begin dismantling wartime import restrictions, sought FBI assistance in 'vigorous' propaganda activity.[27] The Birmingham Branch of the FBI added to the pressure by passing a resolution in favour of amalgamation.[28]

[24] Nugent to Docker, 1 and 6 Mar. 1917, FBI 200/F/3/D1/3/10.
[25] Nugent to Docker, 6 Mar. 1917, ibid.
[26] Nugent to Terrell, 18 Nov. 1918, FBI 200/F/3/S1/35/1, Walker Papers.
[27] Terrell to W. P. Rylands, 8 Jan. 1919, ibid.
[28] H. Parkes to C. Tennyson, 17 Jan. 1919, ibid.

Nugent was, however, now becoming less interested in an accord, although it is important to notice that his change in attitude had little to do with fiscal politics, but rather with the way NUM tactics were undermining the FBI's claim to premier status amongst businessmen's organizations. Even in 1917, he had noticed that NUM propaganda implied a closer relationship with the FBI than actually existed. Now his attitude hardened:

We have heard privately from a good many sources, including Mr. Bonar Law, that Mr. Terrell's spokesmanship for us in the House had been doing us a good deal of harm, also our supposed association with the N.U.M. . . . and our name perpetually appearing in conjunction with theirs . . . gave the impression . . . that we were of the same calibre.[29]

Sir Vincent Caillard, president of the FBI in 1918–1919, was naturally sympathetic to NUM objectives. But even he found difficulty in dealing with the smaller body, and like Nugent was annoyed at what he perceived to be attempts to undermine the superior status of the FBI. Receiving in January 1919 an NUM deputation protesting at the reported withdrawal of import restrictions, Sir Albert Stanley at the Board of Trade suggested a committee of manufacturers to collect details. Terrell reported Stanley as requesting an advisory committee of representative manufacturers,[30] and the NUM executive committee proposed it consist of three FBI members, two NUM members, and one representative each of BEAMA, the British Engineers' Association, and the United Tanners' Federation.[31]

Caillard wondered at the need to include the three trade associations when they were all FBI members. Perhaps also suspicious since the Import Restrictions Department of the Board of Trade already had a Consultative Committee whose job was to liaise with businessmen, on which sat a Mr Alexander of the FBI, he checked to see exactly what sort of committee Stanley had in mind.[32] The delay annoyed Terrell, but Stanley's reply doubtless annoyed him even more. As Caillard informed him:

I understand that the Committee which Sir Albert Stanley is asking for is one whose duties will be confined to setting forth the views of the National Union of Manufacturers on the procedure to be adopted in the consideration of the question of Restrictions on Imports. I understood quite clearly that he is not asking for a General Committee set up for advisory purposes, but . . . a Committee of the National Union of Manufacturers only. . . . This being the case, there would not appear to be any useful purpose served by the Federation of British Industries naming Members to serve on the Committee in question.[33]

---

[29] Nugent to Rylands, 13 Jan. 1919, ibid.
[30] Terrell to Caillard, 20 Jan. 1919, ibid.
[31] Terrell to Caillard, 21 Jan. 1919, ibid.
[32] Walker to Terrell, 31 Jan. 1919, ibid. M. A. Stevens, Secretary of the United Tanners' Federation, also had reservations about the proposed committee.
[33] Caillard to Terrell, 28 Jan. 1919, ibid.

This was a poor backcloth to the FBI–NUM meeting held a couple of days later, which few FBI members bothered to attend. Even so, assistant director Douglas Walker was in conciliatory mood after the meeting. A merger would be difficult 'until the Tariff question is more nearly solved, and many of us who cordially support your policy in this matter can only wish you success in your efforts'. Caillard 'naturally would not desire to turn down any proposal of yours without giving it the closest consideration.'[34]

Walker's friendly tone was no doubt grounded partly in his own Tariff-Reform sympathies, but it also took account of the obvious sentiments of many FBI members. Around April several firms wrote asking whether there was any difference between FBI and NUM objectives, and Walker minimized the difference. Indeed, to the Darlaston engineers, Rubery and Owen, he admitted that the NUM had actually been a member association of the FBI until August 1918.[35] In May 1919 the NUM held a conference at Central Hall, Westminster, with speakers including Sir Edward Carson, George Balfour, Neville Chamberlain, and Sir Richard Cooper, all Tariff Reformers. Many provincial FBI members, receiving tickets through the post, 'returned' them to the FBI offices for redistribution. R. Davenport, of Willans and Robinson Ltd., Rugby steam-turbine manufacturers, chided Tennyson for fearing that the NUM was 'stealing our thunder . . . I don't think this matters very much, so long as they are proceeding on lines we approve of '.[36] C. R. Belling, the electrical engineer, made a veiled threat of resignation, citing his own business's critical interest in a tariff.[37]

The threat from the NUM was an important component in the FBI's attempts to obtain a clear picture of its own membership's fiscal proclivities. M. R. Allard, the Leicester district secretary, reported his members' feeling that the FBI was suffering from the 'lack on our part of a definite policy', and asked what had become of the 'plebiscite on tariffs'.[38] But Nugent's attempts to discover members' opinions were not going well, and his difficulties were increased by the fact that parallel negotiations with BEPO were adding the dimension of food taxes and preference to the simpler issue of industrial protection raised by the NUM-FBI talks.[39]

II

There were both ideological and pragmatic reasons for desiring some accord with the NUM. Many FBI members and staff supported NUM aims, whilst the

[34] Walker to Terrell, 31 Jan. 1919, ibid.
[35] Walker to Rubery and Owen, 11 Apr. 1919, ibid.
[36] Davenport to Tennyson, 26 May 1919, ibid.
[37] Belling to Walker, 2 June 1919, ibid.
[38] Allard to Nugent, 16 June 1919, ibid.
[39] Nugent to Allard, 17 June 1919, ibid.

staff realized, with a clarity heightened by Terrell's propaganda, that the two associations recruited from the same constituency. Always claiming to be, and aiming to be, the pre-eminent representative of British industry, they feared that, if no agreement were reached, future growth might be reduced and large-scale defections might even occur. But FBI negotiations with the British Empire Producers' Organization are at first sight harder to understand. BEPO comprised sixty-five or seventy associations, many of them colonial, and a majority of them representing farmers, primary producers, produce merchants, and manufacturers of agricultural machinery or fertilizers.[40]

A main objective of BEPO was to secure imperial preference, which required the prior imposition of protective duties by Britain. Political considerations dictated that the extent to which it wished those duties to fall on the main foodstuffs was not always made clear in BEPO propaganda,[41] a source of some initial confusion in the FBI. There is also fragmentary evidence that some, at least, of the trade associations within BEPO were breakaways from a larger association which had Free-Trade inclinations, or, more likely, took a neutral position. Contemplating amalgamation, FBI director Roland Nugent observed:

We must not be landed . . . into having parallel sections composed of ex-BEPO members to any of our Groups, because in many instances the firms who have joined [BEPO] are firms who disagree with the main Association of their trade on some point, and the main Association . . . is in our Group. The point Tennyson mentions in regard to Protection is, I think, an instance of this.[42]

Proposals for a 'joint committee' of BEPO and FBI members went back at least to late 1916. In October 1917 BEPO was advocating a joint propaganda campaign on fiscal policy, which prompted the FBI Executive Council to initiate an enquiry to discover members' opinions. At this time the FBI felt able to assert, in its reply to BEPO, 'the sympathy of the majority of its Members with the policy indicated in your letter'. But, according to W. Peter Rylands, the proposed joint committee 'died of inanition' and some friction over Tariff Reform, and in March 1918 he suggested, jointly with Docker, that three BEPO representatives should sit on the FBI Executive Council. Sir William Peate (chairman of the Executive Council), Frank Moore, Harry Allcock, F. R. Davenport, and H. G. Tetley agreed, Tetley observing wryly that such a development would force the FBI to formulate a definite policy on Tariff Reform. An opposing amendment was lost heavily.[43]

Negotiations had got very little further by the summer of 1918, by which time the proposal for a joint committee had been resurrected and extended to include

---

[40] See below, Ch. 11.
[41] See below, Ch. 11.
[42] Nugent to Caillard, 25 Jan. 1919, FBI 200/F/3/D1/2/2, Nugent Papers.
[43] Executive Council Minutes, 5 Jan. 1917, 2 Nov. 1917, 13 Mar. 1918, FBI 200/F/1/1/5.

representatives of the British Imperial Council of Commerce.[44] By January 1919 FBI organizers were talking in terms of full amalgamation, an 'excellent thing' according to Nugent. In earlier negotiations BEPO had sought to maintain its independence, but now it was hard up. Though regarding BEPO as 'neither a very powerful nor a very efficient body', he nevertheless favoured 'the removal of anybody else who is competing with us', whilst its dominion and colonial membership would give the FBI a useful 'nucleus' upon which to build an Empire section.[45]

On 29 January the BEPO Council passed a resolution supporting full amalgamation,[46] and shortly afterwards the FBI Executive appointed a sub-committee of Docker, Caillard, Nugent, and Oldham to effect a merger.[47] But, at a meeting in February, BEPO representatives soon discovered the ambivalent position of the FBI negotiators. Being informed that the FBI could not allow its funds to be spent on propaganda for imperial preference, 'a policy to which the Federation does not yet agree', BEPO chairman Colonel Campbell 'said that in conversation with him Mr. Docker and Sir Vincent Caillard said that the F.B.I. accepted the idea of Protection'.[48] The meeting ended recognizing the need for FBI silence until this issue was resolved.

A further meeting in June showed little to have changed, in spite of the introduction of preference in the Finance Act of 1919. BEPO representatives 'presumed that as the Government had adopted the principle and it had now become the policy of the country, it would also be the settled policy of the F.B.I.', but they were informed by FBI negotiators that a resolution at the second FBI annual general meeting committed the Federation only to 'sympathetic' consideration of preference. There was still the need to ascertain the views of FBI members.

It is clear that the actions of Caillard and Docker were based on the strongly held view that the enquiry into FBI members' views would reveal 'that a very big majority' of the members of the Federation were in favour of the policy, though Caillard did indicate that extracting an answer from the Textiles Group was proving difficult. Docker's associate, Edward Hiley, gave him strong support:

It is not a very big fence to take. We have a very fair idea of what the opinion of the members of the Federation is likely to be. The Chancellor of the Exchequer has made

[44] Report of the chairman of the Organisation and Management Committee, 12 June 1918; Executive Council Minutes, 10 July 1918, ibid.

[45] Nugent to Caillard, 25 Jan. 1919, FBI 200/F/3/D1/2/2, Nugent Papers.

[46] Nugent to Caillard, 30 Jan. 1919, ibid.

[47] R. P. T. Davenport-Hines, *Dudley Docker*, 118, notes that Docker took no part in the negotiations, his place being taken by Sir Ernest Hiley of the Metropolitan Carriage, Wagon and Finance Co.

[48] Minutes of a meeting held between representatives of BEPO and the FBI, 7 Feb. 1919, FBI 200/F/3/D1/3/8, Nugent Papers.

Imperial Preference almost a national policy and to my mind the probability is that . . . [at the next] Annual Meeting no one will vote against it.[49]

Shortly afterwards Nugent was informed by Sir Herbert Dixon of the Fine Cotton Spinners' and Doublers' Association that the textile trade would probably support a resolution on preference 'provided that . . . did not imply that they in any way supported or would support any measure of protection'. Nugent interpreted this as supporting Austen Chamberlain's introduction of preference on existing duties only, and, since it was unlikely to satisfy BEPO, 'rather academic'.[50] Nevertheless, it may have been indications of support of this kind that determined Caillard to recommend amalgamation to the FBI Council meeting in October. Several present objected, including Sir Rowland Barran of Leeds, who claimed to support preference and to believe that the 'hard and fast lines' between free trade and protection that existed before the War no longer obtained, but who feared that amalgamation with a 'protectionist organisation' would prevent recruitment in the West Riding textile industry, where the FBI had as yet 'practically no adherents'.[51] He also distrusted the agricultural and merchant elements in BEPO. Several members agreed with him that there was 'a great danger of splitting the Federation on the question of Protection'.[52]

Caillard welcomed the idea of agricultural members, reminding the Council that the Central Chamber had already joined the FBI, whilst 'to regard colonial manufacturers as competitors was taking a very "Little England" view'. It was better, in the event of conflict, to have the representatives of colonial industry[53] inside the FBI rather than outside. He met more serious opposition over his intention to introduce a resolution at the forthcoming AGM urging the government to include 'substantial' imperial preference 'in any economic or commercial policy which may be adopted in the future'.[54] There is fragmentary second-hand evidence that BEPO regarded this as a precondition for a merger.[55] Though Caillard considered his resolution to go no further than one passed at the 1918 AGM, it provoked considerable opposition in the Grand Council, presumably because it gave tacit approval to the a future extension of preference in a form necessitating duties on the main foodstuffs.

The Grand Council Minutes state that the Council recommended the subcommittee's report to the AGM 'for consideration and adoption, but makes

---

[49] Report of a meeting held between representatives of BEPO and the FBI, 13 June 1919, ibid.

[50] Nugent to Caillard, 10 July 1919, ibid.

[51] In some contradiction was George Garnett's opposition to fusion with a 'protectionist body' because the FBI would become too big and unwieldy.

[52] Grand Council Minutes, 15 Oct. 1919, FBI 200/F/1/1/1.

[53] The Canadian Manufacturers' Association and the South African Federated Chambers of Industry were members of BEPO.

[54] Grand Council Minutes, 15 Oct. 1919, FBI 200/F/1/1/1.

[55] Sir Edward Broadhurst, reported in Nugent to Caillard, 5 Nov. 1919, FBI 200/F/3/D1/2/2, Nugent Papers.

no recommendation regarding the resolution', in terms which suggest that it endorsed the amalgamation but assumed neutrality on preference.[56] Nugent's remarks on 20 October confirm that, although amalgamation was still a live issue, tempers were rising both in BEPO and the FBI: 'although the opposition on both sides has been most unfortunate, and will to some extent rob the amalgamation of its value, on the whole it will be best to go on with it.'[57] He was aware of opposition within the FBI to a merger with BEPO, but he envisaged its effects as being limited to 'a certain number of resignations in Bradford and Lancashire':

I am coming to the conclusion . . . that, whilst there very likely may be a campaign run against us in the North on the ground that we have gone 'protectionist' by amalgamating with a protectionist body, and while the Association which is at present being run by Sir Robert Priestley in Bradford (and which has long been trying to get our Wool Trade Members) may no doubt profit from this campaign, a campaign in the other sense run by Mr. Terrell's National Union of Manufacturers on the ground that by turning down the amalgamation we had definitely gone Free Trade would probably do us more harm still.[58]

He had no doubt the amalgamation would go through at the AGM, but was concerned to minimize the after-effects in Lancashire and Yorkshire. To this end he organized a meeting of FBI members in Manchester on 4 November. Before the meeting he found the leading members of the Manchester Branch nervous of widespread opposition, and this was confirmed in the meeting itself. Though Rylands and a Mr Davies of the Bleachers' Association spoke in favour of the amalgamation, and Sir Herbert Dixon was known to be in similar mind, chairman Sir Edward Broadhurst moved a resolution resisting the endorsement of imperial preference, 'which they understood was a necessary portion of the agreement with the B.E.P.O.'. This received powerful support from delegates of the Federation of Master Cotton Spinners' Associations and the Cotton Spinners' and Manufacturers' Association, and from five or six individual speakers, including one or two engineers. The resolution against amalgamation was carried by thirty-one votes to four, with about twelve abstentions.[59]

The Manchester representative of the strongly protectionist BEAMA considered the meeting untypical of broader FBI opinion, and when he introduced a further resolution that no further action should be taken until all FBI members had voiced an opinion, no one opposed him. But the meeting convinced Nugent of the risk attached to pressing ahead with the amalgamation. Broadhurst and Sir Charles Mandleberg were afraid that virtually the entire Manchester membership might resign, and a Mr Armitage of Bradford envisaged a similar situation there.

[56] Grand Council Minutes, 15 Oct. 1919, FBI 200/F/1/1/1.
[57] Nugent to Caillard, 20 Oct. 1919, FBI 200/F/3/D1/2/2, Nugent Papers.
[58] Ibid.   [59] Nugent to Caillard, 5 Nov. 1919, FBI 200/F/3/D1/2/2, Nugent Papers.

Long discussions between Nugent and Caillard followed, during which Nugent gave Caillard some insight into his own impression of the state of opinion in the Northern FBI districts. During these exchanges, which are examined below for the light they shed on the division of opinion within the Federation,[60] it became evident that Nugent had now changed his mind on the advisability of pressing ahead with negotiations. In his view, the number of resignations which might follow upon a merger had risen to an unacceptable level.

Subsequent events are not well recorded in the FBI archives, but the eventual result is clear. The Caillard-Docker committee's report supporting a preferentia-list resolution as well as the merger with BEPO went before a general meeting of the FBI in November 1919. But, with Nugent now disinclined to support the merger, it is not clear how hard Caillard, as president, pressed it; at one point in the poorly recorded meeting he observed that the merger 'did not meet with the *unanimous* support of members'.[61] The merger was referred back to the Organisation and Management Committee, which effectively meant its doom. At the AGM of November 1920, Rylands, the new president, presented a formula for controversial political issues:

Any policy . . . which is in the common interests of industry is supported by the F.B.I., by all the means in its power. Any policy . . . which is in the interests of one industry or group of industries and not against the interests of any other industry or groups, is supported by the F.B.I.

Any policy . . . which is in the interests of one group but is opposed to the interests of another group is not supported officially by the F.B.I., but the F.B.I. will give equal facilities and assistance to both sides in putting forward their case, and in particular will afford them every opportunity for mutual discussion.[62]

Though this 'address' was received with 'applause', it was clearly a ruling: no resolution was put, no vote taken. Acceptance of an embargo on such matters as an item of principle, for this was the way in which Rylands presented the decision and in which it was interpreted in later years, effectively glossed over the difference of fiscal opinion within the membership, and rendered redundant the question of its magnitude and extent.

III

The FBI administration was, in fact, finding considerable difficulty in completing the investigation into members' views, since certain Industrial Groups would not respond. Even a special committee appointed by the Executive made little progress. Nugent discerned that, in certain trades, there were 'strong sections

---

[60] See below, 307–12.
[61] Annual General Meeting, 12 Nov. 1919, FBI 200/F/1/1/211 (my emphasis).
[62] Annual General Meeting, 30 Nov. 1920, FBI 200/F/1/1/211.

which are themselves very divided on the question'. Speaking specifically of imperial preference, he observed that '[w]e are being blocked in the matter chiefly by two big trades, the Cotton trade and certain sections of the Chemicals trade'.[63]

The most detailed information surviving in the FBI archives on the extent of division within the Federation unfortunately concerns that over the proposed merger with BEPO, which specifically raised the question of preference. Carrying with it the corollary of a possible introduction of duties on the main foodstuffs, preference obviously presented a sterner test of the fiscal inclinations of FBI members than did the proposed merger with the NUM. The surprising thing, perhaps, is not that there was so much opposition to the BEPO merger, but that there was so little. At the meeting with BEPO representatives in June 1919 Nugent attributed opposition more or less entirely to the Textiles Group, which he specifically mentioned as having refused to respond to the FBI's fiscal enquiries, and the Chemicals Group, about which he gave even less information. According to the verbatim minutes of that meeting, he spoke not of the Textile Group's outright opposition to the merger, but of '[c]onsiderable division' within it over preference.[64] This was presumably also true of the Chemicals Group, since many branches of the industry, notably dyestuffs, pharmaceuticals, and photographic chemicals, were shortly to apply for key-industry status and safeguarding. Furthermore, the Group included fertilizers and explosives. There were certainly supporters of protection among pre-war manufacturers of agricultural chemicals, such as Sir William Goulding, whilst superphosphate producers themselves filed a safeguarding application in the 1920s, and Nobel Industries was a large contributor to the ostensibly protectionist British Commonwealth Union.[65] Free-Trade sentiment in the chemical industry was almost certainly concentrated in the alkali and soap trades,[66] and to no small extent, therefore, in Brunner Mond and Lever Brothers, and regionally in the North-West. What proportion of the 5 per cent of FBI members who were in the chemical industry such producers constituted is unknown, but it certainly suggests that, in quantitative terms, it was in cotton rather than chemicals that the forces opposing the BEPO merger were massed.

As late as October Nugent was of the opinion that it would be best to push ahead with the scheme, and accept that 'a certain number of resignations' would be the result.[67] The opposition which caused him to change his mind was clearly that encountered in the Manchester meeting on 4 November, when only four

[63] Nugent to Allard, 17 June 1919 (2 letters), FBI 200/F/3/S1/35/1.

[64] Verbatim minutes of meeting between representatives of BEPO and the FBI, 13 June 1919, FBI 200/F/3/D1/3/8.

[65] See above, Ch. 9 and below, Ch. 11.

[66] On the pre-war views of Joseph Crosfield and Sons Ltd., see A. E. Musson, *Enterprise in Soap and Chemicals* (Manchester, 1965), 179.

[67] Nugent to Caillard, 20 Oct. 1919, FBI 200/F/3/D1/2/2.

out of forty-seven supported the merger. In a letter to Caillard written a day later about more widespread opposition, he was more impressionistic. Armitage, the Bradford district secretary, thought that most of his members would resign if the merger went through. Gordon, the Leeds district secretary, found the leaders of the district solid against the merger, but no meeting had been held. Patterson, the Liverpool district secretary, thought that a majority of his members were opposed, but again there is no evidence that this was more than impressionistic. Nugent had visited Nottingham, finding that there 'a certain number are definitely against it and nobody is very much for it'.[68] In a second letter written on the same day Nugent was even more pessimistic, even though he had presumably had little opportunity to gather fresh intelligence. Now he feared a 'landslide' in the North, starting in Manchester and spreading to Bradford, Liverpool, and Leeds, and perhaps Nottingham.[69] A day later in a further letter to Caillard, Nugent mentioned other districts for the first time. In London, the attitude of most members was 'one of indifference'. There was no objection to amalgamation, but on the other hand 'I don't think most of them are very keen about it'. Swansea, Newcastle, and the Scottish districts 'are probably indifferent, but at any rate would probably raise no very strong opposition'. Only Sheffield and Birmingham seemed particularly strongly in favour of the amalgamation.[70]

Nugent considered that opposition to the merger was rooted in opposition to 'the political tendency of the [preferentialist] resolution which is to accompany it'.[71] Certainly, opposition to the merger was dictated by fiscal allegiance, as was the strong support for it in Sheffield and Birmingham. It seems dangerous to conclude from this, however, that indifference elsewhere to the merger signified indifference to Tariff Reform. Since the majority of associations affiliated to BEPO were primary-producing or merchant groups,[72] it is certainly possible that there was reluctance on grounds other than fiscal politics narrowly defined. Like shipowners and bankers, the entry of merchants into the FBI had caused distinct antagonisms only two years earlier, and distrust of middlemen still persisted amongst FBI members.[73] Indeed, Sir Rowland Barran, opposing the merger in the Grand Council on 15 October 1919, dwelt on this. Claiming to support preference, and presumably searching for arguments which would appeal to protectionists, he urged that the merchant and professional elements in BEPO had little interest in common with FBI members.[74] Such an interpretation would also explain Nugent's comment that the failure of amalgamation would 'stop a

[68] Nugent to Caillard, 5 Nov. 1919, ibid.
[69] Nugent to Caillard, 5 Nov. 1919 (2nd letter), ibid.
[70] Nugent to Caillard, 6 Nov. 1919, ibid.
[71] Ibid.
[72] 'British Empire Producers' Organisation: List Of Affilited Associations', FBI 200/F/3/D1/3/8.
[73] Sir Richard Vassar Smith to Tennyson, 27 Sept. 1918, FBI 200/F/3/D1/3/1; Docker to Nugent, 10 Jan. 1917, FBI 200/F/3/D1/2/2.
[74] Grand Council Minutes, 15 Oct. 1919, FBI 200/F/1/1/1.

small amount of recruiting among people such as the shipping lines, etc., who I believe are rather waiting to see if the amalgamation comes off before they join',[75] a comment which would otherwise hold the curious implication that shipping companies favoured the presence of Tariff-Reform groups in associations that they were considering joining, and in that case also prompt the question of why those shipping lines were not themselves members of BEPO. In such a context, it seems quite possible that protectionist members of the FBI were simply less concerned with the preferentialist aims of colonial primary producers and merchants than they were about retaliation and what was later to become the movement for safeguarding. As Nugent admitted, the distinct majority of FBI members were prepared to acquiesce in the merger. But, to that majority, the BEPO controversy may have seemed something of a sideshow. In such circumstances, an adamant minority held the greater weight.

IV

Information on FBI membership by district and Industry Group in 1921 can be used to gain some impression of the potential danger to the Federation posed by the BEPO negotiations. The number of members in each Industry Group is unavailable, but the total subscriptions raised from each group can be taken as a more-or-less perfect proxy. Textiles, the largest single group, provided £24,046 in membership fees, or 18.53 per cent of total FBI income, whilst chemicals, fertilizers, and explosives contributed £6,712, or 5.17 per cent. Manchester, the biggest district after London and Birmingham, could boast 230 members, or 13.21 per cent of the total, and 12.92 per cent of FBI income; Liverpool, Bradford, Leeds and Nottingham together constituted 13.63 per cent of the membership and contributed 18.09 per cent of FBI finance.[76] The full details are given in Appendices IV to VI below.

These figures give some justification for Nugent's increasing alarm at the effects of large-scale defections. But they also confirm the tendency of the written evidence to suggest that, though not unimportant, the opponents to the merger were in a distinct minority. A few conjectures will reinforce this point. Firstly, no Industrial Group or FBI district would have been unanimous. Even at the Manchester meeting, four members supported the amalgamation and twelve or so abstained. It is never entirely safe to speculate on abstention, but it can fairly be argued that in this case it probably signified no particular opposition to the merger, but a certain loyalty to the immediate business community, and a disinclination to stir up local antagonisms. About a third of those who attended the meeting of 4 November, therefore, cannot be safely regarded as opponents

---

[75] Nugent to Caillard, 6 Nov. 1919, FBI 200/F/3/D1/2/2.

[76] Analysis of FBI membership, 1921–6, FBI 200/F/3/S1/7/16–18, Walker Papers.

of the BEPO merger, nor therefore of preference. Furthermore, what of those who did not attend the meeting? There are no figures for Manchester district membership in November 1919, but it would have been less than the 230 of 1921. If we were to assume a figure of 150, probably too low, then still less than one-third attended the meeting. Were the others indifferent? If so, opposition to the BEPO amalgamation would seem to have been centred upon two-thirds of one-third of the Manchester membership, or only just over one in five.

Of the other four districts mentioned by Nugent as problem areas, only Liverpool seems at first sight to pair naturally with Manchester. The other three seem to fit oddly with evidence presented elsewhere. We have seen above how the Nottingham Chamber of Commerce displayed a pronounced Chamberlainite bias in the early stages of the pre-war campaign, and how that tendency stiffened in the period 1908 to 1910, even though the Chamber found it difficult to translate protectionist sympathy into action.[77] In the War, the Nottingham manufacturers were particularly active in pressing for import prohibitions, and in the 1920s they were involved in applications for the safeguarding of lace and embroidery, gloves, hosiery, and light leather goods. Indeed, it is clear from an enquiry instituted in the Chamber as early as January 1919 that protectionist feeling was running particularly strongly.[78] There is the complication that the average size of firm of the Nottingham FBI member may have been somewhat bigger than average firm size in the Chamber, since the larger Nottingham employers were not well-represented in the Chamber. This could be taken to demonstrate a plausible tendency for smaller firms to be more strongly protectionist than larger, but we would need much stronger evidence to establish such a thesis. It is unlikely, however, that this would have skewed the result markedly, and it is any case offset by the fact that membership of the Nottingham Chamber at the end of 1920 was 666, whilst membership of the FBI district in 1921 was only 76.[79] Nottingham almost certainly needs to be reclassified. Indeed, Nugent's own words, that in the district 'a certain number are definitely against it [the BEPO merger] and nobody is very much for it', would seem to place Nottingham squarely amongst those districts he classified as indifferent rather than those which were opposed.[80] If Nottingham businessmen were indifferent to negotiations with BEPO, which is at the least questionable, this would seem to show they were less immediately interested in preference than in other aspects of Tariff Reform, a general tariff or what was later to become safeguarding, and reinforce the suggestion made above that the BEPO merger was associated more tightly with Tariff Reform in the opposing FBI districts than it was elsewhere.[81]

---

[77] See above, 101–3.
[78] NCC, *Annual Report*, 1919, App. E.
[79] NCC, *Annual Report*, 1920.
[80] Nugent to Caillard, 5 Nov. 1919 (1st letter), FBI 200/F/3/D1/2/2.
[81] See above, 308–9.

As far as Leeds and Bradford are concerned, however, Nugent's impressions were probably nearer to the mark. Before the War, the Bradford Chamber of Commerce was not far off being equally divided, with Free Traders having a very slight margin of superiority over protectionists of 120 to 115 in the vote of 1904.[82] It is that even balance of opinion which is surprising, given the prominence of Lister's Bradford in the Fair Trade movement of the 1880s and the susceptibility of Bradford worsteds to French competition, rather than any change between pre-war and post-war opinion. Leeds Chamber of Commerce recorded a vote of seventy-six to sixty-five in favour of protection in 1904, but division was such that only during 1908 did opinion swing clearly in favour of Tariff Reform.[83]

If these trends had remained unaffected by the War, and if indeed the BEPO merger did encapsulate the fiscal issue within those FBI districts, there would seem every reason to have regarded the Bradford and Leeds Chambers as deeply divided over the issue, rather than being heavily opposed. However, the War had effected a remarkable change in the trade conditions facing the woollen and worsted districts. If cotton stood on the brink of the abyss in 1918 and 1919, woollen manufactures seemed to have turned the corner, at least in terms of the threat from abroad. The ratio of imports to exports, peaking at 63.3 per cent in 1895–1899 and still 59.7 per cent in 1900–1904, fell hugely thereafter, and stood at only 12.2 per cent in 1921. It did rise thereafter, though only to 27.5 per cent in 1927. Even this was apparently enough to send the industry scurrying into an application for safeguarding, but in the meantime the situation was, by historical experience, unusually comfortable. Unlike in cotton, the War retarded the growth of capacity abroad, and by and large foreign tariff increases fell below the trend established before 1914.[84] Seldom has it been found in this study that protectionists became converts, or re-converts, to Free Trade. This may have happened in this case, but it is more likely that the tactical position of the Free Traders strengthened in a situation where the protectionist imperative to action receded.

To return once more to conjecture, let us for the moment ignore Nugent's fear of widespread dissent in Nottingham, and regard Bradford and Leeds as having been split fifty-fifty in the BEPO affair. Given the number of those who usually displayed indifference on Tariff Reform, or who played little active part in the meetings of their associations, it is plausible to argue that even this ratio is unduly favourable to the Free Traders. But, on this basis, the whole of the Manchester and Liverpool district memberships, plus half of that of Bradford and Leeds, would total 402 in 1921, or 23.1 per cent of total FBI membership. If we then

---

[82] See above, 112.

[83] See above, 97–101.

[84] Raw figures from Committee on Industry and Trade, *Survey of Textile Industries* (1928), Table 6, 276, and 223–4.

go further, as discussed above, and reduce the Manchester membership to two-thirds or one-fifth to arrive at a plausible estimate of the true strength of the district's opposition to the merger, the figure comes down to around nineteen or even thirteen per cent of FBI membership in 1921.

We should perhaps be wary of estimates as low as these, especially the lower, the more so since Sir Charles Mandleberg, one of those who feared large-scale resignation in the Manchester district if the merger went through, was a protectionist and therefore had no axe to grind.[85] Furthermore, such speculation obviously ignores Free-Trade sentiment in the non-rebellious districts, though it is to be emphasized that Nugent considered indifference rather than opposition to be characteristic of those districts. But a distinct revision upwards of even the highest figure, 23 per cent, would still leave the Free Traders in a distinct minority within the FBI. Indeed, the *total* membership of Manchester, Liverpool, Bradford, Leeds, and Nottingham constituted less than 27 per cent of that of the FBI. All in all, 25 to 30 per cent would not seem an implausible guess at Free-Trade strength amongst the membership. But, whatever the true figure, Manchester's ability to affect FBI policy was certainly not one of sheer numbers.

V

All this must remain a matter of some conjecture. Nugent certainly knew he could carry the day at a general meeting on the BEPO amalgamation, not only because he had sufficient proxies to do so, but also because supporters from the 'engineering and similar trades who can get to London easily' could be counted upon to outweigh the dissenters from the North. The evidence strongly suggests, however, that he had more than mere tactical advantage—in his own words, 'a majority ... [but not] ... a majority in all trades'.[86]

Even so, to act without a majority in each trade would be to 'immediately lose our position of being a national federation'. In Nugent's eyes, the FBI's great strength in negotiation with government was that it represented 'the whole industry of the country'.[87]

In addition to a natural desire to avoid any damage to FBI recruitment in a period of active expansion, there was also a further consideration, the possibility of a 'domino effect', or multiplier contraction, consequent upon even quite a small reduction in membership, through resignation over the BEPO affair or any other reason. In 1927 Nugent confided to N. C. Cookson that the FBI's income and expenditure were very finely balanced. Even a relatively small loss in income of three or four thousand pounds a year would necessitate immediate economies

[85] See below, 320.

[86] Nugent to Caillard, 6 Nov. 1919, FBI 200/F/3/D1/2/2; Nugent to Allard (1st letter), 17 June 1919, FBI 200/F/3/S1/35/1.

[87] Nugent to Allard (2nd letter), 17 June 1919, ibid.

in work and services. There was then, he explained, 'always the danger of starting a rot through this cutting down leading to the resignation of the members most interested in the particular work which was cut down, thus creating further loss of income causing further cutting down, and so on'. Such a process, he reflected, had actually happened in 'the drastic economy years from 1921 onwards'.[88]

Ironically, Nugent exaggerated the FBI's power to influence government, even if the Federation did speak with the whole voice of British industry. On the other hand, though it is not entirely clear how many other objectives existed on which FBI members *were* unanimous, there were certainly some; lower taxation, economies in government expenditure, and, a few years later, opposition to a capital levy. Such considerations effectively subordinated Tariff Reform in the interests of pursuing more widely acceptable FBI objectives. The strategy was prudent from the point of view of the FBI's administrators even if it meant a refusal to recognize the wishes of a majority of the membership. All the evidence suggests that it was administrative expediency, rather than an evenly balanced difference of views on the fiscal question, which led to FBI inaction. The chances of a protectionist revolt were small—there had been no concrete test of opinion, and the ability of any section of the membership to question the qualitative assessments made by the leadership would be limited. Effectively, the administrators could choose the priorities.

As a result of its neutrality, the FBI became rather impotent in responding to the pushy canvassing and recruiting activities of the NUM. FBI headquarters constantly received from members copies of NUM circulars. To the FBI leaders, these indicated that the NUM was exaggerating its own size and power, and taking credit for the FBI's success with government. In one particularly strong circular, the NUM described the FBI as a 'Free Trade body', and claimed itself to be 'the author . . . of the Safeguarding of Industries Act, to get which upon the Statute Book this Union spent over £30,000. The Federation said not one word in support of that Act'.[89]

The NUM's most active and well-run branch was in Birmingham, and hence C. R. Dibben, the FBI's Birmingham district area organizer, was directed to keep an eye on its activities. Dibben made it clear that he thought NUM activity there far from unsuccessful. Components Ltd., the Birmingham motor-vehicle-components manufacturer, resigned from the FBI in late 1922 or early 1923; and its chairman, Charles Sangster, subsequently secured an NUM resolution to press the government to increase protection of the motor industry.[90] In anticipating an NUM meeting which was to debate a resolution that a 'scientific tariff would promote rather than injure exports', Dibben could report to the FBI that he had

[88] Nugent to C. Cookson, 28 Apr. 1927, FBI 200/F/3/D1/6/10.
[89] NUM circular, 5 Oct. 1923, copy in FBI 200/F/3/S1/35/1.
[90] C. R. Dibben to Brig.-Gen. Leggett, 15 Feb. 1923, ibid.

'no doubt that the N.U.M. have succeeded in bringing . . . Protection right to the front here'.[91] After the meeting, he reported an attendance of 100 to 120, and an intention to hold similar meetings elsewhere because of its success. R. G. Rogers, of Buncker and Haseler Ltd., an FBI member which had always resisted NUM advances, had now changed his mind and joined.[92]

At least in the Birmingham area, the NUM was getting a better press than the FBI organizers were prepared to admit. Stung into an attempt to refute NUM allegations, Sir David Brooks of the FBI wrote to Dudley Docker hoping for a denial of the NUM claim that Docker was president of its Midland Branch. He was disappointed. Docker, a founder member of the NUM, neither confirmed nor denied the claim, only expressed his regret at FBI-NUM antagonism. A year later, presumably under some pressure from the FBI, he resigned his presidency of the Midland Branch of the NUM, though not permanently.[93]

At FBI headquarters, annoyance at NUM exaggeration of links with the FBI developed into a certain contempt for the Birmingham organization when discussing its activities with members. In December 1925, anticipating by some months a very similar campaign by the Empire Industries Association,[94] the NUM launched a three-year appeal for £20,000 p.a. to intensify its propaganda on safeguarding and protection and establish a statistical bureau, a publicity department, and a school for training travelling lecturers. Asked for his opinion by an obviously sympathetic London engineering firm, Radiators Ltd., Nugent seemed to take pleasure in denigrating the campaign:

After all, why should they expect, doing it more or less as amateurs and with relatively small financial resources, to succeed in converting the country when the Unionist Party and the various tariff organisations connected with it, with far greater resources and far longer experiences, have hitherto failed?[95]

Within the FBI itself, there was no serious attempt to reopen the issues of protection or preference until the late 1920s. In July 1922, at Nugent's instigation, the FBI pressed the government to appoint a Board of Trade committee to examine the alarming rise in foreign tariffs and 'discover what pressure it would be possible for this country to apply in the course of negotiations with any particular country'. Doubtless, the protectionists within the FBI knew well by now the chances of such a move leading to anything but frustration.[96]

---

[91] Dibben to Tennyson, 17 Oct. 1923, ibid.

[92] Dibben to Tennyson, 19 Oct. 1923, ibid.

[93] Sir David Brooks to Docker, 22 Oct. 1923, Docker to Brooks, 25 Oct. 1923, H. Baker (secretary of the Midland Branch of the NUM) to Docker, 20 Oct. 1924, ibid. Docker had re-assumed the presidency by 1926.

[94] See below, Ch. 12.

[95] Nugent to H. James Yates, 21 Jan. 1926, FBI 200/F/3/51/35/1.

[96] Grand Council Minutes, 19 July 1922, FBI 200/F/1/1/1.

In January 1923 an FBI committee on inter-imperial trade was established, but according to protectionist Harry Allcock its report six months later 'skated over the crucial point at issue', that of preference. In his attempt to resurrect the issue he was supported by Frank Moore, Sir Algernon Firth, and H. Tomlinson. Several Council members spoke against this, but again, the only specific mention of the location of opposition to preference came from the cotton industry and the Manchester district. Allcock, mocked D. Lloyd Howarth, was probably in a minority of one on the Manchester district committee, whilst other Manchester members asserted trenchantly that in the view of the cotton industry, preference was simply 'a form of the protection controversy, and therefore inimical to their interests'. Reminding the Council that preference lay in 'the realm of political controversy', they invoked the agreement at the General Meeting of 1920 when it had been decided that areas of controversy between members should be avoided.[97]

The evidence is even more fragmentary than that surviving on the events of 1919, but again it all points to the Manchester district. Until the late 1920s, the FBI lived under a veil of silence. The decision of 1920 became a matter of form; it was easier to live by it than to question it, and in any case the decision itself was the answer to the question. The divided nature of the membership could become a self-perpetuating myth.

It should not be forgotten, however, that the Manchester district itself was becoming more important to the FBI, a fact which helped to vindicate the decision of 1920 irrespective of the arithmetic. In the years 1921 to 1926 the Manchester district registered a net increase of 112 firms, an increase of 48.7 per cent. Only two other districts experienced similar expansion, Bradford with an increase of thirty-four firms (55.7 per cent), and Newcastle with an increase of thirty-eight firms (44.2 per cent). Manchester and Bradford alone accounted for 146 out of the total net increase of 287 member firms. They provided over half of the new entrants into the FBI in these years. It must remain a matter of conjecture whether the decision to reject the BEPO arrangement encouraged recruitment in the textile districts, whilst discouraging recruitment in the protectionist heartlands. As Table 10 shows, Birmingham demonstrated the largest decline in membership apart from depressed South Wales and protectionist Northampton, whilst Sheffield exhibited a fairly low rate of increase. The argument has an almost impish appeal. Could it be that the conclusion to the BEPO affair, far from being the result of deep division within the ranks of the FBI, was in truth the cause of it?

Obviously, such speculation would be dangerous. Table 10 does reveal some slight tendency for Northern districts to show a more rapid expansion in the first half of the 1920s than Central and Southern districts, but it is well to remember

---

[97] Special meeting of Grand Council, 20 June 1923, ibid.

TABLE 10. *FBI: Numerical Strength According to Districts 1921–1926*

	Percentage Change	Absolute Increase/Decrease
Bradford	+ 55.7	+ 34
Manchester	+ 48.7	+ 112
Newcastle	+ 44.4	+ 38
Glasgow	+ 36.2	+ 25
Nottingham	+ 32.9	+ 25
Home Counties	+ 24.2	+ 15
London	+ 16.3	+ 68
Edinburgh	+ 10.7	+ 6
Sheffield	+ 8.3	+ 6
Liverpool	+ 5.7	–6
Leeds	–1.4	–1
Leicester	–1.7	–1
Birmingham	–7.3	–18
Northampton	–12.9	–4
South Wales	–24.7	–24

Source: FBI 200/F/3/S1/7/16–18, 32, Walker Papers.

that Nugent regarded Newcastle and the Scottish districts as indifferent towards the BEPO merger. Liverpool would scarcely fit the thesis, unless we were to assume, arbitrarily, that the district was suddenly, and very heavily, affected by a shift in sympathy towards imperial preference on the part of the shipping lines, or some such reason. Under such an interpretation, the place of Leeds in Table 9 would be problematical. The place of Nottingham seems to signify little, whilst that of South Wales suggests that the state of trade might be a powerful influence given the fairly high cost of FBI membership. Fairly moderate rates of expansion in much of the Midlands and Southern England may simply be because the FBI became established there at an earlier date than was the case in parts of the North. There were doubtless many other reasons for differential growth-rates between regions, not least the efficiency of local district secretaries in recruiting. Our safest conclusion would seem to be that the failure of talks with BEPO was seen in Manchester and Bradford as having ruled out the possibility of the FBI going protectionist, that in those districts this had some positive effect on recruitment, and that in consequence there is the possibility that Free-Trade strength in the Federation increased slightly during the period to 1926. Given that, in absolute terms, the other districts expanded as much as those two, however, it is very unlikely that any such strengthening would have been significant.

VI

The decision of 1920 to avoid embroiling the FBI in areas of political controversy reflected closely the forces at work in the Chambers of Commerce before the War, forces which had led to an effective veto on positive action in those chambers which had distinct protectionist majorities. Tariff Reform had become political in a way that, somehow, labour and trade-union matters, or local rates, or even national taxation policy, had not. Compared with its effect on working-class living-standards and food prices, on the balance of payments and capital exports, an important but hidden consequence of Free Trade and the liberal international economy has almost entirely escaped notice: its political emascula-tion of the bulk of the British manufacturing interest, its reduction of the legitimate horizon of freedom in discussion, action, and reaction, its delaying of the emergence of business politics, and maybe also its effect in retarding the development of managerial capitalism in Britain. In Baldwin's tariff election, the manufacturer could be out-voted. In his own associations, he was seldom allowed even to vote. If opinions were never counted, it became that much easier for government to discount them.

Ironically, however, this arbitrary distinction over what was political also ensured that the Free Traders within the FBI achieved a less-than-complete embargo on activity in fiscal matters. After the passing of the Safeguarding of Industries Act, the FBI interpretation was that applications under the legislation were a legitimate form of activity, and the FBI service departments were placed at the disposal of any industry making an application. This was not entirely consistent; it neglected the fact that, with both Liberal and Labour Parties opposed to the Act and intent on repeal, it was hard to regard it as apolitical or uncontroversial in any meaningful sense. It may, indeed, be taken to confirm a suspicion that the businessman's definition of a political issue was one on which the Conservative and Unionist Party was divided. Be that as it may, the interpretation was a pragmatic one, and there is no record of Free Traders having attempted to challenge it.

In the early years of the embargo, the FBI attempted to steer a neutral course in its dealings with the Government on fiscal legislation. The introduction of the Safeguarding of Industries Bill into the Commons was recognized as signalling 'a new phase in the situation', and the Executive Committee revived attempts to discover 'the views of the different trades with regard to the Bill', whilst meetings were arranged between different sections whose interests came into conflict.[98]

Subsequently, however, the main emphasis in FBI activity on safeguarding lay in assisting trades in their applications for an order under the Act: there is little evidence of assistance being given to the opponents of applications, or indeed being requested by them. As early as 1923, members were being informed of the 'material assistance' that had been afforded to trades applying for safeguarding, particular credit being claimed for FBI action on the lace trade. By 1924, a time when the whole policy of safeguarding was under threat of imminent abolition

[98] *Fifth Annual Report*, 1920–1, 17, FBI 200/F/4/2/4.

by the new Labour Government, the *Annual Report* could speak of the FBI's 'accepted policy' of assisting trades in their applications for safeguarding.[99]

The Labour Government's promise to repeal the McKenna duties did, however, cause the FBI particular difficulty. In addressing its members, particularly in its *Annual Report* for 1923–1924, it gave the impression that it was prepared to mount a protest in support of those trades which stood in danger of losing protection when Macdonald entered Downing Street. Nugent considered that an earlier Grand Council decision, not to negotiate with government on the McKenna duties in view of the policy of formal neutrality, was an obstacle which could be overcome. In May 1924 a meeting of those interested in the duty on motor vehicles and parts, including Sir Herbert Austin, John Denny of Leyland Motors, Sir George Beharrell of Dunlop, P. F. Bennett of Joseph Lucas, and more than a dozen representatives of the metal, engineering, and components trades, sought at least a delay, and perhaps a phased withdrawal of the duty on a sliding scale over two or three years. Nugent considered the Grand Council would 'afford the trades concerned the full support of the Federation', since this was a 'question of the sudden alteration of conditions created by a Government and affecting the operations of the trade'.[100]

Perhaps fortunately for FBI unity, however, this transparent stratagem did not have to be put to the test. Further meetings revealed a feeling that the political circumstances were unpropitious, and that any attempt at propaganda might be damaging. The participants were convinced that public meetings being held by the motor trades themselves were harming the cause, and that the only hope lay in bringing the full weight of the FBI behind a deputation to the Chancellor. In fact Sir Eric Geddes, FBI president, had already attempted to open negotiations with the Labour Government, but had been unsuccessful. The motor manufacturers decided that no useful purpose would be served by following Geddes's suggestion of summoning the FBI Grand Council to a special session, and they were clearly somewhat reluctant to open the FBI to the dangers of division for no useful purpose.[101]

The appearance of Cunliffe-Lister's White Paper after Baldwin's return to office presented little threat to FBI unity. In 1925 Churchill introduced the silk duties. Though not safeguarding duties, these were effected through the Finance Bill, the same mechanism as envisaged in the White Paper. The result was an immediate flood of imports before the Bill became law. The Federation urged the Chancellor of the Exchequer to devise a method of plugging this loophole,

---

[99] *Seventh Annual Report*, 1922–3, 14; *Eighth Annual Report*, 1923–4, 14, FBI 200/F/4/2/7.

[100] Minutes of Meeting of Trades affected by the McKenna Duties, 20 May 1924, FBI 200/F/1/1/138.

[101] Minutes of Meeting of Special Sub-Committee appointed to consider the question of the McKenna Duties, 27 May 1924; Minutes of Meeting of Trades affected by the McKenna Duties, 25 June 1924, ibid. See also Captain Roberts to R. A. Higinbotham, 7 Sept. 1925, FBI 200/F/3/D2/3/10.

ostensibly to 'prevent a repetition of the loss of revenue which had been incurred', a delicate expression of the expectation that the silk duties would not be the last to be enacted by the current administration.[102]

Indeed, 1925 saw over forty trades and industries apply to the Board of Trade for safeguarding. The FBI reported to its members that the majority had sought FBI assistance in preparing their cases, and that the Federation's Economic Department had been of considerable assistance in advising on procedures and supplying information on conditions of production in competitor countries.[103] There was annoyance that the Federation could not publicly claim more credit for its actions in such matters. As the Sheffield district secretary informed head office in 1925:

So far as Sheffield is concerned you will be aware that the whole of the data and samples used by the Cutlery Trade in the preparation of their case for application under the Safeguarding of Industries White Paper were provided by us, and the whole of the value of that work will be negatived if we allow the N.U.M. to call a meeting with a flourish of trumpets and to claim a credit for what they have not done.[104]

Assistance to trades making safeguarding applications was still being given in 1928, though by then applications were tailing off,[105] probably because of their extremely low success-rate in relation to the cost and inconvenience involved.

If the decision against giving formal support to the motor trade was merely tactical, the silk duties exposed differences of greater substance between members, and again those differences centred around Manchester and the cotton trade, though Yorkshire woollen producers were also involved. In his 1925 budget, Churchill announced import duties of 3*s.* per pound weight on raw and manufactured silk, and import duties of 3*s.* per pound and excise duties of 2*s.* 6*d.* per pound on rayon cloth, yarn, and staple fibre. Churchill sought revenue, but he also aimed at 'deliberately giving a certain advantage to the home producer', whilst treating home silk and artificial-silk producers with an even hand.[106] On 6 May the Joint Standing Committee on the Cotton Trade protested strongly, and Free-Trade propagandists discerned a deep division between the rayon producers and the cotton and woollen manufacturers, who used rayon yarns in mixed fabrics such as dress goods and knitwear.[107]

The whole issue was not quite so simple. A meeting in Manchester on 12 May, representing spinners and manufacturers controlling 5m spindles and 514,000 looms, declared itself 'very strongly opposed' to import and excise duties on rayon, a 'necessary raw material for the cotton trade'. It was also 'opposed' to

---

[102] *Tenth Annual Report*, 1925–6, 17, FBI 200/F/4/2/9.
[103] Ibid.   [104] Deakin to Higinbotham, 7 Sept. 1925, FBI 200/F/3/D2/3/10.
[105] *Twelfth Annual Report*, 1928, 8, FBI 200/F/4/2/11.
[106] Quoted in B. Mallet and C. O. George, *British Budgets*, 3rd ser., *1921–22 to 1932–33* (1933), 130.
[107] D. Abel, *A History of British Tariffs 1923–1942* (1945), 26–7.

any excise duty on mixed fabrics.[108] At the meeting, most concern was expressed about raw-materials costs. Import duties on mixed fabrics seem to have been the subject of less hostility.[109]

A thirty-five-strong meeting at the FBI in London on 13 May found none of the interests represented satisfied with Mr. Churchill, but it did confirm that the 'greatest blot was the duties on raw material'. E. T. Walker of the Hosiery Manufacturers' Association was the only one who wanted all the import duties maintained, his sole objective being to get the excise duties removed from the proposal. Even the Silk Association, according to its representative, wanted 'reductions on all the raw material duties because they felt that there was no possible hope of getting them taken off altogether'. Raymond Drey, a Stockport manufacturer of mixed-textile pile fabrics, hoped the Chancellor might achieve his revenue objectives from the tax on imported mixed cloths alone, without any duties on yarn or staple fibre.[110]

Interestingly, the rayon-yarn producers thought similarly. J. H. Mandelberg, of the Wigan firm of Harben (V.S.M.) Ltd., explained that the specific duty on staple fibre (inappropriately classified as artificial-silk waste) was too high compared with that on yarn,[111] whilst the duties were in general regressive upon the cheaper qualities of rayon. The rayon producers also clearly desired the abolition of any excises. Though no one from Courtaulds attended the meeting, they were reported to it as favouring total abolition of the duties, since they feared that abolition of the excise only was unlikely to find favour with Churchill.[112]

There was thus dissatisfaction on both sides. Users of rayon in cloth resented duties on yarn, but it was less clear that they opposed the duties on cloth. Producers of yarn and rayon cloth disliked the excise and the high tax on staple fibre relative to yarn. Faced with these complex positions, the FBI committee chairman, Lennox B. Lee, found it impossible to act. Oscar Drey, Raymond's father, attempted to draft a motion urging the removal of all duties on raw materials and yarns, but the maintainance of the import duty (and, if necessary for revenue, the excise duty) on knitted and woven fabrics; but there was insufficient support for the motion to be put. Representatives of cotton and finishing concerns, such as J. & P. Coats Ltd., the English Sewing Cotton

---

[108] As reported in Minutes of First Meeting of Members interested in the Proposed Silk Duties (Budget), 13 May 1925, FBI 200/F/1/1/138 (hereinafter FBI Silk Duties Committee).

[109] The meeting was presumably composed of three types of cotton interest: spinners, manufacturers of pure fabrics, manufacturers of mixed fabrics, and (a growing group) manufacturers of both. Woollen interests and merchants were also present.

[110] FBI Silk Duties Committee.

[111] Staple fibre was at this time largely imported. See H. A. Silverman, *Studies in Industrial Organization* (1946), 330.

[112] This supports the contention that Courtaulds favoured abolition of the excise, but covertly hoped for retention of the import duty. See D. C. Hague, *The Economics of Man-Made Fibres* (1957), 32; D. C. Coleman, *Courtaulds: An Economic and Social History* (Oxford, 1969), ii. 260–1.

Company, the Bleachers' Federation, and the Bradford Dyers' Association Ltd., as well as several less-important concerns, may have sat stony-faced through the meeting—there is no record of them contributing to the discussion. The same is true of several of the interests on the other side, for example the British Celanese and the Leicester Hosiery Manufacturers' Association. It was recognized with regret that the textile trades could not present a united case to the Chancellor, and that the FBI could not act until the different trade associations had made further representations to government. The meeting was adjourned.

It was never reconvened. In large part, this was because the duties actually introduced got rid of some of the less-acceptable features of Churchill's initial proposal. The silk duties were unchanged, but the import duty on rayon yarn was reduced from 3s. to 2s. per pound weight, and the excise duty from 2s. 6d. to 1s. per pound. The import duty on staple fibre was reduced from 3s. to 1s. and the excise duty from 2s. 6d. to 6d.[113]

This suited the purposes of the rayon-yarn and fabric producers,[114] by removing the initial negative effective protection caused by an unduly high duty on staple fibre, mostly imported, and by increasing the differential between the excise and import duties. Rayon imports, 40 per cent of home production in 1924, fell to 2 or 3 per cent by 1930. Though the small UK output of staple fibre actually declined, production of rayon yarn was stimulated, albeit at prices which were substantially higher than in Europe.[115] The changes also lowered the tax on the inputs of mixed-cloth producers whilst still affording them protection on the value added.[116] Whether this was of overall advantage to such producers is less clear, however, since at the same time the duties on rayon probably decreased their competitiveness against unmixed cotton and woollen manufacturers. This was probably less important to producers of hosiery, where artificial silk was clearly a different product, than it was to producers of mixed fabrics. As we have seen, the Manchester Chamber of Commerce reacted mildly to Churchill's innovation, refusing to oppose the duties on principle but concerned on the need for adequate rebates on exports.[117] It may be that its membership was too unwieldy an amalgam of pure- and mixed-cloth producers by this time, or alternatively that pure-cloth producers appreciated the competitive advantage the duties might give them over the mixed-cloth producers.

In the FBI committee, the permanent staff made vague reference to contro-versy 'between different sections which were not in entire agreement' over

---

[113] H. A. Silverman, *Industrial Organization*, 329–30.

[114] At this time pure rayon fabric was largely used in the hosiery and underwear trades.

[115] D. C. Hague, *The Economics of Man-Made Fibres*, 32–3.

[116] Import duties on manufactured goods containing silk and rayon were $33\frac{1}{3}$% if silk or rayon content was more than 20% of the cloth by value; 10% if content was 5–20% by value; and 2% if content was less than 5% by value. See D. Abel, *History of British Tariffs*, 27 n.

[117] See above, 266; A. Redford, *Manchester Merchants*, ii. 217.

approaches to government on the implementation of duties.[118] But much of this related to the much earlier period of physical control by licence. In the immediate post-war period, when wartime import restrictions were still in force, the Federation had held meetings between its industrial groups, both to secure agreement and to assist the Department of Import Restrictions of the Board of Trade, by passing information via the FBI representatives on the Import and Export Advisory Council. Furthermore, the most serious disagreements had been in 'those cases where the finished product of one industry is the raw material of another'.[119] Certainly, it seems that the main bone of contention within the FBI silk committee was of this type, rather than any fundamentalist conflict between the purist Free Traders of the traditional textile industries and the protectionist small-wear trades of the East Midlands.

This suggests strongly that the conflicts between groups alluded to so vaguely by the FBI staff contained a substantial proportion which were not truly about the merits of Free Trade or protection in the proper sense at all, nor were they necessarily between ideological Free Traders and arch-protectionists. Given Redford's analysis of the Manchester Chamber of Commerce after 1924,[120] this may even have been becoming more true, to a limited extent, of cotton manufacturers and merchants. Less controversially, perhaps, it can be argued that, since the protective legislation that was enacted between McKenna and 1931 determined that any duties were imposed in an *ad hoc* manner, this had the consequence that even a zealous Chamberlainite could, with consistency, object to a product being safeguarded if his own industry, which used that product as a semi-finished input, was not.

Looked at in this light, the experience of the FBI in the 1920s generally confirms our findings above.[121] Opposition to a particular safeguarding duty did not necessarily imply opposition to an import duty on that same product under the regime of a general tariff, with or without preferential appendices. The tariff history of every protectionist country ever studied reveals constant friction of this kind, but it would be wrong to ascribe it to diametrically opposed interests and beliefs. There was always a *quid pro quo*, whether it was contained in the absurd excesses of the US 'Tariff of Abominations' in 1828 or in that monument of Bismarckian Germany, the 'Alliance of Iron and Rye'.[122]

Manchester Chamber of Commerce's concern with drawbacks on exports reinforces this. Under the safeguarding legislation such facilities were undeveloped. Yet when the general tariff of the 1930s was erected, their necessity was

---

[118] FBI Silk Duties Committee.

[119] *Third Annual Report*, 1918–19, 18, FBI 200/F/4/2/2.

[120] A. Redford, *Manchester Merchants*, ii. 217.

[121] See above, Ch. 9.

[122] R. V. Remini, 'Martin Van Buren and the Tariff of Abominations', *American Historical Review*, 63 (1957–8), 903–117; Ivo. N. Lambi, *Free Trade and Protection in Germany* (Wiesbaden, 1963).

obvious even to one who had been in the forefront of the defence of Free Trade in the pre-war period. As Sir Sidney Chapman, once Professor of Political Economy in the University of Manchester and subsequently at the Board of Trade, observed in his unpublished memoirs of the protection afforded to the iron and steel industry by the Import Duties Advisory Committee, the users of iron and steel were simply 'brought into line' by allowing drawbacks on imports subsequently re-exported.[123] Apart from drawbacks designed to sustain the re-export and entrepot trades, which were surprisingly little used by the merchants involved in such activity, IDAC was eventually to produce thirty-six schemes in which drawbacks were granted on materials imported and subjected to further manufacture before being re-exported.[124]

Indeed, given its *ad hoc* origins, its incomplete nature, its flat rate, its often arbitrary coverage, and its lack of any even minimally sophisticated provisions for blunting extreme effects on particularly disadvantaged users, the very presence of the safeguarding legislation, and the prospect of demeaning public wrangles during safeguarding applications, would inevitably tend to perpetuate the image of fundamental rift. Amongst British businessmen, who feared the opprobrium and contempt of public opinion, who had had that 'curiously holy smell'[125] of Free Trade in their nostrils for a century, this could only serve to delay the forcible expression of Tariff-Reform sentiment and the build-up of protectionist pressure. But in the FBI it was remarkable how little, and not how much, friction of this kind occurred. As Dudley Docker commented in October 1923, the FBI 'probably would like to be a Protectionist party but dare not'.[126]

---

[123] Sidney Chapman, 'Some Memories and Reflections', n.d. but *c.* 1940, 165–70, Mss. EH C91, John Rylands Univ. Library of Manchester.

[124] Sir Herbert Hutchinson, *Tariff-Making and Industrial Reconstruction* (1965), 60–2.

[125] G. Kitson Clark, 'The Repeal of the Corn Laws and the Politics of the Forties', *Economic History Review*, 2nd ser., 4 (1951), 6.

[126] Docker to Sir David Brooks, 25 Oct. 1923, FBI 200/F/3/S1/35/1.

11

Industrialists and Pressure Groups, 1916–1926

In examining the business groups pursuing Tariff Reform in the 1920s, our accent is not on high politics, since there are other studies which, at least to an extent, cover this ground,[1] or their lobbying of politicians and the Board of Trade, since here success was limited; but on their broader objectives and strategies in a situation where there was an increasing consensus of manufacturers on at least a measure of Tariff Reform, but a pronounced government reluctance to accommodate it. This approach, undertaken comparatively, provides an indication of what policy measures appealed to the manufacturers of the 1920s. Emphasis will be put on the three most important organizations, the National Union of Manufacturers, the British Commonwealth Union, and the Empire Industries Association, with brief consideration also of the British Empire Producers' Organization and the Empire Development Union.

I

The First World War, as well as creating the conditions for a proliferation of trade associations, also witnessed the foundation of a number of extra-parliamentary organizations which combined the objectives of lobbying parliament and influencing public opinion in the interests of industry. In trade matters the most important was the FBI. Alongside the National Confederation of Employers' Organizations, set up by the Engineering Employers' Federation and other employers' associations to keep the FBI out of industrial relations,[2] the FBI was destined to become one of the two 'peak' industrialists' groups in the inter-war period. At about the same time were formed the National Union of Manufacturers (initially the British Manufacturers' Association) and the British Commonwealth Union (initially the London Imperialists). Like the FBI, both attempted

---

[1] The secondary treatment is, however, scattered and diverse. See especially R. W. D. Boyce, *British Capitalism at the Crossroads 1919–1932* (Cambridge, 1987), *passim*; K. Middlemas and J. Barnes, *Baldwin* (1969); R. D. Herzog, 'The Conservative Party and Protectionist Politics, 1918–1932', unpubl. Ph. D. thesis, Univ. of Sheffield, 1984; R. C. Self, 'The Conservative Party and the Politics of Tariff Reform', unpubl. Ph. D. thesis, Univ. of London, 1982.

[2] J. Turner, 'The Politics of "Organised Business" in the First World War', in J. Turner (ed.), *Businessmen and Politics* (1984), 40–3; Sir Charles Tennyson, *Stars and Markets* (1957), 147–52.

an inclusive rather than exclusive representation which crossed the boundaries between industries but, unlike the FBI, both espoused some variant of Tariff Reform.

Both the NUM and the BCU combined propagandist with lobbying activity, though the BCU put more emphasis on direct business representation in parliament. On the surface, this reaped dividends. Whereas in the nineteenth century business representation in parliament had tended to be on sectional or industrial lines,[3] by the 1920s the industrial interest in the Commons appeared *itself* to have become an identifiably inclusive formation, mirroring the establishment of business groups wider than trade associations in the world outside. Observers and participants alike now recognized an 'Industrial Group' of MPs within the Commons.

The extent to which the crystallization of the business interest in parliament aided the protectionist cause was limited. The Industrial Group, formally constituted in February 1919, had as its nucleus the BCU's own adopted MPs, but it soon came to incorporate other elements of the 'hard-faced'; Conservative businessmen elected in 1918 without BCU sponsorship, the remnants of the UBC, and members of the short-lived Parliamentary Committee of the FBI.[4] Rather than becoming a precise mirror of BCU policies, the Industrial Group came to provide a broader representation of all Conservative backbenchers with industrial interests. Furthermore, the BCU's own commitment to Tariff Reform was uncertain, a factor reinforced as Free Trader Sir Allan Smith rose to prominence in its ranks and in the Industrial Group.[5] Though the personal inclinations of most members of the Industrial Group were probably protectionist, the group was subject to the same constraints of party loyalty as were other Conservative backbenchers, its incorporation within official Conservativism dictating a gradualist strategy of persuasion and attrition rather than outright revolt. In consequence, any tensions within and between the parent organizations of the Industrial Group were avoided, and the FBI, no less than the BCU, could regard it as its arm in the Commons.

Whilst this might be taken to represent the politics of the lowest common denominator, the Group nevertheless had, and was perceived to have, a collectivity that set it apart from earlier formations. This collectivity seemed to satisfy the desire of both organizations for a formal and concrete *mechanism* of access to Parliament, the desire of the FBI to be the sole mouthpiece of industry, and of the BCU to enjoy a monopoly of business-government communication. Such a mechanism was at least partly achieved; indeed, the failure of the BCU's

---

[3] The classic examples being the railway interest, the brewers, the shipowners, and the coalowners.

[4] J. Turner, ' "Organised Business" ', 45; T. Rodgers, 'Sir Allan Smith, the Industrial Group and the Politics of Unemployment, 1919–24', in R. P. T. Davenport-Hines (ed.), *Speculators and Patriots* (1986), 102–3.

[5] See below, 351–5. For Smith, see T. Rodgers, 'Sir Allan Smith', 100–23.

policy of sponsoring its own parliamentary candidates was in part due to 'the
success with which the Conservative party had already assimilated business
views'.[6] But assimilation did not mean total accommodation: in a reciprocal
process, the 'industrial' MPs of the 1920s, though having a broader concept of
industrial representation than their predecessors, were still under pressure to seek
their own accommodation with the wider requirements of party.

Much of the impetus towards the formation of business groups during the First
World War came from the experience of intervention and control experienced
by the armaments and engineering industries, especially the Controlled Estab-
lishments under the Ministry of Munitions.[7] It is therefore no coincidence that,
like the FBI, both the NUM and the BCU owed much, in inspiration and
finance, to Dudley Docker. The precursors of Docker's 'productioneer' creed lay
in the pre-war controversy, but during the War some variant of 'productioneering' became endemic to the great bulk of the business community. Docker's was
one of the most far-reaching. His central emphases—trade war, the organizational basis of economic efficiency, the need for full-capacity working, industrial
protection, and an imperial tariff—were also central themes of the Tariff
Commission; Docker subscribed to the Commission's guarantee fund of 1917.[8]
His conviction that economic policy should be in the hands of businessmen and
his advocacy of state involvement in scientific research and technical education
were reminiscent of elements of National Efficiency. In their fullest expression,
however, his prescriptions went beyond these to advocate co-operation and
rationalization in industry with government and financial-sector participation,
and formal, institutional co-operation between workers and employers both at
plant level, through works committees, and at national level through an
'industrial parliament'.[9] This came close to corporatism, but of a type giving
primacy to economic efficiency rather than social equity. Though productioneers
were 'second to none' in endorsing Whitleyism, their 'concessions to labor were
calculated means to industrial ends, not "goods" in themselves'.[10] Even Docker's
vision of a joint forum for employers and employed, or the proposals of the FBI
Labour Committee in 1917 for works committees and joint sickness and
unemployment schemes,[11] were conditional on labour first removing restrictions
and co-operating in achieving full-capacity working to minimize costs; there was

[6] J. Turner, 'The British Commonwealth Union and the General Election of 1918', *English Historical Review*, 93 (1978), 529.

[7] J. Turner, ' "Organised Business" ', 333–4.

[8] Complete details of the guarantee fund are given on a loose paper in 'Tariff Commission Account, 1910–1922', 9/1/2, TCP. Any prospect that Hewins might have emerged as backbench leader of the post-war productioneers, as he had led the wartime trade warriors, was blunted by his appointment as Under-Secretary of State for the Colonies in 1917.

[9] R. P. T. Davenport-Hines, *Dudley Docker* (Cambridge, 1984), 114–17.

[10] P. B. Johnson, *Land Fit for Heroes* (Chicago, 1968), 242–4.

[11] R. P. T. Davenport-Hines, *Dudley Docker*, 115–16.

no inconsistency between Docker's support for such schemes and his unsung participation in the virulent campaign against socialism waged by the BCU.[12]

Docker and his fellow productioneers were at their most influential in the period up to about 1920, before the failure of the Ministry of Reconstruction and the collapse of the German threat reduced the relevance and appeal of their prescriptions, and before the forces of *laissez-faire* regrouped. In the FBI, their influence waned as the membership base widened beyond its original nucleus of large engineering firms. In the BCU, almost paradoxically, they lost ground to Allan Smith and the anti-labour forces of the Engineering Employers' Federation.[13]

Nevertheless, something recognizable as the 'productioneer' approach endured, if only because it was divisible and reducible and because, within their organizations, businessmen could jettison some of its aspects. That Docker's policy on labour relations put employer interests first did not make Whitleyism universally acceptable to business interests—productioneering ran the danger that its supporters would splinter on the level of benefits it would be necessary to concede to workers, and on whether such concessions would pay off. Hence, the failure of the National Industrial Conference in February 1919 reduced the potential for conflict between those businessmen who supported Whitleyism and those who feared that, even in its narrow aims, Whitleyism contained the seed for a more radically corporatist framework of industrial relations.[14]

Similarly with rationalization: it was unlikely that businessmen who otherwise shared the objectives of the more extreme productioneers would achieve consensus on rationalization, except perhaps at the level of rhetoric. Indeed, the industrial importance of the most prominent rationalizers—Docker in the immediate post-war period and Sir Alfred Mond and Sir Hugo Hirst in the later 1920s—and the prominence given to their views in the national press made the policy even less attractive to lesser businessmen. These might lament overproduction and surplus capacity, might even approve of mergers or cartels when occurring naturally. But for any business group intent on Tariff Reform, or anything else, to adopt a programme which had an element of rationalization integral to it would have ensured a small membership indeed. As it was, those who found little attraction in rationalization could take comfort from the fact that it was never adopted as policy, and seldom even mentioned, by the leaders of their organizations. This was, of course, no barrier to Docker's continued participation in the NUM and BCU, or Hirst's active role in the EIA. Mond did advocate rationalization in the EIA in the late 1920s, but it was in connection with agricultural reform, and his ideas on industrial rationalization never became identified with EIA objectives.

[12] J. Turner, 'British Commonwealth Union', 533, 538.
[13] Ibid. 537–8, 546.
[14] H. A. Clegg, *A History of British Trade Unions since 1889*, ii. *1911–1933* (Oxford, 1985), 280–2.

Residually, productioneering amounted to a stress on flexible and full-capacity working, and a demand for legislation favourable to industry and active government assistance, whether in protection, in labour relations, in exporting, or in research, without any concomitant government interference in the structure, ownership, or control of industry. It might preach the virtues of a high-wage, high-productivity economy, but in it labour was dependent on the beneficence of industrial capital. Though shorn of the radicalism of the full version, the creed retained enough of its core—the stress on unrestricted high-capacity working to meet foreign competition—to give the appearance of survival, an appearance reinforced by Docker's continued participation and financial support, and to impart a modern, progressive appearance to what in many ways remained essentially conservative objectives. Docker found that he could carry the bulk of protectionist business opinion only by narrower means.[15] But this reduced form of productioneering did allow an operational consensus within the groups being studied here, albeit one which varied in emphasis from group to group, and thus aided the perception and achievement among members of a wider convergence in industrial attitudes as a whole.

Thus, though the FBI avoided taking a position on Tariff Reform because of fears that dissension among its members would restrict its size and limit its influence, the other inclusive groups were less cautious. Though exaggerating the monolithic nature of the manufacturing interest, they were largely vindicated in that the diversity of that interest lessened noticeably as the 1920s wore on. Convergence was aided by technological change. The leading figures in the business groups with which we are mainly concerned here, the BCU, the NUM, and the Empire Industries Association, tended to come from the 'newer' industries, but the imperatives they stressed were increasingly applicable to other, more traditional industries. Changes in production processes and technologies, more important in the present context than differences in product,[16] were spreading beyond that narrow range of industries which we might regard as having been 'new' in the 1880s and 1890s. During and after the War, intense pressure for changes in production technology, some of it representing an effort to catch up with the lead stolen by the USA before 1914, but all of it associated with increased exploitation of more advanced heat-, electricity- and machine-tool-using processes, made industrialists highly conscious of the importance of high and stable output. The option enjoyed by such industries as late-Victorian shipbuilding, where low capital-intensity meant that the cost of depression or downturn could be transmitted to a skilled labour force,[17] became increasingly

---

[15] R. P. T. Davenport-Hines, *Dudley Docker*, 132.

[16] J. A. Dowie, 'Growth in the Inter-War Period: Some More Arithmetic', *Economic History Review*, 21 (1968), 93–112; B. W. E. Alford, *Depression and Recovery? British Economic Growth, 1918–1939* (1972). See also N. K. Buxton and D. H. Aldcroft (eds.), *British Industry between the Wars* (1979), 15–18.

[17] S. Pollard and P. Robertson, *The British Shipbuilding Industry, 1870–1914* (Cambridge, Mass., 1979), ch. 8.

closed. Nevertheless, the heartland of 'reduced-form' productioneering remained the engineering and allied trades, those at the frontier of scientific management and mass production.

The strategy being articulated was not dissimilar to the analysis of 'continuous running' by Hewins and the Tariff Commission.[18] By the 1920s, of course, this was far less novel, even in Britain. But its widespread assimilation by industrialists, even those whose precise conditions of production still exhibited less advanced characteristics and less extreme needs for market stability, was aided by the new turbulence in industrial relations. Labour disputes threatened continuity of output and maximum efficiency. This, in turn, would reverberate upon labour through lower wages, exacerbating labour unrest. To pay high wages, manufacturers demanded, as often pleaded for, labour co-operation and market stability through safeguarding, even though they might fight shy of the corporatist undertones of the full-blooded productioneer approach. In a wider context there was little in this that was new, and even in the outlook of Tariff Reform it had its precursors in the pre-1914 debate. Rather, it was the intensity of immediate circumstances that differed, and its effect on the convergence of manufacturing opinion, as a creed new in degree if not in kind was articulated with a new vehemence.

Closely related to this was the political emergence of Labour, the threat of nationalization, and what almost all businessmen saw as a profligate provision of health and unemployment provision. Before the War, though Tariff Reform attracted wide support in the business community from its effective beginnings in 1903, the Chamberlainite phase to 1906 or 1907 probably effected fewer *conversions* than did the lurch towards Lloyd-Georgian finance after 1907.[19] Again, in the first half of the 1920s, it was external threat to the manufacturing community as much as the positive attractions of the Tariff Reform policy itself which effected conversion. To those who passionately believed in the policy were added those who, increasingly, had nowhere else to go.

II

There had always been the potential for schism within Tariff Reform: even before 1906 it was possible to contrast Empire radicalism with a more 'squalid argument' based on narrow, insular protectionism.[20] Turner paints a stark contrast between the anti-labour BCU's narrow, insular, and self-interested politics, and the radical social imperialism of Chamberlain and Milner.[21] Tomlinson sees increasing concern with unemployment in the 1920s producing a shift in the emphasis of the Tariff Reformers away from the developmental

---

[18] See above, Ch. 5.   [19] See above, esp. Ch. 3.
[20] B. Semmel, *Imperialism and Social Reform* (1960), 92–3.
[21] J. Turner, 'British Commonwealth Union', 544–5.

aspects of trade preferences towards the effect of Empire settlement on domestic unemployment, and tariff revenues as a means of financing unemployment benefits.[22] Clearly, it is possible to construct a thesis that the 1920s witnessed a change in emphasis within the Tariff Reform movement, away from social-imperialism and imperial preference towards the narrower objective of industrial protectionism.

It is naturally difficult to detect such a change when so many millions of words were shed, in speeches and in print, and often carelessly, on Tariff Reform. Of course the 'imperial vision' was kept alive by Milner, and, after his death, by Leo Amery,[23] sustained by many imperial societies which scarcely entered directly into the economic aspects of the controversy at all. Nevertheless, the inescapable imperative of electoral opinion, underlined in Baldwin's 'tariff election', contained the disaffection of imperially minded Conservatives. There is thus considerable strength to the view that the 1920s were a period of convergence, in which the 'whole hoggers' of previous years, the main body of the party, and even many former Unionist Free Traders, came increasingly, albeit reluctantly, to accept a gradualist policy, the principal expression of which was limited safeguarding.[24]

This brought about some convergence with business views, which had almost always been narrower. Before the War the Tariff Commission had put little emphasis on the reform aspects of social imperialism.[25] One could argue that this was in part the consequence of the pre-war Tariff Reformers having developed a specialization of function within the movement—principally the Commission and the League, later the Unionist Social Reform Committee—each grouping speaking from its own particular interest and attempting to maximize its appeal by speaking to different, if overlapping sections (or emotions?) of the electorate. But even the treatment of preference, left for the most part to Hewins without the same close involvement of the business Commissioners, had concentrated on its economic potential rather than its power for social change. This economistic variant of radical imperialism did, of course, entail a belief that an integrated Empire system would bring corollary benefits for wages and employment. And it did allow the business members of the Commission to co-operate with the imperial and agricultural members, and with few public misgivings endorse a programme which included food duties and preference.

Now, in the 1920s, with the downturn of export markets and the greater degree of import penetration, not to mention the ever-increasing charge of the unemployed upon the state, even the economic aspects of radical imperialism were under threat, especially before 1926. It was always the case that, to some

---

[22] J. Tomlinson, *Problems of British Economic Policy 1870–1945* (1981), 110–11, 112–13.
[23] I. M. Drummond, *British Economic Policy and the Empire, 1919–1939* (1972), 36–42.
[24] R. D. Herzog, 'The Conservative Party and Protectionist Politics', 483.
[25] See above, Ch. 7.

degree, the business groups which pushed most ardently for the extension of safeguarding also proclaimed their faith in imperial preference; but, especially within the BCU and NUM, there was undoubtedly an element of lip-service in this. Empire, like virtue and motherhood, was best spoken well of in British society. Generally, the manufacturing community acquiesced to what Turner discerns as the degeneration of a more noble into a less noble policy.[26] In some businessmen, this betrayed a hostility towards food duties and an indifference, certainly a relative indifference, towards the interests of British and Empire farmers. Thus Oswald Moseley, Manchester rubber manufacturer and recent convert from Free Trade, urged that the protection being considered by Baldwin's advisory committee in November 1923 should be denied to agriculture 'to help the working man'.[27] In others, it simply reflected pragmatic recognition of the fact that one objective must be sacrificed in the interests of achieving the other. There was a logical rationale for directing propaganda towards safeguarding: it was the only area of advance politically possible, and, in any case, after the 1919 budget wider safeguarding brought with it an automatic extension of imperial preference. This argument carried greater conviction after the decisive rejection of food taxes in December 1923, but even before this many in the movement remembered only too well the pre-war campaign, and it did not take Baldwin's 'tariff election' to remind them of public hostility towards food duties. It was not a new feeling—as we have seen, it was expressed very clearly and explicitly by ironmaster Alfred Hickman after the 1906 election.[28] Unfortunately, the historical evidence seldom speaks with so clear a voice, and we cannot therefore gauge precisely the relative prevalence of these two attitudes amongst the members of the protectionist organizations, though we might hazard that the former was the more common.

Whilst this ambiguity reminds us of the need for caution, a comparison of the emphasis put on the imperial consideration by the main pressure groups of the 1920s with their numerical and financial strengths suggests that the narrower end triumphed over the broader, especially before the establishment of the EIA. The most stable (yet, in membership terms, expanding) group of the early 1920s, the NUM, put the main emphasis on the narrower issue of domestic protection. The British Empire Producers' Organization had the most idealistic and visionary programme of all, yet its urgent search for amalgamation with the FBI suggests a lack of financial and emotional security. The BCU's problems may simply have been caused by initial over-ambition, but were exacerbated by an equivocal, ambivalent, and essentially limited approach to Tariff Reform. The post-Chamberlainite Empire Development Union, would-be successor to the TRL, fired by a Hewins over-optimistic after his spell in the Colonial Office and

[26] J. Turner, 'British Commonwealth Union', 544–5.
[27] Moseley to Hewins, 14 Nov. 1923, 84/121–3, HP.
[28] See above, 220.

increasingly out of touch with the businessmen with whom he sought to co-operate, simply petered out.

Differences of approach on the balance between preference and safeguarding were not the only characteristics which distinguished the groups of the 1920s, however. There were also important distinctions in their approaches to labour. Given the strong rise of labour in these years, and the general prevalence within these organizations of the reduced form of productioneering, such differences turned more on presentation than on conviction, but they had important consequences. The BCU diluted its Tariff-Reform objectives with explicitly anti-socialist programmes which many of its members found even more attractive, but which, it has been argued, made it unappealing to the wider body of manufacturers and helped to determine that it had become a spent force by the early 1920s.[29] At the other extreme, however, BEPO's initial tendency towards corporatism hindered its acceptability within the wider business community, whilst the existence of an active pro-labour faction within the early EIA caused friction and delay. Indeed, if the BCU's strong anti-labour stance reduced its appeal to businessmen before 1923, the same would scarcely have been true three years later, when anti-labour sentiment was pronounced in the NUM. Nevertheless, ultimately, expediency dictated that within both the NUM and the EIA the labour issue was not allowed to rise to prominence.

The pressure groups with which we are concerned have been the subject of disagreement among historians. Davenport-Hines dismisses the effects of the NUM as 'nugatory',[30] a judgement he would clearly extend to the others. Boyce adopts a less dismissive view of the NUM, and sees the EIA, particularly, as a dynamic force in propaganda.[31] Capie endorses Boyce's view of the EIA.[32] It is notoriously difficult to assess the impact of propagandist groups, but it is at least clear that, until around 1928, the business pressure that the NUM and EIA were able to exert upon government was limited to keeping Baldwin's cabinet sensitive to, and somewhat embarrassed by, the inadequacies of its programme on safeguarding, and thus had more effect on the sympathetic tone of their public pronouncements than on real developments in policy. Its effect on public opinion, however useful in preparing mental attitudes for change, was clearly insufficient until the dramatic downturn heralded by Wall Street came to its aid. Its main influence would seem to have lain in strengthening the resolve of a body of Conservative backbenchers who were already largely sympathetic, and in reinforcing the developing consensus within the manufacturing sector.

[29] J. Turner, 'British Commonwealth Union', 547.
[30] R. P. T. Davenport-Hines, *Dudley Docker*, 104.
[31] R. W. D. Boyce, *British Capitalism*, 111.
[32] F. Capie, *Depression and Protectionism* (1983), 74.

III

In its early years the British Empire Producers' Organization sought a comprehensive productioneer policy combined with an integrated agricultural and imperial policy. Though its emphasis shifted more towards agriculture and preference as the 1920s progressed, individual members such as Ben Morgan and V. A. Malcolmson nevertheless seem to have retained collectivist, perhaps even corporatist, views. Docker, who in the immediate aftermath of the War was similarly attracted to radical approaches within the business community, was so annoyed when the FBI-BEPO merger failed that he considered removing his companies from the FBI.[33] Before the late 1920s, however, BEPO found little support amongst businessmen.

Around 1920, BEPO comprised about seventy organizations, divisible into five groups. Firstly, there were three 'umbrella' organizations representing Empire manufacturers—the Associated Chambers of Manufacture of Australia, the Canadian Manufacturers' Association, and the South African Federated Chambers of Industry. Secondly, there were nine trade associations, mostly British, concentrated in engineering and milling. Thirdly, there were ten organizations of Empire primary producers, especially sugar growers. Fourthly, there were well over thirty British agricultural organizations, including the Central Chamber of Agriculture, the Farmer's Club, and the British Sugar Beet Growers' Association. And lastly there were eleven organizations of brokers and merchants who dealt mainly in Empire agricultural produce.[34]

In a book which can be taken as an early statement of BEPO policy, written usefully at a time when the FBI merger was in the air, vice-chairman Edward Saunders denied any conflict of interest between British and Empire farmers, asserting that agricultural preference offered scope for both groups to gain:

the fostering of British agriculture need not be regarded as implying any restriction of effort in other parts of the Empire which look to the Mother Country as their chief market. They suggest, rather, an Imperial development policy which will encourage every Dominion and every Colony to contribute an ever-growing fraction of the common stock of food . . . in preference to [imports from] other countries.[35]

Whilst it was true that Britain supplied only about 30 per cent of her main foodstuffs,[36] Saunders's generalized approach probably hid the fact that the devil was in the details. Any precise scheme would have contained endless points of

---

[33] R. P. T. Davenport-Hines, *Dudley Docker*, 118.

[34] 'British Empire Producers' Organisation: List of Affiliated Associations', FBI 200/F/3/D1/3/8, Nugent Papers. As far as has been discovered, no list of the individual firms subscribing to BEPO has survived.

[35] E. Saunders, *A Self-Supporting Empire* (1918), 58.

[36] M. Olson, *The Economics of the Wartime Shortage* (Durham, NC, 1963), 117.

friction between British and Empire Farmers,[37] and it may be significant that the covertly protectionist National Farmers' Union was not among BEPO members.

From the British businessman's point of view, even more important was that BEPO tended to be equally imprecise in any commitment to duties on the main foodstuffs. Before Austen Chamberlain's budget of 1919, Saunders insisted that 'every commodity should be dealt with on its own merits, subject to the principle that tariffs should be confined to manufactured and semi-manufactured goods, keeping foodstuffs free *wherever possible*'.[38] It cannot be doubted that this reluctance to be specific about food duties was essentially presentational, dictated by political considerations. Indeed, the principle of free imports of food 'wherever possible' was subordinate to dealing with each commodity 'on its own merits'. A BEPO proposal for developing sugar beet, 'intended as a model for other industries', involved 'a general tariff applicable to neutrals', a 50 per cent Empire preference, a $12\frac{1}{2}$ per cent preference to allied countries, an anti-dumping measure, and penalties *above* the tariff to offset foreign advantages from bounties, cartels, or freight rebates.[39] Thus, it seems, Saunders's objective of avoiding duties on foodstuffs was empty, his proposals less innocent than they appeared.

As we have seen, such imprecision in stating BEPO policy caused some confusion within the FBI between late 1916 and November 1919, when merger was being discussed; but this did not prevent the FBI leaders from discerning BEPO's general drift. BEPO was protectionist and preferentialist, with the accent on preference, and required an FBI commitment to support preference beyond the automatic inclusion of the 1919 budget. However it was dressed up, this meant food duties, and was clearly a main consideration of Sir Henry Barran and the opponents of merger within the FBI.[40]

Many manufacturers opposed food duties in themselves. Many others would probably have accepted them as part of a full Tariff-Reform package but for the fact that they recognized that food duties would hinder further progress in safeguarding. Whichever the reason, taxation of food was little more attractive to most manufacturers in the early 1920s than it was to the electorate. BEPO leaders were clearly sensitive to this. Perhaps partly because of a desperate search for allies caused by the organizational and financial weaknesses discerned by Nugent,[41] their vagueness on the implications of BEPO policy for the taxation of British food tended to persist.

After the 'Tariff Election' of 1923, BEPO had to accommodate itself to the existence of Baldwin's pledge not to introduce duties on wheat and meat.

---

[37] In the 1930s, external constraints (e.g. a government wish to prevent excessive price rises and to preserve relations with important trading partners such as Argentina) frequently resulted in the spoils of preference being inadequate to satisfy both British and Empire farmers. See T. Rooth, *British Protectionism and the International Economy* (Cambridge, 1993), 212–38.

[38] E. Saunders, *A Self-Supporting Empire*, 82–3 (my emphasis).

[39] Ibid. 82.   [40] See above, Ch. 10.   [41] See above, 303.

Encouraged by the Budget of 1925, in which preference was extended to the minor food duties introduced since 1919, on hops, sugar, tobacco, dried fruit and wines,[42] it sought to promote the dubious view that the extension of such limited measures could result in an effective preferential system. At its AGM in July 1925, its officials argued that an increase in Empire food production and the British food supply would best be achieved by the reduction or remission of intra-Empire duties rather than increases in the duties on foreign produce.[43] Few outsiders, however, would have seen this as more than a tactical withdrawal; there could be no doubt that BEPO continued to wait in hope of more congenial political and electoral circumstances.

The factors limiting the acceptability of BEPO policy to the wider body of manufacturers were not limited to its position on agriculture and preference. Apart from Tariff Reform, BEPO's early programme contained most, if not all, elements of the full-blooded productioneer policy, but these included several that other business groups were reluctant to adopt. BEPO might touch a common chord on the need to reduce conflicts between capital and labour 'to abolish the artificial limit on the productiveness of machinery'; or in its distaste for 'cosmopolitan complacency in finance' and the anti-industrial bias of the London capital market; or on the need for an 'Imperial Bank' akin to the British-Italian Corporation and the British Trade Corporation.[44] More questionable was its position on encouraging the wartime trend towards the co-operation of manu-facturers in science, on industry agreements to reduce 'destructive competition', and on product-specialization by agreement. Furthermore, BEPO spoke in terms unusually conciliatory to labour, with a stress on creating conditions in which 'Capital [could] seek an adequate return, and at the same time ... Labour [could] secure much higher wages without working harder', and on Whitley Councils as a way of preventing piece-rate cutting: 'The development of Joint Industrial Councils ... should ... [establish] the State—not the capitalist—as the ultimate controller of the scale of wages, the conditions of labour and of housing, and of facilities for education and social betterment'.[45] Least of all attractive to British manufacturers, perhaps, were proposals for reviving British agriculture through extensive state intervention, by government guaranteed prices, loans, organization, and agricultural education, as well as social measures on housing and education to increase the efficiency of farm labour.

Such support for rationalization, such positions on labour and on agriculture, signalled a predisposition towards a more radical corporatism that most British businessmen, protectionists and Free Traders alike, eschewed. To an extent, BEPO's emphasis changed, so that by 1925 it was predominantly agricultural.

---

[42] H. G. Williams, *Through Tariffs to Prosperity* (1931), 59–60.
[43] *The Times*, 2 July 1925, 8.
[44] E. Saunders, *A Self-Supporting Empire*, 62–6, 85–7, 95–9.
[45] Ibid. 65, 66–7, 69–74.

But this again scarcely aided in increasing BEPO's influence in business circles. Protectionist businessmen in the 1920s tended to display a sympathy with imperial preference when it was clearly a political means to the end of obtaining a more generally protectionist package; but BEPO's approach seemed to give primacy to preference over protection. Its stress on the Empire as an economic unit rather than a mere market, the centrality that this seemed to accord to food duties, and the weight given to agriculture and to a supposedly close symbiosis between industry and agriculture reached beyond the concerns of most manufacturers.

At the Central Chamber of Agriculture in March 1925, V. A. Malcolmson of BEPO, lamenting the Government's reluctance to promote greater co-operation between landowners, farmers, and workers, pressed for negotiations between the political parties to formulate an agricultural policy.[46] Furthermore, much if not most of the press coverage which BEPO attracted was concerned with reporting its activity on the encouragement of Empire sugar and sugar beet, always a main concern and one in which senior members such as Morgan and Malcolmson were personally interested. In 1927 Morgan achieved his ambition of turning the Empire Sugar Section of BEPO, now representing the entire sugar-producing industry of the Empire, into the Empire Sugar Federation to meet the 'highly organized' competition of US and European producers.[47] Similarly, Empire tobacco-growing was also a cherished objective of the Organisation—Britain must be freed from the 'cult of American tobacco' and the habit of 'smoking Imperially' encouraged.[48] Such an orientation resulted in BEPO's displacement from the centre of the businessman's interest in the Tariff Reform movement of the 1920s. When the pressure to obtain some protection of the British sugar-beet industry, in which BEPO was prominent, achieved some success at mid-decade, it is revealing that even Hannon, who had previously been involved in agricultural policy and organization and was one of the representatives of businessmen most predisposed towards the farming community, thought this divisive.[49] Much involved with the BCU and the EIA, he opposed the second reading of the British Sugar (Subsidy) Bill 'not because of the subsidy to agriculture, but because the subsidy was given to one industry at the expense of another'.[50] As a principled opposition, this was a bit thin—consistency would have required him to oppose the extension of safeguarding on precisely the same criterion. Behind his stance lay the complication that the subsidy on beet caused

---

[46] *The Times*, 4 Mar. 1925, 8.
[47] *The Times*, 2 July 1925, 8, 9 Apr. 1927, 9.
[48] *The Times*, 30 Oct. 1925, 9.
[49] Patrick Hannon had been Director of Agricultural Organization in South Africa, 1904–9. He was subsequently President of the Central Chamber of Agriculture, 1930–1. M. Stenton and S. Lees, *Who's Who of British Members of Parliament*, iv (Brighton, 1981).
[50] *The Times*, 19 Feb. 1925, 7.

friction between cane- and beet-sugar refiners;[51] but the incident suggests that other business groups found BEPO's agricultural bias and its support of policies likely to influence raw-materials costs discomforting.

Nugent was correct in considering BEPO only a minor representative of business opinion. Judging from the entries in the official index to *The Times*, BEPO attracted less than 20 per cent of the press coverage of the NUM or the EIA. Its most distinct influence was indirect, through the influence of its more important members in other propaganda groups. The most dramatic example of this, seen in the early debate within the EIA over relations with Labour MPs, nearly resulted in the EIA being torn apart,[52] providing further evidence that BEPO's agricultural and corporatist bias fitted it ill for close co-operation with more orthodox business groups.

Nevertheless, BEPO survived on the flank of the protectionist-imperialist movement, and continued to stage eye-catching dinners and attract major speakers. At the Mansion House in April 1926, Kylsant presided over a gathering of 300, with Amery, Colonial Secretary and responsible in large part for the minor successes of the 1925 Budget, as the major speaker.[53] In November it hosted a luncheon for the delegates to the Imperial Conference in the Goldsmith's Hall.[54] Attracting considerable numbers of Empire dignatories, officials, and politicians, showy occasions like these were perhaps easy to mount, and said little of domestic business support in depth for the Organization before 1926 or 1927, when the imperial ideal was at something of a discount in protectionist business circles. Most of the main industrialists present at the Goldsmith's Hall—Kylsant, Morgan, Sir Edward Manville of Daimler and late of BSA, Sir Hugo Hirst of GEC, and sugar refiner Sir Leonard Lyle—had ownership interests in Empire countries or Empire trade, as did most of the lesser business figures present. BEPO does not appear to have penetrated the British manufacturing community more widely by attracting those for whom the Empire merely represented a potentially expandable market. Thereafter, as support for an Empire economic system grew within the other protectionist business groups, largely on the coat-tails of an increased determination not to be silenced on protection, BEPO's influence seems to have revived, and BEPO members were prominent in the establishment of the Empire Economic Union, founded in November 1929.[55] Even in the favourable circumstances that led to Ottawa, however, BEPO remained a minor force compared with the EIA and the EEU.

---

[51] E. H. Whetham, *The Agrarian History of England and Wales*, viii. *1914–1939* (Cambridge, 1978), 166. This rift was probably not enduring, however, for cane importers and refiners Tate and Lyle continued their association with BEPO.

[52] See below, Ch. 12.

[53] *The Times*, 4 Feb. 1926, 9.

[54] *The Times*, 2 Nov. 1926, 9.

[55] R. W. D. Boyce, *British Capitalism*, 230–1.

IV

The National Union of Manufacturers was more orthodox than BEPO, and more representative of domestic British manufacturing opinion. Originally the British Manufacturers' Association, the Union was established in 1915 around a Birmingham nucleus, with Dudley Docker as a founder member and George Terrell, MP for West Wiltshire and managing director of Tyer and Co., a Dalston railway-signal manufacturers', as its first president.[56] From the start, the BMA 'nailed their colours to the Tariff Reform mast',[57] though its aims were never restricted to this alone. By 1917 it claimed 634 member firms, and had branches in Sheffield and Glasgow.[58]

By the late 1920s membership had increased to around 3,000 firms. The FBI continually deprecated this success by informing its own members that NUM firms were small, belonging to minor industries. Nevertheless, FBI officials were little short of obsessed with preventing NUM poaching, and put pressure on their members to induce them to leave or prevent them from joining the NUM. Since the NUM could not match the services provided by the FBI, there is little doubt that this was often effective, hence slowing down the NUM's expansion. Nevertheless, there were limits to what could be achieved. In the mid-1920s, eleven out of twenty-eight on the FBI Executive Committee and as many as 30 per cent of those on some other FBI committees were also NUM members, and there was a constant trickle of FBI members defecting to the NUM, usually over Tariff Reform. Many firms persisted in belonging to both organizations—some 160, according to an undated list in the FBI archives.[59]

In his monthly surveillance reports on the Birmingham NUM for the FBI leaders, C. R. Dibben recognized the precedence given to protection. But, beyond that, NUM policy was 'most elastic . . . they will take up any question at a moment's notice and without the slightest hesitation, if by doing so they can enhance their popularity'.[60] Dibben expressed surprise at the NUM's ability to sustain such a high level of activity and services to members when its annual subscription was only five guineas, compared with £100 for full three-year FBI membership. Though inclined to doubt the NUM's financial or organizational capacity, Dibben had to admit that 'we have heard no expression of dissatisfaction . . . on this score'. He acknowledged that the NUM had co-ordinated the views of the small trades of Birmingham in connection with the Cave Committee on the Trade Board Acts (1922) 'very effectively', and that it maintained close contact with the Department of Overseas Trade and

---

[56] M. Stenton and S. Lees, *Who's Who of British Members of Parliament*, iii. *1919–1945* (Brighton, 1979).

[57] Nugent to Docker, 9 Nov. 1916, FBI 200/F/3/D1/3/10, Nugent Papers.

[58] Copy of NUM aims and objectives, FBI 200/F/3/D1/3/10, Nugent Papers.

[59] 'National Union of Manufacturers', undated typescript, FBI 200/F/3/D2/3/10.

[60] Dibben to Walker, 3 Oct. 1922, FBI 200/F/3/D2/3/9.

appeared able to provide members with inside information from official sources.[61]

Boyce has observed that the NUM achieved a high degree of unanimity amongst its members on protection and imperial preference.[62] In fact, preference was clearly a subordinate objective. Furthermore, Boyce's claim that the Union's solidarity was due to a narrow base of support from small firms in light engineering and the motor trades must be qualified, though it was more nearly true of the NUM's leaders than of the members as a whole. Of the NUM's eleven vice-presidents in 1927, five represented firms in electrical and mechanical engineering, iron and steel, and the metal trades; there was one manufacturer of rubber goods (including motor tyres); one of artists' materials; one of printing materials; one of paints and varnishes; and one tanner and maker of leather gloves. Nine came from Birmingham and London.[63]

It is in fact very difficult to give a brief breakdown of the economic interests represented by the NUM, since they were so immensely varied. There were around eighty motor-vehicle (car, commercial, and motor-cycle) and component manufacturers in 1927. In addition there was heavy representation of firms making mechanical- and electrical-engineering products and machinery, both light and heavy—capital goods and plant, office equipment and domestic consumer-durables—as well as a miscellaneous group of around 130 mechanical, electrical, constructional, hydraulic, and heating engineers, many of whom combined contracting with manufacturing. Alone, these firms did not, numerically, dominate the NUM, but they should be seen in association with another large group of members from the small metal-working trades (brass, tin, iron, and aluminium), some of which produced goods ancilliary or integral to the engineering trades, but some of which produced light consumer goods.[64]

Also common were a wide variety of other trades, many of them making small equipment and consumer goods. The following description concentrates only on those trades and products where distinct clusterings of a minimum of around ten or twelve firms can be discerned.

A considerable proportion of member firms belonged to trades associated with successful or unsuccessful safeguarding applications, or with the McKenna duties: iron and steel manufacturers and iron-founders; hardware, metal small-wares and hollow-ware producers; manufacturing jewellers; firms connected with processes in the non-ferrous-metals trades; producers of photographic apparatus and chemicals; paper makers; glassware producers; games equipment and toy

---

[61] Ibid. For the Cave Committee, see Board of Trade, *Report of the Committee on the Trade Board Acts*, Cmd. 1645 (1922).

[62] R. W. D. Boyce, *British Capitalism*, 9.

[63] *National Union of Manufacturers (Incorporated): Descriptive and Classified Directory of Members*, Jan. 1927 edn., (hereinafter cited as *NUM Directory*), 18.

[64] Ibid. *passim*.

manufacturers; brush manufacturers; piano and musical instrument makers; dress and clothing, knitted goods, hosiery, smallwear, and haberdashery manufacturers of all types, as well as button and other accessory manufacturers; producers of fabric gloves; leather manufacturers and dressers, leather glove-makers, fancy-leather goods, bag and trunk manufacturers, harness manufacturers, tanners, boot and shoe manufacturers; producers of cutlery and razors, surgical instruments and appliances, dental and medical equipment, and firms connected with electro-plating; and producers of cattle feed, chemical manufacturers and manufacturing chemists.

Also numerous were producers of pens and pencils, stationery, account books, printing machinery and equipment, artists' materials, paper adhesives, inks, and envelopes, as well as large numbers of lithographers, bookbinders, and card manufacturers; brewers, distillers, mineral-water producers, bacon curers, and a variety of food processors, packagers, and preservers; chocolate manufacturers and manufacturing confectioners; furniture-makers; considerable numbers of paint, enamels and varnish manufacturers; industrial-belting manufacturers; and rubber and rubber-goods producers.[65]

It is to be emphasized that this list concentrates only on those trades and products where there were at least ten or twelve firms within the NUM, and the inclusion of smaller groups would make it completely unhandleable. Even so, it is difficult to generalize from the miscellany presented. Two things are clear, however. First, apart from iron and steel and engineering, there was little representation of the relatively homogeneous staple trades of the nineteenth century. Apart from John Thorneycroft and Swan Hunter, there were no shipbuilders. There were only a dozen or so cotton firms, all minor and only one of them a spinner. The twenty or so woollen and worsted firms were somewhat more numerous and considerably more important, but not to the extent that might have been expected from an industry which had just had its first application for safeguarding refused. Even with iron and steel, and in spite of the fact that the industry was now overwhelmingly united on safeguarding, there were few of the large, nationally known bulk-steel producers, and more characteristic of the seventy or so NUM members were crucible- or tool-steel makers and intermediate producers of semis. Many of the chemicals manufacturers in the NUM were concerned less with the bulk alkali trades of the previous century than with specialized products such as pharmaceuticals, photographic chemicals, chemicals used in assaying, electro-chemical processes, non-ferrous metal production, and in rubber technology. Secondly, there was an unwieldy mixture of 'new' industries and trades—motor accessories, aircraft, electrical engineering, consumer durables, lithographic printing, photographic apparatus, and pre-packed foodstuffs—and 'older' consumer goods trades such as buttons

---

[65] *NUM Directory, 18 passim.*

and buckles, leather goods and saddlery, furniture, and metalwares. Thus, the unifying characteristic was often that NUM members produced goods which were, in aggregate, produced in small enough quantities to hold some tangible prospect of a successful safeguarding application. Obviously, the main exceptions to this were producers of capital goods and electrical products. Whilst cotton firms presumably stayed aloof from the NUM on fiscal grounds, the small presence of woollen and worsted firms and the larger steel producers, when both of these groups were elsewhere involved in agitation for safeguarding, was more likely because they were unconvinced that membership would serve a useful purpose.

By the mid-1920s the NUM had far more London than provincial members, and the stamp of its birth was fading, though in 1926 four of its eleven vice-presidents still came from Birmingham and Walsall firms, compared with four from a much bigger London membership. On the Union's three main working committees, however, London dominated. Of twenty-one Council members, ten came from London firms, and none from Birmingham and district. Only five of the thirty-three members of the Administrative Committee came from Birmingham firms, compared with sixteen from London firms. On the fifteen-strong Policy Committee, seven came from London and only four from Birmingham. This understates London's dominance, since it excludes provincial firms with London head offices. The Midland Branch, headed by an impressive thirty-one-strong Midland Council, nevertheless dwarfed the other provincial branches.[66]

After the 1925 White Paper, the NUM undertook a second wave of branch formation, starting with Bristol in December. The Union had been strong there in the early 1920s, due to a 'very able and well-known representative', but had subsequently lost its position.[67] In Leeds, it recruited by claiming sole credit for the abolition of Excess Profit Duty.[68] In Manchester, the FBI claimed the NUM had about twenty members before it formed a local branch, though the NUM membership list for 1926 suggests some sixty-four, not including firms with Manchester branches. To prepare the ground for an inaugural meeting in October 1926, H. P. Gordon, of the 'Propaganda Department', visited another sixty to seventy, mostly engineering firms, using an NUM campaign to buy British goods as a pretext to introduce firms to the activities of the Union. Butler, the FBI district secretary and a Free Trader, was forced to admit that engineering was 'more susceptible in the policy of Protection than any of our other industries in this area', and conspired with the secretary of the Free Trade Union to ensure that NUM methods were exposed 'in their true light'. Explaining this unsanctioned action to London HQ, he apologized that in

[66] *NUM Directory*, Jan. 1926 edn., 16–18.
[67] Swann to Higinbotham, 16 Dec. 1925, FBI 200/F/3/D2/3/10.
[68] Sharpe to Higinbotham, 1 July 1926, FBI 200/F/3/D2/3/10.

Lancashire 'one has to regard things perhaps somewhat differently than would be the case elsewhere'.[69] For its part, the NUM commonly stirred up dissatisfaction with the FBI's 'Free Trade' stance at inaugural meetings, and it was often the case that new NUM members had refused the advances of the FBI in the past, or were determined to be members of both organizations in spite of FBI disapproval. FBI district secretary Harding thought it was the 'disgruntled element such as the sugar refiners' who were behind the inaugural meeting at Liverpool,[70] but prominent on the Liverpool NUM's district committee were representatives of Sir Max Muspratt's Automatic Telephone Manufacturing Co. Ltd., an FBI member; Arnold Fell, a chemical engineer; and W. G. Rimmer of the Vulcan Motor Co., 'a rough sort of customer' whose firm had left the FBI with some acrimony.[71]

In March 1928 Montgomery, the Newcastle district secretary, was anticipating an NUM recruiting drive in his own area. Newcastle had not been a good area for the NUM, largely because of the influence of the coal and shipbuilding trades, but also because the nearest NUM branch was Leeds; and between 1926 and 1928 it had lost six members, including shipbuilders Swan Hunter and Wigham Richardson, whilst gaining only five. This left the NUM with only fourteen firms in the area, the most important of which was Bolckow Vaughan. It may be that Montgomery's fears were based on a sense that attitudes were changing and he anticipated that NUM attention would concentrate on Middlesborough. Urging Head Office that 'we might take a leaf out of their book on the publicity side', he attempted to recruit Sir Holberry Mensforth of Bolckow Vaughan onto the FBI district committee, to 'forestall . . . the N.U.M.', but this only incited Mensforth to join the executive council of the NUM.[72]

The NUM strove to create a sense of brotherhood amongst member firms. It promoted what it called 'inter-trading' between members, and banned merchants from membership. Terrell reminded his members of the 'vast vested interests in this country, strongly evidenced in the chambers of commerce, of the people who import and distribute hundreds of millions of the foreign-manufactered goods which are annually landed on our shores'. He was also critical of the British banking community, which he suspected 'derive[d] its inspiration from the importers of foreign goods'.[73]

The NUM consciously and explicitly stressed its representation of manufacturing, rather than wider business or commercial interests, at the same time as denying any political alignment. On the surface, it claimed a wide range

[69] Butler to Higinbotham, 22 Sept. 1926, FBI 200/F/3/D2/3/10; count of Manchester firms made from *NUM Directory*, Jan. 1926 edn.

[70] For this meeting, see *Liverpool Daily Post*, 8 Dec. 1926, 8.

[71] Harding to Higinbotham, 8 Dec. 1926, FBI 200/F/3/D2/3/10.

[72] Montgomery to Higinbotham, 20 Mar. 1928, FBI 200/F/3/D2/3/11.

[73] *The Times*, 27 Oct. 1926, 9.

of objectives in aid of the manufacturing community. In 1922, these were stated as:

(1) To conduct, on purely business lines, an organization in the interests of British Manufacturers, Producers, and their Employees, without connection with any political party.

(2) To revive and protect the Empire's Trade, thus ensuring good wages and full employment for capital and labour.

(3) To originate, promote, support, or oppose legislative or other measures affecting British Industries.

(4) To secure the appointment of business men on all Committees promoted by the Government which affect manufacturing interests.

(5) To encourage Trade and Industry within the Empire, to assist those trades which suffer through unfair foreign competition, and to safeguard industrial interests by seeing that all Acts of Parliament dealing with industry are properly administered.[74]

As FBI observers discerned, however, 'the main plank in their platform is undoubtedly Tariff Reform'. During the passage of the Safeguarding Act, Terrell welcomed the measure as a stepping stone to Tariff Reform. But there were two Tariff Reforms beyond safeguarding—a 'considered tariff' (a common NUM phrase) on manufactures, and a Chamberlainite system involving food duties and preference. Whilst the NUM continually stressed the need to expand Empire trade, it was in fact cautious about advocating the latter. Discussions were held on a possible alliance between the NUM and the National Farmers' Union[75] but, as the 1920s passed, and more especially after the 1923 election, more emphasis was put on safeguarding and its broadening into a 'considered tariff'.

Partly influenced by the idiosyncratic bimetallist engineer, Arthur Kitson, the NUM voiced its opposition to the return to gold in 1925. But at the next annual meeting Terrell stopped short of mounting a general 'industrialist' attack on the gold standard,[76] and monetary policy never became the central objective of the Union. The NUM was in fact unusual in giving a fairly explicit ranking of its objectives. At the 1926 AGM, Terrell proclaimed the 'main policy' as protection against unfair competition, 'and largely owing to their [NUM] activities they were getting a consensus of opinion in the country'.[77] The inaugural meeting of the Manchester branch unanimously 're-affirm[ed] the fiscal policy of the union, which [was] to impose a "considered" tariff on foreign imports other than food, which are produced under conditions which make competition by British workers an impossibility'.[78] As Terrell explained, as if echoing Hewins's fears of

[74] Dibben to Walker, 3 Oct. 1922, FBI 200/F/3/D2/3/9.
[75] Dibben to Tennyson, 19 Oct. 1923, FBI 200/F/3/S1/35/1, Walker Papers.
[76] R. W. D. Boyce, *British Capitalism*, 64, 75, 93, 111.
[77] *The Times*, 27 Oct. 1926, 9.
[78] *The Times*, 4 Nov. 1926, 11.

the divisive nature of the existing safeguarding legislation, the Union required graduated duties rather than the flat-rate $33\frac{1}{3}$ per cent of safeguarding. Preference was secondary: with such a tariff 'a material contribution to the policy of Imperial preference *might* be made'.[79] Indeed, when similar declarations were made at the Liverpool inaugural meeting, Harold Jaeger complained 'that the union's policy on this matter might have been formulated by a free fooder'.[80]

The NUM expected little of the Labour Government, but expectations of an extension of safeguarding on Baldwin's return ran high. Apparently with the approval of the Board of Trade, the NUM formed a committee of 24 manufacturers' associations to draft a scheme for a new bill. Ignoring the fact that the NUM report was at the printers', Cunliffe-Lister rushed out his White Paper. He also brushed aside the NUM's request for an examination of the effects of a return to gold on industry. The campaign for extended safeguarding was opened with a lunch for 250 businessmen in Birmingham in July 1925. At the AGM in September, Terrell's speech was disillusioned and angry, and urged that the NUM must appeal directly to the people. To this end, he took advantage of the retirement of Sir Henry Gibson, chairman of the Policy Committee, to announce a reorganization in which Sir John Corcoran, previously Director of Army Contracts at the War Office, would join the NUM as Director. Corcoran was something of a celebrity amongst Tariff Reformers, having introduced a policy of preference for Empire goods into army procurement. An executive 'Chief of Staff', his first task would be to organize a large, three-year propaganda campaign, which would require £60,000 to finance fifty trained lecturers.[81] Two months later, Baldwin was informed of an NUM resolution that the White Paper was 'totally inadequate'.[82]

Most NUM members were little attracted by Docker's early corporatist inclination towards the management of labour relations through an 'industrial parliament' of businessmen and workers. Yet, at the same time, they seem to have avoided involvement in the BCU's virulent and covert campaigns against socialism and bolshevism.[83] In periods of high trade-union activity, however, NUM attitudes to labour relations hardened, as when labour unrest grew early in Baldwin's new ministry. Arguing that high coal prices were affecting industrial competitiveness, the NUM urged repeal of the provision in the Coal Mines Act of 1919 which limited the working day to seven hours.[84] The Midland Council, endorsing an impassioned speech by the Duke of Northumberland in which a socialist and communist attack on the coal-owners was portrayed as a prelude to

[79] *The Times*, 4 Nov. 1926, 11. (my emphasis).
[80] *The Times*, 8 Dec. 1926, 28.
[81] *The Times*, 30 Sept. 1925, 6, 19; Corcoran to Radiators Ltd., Jan. 1926, FBI 200/F/3/S1/35/1, Walker Papers; R. W. D. Boyce, *British Capitalism*, 110–11.
[82] *The Times*, 27 Nov. 1925, 11.
[83] R. P. T. Davenport-Hines, *Dudley Docker*, ch. 6.
[84] *The Times*, 23 Jan. 1926, 7.

nationalization, considered the very principle of 'individual ownership' to be at stake.[85] Critical of a government role in industrial relations, the NUM sought a return to district bargaining on 'business principles' in the coal industry: government intervention and a national mechanism only stiffened resistance and raised the hopes of workers.[86] Welfare expenditure was also too generous. The heavy surplus on the Health Insurance Valuation of 1923 showed that the scheme was 'over-financed' and sickness provisions too favourable.[87] In voicing the NUM's demand for a reduction of the burden of the insurance acts, Terrell railed against excessive 'sobstuff' legislation.[88]

NUM policy on labour was typical of the way in which the quasi-corporatist strands within wartime productioneering were discarded in favour of an approach more universally acceptable to businessmen—a patronizing, supposedly benevolent, quasi-paternalist approach which saw working men as having been deluded into believing that they could buck business principles and economic realities, and needing to be shown that only with unstinting trade-union co-operation to achieve high and stable output could high wages be paid. It remained recognizably 'productioneer' in its stress on the imperative of full-capacity working, but at its root was a desire to weaken trade-union power at plant, branch, and national level that most businessmen could share. It was all summed up by Docker: 'The men were really good fellows, but they were spoilt by rotten leadership'.[89] The great majority of firms were not touched by industrial unrest; rather, the problem was one of 'irresponsible agitators'.[90] The NUM urged repeal of the Trades Disputes Act, maintaining that if the individual freedoms of workers were protected against picketing, strikes would be rare. The Policy Committee urged members to give preference to those unions which took a 'non-political' approach to negotiation.[91]

V

The early history of the British Commonwealth Union has been excellently told, and it is unnecessary to give a full account of the Union here.[92] Tariff Reform bulked large in the objectives of the 'London Imperialists', the Union's predecessor organization, formed in December 1916 at a meeting of nine prominent industrialists, no less than four of them from Vickers and several with interests in shipping (mostly with a Canadian link) and shipbuilding. Indeed, the history of negotiations for a relationship with the FBI, in which Roland Nugent feared splitting his membership and was supported by Herbert Dixon of the FCSDA, suggests a similar Tariff Reform dimension to those of the abortive NUM and

---

[85] *The Times*, 12 Feb. 1926, 9.   [86] *The Times*, 14 Sept. 1926, 14.
[87] *The Times*, 23 Jan. 1926, 7.   [88] *The Times*, 1 July 1926, 11.
[89] *The Times*, 11 Jan. 1927, 11.   [90] *The Times*, 27 Oct. 1926, 9.
[91] *The Times*, 25 Jan. 1927, 14.   [92] J. Turner, 'British Commonwealth Union', 528–59.

BEPO mergers examined above.[93] When the London Imperialists took the name of 'Industrial and Agricultural Legislative Union' in June 1917, their constitution put Tariff Reform, or more literally imperial preference, above all other.[94]

But the BCU was not a good vehicle for the pursuit of Tariff Reform objectives. Its object of sponsoring its own MPs, of promoting 'a powerful Industrial Party in the House of Commons' was precocious. '[I]ts members, being for the most part businessmen, were not yet ready to compete in politics on equal terms with professional politicians', and its very attempt to monopolize business–government relations caused frictions.[95] Furthermore, the BCU's harsh variant of the productioneer outlook on labour increasingly tended to dominate. In April 1917 the London Imperialists' Executive considered negotiating with the Labour Party, and urged that Labour, in exchange for wages sufficient for 'reasonable comfort and enjoyment', should 'accept the principle that there should be no restriction of output and that the safeguarding of the interests of industries should be their common object in Parliament'.[96] The prospect of productioneer-domination of industrial relations obviously made the likelihood of securing allies in the Labour Party minimal, and it is predictable that the new association's main attempts at such negotiations were with 'patriotic labour bodies' such as the British Workers' League of Hyndman and Victor Fisher, the Merchant Seamen's League, and the Trade Union Labour Party.[97] Nevertheless, the very desire for some kind of compact with labour did imply a limit to the enthusiasm with which the case for Tariff Reform could be pressed. Finally, in adopting a strenuous policy on capital–labour relations, the BCU developed a close association with employers' associations such as the EEF and the Shipbuilding Employers' Federation. Whilst the 'right to manage' had an appeal for probably the heavy majority of Tariff Reform businessmen, the EEF had no declared outlook on Tariff Reform, whilst the post-war attitude of the shipbuilders was at best uncertain and probably still hostile. Post-war industrial unrest compounded the lessons of the Bolshevik Revolution, so that the establishment of a productioneer framework for industrial relations soon became the dominant industrial objective of the BCU, just as the fight against socialism became the main plank of the BCU's business candidates in the 1918 election. The establishment of a BCU council and committee structure saw the displacement of the original London Imperialists by newcomers such as Allan Smith of the EEF, Sir Ernest Hiley of British Westinghouse, Sir Hallewell Rogers of BSA, and Sir Richard Vassar-Smith of the Midland Bank. Whilst many of these were Tariff Reformers, and whilst the inclusion of Sir Joseph Lawerence and Patrick

[93] J. Turner, 'British Commonwealth Union', 533–5; cf. above, ch. 10.
[94] The constitution is quoted in J. Turner, 'British Commonwealth Union', 535.
[95] Ibid. 529.
[96] London Imperialists, Executive Committee Minutes, 19 Apr. 1917, Hannon Papers.
[97] BCU Executive Committee Minutes, 5 Sept. 1918, Hannon Papers.

Hannon strongly reinforced this, it is nevertheless clear that Tariff Reform had become distinctly diluted in comparison with a strong posture on industrial relations: 'Although Tariff Reform was always a fundamental element of its programme, most of the Union's passion, organization and money went into the struggle against the Labour party'.[98]

The BCU was 'interested' in fifty-seven candidates in the election of December 1918, but probably only gave actual assistance to twenty-four. Though eighteen of these were elected, their impact is debatable, since their views on Tariff Reform, post-war relations with Germany, a strong labour policy, and closer business–government relations were similar to those of the Unionist MPs elected who were not connected directly with the BCU; 'in its industrial policy the Union was swimming strongly and enthusiastically with the tide'.[99] What is much clearer is that subsequently the Union failed to live up to the expectations of its founders. In October 1918 the Union expected, on the basis of 'present membership', an income of £50,000 p.a. for three years, anticipated to rise as a massive postal appeal to 25,000 leading firms bore fruit.[100] There are indeed indications that funds flowed in quite liberally before the election, and in its immediate aftermath the rate was largely maintained, with contributions being received at over £3,000 per month in January and February 1919. In April contributions plummeted to £364, provoking the GPC to comment, 'There appears to be serious difficulty in convincing British manufacturers of the importance to them of having their own parliamentary machine actively at work';[101] but over the summer there was a recovery, funds flowing in at over £2,500 per month, a rate maintained until February 1920. These were large

TABLE 11. *British Commonwealth Union: Income 1918–1923*

	£	Approx. Monthly Rate
July 1918–Nov. 1918[a]	22,655	4,531
July 1918–Jan. 1919[a]	19,639	2,805
Jan. 1919–Feb. 1919	6,455	3,227
July 1919–Feb. 1920[b]	17,912	2,388[b]
July 1920–June 1921	17,995	1,499
July 1921–Dec. 1921	9,168	1,528
Jan. 1922–June 1922	2,476	412
July 1922–June 1923	17,551	1,462

[a] These figures are obviously inconsistent.
[b] $7\frac{1}{2}$ months.
Sources: BCU Executive Committee Minutes, 5 Dec. 1918; 6 Feb. 1919; 6 Mar. 1919; 12 Feb. 1920; BCU Subscription Lists, July 1920–June 1921; July–Dec. 1921; Jan.–June 1922; July 1922–June 1923; BCU (Hannon) Papers.

[98] J. Turner, 'British Commonwealth Union', 539.
[99] Ibid. 544.
[100] BCU Council Minutes, 31 Oct. 1918, Hannon Papers.
[101] BCU Executive Committee Minutes, 1 May 1919, Hannon Papers.

figures, even when adjusted for wartime inflation, but they never satisfied the
expectations of the early months. By mid-1920 income had fallen to a monthly
rate of around £1,500, less than 40 per cent of the original expectation, and half
that of a few months earlier.[102]

Detailed information on subscriptions, available from mid-1920 to mid-1923,
shows the financial dependence of the BCU on a relatively small number of
firms. Of just over 180 contributors in the year to 31 June 1921, forty-three firms,
mostly with a national reputation and each contributing £100 or more, provided
£15,058 out of total receipts of £17,995. Thirty of these forty-three came from
steel, mechanical engineering, locomotive- and ship-building, from electrical
engineering, or from food processing and the liquor trade.[103] These sectors also
contained four of the eight firms which contributed over £500—Docker's
Metropolitan Wagon, Carriage and Finance Co. Ltd. (£2,500); Caillard's
Vickers Ltd. (£2,500 plus £250 from Metropolitan-Vickers); Hannon and
Manville's BSA Ltd. (£1,000); and the British Sugar Refiners' Association
(£500). Less expected amongst this group were Nobel Industries Ltd.
(£1,000); the National Gas Council (£1,000); Sir Robert McAlpine and Sons
Ltd. (£500); and Francis Willey and Co. Ltd., a Bradford wool and tops
merchant (£500).

Lesser contributors were not necessarily small or little-known firms, however.
They included brewers such as Charringtons Ltd. and Allsopps Ltd.; collieries
such as Cambrian Collieries Ltd. and the Naval Colliery Co. Ltd.; Sheffield steel
and edge-tool firms such as Spear and Jackson Ltd., Arthur Balfour and Co. Ltd.,
and Edgar Allen and Co. Ltd.; Walker and Hall Ltd.; Vauxhall Motors Ltd.; the
hosiery firm, Wolsey Ltd.; the British Oxygen Co. Ltd.; Joseph Rank Ltd.; and
the rapidly growing seed firm, Sutton and Sons of Reading. In subsequent years
they were joined by prominent firms such as General Electric, Joseph Lucas Ltd.,
Babcock and Wilcox Ltd., Sir Wm. Arrol and Co. Ltd., Wm. Denny and Bros.
Ltd., John Thorneycroft and Co. Ltd., the Bristol Aeroplane Co. Ltd., Tate and
Lyle Ltd., the Britannic Merthyr Coal Co. Ltd., and Debenhams Ltd.[104]

Of particular significance are a group of contributors which, on pre-war
criteria, seem out of place in a protectionist organization—six electricity-power-
supply companies, together with their UK trade association; four collieries; two
shipowning firms; and no less than nine shipbuilding concerns (besides Vickers).
More surprising still is the appearance of Brunner, Mond and Co. Ltd. (£52) in
November 1922. Most surprising of all, however, is the simultaneous appearance
of the three great textile-engineering firms, Howard and Bullough Ltd. (£105),
Platt Bros. and Co. Ltd. (£1,000), and Dobson and Barlow Ltd. (£250), also in
November 1922.

---

[102] BCU Subscription List, July 1920–June 1921, Hannon Papers.   [103] Ibid.
[104] BCU Subscription Lists, July–Dec. 1921, Jan.–June 1922, July 1922–June 1923, Hannon
Papers.

Just as disappointing as finance to the BCU leadership was the failure to realize their expectations on membership. In November 1918 there were 192 members. In February 1919 total membership was 210, and by February 1920 the figure had grown to 336.[105] Though membership had increased by 50 per cent in a year, the response to the massive postal appeal had been poor. More important, it was not sustained. From mid-1920, the BCU began a long process of stagnation that only ended when, largely inert, it was amalgamated into the EIA in 1926. As early as January 1922, the information and propaganda activities of the BCU were being cut down, most importantly in the abolition of the Union's Economic Research Branch, which saved about £3,000 p.a., as the Union decided to concentrate most of its resources on parliamentary activity.[106]

Turner offers three explanations for the BCU's failure to meet its founders' expectations, the survival into the post-war period of substantial business support for Free Trade, the reluctance of businessmen to associate themselves with BCU policy on labour, and the perception of the wider business community that the BCU too narrowly sought advantage for one sector of industry, heavy engineering.[107]

In as far as it interprets failure as the failure to recruit more firms favourable to Tariff Reform, the first explanation seems inadequate. With a peak membership of less than 400 firms, the BCU tapped only a tiny part of the protectionist sentiment within the business community. The NUM, and even the FBI, had far more protectionists among their members than did the BCU. The BCU's failure was clearly an inability to mobilize already-existing protectionist sentiment rather than a manifestation of the continuing strength of Free Trade, as real as that may have been in the 1920s.

In part this represents a problem common to all Tariff-Reform pressure groups; protection was a public good, and if granted by government it would have been available to all businessmen, whether they had been members of such organizations or not. According to the 'logic of collective action',[108] the rational businessman would wait on the sidelines, allowing others to incur the expense, inconvenience, and (we might add) the public opprobrium of participation. Late in 1918, 151 out of 192 firms which had joined the BCU as a result of the postal appeal had still made no contribution.[109] In February 1920 a membership of 336 firms was claimed, yet only 185 contributed to the funds between July 1920 and June 1921.[110] The BCU's process of sponsoring parliamentary candidates was

---

[105] BCU Executive Committee Minutes, 7 Nov. 1918, 5 Dec. 1918, 6 Feb. 1919, 6 Mar. 1919, 1 May 1919, 2 Oct. 1919, 12 Feb. 1920, Hannon Papers.

[106] R. D. Herzog, 'The Conservative Party and Protectionist Politics', 483.

[107] J. Turner, 'British Commonwealth Union', 547.

[108] M. Olson, *The Logic of Collective Action* (Cambridge, Mass., 1965), *passim*; and *The Rise and Decline of Nations* (New Haven, 1982), esp. ch. 2.

[109] J. Turner, 'British Commonwealth Union', 548 n. 3.

[110] BCU Subscription List, 1 July 1920–30 June 1921, Hannon Papers. See BCU Council Minutes, 4 July 1918, for an attempt to institute a payroll levy on members.

expensive and uncertain in its results, not only in the chances of defeat but also in guaranteeing the product once in Parliament. To many protectionist business-men, still expecting the Coalition to deliver on safeguarding, there was probably little enthusiasm for a separate businessman's party. Or, if there was, the business could safely be left to someone else. The relationship between an organization's membership and the wider sympathy for its goals was clearly very indirect. Furthermore, to use the impressive growth of the FBI as a comparator for the BCU is misleading.[111] It should not be too easily assumed that FBI refusal to become involved in the Tariff-Reform controversy facilitated its growth when there were those in the FBI—leaders, canvassers, and members alike—who thought the very reverse.[112] In addition, the FBI was distinct from the BCU in offering services to its members.[113] These were an important consideration for business firms, as was shown when economy cuts provoked resignations.[114] In this respect, the FBI was more akin to a trade association, or to today's Chambers of Commerce, than to the BCU, and a comparison of the membership growth of the two reveals little.

How important to potential recruits with Tariff-Reform sympathies was Turner's second explanation, that businessmen were reluctant to identify them-selves with the BCU's strong position on labour? Under Chamberlain, Tariff Reform had symbolized regeneration through unity, an alternative to Liberal collectivism. In a period when both the Liberal and the Unionist Parties had been concerned to prevent politics from polarizing along class lines, Tariff Reformers had rejected the assumption that their policy would divide the classes—it was a national policy, and should stand above politics. But even before 1914 the businessmen of the Tariff Commission did not act according to such an organic conception of society. Division between members over how critical of the trade unions their report on iron and steel should be did not arise because of any dispute over the facts of the matter—the Commission's emphasis on 'continuous running' suggests the desire for an American-style 'hard-driving' approach and the assertion of tighter managerial control over the labour process. Rather, the consideration was whether it was politically expedient to alienate the trade unions.[115] It seems likely that such considerations still operated in the early 1920s. Whilst no doubt ultimately sympathizing with the harder stance of employers within the strife-torn industries, many businessmen came from industries relatively unaffected by industrial unrest, and would have seen a BCU policy on labour dominated by Allan Smith and the EEF as publicly and politically uncongenial.

There were even such sentiments within the BCU itself. After the 1918 election campaign, Caillard wondered whether the BCU's emphasis on industrial

---

[111] See J. Turner, 'British Commonwealth Union', 547.   [112] See above, ch. 10.
[113] A factor also stressed by M. Olsen; *Logic*, 132–67, and *Rise and Decline*, 23.
[114] See above, 312–13.   [115] See above, 144–5.

strife had not done more harm than good. Caillard was not pro-labour. In 1904 he had been one of the sterner critics of the trade unions on the Commission. Subsequently, in 1925, he was to oppose violently a move in the EIA to reach an accord with sympathetic elements in the Labour Party.[116] Yet there was undoubtedly within him the tendency of the old-style Tariff Reformers to play down any confrontation with labour.

Within the BCU, however, Allan Smith was sanguine: the issue had to be faced.[117] In some quarters his EEF-determined approach probably increased the popularity of the BCU. For instance, even if the cosmopolitanism of their trade was weakening, it seems likely that the great textile engineers, Platts, Howard and Bullough, and Dobson and Barlow, were attracted more to the BCU for its labour policy than for its protectionism, especially in 1922, after the engineers' lockout in which 17m working days had been lost and the bargaining position of the Amalgamated Society of Engineers strengthened.[118] But to those primarily interested in protection or preference, this was at best a diversion, at worst harmful.

Even so, productioneer-inclinations were very common among Tariff Reformers, and we would doubt that BCU policy on labour put a serious brake on recruiting more. In fact, it is Turner's third explanation for the BCU's failure that comes closest to the mark in explaining the failure to recruit more Tariff-Reform firms, though for decidedly unexpected reasons. Amongst manufacturers, the BCU was perceived to be the tool of a small group of large heavy-engineering firms. And largely it was. Given the general fervour within engineering for productioneering, and in its newer sectors for 'key' or 'infant-industry' protection, it might seem that this would make it particularly attractive to protectionist businessmen. But, ironically, the large engineering firms which formed the BCU's backbone ensured that the BCU's commitment to Tariff Reform was much less 'fundamental' than Turner recognizes.

Smith was a Free Trader, and his dominance within the BCU until 1923 clearly reduced its profile as a Tariff-Reform organization. But he was not unsupported. Vickers apart, many of the shipbuilding and shipping members of the Union probably still hoped for a revival of export business. Collieries, textile engineers, and electricity-supply companies were unlikely enthusiasts for protection. There may also have been a carefully concealed split in the BCU between engineering firms which undertook large, one-off contracting work overseas and firms which did repetition work or mass production—the same split which had been noticed by the Balfour of Burleigh Committee some years earlier. There is certainly evidence that some export-orientated engineering firms within the BCU were concerned that their specific overseas interests should not be jeopardized.

[116] See above, ch. 5 and below, ch. 12.
[117] J. Turner, 'British Commonwealth Union', 546.
[118] A. Shadwell, *The Engineering Industry and the Crisis of 1922* (1922), ch. 6.

In the early years after the War, the Union sought 'adequate protection' for the motor industry, and made protestations to the Government over the Imports and Exports Regulation Bill. But the GPC's reaction to the Safeguarding Bill in November 1920 betrayed an equivocal position. The number of key industries should be kept as small as possible, and the Government should recognize 'that the vital need of the moment was to tide over the difficult time of the re-establishment of industry, during which safeguarding was necessary, bearing in mind the fact that efficient industrial organization would effectively deal with the foreign competition in a comparatively few years'.[119]

Though the BCU advocated government assistance in trade, this was sought mostly on the export side. The BCU's concerns ranged from the traditional demands for reforms in the consular service and improvements in commercial intelligence to pressing for direct government aid in securing export contracts, mostly in the form of subsidized interest rates to finance large export contracts. Particular efforts were made to secure government participation in schemes to secure a monopoly of the contracts on offer for the post-war reconstruction of Poland and Romania.[120]

It seems, therefore, that the BCU's conception of Tariff Reform was closely tailored to the specific interests of the large engineering firms which formed its backbone. Its support for protection was selective, being conditioned by a belief that, overall, the imposition of tariffs should be limited in order to have a minimum effect on export recovery. This was a far narrower definition of safeguarding than had been proposed by the Balfour of Burleigh Committee.

Similar characteristics were evident in the BCU's approach to imperial preference. Though an 'Imperial Economic System' was first among the objectives of IALU in 1917,[121] this had clearly ceased to be such a high priority by May 1920, when there is a vague reference in the executive council minutes to a change in policy on preference.[122] In 1922 Hewins put to the BCU a scheme for a campaign to educate British public opinion on the expansion of inter-imperial trade in accordance with resolutions passed at the Imperial Conference of 1918, a scheme in which he purposely played down the role of tariffs and trade preferences.[123] With Caillard enthusiastic, Hannon initially responded positively to Hewins's scheme; it provided an 'immense opportunity' to develop imperial trade, as well as the 'political text for an appeal to this country of the very greatest value'.[124] But he was playing a double game. To Docker he

[119] BCU GPC Minutes, 10 Nov. 1920, Hannon Papers.
[120] 'Reconstruction of Poland: Memorandum by the General Secretary', [n.d.], Box 12 Folder 2, BCU (Hannon) Papers.
[121] IALU Council Minutes, 25 Oct. 1917, Hannon Papers.
[122] BCU Executive Committee Minutes, 7 Apr. 1920, Hannon Papers.
[123] 'Development of Imperial Trade: Memorandum by the Director of the British Commonwealth Union', [n.d.], Hannon Papers.
[124] Hannon to Caillard, 3 July 1922, Box 12 Folder 5, BCU (Hannon) Papers.

confided Leo Amery's opinion that Hewins was not highly regarded by the Dominion governments. Docker shared his reservations, and was also unimpressed by the scheme on the ground that any encouragement of imperial trade might be detrimental to the expansion of Britain's foreign trade in general.[125]

Discussing the proposal in July, the GPC decided to 'take steps to give immediate effect to the Imperial Preference provision of the Constitution of the B.C.U.'.[126] This decision in itself suggests that preference had become dormant in BCU policy. A sub-committee comprising Allan Smith, Caillard, Rogers, and Sir Henry Cowan was established to consider Hewins's scheme. The sub-committee held a friendly meeting with Hewins, but, as is clear from Hannon's post-mortem of it, the extent to which the BCU was prepared to press actively for an expansion of imperial trade was very limited. Hewins's scheme might embroil the BCU:

in difficulties and misunderstandings with many of its members, whose interests are mainly concerned with foreign markets, more especially China, Japan and South America, and that therefore it would be unwise to identify ourselves with a movement definitely committed to an Empire policy as against all other considerations.[127]

In the lull after the labour troubles of the early 1920s, BCU interest in Tariff Reform revived a little. In January 1923, it was unanimously decided at the AGM that 'the principle of Imperial Preference, as being one of the cardinal principles on which the Union was founded, should continue to receive the full support of the Union'. There was a corollary emphasis on 'impressing on Members of the Industrial Group the *paramount* necessity' of securing a reduction of taxation on industry, and of funding pensions on an annuity basis.[128] It may be that, now eighteen months after the Safeguarding Act, there was mounting annoyance that so little had been achieved. Furthermore, Allan Smith was becoming a liability to the Union, because of the difficulties created by his strong antipathy towards Baldwin. Shortly afterwards, he incensed the Conservative Party by standing as a Unionist Free Trader in Glasgow.[129]

But the revival was small. Alarmed by Baldwin's decision to go to the country on Tariff Reform, the Union held a special meeting. Docker was unconvinced that a tariff policy could operate quickly enough to alleviate the looming winter unemployment. '[I]mmediate policies' were necessary, and a government 'as yet comparatively unknown, and lacking the full confidence of the country' would 'in the circumstances . . . create distrust, suspicion and uncertainty among the

---

[125] Hannon to Docker, 3 July 1922, Docker to Hannon, 3 July 1922, Box 12 Folder 4, BCU (Hannon) Papers.
[126] 'Conference Relating to Inter-Imperial Trade: Memorandum by the Director of the British Commonwealth Union', [n.d.], Hannon Papers.
[127] Hannon to Docker, 19 July 1922, Box 12 Folder 5, BCU (Hannon) Papers.
[128] BCU, Fourth AGM, 10 January 1923, Box 13 Folder 1, BCU (Hannon) Papers (my emphasis).
[129] Rodgers, 'Sir Allan Smith', 117.

industrial community' with such proposals.[130] In reporting the resolutions of the meeting to Baldwin, Hannon urged postponement. BCU alarm was couched not in terms of hostility to Tariff Reform—indeed, there was an indication that the Union was prepared to accept food duties as long as they excluded wheat and meat—but at its timing. Postponement would allow time 'for the cultivation of public opinion on the need of a Tariff'; in the meantime the BCU wanted an extension of safeguarding. As Hannon reported, BCU intelligence suggested 'very grave differences of opinion are apparent [in industry] on the subject of the *immediate* imposition of a General Tariff on manufactured goods'.[131]

In itself this reaction was not surprising. Baldwin's decision shocked many avid Tariff Reformers, and even zealots like Amery and Hewins opposed it.[132] There are also signs that BCU ineffectiveness on Tariff Reform was at least in part due to its close association with the Industrial Group.

Before December 1923, the Industrial Group had of course been subject to the same dominance of Allan Smith as had the Union, but its uncertainty on Tariff Reform persisted both after his departure[133] and after the reverses it experienced during the election. The Group suffered heavily in the election, some 40 of its members being defeated, including leading figures such as Sir Phillip Dawson, Sir Edward Manville, and Basil Peto. The Group was reorganized, with Sir Arthur Shirley Benn as chairman and Hannon as secretary, and was now kept more closely under the eye of Conservative Central Office.[134] But Smith's departure did not cure the Group's ambivalence towards Tariff Reform. In February 1924 it wrote to MacDonald opposing the abolition of the McKenna duties, and in March it opposed the Labour Government's reduction of the German Reparations duties.[135] But it was fundamentally divided over how to respond to the Government's decision not to implement the resolutions of the 1923 Imperial Conference. A meeting of thirteen of the Group was unable to agree, and adjourned in the hope of securing 'a larger and more representative attendance'. The second attempt attracted only five of those at the first meeting, and five others. It was a dubious basis for the unanimous resolution that the 'policy of extended Imperial Preference demands increasing support'.[136] Then, in February 1925, Cunliffe-Lister addressed a large attendance of the Industrial

---

[130] 'Special Conference of the Representatives of Industry and Finance', 8 Nov. 1923, Box 13 Folder 3, BCU (Hannon) Papers.

[131] Hannon to Baldwin, 9 Nov. 1923, Box 13 Folder 3, (BCU) Hannon Papers (my emphasis).

[132] J. Ramsden, *The Age of Balfour and Baldwin 1902–1940* (1978), 179; W. A. S. Hewins, *The Apologia of an Imperialist* (1929), ii. 23.

[133] Smith fell out with his South Croydon constituency party in November when they refused him the freedom to fight the election as a Free Trader. Shortly afterwards, he resigned as chairman of the Industrial Group.

[134] T. Rodgers, 'Sir Allan Smith', 117.

[135] Industrial Group Minutes, 14 Feb. 1924, 6 Mar. 1924, Box 13 Folder 3, BCU (Hannon) Papers.

[136] Industrial Group Minutes, 19 and 23 June 1924, Box 13 Folder 3, BCU (Hannon) Papers.

Group on safeguarding and the White Paper. After a lengthy discussion, the meeting 'failed to arrive at any definite conclusion as to the policy that the Group should adopt and the matter generally was deferred for future consideration'.[137]

Subsequently, Hannon wrote to Churchill urging the reimposition of the McKenna duties and expressing the BCU's hope:

that a sufficient number of reports will be received under the Safeguarding of Industries procedure to enable certain Safeguarding Duties to be incorporated in the Budget and this should have the effect of materially adding to the prospective [budget] surplus. On the other hand, it is appreciated that the increased preferences to Empire produce will absorb at least some part of this surplus.[138]

By now, however, the BCU had been in terminal decline for some time. Any slight strengthening of its position on Tariff Reform with the eclipse of Allan Smith had to be set against its waning strength. The BCU's war against socialism might continue to be something of a thorn in the flesh of Joynson-Hicks and the Home Office,[139] but its demands on Tariff Reform did not add significantly to the pressure that was being exerted by Conservative backbenchers—a pressure that the Government was containing without great difficulty.

VI

BEPO's programme proved too broad and too corporatist to be widely acceptable to the domestic British manufacturer. Though, almost paradoxically, the Organization survived because of a high level of cohesion amongst its members, it showed little capacity for growth until late in the 1920s. On Tariff Reform, the dominance of the BCU by Allan Smith and a few large engineering firms with specific export interests resulted in an ambivalent posture which stood to damn it in the eyes of Free Traders and Tariff Reformers alike, and the Union was not able to survive the difficult first half of the 1920s, even after the departure of the abrasive Smith. Of the business groups active before 1926, the NUM proved the most successful in terms of membership and stability. It never seems to have experienced financial or membership crisis, and indeed expanded healthily throughout the period. Much of its success in attracting and retaining the support of both large- and small-scale manufacturers was due to its pursuing the narrower policy of safeguarding and a general industrial tariff right from its inception in 1916 to the early 1930s. At times, reflecting general business sentiment, anti-labour or at least anti-union feeling was pronounced in the NUM, but it seldom dominated. NUM unity was in one sense ensured by its

---

[137] Industrial Group Minutes, 26 Feb. 1925, Box 13 Folder 3, BCU (Hannon) Papers.

[138] Hannon to Churchill, 6 Apr. 1925, Box 13 Folder 2, BCU (Hannon) Papers.

[139] On the BCU's intemperate reaction to the Zinoviev affair, see Joynson-Hicks to Hannon, 15 Oct. 1925, Box 13 Folder 2, BCU (Hannon) Papers.

definite and unequivocal aims: firms knew exactly what they were joining. In the early years it was aided by somewhat limited regional representation—Birmingham, London, and the Midlands, rather than Birmingham alone—but this was continually extended into the North, especially as industrialists' frustration mounted after Cunliffe-Lister's White Paper in 1925. Industrially, many NUM members came from small industries or branches of industry where there was, at least on the surface, some hope of a safeguarding enquiry being granted, and many were indeed actively involved in making applications. In that limited number of cases where applications were successful, it is interesting to note that firms tended to remain members of the Union.

12

The Empire Industries Association

After 1925 the NUM was joined by another stable group, the EIA, whose position in the spectrum between safeguarding and preference was less defined. Initially, faced with some internal conflict over the two semi-alternatives, the EIA elected, on the surface, to go for both, and never gave such clear indications as did the NUM that safeguarding had primacy over preference. Earlier in the decade this might have caused misgivings amongst business supporters. But, as a latecomer, the EIA's choice was relatively easy. Manufacturing reaction to the inadequacies of the White Paper of 1925 was increasingly impatient, whilst the prospect of Empire markets at a time when the visible trade balance was worsening appeared to give the Empire a strategic importance in British trade that it lacked in the Edwardian period. After 1926, an apparently heightened emphasis on imperial policy was unlikely to lose the EIA significant business support amongst those demanding an extension of safeguarding.

It is essential to recognize, however, that EIA policy on Empire remained limited. To increase the acceptability of its policy to electorate and government, it did not seek to undermine Baldwin's pledge that there should be no import duty on the main foodstuffs. Before the 1929 election, the EIA, like the NUM, accepted and promoted a narrower definition than did the businessmen of the Tariff Commission before 1914. This might appear to show that it had grown beyond the tutelage of mentors like Chamberlain and Hewins, that industry could now assert its own brute position, rather than riding on the coat-tails of something prettier. But, in truth, with the imperial star rising as Britain's manufacturers finally gave up on European recovery, the business members of the EIA were less discomforted by a wider imperial policy than their predecessors in the NUM and BCU, and there is little doubt that, without political constraints, they would have acquiesced in the introduction of food taxes. EIA policy was not, in fact, dominated by business considerations but by political ones, and it was politicians who determined its agenda. Hence, in an important way, the position of the businessman in Tariff-Reform politics had changed little. If the Tariff Commission's broader vision was largely, though not entirely, impressed upon it by a relatively small group of committed imperialists—Chamberlain, Hewins, Caillard, Birchenough—the EIA's less-radical approach reflected a willingness to work within the confines of official Conservative policy. In their different ways, businessmen within both organizations knelt in a position of subservience to the politicians.

Before examining the EIA, however, it will be useful to give brief consideration to the much-less-successful Empire Development Union. In its attempt to harness the power and influence of businessmen for the wider rather than the narrower ends of Tariff Reform, the EDU was in some respects similar to the EIA. Furthermore, together with the BCU, it was seen as an ancestor of the EIA. Since it was also the lineal descendant of the Tariff Commission, and, to an extent, the successor to the TRL, it contained the potential to form a bridge between the pre-war and post-war movements. But, founded at a difficult time in the early 1920s, when the imperial ideal was not the first consideration of protectionist businessmen, and maladroitly led, it never proved capable of fulfilling this role.

I

Even more dramatically than the BCU, the Empire Development Union did not live up to initial expectations. Its primary object, to 'promote the Trade Relations of the United Kingdom within the Empire on the lines of Resolutions unani-mously adopted at [the] successive Imperial Conferences [of 1917 and 1918]',[1] was seen almost as a personal crusade by Hewins, the EDU's chairman, and only slightly less so by Walter Long, its president. As Long's Under-Secretary for the Colonies, Hewins had chaired the Economic Committee of the Conference of 1918, and he subsequently regarded the resolutions in favour of preference passed in these years as standing pledges upon which Lloyd George had defaulted.[2] Significantly, the EDU was formed in September 1922, during the death-throes of the Coalition.

Hewins envisaged a large organization comparable to the TRL, but with more explicit links with the business world. When he and Caillard approached the BCU with their scheme to promote imperial trade, they were apparently contemplating even more—a full merger of the Tariff Commission, the TRL, and the BCU. According to Lord Gisborough, chairman of the TRL Finance Committee, they had been 'authorised to see Hannon & others & find out if they were prepared to amalgamate under the new name [of Imperial Development Union]'.[3] When the BCU declined even the trade scheme, they determined to go it alone.[4]

---

[1] EDU Minutes, 11 Sept. 1922, Box 33, HP.
[2] W. A. S. Hewins, *Apologia of an Imperialist* (1929), ii. 139–43 and chs. 19 and 22. Long was Colonial Secretary at the time of these Imperial Conferences.
[3] Gisborough to Hewins, 12 Sept. 1922, 80/145–6, HP.
[4] Hannon to Docker, 19 July 1922, Box 12, BCU Papers.

Both the Tariff Commission and the TRL were finding the climate harsh in the early 1920s. By 1921 the Commission was in a terminal state of decline, partly due to Hewins's neglect of it after his appointment to the under-secretary-ship. The TRL was still uncertain of its post-war role. As early as 1917 Victor Fisher, resisting suggestions that the British Workers' League should join the TRL, argued that '[t]he name is too redolent of our pre-war controversies, and "Reform" is stamped with the hall-mark of Victorian radicalism'.[5] After the War, there was internal dispute over reparations—should the TRL press for a settlement that might disrupt European trade and recovery, or concede that Germany could not pay and that trade war was at an end? Furthermore, some desired closer harmony with the leaders of the Coalition to counter the attempts of Lord Derby and the FTL to undermine the TRL—the Lanca-shire and North-Western Committee of the League was openly debating a change of name—whilst other members regarded such moves as a betrayal, lamenting that the trade policy of the TRL was as uncertain as that of the Government.[6]

Prevailed on to become temporary chairman, Hewins had found that that the War had 'extinguished' some branches, and that, although the regional federa-tions were still intact, there was a financial crisis, due less to a decline in small subscriptions than to 'a great decline in the contributions received from wealthier people'. In March there were only funds for a few weeks.[7] At a meeting in July 1921 the League's leaders were attacked for lethargy in raising funds, the lack of a definite policy, even for 'sacrific[ing]' the principles of Tariff Reform. The launch of a £10,000 appeal, initiated by London solicitor Sir Charles Cottier's announcement that he would contribute £1,000, had little effect in attracting new funds.[8] The unsuccessful approach to the BCU, followed almost immedi-ately by the formation of the EDU, represented successive attempts to rejuvenate the organizational basis of Tariff Reform propaganda.

Regarding the business community as central to the membership and finances of the Union, the organizers made a large postal appeal to leading firms and chambers of commerce.[9] They compiled a list of thirty-one known sympathizers, half of them titled, perhaps with a view to forming an EDU council. The great majority were important businessmen, some of an industrial protectionist or productioneer persuasion, but many more with prominent imperial interests, especially in oil, shipping, and merchant banking.[10]

---

[5] Fisher to Austen Chamberlain, 25 Oct. 1917, 12/86, Austen Chamberlain Papers.

[6] H. Sowler to Hewins, 30 May 1921, 77/168–9, HP.

[7] TRL circular, 4 Mar. 1921, 77/83, HP.

[8] Report of a Special Meeting of the Tariff Reform League, 22 July 1921, in *A Call to Action* (TRL Pamphlet, London, 1921).

[9] Unheaded typescript, 27 Mar. 1923, 33/19e, HP.

[10] Unheaded and undated typescript list, 33/2b–2c, HP.

This orientation towards the imperial rather than the domestic aspects of Tariff Reform distanced the EDU from the BCU, and accommodated the prospect of a substantial middle-class and professional influx if the TRL were wound up. It also raised the question of food taxes, which was handled gingerly by the EDU organizers. Long was concerned to use the EDU to promote at least a degree of agricultural protection.[11] As the 1923 election approached, however, Hewins denied that Empire preference would require duties on wheat and meat, claiming that in any case the 'surplus production of the Dominions' would ensure that a duty would not increase British food prices.[12] After the election defeat, he returned to his more consistent long-term position, advocating 'slightly protective ... revenue duties', and 'very moderate' aid to agriculture by bounty or subsidy in line with the Tariff Commission's pre-war report.[13]

There was little enthusiasm for the new Union, either among the firms contacted or the would-be council members, none of whom mentioned the EDU in his *Who's Who* entry. Only Long, Hewins, Cottier, and Caillard attended meetings, and the EDU remained the organ of this small group.[14]

Cavalierly, Hewins was awarded a salary of £2,000 p.a. when the EDU's assets were only £500, entirely provided by Cottier. There were plans for an EDU bulletin and a network of expert committees.[15] Consideration was given to an optimistic proposal by Victor Fisher, now of the Empire Workers' Council, to carry Empire propaganda into the heartland of 'rampant' Cobdenism, the trade-union lodges, working-men's clubs, adult schools, and nonconformist church brotherhoods.[16] Beaverbrook co-operated with Long in publishing EDU material in his newspapers,[17] and Hewins continued to write for the imperial cause in *The Morning Post* and elsewhere. An imposing meeting was held at the Mansion House on St George's Day, 23 April 1923,[18] and in the run-up to the Imperial Conference in October the EDU gained some support in Empire countries. E. Jowett, president of the 'Victoria Branch', told an audience which included premier Bruce that a petition of 100,000 trade associations, companies, and individuals had been collected under EDU auspices.[19] But at home the EDU never had the funds to develop a propaganda organization on the scale of the TRL. Even the impressive Mansion-House meeting only brought in £1,000, and when the EDU was finally absorbed by the EIA there were difficulties in

[11] Long to Hewins, 13 and 19 Aug. 1922, 80/99–101, 80/125, HP.

[12] 'The Case for Protection', *Evening Standard*, 26 Oct. 1923.

[13] W. A. S. Hewins, *Trade in the Balance* (London, 1924), 91–101, 157–8.

[14] EDU Minutes, 11 Sept. 1922, Box 30, HP; see also EDU Minutes, 11 Sept. 1922, Box 30, HP; Hamilton to Hewins, 14 Aug. 1922, 80/104–110, HP; Caillard to Long, 5 and 10 Oct. 1922, 80/246, 80/248–50, HP.

[15] Ibid.   [16] Fisher to Hewins, 19 Dec. 1922, 83/107, HP.

[17] Beaverbrook to Long, 20 Dec. 1922, 83/119, HP.

[18] *Our Imperial Opportunity: Importance of the Coming Economic Conference* (EDU pamphlet, London, 1923).

[19] *Melbourne Argus*, 23 Aug. 1923.

establishing and settling its debts. Through its limited activities in education and in the press, it became the vehicle for attempts to secure Hewins's re-entry into politics—whilst its chairman, he unsuccessfully fought Alfred Mond for Swansea West in 1922, 1923, and 1924, and wrote his lucid *Trade in the Balance* (1924). Such attempts were unsuccessful, according to Hewins largely because of prejudice against his Catholic conversion.[20] He was still held in sufficient regard for Baldwin to include him in Milner's Tariff Advisory Committee in November 1923.[21] But he may have acted in such a way as to diminish his own standing with the Conservative leadership. According to his memoirs, he was critical of the TAC's proceedings, refusing to allow the committee access to Tariff-Commission material, and was generally appalled at the prospect of fighting an election on the tariff issue.[22] Whilst there is no contemporary record of his disaffection in the few surviving records of the TAC, there is substance to the view that, in his later career, Hewins saw himself as 'a kind of Warwick, a maker and destroyer of governments'.[23] Long, Caillard, and Cottier appear to have shared this delusion; they were in no doubt that he was the country's 'best exponent' of schemes for imperial development.[24] But in the eyes of potential supporters the accession of Labour destroyed any immediate prospect of extended preference, and the EDU struggled from hand to mouth until absorbed by a reluctant EIA in 1925.

II

The Empire Industries Association is commonly regarded as the most dynamic and influential Tariff Reform group of the period 1925–1929. Leo Amery maintained that it 'was destined to do invaluable work in keeping our policy before the country, and to exercise a decisive influence in Parliament when Free Trade was finally swept away by the great depression in 1931'. Forrest Capie has endorsed this view of 'this most powerful pressure group', whilst Robert Boyce has credited the EIA with being 'a major factor' in the revival of imperial protectionism.[25]

The origins of the EIA lay in the desire of Leo Amery and Neville Chamberlain to establish a 'Fair Trade union' to replace the defunct TRL and maintain the momentum of Tariff Reform in the aftermath of Baldwin's election defeat. Early in 1924 Sir Henry Page Croft joined their plan, and cast about for

[20] Hewins to Baldwin, 9 Apr. 1929, 92/91–4, HP.
[21] For the Tariff Advisory Committee, see below, Ch. 13.
[22] K. Middlemas and J. Barnes, *Baldwin* (1969), 219, 233.
[23] Sir Keith Hancock, *Survey of British Commonwealth Affairs 1918–1939*, ii. I, *Problems of Economic Policy 1918–1939* (1942), 137–8.
[24] Long to Austen Chamberlain, 19 Feb. 1922, 33/1/32, Austen Chamberlain Papers.
[25] L. S. Amery, *My Political Life*, ii (1953), 291; F. Capie, *Depression and Protectionism* (1983), 74; R. W. D. Boyce, *British Capitalism at the Crossroads, 1919–1932* (Cambridge, 1987), 111.

financial support. When Baldwin pledged to abandon food taxes and a general tariff, Amery and Chamberlain, both on the opposition front bench, recognized that they could not take a formal role in any organization which disagreed with official party policy. Hewins, Caillard, and Cottier were annoyed at the foundation of a rival to the EDU, but a meeting in December secured agreement that not only the EDU, but also the BCU, should be merged into the new organization.[26]

It was not until the summer of 1926 that EIA propaganda developed the scale that was to be characteristic of the period 1927–1931. There was an unusually long gestation period compared with organizations like the TRL and Tariff Commission, let alone with more ephemeral pressure groups, which would often spring up overnight. The explanation is threefold—initial differences over policy, financial constraints, and delays caused by an attempt to secure the co-operation of Labour representatives.

In January 1925, Hewins produced a memorandum on Baldwin's statement outlining the limits of the Government's policy on safeguarding and preference in the House of Commons on 17 December 1924.[27] Less disappointed than Hannon and other members of the Industrial Group,[28] he claimed it would afford 'ample means for the protection of British enterprise against unfair foreign competition' and for 'creating a practical working basis for the steady extension of preferential trading'. But he stressed that the industrial community would demand 'a broad and generous interpretation' of what constituted 'unfair foreign competition', the phrase used by Baldwin. The new association, the 'proposed "Fair Trade" Organisation', should focus attention on the uneven incidence of taxation at home and abroad, differences in labour conditions, wage rates, and hours, and state assistance and subsidies. It should be London-based, complete with an 'Economic Intelligence Staff' and branches in the industrial centres, and should act as the 'G.H.Q. of British industry'.[29] Trusting to a literal interpretation of Baldwin's policy outline, Hewins saw the EIA as a reborn Tariff Commission, proving the case for safeguarding applications under a process of 'reduction' or 'isolation' now legitimized by the Prime Minister.

Hannon was less convinced, but he recognized that the need for loyalty towards the Government meant that the new 'Association should operate within the four corners of the Prime Minister's statement'. In operational terms, therefore, there was no difference between Hewins's position and his own.[30] Both envisaged the Association's function to be to campaign for the utilization of the new safeguarding criteria to the full, and to exert pressure for relaxing their interpretation.

---

[26] R. D. Herzog, 'The Conservative Party and Protectionist Politics, 1918–1932', unpubl. Ph. D. thesis, Univ. of Sheffield, 1984, 493–6.

[27] *Parliamentary Debates*, 5th ser., clxxix (1924–5), cols. 1058–68.

[28] Hannon to Amery, 17 Feb. 1925, 88/39, HP.

[29] 'Proposed "Fair Trade" Organisation', 6 Jan. 1925, 88/2, HP.

[30] Hannon to Amery, 17 Feb., 1925.

Preliminary meetings were held in January and February. Early versions of the EIA's objectives put the main emphasis on safeguarding: on 15 January the title being canvassed was the 'British Industries Defence Association'. Some, however, desired greater emphasis on preference. Caillard preferred the name 'Empire Economic Development Association', which put the emphasis on development and also gave scope for the inclusion of Empire Settlement.[31] His sentiments were shared by Lord Hunsdon, merchant banker and brother of former Tariff Commissioner Vicary Gibbs,[32] who reluctantly agreed to be chairman after the ex-president of the Board of Trade and Chancellor of the Exchequer, Sir Robert Horne, had declined for fear of upsetting his constituents at Glasgow, Hillhead.[33] Believing that 'unless we give the Colonies a preference on foodstuffs including wheat it is not going to get us very far', Hunsdon registered his 'alarm' on reading an early draft of the EIA's objectives. Further consultation with Hewins seems to have reassured him, perhaps excessively:

I now understand from you that the *whole* object of the Empire Industries Association is the extension of Empire Preference and that it is not to be mixed up with the Safeguarding of Industries or Protection except so far as import duties are necessary for Empire preference.

I hope that the Appeals and statements will make this clear also.

Empire Preference is a big enough question by itself.[34]

V. A. Malcolmson, stockbroker and, as he called it, 'co-founder' of the EIA, thought similarly. Important to the EIA on account of a large subscription of £3,000, he considered that a policy stressing preference whilst leaving safeguarding in the background would be beneficial 'from the point of view of public support, especially in the provincial press'.[35]

In reassuring Hunsdon, Hewins may have argued that preference would follow automatically from an extension of safeguarding, because of the commitment in the 1919 Finance Act to allow preference on duties then existing or thereafter imposed. Certainly, Hunsdon did not always catch the drift of what he was told.[36] In any case, his vision of the EIA's purpose was unrealistic. Its members were annoyed and frustrated by Baldwin's timorous approach. Hannon wanted the speeding-up of the application process, and Board of Trade information on industrial conditions abroad made available to applying industries. John Gretton, chairman of the 'safeguarding committee' in the Commons, feared that Baldwin

---

[31] Paper in 88/5, HP. See also R. S. Keary (P. S. to Caillard) to Hewins, 24 Jan. 1925, 88/8–9, HP. Empire settlement had also been a concern of the EDU. See EDU Minutes, 11 Sept. 1922, Box 33, HP, and, more generally, I. M. Drummond, *Imperial Economic Policy 1917–1939* (1974), chs. 2–3, and G. F. Plant, *Oversea Settlement* (1951), pt. III.

[32] *Who Was Who*, iii.

[33] Hunsdon to Hewins, 7 July 1925, 88/77–8, HP. See also F. Capie, *Depression and Protectionism* 73.

[34] Hunsdon to Hewins, 31 July 1925, 88/133–4, HP (my emphasis).

[35] *Who Was Who*, iv; Malcolmson to Hewins, 10 Aug. 1925, 88/141–2, HP.

[36] See below, 367.

and Cunliffe-Lister intended to do the 'least possible' under the Act. Croft observed that 'in no single instance yet has the Board of Trade made up their minds'. Carlyon Bellairs saw the 'ridiculous white paper' as evidence that 'it seems to be a craze among our leaders to tie their policy up in knots to satisfy opponents' criticism and to end by satisfying nobody'. As A. E. Hills, a Birmingham manufacturer of stainless steel tubing, saw it, 'The weakness of the Conservative Government makes it doubly necessary for manufacturers to become strong'.[37]

It was thus scarcely realistic that the fledgeling association should restrict its campaign to preference. This did not mean, however, that EIA members wished to exclude preference, the more so since most, like Hewins, saw the two as linked. Subsequent discussions allowed some redress in the balance between safeguarding and preference to suit Hunsdon's taste, without backtracking on the former; a manifesto produced in September gave the two objectives more equal treatment than had earlier versions.[38] Nevertheless, Hunsdon's nervousness on safeguarding, and his desire for a policy with greater popular appeal, explains much about his weak chairmanship in the subsequent crisis within the EIA over Labour representation.

There was concern within the EIA that the negativism of Cunliffe-Lister's White Paper made the prospects of success so remote that it would limit the Association's ability to raise funds and destroy the effectiveness of its propaganda. This was of particular significance since the EIA's plans were ambitious and likely to prove expensive. In August 1925 the General Purposes Committee was considering a large weekly campaign in the provincial press on imperial trade. There would be an 'Imperial and Economic Service Bulletin' published at regular intervals, and a country-wide programme of lectures and addresses by specially trained speakers. EIA publications would need to be substantial pamphlets; it 'would serve no useful purpose' merely to duplicate the short, cheap leaflets being produced by Unionist Central Office on similar lines. When parliamentary activity and co-operation with trade associations such as the Federation of Iron and Steel Manufacturers on safeguarding were added, the EIA's projected activities involved considerable outlay.[39]

Finance was indeed a restraining factor. Being formed out of the remnants of the BCU and the EDU, both now 'semi-moribund',[40] the EIA was exposed to the danger of inheriting their liabilities, which in the EDU's case were undetermined. In its infant year the Association was paying the salaries of some former

---

[37] Hannon to Amery, 17 Feb. 1925; Gretton to Hewins, 20 Mar. 1925, 88/61, HP; Page Croft to Hewins, 5 Apr. 1925, 88/66, HP; Bellairs to Hewins, 19 Sept. 1925, 88/187, HP; Hills to Hannon, 5 Oct. 1925, 88/208, HP; 'Draft Letter of Appeal', July 1925, 88/135–6, HP.

[38] EIA Manifesto, 22 Sept. 1925, 88/192, HP.

[39] GPC Minutes, 5 and 13 Oct. 1925; EIA Minute Book, Hannon Papers.

[40] R. W. D. Boyce, *British Capitalism*, 111.

employees of both organizations; and, as late as October 1925, uncertainty over the state of EIA funds and staffing needs led to a decision to continue employing office staff 'on the weekly basis on which they had been for several months'. Furthermore, whilst the EIA was reluctant to recognize quite large EDU liabilities which probably represented salary arrears due to Hewins, it did in effect inherit the EDU's £1,000 overdraft, since Caillard reduced his contribution to the EIA to pay this off. Since the large inaugural meeting planned for the Queen's Hall, which would have had as a main purpose an appeal and the raising of subscriptions, was being continually postponed in this period, it is clear that the GPC was watching every penny. Offers to form branches were welcomed, but it was made clear that the Association could not undertake financial assistance. On the other hand, the EIA was quite prepared to absorb G. A. Malcolm's Imperial Commercial Association, with 685 members, annual subscriptions of £1,650, a bank balance of over £500, and 'no liabilities of any kind', without pausing to enquire into whether EIA policy was acceptable to ICA members. This was of some embarrassment subsequently when it was discovered that it was not.

In spite of Hannon's insistence that £13,000 had been guaranteed, subscriptions actually received rose from £2,867 on 28 October to only £3,714 on 31 December, so that funds were coming in at less than £500 per month. In the same period, the EIA's net balance in hand fell by rather more than this, from £2,673 to £1,477.[41] Originally it had been anticipated that some £25,000 p.a. would be necessary to fund the EIA; and some of the early guarantees, such as the £1,000 offers made by Caillard's Vickers and Sir Otto Beit, had been conditional on this sum being reached.[42] By July 1925 it was recognized that this was unrealistic, but the Executive Committee still thought £15,000 p.a. attainable. By December the bulk of the guarantees promised to the EIA had not materialized, and efforts were being made to persuade conditional subscribers to relax their demands. Hunsdon, alarmed by the EIA's overdraft, constantly urged conservatism in expenditure.[43]

The most important rift between EIA members was that on Labour representation. Ben Morgan, a BEPO representative on the EIA, raised the possibility of co-operation with the Labour and Liberal Parties in July 1925. To Malcolmson, also a BEPO member, the EIA 'bears too definitely the impress of a Party Political organisation and even at that, [is] too closely identified with *one section* of that political party'. A wider membership, 'a *wholly British* movement, entirely

[41] GPC Minutes, 13 and 28 Oct., 10 and 17 Nov., 1, 15 and 31 Dec. 1925, EIA Minute Book, Hannon Papers.
[42] This practice was identical to that involved in some of the Tariff Commission's guarantee funds, and may have been common elsewhere.
[43] Consultative [Executive] Committee Minutes, 23 June 1925, 221/1/2/1, EIA Papers; Caillard to Hewins, 2 Sept. 1925, 88/177, HP; Arthur Dearle to Hewins, 17 Sept. 1925, 88/185, HP; Hunsdon to Hewins, 30 Oct. 1925, 88/221–2, HP.

divorced from sectional interests', would appeal both to the electorate and to subscribers. It would be *'much better* to have *no Members of Parliament at all* than to have only Unionists. Everything the E.I.A. does or says will come before the electorate *in an entirely different light,* if it is equally supported by prominent members of the Labour Party'.[44]

In August Malcolmson suggested that four Labour representatives, J. H. Thomas, Dr Haden Guest, Frank Hodges, and Robert Young, all Labour MPs who appear to have had some connection with BEPO and were believed by the Tariff Reformers to support the extension of safeguarding, be added to the EIA Executive. He claimed support from Amery, Neville Chamberlain, and 'some of the "young party" of Unionist MPs'.[45]

Hewins, less than lukewarm at the proposal, suggested instead W. A. Appleton, right-wing secretary of the Lace-Makers' Union between 1896 and 1907 and secretary of the General Federation of Trade Unions thereafter. Appleton had supported the safeguarding application by the Federation of Lace and Embroidery Employers' Associations earlier in the year,[46] and was widely known to 'prefer . . . a policy of industrial co-operation to one based on class warfare'.[47] But Malcolmson, who knew him well, realized that by joining the EIA on his own Appleton would lose credibility and influence, and continued to press for 'some definitely "Labour" man of eminence', even suggesting an approach to Ramsay Macdonald. In December he complained that a circular letter to MPs had betrayed 'an attitude towards political affairs which was not contemplated on the formation of the Association'. His hand was strengthened by the news that the ICA had taken strong exception to the proposed take-over by the EIA, which in ICA opinion 'held such definite and pronounced political views'.[48]

Approval being given for preliminary negotiations, Sir Hugo Hirst had by mid-December consulted Guest, Young, Hodges, and Major A. G. Church, replacement for an unreceptive Thomas, and had drafted alterations to the EIA manifesto which would allow them 'to come on to the E.I.A. platform'. A meeting between the four Labour representatives and Hirst, Morgan, and Herbert Williams established that Guest and his companions preferred prohibitions to import duties and an extension of safeguarding, 'but it was suggested that

[44] EIA Minutes, 15 July 1925, copy in 88/81, HP; Malcolmson to Hewins, 10 Aug. 1925, 88/141–2, HP; Malcolmson to Hewins, 17 Sept. 1925, 88/183–4, HP (Malcolmson's emphasis).

[45] Malcolmson to Hewins, 10 Aug. 1925. On the BEPO connection, see *The Times,* 2 Nov. 1926, 9. The debate on Cunliffe-Lister's new safeguarding procedure in Feb. 1925 touched a raw nerve in a Labour Party sensitive to imports made with sweated labour. Only Guest, however, went so far as to support the Conservative Government. See R. W. D. Boyce, *British Capitalism* 83–4. It should be observed that the EIA papers clearly mention Frank Hodges of the Miners' Federation when John Hodge of the Iron and Steel Trades Confederation might seem a more likely candidate.

[46] Board of Trade, *Report of the Lace and Embroidery Committee,* Cmd. 2403 (1925), 2.

[47] A. Prochaska, *History of the General Federation of Trade Unions 1899–1980* (1982), 157–63, esp. 162.

[48] Malcolmson to Hewins, 17 Sept. 1925, 88/183–4, HP; GPC Minutes, 1 and 15 Dec. 1925, Hannon Papers.

some common ground might be found'. Hirst felt it necessary for any further decision to rest on a meeting between the Labour men and the full EIA General Purposes Committee, but in the event the main task of further revisions to the manifesto was left to Hunsdon, Hannon, and Williams.[49] The result, a remarkably bland document, dwelt on unemployment, wages, and unfair foreign competition. Empire preference was mentioned only twice, each time alongside 'the employment of non-tariff preferences, which should be used to the full'.[50]

This put both the main objectives of the EIA, safeguarding and preference, at a considerable discount, and it is surprising that so many on the Executive were prepared to countenance the document. But on 1 February 1926 'approval of the labour scheme' was carried *nem con*,[51] and the Committee placed their resignations in the hands of the chairman, who, with the assistance of Morgan and Hirst, was to reconstitute it with a free hand.[52] Meeting with Guest on 4 February, these three agreed with his desire to 'balance[e] the political elements [on the new Executive] as far as possible', and invitations were sent to Caillard, Gretton, Hannon, Hewins, Hills, Hirst, Machin, Malcolmson, and Morgan, together with Guest, Church, Hodges, and Young. Furthermore, it was agreed that Guest should be appointed co-secretary, to avoid the 'distinctly Conservative colour' imparted by Williams being the EIA's only executive officer. In Hunsdon's words, 'the Conservative MPs should be drastically cut down in order not to swamp the Labour men'.[53]

Reaction was dramatic, and to Hunsdon baffling. Hewins, Cottier, and Peto resigned from the EIA before the meeting of 4 February, Gretton and Caillard shortly afterwards. Hunsdon initially ascribed this to a misunderstanding. He had evidently been misled by the silence of opponents to the scheme at the meeting of 1 February; as he wrote to Hewins, 'I thought you were in favour of the new scheme and . . . that your silence on Monday gave consent to all that we were doing'. To Cottier, he admitted that he did not understand 'your point that the new scheme is not in harmony with the objects for which the EIA was formed and is against the considered policy of the Conservative Party'.[54]

Whilst Hunsdon insisted that his role was merely to carry out the wishes of the Executive, and whilst he recognized that the new policy would have to come before a general meeting of members and subscribers, his stance was naïve, just

[49] GPC Minutes, 15 Dec. 1925, 19 and 26 Jan. 1926, Hannon Papers.

[50] 'Draft Manifesto. Empire Industries Association. As revised at Conference between Lord Hunsdon, Dr. Haden Guest, M.P., Major Church, Mr. P. J. Hannon, M.P., and Mr. H. G. Williams, M.P.', 23 Jan. 1926, 89/204–5, HP.

[51] Hunsdon to Hewins, 4 Feb. 1926, 89/222–3, HP.

[52] Letter from Herbert Williams inviting certain EIA members to serve on Provisional Executive Committee, 5 Feb. 1926, copy in 89/227–8, HP.

[53] Special Sub-Committee Minutes, 4 Feb. 1926, 221/1/2/1, EIA Papers; Hunsdon to Hewins, 4 Feb. 1926; 89/224–5, HP.

[54] Hunsdon to Hewins, 4 Feb. 1926, 89/222–3, HP; Hunsdon to Cottier, 4 Feb. 1926, 89/218–21, HP.

as his hope that Hewins, who 'knows most about these things', would continue to 'direct the policy' of the EIA was short-sighted.[55] The very letter-heading of the Association bore the legend, 'For the Extension of Empire Preference and the Safeguarding of Home Industries'. Protectionists who pressed for increased safeguarding provision would scarcely have retained any credibility with a reluctant government had they muted their demands. Furthermore, Hunsdon's understanding 'that both Amery and N. Chamberlain desired and still desire to see our Assn. as the organising head of a national and non-party movement' was deficient if he imagined that such committed Tariff Reformers would concede to any retreat of this kind. Rhetoric aside, the national and non-party movement desired by Amery[56] had to be based on Chamberlainite principles, not diluted out of recognition merely to achieve consensus. One did not achieve Tariff Reform by abandoning it.

Immediately he learned of the results of Hirst's early meeting with the Labour representatives, a meeting held, significantly, at GEC's Magnet House rather than the EIA offices to avoid compromising them, John Gretton discerned the basic incompatibility between the two sides:

> The Labour people require that all measures of safeguarding and protection shall be eliminated from any statement of objects . . . and . . . they strictly limited their adhesion to preference for Colonial goods . . . to preference on existing duties. Nothing was indicated by them to replace the proposals and objects to which they raise objection.[57]

His opinion that 'there is nothing yet for the Empire Industries people to consider', his reflection that it was 'futile to agree upon a formula of words without considering what is to be done to carry them into effect', were correct.[58] The new Provisional Executive Committee met three times between February and April. Immediately, Hunsdon and Young clashed over the interpretation of the revised manifesto. Young held 'that it was not the intention of the Association to advocate the imposition of Tariffs with a view to giving preferences to the Dominions', but merely to give preference if tariffs were imposed. To Hunsdon, the manifesto showed that the EIA advocated the imposition of tariffs for the purpose of imperial preference. It was left to the two co-secretaries to come up with a proposal outlining concrete methods acceptable to both sides.[59] By the third meeting, it was evident that the attempt had failed. The Unionist members of the Committee insisted that the introduction of tariffs and preference must form the 'principal plank' of EIA policy, whilst the Labour members were well

[55] Hunsdon to Hewins, 4 Feb. 1926, 89/222–3, HP.

[56] Hunsdon to Hewins, 4 Feb. 1926, 89/224–5, HP. Amery's diary for 20 Jan. recorded that Hirst and Morgan had signed a statement of policy with the Labour group 'which, with only a word or two altered, is the one we drafted at the meetings at Neville's house 18 months ago'; J. Barnes and D. Nicholson (eds.), *The Leo Amery Diaries*, i. *1896–1929* (1980), 439.

[57] Gretton to Hewins, 26 Jan. 1926, 89/208, HP.

[58] Ibid.   [59] Provisional Executive Committee, 24 Feb. 1926, 221/1/2/1, EIA Papers.

aware that 'even if they themselves were willing to go a long way in this direction, they could not hope to gain any volume of support from the Labour Party'.[60]

Even this was not quite the end of the matter. Serious attempts were still being made to accommodate the Labour group at this last meeting, and the hope was expressed 'that at some future time it might be possible to come together again'.[61] After this, Croft maintained, certain EIA members 'still wished to angle for Socialist support', and in his memoirs he gave this as his reason for resigning from the EIA at the end of July.[62] Gretton's version of Croft's resignation was consistent with this, but more revealing. Apparently prompted by Morgan, Hunsdon wrote to Croft suggesting 'that he should not be a member of the Council, but that he might serve on a secret propaganda committee; the names of the members of this body not being published'. Croft, from the days of his National Party onwards well known for his anti-union and anti-socialist beliefs, may well have been anathema to those who still hoped for some rapprochement with Labour; and Morgan's was clearly a thinly veiled attempt to marginalize him.[63]

There was clearly an affinity between Malcolmson's plan to recruit Labour members to the EIA and the 'progressive' outlook of the more pro-labour productioneer or the corporatist—the ideal of co-operation between labour, capital, and the state in the formulation of an economic policy which denied antagonistic interests between classes. Malcolmson, with interests in stockbroking, agriculture, sugar beet, and flax-growing, was a founder member of the Industrial Peace Union. Morgan, his close associate, was an engineer with an interest in the technical aspects of labour management, and had been a technical adviser to Lloyd George's wartime Ministry of Munitions. Hirst was to be one of Alfred Mond's 'co-adjutors' in the Mond–Turner talks which began in 1927. All three were fervent and active imperialists prominent in BEPO, Malcolmson being a 'co-founder' and Morgan being chairman throughout the 1920s. As we have seen, immediately after the War BEPO's programme had integrated the themes of Empire economic unity, agricultural expansion, and co-operation between labour and capital into a collectivist package with corporatist undertones.[64] Whether such influences adequately explain the support of Hannon is more doubtful. It is true that he was in close orbit with Docker and the similarly inclined Sir Edward Manville—he was appointed a director of BSA in

[60] Provisional Executive Committee, 19 Apr. 1926, 221/1/2/1, EIA Papers.
[61] Ibid.   [62] Lord Croft, *My Life of Strife* (London, n.d.), 178.
[63] Gretton to Hewins, 28 July 1926, 90/75, HP. Croft opposed radical trade unionism and abhorred socialism. See W. D. Rubinstein, 'Henry Page Croft and the National Party, 1917–22', *Journal of Contemporary History*, 9 (1974), 139–42.
[64] For Malcolmson, see *Who Was Who*, iv; also *The Times*, 7 Dec. 1926, 12. For Morgan, see *Who Was Who*, iii. For Hirst, see K. Middlemas, *Politics in Industrial Society* (1979), 208; H. F. Gospel, 'Employers' Labour Policy: A Study of the Mond-Turner Talks 1927–33', in R. P. T. Davenport-Hines (ed.), *Business in the Age of Depression and War* (1990), 206–23.

1924—and had connections with agriculture, but he was also associated with the BCU and NUM, where pro-labour sentiments were less in evidence.[65] A political animal, he seems to have been capable of occupying any position within the productioneer-corporatist spectrum according to circumstance.

The opponents of Malcolmson's scheme were, naturally, not opposed to the vision of high wages through high output. Caillard and Hewins had after all been pioneers of many of the ideas central to the 'trade-warrior' and productioneer mentalities. In 1918 and 1919 Caillard had feared that Allan Smith's anti-labour posture in the BCU was counter-productive. Croft had even shown some brief sympathy with corporatist ideas. After the War, *National Opinion*, the organ of his National Party, had regularly gone beyond an emphasis on high output and productioneering to advocate that each industry should be organized into a trade association with a joint council of employers and employees.[66] But Caillard had been critical of trade unions before 1914, and Croft's attitude to labour hardened as the War receded.[67] Peto and Gretton had interests in industries not noted for enlightened labour relations,[68] and belonged to the 'die-hard' wing of the Conservative Party. Broadly, those who opposed Malcolmson seem to have had less 'progressive' attitudes towards organized labour than those who supported him. More generally, this suggests that the opposing factions on the EIA Executive may have responded differently to the labour troubles of 1925 and 1926, the one seeking conciliation and the other proclaiming constitutionalism in the face of bolshevism.

But in a sense the rift was less complicated, centring on the practical possibilities of an accord with parliamentary Labour and the consequences for the EIA's awkward relationship with the Conservative Party. The Labour issue exposed an underlying difference in political realism. It was perhaps inherent in the 'progressive' outlook that its adherents should underestimate the political difficulties, but support from Chamberlain and Amery shows that they were not alone.

All the opponents of the scheme, with the exception of Cottier, had experience of the pre-war tariff controversy. Generally, they were more conservative than their adversaries in their desire to work within the framework of the official Party. Croft, Gretton, Peto, and Hewins in particular would have felt their position compromised by an institutional association with Labour MPs. Before the War, it had been union leaders, not Labour MPs, whom the Tariff Reformers had attempted to recruit into a national and imperial movement intended to rise

---

[65] *National Union of Manufacturers (Incorporated): Descriptive and Classified Directory of Members*, 1926 edn.; R. P. T. Davenport-Hines, *Dudley Docker* (Cambridge, 1984), 218–19.

[66] W. D. Rubinstein, 'Henry Page Croft', 141–2.

[67] I am indebted to Alan Sykes for information on Croft. For Caillard, see above, Ch. 5.

[68] Basil Peto had interests in civil and railway contracting. Gretton was chairman of the highly capitalized brewers, Bass, Ratcliffe and Gretton, with an issued capital of £2.7m in 1916.

above politics. A formal relationship with the political expression of Labour, especially now that it had become the main opposition party, was quite different.

If this was not enough, there was also the tactical realism of the proposal. The Tariff-Reform veterans had already lived through earlier attempts to convert labour, and had suffered the delusion that the organized labour movement was out of touch with working people. In private, Chamberlain and the Tariff Commission had tried to convert moderate union leaders. In the country, the TRL's message had centred on wages and employment. In the press, Tariff Reform had meant 'work for all' and an Empire family. More with an eye towards Labour than towards entrenched Liberalism, they had sought to raise the tariff above politics, to transcend party with a great and noble national policy. And they had failed. To them, the EIA's efforts to secure co-operation with Labour politicians were nothing but a futile re-run of earlier disappointments. As Croft remembered, 'Weary months were wasted'.[69]

At a time when there were some indications that Labour was becoming less hostile to safeguarding and imperial policy,[70] it is unremarkable that those with corporatist or quasi-corporatist inclinations should have underestimated the difficulties. More surprising is the lapse of judgement by Chamberlain, Amery, and Hannon, all of whom, of course, were well-used to the exigencies of Tariff Reform politics. It seems likely that, having deliberately distanced themselves from the day-to-day affairs of the EIA because of their position in the official opposition, and then the Government, Chamberlain and Amery simply blundered, imagining that a national movement could be forged without the sacrifice of long-standing Chamberlainite principles. Afterwards, Amery conceded that the negotiations with Labour had been a 'mistake'.[71] Hannon, too, had experienced Tariff Reform politics before the War,[72] and in other respects he kept within the bounds of Party propriety. But, a lover of intrigue, he was always able to face both ways. Momentarily, his political opportunism faltered, and he simply backed the wrong side. As with his later flirtation with Beaverbrook's Empire Crusade, it did him little long-term harm.

Though it was no intention of any of the supporters of the Labour scheme to estrange the EIA from the official Conservatism, the defeat of that scheme was necessarily a factor in the process whereby the EIA recognized the umbilical cord which joined it to the Conservative Party. In one sense the metaphor is not apt, for the infant showed definite signs of adolescence. But the Labour issue cleared EIA minds wonderfully, led directly to the ascendancy of Croft within the Association, and thus helped to define and limit the extent to which the EIA

---

[69] Croft, *My Life of Strife*, 178.

[70] See R. W. D. Boyce, *British Capitalism*, 83–90.

[71] According to Hewins. See R. D. Herzog, 'The Conservative Party and Protectionist Politics', 500.

[72] Hannon was a vice-president of the TRL, 1910–14.

would be an embarrassment to the Baldwin Government's limited policy on Tariff Reform.

<h2 style="text-align:center">III</h2>

Estranged from the EIA over the Labour issue, Hewins was also convinced that its intended tactics of large-scale propaganda on safeguarding were misconceived. In the public mind, safeguarding seemed a procedure established in statute and practice. An appeal to the country was 'cut from under our feet when . . . the Government in office is carrying out the policy, and the obstacles in the way of further development are mainly of a technical character which are not very suitable for popular exposition'. Since the passing of the 1921 Act, he had found 'no great demand for propagandist meetings in the country'.[73] The EIA would therefore be more useful as a research and information bureau, giving technical assistance to industries in their safeguarding applications, and high-powered lectures to informed audiences. Industry's need for such assistance was increased by the Anglo-German treaty of 1925, which blocked safeguarding against currency depreciation and threw the onus of any application onto the other criteria in the White Paper—subsidies, bounties, and 'inferior conditions of employment and labour' abroad.[74]

Hewins's assessment of the implications of the 1925 treaty was accurate, and shared by the Board of Trade.[75] His belief that the SIA took the wind out of the Tariff Reformers' sails in their public appeals was also probably not without foundation. Nevertheless, he was over-optimistic about the Baldwin Government's willingness to extend safeguarding. Following a meeting with Baldwin late in 1925, he discerned 'widespread agreement' that safeguarding 'should be carried out only when and where it is really desirable, taking the trades or groups of trades seriatim'.[76] Baldwin having apparently endorsed a pragmatic and empirical approach, Hewins's main fear was that now the indiscriminate application of the crude, flat-rate $33\frac{1}{3}$ per cent of the Safeguarding Act would 'create quite as many enemies as friends, and may lead to the indefinite postponement of remedial measures' when applied to large, complex industries.

---

[73] 'Mr. Hewins' Promised Statement', n.d., 89/141–7, HP.

[74] Ibid.; see also Board of Trade, *Safeguarding of Industries: Procedure and Enquiries*, Cmd. 2327 (1926), 3.

[75] In more precise terms, the Board of Trade's legal advisers considered that a treaty with a most-favoured-nation clause was not infringed if a duty was confined to goods actually dumped, since the 'special conditions' of dumping could be avoided by the exporter. But the pre-1924 anti-dumping duties were levied on whole classes of (usually German) goods because of exchange depreciation, and this would not be possible under a treaty with a most-favoured-nation clause because currency depreciation would not be considered an avoidable special condition in which the exporter was culpable. See 'Anti-Dumping Legislation. Note by the President of the Board of Trade' and accompanying memorandum, dated June 1931, BT 55/58/9, PRO.

[76] Hewins to Baldwin, 3 Nov. 1925, 4, 88/243, HP.

A safeguarding application based on a flat-rate tariff would lead to the applying industry being riven by internal division and antagonism, which would bring the whole safeguarding policy into public disrepute. His experience of Milner's Tariff Advisory Committee in 1923 led him to believe the Board of Trade incapable of designing a more sophisticated tariff, based on labour content or degree of manufacture. Manufacturers, too, were ill-equipped, since a safeguarding application required 'information which it is not in their power to obtain, which in fact can only be obtained ... by ... Government'.[77] In short, rather than mistrusting Baldwin, Hewins feared that the main threat to safeguarding was its own intrinsic divisiveness in preventing the build-up of a consensus in manufacturing industry.

Gretton's opinion that Hewins's technical bureau might be an alternative forced on the EIA because 'funds are insufficient for the original intention',[78] and Hannon's appreciation of the constraints imposed on the EIA by Government policy,[79] indicate that there was some early sympathy on the EIA Executive for Hewins's approach. However, that Hewins's confidence in Baldwin was to prove misplaced goes a considerable way in vindicating the EIA's aim of escalating Tariff Reform propaganda. At the same time, Hewins's own preferred strategy was to a considerable extent self-seeking, tantamount to resurrecting the Tariff Commission in the clothes of the EIA. But he was to find the EIA unreceptive. When he had had Chamberlain's ear, there had been little difficulty in impressing his own plans, methods, and objectives on the Commission. Now, with his strongest supporters, Caillard and Cottier, embroiled in the resignations over the Labour issue, he was at his weakest. The businessmen in whose hands lay the direction of the EIA might defer to him on items of technical complexity, but they no longer felt that degree of dependence and need for guidance that had ensured for the Tariff Commission such a long period of internal harmony. If the businessmen of the 1920s were still subordinate to the politicians, they had at least escaped the schoolroom.

For some time there was confusion within the EIA over what exactly Hewins was about; his cryptic talk of 'a great scheme in preparation'[80] fuelled speculation that he was undertaking work for Unionist Central Office, particularly undesirable at the time of the negotiations with the Labour group in view of the 'new non-party character' of the Association.[81] In fact, however, Hewins was now a spent force. For some years he had been attempting to find a buyer for the collected papers of the Tariff Commission, which he regarded as his own personal property. But successor propaganda groups had been uninterested, not

[77] Ibid. 5–8, 88/244–7, HP.
[78] Gretton to Hewins, 6 Feb. 1926, 89/229–32, HP.
[79] See above, 362.
[80] Quoted in Hunsdon to Cottier, 4 Feb. 1926, 89/218–21, HP.
[81] H. G. Williams to Hewins, 25 Feb. 1926, 89/251, HP.

surprisingly since the price was high and, in spite of Hewins's blustering, much of the information on offer must have been very dated. A career propagandist, it seems likely that he had little provision for old age. His actions became increasingly desperate, even to the extent of a violent attack on Caillard, his most loyal and generous supporter, for 'betraying' him. He was saved by Cottier, who secured him a directorship of the Victoria Wine Company at £1,000 p.a., which at least allowed him to write his memoirs in peace.[82]

Under Croft, called in to chair the Association after the Labour débâcle, the campaign for safeguarding and preference escalated. Most of those resigning over the Labour issue rejoined. Staunch Tariff Reformers Lord Lloyd and Shirley Benn were appointed to the Executive, serving alongside Hannon, Hirst, Cottier, and Sir Harry McGowan of ICI. Effort was concentrated in the centre, the formation of provincial branches being suspended to conserve resources.[83] In the provinces, meetings were usually hosted by local Party associations, the Primrose League, and various debating societies and imperial organizations,[84] though certain areas were singled out for intensive campaigns, such as the Midlands (thirty-seven meetings) and Manchester (twenty-five meetings) in 1927, and a 'special series' in Yorkshire in 1928, whilst the successful open-air meetings in nine London parks in the summer of 1927 was extended to Manchester in the late summer of 1928. By 1929 EIA speakers were addressing sixty meetings in Manchester and the North-West each month. Under Herbert Williams the publicity department was expanded, until in 1929 four million pamphlets were issued.[85]

Croft's own role in this activity was little short of immense. An indefatigable speaker, he appeared on platforms throughout the country as many as three or four times a week. His letters to the press from the EIA's offices, presumably ghosted by Williams and his staff, appeared nearly as frequently. Above we have suggested that in *The Times* the EIA was accorded at least five times the coverage that BEPO was.[86] The inclusion of Croft would double or treble that differential; and in the provincial press the disparity was even greater.

Croft's message was essentially simple and centred upon unemployment. He highlighted the growing imbalance of visible trade, from £124m in 1924 to £465m in 1926.[87] Was it not absurd to suffer unemployment of 1.4m at the same

[82] Caillard to Hewins, 28 Feb. and 3 Mar. 1927, 91/1–2, HP. See also F. Bromwick to Hewins, 3 Aug. 1927, 91/50, HP. There is some uncertainty about the precise remuneration. At the AGM in May 1928, the shareholders voted Hewins and Cottier £2,500 each after tax. But it may be an indication of the obligation he felt to the Company that Hewins only accepted some £500 p.a. See Victoria Wine Co. to Messrs. Ogden, Hibberd Bull and Langdon (their auditors), 91/182, HP.

[83] EIA Executive Committee, 28 Oct. 1926, 17 Feb. 1927, 221/1/2/1, EIA Papers.

[84] Croft, *My Life of Strife*, 179.

[85] EIA, *Annual Reports*, 1927, 1928, and 1929.

[86] See above, 337.

[87] Croft to Ed., *Evening News*, 15 Jan. 1927. Whilst the 1926 figure was obviously based on the *Board of Trade Journal*'s estimate of £466m, the origin of the 1924 figure is unknown. Both were higher

time as manufactures flooded in from abroad? The best solution, in the prevailing political circumstances, was to extend safeguarding and preference to the limits of Baldwin's election pledge. Indeed, how much worse would unemployment be but for the safeguarding provisions that had already been introduced?

Croft took as his text those industries which were held to have made strong progress under safeguarding. Pre-eminent amongst these was the motor industry. The car producers had expanded steadily whilst effecting marked price reductions throughout the safeguarding period, a fact which had long been used by the Association of British Motor Manufacturers and Traders in their protectionist propaganda.[88] Of course, the possibility that protection only served to lessen the price reductions made possible by technical and organizational progress was, in terms of the public debate, a refinement so complex that the Tariff Reformers could ignore it with impunity. As Sir Robert Horne recognized, when defending safeguarding and the McKenna duties against the threat of abolition by the incoming Labour Government in October 1929, the industry 'provides our best illustration'.[89] Even Churchill tacitly admitted the same point when extending the McKenna duties to include commercial vehicles in 1926:

The motor-car associations, bodies representative of the users of these vehicles, commercial and otherwise, have made no sort of protest. On the contrary, he had received a deputation at which the representatives of the users said they were making no opposition to this particular proposal. If they looked at the effect of the McKenna duties, which were re-imposed last year, on the motor-car trade, it was quite clear that there had not been that rise in price which would be the necessary foundation for all the arguments which were used about the hardships to the farmer, of the difficulty of carrying wool from the docks, and the troubles of the brewer.[90]

It was also an industry whose leaders were virtually unanimous on the benefits of protection—only Sir Percival Perry of the Ford Motor Co. Ltd. professed to be unconcerned at the threat from Snowden in 1929, and of course he was vulnerable to the criticism that his real desire was the free importation of component parts from his parent company in the USA.[91] Furthermore, both William Morris, who had become very despondent when the McKenna duties were allowed to lapse under the first Labour Government,[92] and Herbert Austin

than the estimates currently accepted, on account of their valuing imports c.i.f. instead of f.o.b. See B. R. Mitchell, *Abstract of British Historical Statistics* (Cambridge, 1962), Table 16B, 335 for the Board of Trade series; B. R. Mitchell, *British Historical Statistics* (Cambridge, 1988), Table 15B, 873, for currently accepted estimates.

[88] Association of British Motor Manufacturers Ltd., 'The British Motor Car Industry: The Progress of Touring Car Manufacture under a Protective Tariff' (1923), esp. sections 9–10.
[89] Horne to Croft, 4 Oct. 1929, 1/14, Croft Papers.
[90] Churchill in House of Commons, as quoted in *The Times*, 8 June 1926, 8–9.
[91] Croft to Ed., *Yorkshire Post*, 10 Mar. 1930.
[92] R. C. Whiting, *The View from Cowley* (Oxford, 1983), 33–7.

were firm advocates of protection beyond the motor industry. Croft arranged for their views to be aired in the press at regular intervals. Since the re-imposition of the McKenna duties, announced Morris, passenger-car output had increased by 35 per cent, exports by 167 per cent, and prices had fallen by 22 per cent. Lower wages to meet continental competition were not the answer: 'I am strongly in favour of safeguarding all round'.[93] Austin took an even longer view. Since 1915 turnover had increased sixfold, employment and exports fivefold, average earnings by 150 per cent, and prices had fallen by 62 per cent. The McKenna duties and the stability and security they bred had transformed attitudes in the industry. Austin '[could not] understand' why safeguarding was not extended more widely—other industries were 'entitled . . . to demand such equality'.[94]

Even more important to Croft than propaganda, however, was the mobilization of support in the Party and amongst MPs. At its conferences at Scarborough in 1926 and Cardiff in 1927 the delegates of the National Union gave him solid support. At Yarmouth in 1928 he secured a National Union resolution in favour of safeguarding iron and steel, always a main objective of the EIA. His 'direct challenge to our leaders' was carried with only a handful of dissentients. By July 1927 the EIA had 160 members sitting in the Commons, and by the 1929 election the 'large majority' of Unionist MPs sat on its parliamentary committee. By late 1928, an EIA memorial on the steel industry attracted the signatures of 200 MPs and was accompanied by a large meeting at the Albert Hall led by Sir Robert Horne.[95]

IV

What, then, was the nature of the phoenix that rose from the ashes of the Labour crisis? Clearly, the EIA's organizers were intent on a large, national propaganda. Hewins's narrower conception of a technical bureau offering assistance to industries applying for safeguarding did not satisfy the aspirations of the bulk of the EIA's members, though if Hewins had rejoined there might well have been some subsidiary activity of this kind. Croft did press Hewins to rejoin the EIA, but not until July 1928, well after the higher-profile activities that he disparaged had become irreversible.[96]

But what kind of high-profile organization should the Association be? As the EIA regrouped after the departure of Haden-Guest and his colleagues, there was still sufficient representation of BEPO and the defunct BCU on its Executive to raise the possibility that its future development would bear a marked similarity

[93] Morris to Croft, in *Daily Mail*, 16 Sept. 1927.
[94] *Birmingham Post*, 21 Aug. 1928.
[95] Croft, *My Life of Strife*, 179–82.
[96] Croft to Hewins, 27 July 1928, 91/131, HP.

to one or other of them. It did not. The experience of both these organizations had provided lessons in what to avoid. In spite of the continued participation of Morgan and Malcolmson, the EIA avoided those large and insubstantial conceptions of imperial integration that were associated with the primary producers of BEPO. On the other hand, the BCU's experience showed that the new body stood to gain little and risked losing much if it adopted the Union's harsh anti-labour stance. The BCU strategy of developing a truly independent wing of industrial MPs within the Commons was similarly unattractive. In spite of running its own candidates at elections, the BCU had not achieved any monopoly of influence over the Industrial Group, and ultimately it had been forced to work within the orbit of backbench parliamentary Conservatism. In large part the EIA would do the same.

Amery and Neville Chamberlain had originally envisaged the EIA as akin to the old TRL. Certainly the underlying motives behind EIA policy were less sectional than those of the BCU and NUM. But, in spite of its very title, the activities of the Association were, until well into 1930, less overtly imperial than those of the Edwardian TRL. The higher proportion of industrial MPs in the Conservative Party than before the War reduced the importance of Free Traders within the Party—a new-style TRL would be from the start a stronger force within the parliamentary Party than the old. But at the same time the attempt to proselytize the broader social-imperialist collectivism of the Milnerite TRL stood in danger of arousing tensions within the narrower parliamentary Conservatism of the 1920s, that narrowness in part forced by electoral considerations, but in part also autonomous, being itself closely related to the continuing rise of the industrialist within the parliamentary Party.

Croft originally intended to tap the pockets of 'a dozen or so of the biggest men'.[97] The only surviving evidence on the precise sources of EIA funds, relating to the period from July 1926 to June 1927, shows that seventeen contributors of over £100 furnished £3,525, or 68.4 per cent of income.[98] Whilst the list did not suggest that the EIA had at this time broken into radically new areas of support for Tariff Reform, it did reflect a character more akin to the wider approach of the Tariff Commission and the League than to the narrower approach of the NUM and the BCU. The imperial interest was highlighted by contributions from the British Sugar Refiners' Association (£100), reflecting the influence of Morgan, Malcolmson, and BEPO; Sir James Mills, chairman of the Union Steamship Co. of New Zealand (£100); and Sir Arthur Myers, London director of the National Bank of New Zealand (£100). Within a more domestic orbit, there were those Tariff Reformers who had long stood on the imperial wing of the movement—Sir Joseph Lawrence's Linotype and Machinery Ltd. (£100); G. Holt-Thomas, newspaper proprietor, agriculturalist, founder of the Associ-

[97] Croft to Amery, 29 Jan. 1924, 1/2, Croft Papers.
[98] 'EIA Subscriptions, July 1926–June 1927', 221/1/4/1, EIA Papers.

ation of British Motor Manufacturers 'to demand a duty on foreign cars'[99] and of Imperial Airways (£100); Sir Otto Beit (£500); Sir Hugo Hirst (£500); and Sir Charles Cottier (£500). More narrowly domestic considerations were probably stronger with other well-known protectionists—Sir Richard Cooper, chemical manufacturer and earlier supporter of Croft's National Party (£100); Sir Robert Horne (£100); A. E. Hills (£500); the Morgan Crucible Co. (£125); the Millom and Askham Hematite Iron Co. (£100); and the Wine and Spirit Trade Defence Fund (£100). Less predictable, perhaps, was the inclusion of Harold Sanderson, a shipowner with largely North Atlantic interests (£100); James Nelson and Co., Nelson cotton manufacturers (£100); and J. and A. Scrimgeour, City stockbrokers (£300).[100]

The short period covered by this list may give rise to some distortion; the omission of Caillard and Vickers stands out immediately. Nevertheless, it is noticeable that nearly 40 per cent of funds during these months came from four individuals—Beit, Cottier, Hills, and Hirst. Doubtless these were not the last large subscribers to enter the lists: in October 1927 the Society of Motor Manufacturers and Traders agreed to subscribe £200 or £250 through Sir Edward Manville.[101]

More importantly, we cannot know whether financial support widened as the Association grew in the late 1920s. The EIA never had that closed, conspiratorial image that did so much to ensure that the BCU's finances remained highly concentrated, and it may even have attracted contributions from the professional middle classes and minor country society that had supported the old TRL. Open-air rallies and summer events gave the EIA a pleasant social aspect—the BCU could never have held afternoon tea dances in the Pump Room at Bath.[102] By the same token, it is doubtful that the EIA was as attractive to small firms as was the NUM. The social composition of its council was broader than that of the NUM, and included landowners, statesmen, and imperialists amongst whom lesser and provincial industrialists might feel uneasy. Its imperial aims were wider than those of the NUM, and its industrial aims narrower. It provided no services to members beyond political support for the extension of safeguarding. There was no willingness to step far beyond tariffs and engage in the promotion of sectional industrial interests over a wide field of political activity (taxation, labour issues, export promotion, etc.), no provision of services to members, and no close relationship with employers' associations on labour matters. Thus, the EIA may have been to an extent successful in attracting funds from a wider constituency. But even if it was not, and remained dependent on large per capita contributions

[99] *Who Was Who*, iii. 1929–1940.
[100] *Sell's Directory of Registered Telegraphic Addresses* (1927 edn.) also lists a J. Scrimgeour and Sons Ltd., Dundee produce importers. The City firm seems the more likely, but in any case there may have been a connection.
[101] Finance Committee Minutes, 12 Oct. 1927, 221/1/4/1, EIA Papers.
[102] Executive Committee Minutes, 24 Nov. 1925, 221/1/2/1, EIA Papers.

from a relatively small number of firms,[103] its character and its policies avoided being obviously coloured by any such dependency.

Thus, under Croft, a hybrid was produced. The EIA was distinctly more of an industrial group than the TRL had been, but distinctly less of one than the BCU and NUM. If its funds were as narrowly based as those of the BCU, it did not apply them to the same narrow, sectional ends. Its accent was more imperial than that of the BCU and NUM, but less than that of the TRL. Its strategy of gaining support in Parliament was less radical than that of the BCU, but more pervasive and persistent. The EIA caught the flood tide, and its policies and tactics can be seen as an essay in pragmatism. In this process, though arguably the most successful pressure group in the history of Tariff Reform, the EIA was nevertheless the most accommodationist of them all. Even with overwhelming parliamentary support, the businessmen and imperialists of the EIA remained impotent to effect a radical change in British politics. The history of the EIA can be analysed in two different ways, both equally valid. Here was the assembly of a broad coalition for the final assault, an assault to be launched on increasingly favourable terrain. But here also was the last act in a drama of business subservience to politics.

Nevertheless, industrial representation dominated the EIA council, many important industrialists were its allies both in and out of Parliament, and its campaigns for safeguarding were unremitting. Furthermore, those campaigns could be specific to certain industries, as with steel; though it is important to recognize that the prominence given to this industry in EIA propaganda was as much, if not more, due to its symbolic and strategic importance in advancing the whole policy of safeguarding as it was to promoting its own sectional interest. Other industries, too, such as lace and embroidery, received consistent EIA support. In June 1927 the EIA agreed to a propaganda campaign on behalf of the match, motor, and glove industries. This would be 'nominally' conducted by the Association, which would 'benefit by the publicity accorded to their name', but would be financed by the industries concerned and handled by an advertising agency.[104]

This heavy accent on industrial representation and industrial objectives was a pragmatic response to political circumstances. It was not an indication that the spirit of insular protectionism so feared by Amery and Hunsdon[105] dominated within the EIA. When the council members were announced in October 1926 *The Observer* split them into four categories. There were 'statesmen' such as Sir Robert Horne, Sir Hamar Greenwood, Sir George Courthope, Selborne, Londonderry, and Desborough—it might be added that the last four were also prominent agricultural protectionists. There were 'captains of industry' such as

[103] Certainly this seems to have been the position in 1930. See below, 417–18.
[104] Special Executive Committee Meeting, 1 June 1927, 221/1/2/1, EIA Papers.
[105] See above, 363, and R. D. Herzog, 'The Conservative Party and Protectionist Politics', 493.

Waring, Invernairn, Sir Felix Pole, Sir Ernest Petter, Muir Ritchie, and Sir Herbert Cayzer. There were 'city magnates' such as Hunsdon, Sir Stanley Machin, Sir Edward Stern, and Sir Arthur Shirley Benn. And there were 'imperialists', among whom were Sir Thomas MacKenzie, Sir George MacLaren Brown, Angus McDonnell, Archibald Weigall, Charles Bright, and Charles McLeod.[106] Omitted by *The Observer* was a fifth group, small but significant. Retired servicemen such as Carlyon Bellairs, Lt.-Gen. Sir Arthur Holland and Col. Sir Charles Warde were appointments reminiscent of the southern counties 'manor-house' flavour of the provincial TRL.

Few of the 'imperial' members had the same degree of metropolitan-based self-interest in expanding trade links with the Empire as McLeod, an East-India merchant. They were more reminiscent of those 'imperial' members appointed to the Tariff Commission in 1904. MacKenzie had been High Commissioner of New Zealand after an illustrious career in dominion government, culminating briefly in the premiership. McDonnell, a United Empire loyalist, had been a Canadian barrister before entering British politics. Weigall had been Governor of South Australia. Where there were business interests, they were typically not simply those of the metropolitan businessman seeking sheltered Empire markets. They were those of men who had spent a lifetime in the development of colonial resources or communications—Brown in the service of the Canadian Pacific Railway, Bright in imperial telegraph communications.

Funds were not plentiful, and it has been argued that this resulted in the EIA's main effort being parliamentary, where money was of less 'overriding import-ance'. This is perhaps misleading—the Association conducted extra-parliamen-tary propagandist activity on a large scale—but as a statement of relativities it is buttressed by Croft's own testimony that the 'most important objective . . . was to enthuse, educate, and, if necessary, convert' Unionist MPs and candidates.[107]

The result of these interacting forces was a creature different from the BCU or the NUM. The EIA would not step beyond its platform of safeguarding and preference to that constellation of related issues that concerned the businessmen of those organizations. In 1928, the Executive Committee refused a request from the Research Association of the British Rubber and Tyre Manufacturers to assist the Rubber Industry Bill as being beyond the EIA's scope, even though it favoured the measure.[108] More generally, Tariff Reform was proclaimed to be the only solution to unemployment. This had the effect of removing many of those employer concerns which were so uncongenial to labour. Relatively little emphasis was put on national economy and the need to reduce the general level

---

[106] *The Observer*, 17 Oct. 1926, omitting Bright and McLeod; see also list of council members in *The Times*, 17 Dec. 1926, p. 9.

[107] R. D. Herzog, 'The Conservative Party and Protectionist Politics', 501–2; Croft, *My Life of Strife*, 181.

[108] Executive Committee Minutes, 24 Oct. 1928, 221/1/2/1, EIA Papers.

of taxation in the interests of industrial survival, social benefits did not come under attack, and where the EIA touched upon productioneering it was to stress the benefits of a high-wage, high-volume industry rather than the industrial discipline necessary to achieve it. Thus the Association memorialized Baldwin that industrial unrest was aggravated by unemployment, short time, and wage reductions, and that industrial goodwill demanded a secure market with fair wages.[109] The contrast with the BCU, whose accent on the extreme form of the productioneer creed betrayed so clearly its sectional representation, and even with the more moderate NUM, was marked.

The EIA was also careful not to step too far beyond the confines of official Conservative policy or endanger the Government. In February 1928 Croft wrote to Baldwin urging the widest extension of safeguarding 'within the limits of the election pledge'.[110] It joined the NUM in new attempts to persuade Baldwin to reconsider safeguarding iron and steel, and in May held a large meeting at the Albert Hall. But in July EIA MPs resisted the temptation to divide the House on safeguarding the industry after a critical speech by Croft.[111] Probably deliberately to cap the escalating pressure from the EIA and NUM on iron and steel, MacDonald tabled a motion of censure to expose the inadequacy of government policy on unemployment on the 24th. Opportunistically, EIA MPs tabled an amendment in favour of safeguarding iron and steel. But Croft remained insistent that the EIA had never stepped beyond Baldwin's election pledge, nor acted in any way to damage the Party. To a member who threatened resignation he replied loftily, 'You are no doubt aware that *we* approached the Whips and tabled the modified amendment to the Vote of Censure, which apparently had the full support of the Party and upon which the Whips told.'[112] To Baldwin he wrote:

When Mr. Churchill goes out of his way to say [in speeches in the City and the Commons] that my friends and I were advocating 'protective duties placed on all foreign imports', he must know that is untrue ... whatever our personal feelings might be, not one of us has ever varied from the plan which you adopted on behalf of the Party, namely, that no industry should be protected unless it applies for protection and is granted it after consideration by some committee or tribunal.

... even if the meeting [of the National Union in September?], as I expect it will, decides to reaffirm its belief that the safeguarding of iron and steel is an urgent necessity, I appreciate the fact that you, and you alone, must dictate the strategy of the Party. Although I respectfully think that that strategy is wrong, and the advice you have received from the Central Office is deplorable, I shall do all in my power, as also I think will most of my associates, to prove my loyalty to yourself.[113]

[109] *The Times*, 17 Dec. 1926, 9.
[110] Executive Committee Minutes, 8 Feb. 1928, 221/1/2/1, EIA Papers.
[111] R. D. Herzog, 'The Conservative Party and Protectionist Politics', 503.
[112] Croft to R. A. Sanders (MP for Wells, Somerset), 26 July 1928, 1/18, Croft Papers.
[113] Croft to Baldwin, 27 July 1928, 1/3, Croft Papers.

The difference between Baldwin and the EIA was simple. Croft and his supporters wanted Baldwin to work to the limit of his election pledge. Baldwin counted electoral reasons in wishing to stay very much inside it. Ultimately, by its own lights, the EIA stayed loyal, seeing the difference as a legitimate discussion over future Party strategy within the limits of the pledge.

And loyalty was the way in which Croft portrayed it. 'I do not think the Whips ever quite appreciated the strength of feeling in the House of Commons over Iron and Steel last session,' he informed Baldwin in September. 'It was only with the greatest difficulty that our people could be restrained . . . If the Engineers, Shipbuilders, the Motor trade and other [trades] opposed it, that would be a satisfactory explanation, but we all know that serious opposition no longer exists.'[114]

In this sense, even the victory of Croft's resolution on the safeguarding of iron and steel at the National Union conference in September, his 'direct challenge to our leaders',[115] was scarcely more of an exception to this reluctance to step too far beyond the pale. Protection of the industry might be against the hidden agenda of the Government, but it did not contravene official policy as given in the White Paper. The resolution was a slap in the face, rather than a stab in the back.

Of course the EIA's action on iron and steel was a source of considerable embarrassment and annoyance to Baldwin. But even more serious would have been a similar waywardness on food duties and preference, for here the earlier election pledge did not contain the same elasticity and ambiguity that it did on industrial safeguarding. On this, the EIA was even more scrupulous in avoiding a rupture with the Front Bench.

Early in its history, the EIA rejected a close working relationship with the NUM, because the NUM's programme 'did not include the Extension of Imperial Preference or the introduction of a Tariff on the same lines as those indicated in the Constitution of the E.I.A.'[116] Privately, the EIA had no objection to the introduction of substantial preference beyond its mere extension through safeguarding under the 1919 Act, the NUM approach. In spite of this, however, its official posture on food duties remained even more within the limits of government policy than did its position on safeguarding. Until Labour's accession to power in 1929, the main weight of EIA activity in Parliament, at the National Union, and in propaganda, was centred on safeguarding. Since, ostensibly, the Government favoured the extension of safeguarding where appropriate, and had created the machinery for this, this emphasis clearly held less potential for undermining the Government than a high-profile campaign on preference when Baldwin was pledged not to introduce food taxes.

[114] Croft to Baldwin, 17 Sept. 1928, 1/3, Croft Papers.
[115] Croft, *My Life of Strife*, 180.
[116] GPC Minutes, 30 Sept. 1925, EIA Minute Book, Hannon Papers.

It has recently been claimed that 'many progressive industrialists' within the EIA were becoming increasingly aware that the fortunes of agriculture and industry were linked, and that agriculture must be reintegrated into the Tariff-Reform process and must no longer be regarded as a special case when it came to safeguarding. Such were the views of Alfred Mond, who joined the EIA after his spectacular defection from the Liberals over land reform, and of Hugo Hirst. Both recognized the growing importance of the more progressive sectors of British agriculture as a market for the artificial fertilizers and feeds of ICI and the electrical farm equipment of GEC.[117]

Before the EIA in 1927, Mond raised a scheme in which Empire needs would be supplied by the lowest-cost Empire producers.[118] Such rationalization, however, offered a bleak prospect to all British farmers except dairy, fruit, and vegetable producers: Tariff Reformers had recognized the difficulties inherent in Empire free trade in food ever since the Tariff Commission had modified Chamberlain's Glasgow scheme to afford British farmers some low protection against colonial grain and meat.[119] In general, therefore, Mond took a more attainable and pragmatic approach, advocating subsidies, organizational improvements, and unilateral preferential treaties in a *movement towards* Empire free trade in food. Nevertheless, the element of rationalization that he brought from industry into agriculture was not abandoned.[120]

In fact, there seems to have been scant support within the EIA for Mond's vision, which was somewhat heroic in its belief in harmonic balance, not only between British agriculture and industry, but also between British and Empire agriculture and industry. Initially uncertain of its stance, the Association set up an informal committee on agricultural policy in 1927, chaired by Mond. Shortly afterwards, Hannon tried unsuccessfully to organize joint action between 'centralised industries and agriculturalists' through the Central Chamber of Agriculture.[121] No record of his attempts has survived, but at about the same time Croft became embroiled in a controversy with the National Farmers' Union which suggests that there were intractable obstacles to such an alliance.

Though he said little about agricultural protection before the 1929 election, Croft was on occasion candid enough to admit that he favoured it. On home ground, in the partisan *National Review*, he dismissed agricultural subsidies as

[117] A. F. Cooper, *British Agricultural Policy 1912–36* (Manchester, 1989), 82–3. It should be noted, however, that much of Cooper's evidence comes from the mid-1930s.

[118] *The Times*, 3 Nov. 1927; also A. F. Cooper, *British Agricultural Policy*, 87.

[119] A. J. Marrison, 'The Tariff Commission, Agricultural Protection and Food Taxes, 1903–1913', *Agricultural History Review*, 34 (1986), 171–87.

[120] A. Mond, 'The British Empire as an Economic Unit', in *Industry and Politics* (1927), 285–9; Lord Melchett, *Imperial Economic Unity* (1930), 79, 83–4. Melchett's insistence in 1930 that domestic prices would not rise because Empire food supply was in surplus reinforces the view that his objective of substantial rationalization had not changed.

[121] A. F. Cooper, *British Agricultural Policy*, 88.

politically unacceptable, and cheap credits as merely 'prolonging the agony', and stated his own conviction that safeguarding was the only solution to the British farmer's difficulties. He stressed that this was a personal view, and reminded his readers that 'it is most unfair to blame the Government for not doing what they had no mandate to do'.[122] Thus J. F. Wright, the East Anglian county secretary of the National Farmer's Union, was clearly mistaken in claiming that Croft supported the NFU's interpretation that agriculture had been included in Baldwin's pledge to extend safeguarding on merit. Rebutting the charge, Croft turned on the NFU. According to Wright, the NFU had supported safeguarding since 1922:

I was under the impression that certain officials of the N.F.U. were declared Free Traders, and I am glad to be assured that this is not so, and that henceforward the National Farmers' Union will come into the open for a policy of protection for British agriculture which I have always advocated.[123]

Croft's sarcasm was patent. And it was directed, of course, not at the attitude of the NFU to agricultural protection, nor even its interpretation of the content of Baldwin's pledge, but at NFU opposition to any safeguarding of industry as long as food duties remained politically untouchable.

Thus, before 1929, it cannot be claimed that there was any marked sensitivity towards agricultural protection on the part of the industrialists within the EIA—the evidence is meagre, but it rather suggests tensions than sympathies. Mond's views were almost certainly shared by only a minority of industrialists within the EIA. In any case, the EIA was led by politicians, its agenda determined by the situation of the Party. To the extent that, tacitly, it favoured food duties, the impetus came less from an increasing awareness on the part of the industrialists within the EIA of a symbiotic relationship between agricultural and industrial prosperity than from considerations of imperial preference, and from the Association's political wing. When forced to do so, the EIA denied the charge of agricultural protectionism. As late as July 1928, a correspondent in the press, aware that Croft himself was 'notoriously' in favour of food taxes, demanded a clarification of EIA policy.[124] Croft was unequivocal:

I desire to say definitely that the Empire Industries Association is not in favour of any variation of [i.e. from—AJM] the Prime Minister's pledge, and is therefore opposed to any form of agricultural protection until a mandate has been given by the electorate for such a policy.[125]

[122] Croft, 'The Plight of Agriculture and Safeguarding', in *National Review*, Aug. 1927.
[123] Croft to Ed., *Eastern Daily Press*, 3 Oct. 1927. See also *East Anglian Daily Times*, 23 Sept. 1927; Croft to Ed., *Eastern Daily Press*, 22 Sept. 1927; Wright to Ed., *Eastern Daily Press*, 24 Sept. 1927.
[124] Geoffrey Mander to Ed., *Express and Star*, 5 July 1928.
[125] Croft to Ed., *Express and Star*, 11 July 1928.

Before the 1929 election, and even for some time after it, the main thrust of the EIA's agricultural policy remained the long-term one of educating farmers on the advantage a of 'step-by-step' safeguarding policy, and emphasizing the importance of urban–industrial prosperity to the agricultural community.[126] It is doubtful that farmers were convinced,[127] but in this approach lay no disloyalty to the Party.

When Mond effectively defected from the EIA to join the Empire Crusade, the EIA refused to endorse Beaverbrook's movement. This troubled the conscience of the EIA, even to the extent that it remonstrated with Unionist Central Office over its refusal to give official endorsement to Sir John Ferguson, the Unionist candidate at the Twickenham by-election in July 1929, who had declared for Empire Free Trade.[128] Indeed, the Empire Crusade posed particular difficulties for the EIA. It was launched at a time when the international situation was causing the beginnings of a sea change in British public opinion. Support for Ferguson suggests that, by Twickenham, the majority of EIA members were personally in favour of food duties, but reluctant to support them openly if that meant taking the Association further outside the orbit of official Party policy, or harming the electoral prospects of EIA members. Still, in February 1930, with the tide of protectionist sentiment ever swelling, the Executive Committee saw the value of bending the presentation of their beliefs to suit electoral circumstances; 'speakers from the Association should advocate the widest extension of Empire preference but should not speak in Constituencies where the Members or Candidates were Members of the E.I.A. and were anxious to avoid the discussion of food taxes'.[129] By now, however, the EIA was becoming impatient of containment. To Croft, the election had removed Baldwin's previous election pledge. The Party was now at liberty to campaign on a new platform. The situation with regard to food duties was now analagous to that of iron and steel before the election.

V

In 1925–1926 the EIA had deliberately rejected a plan which at root accepted rather than challenged government policy: Hewins's plan for a technical bureau which would assist industries in their applications for safeguarding. In spite of this, to a large extent it compromised thereafter. In April 1926 Amery confided to Cottier that, unless Baldwin could prevail over Churchill and enter the next

[126] A. F. Cooper, *British Agricultural Policy*, 88; R. D. Herzog, 'The Conservative Party and Protectionist Politics', 513.
[127] Farmer antagonism towards industrial safeguarding was to emerge again in 1930 as Beaverbrook's Empire Crusade shifted its accent more heavily towards agricultural protection. See Beaverbrook to Croft, 10 May 1930, 3 Dec. 1930, 1/4, Croft Papers. See also below, Ch. 13.
[128] R. R. James (ed.), *Memoirs of a Conservative* (1969), 318.
[129] Executive Committee Minutes, 18 Feb. 1930, 221/1/2/1, EIA Papers.

election 'free from the present restrictions as regards protection and preference
... [he] might be compelled to break off and force the issue single-handed'.[130]
Effectively, he decided not to do this when, warning Baldwin but under advice
from Neville, he declined to address the Albert Hall meeting on iron and steel
in May 1928.[131] Had he done so, the EIA would have been in an exquisitely
difficult position. It would have lamented a rift in the Cabinet when an election
was in sight, but it could have scarcely disowned Amery when the cause of the
rift was his appearance on an EIA platform.

With prominent publicists such as Croft and Mond, the EIA received a large
amount of press exposure, and probably did more to influence public opinion
than similar organizations. But the inclusion within the EIA of major industrialists of the calibre and reputation of Mond and Sir Harry McGowan of ICI, Lord
Weir, Sir Hugo Hirst of GEC, and Sir Herbert Austin, and of a large number
of industrialists of only slightly lesser rank, did not change the fact that in certain
senses the Association represented a step backwards from that radical conception
of the businessman in politics which the BCU had seemed to promise. Doubtless,
this recognized reality. As when after 1926 J. C. C. Davidson set about
revitalizing the Conservative Party organization, the 'big money' forthcoming
from the business community, not least from City firms 'thoroughly frightened
of a Socialist government' contrasted starkly with the funds available to the
EIA.[132] But fear of socialism was, of course, not confined to the City, and hence
the need for unity reinforced any natural tendency within the EIA towards
accommodation. Thus an apparently huge number of parliamentary allies, over
280 by 1929, according to Croft,[133] did not affect the EIA's ability to influence
events. Whilst the business membership was more than a façade, Croft's control
of the organization reflected the original intentions of Chamberlain and Amery,
ensuring that the EIA's objectives were essentially party objectives, and in many
ways less radical than those of the old TRL. Both behind and in front of the
scenes, it was led by politicians determined not to split the Conservative Party,
and supported by industrialists who readily acquiesced in that strategy. 'There is
no revolt,' claimed Croft,[134] and before the election he was right, though on iron
and steel the EIA had come close.

---

[130] Amery diary, 22 Apr. 1926, in J. Barnes and D. Nicholson, *The Leo Amery Diaries*, i. 449.
[131] Amery diary, 7 May 1928, ibid. 542–3.
[132] Davidson, quoted in J. Ramsden, *The Age of Balfour and Baldwin, 1902–1940* (1978), 220.
[133] Croft, *My Life of Strife*, 181.
[134] *Morning Post*, 30 July 1928. See also *Financial News*, 27 July 1928; *Yorkshire Post*, 27 July 1928.

13

The Outer Courts of the Temple

During the debate on the Import Duties Bill in February 1932, Clement Attlee likened Neville Chamberlain to the 'chief priest' at the sacrifice of Free Trade, sitting flanked by his new acolytes, Runciman and Sir John Simon. 'The real prophets of the new era,' he observed sardonically, referring to Croft and Amery, 'have to be content with the outer courts of the temple.'[1] As the world toppled into depression after 1929, the last resistance to protectionism within the British business community crumbled. Croft's backbench forces now dominated the Conservative Party. Yet, as ever, business waited upon politics. And politics sought a way in which protection might be introduced as a national policy—in political rhetoric a policy to unite and not divide, but in the eyes of the cynical or the calculating, a policy for which the Conservatives could not be held solely responsible.

I

Even without Churchill, there would have been little inclination within the cabinet towards an orgy of safeguarding between 1925 and 1929. The only time when a protectionist defection threatened was when Amery briefly considered allying himself openly with the EIA in demanding protection for iron and steel in 1928.[2] Industrial divisiveness was not the main concern. In March 1928 D. A. Bremner of the British Engineers' Association informed Sir William Larke of the NFISM that the engineers were now 'sympathetic' to the safeguarding of steel.[3] In April the Heavy Steelmakers' Safeguarding Committee reinforced this in their memorial to Baldwin. Consultation with consumers of steel now indicated 'a large body of opinion . . . which views with grave apprehension the present position and future prospects of the Steel Industry and the effect on their own future'. The engineering industry, a large proportion of coal-owners, and many prominent shipbuilders, would not oppose the safeguarding of steel. The motor industry would 'undoubtedly give active support'.[4]

[1] *Parliamentary Debates*, 5th ser., cclxi (1931–2), col. 297.
[2] See above, 385–6.
[3] Quoted in T. Rooth, 'The Political Economy of Protectionism in Britain, 1919–32', *Journal of European Economic History*, 21 (1992), 60.
[4] C. H. Peat to Baldwin, 2 Apr. 1928, fols. 10–17, Ms. Eng. Hist. 896, Worthington Evans Papers.

The crucial reason for inertia on safeguarding was electoral. In July 1928, the month in which EIA agitation on iron and steel reached its peak, Baldwin's cabinet policy committee discussed strategy for the forthcoming election. Though an extension of safeguarding would win votes in Yorkshire, it would lose them in Lancashire. Overall, 'few votes would be lost . . . [by] doing nothing for our friends'. Any amendment of the safeguarding procedure should be 'relegated to the background'.[5]

To allay any concern that a Conservative victory would mean a wide extension of safeguarding, the committee even considered publishing an amended draft White Paper before the election, to show that the proposed changes would be inconsiderable. Beyond replacing the troublesome phrase 'abnormal competition' with one easier for the Board of Trade to interpret,[6] 'it would be better . . . to leave the rest of the White Paper unaltered'.

The near crisis on iron and steel subsided. As winter approached, there was still lingering support for reopening the question. Amery and J. C. C. Davidson believed that an enquiry might yield electoral advantages in northern industrial constituencies, and have the additional benefit of postponing any action until after the election. Their arm was strengthened by the support of Arthur Pugh and the ISTC.[7] But even Chamberlain, who in August had supported Amery's proposal that there should be a positive declaration on safeguarding before the election,[8] now agreed with Baldwin that the Amery-Davidson scheme was impracticable: 'there are many obvious dangers about it which have no doubt been foreseen by the Labour Party'.[9] The cabinet did yield, however, to demands for a second safeguarding enquiry into woollens and worsteds, demands made by Bradford and Keighley manufacturers' associations and supported by associations from Huddersfield, Leeds,[10] Yeadon, Guiseley, and Calder Vale. The choice of chairman, no less than Sir Hubert Llewellyn Smith, shows a cabinet appreciation of the high sensitivity of the enquiry. And in January 1929 Baldwin informed Arthur Pugh of the ISTC that, if the Conservatives were returned, the steel industry would be allowed to make an application for safeguarding on the same footing as other industries,[11] a concession that was laced with some ambiguity.

---

[5] Cabinet Policy Committee Minutes, 16 July 1928, fols. 27–32, Ms. Eng. Hist. 896, Worthington Evans Papers.

[6] '[S]ubstantial consumption of foreign imported goods' was suggested.

[7] The ISTC's request for an enquiry into the industry was couched in sufficiently broad terms for the National Executive of the Labour Party to support it. See [Sir Arthur Pugh], *Men of Steel* (1951), 442.

[8] J. A. Cross, *Lord Swinton* (Oxford, 1982), 88.

[9] Chamberlain to Cunliffe-Lister, 8 Jan. 1929, 174/2/1, Swinton Papers.

[10] In September 1928 the Council of the Leeds CC abandoned its embargo on discussion of safeguarding, and supported Birmingham's campaign for extension and simplification. See M. W. Beresford, *The Leeds Chamber of Commerce* (Leeds, 1951), 163–4.

[11] [Pugh], *Men of Steel*, 442; J. C. Carr and W. Taplin, *History of the British Steel Industry* (Oxford, 1962), 467.

By now, safeguarding bit both ways. It was no longer certain that the widespread expectation that Labour would abolish, as it had done in 1924, would carry electoral advantage. As the election approached, Croft's tireless propaganda continued.[12] In the spring came reports of strong support for safeguarding in the textile districts of the West Riding, and in Gloucester and Stroud. The Liberal and Labour candidates for Nottingham East and West were divided over how to respond to an incongruous alliance between laceworkers and miners in support of safeguarding.[13] The Conservative position was strengthened in March by the release of the final report of the Balfour Committee on Industry and Trade. A committee set up by Labour in 1924 and largely composed of Free Traders now reported in favour of continuing the safeguarding and McKenna duties.[14] The cabinet's holding action made sense.

In May, Labour's vulnerability to embarrassment over safeguarding erupted into burlesque. The press reported Sir Herbert Austin as threatening to close his Longbridge works if the McKenna duties were repealed. Unwisely, MacDonald and Snowden rose to the bait. Austin's 'threatening and blackmailing' reminded Snowden of 1923, when William Morris had prompted his workers to deluge the Treasury with printed postcards claiming that they had been given notice. Then, Morris's claim that the abolition of the duties would lead to a million job losses had been seen by Snowden as a 'ramping, raging, lying campaign'.[15] Snowden's intemperance persisted in 1929. His threat to consider effective nationalization under the Emergency Powers Act allowed the Conservatives to wheel out Birkenhead (F. E. Smith) in defence of Law and Constitution. In ridiculing Snowden's legal knowledge, Smith also made mockery of the Labour leaders' own past record: 'all I can say is that Mr. Snowden and his friends are very lucky to have avoided imprisonment at the time of the general strike. If ever there was a conspiracy against trade it was that'. Had Austin not a right to close down operations which lost money? And what of the prospect of Labour politicians running Longbridge? There was not one of them, J. H. Thomas apart, 'whom I would entrust to let out push cycles'.[16]

Late in April 1929, the results of Llewellyn Smith's investigation into woollens and worsteds were filtering through to members of the Government. Churchill feared that recommendation of even a small duty would allow the Liberals to make great play upon the 'immense' extension of safeguarding that this portended. '[T]he last thing in the world we want to do is to disturb the

---

[12] Croft to Ed., *The Times*, 8 Jan. 1929, 8; *The Times*, 14 Jan. 1929, 8; 6 Feb. 1929, 10; 19 Mar. 1929, 9; 30 Mar. 1929.

[13] *The Times*, 21 May 1929, 7; 23 May 1929, 7.

[14] *Final Report of the Committee on Industry and Trade*, Cmd. 3282 (1929), 275–81.

[15] R. J. Overy, *William Morris, Viscount Nuffield* (1976), 108. On Austin's poor opinion of politicians, see R. Church, *Herbert Austin* (1979), 137.

[16] Snowden at Morley, 22 May 1929, Churchill at Woodford, 23 May 1929, both in *The Times*, 24 May 1929, 8. Also Birkenhead at Liverpool, 23 May 1929, in *The Times*, 25 May 1929, 6.

comfortable position into which the fiscal controversy has now got.' At the Board of Trade, however, Cunliffe-Lister was incensed by Churchill's suggestion that Llewellyn Smith should be persuaded to delay his report, 'by raising various points of detail, or by simple inertia', until after the election. In asserting the independence of Board of Trade committees, he made it clear to Baldwin that Chamberlain stood on his side. Churchill was not shaken; the experienced Llewellyn Smith would regard a request over timing as perfectly reasonable, just as Norman at the Bank of England would recognize that an election campaign was an inopportune time for a change in bank rate.[17]

Churchill's wish prevailed. Although Llewellyn Smith's report advocating a safeguarding duty of 10 to 15 per cent on women's dress fabrics was dated 30 April and presented to the Board of Trade before the election, its contents were not disclosed until afterwards.[18] That Baldwin refused to leak its findings when speaking in Leeds and Bradford has been portrayed as 'excessive scrupulousness', a refusal to 'take advantage of the most elementary electioneering techniques'.[19] There is of course a less charitable interpretation.

The wish to stand still on safeguarding both reinforced and was reinforced by Baldwin's 'safety-first' formula. The cabinet endorsed a strategy of denying the efficacy of spectacular, radical approaches such as that being offered by Lloyd George,[20] of convincing the public that trade recovery must necessarily be long and soundly based, and of making its appeal on its past record. Effectively, this put the weight of the campaign on Baldwin's character—on his honesty, his integrity, his pragmatism, his cautious judgement, his embodiment of English values.[21]

The Conservative manifesto renewed Baldwin's pledge against food taxes and a general tariff,[22] but its ambivalence on safeguarding made it easy for opponents to assert there was a hidden agenda. A phalanx of twenty-one Liberal candidates for North-Western constituencies signed a 'Back to Free Trade' manifesto

---

[17] Churchill to Cunliffe-Lister, 25 Apr. 1929, Cunliffe-Lister to Churchill, 25 Apr. 1929, Churchill to Cunliffe-Lister, 28 Apr. 1929, 313/1/3, Swinton Papers.

[18] H. G. Williams, *Through Tariffs to Prosperity* (1931), 58–9. Duties were also recommended on made-up garments, whether for men or women. After the election, Mackinder, Peto, and Croft attempted to embarrass the Labour Government by claiming that its shelving of the report was a rejection of the wishes of organized labour. In fact, though 15 textile unions supported the safeguarding application, their membership was only about a quarter of that of the nine unions which opposed it. See Board of Trade, *Report of the Woollen and Worsted Committee*, Cmd. 3355 (1929), paras. 106–8; *Parliamentary Debates*, 5th Ser., vol. ccxxix, cols. 232–3; Board of Trade memorandum, 'Safeguarding Etc. Duties', July 1929, BT 55/58/12.

[19] K. Middlemas and J. Barnes, *Baldwin* (1969), 524.

[20] Such proposals originated in the Liberal Industrial Inquiry of 1927 and were embodied in the election manifesto, *We Can Conquer Unemployment*. See M. Freeden, *Liberalism Divided* (Oxford, 1986), 105–26.

[21] P. Williamson, ' "Safety First": Baldwin, the Conservative Party, and the 1929 General Election', *Historical Journal*, 25 (1982), 385–409, esp. 405–9.

[22] A. Thorpe, *The British General Election of 1931* (Oxford, 1991), 32.

claiming that Baldwin, if returned to power, would extend safeguarding to such an extent that it would be tantamount to a general tariff.[23] Predictably, therefore, the unexpected defeat of May 1929 was interpreted differently by Baldwin and the advanced Tariff Reformers. To Baldwin, the need was for caution. In the early months, fearing that Labour might hold a snatch second election to secure an overall majority whilst its standing was still high, he was reluctant to declare any advance in policy. To Croft and the EIA, to Gretton and the 'die-hards', and to an increasing number in the moderate centre of Conservative opinion, however, the election result suggested that a bolder position on tariffs would have had a positive electoral appeal. As Amery reminisced sadly, if the Baldwin government had protected steel and several other important industries, 'all of which we could have done within our pledges', the benefits would now be apparent. It was now necessary to 'get back to a real fighting spirit'.[24]

Conflict over safeguarding still continued, but it was eclipsed by disagreement over imperial preference and food duties. Those wishing for a 'forward' policy received wide support from the activists in the constituency associations, as shown in the surviving responses to Davidson's enquiry into the causes of defeat.[25] Baldwin, however, feared that Tariff-Reform policies sufficiently advanced to satisfy the more secure southern constituencies would further alienate the floating voter in the north. An election which had seen a leftward shift in voting behaviour but a rightward shift in the Conservatives returned clearly made it difficult to reconcile conviction with pragmatism. Here lay the essential tensions of 1929 to 1931.

These tensions were aggravated by Beaverbrook's Empire Crusade, and the formation of his United Empire Party.[26] Beginning as a movement for utopian Empire Free Trade, but shifting later towards straight agricultural protectionism, the policy was essentially impractical; but it struck a chord with the southern constituency associations. Beaverbrook had little sympathy with industrial protectionism. He had declined to support Baldwin's 'insular' campaign in the 1923 election and was 'not greatly interested in safeguarding. I wouldn't take very much trouble to help that cause.' To Croft, he even threatened to oppose duties on manufactures if there was no quid pro quo.[27] Nevertheless, he attracted sympathy and support from many EIA and die-hard MPs, whose leaders used him to press Baldwin for a definite advance in policy. After much skirmishing, Baldwin agreed in March to submit food duties to a referendum when the Conservatives regained office.

---

[23] *The Times*, 18 Mar. 1929, 16.

[24] Amery to Croft, 6 June 1929, 1/2, Croft Papers.

[25] S. Ball, *Baldwin and the Conservative Party* (New Haven, 1988), 32.

[26] Ibid. chs. 3–6; A. J. P. Taylor, *Beaverbrook* (1972), chs. 11–13; K. Middlemas and J. Barnes, *Baldwin*, ch. 21.

[27] Beaverbrook to Croft, 16 Apr., 10 May, 3 Dec. 1930, 1/4, Croft Papers.

The 'uneasy truce' which followed was sustained only by differing interpretations of this concession, Beaverbrook thinking food taxes were now accepted as party policy, but Baldwin regarding them as removed from immediate consideration by the referendum.[28] The threat from Croft's 187 EIA MPs and Gretton's die-hards was ever present; Croft's tactics, 'half of pulling [Beaverbrook's] teeth, and half of using him to frighten the Party on',[29] were similar to those of Amery and Neville Chamberlain, though he sailed closer to the wind in pursuing them.

The truce was effectively dead by June, in spite of Baldwin's vague proposal, made at Glenham Park, for price guarantees for grain farmers and safeguarding against Russian dumping.[30] Reviving the UEP, Beaverbrook attempted to subvert the local constituency associations. In the short run, this allowed Baldwin to play the card of party loyalty, Gretton and Croft's move to replace the referendum with a 'free hand' failing heavily at Caxton Hall on 24 June. But by September it was increasingly obvious that northern Conservatives were swinging into line astern behind southern, and that the local organizations were 'within a hair's breadth of . . . open revolt'.[31]

Neville Chamberlain now stepped in. In May, when he had been put in charge of the Conservative Research Department, he had immediately put its Agricultural Research Committee to the construction of a coherent agricultural policy. Maybe inspired by Addison, who had been pressing similar ideas in the Labour cabinet since February, the ARC recommended a wheat quota in July.[32] This course was obviously attractive, since it concealed to some extent the protection of that most politically sensitive of all commodities. Impeccable Tariff Reformer, loyal without question in spite of being widely regarded as the heir apparent, chairman of the Party, Chamberlain possessed all the initiative.

At the Crystal Palace on 20 September, Chamberlain, echoing his father's 'unauthorized programme' of 1885, outlined a policy of expenditure cuts, an emergency tariff, a wheat quota, and a 'free hand' on other food duties. Baldwin agreed to the policy change and summoned a Unionist business committee (a shadow cabinet) for 7 October. Difficulties with Churchill led to an adjournment. On the 8th, premier Bennett of Canada made his famous offer at the Imperial Conference, 'a preference in the Canadian market in exchange for a like preference . . . based upon the addition of a ten percentum increase in prevailing general tariffs, or upon tariffs yet created'.[33] With no little justice, J. H. Thomas could describe the offer as 'humbug', but Labour could not respond and the Conservatives could; to Neville Chamberlain it was 'Heaven-sent', and before

[28] S. Ball, *Baldwin and the Conservative Party*, 62–3.
[29] Ibid. 69.   [30] Ibid. 87.   [31] Ibid. 97.
[32] A. F. Cooper, *British Agricultural Policy 1912–36* (Manchester, 1989), 103; P. Williamson, *National Crisis and National Government* (Cambridge, 1992), 97.
[33] A. Thorpe, *The British General Election*, 34.

the business committee reconvened he had secured a press statement from Baldwin. Beaverbrook's crusade continued, but now with less sympathy from Amery and Croft. Gretton mounted a further attack on Baldwin, but on 30 October at the Caxton Hall he was defeated. Discontent still smouldered until May 1931, but Baldwin was now secure. Gretton at least had the consolation that the Party now stood for what was in effect a general tariff on manufactures, imperial preference, a wheat quota, and a 'free hand' on other food duties.[34]

II

During the winter of 1929–1930 trade downturn became visible. The Board of Trade's seasonally adjusted index of industrial production (1924=100) fell from 115 in the third quarter of 1929 to 104 in the second quarter of 1930. The percentage of insured workers unemployed rose from under 10 per cent in the summer of 1929 to 15 per cent in May 1930, the increase being particularly marked in the export-sensitive trades.[35] The late spring and early summer of 1930 saw a new and more assertive articulation of protectionist sentiment within the business community. Several important Chambers of Commerce conducted polls of members, a group of prominent bankers and financiers created a press sensation in calling for protection and preference, and the FBI leaders finally consented to a plebiscite. The embargo that had operated even in organizations predominantly sympathetic to Tariff Reform was crumbling. Though sensitive to the struggle going on within the Conservative Party, protectionist businessmen no longer had to fear embarrassing or endangering a Conservative Government by voicing their prescriptions; they might, on the other hand, strengthen the resolve of a timid opposition leadership.

Business anxiety was fuelled particularly by the fear that the Labour Government would commit itself to an unequal agreement in an internationally negotiated tariff truce. This was felt widely, but perhaps nowhere was it a more important factor in conversion than in the Manchester Chamber of Commerce.

In the 1920s, the Chamber had been generally pessimistic about the chances of international agreement to reduce tariffs.[36] Nevertheless, it gave its approval to the resolutions of the World Economic Conference at Geneva in 1927, President W. E. Thompson maintaining that 'nobody was better adapted than the Manchester Chamber to play a leading part' in securing their adoption.[37] He treated a sceptic, who argued that the resolutions were 'pious' and doomed to

[34] R. Skidelsky, *Politicians and the Slump* (Harmondsworth, 1970), 276; P. Williamson, *National Crisis*, 130–2; S. Ball, *Baldwin and the Conservative Party*, 132–50; A. Thorpe, *The British General Election*, 37.

[35] F. Capie and M. Collins, *The Inter-War British Economy: A Statistical Abstract* (Manchester, 1983), 27, 63, 66–7.

[36] *Manchester Evening Chronicle*, 19 Oct. 1924.

[37] Manchester Chamber of Commerce, *Monthly Record*, June 1927, 172–5.

be ignored, with contempt. Manchester's delegates to the International Chamber of Commerce at Stockholm had already begun the work of persuasion. '[M]any at Stockholm [were] of the same mind as themselves,' and 'I believe we can exert such an influence that these two Conferences will be looked upon in years to come as veritable turning points.'[38]

The sceptic was of course correct. Whilst the WEC was well-attended by 194 delegates from 50 countries, few had authority to negotiate for their governments. The USA sent only observers, and the Conference centred largely upon intra-European frictions, with little result.[39] But the internationalist Willie Graham, President of the Board of Trade in the Labour Government, persisted. At the League of Nations in September 1929, and against a background of Aristide Briand's efforts to encourage European union through some kind of embryonic common market, he proposed a two- or three-year tariff truce as a prelude to real reductions. This led to the clumsily titled 'Preliminary Conference with a view to Concerted Economic Action', which opened in February 1930.[40]

Thompson's blustering disguised growing doubts in the Manchester Chamber. Though the directors still held the Free Trade line in the opening months of 1929, they did discuss the issue in February, March, and April, apparently without informing the membership.[41] A safeguarding resolution, drafted by Robert Waddington, cotton spinner and manufacturer and MP for Rossendale, was withdrawn because of the impending election, but surprised its author by the support it attracted.[42] By now the Manchester Chamber's resistance to safeguarding rested on little more than political expediency and timing. In March Thompson tried unsuccessfully to secure a postponement of the ABCC's report on safeguarding procedure, revealing that Churchill had advised him that he 'deprecated any public agitation on the question of free trade or protection' so close to an election.[43]

The Conservative defeat in May lifted the constraints masking the changing mood of the Chamber. At the Edinburgh meeting of the ABCC on 3 October, R. C. Rodgers of Birmingham secured a resolution opposing the abolition of safeguarding, and demanding its extension. The Manchester delegates, president

[38] Presidential address, 18 July 1927, in *Monthly Record*, July 1927, 210–11.

[39] R. W. D. Boyce, *British Capitalism at the Crossroads, 1919–1932* (Cambridge, 1987), 222. Boyce has suggested that the failure of the WEC was partly due to Britain's intractability on her own tariffs (especially on dyestuffs, lace, and wines), and to Britain's insistence on most-favoured-nation principles which restricted Europe's ability to effect bilateral or trilateral tariff reductions and to erect a European economic bloc in countervailing power to the USA (119–22, 125–33). It is well to remember, however, that Britain's commercial policy was still far more liberal than her trading partners', and much European annoyance was probably orchestrated deliberately in an attempt to find a negotiating lever.

[40] Ibid. 219–23, 235.

[41] There is no mention in MCC, *Monthly Record*, February–April 1929.

[42] T. Rooth, 'Political Economy of Protectionism', 61–2.

[43] ABCC, Executive Council Minutes, 6 Mar. 1929.

Sir Kenneth Stewart and secretary Raymond Streat, reported Rodgers's case as 'careful and well-reasoned . . . Nothing of equal force or logic was said on the other side . . . The resolution was adopted by quite a considerable majority and with much less debate than similar resolutions have elicited on previous occasions'.[44] Interestingly conceding that the ABCC had 'always had a small majority on the side of Protection', the Manchester observers found it 'unusual . . . to find the Free Trade side so quiescent'. Their report essentially discounted any hope of an internationalist solution; rather, Empire preference was the 'dominating issue' at the meeting, a resolution favouring its extension securing a large majority. There had been some sympathy for a 'European Economic Union' as a countervailing force to the USA, but most delegates had shared Sir Gilbert Vyle's preference for an Empire union over a European union. If Vyle's speech had a weakness, the Manchester delegates felt it 'lay in treating the idea of a European Union as though it were far more advanced than it actually is'.[45] Manchester's leaders no longer condemned protectionist opinion.

As the tariff-truce conference drew near, it became clear that British business opinion in general was hostile. The Dominions, intent on tariff increases rather than reductions, would not attend. As in 1927, the USA would only send observers. Convinced that Britain would get a poor bargain in any tariff truce, the FBI, the ABCC, and the London Chamber, all of which had some kind of embargo in operation on the discussion of Tariff Reform, joined the protectionist EIA, NUM, and NFISM in opposing British participation.[46] More cautiously, Manchester's board of directors determined on a neutral approach. In its new year report, it protested that the Chamber 'ha[d] done nothing to hinder the accomplishment of a tariff truce', but it did stress that many other British chambers were hostile to the impending conference.[47] In February 1930 the large European and United States Section of the Chamber, composed largely of export-orientated cotton merchants and manufacturers, passed a resolution protesting against a tariff truce. The board of directors met on 5 February and agreed to forward the Section's resolution to the Board of Trade without comment. The air was pregnant with expectation, since some of the press interpreted the directors' meeting as a sign that a sensational announcement on the Chamber's fiscal stance was imminent. At the annual meeting, cotton spinner H. P. Greg criticized the directors for their 'lack of honesty' in forwarding the resolution to the Board of Trade.[48] The EIA sought to capitalize on this with a big show at the Free Trade Hall. As Croft wrote gleefully,

[44] Manchester Chamber of Commerce, *Monthly Record*, Oct. 1929, 304–5. [45] Ibid.
[46] FBI, *Fourteenth Annual Report*, 1930, 37, 200/F/4/2/13, FBI. Also LCC, Council Minutes, 10 Dec. 1929.
[47] Manchester Chamber of Commerce, Directors' Report for 1929, in *Monthly Record*, Jan. 1930, p. vi.
[48] President Herbert Lee at the annual meeting, 10 Feb. 1930, in *Monthly Record*, Feb. 1930, 36–7, 42, 44.

'Manchester . . . is the key position, and today as I expected they are gasping for breath as the strangulation of competition goes on and they are clutching for any straw.'[49]

It was only the extreme optimist who could have been disappointed by the results of the tariff-truce conference. Only thirty nations were represented, and only eighteen signed the convention and protocol in March.[50] Those who remembered 1927 knew well that the prospect of widespread ratification was remote. Furthermore, the USA's refusal to participate actively destroyed any lingering hopes in Europe that Congress might step back from implementing the new rates of the Hawley-Smoot Tariff Bill. Hearings dated back to December 1928, and the tariff was anticipated with anxiety, anger, and frustration in Europe. This was justified: meeting no organized resistance, the lobbyists did their work well, and the new rates were swingeing. Average *ad valorem* rates on chemicals and paints (33.4 per cent) were moderate when compared with those on cotton manufactures (46.4 per cent) and woollen goods (59.8 per cent).[51] To add insult to injury, the tariff seemed monstrously unnecessary. The 1920s had seen US penetration of the world economy unparallelled before 1914. Much of the conflict between American and British interests over raw materials—rubber, oil, nickel, and copper—took place at least partly hidden from the public eye, but this was much less true of the overseas expansion of the US automobile, electrical, and communications industries. Such penetration had been recognized by prominent protectionists like Hirst, Morris, and Austin since the early 1920s, and had been a factor in the conversion of Sir Alfred Mond. By 1928 even Montagu Norman was attempting arrangements to prevent US takeovers of British overseas banks in the artificial conditions created by the Wall Street bubble, and politicians like Baldwin and Churchill were barely concealing their distaste for US ventures overseas.[52] When Hoover, at the Department of Commerce since 1921 and the official personification of US economic expansionism,[53] became president in March 1929, the USA led the world handsomely in manufactured exports and foreign lending, and had an immensely strong balance of payments. His election promises of increased agricultural protection were hard enough to bear, but the subsequent proposals for large increases in duties on manufactures seemed totally excessive, creating an impression that the US was intent on dominating the world whilst remaining insulated at home.[54] In

---

[49] Croft to Beaverbrook, 12 Mar. 1930, 1/4, Croft Papers.

[50] A second conference, opening in November, was even less successful, only 12 countries finally ratifying the convention in March 1931. See Boyce, *British Capitalism*, 235–40, 275–6, 309–10; H. Liepmann, *Tariff Levels and the Economic Unity of Europe* (1938), 349–53.

[51] P. W. Bidwell, *Our Trade with Britain* (New York, 1938), 22–5; E. E. Schattschneider, *Politics, Pressures and the Tariff* (New York, 1935), *passim*.

[52] R. W. D. Boyce, *British Capitalism*, 178–82.

[53] J. Brandes, *Herbert Hoover and Economic Diplomacy* (Pittsburg, 1962).

[54] For French and Italian reaction, see R. W. D. Boyce, *British Capitalism*, 199–200.

May 1930, one thousand American economists petitioned Hoover to veto the tariff bill. He refused.[55]

In the Manchester Chamber, the European and US Section's protest unleashed agitation on the fiscal issue from a number of individuals and trade sections. In April, the directors decided in favour of a referendum.[56] Drafting a questionnaire with care, they offered members six policy-choices, directing them to choose only one. Empire preference, the use of tariffs as negotiating weapons, and a royal commission were all rigorously excluded. As president Herbert Lee explained, the intention was to discover 'what fundamental fiscal policy the members of the Chamber now support', without the complication of ranked or 'conditional' answers.[57]

The questionnaire was issued on 16 May to 3,941 members. The response rate was respectable, 2,343 voting and only 38 spoiling their papers by voting for more than one option. Of those replying, 607 clung to Free Trade, 986 favoured safeguarding as a 'settled policy', 232 supported an all-round general tariff, 196 wanted a general tariff on everything except raw materials, 27 preferred a general tariff on all imports except food, and 295 required a general tariff on all but food and raw materials.[58]

The president received the result on 2 June and it was issued to the press immediately. To the *Daily Dispatch*, the result represented 'a big majority against Free Trade'. *The Manchester Guardian*, however, thought differently: 'If Manchester had been "converted" to tariffs, it had only been "converted" to a few unspecified tariffs, and not to a complete system. It is a purely psychological reaction.'[59]

There was indeed ambiguity in the result. Of the 1,736 who favoured protection of manufactures (986 + 232 + 196 + 27 + 295) over half only committed themselves to safeguarding. But what did safeguarding mean in the context of 1930? It is important to notice that in January 1930, responding to the discussion in the ABCC the previous October, Manchester's directors had passed a resolution opposing abolition of the McKenna and safeguarding duties. That the directors were more cautious in declaring an apostasy on Free Trade than were members is shown by their reaction to the European and US Section's resolution on the tariff truce.[60] It is unlikely that Manchester was endorsing an empty Baldwinian strategy of safeguarding when the great bulk of businessmen had accepted Birmingham's demand for a wholesale extension based on economic need. In the economic blizzard, just about everything qualified, and

[55] P. W. Bidwell, *Our Trade*, 214.

[56] Manchester Chamber of Commerce, *Monthly Record*, Apr. 1930, 119.

[57] Manchester Chamber of Commerce, *Monthly Record*, May 1930, 140–1.

[58] Manchester Chamber of Commerce, *Monthly Record*, June 1930, 172.

[59] *Manchester Guardian*, 3 June 1930 (editorial). A. Redford, *Manchester Merchants and Foreign Trade*, ii (Manchester, 1956), 239–40, supports this interpretation.

[60] A. Redford, *Manchester Merchants*, ii. 239.

to make much of the distinction between safeguarding and general protection was unreal.[61]

On 23 June the directors approved the submission of the result to the Government. In July, Greg attempted a vote of censure, but received scant support. In September the Manchester Chamber joined in the general business protest at the Labour Government's threat to the McKenna, safeguarding, and silk duties, and in October it explicitly cited the referendum as effective proof that a majority of members would support an extension of imperial preference. In November the directors urged the Government not to ratify the tariff truce.[62] They were ignored, Snowden and Graham prevailing over a Labour cabinet to reverse a decision made in July against ratification. In the event only seven countries joined Britain in the agreement: Belgium, Switzerland, and five Baltic states with whom Britain already had relatively good trade relations.

Manchester's referendum was certainly the most sensational event in the chambers of commerce in May and June 1930. But there were also signs of a more general mobilization. In February Sir Walter Raine led an ABCC delegation of twenty-two chambers to Snowden. Ostensibly they merely sought clarification of government policy on safeguarding, but they did remind the Chancellor of the rise in employment under the McKenna and silk duties. Notable was the presence of Liverpool, Bury, Oldham, and Bolton.[63] Around the time of the Manchester referendum, votes were also taken in Sheffield, Huddersfield, Bradford, Leeds, Leicester, and Liverpool. In Bradford protectionists outnumbered Free Traders by seven to one, in Leeds by 497 to thirty-seven, in Kidderminster by twenty-eight to two. All testified to the torrent of business opinion in favour of fiscal change, even Liverpool supporting 'protective import duties of one kind or another' by an 'overwhelming majority'.[64]

There were still holding actions. In April the secretary of the London Chamber was instructed to inform members that the Chamber's attitude towards the McKenna duties was one of 'strict neutrality and that it saw no reason for departing from it'. It was not until October 1931 that a referendum, the first allowed since 1907, showed over 90 per cent of members to favour the immediate imposition of duties.[65] The Executive Council of the ABCC, operating under a similar embargo, kept an eye on the referenda being conducted elsewhere, but the President's Advisory Committee recommended that the

---

[61] More real was the ambiguity on food taxes. Only 428 (232 + 196) explicitly approved of these. What was not clear was how many of the 986 who opted for safeguarding considered agriculture a legitimate candidate.

[62] Manchester Chamber of Commerce, *Monthly Record*, July 1930, 215; Aug. 1930, 238–9; Sept. 1930, 269; Oct. 1930, 299; Nov. 1930, 333.

[63] *BCCJ*, 15 Mar. 1930, 210–11.

[64] *BCCJ*, 15 July 1930, 564. See also T. Rooth, 'Political Economy of Protectionism', 62.

[65] LCC, Council Minutes, 8 Apr. 1930, 13 Oct. 1931.

Chamber take no action.[66] In spite of their changed position, the directors of the Manchester Chamber did not press hard upon government until September 1931, when they protested that talk in Parliament of an 'immediate restriction of luxury imports' did not go far enough.[67] Indeed, it was only when Labour had fallen that the remnants of embargo finally collapsed. Committing the Lincoln meeting of the ABCC on 24 September to his diary, Raymond Streat recorded a 'practically solid vote for tariffs. London and Manchester, the pillars of Free Trade in years gone by at the Association Meetings came round'.[68]

III

In July 1930 a meeting of fourteen prominent bankers at Hambro's Bank led to the publication of the sensational 'bankers' manifesto', a document endorsed shortly afterwards by nine more leading City figures.[69] Some had been associated with a public plea for the removal of world trade barriers in 1926.[70] Now, like the Manchester Chamber of Commerce disillusioned with the failure of the tariff truce conference, and angered by Hawley-Smoot, they recognized 'the hopes expressed four years ago . . . have failed to be realised'. As trade barriers grew and Britain became the world's dumping ground, it was necessary to secure home and export markets by an Empire policy, with duties on '*all* imports from all other countries'.[71]

---

[66] ABCC, Executive Council Minutes, 7 May 1930, 2 July 1930.

[67] M. Dupree (ed.), *Lancashire and Whitehall: The Diary of Sir Raymond Streat* (Manchester, 1987), i. 90; A. Redford, *Manchester Merchants*, 242. The directors continued to be reluctant to intervene in political issues, lest they inflame Indian opinion. Indian cotton duties had been increased and the boycott on cotton goods, begun in April 1930, was still unofficially in operation in summer 1931. There was also a reluctance to deal with a Labour Government of whose policy on India the Chamber was increasingly critical. See A. Redford, *Manchester Merchants*, 280–4.

[68] M. Dupree (ed.), *Lancashire and Whitehall*, 94–5.

[69] The original signatories were Sir Eric Hambro (Hambro's Bank Ltd.); Walter Wigham (director, Bank of England); Sir Herbert Lawrence (chairman, Glynn, Mills and Co.); Sir Harry Goschen (late chairman, National Provincial Bank Ltd.); R. H. Tennant (chairman, Westminster Bank); Sir George May (Prudential Assurance Co.); Lord Ashfield [Sir Albert Stanley] (director, Midland Bank Ltd.); Beaumont Pease; Vivian Hugh Smith (Morgan, Grenfell and Co.); Lord Glenconner (Hambro's Bank Ltd.); Sir Alan Anderson (director, Bank of England); Reginald McKenna (chairman, Midland Bank Ltd.); Sir Harold Snagge (director, Barclay's Bank Ltd.); and Viscount Bearsted (director, Lloyd's Bank Ltd.). These were soon joined by F. C. Goodenough (chairman, Barclay's Bank Ltd.); Sir Cecil Budd (Vivian, Younger, and Bond Ltd., metal merchants); Sir Guy Granet and Alfred Wagg (directors of the Bankers' Industrial Development Corporation); R. S. Guinness (Standard Trust; Guinness, Mahon and Co.); Arthur Gairdner (chairman, British Overseas Bank Ltd.); T. Gilbert Scott (stockbroker; director, United Dominions Trust); John Hugh Smith; and J. Gibson Jarvie (chairman, United Dominions Trust).

[70] See 'A Plea for the Removal of Restrictions upon European Trade', *The Economist*, 23 Oct. 1926; P. Williamson, 'Financiers, the Gold Standard and British Politics, 1925–1931', in J. Turner (ed.), *Businessmen and Politics* (1984), 112.

[71] 'Bankers and Fiscal Policy', *Bankers' Magazine*, Aug. 1930, 175–6 (my emphasis).

A public announcement from such a source might be 'unusual',[72] but it was not seriously challenged. A Free-Trade counterblast quickly appeared, but this was soon discovered to have been organized by the National Association of Merchants and Manufacturers. Its signatories were minor figures, and most were not bankers.[73] Furthermore, in the succeeding weeks and months the original manifesto attracted support from other leading bankers—W. W. Paine of Lloyds Bank, Sir George Touche of the Trustees Corporation, and R. Holland Martin, president of the Institute of Bankers.[74]

The most sensational conversion was that of Sir Felix Schuster in October. He had for years been unusual among bankers in openly opposing protectionism in the press. Now, though 'still of the opinion that Free Trade would be best for us—best for the world', he swung towards retaliation. Attacking a speech by Snowden at Manchester, he denied that the protectionist strategy was to reduce wages. Rather, Britain's industrialists had in recent years and 'at great sacrifice . . . carried on at a loss in order to keep their workmen in employment'. Conditions abroad were so unfair that safeguarding was 'not only justifiable but inevitable'.[75] Schuster's address, though making those customary obeisances to Cobden that were ironically just as much a part of Fair-Trade as of Free-Trade speeches, suggests that even for Free Traders the elastic limit had been reached.

Beneath the manifesto lay a deeper context of political and economic considerations, all tightly interwoven, which merit consideration. Firstly, the more-or-less simultaneous appearance of a Labour Government and economic downturn raised the spectre of serious political intervention in the financial sector. This vulnerability did not develop overnight. 'That the banker is unpopular, not only in Labour circles but amongst the business community also, admits today of no dispute,' wrote T. E. Gregory in 1927.[76] At this time discontent focused largely on general credit and currency policy, and hence directly or indirectly on the gold standard and on the Bank of England's management of it. Partly because he considered that the pressure on sterling was

---

[72] 'Bankers and Fiscal Policy', *Bankers' Magazine*, Aug. 1930, 178.

[73] Ibid. 176. Those signing the counter-manifesto were Henry Bell (director, Lloyd's Bank); Sir Hugh Bell (ironmaster and coal-owner); Sir Ernest Benn (publisher); Viscount Cowdray; F. D'Arcy Cooper (chairman, Lever Bros.); Harold Cox (economic journalist); Sir Charles Harris (late of War Office Finance Department); Viscount Leverhulme; Sir Charles Mallet (economist); Dr. T. E. Page; and Sir Alexander Roger.

[74] W. W. Paine to Ed., *The Times*, 18 July 1930; *Bankers' Magazine*, Aug. 1930, 181; Martin before Institute of Bankers, *Bankers' Magazine*, Dec. 1930, 851–2.

[75] Schuster also suggested that he had always been sympathetic to imperial preference, and claimed that a 'new atmosphere' and a desire by the Dominions for closer ralations now made the prospect more favourable than in the days of Joseph Chamberlain and Rosebery. Speech before Lincoln Chamber of Commerce; *Bankers' Magazine*, Nov. 1930, 822–4.

[76] *Financial Times*, 3 Oct. 1927, quoted in S. E. Thomas, *British Banks and the Finance of Industry* (1931), 15.

caused more by international distortions than by domestic weaknesses, but partly also to avoid the Churchillian temper, Montagu Norman resorted to endless expedients to avoid raising Bank Rate between December 1925 and February 1929. By then he could contain the pressure no longer. The speculation on Wall Street forced upward movements in February and August and led to renewed outcry from several trade associations and from Labour. Nationalization of the Bank, insinuated into Labour's official programme by Brailsford and the ILP, was not seriously on the agenda; but even Snowden, the Bank's principal Labour ally, wanted some change in the interests of trade and employment. After the election Norman had no wish to embarrass Snowden in his dealings with the Bank's 'more threatening Labour critics'.[77]

If criticism of general monetary policy fell mainly upon Norman and the Bank, the commercial bankers were more directly implicated in the charge that the British financial sector provided little 'practical financial assistance' for industrial development and restructuring, and had no counterpart to Germany's system of industrial banking.[78] Such complaints were not novel when they came from the NUM and BEAMA. They took on a more serious aspect when they appeared to be spreading from industrialists to politicians, and not only to Labour politicians.

In September 1928, Steel-Maitland spoke in cabinet of the 'individualism run riot' of the five major clearing-banks.[79] At the National Union Conference in November 1929, Wardlaw-Milne, Conservative MP for Kidderminster, complained that, in setting up the Macmillan Committee, Snowden had shown too tender a concern for the interests of the banking establishment. He also demanded that the Committee should discuss provision of 'reasonable credit facilities . . . for the development of existing undertakings and for assisting in the inauguration of new enterprises'.[80] In May 1930, shortly before the meeting at Hambro's Bank, the TUC and FBI met to discuss their submissions to the Macmillan Committee. Initial reactions were that their views 'very largely co-incide[d]'. Subsequent discussions showed this to be illusory, partly because the two organizations disagreed over the proper role of the banks and the state in industrial rationalization. But neither held the bankers blameless, and at the time of the bankers' manifesto it seemed quite possible that a joint FBI-TUC attack on the bankers might emerge to be incorporated into the criticisms circulating amongst politicians.[81]

[77] W. A. Brown, *England and the New Gold Standard 1919–1926* (1929), 251–4; P. Snowden, *An Autobiography* (1934), ii. 839–42; C. Cross, *Philip Snowden* (1966), 241–2; P. Williamson, *National Crisis*, 112–16.
[78] S. E. Thomas, *British Banks*, 13.
[79] Quoted in K. Middlemas, *Politics in Industrial Society* (1979), 180n.
[80] Quoted in *Financial News*, 21 Nov. 1929; S. E. Thomas, *British Banks*, 30.
[81] M. Dintenfass, 'The Politics of Producers' Co-operation: the FBI-TUC-NCEO Talks, 1929–1933', in J. Turner (ed.), *Businessmen and Politics*, 80–2.

Many historians have endorsed the contemporary view of a failure of the banks to accommodate the long-term needs of industry.[82] Even those who argue that the accusation has been overdrawn, and that by the 1920s the banks regularly did accommodate industry in ways which went beyond orthodox principles of short-term lending, acknowledge that the banks could not admit this openly, since this would have blighted the borrower's reputation of credit-worthiness and undermined public confidence in the banks themselves.[83] Hence, whether the prevailing criticism was justified or not, it made sense for bankers to endorse policies ostensibly in the interests of industry—if those policies cut across the historic interest of the bankers that only increased the dramatic value of the gesture. This would not only appease supporters of protection within the Labour Party; it would also serve to convince Labour opponents of protection that the parasitic money-interest was now at least aligned with the real forces of production, even if misguidedly so. The change in direction would also placate dominant opinion within the Conservative Party. Indeed, Macdonald's election might impel the bankers to go some way towards appeasing Labour opinion, but it also, paradoxically, produced a heightened need for them to ensure their position within the main-stream ranks of parliamentary and constituency Conservatism. To argue that industrial and political discontent with the financial community had risen to such levels that a Conservative Government might have been 'forced . . . for the first time seriously to examine its inbuilt prejudice in favour of the bankers'[84] would, in retrospect, seem exaggerated. Nevertheless, with the cautious Baldwin now heavily on the retreat within the Party, it served the bankers little to delay any longer the choice between their preference for Free Trade and their Conservatism. Before the manifesto was signed, F. C. Goodenough of Barclays Bank had become treasurer of the EEU, and McKenna of the Midland had expressed sympathy with the Empire Crusade.[85]

Secondly, we must bear in mind the question of direct economic self-interest. Whilst the bankers were clearly concerned about the deteriorating trade- and payments-balances, it is doubtful that they were prompted by fear of an imminent collapse of sterling, as in the midst of the later crisis of September 1931, when Henry Clay produced an internal Bank-of-England memorandum advocating a tariff 'purely as a measure of defence of the currency'.[86] Indeed, the clearing banks would not have been afraid of devaluation *in itself* because both sides of their balance sheets were denominated in sterling, and the hot-money

[82] See esp. M. H. Best and J. Humphries, 'The City and Industrial Decline', in B. Elbaum and W. Lazonick (eds.), *The Decline of the British Economy* (Oxford, 1986), 229–34; G. Ingham, *Capitalism Divided?* (1984).

[83] D. M. Ross, 'The Clearing Banks and Industry: New Perspectives on the Inter-War Years', in J. J. van Helten and Y. Cassis (eds.), *Capitalism in a Mature Economy* (Aldershot, 1990), esp. 57–8.

[84] K. Middlemas, *Politics in Industrial Society*, 180.

[85] P. Williamson, 'Financiers the Gold Standard, and British Politics', 119.

[86] R. S. Sayers, *The Bank of England, 1891–1944* (Cambridge, 1976), ii. 403n.

balances which would react to sterling crisis were more probably invested in sterling bills, or deposited at acceptance houses rather than clearing banks. Admittedly, the issuing houses would have been somewhat more vulnerable to this fear, but subsequent events proved that the main threat to their stability lay in crises in non-British currencies which prevented their foreign debtors from discharging their acceptance liabilities. Furthermore, in the summer of 1930 there was no strong reason to fear a dramatic fall in the exchanges. Though chronically weak, the balance of trade was 'not catastrophically' so, and had not prevented Montagu Norman from easing the slump by reducing the Bank Rate in the easier conditions after Wall Street.[87] Indeed, Norman took pains to distance the Bank from a manifesto that two of its directors had signed, arguing that protection would distract industry from the need to rationalize and put its own house in order.[88]

But the *indirect* effects on the commercial banks, the effects of an adverse trade balance on interest rates and therefore on industry, were more serious. In November 1929 Holland Martin reminded the Institute of Bankers that 'Finance cannot for long be successful if industry and trade are not prosperous. The financial pre-eminence of the City of London . . . would crumple up like a house of cards'.[89] Doubtless, as rhetorical devices, such statements were common; but by 1930 it was indeed true that the banks were more vulnerable to industrial failure than at any time since at least the 1870s. During the late 1920s the commercial banks had become sucked into an unusually close relationship with industry. War and post-war boom, together with subsequently unfulfilled expectations of a return to normalcy, led to a liberal provision of overdrafts and advances, and to a lesser extent of debenture capital. The banks' reluctance to write off these debts as trade depression continued sometimes resulted in their becoming enmeshed in the provision of long-term capital—the classic case was the process whereby the Lancashire banks found themselves holding a substantial part of the share capital of new cotton companies formed in the euphoria of 1919 to 1920—whilst at the very least bankers were forced to accept the rollover of short-term credits as more routine.[90] The banks had gone 'far beyond their usual practice in their advances to trade', warned Schuster. 'Trading at a loss . . .

---

[87] Ibid. 389. It is difficult to be certain of this judgement. In the spring, the New York exchange remained somewhat stronger than the Berlin, and in late May there was the beginning of a major gold movement to Paris. Yet in August the Bank was still managing to hold the line and it was only as the autumnal drain developed that the expectation arose that 'fundamentally deflationary measures' would be required. Nevertheless, throughout the year, London's short-term liabilities greatly exceeded the Bank's gold and foreign currency reserves. See D. E. Moggridge, *British Monetary Policy, 1924–1931* (Cambridge, 1972), 139.

[88] H. Clay, *Lord Norman* (1957), 368.

[89] Quoted in S. E. Thomas, *British Banks*, 131–2.

[90] For the best treatment, see S. Tolliday, *Business, Banking and Politics: The Case of British Steel, 1918–1939* (Cambridge, Mass., 1987), ch. 7. Also, M. H. Best and J. Humphries, 'The City and Industrial Decline', 229–34; B. Bowker, *Lancashire under the Hammer* (1928), esp. ch. 3.

cannot be carried on indefinitely.'[91] Some of the major issuing houses, too, had moved closer to British industry in the 1920s; the relatively low demand abroad for issuing in London compared with the Edwardian years resulted in a new attention to domestic industrial issues.[92]

There was little voluntarism in this tendency, still less a deliberate trend towards finance-capitalism,[93] with its associated features of interlocking directorships and co-ordinated management decision-making. If anything, bankers were even less attracted by the prospect of getting dragged into industrial management than they were by the prospect of financing rationalization.[94] Rather, the involvements of the 1920s were generally of an accidental and contingent nature, in which bankers had little choice. In the 1920s, the Bank of England had become extensively involved in schemes to rationalize and modernize steel and cotton. The Newcastle branch's efforts to aid its largest customer, Armstrong Whitworth, led to Bank promotion of the Vickers-Armstrong merger in 1928 and the Lancashire Steel Corporation early in 1930. Also in 1928 Norman threw his support behind a scheme for a Lancashire Cotton Corporation to rationalize the American-spinning section of the industry.[95] But he found the commercial banks reluctant to participate, despite their earlier extension of credit to industry.

Persisting partly on account of his genuine belief in the necessity of bank participation, and partly to improve relations with the new Labour Government,[96] Norman set up Securities Management Trust Ltd., essentially an advisory body and a channel for finance, in November 1929. In April 1930 the Bankers' Industrial Development Company was formed with a nominal capital of £6m, £4.5m of which was provided by the commercial banks, though this was not all called up, 'remaining in effect as a guarantee fund'.[97]

The bankers' manifesto appeared only weeks after the establishment of BIDCo, and many of its signatories were associated with Norman's new creation. Two, Sir Guy Granet and Alfred Wagg, sat on BIDCo's board. Granet, Norman's deputy at the Bank, was a prominent rationalizer in railways and the electrical industry. Wagg was closely involved in the Lancashire Steel Corporation. Three more sat on BIDCo's advisory council—Lord Bearstead; Sir Eric Hambro; and Sir Herbert Lawrence, who, together with interests in private banking, was also managing director of Vickers. Like these five, three other

[91] Speech before Lincoln Chamber of Commerce, in *Bankers' Magazine*, Nov. 1930, 823.

[92] R. J. Truptil, *British Banks and the London Money Market* (1936), 143, 150; T. Balogh, *Studies in Financial Organization* (Cambridge, 1947), 256–9.

[93] The classic statement is in R. Hilferding, *Finance Capital: A Study of the Latest Phase of Capitalist Development* (Vienna, 1910; Eng. edn. ed. T. Bottomore, transl. M. Watnick and S. Gordon, 1981).

[94] See e.g. J. W. Beaumont-Pease, in Committee on Finance and Industry, *Minutes of Evidence*, (1931), i. Q.2203–2206.

[95] H. Clay, *Lord Norman*, ch. 8; R. S. Sayers, *The Bank of England*, i. ch. 14; S. Tolliday, *Business, Banking and Politics*, ch. 8.

[96] R. S. Sayers, *The Bank of England*, i. 324.

[97] Ibid. 326.

signatories represented merchant banks and issuing houses associated with BIDCo—Lord Glenconner, V. H. Smith, and R. S. Guinness. Another seven had connections with the London clearing banks, all of which were subscribers to BIDCo shares—Sir Harry Goschen of the National Provincial; Goodenough and Sir Harold Snagge of Barclays; Beaumont Pease of Lloyds (and the family steel firm); and McKenna and Lord Ashfield (Sir Albert Stanley) of the Midland, for long the clearing bank having the closest links with industry.

Of the other nine signatories, we might note that Walter Wigham and Sir Alan Anderson were both directors of the Bank, the latter having 'rather more . . . knowledge of industrial matters' than was usual in Threadneedle Street.[98] Sir George May of the Prudential was later to be chairman of the Import Duties Advisory Committee. J. Gibson Jarvie and T. Gilbert Scott represented United Dominions Trust. An unusual institution in the British context, this was formed in 1922 to provide long-term credit to British manufacturers and distributors so that they could extend hire-purchase facilities to their customers. In January 1930 the Bank of England trebled the capital of UDT by providing £500,000, of which half was paid up.[99]

It is tempting to connect the appearance of the manifesto with the formation of BIDCo. Irrespective of wider opinion in the City, were the signatories a group which shared Norman's enthusiasms and which was fully committed to a closer relationship between finance and industry, constituting an alliance such as Schumpeter had discerned in pre-war Germany?[100] Was this the reason why, unlike Norman, they now forsook the traditional cosmopolitanism of their profession and embraced protection?

To argue thus would be unwise. The non-Bank capital of BIDCo was distributed amongst 'practically all the joint stock banks and issuing houses of importance in the country'.[101] Any important group of bankers, such as signed the manifesto, would have inevitably included a high proportion who were associated with BIDCo. More importantly, even if the association was significant, it would not reveal the precise motivation of those bankers who were led to signing the manifesto because of their association with BIDCo. In particular, it would not distinguish between those who saw the future leading inevitably to a convergence between financial and industrial interests, those who considered immediate economic conditions so severe that a tariff was vital in the interests of both industry and the wider economy, and those who would have resisted a tariff but for the cynical calculation that it would raise industrial profitability in the short term and allow time for bank disengagement.

Whilst some of the signatories may have been proponents of closer long-term links between finance and industry, it is important to notice that

---

[98] Ibid. 324.   [99] S. E. Thomas, *British Banks*, 156–8.
[100] J. A. Schumpeter, *Imperialism and Social Classes* (Oxford, 1951), 106–7.
[101] S. E. Thomas, *British Banks*, 151.

Norman and Granet, the leading lights in BIDCo, were not. In their evidence before the Macmillan Committee, both saw BIDCo and SMT as a temporary solution to emergency conditions, to be wound up when industry's circumstances improved. They gave no indication that evolutionary change was dictating a closer involvement of finance in industry, or that they would have welcomed it if it had been. One at least of Norman's motives in becoming so involved in industrial finance was to keep the Labour Government out of it.[102]

It would perhaps be unduly cynical to believe that any of those signing the bankers' manifesto did so merely in the hope that a tariff would raise short-term industrial profitability enough to allow bank disengagement. In the 1930s the commercial banks *did* seek to disentangle themselves from long-term commitments to industrial finance, though in the dearth of foreign business after 1931 the issuing-houses headed in the opposite direction, perhaps encouraged by the effects of the tariff and depreciation on industrial profitability.[103] Bankers are a secretive group, seldom leaving reasons for their actions to posterity, but most of the signatories probably reacted to the immediacy of the industrial crisis, seeing a tariff as necessary to industrial survival, made more aware than in years past of the mutual interdependence of the two sectors for prosperity, and yet still having little predisposition towards close long-term links between finance and industry.[104]

In any case, if some did advocate a tariff with the hidden motive of using it as a temporary device to aid bank disengagement, their operational requirements coincided in the short term with those of more genuine believers in the restorative effects of a tariff on industry and the economy. In addition, the depression threw into sharp relief the common interest shared by virtually all businessmen in economy and retrenchment, an interest which threatened to make differences over protection of secondary importance. Indeed, it is important to recognize, and has hitherto gone unnoticed, that the Free-Trade counter-manifesto did not so much damn protection out of hand as argue that it was irrelevant to the main problems facing British industry:

No present party takes any serious interest in economy: all appear to accept as inevitable a continuance of public expenditure on something like the present scale . . . British industry, *protected or unprotected*, cannot survive a continuance of the present burden of taxation . . . *Protection even to the point of prohibition of imports cannot save it*, while these major

---

[102] Committee on Finance and Industry, *Minutes of Evidence*, (1931), ii. Qu. 9127, 9137, 9140–1, 9151–2.

[103] S. Tolliday, *Business, Banking and Politics*, 184; T. Balogh, *Financial Organization*, 288–9.

[104] This interpretation would carry two important implications. First, the signatories of the bankers' manifesto were not committed fundamentally to a regime of long-term industrial protection. Secondly, if they are not seen as a small group who embraced finance-capitalism, it is more likely that they can be regarded as representing wider City opinion in 1930. This is compatible with the senior positions many of them held within their own institutions.

troubles remain, and protectionist propaganda at this moment only serves to divert attention from them.[105]

The counter-manifesto criticized the Conservatives for their protectionism and the Liberals for succouring Lloyd George's collectivist schemes. It was thus the 'curious condition of present-day politics that free trade may have to look for its chief standard bearer to a [Labour] party which, while professing to believe in freedom for the foreigner, denies any vestige of it to the trader or worker at home.'[106]

This caused some mirth amongst protectionists. Tariff Reformers had never urged a tariff because British industrialists were intrinsically inferior. They had always used the fact that British industry was more heavily taxed than its competitors to justify their policy. Responding to the counter-manifesto, Paine could of course admit that labour legislation and trade-union restrictionism resulted in British wages being 40 to 50 per cent above those in Europe, and that in addition there was 'enormous expenditure upon social services [and] unemployment doles' which fell upon the productive sector. But where, he jeered, was the Free-Trade solution?

by artificially protecting one of the essentials of production we have rendered inevitable the protection of the product against competition which otherwise we are powerless to meet . . . Of course, if this artificial protection of labour could be removed, and we could revert to the conditions with which Peel, Bright, and Cobden had to deal, the way might be open to us to revert to our former faith, but is there the remotest prospect of that being done before the ruin of our trade is accomplished?[107]

It was an argument used by Tariff Reformers for over thirty years. Now it had become accepted by all but a handful of former Free Traders. But, in truth, the business community did not, as Paine's riposte might be taken to imply, see protection and retrenchment as alternative policy-options. The depression increased their determination to press for both. To a certain extent it can be argued that during the depression the difference between Tariff-Reform and former Free-Trade businessmen merely became one of the *priority* accorded to protection or economy. Even that is not entirely accurate—sensing that protection had been won within the Conservative Party, some protectionist businessmen changed their emphasis to retrenchment, determined to maximize their position on both fronts.

Indeed, in the same month as the bankers' manifesto appeared, a group of 'old-fashioned Liberal businessmen' led by Hugh Bell and Ernest Benn founded the Friends of Economy movement for Free Trade and retrenchment. Almost immediately, they found that retrenchment attracted such a following amongst protectionist businessmen that they shifted their emphasis towards it and away

---

[105] *Bankers' Magazine*, Aug. 1930, 177 (my emphasis).   [106] Ibid.
[107] W. W. Paine to Ed., *The Times*, 18 July 1930.

from Free Trade.[108] The attraction for Tariff Reformers is not surprising—even the most protectionist Chambers of Commerce had been quick to denounce rising public expenditure throughout the 1920s. In the Conservative Party, those who saw protection as a way of *sustaining* public expenditure were rare enough, and indeed in December Baldwin and Chamberlain were pushed into taking steps to correct the impression that the Party was uninterested in economy.[109] Businessmen who thought similarly were even rarer. What is more surprising than the Conservative reaction is that the founders of the Friends of Economy were prepared to soft-pedal on Free Trade, and sit in council with the likes of arch-protectionist Sir Robert Horne. Their action, like the rhetoric of the Free-Trade counter-manifesto, suggests that the Free-Trade citadel had already been given up as lost.

IV

The FBI, now overwhelmingly protectionist, spent the first months of the Labour Government with its heart in its mouth. Most Free Traders in the FBI no longer supported the removal of the safeguarding duties, and a resolution was passed that such action would be 'most damaging' to industry. Even so, the leaders remained wary of publicizing any differences, however slight, and the embargo on discussion of Tariff Reform remained in place.[110]

Yet the FBI leaders' dilemma now became more acute. Neutrality had been pursued to maintain internal cohesion and give credence to the FBI's claim to be undisputed representative of industrial opinion. Any sign that some other organization might place itself in the van of business opinion was always to be feared: not responding to the taunts of the NUM in the 1920s had been a calculated risk. The bankers' manifesto provided the spur. Within days of its announcement, Sir Peter Rylands demanded in the Grand Council that FBI opinion be tested. His opponents, expecting serious division, raised no objection.[111] Doubt was cast on their sanguinity shortly afterwards when a poll of the British Engineers' Association reported 96 per cent of respondents in favour of Tariff Reform.[112]

A Fiscal Policy Enquiry Committee was established. This polled both the Industrial Groups and individual firms, with careful procedures to prevent double-counting.[113] Before its report could be completed, however, there came further news of the FBI's increasing danger of being outflanked. At the beginning

---

[108] P. Williamson, *National Crisis*, 139, 144; D. Abel, *Ernest Benn* (1960), 65–82.
[109] P. Williamson, *National Crisis*, 173.
[110] Grand Council Minutes, 12 Mar. 1930, 200/F/1/1/2, FBI.
[111] Grand Council Minutes, 9 July 1930, 200/F/1/1/2, FBI.
[112] T. Rooth, 'Political Economy of Protectionism', 62.
[113] FPEC Minutes, 9 and 16 July 1930, 200/F/1/1/74, FBI. The membership of the FPEC comprised Sir James Lithgow (president); O. C. Armstrong; Lord Barnby (Francis Willey); Lord

of October, president Sir James Lithgow registered alarm at the 'multiplicity of bodies that were being created' to represent business opinion in the depression. He was particularly concerned by Sir William Morris's new National Council of Industry and Commerce, a body of about 100 prominent businessmen whose leaders initially flirted with ideas of running business candidates and establishing a business party similar to those of the early BCU, and which FBI members felt was taking advantage of the FBI's inertia on the tariff issue.[114]

Whilst FBI leaders attempted to formulate working arrangements and demarcations to present to the NCIC, the results of the plebiscite were analysed. They confounded any belief that members were still seriously divided over the fiscal issue; 7.4 per cent reported a divergence of view on their boards which precluded a 'unanimous' decision, whilst others abstained 'on the ground that their industries would not be directly affected'. But, of the 72 per cent of firms which recorded a definite vote, over 96 per cent favoured a 'more general application of safeguarding duties' and a 'wide extension' of imperial preference. The result was virtually unchanged when firms were weighted by employment, and no Industrial Group still recorded a majority for Free Trade. Indeed, the coal industry, even the export sector, endorsed change overwhelmingly, 99 per cent being in favour. W. A. Lee, of the Mining Association of Great Britain, 'had not received one single vote from any export district in favour of the present system'.[115] The BEA poll had been mirrored almost precisely.

Aided by the knowledge that the Conservative Party was now coming to an accord on a definite and unambiguous fiscal policy, and meeting only five days after Bennett had made his offer of increased preference, the Grand Council reacted quickly to the plebiscite. Passing a series of resolutions drafted by past president Sir Eric Geddes,[116] it determined that the Federation would 'press by every means in its power' for protection and preference.[117] The Fiscal Policy Enquiry Committee, now re-styled the President's Advisory Committee on Fiscal Policy, was left in overall control, whilst a Fiscal Policy Committee was established to draft the FBI's tariff requirements, and a Co-ordinating Committee was set up to liaise with other business groups. By this time the Conservative Party had declared that it would be necessary to pass an emergency tariff in

Gainford (J. A. Pease); Lennox B. Lee; Sir Max Muspratt; Sir Peter Rylands; Sir Eric Geddes; and Sir Dudley Docker. Later members included Sir Arthur Duckham and Lord Weir.

[114] Grand Council Minutes, 1 Oct. 1930, 200/F/1/1/2, FBI. On the NCIC, see P. Williamson, *National Crisis*, 63–4, 138–9.

[115] 'Report of the Special Committee on Fiscal Policy', n.d., 200/F/1/1/74, FBI; Grand Council Minutes, 13 Oct. 1930, 200/F/1/1/2, FBI.

[116] One resolution re-affirmed the FBI's 'policy of abstention from party politics' except at a time of 'grave national peril'. Another recognized that protection would not be sufficient in itself and went on to list additional measures.

[117] Grand Council Minutes, 13 Oct. 1930, 200/F/1/1/2, FBI.

order to forestall anticipatory dumping; but operating in the public eye still held dangers for the FBI, since any internal squabbling over grading would be damaging if played upon by the Free Trade press.[118]

V

The FBI's investigation of a tariff structure was almost immediately eclipsed by the Conservative Party's own. Chamberlain's assumption of the chairmanship of the Conservative Research Department led to the establishment of Cunliffe-Lister's Tariff Committee. This, it has been claimed, broke with the Conservative tradition of *ad hoc* empiricism and 'muddling through':

[T]he basis for the tariff legislation of the National Government, including both the Abnormal Importations Act of 1931 and the Import Duties Act of 1932, was provided by the detailed proposals of the Cunliffe-Lister committee. Few British Governments have taken office equipped with such thorough and programmatic preparation for a major innovation in public policy.[119]

Cunliffe-Lister would have agreed. The Tariff Committee 'worked for eighteen months. We received a mass of evidence from many trades and industries, and produced a report covering the whole structure and operation of a general tariff'.[120]

Such remarks exaggerate the thoroughness of the Committee's enquiries, and overlook the differences between its recommendations and the protective legislation eventually introduced by the National Government. Nevertheless, Cunliffe-Lister's work was highly important. In giving tangible shape to the protectionist consensus within the Conservative Party, it laid down objectives that simply could not be ignored by the body finally empowered to implement the Import Duties Act.[121]

In fact the Committee met only twenty-five times, and only for a period of approximately six months. Cunliffe-Lister 'soon became impatient with the lack of application—and even of knowledge—of his colleagues', whilst secretary Henry Brooke's opinion of them was even less charitable. In consequence these two shouldered the brunt of the work.[122] This may have been partly the result of keeping the Committee small and restricting its enquiries in a deliberate attempt to avoid the charge that it was a vehicle for pushing vested interests. Apart from the chairman himself, the only major business representatives were Sir Basil Blackett, director of the Bank of England and of several telegraph and wireless

---

[118] FPC Minutes, 23 and 29 Oct. 11 Nov. 1930, 200/F/1/1/75, FBI.

[119] S. H. Beer, *Modern British Politics* (1965; 1969 edn.), 288.

[120] Lord Swinton, *I Remember* (1948), 38; also cited ibid.

[121] Sir H. Hutchinson, *Tariff-Making and Industrial Reconstruction* (1965), 21–2.

[122] Minutes of Tariffs Committee, CRD, 1/2/6; J. A. Cross, *Lord Swinton*, 95; J. Ramsden, *The Making of Conservative Party Policy* (1980), 53.

companies, and Herbert Williams. Though Williams had given up his position as secretary of the Machine Tools Association in 1928, he still had extensive knowledge of industrial structure and business opinion, and, like Amery, he brought with him links with the EIA and EEU onto the Committee.[123] Even so, there was no attempt to secure the wide base of industrial representation that the Tariff Commission, by its working philosophy, would have considered necessary to the construction of a tariff. The Committee's draft report made clear the extent to which it worked independently, even secretly, through 'private enquiry from experts. We also gave due consideration to *several unsought* memoranda sent in to the Research Department by representatives of various trades *who had noticed* Mr. Baldwin's references in his speeches to the existence of the Committee'.[124]

Even this may exaggerate. Enquiries do not appear to have been formal or extensive—for the most part, no record of them remains in the Committee's papers. With the exception of iron and steel, 'regarded as of such special importance that it was worthwhile making an effort to secure agreement with the leaders as to the rates of duty to be imposed', consultations were undoubtedly minor. The Committee was clearly anxious to avoid the accusation that Conservative tariff policy would degenerate into a 'profiteer's paradise' or a 'crook's corner', and it devoted a substantial part of its report to the establishment of a judicial tariff board, insulated from political and business pressure, with a 'power of quick suspension' should a particular duty work against the public interest.[125]

In their work on the actual structure of a protective tariff Cunliffe-Lister and Brook built upon the work of Milner's Tariff Advisory Committee of 1923. This was a hastily convened but heavyweight group of Tariff Reformers comprising Milner, Kylsant, Sir William Ashley, Sir Algernon Firth, Hewins, Sir Arthur Pugh of the ISTC, and Sir Peter Rylands. Holding ten meetings in November and December 1923, it disbanded itself shortly after Baldwin's election defeat, leaving only an informal report on its 'necessarily imperfect and provisional . . . [and] interrupted labours'.[126] Even so, as the organ of a government in power, the TAC was able to tap the experience of the relevant departments, especially the Board of Trade and Customs and Excise.[127]

The early meetings of the CRD bore a strong resemblance to the unfinished labours of the TAC. Both favoured an initial *ad valorem* tariff, gradually changed to specific where appropriate; both recommended a full-time Tariff Board to

[123] The other members were ex-diplomat Lord Lloyd, and ex-military Tory MP Herbert Spender Clay.

[124] 'Tariffs Committee: Draft Report', 3, CRD 1/2/10 (my emphasis).

[125] S. Baldwin, 'The Conservative Tariff Policy: Text of Address given at Hull on July 18th. 1931', copy in CRD 1/2/13; Joseph Ball's summary of the Report of the CRD Tariff Committee, 4, CRD 1/2/11.

[126] 'Tariff Advisory Committee Report', Dec. 1923, copy in CRD 1/2/1.

[127] 'Tariff: Report of Inter-Departmental Conference', 485/1–31, Milner Papers.

hear disputes over classification, applications, and appeals; and both favoured the continuance of existing provisions—the one-third preference on Empire products and the rates applying under existing legislation such as the key-industry provisions and the Dyestuffs Act. There were differences, however, in the levels of duties recommended. Most members of the TAC favoured rates of 5 per cent on raw materials, $12\frac{1}{2}$ per cent on semi-manufactures, and 20 per cent on finished goods. But Firth and Rylands pressed for higher duties, and Ashley conceded that these would be necessary if dumping affected the home market. Thus it was recommended that the $33\frac{1}{3}$ per-cent rate of the safeguarding legislation be extended to any industry of 'national interest' if trading conditions were abnormal.[128] This was clearly tantamount to trans-planting the troublesome safeguarding hurdle into a general tariff, though how rigorously the TAC intended it should be applied must remain a matter of conjecture. Cunliffe-Lister's later rates of 10 per cent, $16\frac{1}{2}$ per cent, and 33 per cent, as well as representing a general shift upwards, also escaped that trap, applying the safeguarding rate without test to all fully manufactured goods.[129]

Though higher than those contemplated by Milner's TAC, these rates did not represent any failure to insulate the Tariff Committee from business pressure and log-rolling. The FBI's Fiscal Policy Committee met several times whilst Cunliffe-Lister's enquiry was under way, and the fact that the CRD archive contains copies of the FPC's draft report as well as its final report suggests that Cunliffe-Lister was kept informed of FBI thinking.[130] Furthermore, the chairman of the FPC, Sir William Larke, kept contact with Cunliffe-Lister on iron and steel in his position as director of the NFISM. But the FPC itself exercised little pressure on the CRD. It made clear its requirement that Chamberlain's 'emergency tariff' should not be flat-rate: beyond this, it was reluctant to press a detailed scheme, since the Government would be 'chary about accepting a ready-made policy'. Furthermore, the FPC expected the emergency tariff to be crude and liable to heavy criticism. Since the Conservative Party favoured a permanent tariff board to convert the emergency tariff piecemeal into a permanent tariff, the FBI should sit on the sidelines, consulting its Industrial Groups and advising the tariff board. At least in its rhetoric, the FPC was as concerned to create a mechanism for removing a tariff if it was abused by the protected industry as was Cunliffe-Lister.[131] Only if the FBI were pressed by government to recommend rates should a five-tier tariff of zero, 10 per cent, 15 per cent, 25 per cent, and $33\frac{1}{3}$ per cent be suggested. A joint meeting of the FPC and the EEU affirmed 'the desirability of not consulting individual

[128] TAC Minutes, 22 Nov. 1923, 486/9–14, Milner Papers.
[129] Tariff Committee Minutes, 19 Dec. 1930, CRD 1/2/6.
[130] FPC Minutes, 200/F/1/1/75, FBI; TC/7 and TC/24, CRD 1/2/7.
[131] FPC Minutes, 23 and 29 Oct. 1930, 11 Nov. 1930, 200/F/1/1/75, FBI.

industries in regard to the emergency schedule, but of leaving it to the Board of Trade'.[132]

Thus, within the FBI there was consensus that heavy lobbying was unnecessary and confidence that Conservative intentions were broadly acceptable. The creation of a tariff board would provide the forum for tariff negotiation by individual industries, and the politicians should be left to bear the brunt of the criticism that the first attempts at a protectionist tariff would attract. The first objective was the establishment of a protectionist *regime*. That accomplished, lobbying the Board of Trade would lose its odium and its sensitivity. At the same time, the FBI would be displaced from the storm-centre of inter- and intra-industry conflicts over free lists, export drawbacks, and grading structures.

There were doubtless informal and unrecorded consultations between Cunliffe-Lister and FBI leaders, but they probably did not extend beyond generalities and certainly did not amount to anything in the nature of sustained lobbying or log-rolling. With iron and steel, however, that industry of 'special importance', Cunliffe-Lister took greater care. Little had come of the Baldwin cabinet's hopes that the banks might be the vehicle to promote thoroughgoing rationalization in the industry. In the summer of 1930, Norman, who persisted in the belief that a tariff would reduce the industry's incentive to rationalize voluntarily, was alarmed to find that the Conservatives were becoming more willing to concede protection without prior rationalization; 'Cunliffe-Lister would go no further than undertaking to stress to his steel friends that the *amount* of protection they would get would depend on their efforts to rationalise'.[133] Neville Chamberlain, also, was now prepared to grant protection before rationalization. A subcommittee of the Committee for Civil Research, reporting in May 1930, thought the state of the industry so serious that 'in return for a measure of protection the industry is in a mood to pledge itself to almost anything', and might be induced to produce concrete plans rather than vague promises. 'Safeguarding *by itself* might do good or . . . even do harm. Its effect on the minds of those in high places in the industry is what matters'.[134] Chamberlain, too, considered that a psychological boost was vital, and that protection would be necessary to secure the large amounts of capital necessary for improvement.[135]

When Williams undertook to enquire into the industry for the Tariff Committee in January 1931,[136] he could scarcely have done so at a more dramatic time. The industry was working at 30 per cent of capacity. In the same month, the NFISM Executive determined to 'force a decision' against the 'small minority'

[132] Report of Joint Meeting of Representatives of the EEU and the FBI Fiscal Policy Sub-Committee, 28 Nov. 1930, 200/F/1/1/75, FBI.
[133] S. Tolliday, 'Tariffs and Steel, 1916–1934: The Politics of Industrial Decline', in J. Turner (ed.), *Businessmen and Politics*, 60–1.
[134] 'Summary of Report on the Iron and Steel Industry', 29 May 1930, CRD 1/4/3.
[135] CRD Memorandum on the Iron and Steel Industry, 16 June 1930, CRD 1/4/3.
[136] Tariff Committee Minutes, 21 Jan. 1931, CRD 1/2/6.

of its members who still clung to Free Trade. A protectionist resolution was passed with only two dissentients—K. D. MacKenzie, a Scottish sheet roller, and H. Spence Thomas of the Melingriffith Tinplate Co.[137]

The Tariff Committee trod carefully, not because the Free-Trade residue within the industry was important in itself, but because even small divisions would be magnified by political opponents. It was the progressive steel roller, L. D. Whitehead,[138] who established a basis for consensus. Belonging to that section where Free Traders had been most common, Whitehead nevertheless believed that once imports had destroyed the heavy steel-makers the finishing trades would be next in line. Fearful that a flat-rate emergency tariff of 10 per cent[139] would be of 'little use in the more finished trades' because of the disparity of British and European labour costs, he proposed a schedule with 5 per cent on pig, 10 per cent on semis, 15 per cent on heavy finished steel, 20 per cent on light rolled sections, and 25 per cent on wire and tubes. Such rates would be greeted by the industry 'with virtual unanimity'.[140] Larke of the NFISM endorsed these proposals, even though they afforded lower protection to semis and heavy finished products than his own.[141] By 13 February he had secured the approval of four of the main heavy-steel producers,[142] and had been led to believe that the largest tinplate maker, Richard Thomas and Co., and the large sheet-maker, John Summers and Sons Ltd., would also give their support.

This was as far as Cunliffe-Lister could go. To secure the agreement of the entire industry would require a meeting of some 300 people, which would 'necessarily become public' and be 'most undesirable'. It would also be superfluous.[143] Whilst he clearly felt vulnerable to criticism that the steel industry had been singled out for special consultation, he could with some justice claim that the result had not been a victory for log-rolling. The five-tier iron-and-steel schedule afforded lower protection to the industry than if the three-rate principle had been applied. This was 'a complete answer to any charge that the steel manufacturers have been able to manipulate the tariff in their own interests'.[144]

---

[137] J. C. Carr and W. Taplin, *The British Steel Industry*, 469.

[138] Whitehead introduced the Morgan semicontinuous mill into Britain at Tredegar in 1906–7. See D. Burn, *Economic History of Steelmaking 1867–1939* (Cambridge, 1940), 198; J. C. Carr and W. Taplin, *The British Steel Industry*, 225.

[139] Presumably the 'revenue tariff' which received some exposure in the press.

[140] Whitehead to Cunliffe-Lister, 13 Feb. 1931, TC/23, CRD 1/2/7.

[141] Larke to Williams, 27 Jan. 1931, TC/15, CRD 1/2/7.

[142] Sir John Craig, chairman and managing director of David Colville and Sons; Arthur Dorman of Dorman, Long and Co.; Sir John Beale of Guest, Keen, Baldwins, Ltd. (and chairman of GKN); and R. S. Hilton, managing director of United Steel Companies Ltd. By the time Cunliffe-Lister's report was completed the iron and steel provisions had also been endorsed by H. C. Bond of Colville's; E. J. George of the Consett Iron Co.; Sir Peter Rylands of Rylands Bros.; and B. Talbot of the Cargo Fleet Iron Co.

[143] Memo by Cunliffe-Lister, TC/23, CRD 1/2/7.

[144] Ball's summary of CRD Tariff Committee Report, 2, CRD 1/2/11.

VI

Just as the FPC's preferred strategy was to stand aside whilst the politicians drafted the emergency tariff, so the FBI's leaders hoped to avoid public propaganda, which should be the province of its new partners on the Co-ordinating Committee. The representatives of the EIA, NUM, NCIC, and EEU, none of which had any aversion to standing in the spotlight, had no objection to the FBI playing a backstage role. They also thought it possible, at least to some extent, to achieve the rough division of labour sought by the FBI. The NCIC should concentrate on the persuasion of working men through its League of Industry, the EIA and NUM on propaganda and parliamentary work, the EEU on imperial economic relations. More problematic was the FBI's hope that the Co-ordinating Committee could be used to prevent the other organizations issuing material in conflict with its own objectives.[145] The main areas of potential disagreement were preference and agriculture.

On preference, the motor manufacturers were almost certainly a minority within the FBI in advocating free entry of colonial primaries; more typical was the BEA's view that this would throw away a bargaining counter with the Empire.[146] During the 1920s the FBI's Overseas Committee had found existing preferential arrangements unsatisfactory.[147] In autumn 1929 attention became fixed on increases in the Australian tariff and Canada's raising of the Empire content of goods eligible for preference from 25 to 50 per cent. A year later, FBI shoe manufacturers were angered when Bennett, whose accession to power had been expected to liberalize Anglo-Canadian trade, announced that Canadian producers would be protected from the 'cheap labour' of the mother country.[148] Against this background, FBI leaders were determined to exclude the Federated Chambers of Commerce of the British Empire from the Co-ordinating Committee.[149]

The FBI was thus in ungenerous mood, and it remained to be seen whether it could co-operate on the Co-ordinating Committee with Croft's EIA, or the EEU of Mond and Amery. In more normal times such concerns would have daunted the FBI leaders, but they no longer did so, and boldness was justified. In November 1930 Herbert Williams informed the Co-ordinating Committee that the EEU had 'not yet consider[ed] the tariff which was desirable for British industry'.[150] This was meant to reassure FBI representatives that the EEU's imperial vision did not extend to a generosity which would preclude real

---

[145] PAC Minutes, 5 Nov. 1930, 200/F/1/1/74, FBI. Sir Arthur Duckham feared that co-operation with the other organizations would jeopardize the FBI's new-found relationship with the TUC, but Lithgow had already taken soundings and found the TUC chairman and secretary amenable.

[146] FPC Minutes, 29 Oct. 1930, 200/F/1/1/75, FBI.

[147] Overseas Committee Minutes, 26 Feb. 1925, 24 June 1926, 1 Mar. 1928, 6 Dec. 1928, 200/F/1/1/65-6, FBI.

[148] Overseas Committee Minutes, 26 Sept. 1930, 200/F/1/1/66, FBI.

[149] PAC Minutes, 5 Nov. 1930, 200/F/1/1/74, FBI.

[150] Co-ordinating Committee Minutes, 12 Nov. 1930, 200/F/1/1/74, FBI.

bargaining. Amery favoured negotiations direct with Australian and Canadian manufacturers to discover which industries the Dominions really wanted to protect, and which represented 'merely a political desire to foster [indigenous] industry generally'.[151] Croft, also, was insistent that the Co-ordinating Committee should work to a common formula. As trust grew, the FBI raised no objection when Sir Ben Morgan, a representative of the EEU on the Committee, secured the inclusion of BEPO upon it.[152]

But this still left agriculture. Determined to improve imperial markets for UK manufactures, the FBI, EEU, and EIA recognized that the leverage of preference on food duties was central. In a sense, therefore, the FBI had to have an agricultural policy, and this made it difficult to avoid the awkward question of food duties. Recognizing, in Weir's dismissive phrase, that agriculture should 'receive some assistance', the FBI was nevertheless reluctant to get embroiled in agricultural protection, and a meeting with NFU representatives convinced Lithgow that it would not be 'suitable' for the NFU to join the Co-ordinating Committee.[153] Shortly afterwards the FBI was pressed by the Central Chambers of Agriculture to endorse a memorandum on agricultural policy. It found the document 'open to serious objection' from an industrial perspective. Yet fear that the FBI's partners might be overly sympathetic to agriculture was overborne by the desire to delegate the responsibility for formulating an agricultural policy to someone else. Against all precedents of FBI cautiousness, and almost before the Co-ordinating Committee was fully in operation, Nugent and Walker were exploring the possibility that the EEU might take over this aspect of the work and produce a joint EEU-FBI policy. The EEU representatives, led by Amery, took on the task with alacrity.[154]

The EEU's solution was to adopt the wheat quota-scheme of the CRD's Agricultural Research Committee. Williams had attended the ARC's meeting with grain merchants and millers in July, and the EEU had declared its support for the quota soon after the Crystal Palace speech.[155] Subsequently, it had established a joint committee with the CCA, both organizations being concerned to demonstrate 'the possibility—previously doubted—of representatives of industry and of agriculture agreeing upon a common policy for agriculture'. The committee's report, available to the FBI in the summer of 1931 though not published until October, repeated the call for a wheat quota whilst preferring tariffs for other agricultural goods.[156]

[151] Report of joint meeting of representatives of EEU and FPC, 28 Nov. 1930, 200/F/1/1/75, FBI.

[152] Co-ordinating Committee Minutes, 12 Nov. 1930, 200/F/1/1/74, FBI.

[153] PAC Minutes, 5 Nov. 1930, 200/F/1/1/74, FBI.

[154] Co-ordinating Committee Minutes, 12 Dec. 1930, 27 Jan. 1931, 200/F/1/1/74, FBI.

[155] A. F. Cooper, *British Agricultural Policy*, 101–3. The EEU's *Preliminary General Report of the Research Committee* was circulated to the delegates at the Imperial Conference in October.

[156] EEU, *Agricultural Policy: Past, Present and Future* (1939), 7. A summary of the joint EEU-CCA report is given on 9–12.

Once again following the trend of Conservative Party policy, and like others seeking ways of making the introduction of tariffs more palatable, all but one of the FBI's industrial groups approved. Dissent came from the millers, who sought to mobilize the FBI in their defence. Already in a situation of over-capacity, in part the consequence of government control during the War and decontrol after it, and mindful of some sentiment within Labour ranks for nationalization,[157] the millers were highly sensitive to government intervention. More specifically, the millers were opposed to early schemes for a wheat quota—Addison's scheme, and even more so that of the ARC—because they required the millers to use home and Dominion wheat in specified proportions. This would increase the price of the former to the British miller, since the very object was to call forth an additional supply, and perhaps also that of the latter. But having avoided the implementation of any duty on wheat in requiring the quota, both the Labour and Conservative versions then avoided the introduction of any import control upon foreign or Dominion *flour*, since this would destroy the façade of duty-free bread.[158] It was a classic but beautifully concealed example of negative protection of the milling industry.

The long history of the wheat quota stretches well beyond Ottawa, and is beyond the scope of this study. What is significant here is that, in its concern to brush past the agricultural problem, the FPC displayed only ritual sympathy with the millers, and was clearly reluctant that the scheme should falter on their account. As the National Government formulated proposals for a quota some months later, the millers found them no more acceptable than those of the EEU, and sought FBI aid. There was some sympathy, but as late as January 1932 the FBI had made no commitment of support beyond the 'ordinary assurance of industrial solidarity'.[159] The affair suggests, once more, that British manufacturers were less opposed to agricultural protection in itself than they were fearful that food duties would prevent the attainment of an industrial tariff. Once protection of wheat had been hidden by a quota, the need was to push ahead.

VII

At the second meeting of the Co-ordinating Committee, Croft appealed for financial assistance. Though Amery considered that the bankers' manifesto had given Tariff Reform its 'biggest leg up since 1903',[160] any effect on EIA finances had been far from dramatic. In the third quarter of 1930 new subscriptions and

[157] A. F. Lucas, *Industrial Reconstruction and the Control of Competition* (1937), 136–9.
[158] FPC Minutes, 14 May 1931, 200/F/1/1/75, FBI.
[159] FPC Minutes, 19 Jan. 1932, 200/F/1/1/75, FBI. For details of the introduction and subsequent history of the wheat quota, and of agricultural policy more generally, see A. F. Cooper, *British Agricultural Policy*, and T. Rooth, *British Protectionism and the International Economy* (Cambridge, 1993), ch. 8.
[160] Quoted in R. W. D. Boyce, *British Capitalism*, 254.

renewals together totalled only £537; in July there was a danger that meetings in the critical North-West might have to be discontinued for want of a mere £60. A dinner in Croft's honour in October and an appeal brought in £3,549, but the Association still 'lived from hand to mouth'. New subscriptions in December dropped to £3.[161]

Nugent thought a contribution possible from the FBI's own small fund;[162] the NUM and EEU were in no position to help. But Morris, who had donated £1,000 to the EIA in January 1929 in recognition of Croft's 'invaluable work' on safeguarding,[163] stepped in immediately, attracted by Croft's suggestion that the EIA's appeal to workers might be integrated with the work of the League of Industry. The NCIC had as yet made no appeal for funds of its own, but Morris himself guaranteed £5,000. With this, Croft promised a doubling of propaganda, and a week later the EIA undertook to supply speakers for the League of Industry's incursions into the factories.[164]

The best estimate of EIA income for the ten months from January to October 1931 is £9,340.[165] If this is correct, Morris provided over half, and did indeed enable Croft to double EIA effort. In the year ended 30 September 1930 the EIA had organized 1,540 meetings. In January 1931 it stepped up its meetings in Lancashire from 60 to 140 per month, and increased those in Yorkshire to 40 per month, in Durham to 30 per month, and in London to 320 per month. There were three separate campaigns in the South West: 'for the first time tariff speakers were being welcomed in the Cornish constituencies'. Press activity was also doubled. This quickening of pace was sustained. By the end of September 1931 the yearly total of meetings stood at 2,620, of which 1,140 had been held in the North West.[166]

In December 1930 the existence of the Co-ordinating Committee was leaked to the press, but even FBI members acknowledged that little harm had been

---

[161] EIA, Finance Committee Minutes, 7 July 1930, 20 Nov. 1930, EIA Papers; EIA, *Fourth Annual Report 1930*; Croft, *My Life of Strife*, (London, n.d.), 183.

[162] In fact, the propaganda fund stood at *c.* £7,000, a substantial sum compared with the other groups on the Committee. See FPC Minutes, 11 Dec. 1930, 200/F/1/1/75, FBI.

[163] On this occasion Morris was generally 'opposed to the existence of Associations and Societies which seek ... to procure certain advantages in return for the money which is subscribed', largely because they had little chance of success unless 'organised and controlled on economical business lines'. Noting with alarm the proliferation of societies as the general election drew near, he advocated some attempt at co-ordination and amalgamation: the businessman would be more generous 'if the appeal emanated from one source which he knew to be reliable'. See Morris to Croft, 9 Jan. 1929, 1/16, Croft Papers.

[164] Co-ordinating Committee Minutes, 20 and 28 Nov. 1930, 200/F/1/1/74, FBI.

[165] Figures for February and March are unavailable, so the total of £7,472 has been increased proportionately. More importantly, it is not certain that donations are fully recorded before Aug. 1931. See EIA, Finance Committee Minutes, 20 Nov. 1930, 25 June 1931, 9 Sept. 1931, 5 Nov. 1931, EIA Papers.

[166] EIA, *Fourth Annual Report 1930*; *Fifth Annual Report 1931*; Co-ordinating Committee Minutes, 27 Jan. 1931, 200/F/1/1/74, FBI.

done, and over the next months any FBI reserve at a more public position melted away. Nugent pursued the rather bizarre scheme of preparing material for the commercial travellers of FBI firms to distribute to their customers. Much emphasis was put on a series of colour posters with the EIA's imprint. By mid-February 1931 the FBI itself had issued 700,000 leaflets, 15,000 posters, and 10,000 pamphlets. In March the Federation published 60,000 copies of 'Industry and the Nation', a report by the FPC with some assistance from the Industrial Policy Committee. It recommended an emergency tariff, to be replaced by a 'scientific tariff' constructed by an independent tariff board, together with imperial preference and 'any reasonable method' of safeguarding British agriculture.[167] Only in two areas did the Co-ordinating Committee exercise restraint: the other groups resisted, as too 'political', the EIA's call for mass demonstrations in industrial centres, and the Committee avoided issuing propaganda on particular industries, reluctant to be identified with any narrow, sectional appeal.

The EEU did not develop the national propaganda machine envisaged by its founders the previous July: with Mond's failing health and death in December 1930 the 'wider organization . . . faded out', and Amery and Williams concentrated on their 'research' into agricultural policy and preference.[168] BEPO contributed little to the effort. Otherwise, activity was at a high level, and harmony on the Committee was increased by the knowledge that it had caught the flood tide of public opinion. A large proportion of the activity overseen by the Co-ordinating Committee was directed at workers, just as the EIA's propaganda concentrated on working-class constituencies. In the new year, twenty-eight branches of the League of Industry were formed; according to Cambray of the NCIC, very little opposition was encountered in the factories. By June there were 200 branches grouped into eight area organizations. Whereas in November 1930 the district secretaries of the FBI had found members reluctant to inflict propaganda upon their workforces, by March 1931 some 500 firms were distributing material. The summer saw an attempted Free Trade revival, but the campaign was shadowed by the EIA, which anticipated Liberal meetings by a week, and then remained in the locality afterwards, inundating the hapless populace with speeches and literature. At the time Croft thought the Free Trade effort unimpressive; retrospectively he considered it 'a fiasco and no special effort was needed to counter it'.[169] By June the Committee sensed that the public was tiring of the onslaught, and a pause was suggested. Significantly,

---

[167] Co-ordinating Committee Minutes, 28 Nov. 1930, 12 Dec. 1930, 18 Dec. 1930, 18 Feb. 1931, 200/F/1/1/74, FBI; FBI, *Fifteenth Annual Report 1931*, copy in 200/F/4/2/14, FBI; 'Industry and the Nation' endorsed the joint report of the EEU and CCA on agriculture, subject to expressing reserve on the wheat quota and reporting the milling industry's opposition to it.

[168] L. S. Amery, *My Political Life* (1955), iii. 19–20.

[169] Co-ordinating Committee Minutes, 27 Jan. 1931, 17 June 1931, 200/F/1/1/74, FBI; PAC Minutes, 5 Nov. 1930, 11 Mar. 1931, 200/F/1/1/74, FBI; EIA, *Fifth Annual Report 1931*.

it did not meet again until December, by which time the Abnormal Importations Bill lay before Parliament.

VIII

From about May 1931, the Conservatives became increasingly confident of a return to power. Public opinion had clearly moved rapidly towards tariffs in the previous year.[170] At Hull in July, Baldwin endorsed the proposals of Cunliffe-Lister's CRD committee, referring to an 'emergency' tariff which would be imperfect in the first instance and would require 'adjustment' by a permanent Tariff Commission.[171]

In its lack of specific detail, Baldwin's announcement might formerly have led businessmen to doubt that the industrial tariff was yet secure, but there was now a clear feeling that the mandate imposed on the Conservative leaders by their Party was inescapable. More fundamental to the uncertain position of the industrial tariff was the increasingly widespread support for crisis measures by erstwhile Free Traders. There was an *ex ante* possibility that Labour might pre-empt the Conservatives by introducing a revenue tariff in a package designed to rectify the budget and restore the trade balance. Ever since December 1929 there had been some support for a tariff in the cabinet, but the brooding presence of Snowden had limited the infection. By August 1931, fifteen out of twenty-one cabinet members favoured a revenue tariff—some, like MacDonald himself, as a way of avoiding a rise in direct taxation which would hit confidence in the financial markets, others as a course preferable to expenditure cuts. At this time a revenue tariff seemed to be upon everyone's lips. Anticipating MacDonald's remarkable three-party meeting on 18 September to discuss a consensus on the May Committee's proposals, Baldwin and Bridgeman, and even Amery and Horne, urged Conservative representatives Chamberlain and Hoare to press for a revenue tariff. Liberal Sir Herbert Samuel discerned a Conservative attempt to secure protection 'under the name of an Emergency Tariff for revenue'.[172]

But Chamberlain was playing a long game—longer, as it turned out, than he knew himself. At the inter-party meeting he stressed retrenchment, determined that the Labour cabinet should not avoid economy by resort to a tariff. His strategy was to force Labour to bear the unpopularity of expenditure cuts, allowing the Conservatives to return after an election with a progressive programme of protection and preference. The formation of the National Government, at first intended to last only a few weeks, did not fundamentally

---

[170] P. Williamson, *National Crisis*, 242; S. Ball, *Baldwin and the Conservative Party*, 154, 169–71.

[171] S. Baldwin, 'The Conservative Tariff Policy: Text of Address given at Hull on July 18th. 1931', copy in 1/2/13, CRD.

[172] P. Williamson, *National Crisis*, 308 (Samuel cited, 300).

alter this strategy. But the National Government proved unexpectedly popular. To bring it down might backfire on the Conservatives. After unpopular spending cuts, non-National Labour might be in a stronger position, requiring continued coalition to meet it. It soon became clear that the National Government might last longer than anyone thought.[173]

The Conservatives' new allies, many recent and reluctant converts to a tariff, required careful handling as long as the Conservatives wished to avoid exercising *force majeure* within the National Government. Hence, it was early recognized that tariffs must be postponed. Amery was incensed, but Croft's role as marshall of backbench protectionism was critical. He demanded from Baldwin an assurance that 'a mandate is sought from the Country for a tariff policy directly the immediate financial problem is solved . . . [and that] nothing will be done to compromise the position of the Party with regard to Protection and Preference'. Baldwin's reply was simple: 'Politically we are as velvet'.[174]

'Revenue' tariffs, or 'emergency' tariffs, or tariffs to correct the 'balance of trade', the very tariffs that former Free Traders were likely to accept, were clearly insufficient for industrial protectionists. A revenue tariff would probably be too low to be protective, might encompass raw materials, and would probably be flat rate. It is important to notice that, as it appeared in the crisis of 1931, the 'balance of trade' argument for a tariff was not the same as that used by Croft in his EIA speeches. Croft stressed the merchandise balance, arguing that rectification would lessen unemployment.[175] This naturally implied a permanent tariff, since Britain's need for food and raw-material imports predisposed her to a permanent deficit. But, by the summer of 1931, the term was used less specifically, advocates of such a measure intending it to redress imbalance on current account, or even to redress the overall balance of payments, including capital account. This, alongside the need to balance the budget, was the objective of those within the Bank of England who urged a tariff in the September crisis.[176] The term 'emergency' tariff encapsulated the protectionists' problem. Tariffs for revenue and 'balance-of-trade' purposes might not only be unsuitable for industrial purposes; they might also be impermanent.

The devaluation of September 1931 was a serious complicating factor, since it afforded the Free Traders a strong case for arguing that a tariff was no longer necessary.[177] Furthermore, the uncertainty introduced by this new factor increased the logic behind a temporary rather than a permanent tariff solution. There were signs of this even among a minority of FBI representatives—Boyd of the shipbuilders and Lee of the coal-owners still regarded devaluation highly

[173] Ibid. 302, 342–3, 390–1.
[174] Croft to Baldwin, 25 Aug. 1931, Baldwin to Croft, 26 Aug. 1931, 1/3, Croft Papers.
[175] e.g. Croft to Ed., *The Times*, 31 May 1927, 12.
[176] R. S. Sayers, *The Bank of England*, ii. 403 n.; T. Rooth, 'Political Economy', 84.
[177] L. Robbins, *Autobiography of an Economist* (1971), 156.

in relation to protection. On 25 September Alexander Ramsay[178] and Sir William Larke informed the FBI's Economic Emergency Committee that there was in some quarters 'undue optimism' on the effects of devaluation. Most within the FBI doubted that devaluation would cure the trade balance on its own, or have a permanent effect, but the EEC found it difficult to draft a press release which would stress the need for a tariff without implying that depreciation would be unhelpful.[179]

Though, after the election, the reconstituted National Government acted quickly to introduce the Abnormal Importations Act in November, the measure was uncertain in its provenance. In September its architect, Runciman, had 'suggested that a high tariff on a few selected luxuries might help the balance of trade'.[180] It had been Snowden's suggestion that Runciman be President of the Board of Trade when Baldwin insisted that Chamberlain be given the Exchequer instead of Health.[181] Now, Runciman had power by Order in Council to impose, at his own discretion, duties of up to 100 per cent on manufactures imported in 'abnormal' quantities for a twelve-month period. The reappearance of the word 'abnormal' chilled those who remembered the history of safeguarding under the 1925 White Paper. Immediately the NUM contacted all MPs with the demand that it should be interpreted liberally.[182]

But now there was an important difference. Before 1929 Croft would have destroyed the party he loved. Now he still stood behind Baldwin, sword sheathed, hand on hilt. But the thrust would no longer be for Baldwin's back. At the end of October he none too subtly reminded the country that the EIA were 'not only a considerable majority of the Conservative Party, but an actual majority of the new House'.[183] Beaverbrook, like Amery exasperated with Conservative procrastination in joining the National Government, reported gains in EIA membership with glee in his newspapers—one cartoon depicted terrified Labour ministers on the back of the vast, rampaging tiger of 'Page Croft's Absolute Majority Tariff Group'.[184] Furthermore, Runciman acted quickly. His first Order was made on 20 November—previously failed safeguarding applications like domestic pottery and glassware, cutlery, woollen manufactures, carpets, and tyres came tumbling home among seventeen product groups subjected to 50 per cent duties. The second Order, on 30 November, included a further eight groups, and the third,

---

[178] Author of *The Economics of Safeguarding* (1930).

[179] Economic Emergency Committee Minutes (hereinafter EEC), 25 Sept. 1931, 200/F/1/1/74, FBI.

[180] L. Amery, *My Political Life*, iii. 65. Runciman's announcement, made in the debate on Snowden's supplementary budget on 10 September, was widely anticipated in the Commons and attracted widespread attention in the country; B. Mallet and C. O. George, *British Budgets*, 3 ser. *1921–22 to 1932–33* (1933), 376–7.

[181] P. Snowden, *An Autobiography*, ii. 999; T. Rooth, *British Protectionism*, 63.

[182] Co-ordinating Committee Minutes, 18 Nov. 1930, 200/F/1/1/74, FBI.

[183] *Liverpool Post and Mercury*, 31 Oct. 1931.

[184] *Evening Standard*, 12 Nov. 1931.

on 17 December, another twelve. Altogether, some £50m of imports were covered by the new duties.[185] The *Morning Post* reported 'praise' from Conservative backbenchers, whilst Beaverbrook's *Evening Standard* gave emphasis to Croft's demand for an immediate declaration of policy on agriculture.[186]

The FBI took these events coolly. Larke and Sir George Beharrell of Dunlop thought that a tariff imposed by hitherto Free-Trade ministers 'would be more firmly established than in any other way'.[187] The EEC recognized difficulties in negotiation with government when Runciman's criteria for 'excessive imports' were unclear, but it was comforted by his apparent belief that 'a considerable restriction of imports' was necessary to restore the balance of trade. It supported chairman W. J. U. Woolcock's view that 'the Federation could render only general support', and that in making cases 'each industry would have to do this for itself'. The Federation could act as a medium between its members and the Board of Trade—indeed, it had been doing so for some weeks—but ultimately 'all industries should watch their own interests'.[188]

FBI president Sir James Lithgow was less sanguine. In October and November 1930 the FPC had decided that the emergency tariff should be left to government, and that it should be the role of an official tariff board to refine that emergency tariff into a permanent tariff. But it expected that emergency tariff to be graduated, and especially to compensate manufacturers of finished goods for any duties imposed on semi-manufactures. By the summer of 1931, when 'Industry and the Nation' appeared, the FPC evidently anticipated that the three- or five-tier tariff of the CRD Committee would form the basis of the emergency tariff; it was largely because of Cunliffe-Lister's enquiry that the FBI had abandoned its original intention of drafting a detailed tariff. Lithgow, concerned that many of the products being imported in 'abnormal quantities' were semi-manufactures, feared that the AIA might result in negative effective protection for finished products. The FBI should therefore supply the Board of Trade with details of the 'precise duties' required by industry, 'based on information which ought to be in the possession of the staff'.[189]

Similar criticisms of the AIA had been aired at the Co-ordinating Committee on 18 November, when Nugent had urged that it was more important to secure a satisfactory permanent general tariff than to worry over the details of the emergency tariff.[190] Nevertheless, the FPC was hastily summoned to a meeting on 27 November. Probably to test opinion, Lithgow's intervention was initially withheld. Nugent, as the impartial Federation official, reminded members that

[185] R. M. Findlay, *Britain under Protection* (1934), 15–16.
[186] *Morning Post*, 23 Nov. 1931; *Evening Standard*, 25 Nov. 1931.
[187] EEC Minutes, 17 Nov. 1931, 200/F/1/1/74, FBI.   [188] Ibid.
[189] EEC Minutes, 24 Nov. 1931, 200/F/1/1/74, FBI.
[190] Co-ordinating Committee Minutes, 19 Nov. 1931, 200/F/1/1/74, FBI.

the AIA violated the 'cardinal' principle that any tariff on semi-manufactures should be 'carried through the various stages of production . . . to the complete article, in order to protect the home manufacturer', and was thus at variance with 'Industry and the Nation'. Larke was less dispassionate. Of course he preferred the FBI scheme, but industry must 'make the best' of the AIA. He doubted the AIA would seriously prejudice industry as long as the Board of Trade was advised of difficulties. He 'deprecated any representation to the Government in regard to the . . . Act', which, after all, was mainly aimed at restoring the balance of trade and protecting the exchange rate. Other members went further. Whereas Larke thought 'hard cases were bound to arise', George Mullins thought that a duty on semis would not necessarily have serious effects on finished-product prices. And Bremner, who represented the engineers for whom a tariff on steel semis should have been of particular concenr, reminded the FPC that their own emergency tariff would doubtless have caused initial difficulties of its own. Already the BEA had approached the Board of Trade on the need to proceed quickly from the AIA to a 'considered tariff'. It was clear that Larke carried the meeting with him in his determination that industry's response to the AIA should not be carping; 'it would have a very bad effect if the Federation openly expressed any dislike of the present procedure, especially as the present House of Commons showed an unusually disinterested determination to remedy the national position'.[191]

Only then was Lithgow's intervention revealed. To Larke, Lithgow had 'misconceived' a measure whose purpose was not to protect but to rectify the balance of trade. Furthermore, to submit actual tariff schedules would be to go against earlier FPC and Council decisions—it had already been established that 'it was not possible for the Federation to recommend actual rates of duties required by the various industries, but that each industry should make its own representations direct'. This did not preclude the FBI from giving assistance. Nugent indicated that, after consultation with the Board of Trade, the FBI staff had already compiled a checklist to aid industries in their applications. In support, the representatives of fourteen trade associations on the FPC (more or less the entire attendance) indicated that their industries had set up committees to prepare tariff applications.[192]

There was no dissent. The FPC was of one mind in seeing the future in two stages—the replacement of the AIA by an emergency tariff (presumably based closely on Cunliffe-Lister's tariff, modified by individual industry-representations to the Board of Trade), and the subsequent replacement of the emergency tariff by a permanent tariff, in which the onus was on the trade associations to prepare detailed cases. The FBI would provide advice on the general form of applications and intermediation when the interests of two groups conflicted. But this strategy

---

[191] FPC Minutes, 27 Nov. 1931, 200/F/1/1/75, FBI.   [192] Ibid.

would at least partially insulate the FBI from the 'invidious position' of 'having to decide upon the claims of respective industries'.[193]

The EEC and the FPC were thus agreed. Further discussions, on 4 January 1932, showed a similar acceptance of the shortcomings of the AIA. Problems arising for certain firms which had contracted for imports since made dutiable were discounted. Davidson Pratt, representing chemicals, 'advised against any hasty action regarding isolated cases as unfortunate repercussions might ensue'. More importantly, the FBI should exert its influence to prevent manufacturers increasing prices under the AIA 'as this would weaken the case for tariffs generally'. By the time the meeting's minutes had been circulated, on 19 January,[194] Lithgow had been converted. At a meeting of the EEC, he acknowledged that it was unwise to press the Government on policy, especially on the AIA.[195]

The FPC still expected a graduated emergency tariff—the Cunliffe-Lister tariff—to replace the AIA. On 8 February 1932 the FPC discussed a preliminary government announcement that the Import Duties Bill would be based on a 10-per-cent revenue tariff, in which protection would be incidental and offset by the fact that raw materials were included. Nevertheless, it was the Government's intention to erect 'a superstructure of protection' on this basic framework. For Larke, this was enough; the FBI's prime interest lay in supporting the Government.[196] Less than a week later, the Import Duties Bill was published. The Cunliffe-Lister tariff did not appear in it. Beyond the basic 10 per cent, no rates or structure were mentioned. The Tariff Board had become the new master. Larke's committee reviewed the Bill section by section, and found it of a 'generally . . . satisfactory nature'.[197]

The FBI had accepted the impracticability of a business-designed tariff structure. Whilst it still anticipated a tiered and structured general tariff, it accepted the primacy of the tariff board, and expected Conservative dominance of the National Government to produce an industrial tariff in piecemeal stages. The Tariff Commission's conception of a predetermined blueprint was finally dead.

Heavy pressure continued to come from Croft, principally on agriculture and steel. *The Daily Express* discerned the hand of the EIA behind the 'formidable revolt' that threatened in the Commons on 7 December.[198] Emboldened by such support, the steelmakers were not so philosophical or so patient as the FBI. Now confident that a long-term 'scientific' tariff would be implemented, the NFISM

---

[193] EEC Minutes, 24 Nov. 1931, 200/F/1/1/74, FBI.
[194] FPC Minutes, 4 Jan. 1932, 200/F/1/1/75, FBI.
[195] EEC Minutes, 13 Jan. 1932, 200/F/1/1/74, FBI.
[196] FPC Minutes, 8 Feb. 1932, 200/F/1/1/75, FBI.
[197] FPC Minutes, 15 Feb. 1932, 200/F/1/1/75, FBI.
[198] *Daily Express*, 8 Dec. 1931.

set its tariff committee to produce a schedule.[199] The Electrical Industries'
Council and the Society of Motor Manufacturers and Traders supported the
NFISM, and it is notable that the only criticism that now came from previously
Free-Trade groups like the independent tinplate makers, the structural engineering industry, and the shipbuilders, was that arrangements for drawback on export
were inadequately specified. None thought it realistic to stem the tide of
protection. Clearly the era of negotiation, of claim, counter-claim, and compromise, had begun. Against this background, the heavy steelmakers were
dissuaded from pressing their objection in the interests of securing acceptance of
protection in principle. They were amply rewarded by the Import Duties
Advisory Committee in April 1932.[200]

X

The business community was clearly well-briefed to exercise patience. All now
knew the realities of power within the National Government, and that it was best
to leave the strategy for overcoming the residual sentiments of Free Trade within
it to Neville Chamberlain.[201] All knew, also, that Runciman had embarked upon
Asquith's 'inclined plane', and would have little opportunity to draw back. The
prompt implementation of the AIA was the acid test, the untested might of the
EIA the insurance against recidivism.

Tariff Reform zealots were less than satisfied. As well a graduated tariff
structure, Cunliffe-Lister's report had made recommendations on imperial
preference, had supported a continuation of the McKenna, safeguarding, and
silk duties, and had made concrete proposals for some specific duties on raw and
processed foodstuffs.[202] Beyond imposing an across-the-board tariff of 10 per cent

[199] J. C. Carr and W. Taplin, *The British Steel Industry*, 475–7.

[200] Sir H. Hutchinson, *Tariff-Making*, 31–2, 186. The steelmakers' only major disappointment was
that the shipbuilders secured the exemption of steel used for shipbuilding in the Import Duties Act.
Cunliffe-Lister had found the great bulk of the steel industry heavily opposed to a 'universal' system
of drawbacks, and was inclined to brush aside the objections of the shipbuilders, whilst encouraging
them to negotiate special arrangements with the steelmakers. Essentially, he considered drawbacks
legitimate only where imported components were essential for export-destined goods; mere cheapness
was not a consideration. In particular, drawbacks would make duties on sheet bars and other
semi-finished steel almost useless. Nevertheless, he found Larke and the NFISM willing to accept that
'special claim[s]' might be brought before the Tariff Board. In fact, exemption of all materials used
in 'shipbuilding yards' was built into the Import Duties Act itself. See 'Tariffs Committee: Draft
Report', 7, 18–20, CRD 1/2/10; memo by Cunliffe-Lister, 13 Feb. 1931, TC/23, CRD 1/2/7;
Hutchinson, *Tariff-Making*, 20, 58–9.

[201] For the impact of the financial crisis, the policymakers' increasing fears that depreciation
without a tariff would lead to a spiral of inflation and further depreciation, and for Neville
Chamberlain's manipulation of the Cabinet Committee on the Balance of Trade (Dec. 1931–Jan.
1932), see B. Eichengreen, 'Sterling and the Tariff, 1929–1932', *Princeton Studies in International Finance*,
48 (1981), repr. in *Elusive Stability*, (Cambridge, 1990), 180–214.

[202] Ball's summary of CRD Tariff Committee Report, 2, CRD 1/2/11.

and making a start at a free list which included important foodstuffs, the Import Duties Bill 'made no mention of constructing a system of protective duties, beyond [a] reference to the desirability of restricting imports'.[203] Though Empire goods were admitted free, a final decision on preference was effectively shelved pending negotiations at the Imperial Conference to be held in the summer. Amery protested that the Government was shedding too much responsibility and laying it on the tariff board:

[I]t would have been infinitely simpler for the Government to have done what we in the Opposition contemplated doing—to impose a general emergency industrial tariff of two or three or four grades. It could have been very easily adjusted to whatever standard and appropriate rate for the highest duties on fully manufactured goods the Government decided upon. And then we could have left the committee to rectify mistakes . . . It would have been far easier for these five gentlemen to deal with 5 per cent. of the field of industry than to deal with 100 per cent.[204]

Amery was correct. In the words of Herbert Hutchinson, secretary of the Import Duties Advisory Committee, 'Parliament had passed the buck to the Committee'. But the consequences were of little importance. As Hutchinson knew full well, this reflected nothing more than 'a desire to make the legislation . . . a little easier for the Free Trade minority of the Cabinet. There was no doubt . . . as to what Parliament and public opinion wanted'.[205]

[203] Sir H. Hutchinson, *Tariff-Making*, 21.

[204] *Parliamentary Debates*, 5th ser., cclxi (1931–2), cols. 305–16, esp. 312.

[205] Sir H. Hutchinson, *Tariff-Making*, 22. Until recently, Hutchinson's account of IDAC, essentially administrative, has been the only in-depth study of the management of Britain's tariff regime in the 1930s. The more complete story remains to be told, but important beginnings have been made in T. Rooth, *British Protectionism*; and C. Wurm, *Business, Politics and International Relations* (1988; Eng. edn. Cambridge, 1993).

Conclusion

As British history before 1880 and US history since 1945 both show, nations in the economic ascendant are prone to patronize the world with their belief in economic liberalism. The coincidence suggests that the belief is seldom pure, but contains an underlying core of self-interest. In the world of nineteenth-century business, Free Trade as an *ideal* probably weighed less heavily than it did amongst the professional, political, or literary middle classes. Businessmen are not attracted to remote or abstract arguments which balance broad, indirect effects of the second order against narrow, direct effects of the first. In the context of Britain's pre-eminence in manufacture in the 1840s, the first-order effects were cheaper raw materials and unimpeded access to foreign export markets, rather than protection from the—as yet slight—competition of foreign manufactures. To the industrialist who fought against the Corn Laws, the Ricardian theory of comparative costs related to a world whose stable resource-bases and factor endowments assigned Britain a fixed place as workshop of the world. International specialization, as it passed into the legend of the twentieth-century textbook, was about iron and bananas, wheat and manufactures; it was not, or so it must have seemed to the many, about international rivalry between advanced industrial nations. Few of those industrialists who campaigned against the Corn Laws would have accepted that the remorseless laws of the market should apply, unfettered, in less fortunate times. In any case, they espoused Repeal as much to promote a class-political interest—against the landed élite—as to promote their direct business interest. But the two had a convenient symmetry: the sacrifices necessary to allow increased manufactured exports and a constant real wage at reduced money-wage levels would be made mainly in the counties and the shires.

The veneer of principle which overlay this position was not tested for a generation, not tested seriously for over half a century. By the 1900s, Liberal academics, politicians, and journalists may have regarded the long-term rise and decline of industries with equanimity or quiet resignation, but businessmen were seldom so detached. Schumpeter's belief that the manufacturer had a natural predisposition towards protectionism rested on his knowledge of business behaviour in countries whose initial industrial inferiority to Britain forced them from the start to conceive of world trade in manufactures mainly in terms of international rivalry among manufacturing nations. But his view applies to

Britain too. Free Trade was, in an important sense, self-fulfilling. Irrespective of its effect on British growth-rates and welfare-levels, it did contribute to a high degree of export-orientation, and to the growth of merchanting, banking, shipping, and capital export. Cosmopolitanism created vested interests just as surely as did protectionism. If there was justice in the protectionist case—and surely there was, in a situation where after 1870 the rest of the world became increasingly protectionist whilst Britain did not—that made no difference to those interests. And they included manufacturers whose commitment to Free Trade was essentially pragmatic—the tinplate manufacturers, the steel rollers, and the shipbuilders, with their perceived dependence on free competition in their raw-material markets, and the cotton spinners and manufacturers with their clear dependence on exports. These last, long exposed to the higher culture of the Manchester intelligentsia, may be forgiven for having found it difficult to separate principle from personal interest. They hardly seemed to notice that in their support for one tenet of liberalism, free markets, they were willing to trample on a greater one—the right of self-determination of the Indian sub-continent.

Export and import merchants had a clear and easily defined position; trade was their function. Elsewhere, vested interests, on both sides, were seldom so simple as to define an industry's contours clearly. Within the manufacturing sector, cotton came closest to unanimity on Free Trade, but probably not by the ten-to-one margin asserted by the Liberal press. Even in heavily Free Trade industries, the *degree* of commitment to Free Trade had to be balanced against political loyalties in a period when the historic balance was changing. If historic Liberalism had created vested interests in Free Trade, contemporary Liberalism seemed to contradict the interest of business in low taxation and social spending. By 1910 this was appreciated by many cotton masters. Before 1900, the broad political alignments of the bankers of the City of London were different from those of Lancashire businessmen, but the tensions they felt were broadly the same. For them, like the cotton masters, the logically preferred solution would have been the rise of the Unionist Free Traders to dominance within the Unionist Party. That frustrated, the bankers would eventually have to choose; but in the meantime most elected to keep their silence on Tariff Reform.

In most manufacturing industries, majority opinion was probably more evenly balanced, and already inclining in 1903 towards protectionism. This certainly seems to have been true by 1905, when ACCUK, a body which included merchants alongside manufacturers, could count a majority in favour of Tariff Reform. But the situation, and indeed the historian's ability to analyse it, was clouded by three factors. Firstly, the intellectual hegemony and moral high ground occupied by Free Trade made protectionist opinion hard to articulate: it made the protectionist appear grasping and corrupt—if not that, then stupid, which was probably even worse. Declaring one's protectionism was an act of personal exposure, not only unpleasant, but also fruitless unless others in their thousands joined suit. Secondly, the protectionism offered was less than ideal. Stemming from Joseph Chamberlain's 'constructive imperialism', it proclaimed the possibility of expanding empire markets. Of that, the manufacturer could approve, at the same time that he appreciated the popularity of the imperial appeal in British society and the value that a political leader of national stature imparted to Tariff Reform. But most doubted the willingness of the dominions to revert to a colonial economic system, and were even more troubled over the necessary corollary of food duties, not because of any lingering attachment to anti-landlordism amongst the manufacturers of the new century, but rather because those duties would inflame working-class antagonism and frustrate attainment of an industrial tariff. Thirdly, such businessmen's organizations and associations as there were had grown up under a regime where there was little difference between the economic policies of the two political parties. The culture of *laissez-faire* itself meant that those organizations fitted only uncomfortably into the prevailing institutional structure, whilst, with business conditions of little relevance, individual businessmen's politics could remain divergent. Membership, too, always mattered to the leaders and secretaries of such groups: numbers meant prestige and subscriptions. If membership translated into influence in non-political matters, the reverse was almost true in political. There was a dread in such organizations of 'political' issues. But these were already, by 1900, defined in a slanted way. With the rise of Labour and the emergence of the employers' association, it was clear that industrial relations would not be so counted. As Liberal collectivism emerged into the 'New Liberalism' in the new century, in the prelude to welfare reform, taxation and the politics of redistribution stood poised to follow in the same path. Businessmen did make the attempt, before 1906, to avoid areas of controversy between Liberals and Unionists, but this became increasingly difficult as party differences over policies with profound economic implications became more fundamental, and as the consensus over Gladstonian principles of public finance crumbled.

In the short term, the growth of protectionism could be hidden, even denied. Within the Chambers of Commerce, members were reluctant to admit division. This attitude favoured the status quo, and could be played upon by the Free Traders, so that the consequent reluctance to count votes kept the size of the opposing forces relatively hidden. Before 1907, this reluctance was reinforced by conflict within the Unionist Party itself. Already it was the case that businessmen would follow the agenda of politics, rather than set it.

The trade recovery of 1905–1914, punctuated only by the downturns of 1907–1908 and 1911, might be thought to have blunted the growth of protectionist sentiment. In fact, such a tendency was more than offset by political considerations related to public finance. After Valentine and Balfour's partial conversion, the embarrassments caused by Unionist division appeared to recede.

At the same time the budgets of Asquith and Lloyd George made explicit the partially hidden trends of the previous decade. Welfare reform threatened to loosen the hold of employers on their workers, and at the same time demanded that they were main contributors to the process. But if this seemed a dark hour for the manufacturer, he might now count on new allies. The Unionist Party was uniting under the new developments. Bankers, merchants, and rentiers were as exposed to the tax-man as were manufacturers. Opinion in the Chambers of Commerce was tilting more clearly in favour of fiscal reform. In 1903 Chamberlain had tapped a protectionist sentiment that had been latent for twenty years, since the Fair Trade movement. In 1907–1910 his successors probably witnessed a far more significant influx of new believers. An achievement for the Tariff Reformers on the surface, this allowed a good showing in the general elections of 1910, good at least compared to the magnitude of defeat in 1906. But, in the longer run, the new wave of conversions had a scarcely understood significance. For many, now, Tariff Reform was desired less in itself than for what it allowed the nation to avoid. When the Conservatives regained the chance to govern, Tariff Reformers would consider the survival of a Conservative Government as more important than the policy itself. After the War, the imperative was to keep Labour out of office. Few protectionist Conservative businessmen had sufficient confidence in the electoral attractions of tariffs to challenge seriously their political leaders' assessment of Party necessity.

A period when business opinion on economic issues was almost irrelevant to party conflict was being replaced by one in which business views were being incorporated into mainstream Conservatism. For protectionists, this meant the tailoring of their creed to suit wider Conservative strategies, albeit strategies which they themselves supported. The Great War was perhaps something of a diversion. It was fertile ground both for the formation of new business groups and for the spread of protectionist feeling. The German threat was exposed, and of course magnified and distorted. More clear-headed, some businessmen rediscovered an American threat that had been almost forgotten since the depression after the Boer War. Merchants and shippers, with cargoes, capital, and employees at risk on the high seas, now seemed determined that things should never again be allowed to come to such a pass. Trade war demanded an active trade policy. For all this, the Balfour of Burleigh Committee knew that there was no political consensus on food duties, no certainty of long-term consensus on punitive measures against Germany if they conflicted with the interests of domestic trade, and no solidarity of resolve in Britain should the Americans threaten reprisal against the Paris Resolutions.

In spite of this, the Committee uncovered an essential consensus within the British manufacturing sector in favour of the widespread safeguarding of industry. This meant more than the protection of 'key' industries, more than anti-dumping duties. It meant protection against abnormal imports, against lower taxes, against lower labour-costs—it came close to meaning protection against foreign protectionism itself. In the 1920s, few British manufacturers spoke out against extension of the Act of 1921. Opposition to safeguarding still persisted amongst steel-rollers and shipbuilders, determined to maintain free access to the world market in semi-products. Here, margins were low, competition intense. Cotton spinners feared that duties on fabric gloves would damage the German demand for British yarn, whilst the industry in general was disturbed by duties on artificial silk. But, mostly, it was merchants who orchestrated the business opposition to the new legislation.

More hidden to the modern eye, but glimpsed in the history of the BCU, certain large engineering companies, involved less in domestic mass-production or precision-work than in overseas projects and contracting, still clung to internationalist hopes of trade revival. What is significant, however, is that the BCU remained nominally protectionist. The FBI had almost the reverse problem. Public neutrality on the fiscal issue concealed a substantial protectionist majority among the membership, and a widespread jealousy among the leadership that the NUM could campaign on a positive policy. If the BCU was reluctant to disown protectionism, there were many in the FBI who would have liked to proclaim it. Contradictory only on the surface, both examples show where the inter-war manufacturer's sympathy lay.

Thus, amongst industrialists, the wartime consensus for a full-blooded policy of safeguarding, little short of a general tariff on manufactures, was not dissipated in the first half of the 1920s. Beyond this, however, the attitude of most industrialists to Joseph Chamberlain's original conception of Tariff Reform, incorporating imperial preference and the food duties necessary to implement it, was more equivocal. In the transition from war to peace, there was a perhaps surprising amount of support within the cautious FBI for amalgamation with BEPO, even though food duties were a hidden precondition. If BEPO had its supporters in the FBI, more were not sufficiently interested and, as a result, vehement opposition, centred in Manchester and based upon surviving Free-Trade values, carried the day. Thereafter, Austen Chamberlain's formula in the 1919 budget was used by protectionist business groups such as the BCU and the NUM to sideline the issue of food taxes. Like those of their political counterparts in the Conservative Party, the main motives of businessmen revolved around a fear of antagonizing the electorate at a time when Labour was emerging as the principal political opposition. If protectionist businessmen had sensed that preference and agricultural protectionism would have increased the acceptability of extended safeguarding, they would have embraced it. Food duties would, after all, have relieved some of the heavy post-war pressure on direct taxation, and provided some lever, however small, for negotiation with the dominions on manufactures. Those historians who have discerned a narrowing of Tariff Reform in the 1920s, a retreat from Chamberlain's constructive imperialism to a more sectional industrial programme, are correct. But it is well to remember that this transition began much earlier, with Balfour's espousal of Tariff Reform as a way of avoiding the redistributive effects of a recourse to direct taxation from 1908–1910, and with Bonar Law's abandonment of food duties in 1913. It was only reinforced as the industrialist rose in prominence in the parliamentary Party of 1918–1925, and the protectionist business groups of the 1920s accepted the short-term subordination of their objective to wider Conservative aims and strategies.

McKenna, dyestuffs, and key-industry duties apart, safeguarding before 1925 was largely an illusion, maintained by a political and electoral willingness to punish Germany, and sustained, amongst protectionist manufacturers, by the hope that things would change, promises be kept. This was a period when protectionist business opinion was best represented by the simple programme of the NUM, in which the fashionable productioneer solution of full-capacity working was relatively unmodified by corporatism, collectivism, or rationalization, rather than the prescriptions of the more radical and collectivist BEPO and the more politically ambitious and devious BCU.

In the short run, and ironically, Baldwin's defeat in the 'tariff election' of 1923 probably deflated mounting protectionist discontent as, once again, Conservatives had to unite in the face of a greater threat. But 1925 saw resumption of the pressure, and what businessmen saw as new promises in Cunliffe-Lister's White Paper. By the mid- to late 1920s unmodified Free Trade opinion had become a minor force in business circles; in manufacturing, believers in the old orthodoxy were increasingly isolated, whilst the cosmopolitan merchant community, however wealthy were some of its members, had few great names to weigh against the great industrialists who were latent protectionists or active members of the EIA.

Yet, seen in the context of organized business as a force in politics, the EIA was in one sense a step backwards, compared at least with the ambitions of the BCU. If the business voice was more persistent, more organized, better articulated, than before the Great War, it was scarcely more powerful. Almost paradoxically, the EIA's relative success lay in a reversion to the ideals and the organizational characteristics of the Edwardian TRL. Sectionalism was rejected and a social dimension reintroduced into campaigning. Here was an attempt to capture, at least in some of its dimensions, one-nation Toryism. The EIA did achieve some limited movement towards a fusion of business and politics, but the impetus and the dynamic came from the politicians within it rather than the businessmen. Those politicians played a waiting game. Before 1930, unwilling to distance the EIA too far from official Conservative policy, and perhaps still reluctant to alienate industrialists whose main interest in Tariff Reform was confined to domestic protection, they avoided an advanced or a clear position on imperial preference and food duties.

By Baldwin's fall in May 1929, the shrinkage of Free-Trade business opinion had gone far, by the summer of 1930 about as far as it was ever likely to go. A few unrepentant steel-rollers remained, an unbowed Rowntree or Lever. But the coal-owners, like most of the dwindling band of Free Trade businessmen, had come to accept the approaching victory of their opponents, whilst the shipbuilders' resistance would now be limited to fighting for the exemption of duties on semi-finished steel for use in ships. Labour's first winter saw a heavy deterioration in Britain's economic position, and there were renewed fears that a government with a naïve attachment to internationalism would be hoodwinked into the one-sided diversion of a tariff truce. But the protectionist declaration of the FBI, and perhaps even that of the bankers, were not fundamentally the product of immediate economic circumstances. They were rather a recognition that Baldwin's rearguard had run its course and a reformulation of Conservative policy was pending. It was only the absence of this reformulation that allowed embargo to contain protectionism within the FBI for so long, and which obviated the need for the City to demonstrate its alignment with Conservatism.

If, within the Conservative Party, protectionism was subordinated to the wider political imperative of keeping Labour out, it was an imperative that most protectionists shared. This subordination of business interest to political leadership had its counterpart in attempts at formulating a tariff blueprint. Before the War, the Tariff Commission, in its early years one of the most theoretically innovative business groups that Britain has ever seen, nevertheless faced immensely complex problems in its objective of designing a 'scientific' tariff. Official information was poor. The bureaucratic and technical knowledge of the process was lacking in Britain, and in consequence the Commission made life harder for itself by failing to appreciate the crude and often arbitrary way in which foreign tariffs came into being. But politics also mattered here. Unable to institute in the real world an initial tariff which could then be refined in a process of learning-by-doing, Chamberlain and Hewins had to promise an integrated and harmonious tariff in which frictions would be minimized and antagonisms overcome. Such an idealized tariff, a tariff that *in itself* had to be a means of political conversion, was impossible to realize. Without pressure from the political presence on the Commission, the business members, in legend hard-faced, brazen, and grasping, would almost certainly have been too timid to produce any tariff schedules at all. After 1906, without Chamberlain to stiffen resolve, difficulties mounted. Technical difficulties persisted, cracks appeared in the harmonious sphere, critical groups refused to co-operate. And, ultimately, the switch from a Chamberlainite accent on preference and protection to a Balfourite emphasis on revenue pushed the precise structure of the Unionist tariff out to the periphery of even the Commission's political agenda.

The Balfour of Burleigh Committee concerned itself with broad principles rather than the construction of detailed tariff structures, and even here found difficulties in interpreting its ambiguous terms of reference and the intentions of its political masters. Baldwin's Tariff Advisory Committee of 1923 was redundant almost before it made a start. The FBI's attempt to draft a tariff was almost immediately laid aside when it was realized that a similar attempt was to be made in the Conservative Research Department. Businessmen were only too pleased to pass the burden to others—the politicians were more proficient and less self-conscious.

At the CRD, Cunliffe-Lister was faced with a situation that his predecessors in tariff formulation would have envied—a high probability that a Tariff-Reforming government would be elected to office. Unlike the Tariff Commission, he could proceed on the reasonable assumption that to make an omelette it was necessary to break eggs. Niceties were discarded, inaccuracies unconsidered, close consultations mostly avoided. For a moment, it appeared that the power-politics of real tariff-formulation had arrived. But even this was premature. The need to demonstrate the unity of National government led at the last moment to the appointment of an ex-Liberal as president of the Board of Trade. More importantly, it led to the introduction of a Tariff Act in a form designed to propitiate the vestigial interests of Free Trade, a form which on the surface violated cardinal principles long held by the Tariff Reformers, and to the creation of a tariff board supposedly immune from political pressure. Even now, the uncertain permanence of public opinion made the Conservatives wary of too closely identifying themselves with the politics of sectoral interest. And Neville Chamberlain had effectively maintained a long-established independence from business dictation, an independence which would allow flexibility in the conduct of commercial policy and commercial diplomacy in the 1930s.

Appendix I

Tariff Commission Members, 1904

Charles Allen	Sir Henry Bessemer and Co. Ltd. (C) [700]
	Ebbw Vale Steel, Iron and Coal Co. Ltd. (MD) [2,500]
	Sheffield and Hallamshire Bank (VP)
Frederick Baynes	Cotton manufacturer (Blackburn)
	Baynes and Dixon, cotton merchants (Ptnr)
	London and North Western Railway Co. (D)
J. Henry Birchenough	John Birchenough and Sons, silk manufacturers
	Macclesfield Chamber of Commerce (C)
	Imperial Continental Gas Association Ltd. (D)
	British Exploration of Australia Ltd. (D)
Rt. Hon. Charles Booth	Alfred Booth and Co. (Senior Ptnr)
	Booth Steamship Co. (C)
	Manaos Harbour Ltd. (D)
Henry J. Bostock	Edwin Bostock and Co. Ltd., boot and shoe manufacturers (D) [1,100]
Samuel Bagster Boulton	Burt, Boulton and Heywood Ltd., chemical manufacturers and timber importers (C and MD)
	Tar Distillers' Association (P)
	British Australian Timber Co. Ltd. (C)
	Dominion Tar and Chemical Co. Ltd. (C)
	Former (P), West Ham Chamber of Commerce
	Former (VP), London Chamber of Commerce
Richard Burbidge	Harrod's Stores Ltd. (MD) [3,000]
	Hudson's Bay Co. (D)
Sir Vincent H. P. Caillard	Vickers, Sons and Maxim (D)
	Wolseley Tool and Motor Car Co. (D)
	G. F. Milne's and Co. Ltd., tramway and railway carriage manufacturers (C)
	Daira Sanieh Co. (C)
	National Bank of Egypt (C, London Committee)
Joseph John Candlish	Robert Candlish and Son Ltd., glass bottle manufacturers (C) [487]
	British Association of Glass Bottle Manufacturers (C)
	Daily Express (D)
	Evening News and Hampshire Telegraph (D)
	Northern Daily Mail (D)
	Sunderland Echo (D)

Henry Chaplin MP	Ex-landowner, Lincolnshire
	Conservative MP, Sleaford Division of Lincolnshire (to 1906)
	Conservative MP, Wimbledon (1907–1916)
	Former (P), Local Government Board
	Former (P), Board of Agriculture
Hon. Sir John A. Cockburn	Former Premier, South Australia
	Former Minister of Education, South Australia
	Former Minister of Agriculture, South Australia
	Former Agent-General for South Australia
J. Howard Colls	Colls and Sons, builders and contractors (C?) [3,300]
J. G. Colmer	Coates, Son and Co.
William Cooper	Dead meat wholesaler
	London Chamber of Commerce, Cattle and Meat Trades Section (C)
John A. Corah	Cooper, Corah and Sons, hosiery manufacturers [1,700]
John W. Dennis	W. Dennis and Sons, farmers and agricultural produce merchants
Charles Eckersley	Caleb Wright and Co., cotton spinners.
	Fine Cotton Spinners' and Doublers' Association (D) [30,000]
	Société Cotonnière de l'Hellennes, Lisle (D)
Francis Elgar	Fairfield Shipbuilding and Engineering Co. (MD) [6,000]
	Institute of Naval Architects (VP)
Sir Charles Elliott	Former Lieutenant-Governor, Bengal
Lewis Evans	John Dickinson and Co., paper manufacturers (D) [2,850]
	North Wales Paper Co. (D)
	Paper Makers' Association (MC)
George Flett	Dick, Kerr and Co. Ltd., engineers and contractors (MD) [3,850]
Sir Charles Follett	Former Solicitor to HM Customs and Excise
Thomas Gallaher	Gallaher Ltd., tobacco manufacturers (Founder and C)
	Belfast Steamship Co. (C)
Hon. Vicary Gibbs	Antony Gibbs and Sons, merchants and bankers (Ptnr)
Alfred Gilbey	W. and A. Gilbey, wine and spirit merchants [1,200]
Sir William J. Goulding	W. and H. M. Goulding Ltd., chemical manure manufacturers (C)
	Great Southern and Western Railway of Ireland (C)
W. H. Grenfell MP	Landowner (12,000 acres)
	Conservative MP for Wycombe Division of Buckinghamshire (1900–1905)
F. Leverton Harris MP	Harris and Dixon, shipowners
	National Discount Co. Ltd. (D)
	Indian Collieries Syndicate Ltd. (D)
	Metropolitan Electric Supply Co. Ltd. (D)

	Conservative MP for Tynemouth (1900–1906), Stepney (1907–1910), East Worcestershire (1914–1918)
J. Mitchell Harris	Charles and Thomas Harris and Co., bacon curers [246]
	West of England Bacon Co. (MD) [28]
W. Harrison	Harrison, Macgregor and Co. Ltd., agricultural engineers (C)
	Agricultural Engineers' Association (P)
Sir Alexander Henderson MP	Greenwood and Co., stockbrokers (Senior Ptnr)
	Great Central Railway (C)
	Liberal Unionist MP for West Staffordshire (1898–1906)
Sir Robert Herbert	Former Permanent Under-Secretary for the Colonies
	Former Premier of Queensland
	Former Agent-General for Tasmania
	Telegraph, Construction and Maintenance Co. (C)
	Eastern and South African Telegraph Co. (D)
	Union Castle Mail Steamship Co. (D)
	P and O Steam Navigation Co. (D)
	Union Bank of Australia (D)
Sir Alfred Hickman MP	Alfred Hickman and Co. Ltd., iron and coal masters (C) [4,500]
	Former (P), British Iron Trade Association
	Iron and Steel Institute (MC)
	Mining Association of Great Britain (MC)
	Conservative MP for Wolverhampton West (1892–1906)
Sir Alfred L. Jones	Elder, Dempster and Co., shipowners (C)
	African Steamship Co.
	British and African Steam Navigation Co.
	Elder Navigation Collieries Ltd.
	British Bank of West Africa (C)
	Liverpool Chamber of Commerce (P)
	Liverpool Steamship Protection &c. Association (P)
	British Cotton Growing Association (P)
Arthur Keen	Guest, Keen, and Nettlefolds Ltd. (C and MD) [17,715]
	Bolckow Vaughan and Co. (D) [14,700]
	London, City and Midland Bank (C)
	Institute of Mechanical Engineers (VP)
	Iron and Steel Institute (VP)
J. J. Keswick	Jardine, Matheson and Co. (Ptnr)
	Rio Tinto Co. (C)
	Bengal Iron and Steel Co. (D)
	East India Coal Co. (D)
	Former member, Legislative Council of Hong Kong
Ivan Levinstein	Levinstein Ltd. (MD)
	Former (P), Manchester Chamber of Commerce

	Former (P), Society of Chemical Industry
	Society of Dyers and Colourists (VP)
Sir W. T. Lewis	Various South Wales Colliery Cos. (Prop and C)
	Former (P), Mining Association of Great Britain
	Former (P), Institute of Mining Engineers
	Former (P), South Wales Institute of Engineers
	Iron and Steel Institute (VP)
	Institute of Mechanical Engineers (MC)
	Mellingriffith Tinplate Works (C)
Robert Littlejohn	African Banking Corporation (D)
Charles Lyle	Abram Lyle and Sons, sugar refiners (C)
	Lyle Shipping Co. Ltd., shipowners
A. W. Maconochie MP	Maconochie Bros. Ltd., meat preservers and packers (MD)
	Maconochie's Solderless Tinning Syndicate Ltd. (C)
	Liberal Unionist MP for East Aberdeenshire (1900–1906)
Henry D. Marshall	Marshall, Sons and Co., agricultural engineers (MD) [*c*.3–4,000]
	British Engineers' Alliance Ltd. (D)
	J. and H. Gwynne (Engineers) Ltd. (D)
	Shireoaks Colliery Co. (D)
	Institute of Mechanical Engineers (MC)
	Agricultural Engineers' Association (MC)
William H. Mitchell	William Fison and Co. Ltd., worsted spinners and manufacturers (D)
	Bradford Chamber of Commerce (VP)
	Association of Chambers of Commerce of the UK (EC)
	Bradford Piece Dyeing Board (C)
Alfred Mosely	Diamond merchant
Sir Andrew Noble	Sir W. G. Armstrong, Whitworth and Co. Ltd. (C) [22,395]
Hon. Charles Parsons	C. A. Parsons and Co. Ltd. [880]
	Parsons Marine Steam Turbine Co. (MD) [300]
	Newcastle and District Electric Lighting Co. (D)
	Cambridge Electric Supply Co. (D)
	Scarborough Electric Supply Co. (D)
Sir Walter Peace	Agent-General for Natal
	Former merchant and shipper
C. Arthur Pearson	*Daily Express* (Prop)
	Standard (Prop)
Sir Westby Perceval	Former Agent-General for New Zealand
	Former Agent-General for Tasmania
C. J. Phillips	Watney, Combe, Reid and Co. (DC) [1,430]
Joseph Rank	Joseph Rank Ltd., flour millers (GD) [326]
	National British and Irish Millers' Insurance Co. (D)
R. H. Reade	York Street Flax Spinning Co. Ltd. (C and MD) [4,385]
	Belfast Chamber of Commerce (VP)

	Belfast and Northern Counties Railway Co. (D)
	Midland Railway (member of Northern Ireland Committee)
Sir George Lisle Ryder	Former (C), Board of Customs and Excise
Sir Cecil Clementi-Smith	Former Governor, Straits Settlements
	High Commissioner for North Borneo and Sarawak
	Lieutenant-Governor of Ceylon
Sir Charles Tennant	Charles Tennant, Sons and Co., chemical manufacturers
	United Alkali Co. (P)
	Union Bank of Scotland (C)
Francis Tonsley	National Association of Master Bakers and Confectioners (P)
Sir John Turney	Turney Brothers Ltd., leather manufacturers (C and MD) [675]
	Burrough's Adding and Registering Machine Co. Ltd. (C)
	Raleigh Cycle Co. Ltd.
	Hall's Glue and Bone Works Ltd. (C)
S. J. Waring	Waring and Gillow, furniture manufacturers
W. Bridges Webb	Baltic Marine and Shipping Exchange (C)
	Dewar and Webb, grain merchants (Senior Ptnr)

Notes:

C	Chairman
D	Director
DC	Deputy Chairman
EC	Executive Committee Member
GD	Governing Director
MC	Member of Council
MD	Managing Director
P	President
Prop	Proprietor
Ptnr	Partner
VP	Vice-President
[700]	Approximate employment of company in 1903–4, if known, is given in square brackets.

Public appointments, membership of official government inquiries and commissions, etc., have been omitted. More complete information on these, and on the changing business interests of Commission members, can be found in source (b) below.

Sources: (a) *Report of the Tariff Commission*, vol. i. *The Iron and Steel Trades* (1904), para. 1; (b) A. J. Marrison, 'British Businessmen and the "Scientific Tariff": A Study of Joseph Chamberlain's Tariff Commission, 1903–1921', unpubl. Ph. D. dissertation, Univ. of Hull, 1980, biographical appendix.

Appendix II

British Iron and Steel: Output and Imports 1896–1925

	Pig Iron	Puddled Iron	Steel Ingots & Castings	Total	Total Iron and Steel Imports	
	(a)	(b)	(c)	(d)	(e)	(f)
	'000 tons	'000 tons	'000 tons	'000 tons	'000 tons	%
1896	8660	1214	4132	14006	—	
1897	8796	1238	4486	14520	516	3.55
1898	8610	1116	4566	14292	591	4.14
1899	9421	1202	4855	15478	645	4.16
1900	8960	1163	4901	15024	800	5.32
1901	7929	974	4904	13807	924	6.69
1902	8679	998	4909	14586	1131	7.75
1903	8935	950	5034	14919	1304	8.74
1904	8694	936	5027	14657	1292	8.81
1905	9608	939	5812	16359	1356	8.29
1906	10184	1010	6482	17656	1216	6.89
1907	10114	975	6523	17612	935	5.31
1908	9057	1168	5296	15521	1119	7.21
1909	9532	1129	5882	16543	1193	7.21
1910	10012	1119	6374	17505	1367	7.81
1911	9526	1191	6462	17179	1762	10.26
1912	8751	1327	6796	16874	1997	11.83
1913	10260	1207	7664	19131	2220	11.60
1914	8924	—	7835	16759	1618	9.65
1915	8794	943	8550	18287	1182	6.46
1916	9048	960	8992	19000	776	4.08
1917	9322	816	9717	19855	497	2.50
1918	9086	647	9539	19272	337	1.75
1919	7398	540	7894	15832	509	3.22
1920	8035	589	9067	17691	1108	6.26
1921	2616	218	3703	6537	1640	25.09
1922	4902	220	5881	11003	881	8.01
1923	7441	332	8482	16255	1322	8.13
1924	7307	309	8201	15817	2429	15.36
1925	6262	210	7385	13857	2720	19.63

Source: B. R. Mitchell and P. Deane, *Abstract of British Historical Statistics* (London, 1962), 134–7, 142–3. Columns (d) and (f) are simply derived from the others. Column (d) = (a) + (b) + (c). Column (f) is (e) as a percentage of (d): that is, it does *not* equal the import content of home consumption, but rather the shortfall of home production due to imports, assuming that (i) consumers in Britain would not have reduced consumption if foreign imports had ceased, and (ii) that exports would have remained unchanged even though imports had been curtailed.

Appendix III

Support for and Opposition to Safeguarding Applications: 1925–1929

Support	Opposition
Lace and Embroidery	
Federation of Lace and Embroidery Employers' Associations	Lace and Embroidery Group of London Chamber of Commerce
British Plain Net Manufacturers' Association	Lace Executive Committee of the Wholesale Textile Association
	Embroidery Buyers' Association
Superphosphates	
Fertiliser Manufacturers' Association	National Farmers' Union
	National Farmers' Union of Scotland
	Ulster Farmers' Union
Aluminium Hollow-Ware	
British Aluminium Hollow-Ware Manufacturers' Association	5 or 6 firms of wholesale import merchants
Gloves	
Joint Industrial Council of the Glove Making Industry	Group of London and Manchester wholesale distributing houses
National Association of Fabric Glove Manufacturers of the UK	
Glove and Fabric Warp Makers' Association	
Gas Mantles	
Manufacturer	Gas mantle importers and wholesalers organized by members of London Chamber of Commerce

APPENDIX III (continued)

Support	Opposition
Packing and Wrapping Paper	
Union of Wrapping Paper Makers British Paper Bag Federation	Group of London Chamber of Commerce, including merchants, importers, agents, and industrial users Employers' Federation of Envelope Makers and Manufacturing Stationers Manufacturing Confectioners' Alliance
Cutlery	
Sheffield Cutlery Manufacturers' Association	Cutlery Import Group Committee of the London Chamber of Commerce
Brooms and Brushes	
British Brush Manufacturers' Association	Group of importers from the London Chamber of Commerce
Enamelled Hollow-Ware	
Wrought Hollow-Ware Trade Employers' Association (Enamelled Hollow-Ware Section)	3 large retailers and 5 importers and merchants
Worsteds	
Bradford and District Manufacturers' Association Keighley and District Manufacturers' Association Textile Commission Manufacturers' Association Bradford Merchants' Association Other manufacturers, makers-up and merchants, (including approx. 90 per cent of Bradford worsted merchants) Executive Council of London Employers' Association[a] Wholesale Mantle and Costume Manufacturers' Federation[a]	Textile Trade Section of London Chamber of Commerce 3 (small) cloth manufacturers 2 garment makers National Association of Unions in the Textile Trades
Hosiery	
Joint Industrial Council of Hosiery Trade Federation of Hosiery Manufacturers' Associations	Hosiery Trade Group Committee (largely importers, warehousemen, general textile merchants, retail drapers) many of

whom were members of the Textile
Trade Section of the London Chamber
of Commerce

Light Leather Goods and Metal Fittings

National Leather Goods and Saddlery
    Manufacturers' Association
British Fitting Manufacturers' Association

Not stated, but claimed by the applicants
to be 'representatives of foreign
manufacturers or . . . merchants'

Translucent Pottery

British Pottery Manufacturers' Federation
English China Manufacturers' Association
10 non-member manufacturing firms
4 firms of merchants and dealers

China and Glassware Section of London
    Chamber of Commerce, 'whose
    members are substantially imterested in
    the matter as importers and wholesale
    distributors'

Hosiery (Second Enquiry)

Joint Industrial Council of the Hosiery
    Trade
Scottish hosiery manufacturers

Hosiery Trade Group Committee, many of
    whose members were from the Textile
    Trade Group of the London Chamber
    of Commerce

Monumental and Architectural Granite

Aberdeen Granite Manufacturers'
    Association
Cornish Granite Merchants and
    Quarrymasters' Association

Importers and merchants

Button, Pins, Hooks and Eyes, Snap Fasteners

British Button Manufacturers' Association
Pin, Hook and Eye, and Snap Fasteners
    Employers' Association

Group of importers and wholesalers
Wholesale Textile Association (all
    merchants with the exception of one
    merchant-manufacturer)

Handkerchiefs and Household Linens

Handkerchief and Embroiderers'
    Association of Belfast
Dunfermline manufacturers
2 trade unions

Group of importers and wholesalers
Wholesale Textile Association
Tootal, Broadhurst, Lee Co. Ltd.
Calico Printers' Association Ltd.

Enamelled Hollow-Ware (Second Enquiry)

Wrought Hollow-Ware Trade Employers'
    Association (Enamelled Hollow-Ware
    Section)
2 trade unions

Merchants, importers and wholesalers (all
    but one with EC1 addresses)

APPENDIX III (continued)

Support	Opposition

Woollens and Worsteds

Support	Opposition
Bradford and District Manufacturers' Federation (worsteds)	Group of manufacturers and merchants (about 5 manufacturers called as
Keighley and District Manufacturers' Federation (worsteds)	witnesses, alongside 9 merchants, drapers, and textile agents)
Textile Commission Manufacturers' Association (worsteds)	
Huddersfield Woollen Safeguarding Association	
Heavy Woollen District Manufacturers' Association	
Leeds and District Woollen and Worsted Manufacturers' Association	
Yeadon and Guiseley Manufacturers' Association	
Calder Vale and District Woollen and Worsted Manufacturers and Spinners' Association	
British Wool Federation	
Worsted Spinners' Federation	
Bradford Dyers' Association	

[a] The support of the Executive Council of the London Employers' Association and the Wholesale Mantle and Costume Manufacturers' Federation for the application from the worsted manufacturers was conditional on the *quid pro quo* of safeguarding of finished garments.

Sources: Board of Trade, *Report of Lace and Embroidery Committee*, Cmd. 2403 (1925), 1; *Report of the Superphosphate Committee*, Cmd. 2475 (1925), 5–6; *Report of the Committee on Aluminium Hollow-Ware*, Cmd. 2530 (1925), 4; *Report of the Committee on Leather Gloves, Fabric Gloves, and Glove Fabric*, Cmd. 2531 (1925), 3; *Report of the Committee on Gas Mantles*, Cmd. 2533 (1925), 3, and App.; *Report of the Committee on Packing and Wrapping Paper*, Cmd. 2539 (1925), 3 and App. IV; *Report of the Committee on Cutlery*, Cmd. 2540 (1925), 3; *Report of the Committee on Brooms and Brushes*, Cmd. 2549 (1925), 3; *Report of the Committee on Enamelled Hollow-Ware*, Cmd. 2634 (1926), 3; *Report of Worsted Committee*, Cmd. 2635 (1926), 3–4; *Report of the Committee on Hosiery*, Cmd. 2726 (1926), 3–4 and App. C; *Report of the Committee on Light Leather Goods and Metal Fittings*, Cmd. 2837 (1927), 16; *Report of the Committee on Table-ware of Translucent Pottery*, Cmd. 2838 (1927), 3 and App. C; *Second Report of the Committee on Hosiery*, Cmd. 3078 (1928), 11; *Report of the Committee on Monumental and Architectural Granite*, Cmd. 3079 (1928), 3; *Report of the Committee on Buttons, Pins, Hooks and Eyes and Snap Fasteners*, Cmd. 3080 (1928), 3, 24–5; *Report of the Committee on Handkerchiefs and Household Linen Goods*, Cmd. 3096 (1928), 3 and App. H; *Second Report of the Committee on Enamelled Hollow-Ware*, Cmd. 3115 (1928), 3, 10; *Report of the Woollen and Worsted Committee*, Cmd. 3355 (1929), 3–4, 32–3.

Appendix IV

FBI Main Group Analysis of Membership by Total Subscriptions: 1921–1926

[Entries in pounds: shillings and pence omitted]

INDUSTRIAL GROUP	1921	1922	1923	1924	1925	1926
6 Textiles	24,046	21,454	20,417	20,676	20,301	21,293
5 Iron and Steel, etc.	19,333	16,333	14,560	13,189	12,757	12,289
2 Mechanical Engineering	19,063	16,855	14,438	14,581	14,636	14,636
13 Rubber, Asbestos, etc.	7,748	6,382	6,121	6,070	5,863	5,598
9 Chemicals, Fertilizers, and Explosives	6,712	5,700	4,962	5,109	5,031	4,953
10 Foodstuffs and Liquors	6,127	5,102	4,733	4,731	5,060	5,020
3 Shipbuilding, Marine Engineering, etc.	5,679	5,568	4,641	4,451	4,079	3,786
4 Electrical Engineering	5,092	5,137	4,570	4,785	5,206	5,382
16 Non-Ferrous Metals	4,686	4,140	3,613	3,718	3,603	3,534
1 Mining, Quarrying, etc.	4,615	3,873	3,701	3,535	3,146	3,064
11 Miscellaneous	3,312	2,735	2,869	3,108	3,041	3,479
12 Public Utilities	3,142	2,806	3,029	2,625	2,715	2,176
22 Brewing, Distilling, etc.	2,910	2,781	3,050	3,168	3,232	3,315
18 Papermaking, Stationery, etc.	2,766	2,584	2,482	2,478	2,343	2,268
19 Banking and Insurance	2,410	2,380	2,420	2,180	2,080	2,460
7 Glass and Clay Products	2,351	2,484	2,111	2,362	2,429	2,154
17 Oils and Fats	2,146	2,105	2,081	2,086	2,193	2,291
12 Building Trades	1,915	1,585	1,529	1,407	1,463	1,424
20 Woodworking	1,728	1,337	1,213	1,143	973	972
8 Printing, Printing Ink, Typefounders, etc.	1,416	1,246	1,478	1,578	1,498	1,501
21 Cutlery, Jewellery, Electro-plating, etc.	1,383	969	813	754	855	1,087
11 Agriculture	192	180	180	196	196	125
23 Fisheries	—	100	100	115	135	132

Note. The Industry Groups have been ranked in size order (in 1921). The number in the left hand column is the FBI's internal Industry Group Number.
Source. FBI 200/F/3/S1/7/16–18 (Walker Papers).

Appendix V

FBI Numerical Strength According to Districts: 1921–1926

	1921	1922	1923	1924	1925	1926
London	418	446	455	451	449	486
Birmingham	247	244	226	228	222	229
Manchester	230	274	291	309	321	342
Liverpool	105	101	103	105	111	111
South Wales	97	98	87	81	78	73
Newcastle	86	89	102	113	129	124
Nottingham	76	94	97	101	95	101
Leeds	73	79	77	75	75	72
Sheffield	72	78	73	74	73	78
Glasgow	69	95	100	98	95	94
Home Counties	62	73	77	79	80	77
Bradford	61	74	85	89	87	95
Leicester	58	61	60	60	58	57
Edinburgh	56	69	69	67	61	62
Northampton	31	29	26	26	27	27
TOTAL MEMBERSHIP	1,741	1,904	1,928	1,956	1,961	2,028

Note: Ranked in size order (in 1921).
Source: FBI 200/F/3/S1/7/16–18 (Walker Papers).

Appendix VI

FBI Financial Strength According to Districts: 1921–1926

[Entries in pounds: shillings and pence omitted]

	1921	1922	1923	1924	1925	1926
London	35,215	29,905	27,678	27,291	27,169	28,011
Manchester	16,782	16,528	15,300	15,482	15,375	15,555
Birmingham	16,152	12,276	10,256	10,729	10,901	11,261
Liverpool	8,163	6,780	6,470	6,534	6,408	6,358
Newcastle	7,278	7,177	6,472	6,667	7,093	6,475
South Wales	6,555	4,983	4,360	4,180	3,907	3,755
Glasgow	5,979	6,188	5,982	5,985	5,925	5,783
Leeds	5,681	4,860	3,920	3,577	3,452	3,262
Nottingham	5,334	5,190	4,888	5,002	4,868	4,635
Sheffield	5,204	4,607	3,702	3,502	3,422	3,547
Bradford	4,562	4,380	4,235	4,482	4,405	4,632
Leicester	4,098	3,512	3,303	3,269	3,028	2,962
Home Counties	3,853	3,260	3,247	3,380	3,220	3,133
Edinburgh	3,438	3,310	3,218	2,945	2,707	2,630
Northampton	1,630	1,053	900	920	935	940
TOTAL	129,924	114,009	103,931	103,945	102,815	102,939

Note. Ranked in order of size of total district subscriptions (in 1921).
Source. FBI 200/F/3/S1/7/16–18 (Walker Papers).

Bibliography

(A) Manuscript Sources

(i) *Private Papers and Papers of Non-Governmental Institutions and Associations*

First Viscount Addison (Christopher Addison) Papers (Bodleian Library)

Earl of Oxford and Asquith (Herbert Henry Asquith) Papers (Bodleian Library)

Associated Chambers of Commerce of the United Kingdom (Guildhall Library)

Association of British Chambers of Commerce (Guildhall Library)

Arthur James Balfour Papers (British Library, Additional Manuscripts)

Birmingham Chamber of Commerce (at the Chamber's Offices)

British Commonwealth Union Papers (materials contained in Hannon Papers, House of Lords Record Office)

British Engineers' Association Papers (Modern Records Centre, University of Warwick)

Sir William Bull Papers (Churchill College, Cambridge; House of Lords Record Office)

Sir Austen Chamberlain Papers (Birmingham University Library)

Joseph Chamberlain Papers (Birmingham University Library)

Sir Sidney Chapman Papers (British Library of Political and Economic Science)

Conservative Research Department Papers (Bodleian Library)

First Baron Croft (Henry Page Croft) Papers (Churchill College, Cambridge)

Empire Development Union Papers (contained in Hewins Papers, Sheffield University Library)

Empire Industries Association Papers (Modern Records Centre, University of Warwick; Hannon Papers, House of Lords Record Office)

Federation of British Industries Papers (CBI Predecessor Archive, Modern Records Centre, University of Warwick)

Sir Patrick Hannon Papers (House of Lords Record Office)

W. A. S. Hewins Papers (Sheffield University Library)

Hull Chamber of Commerce (Hull Central Library)

Industrial Group Papers (some survivals contained in Hannon Papers, House of Lords Record Office)

Leeds Chamber of Commerce (Brotherton Library, University of Leeds)

London Chamber of Commerce (Guildhall Library)

Manchester Chamber of Commerce (Manchester Central Reference Library)

Alfred Lord Milner Papers (Bodleian Library)

National Union of Manufacturers Papers (some survivals contained in FBI Papers, Modern Records Centre, University of Warwick)

Nottingham Chamber of Commerce (at the Chamber's Offices)

Sheffield Chamber of Commerce (Sheffield Central Library)

First Earl of Swinton (Philip Cunliffe-Lister) Papers (Churchill College, Cambridge)

Tariff Commission Papers (British Library of Political and Economic Science)

Sir Laming Worthington-Evans Papers (Bodleian Library)

(ii) Official

BT 13/120	Safeguarding of Industries: Lace and Embroidery Committee.
BT 55/8	Committee on Commercial and Industrial Policy (Balfour of Burleigh)
BT 55/13	Committee on Commercial and Industrial Policy (Balfour of Burleigh)
BT 55/43/2	Safeguarding of Industries Act: key Industries Committee. Notes.
BT 55/49/7	Board of Trade Policy Committee: Sub-Committee on Industry and Trade, 1927, Draft Conclusions, 12 December 1927.
BT 55/57/7	Safeguarding of Industries: Informal (Chadwick) Committee, 1925–26.
BT 55/58/9	Safeguarding of Industries: Committee Papers.
BT 55/58/11	Safeguarding of Industries Informal Committee on Schedules.
BT 55/58/12	Safeguarding of Industries, 1929.
BT 55/78	Safeguarding of Industries: Lace and Embroidery Committee.
BT 55/89	Safeguarding of Industries: Worsted Committee, 1925.
BT 55/95	Safeguarding of Industries: Woollen and Worsted Report, 1929.
BT 55/98/170	Safeguarding of Industries: Machine Tools Association Application.
C.P. 355(23)	Cabinet Memorandum on Safeguarding of Industry by President of Board of Trade, 27 July 1923.
C.P. 18(25)	Cabinet Memorandum on Safeguarding of Industry by President of Board of Trade, 14 January 1925.
C.P. 137(29)	Cabinet Memorandum on the Report of the Safeguarding Committee on Woollens and Worsteds, 2 May 1929.

(B) Official Publications

House of Commons Debates.
House of Lords Debates.
Annual Statement of Trade of the United Kingdom, Sessional Papers, House of Commons.
Statistik des Deutschen Reichs.
Board of Trade Journal.
Diplomatic and Consular Reports, Annual Series, no. 3140 (1904).
Statistical Abstract for the United Kingdom, 1896–1910, Cd. 5841 (1911).
Statistical Abstract for the United Kingdom, 1919–1932, Cmd. 4489 (1934).
British and Foreign Trade and Industry: Memoranda, Statistical Tables, and Charts Prepared in the Board of Trade, with Reference to Various Matters Bearing on British and Foreign Trade and Industrial Conditions, Cd. 1761 (1903).
Report of the Committee on the Board of Trade and the Local Government Board, Cd. 2121 (1904).
Report of the Sub-Committee of the Advisory Committee of the Board of Trade on Commercial Intelligence with Respect to Measures for Securing the Position, after the War, of Certain Branches of British Industry, xvi. Cd. 8181 (1916); *Summaries of Evidence*, Cd. 8275 (1916).
Committee on Commercial and Industrial Policy, *Resolutions and Letter to the Prime Minister on Imperial Preference*, Cd. 9482 (1917).
Committee on Commercial and Industrial Policy, *Interim Report on Certain Essential Industries*, Cd. 9032 (1918).
Committee on Commercial and Industrial Policy, *Interim Report on the Importation of Goods from the Present Enemy Countries after the War*, Cd. 9033 (1918).

Committee on Commercial and Industrial Policy, *Interim Report on the Treatment of Exports from the United Kingdom and British Overseas Possessions and the Conservation of the Resources of the Empire during the Transitional Period after the War*, Cd. 9034 (1918).

Committee on Commercial and Industrial Policy, *Final Report*, Cd. 9035 (1918).

Report of the Departmental Committee appointed by the Board of Trade to consider the position of the Textile Trades after the War, Cd. 9070 (1918).

Report of the Departmental Committee appointed by the Board of Trade to consider the position of the Iron and Steel Trades after the War, Cd. 9071 (1918).

Report of the Departmental Committee appointed by the Board of Trade to consider the position of the Electrical Trades after the War, Cd. 9072 (1918).

Report of the Departmental Committee appointed by the Board of Trade to consider the position of the Engineering Trades after the War, Cd. 9073 (1918).

Report of the Departmental Committee appointed by the Board of Trade to consider the position of the Coal Trade after the War, Cd. 9093 (1918).

Final Report of the Departmental Committee appointed by the Board of Trade to consider the position of the Shipping and Shipbuilding Industries after the War, Cd. 9092 (1918).

Board of Trade, *Report of the Committee on the Trade Board Acts*, Cmd. 1645 (1922).

Board of Trade, *Safeguarding of Industries: Procedures and Enquiries*, Cmd. 2327 (1925).

Board of Trade, *Report of Lace and Embroidery Committee*, Cmd. 2403 (1925).

Board of Trade, *Report of the Superphosphate Committee*, Cmd. 2475 (1925).

Board of Trade, *Report of the Committee on Aluminium Hollow-Ware*, Cmd. 2530 (1925).

Board of Trade, *Report of the Committee on Leather Gloves, Fabric Gloves, and Glove Fabric*, Cmd. 2531 (1925).

Board of Trade, *Report of the Committee on Gas Mantles*, Cmd. 2533 (1925).

Board of Trade, *Report of the Committee on Packing and Wrapping Paper*, Cmd. 2539 (1925).

Board of Trade, *Report of the Committee on Cutlery*, Cmd. 2540 (1925).

Board of Trade, *Report of the Committee on Brooms and Brushes*, Cmd. 2549 (1925).

Board of Trade, *Report of the Committee on the Safeguarding of Industries Act, 1921, Part I*, Cmd. 2631 (1926).

Board of Trade, *Report of the Committee on Enamelled Hollow-Ware*, Cmd. 2634 (1926).

Board of Trade, *Report of the Worsted Committee*, Cmd. 2635 (1926).

Board of Trade, *Report of the Committee on Hosiery*, Cmd. 2726 (1926).

Board of Trade, *Report of the Committee on Light Leather Goods and Metal Fittings*, Cmd. 2837 (1927).

Board of Trade, *Report of the Committee on Table-ware of Translucent Pottery*, Cmd. 2838 (1927).

Board of Trade, *Second Report of the Committee on Hosiery*, Cmd. 3078 (1928).

Board of Trade, *Report of the Committee on Monumental and Architectural Granite*, Cmd. 3079 (1928).

Board of Trade, *Report of the Committee on Buttons, Pins, Hooks and Eyes and Snap Fasteners*, Cmd. 3080 (1928).

Board of Trade, *Report of the Committee on Handkerchiefs and Household Linen Goods*, Cmd. 3096 (1928).

Board of Trade, *Second Report of the Committee on Enamelled Hollow-Ware*, Cmd. 3115 (1928).

Board of Trade, *Report of the Woollen and Worsted Committee*, Cmd. 3355 (1929).

Non-Parliamentary, Board of Trade, Committee on Industry and Trade, *Factors in Industrial and Commercial Efficiency* (1927).

Non-Parliamentary, Board of Trade, Committee on Industry and Trade, *Further Factors in Industrial and Commercial Efficiency* (1928).

Non-Parliamentary, Board of Trade, Committee on Industry and Trade, *Survey of Textile Industries: Cotton, Wool, Artificial Silk* (1928).

Board of Trade, *Final Report of the Committee on Industry and Trade*, Cmd. 3282 (1929).

Non-Parliamentary, Committee on Finance and Industry, *Minutes of Evidence* (2 vols., 1931).

(C) Reports and Selected Memoranda of the Tariff Commission

(i) Reports

Report of the Tariff Commission, i. *The Iron and Steel Trades* (London, 1904).

Report of the Tariff Commission, i. *The Iron and Steel Trades: Popular and Abridged Version* (London, 1905).

Report of the Tariff Commission, ii. *The Textile Trades*, part 1, *The Cotton Industry* (1905).

Report of the Tariff Commission, ii. *The Textile Trades*, part 2, *Evidence on the Woollen Industry* (1905).

Report of the Tariff Commission, ii. *The Textile Trades*, part 3, *Evidence on the Hosiery Industry* (1905).

Report of the Tariff Commission, ii. *The Textile Trades*, part 4, *Evidence on the Lace Industry* (1905).

Report of the Tariff Commission, ii. *The Textile Trades*, part 5, *Evidence on the Carpet Industry* (1905).

Report of the Tariff Commission, ii. *The Textile Trades*, part 6, *Evidence on the Silk Industry* (1905).

Report of the Tariff Commission, ii. *The Textile Trades*, part 7, *Evidence on the Flax, Hemp and Jute Industries* (1905).

The Tariff Commission, iii. *Report of the Agricultural Committee* (1st edn., 1906).

Report of the Tariff Commission, iv. *The Engineering Industries: Including Structural, Electrical, Marine and Shipbuilding, Mechanical and General Industrial Engineering* (1909).

Report of the Tariff Commission, v. *The Pottery Industries* (London, 1907).

Report of the Tariff Commission, vi. *The Glass Industry* (London, 1907).

Report of the Tariff Commission, vii. *Sugar and Confectionery* (London, 1907).

(ii) Memoranda Cited in Text

(Copies held in Tariff Commission Papers, British Library of Political and Economic Science. A full list of the fifty pre-1914 titles is given in Marrison, 'British Businessmen and the "Scientific" Tariff', 602–4).

Tariff Commission, 'Summary of Evidence Contained in Answers to Forms of Inquiry No. 1 Issued to Manufacturers', Memorandum 5, 14 March 1904 (working memorandum, for internal circulation only).

Tariff Commission, 'Memorandum on the Evidence Respecting the Iron and Steel Trades', Memorandum 9, 16 March 1904 (working memorandum, for internal circulation only).

Tariff Commission, 'Memorandum on the Work of the Tariff Commission', *Memorandum No. 21,* 11 February 1905.

Tariff Commission, 'Unemployment', *Memorandum No. 37,* 23 March 1908.

Tariff Commission, 'The Trade Relations of India with the United Kingdom, British Possessions and Foreign Countries—Part I', *Memorandum No. 38*, 9 November 1908.

Tariff Commission, 'Preference and the New Canadian Tariff Arrangements with France, Germany and the United States', *Memorandum No. 41*, 7 May 1910.

(D) Reports, Journals, etc., of Other Non-Governmental Organizations

Associated Chambers of Commerce of the United Kingdom, *Official Programmes of Meetings*

Association of British Chambers of Commerce, *Reports*

Association of British Chambers of Commerce, *Proceedings*

Birmingham Chamber of Commerce Journal

London Chamber of Commerce, *Chamber of Commerce Journal*

Empire Industries Association, *Annual Reports*

Federation of British Industries, *Annual Reports*

Hull Chamber of Commerce, *Annual Reports*

Leeds Chamber of Commerce, *Annual Reports*

London Chamber of Commerce, *Second Report of the Special Committee on Trade during and after the War* (1916)

Manchester Chamber of Commerce, *Monthly Record*

Nottingham Chamber of Commerce, *Annual Reports*

Sheffield Chamber of Commerce, *Annual Reports*

(E) Reference Works, Directories, etc. (Contemporary and Secondary)

H. H. BASSETT (ed.), *Men of Business at Home and Abroad, 1912–1913* (n.d.).

Dictionary of National Biography.

Federation of British Industries, *F.B.I. Register of British Manufacturers* (1930–31 edn.).

P. and G. FORD, *A Breviate of Parliamentary Papers, 1900–1916* (Shannon, 1969 edn.).

P. and G. FORD, *A Breviate of Parliamentary Papers, 1917–1939* (Shannon, 1969 edn.).

A. S. HARVEY, *The General Tariff of the United Kingdom: Law and Regulations* (1933).

D. J. JEREMY and C. SHAW (eds.), *Dictionary of Business Biography: A Biographical Dictionary of Business Leaders Active in Britain in the Period 1860–1980* (5 vols., 1984–6).

Kelly's Directory of Cheshire (1902 edn.).

National Union of Manufacturers, *National Union of Manufacturers (Incorporated): Descriptive and Classified Directory of Members* (1926, 1927, and 1937 edns.).

W. W. RICH (ed.), *Handbook of the United States Tariff: containing the Tariff Act of 1913* (New York, 1913).

Sell's Directory of Registered Telegraphic Addresses (1927 edn.).

T. SKINNER, *Directory of Directors* (various edns.).

M. STENTON and S. LEES, *Who's Who of British Members of Parliament*, iii. and iv. (Brighton, 1979, 1981).

White's Directory of Sheffield and Rotherham (31st edn., 1909).

Who Was Who, i, *1897–1915* (London, 1920, 3rd edn., 1935); ii, *1916–1928* (London, 1929); iii, *1929–1940* (London, 1941); iv, *1941–1950* (London, 1952).

(F) Newspapers, Journals, Periodicals, etc.

Bankers' Magazine
Birmingham Post
Daily Express
Daily Mail
Daily Telegraph
East Anglian Daily Times
Eastern Daily Press
Echo
Economic Journal
The Economist
Evening Standard
Express and Star
Financial News
Financial Times
Free Trader
Iron and Coal Trades' Review
Ironworkers' Journal
Liverpool Daily Post
Liverpool Post and Mercury
Macclesfield Courier
Manchester City News
Manchester Evening Chronicle
Manchester Guardian
Monthly Notes on Tariff Reform
Morning Post
National Review
Nottingham Daily Express
Nottingham Daily Guardian
Observer
Quarterly Journal of Economics
Sheffield Daily Independent
Sheffield Daily Telegraph
Standard
Tariff Reformer and Empire Monthly
Textile Mercury
Textile Recorder
The Times
Trader
Transactions of the Manchester Statistical Society
War Notes for Members of the Tariff Reform League
Western Mercury
Westminster Gazette
Yorkshire Post

(G) Autobiographies, Memoirs, Diaries, Biographies

D. ABEL, *Ernest Benn: Counsel for Liberty* (1960).

J. AMERY, *Life of Joseph Chamberlain*, v., vi., *Joseph Chamberlain and the Tariff Reform Campaign* (1969).

L. AMERY, *My Political Life* (3 vols., 1952–4).

M. BALFOUR, *Britain and Joseph Chamberlain* (1985).

J. BARNES and D. NICHOLSON (eds.), *The Leo Amery Diaries*, i. *1896–1929* (1980).

SIR HENRY BESSEMER, *An Autobiography* (1905).

R. BLAKE, *The Unknown Prime Minister: The Life and Times of Andrew Bonar Law, 1858–1923* (1955).

R. D. BLUMENFELD, *R. D. B.'s Diary, 1887–1914* (1930).

SIR AUSTEN CHAMBERLAIN, *Politics from Inside: An Epistolary Chronicle, 1906–1914* (1936).

R. CHURCH, *Herbert Austin: The British Motor Car Industry to 1941* (1979).

H. CLAY, *Lord Norman* (1957).

J. M. COHEN, *Life of Ludwig Mond* (1956).

LORD CROFT, *My Life of Strife* (London, n.d.).

C. CROSS, *Philip Snowden* (1966).

J. A. CROSS, *Lord Swinton* (Oxford, 1982).

S. DARK, *Life of Sir Arthur Pearson* (London, n.d.).

R. P. T. DAVENPORT-HINES, *Dudley Docker: The Life and Times of a Trade Warrior* (Cambridge, 1984).

P. N. DAVIES, *Alfred Jones: Shipping Entrepreneur Par Excellence* (1978).

D. DILKS, *Neville Chamberlain*, i. *Pioneering and Reform, 1869–1929* (Cambridge, 1984).

M. DUPREE (ed.), *Lancashire and Whitehall: The Diary of Sir Raymond Streat* (Manchester, 1987).

D. DUTTON, *Austen Chamberlain: Gentleman in Politics* (Bolton, 1985).

P. FRASER, *Joseph Chamberlain: Radicalism and Empire, 1868–1914* (1966).

A. M. GOLLIN, *The Observer and J. L. Garvin, 1908–1914: A Study in a Great Editorship* (1960).

A. M. GOLLIN, *Proconsul in Politics: A Study of Lord Milner in Opposition and in Power* (1964).

P. J. GRIGG, *Prejudice and Judgement* (1948).

W. A. S. HEWINS, *The Apologia of an Imperialist: Forty Years of Empire Policy* (2 vols., 1929).

R. P. T. DAVENPORT-HINES (ed.), 'Two Autobiographical Fragments By Hugo Hirst', *Business History*, 28 (1986).

B. HOLLAND, *Life of Spencer Compton, Eighth Duke of Devonshire* (1911).

R. R. JAMES (ed.), *Memoirs of a Conservative: J. C. C. Davidson's Memoirs and Papers, 1910–37* (1969).

R. JAY, *Joseph Chamberlain: A Political Study* (Oxford, 1981).

S. H. JEYES and F. D. HOW, *Life of Sir Howard Vincent* (1912).

T. JONES, *Whitehall Diary* (3 vols., 1969).

S. E. KOSS, *Sir John Brunner: Radical Plutocrat, 1842–1919* (Cambridge, 1970).

S. E. KOSS, *Asquith* (1976).

Marchioness of Londonderry, *Henry Chaplin: A Memoir* (1926).

S. McKENNA, *Reginald McKenna, 1863–1943: A Memoir* (1948).

K. MIDDLEMAS and J. BARNES, *Baldwin: A Biography* (1969).

W. H. MILLS, *Sir Charles Macara* (Manchester, 1917).

A. H. MILNE, *Sir Alfred Lewis Jones* (Liverpool, 1914).

K. and J. MORGAN, *Portrait of a Progressive: The Political Career of Christopher, Viscount Addison* (Oxford, 1980).

R. J. OVERY, *William Morris, Viscount Nuffield* (1976).

SIR CHARLES PETRIE, *Life and Letters of the Right Hon. Sir Austen Chamberlain*, (2 vols., 1939).

A. C. PIGOU (ed.), *Memorials of Alfred Marshall* (1925).

L. ROBBINS, *Autobiography of an Economist* (1971).

S. SALVIDGE, *Salvidge of Liverpool* (1934).

P. SNOWDEN, *An Autobiography* (2 vols., 1934).

LORD SWINTON, *I Remember* (1948).

A. J. P. TAYLOR, *Beaverbrook* (1972).

SIR CHARLES TENNYSON, *Stars and Markets* (1957).

C. TREBILCOCK, *The Vickers Brothers: Armaments and Enterprise, 1854–1914* (1977).

B. WEBB, *Our Partnership* (1948).

K. YOUNG, *Arthur James Balfour* (1963).

S. H. ZEBEL, *Balfour: A Political Biography* (Cambridge, 1973).

(H) Contemporary Works (Books, Speeches, Articles, Pamphlets)

P. ASHLEY, *Modern Tariff History* (1st edn., 1904; 3rd edn., 1920).

W. J. ASHLEY, *The Tariff Problem* (1903).

H. H. ASQUITH, *Trade and the Empire: Mr. Chamberlain's Proposals Examined in Four Speeches and a Prefatory Note* (1903).

—— *Speeches by the Rt. Hon. H. H. Asquith from his First Appointment as a Minister of the Crown in 1892 to his Accession to the Office of Prime Minister, April 1908: Selected and Reprinted from The Times* (n.d. but 1908).

A. J. BALFOUR, *Economic Notes on Insular Free Trade* (1903).

—— *Fiscal Reform: Speeches Delivered by the Right Hon. Arthur James Balfour M. P. from June 1880 to December 1905* (1906).

M. V. BERARD, *British Imperialism and Commercial Supremacy* (Eng. edn. 1906).

S. L. BESSO, *The Cotton Industry in Switzerland, Vorarlberg and Italy* (Manchester, 1910).

SIR WILLIAM BEVERIDGE et al., *Tariffs: The Case Examined* (2nd edn., 1932).

C. F. BICKERDIKE, 'The Theory of Incipient Taxes', *Economic Journal*, 16 (1906).

P. BIDWELL, *Our Trade with Britain: Bases for A Reciprocal Tariff Agreement* (New York, 1938).

—— *Trading Tariffs with the English* (Economic Policy Committee, Des Moines, n.d. but 1938).

C. BOOTH, 'Fiscal Reform', *National Review*, 42 (1903–4).

—— 'Trade and Tariffs', *National Review*, 49 (1907).

R. BOOTHBY et al., *Industry and the State: A Conservative View* (1927).

B. BOWKER, *Lancashire Under the Hammer* (1928).

C. W. BOYD (ed.), *Mr. Chamberlain's Speeches* (2 vols., 1914).

LORD BRASSEY, *Sixty Years of Progress; and the New Fiscal Policy* (2nd edn., 1906).

British Iron Trade Association, *Report of the Delegation . . . on the Iron and Steel Industries of Belgium and Germany* (1896).

—— *American Industrial Conditions and Competition* (1902).

458 *Bibliography*

W. A. Brown, *England and the New Gold Standard, 1919–1926* (1929).

G. Byng, *Protection: The Views of a Manufacturer* (1901).

V. H. P. Caillard, 'Foreign Trade and Home Markets', *National Review*, 39 (1902).

—— 'Some Suggestions Toward an Imperial Tariff', *National Review*, 39 (1902).

—— ' "The Dream of a British Zollverein": A Reply to Sir Robert Giffen', *National Review*, 39 (1902).

—— *Imperial Fiscal Reform* (London, 1903).

J. Chamberlain, *Imperial Union and Tariff Reform: Speeches Delivered from May 15 to Nov. 4, 1903* (1903).

S. J. Chapman, *The Lancashire Cotton Industry: A Study in Economic Development* (Manchester, 1904).

—— *The Cotton Industry and Trade* (1904).

—— 'The Report of the Tariff Commission on the Iron and Steel Trades', *Economic Journal*, 14 (1904).

—— 'The Report of the Tariff Commission [on the Cotton Industry]', *Economic Journal*, 15 (1905).

—— *A Reply to the Report of the Tariff Commission on the Cotton Industry* (Manchester, 1905).

C. H. Chomley, *Protection in Canada and Australasia* (1904).

J. H. Clapham, *The Woollen and Worsted Industries* (1907).

Cobden Club, *Report of the Proceedings of the International Free Trade Congress, London, August, 1908* (n.d. but 1908).

J. Collings, *Land Reform* (1906 edn.).

Compatriots' Club, *Compatriots' Club Lectures: First Series* (1905).

M. T. Copeland, *The Cotton Manufacturing Industry of the United States* (Cambridge, Mass., 1912).

H. Cox, *Mr. Balfour's Pamphlet: A Reply* (1903).

—— (ed.), *British Industries under Free Trade* (1903).

W. Cunningham, *The Rise and Decline of the Free Trade Movement* (Cambridge, 1904; 2nd edn., 1905).

—— *The Wisdom of the Wise: Three Lectures on Free Trade Imperialism* (Cambridge, 1906).

—— *The Case Against Free Trade* (1911).

Daily Telegraph, *Imperial Reciprocity: A Study of Fiscal Policy* (1903).

W. H. Dawson, *Protection in Germany* (1904).

H. Dietzel, *Retaliatory Duties* (1906).

W. E. Dowding, *The Tariff Reform Mirage* (1913).

Empire Development Union, *Our Imperial Opportunity: Importance of the Coming Economic Conference* (1923).

Empire Economic Union, *Agricultural Policy: Past, Present and Future* (1939).

M. G. Fawcett, *Political Economy for Beginners* (9th edn., 1904).

Federation of British Industries, *Industry and the Nation* (1931).

R. M. Findlay, *Britain under Protection* (1934).

J. L. Garvin, *Tariff or Budget? The Nation and the Crisis* (n.d. but 1909).

R. Giffen, *Essays in Finance: First Series* (1877).

—— 'Are We Living on Capital?', repr. in *Economic Inquiries and Studies*, ii. (1904).

T. L. Gilmour (ed.), *All Sides of the Fiscal Question* (1903).

H. B. Gray and S. Turner, *Eclipse or Empire?* (1916).

T. E. GREGORY, *Tariffs: A Study in Method* (1921).

R. HAGGARD, *Rural England: Being an Account of Agricultural and Social Researches carried out in the Years 1901 and 1902* (2 vols., 1906 edn.).

H. HAUSER, *Germany's Commercial Grip on the World* (New York, 1918 edn., repr. 1983).

E. HELM, 'The Middleman in Commerce', *Transactions of the Manchester Statistical Society* (1900–1).

W. A. S. HEWINS, *English Trade and Finance, chiefly in the Seventeenth Century* (1892).

—— *Trade in the Balance* (1924).

H. B. HEYLIN, *Buyers and Sellers in the Cotton Trade* (1913).

R. HILFERDING, *Finance Capital: A Study of the Latest Phase of Capitalist Development* (1st Austrian edn., Vienna, 1910; English edn., ed. T. Bottomore, transl. M. Watwick and S. Gordon, 1981).

F. W. HIRST, *Safeguarding and Protection in Great Britain and the United States* (1927).

—— and J. E. ALLEN, *British War Budgets* (1926).

J. A. HOBSON, *International Trade: An Application of Economic Theory* (1904).

—— *The New Protectionism* (1916).

B. HOLLAND, *The Fall of Protection, 1840–1850* (1913).

J. S. JEANS, *The Iron Trade of Great Britain* (1906).

J. JENKS and W. E. CLARK, *The Trust Problem* (New York, 4th edn., 1920).

H. S. JEVONS, *The British Coal Trade* (1915, 2nd edn., Newton Abbot, 1969).

J. M. KEYNES, *The Economic Consequences of the Peace* (1919).

J. L. LAUGHLIN and H. P. WILLIS, *Reciprocity* (New York, 1903).

A. BONAR LAW, 'Tariff Reform and the Cotton Trade', *National Review*, 56 (1910–11).

H. B. LEES SMITH, *India and the Tariff Problem* (1909).

—— *Studies in Indian Economics: A Series of Lectures Delivered for the Government of Bombay* (1909).

SIR ROPER LETHBRIDGE, *The Indian Offer of Imperial Preference* (1913).

LIBERAL PARTY, *We Can Conquer Unemployment: Mr. Lloyd George's Pledge* (1929).

F. LIST, *The National System of Political Economy* (1st Eng. edn., transl. S. S. Lloyd, 1885; 2nd Eng. edn., with introduction by J. S. Nicholson, 1904).

D. LLOYD GEORGE, *The People's Budget: Explained by the Right Honourable D. Lloyd George, M.P.* (n.d. but 1909).

A. M. LOW, *Protection in the United States* (1904).

J. LYSAGHT, 'Preferential Tariffs in the Sheet Iron Business', *Economic Journal*, 13 (1903).

SIR C. MACARA, *Trade Stability and How to Obtain It* (1925).

—— *Modern Industrial Tendencies* (1926).

F. L. McDOUGALL, *Sheltered Markets: A Study of the Value of Empire Trade* (1925).

T. J. MACNAMARA, *Tariff Reform and the Working Man* (1910).

H. W. MACROSTY, *The Trust Movement in British Industry: A Study of Business Organisation* (1907).

B. MALLET and C. O. GEORGE, *British Budgets*, 2nd ser., *1913–14 to 1920–21* (1929).

—— *British Budgets*, 3rd ser., *1921–22 to 1932–33* (1933).

A. MARSHALL, *Industry and Trade: A Study of Industrial Technique and Business Organization; and of their Influences on the Conditions of Various Classes and Nations* (London, 1919; 1927 edn.).

H. W. MASSINGHAM (ed.), *Labour and Protection: A Series of Studies* (1903)

LORD MELCHETT [A. Mond], *Imperial Economic Unity* (1930)

H. O. MEREDITH, *Protection in France* (1904).

M. MILLIOUD, *The Ruling Caste and Frenzied Trade in Germany* (1916).

VISCOUNT MILNER, *Constructive Imperialism: Five Speeches* (1908).

LORD MILNER, *The Nation and the Empire: Being a Collection of Speeches and Addresses* (1913).

SIR GUILFORD MOLESWORTH, *Economic and Fiscal Facts and Fallacies* (1909).

A. MOND [Lord Melchett], *Industry and Politics* (1927)

L. G. CHIOZZA MONEY, *Elements of the Fiscal Problem* (1903).

—— *Money's Fiscal Dictionary* (1910).

A. MOSELY (ed.), *Mosely Industrial Commission to the United States of America, Oct.–Dec., 1902: Reports of the Delegates* (Manchester, 1903).

E. S. MONTAGU and B. HERBERT, *Canada and the Empire: An Examination of Trade Preferences* (1904).

T. W. PAGE, *Making the Tariff in the United States* (New York, 1924).

G. PEEL, *The Tariff Reformers* (1913).

F. PIERCE, *The Tariff and the Trusts* (New York, 1907).

A. C. PIGOU, *The Riddle of the Tariff* (1903).

—— *Protective and Preferential Import Duties* (1906, repr. 1968).

E. PORRITT, *Sixty Years of Protection in Canada, 1846–1907, Where Industry leans on the Politician* (1908).

E. A. PRATT, *Trade Unionism and British Industry* (London, 1904).

L. L. PRICE, 'Economic Theory and Fiscal Policy', *Economic Journal*, 14 (1904).

A. RAMSAY, *The Economics of Safeguarding* (1930).

R. REA, *Free Trade in Being* (1908).

J. M. ROBERTSON *Trade and Tariffs* (1908).

—— *The Collapse of 'Tariff Reform': Mr. Chamberlain's Case Exposed* (1911).

—— *The New Tariffism* (1918).

—— *The Political Economy of Free Trade* (1928).

—— *Fiscal Fraud and Folly: A Study of the Propaganda of 'Empire Free Trade' and other Programmes* (London, n.d., but *c.* 1930).

E. SAUNDERS, *A Self-Supporting Empire* (1918).

A. SHADWELL, *The Engineering Industry and the Crisis of 1922* (1922).

A. SHORTT, 'The Anti-dumping Feature of the Canadian Tariff', *Quarterly Journal of Economics*, 20 (1906).

F. E. SMITH [Lord Birkenhead], *Speeches Delivered in the House of Commons and Elsewhere, 1906–1909* (Liverpool, 1910).

SIR JOSIAH STAMP, *The Fundamental Principles of Taxation in the Light of Modern Developments* (1921).

THE STANDARD, *How to Capture German Trade* (1914).

J. STURGIS, *The Prime Minister's Pamphlet* (1903).

TARIFF REFORM LEAGUE, 'A Policy for Agriculture: Tariff Reform and Imperial Preference', *TRL Leaflet 116* (n.d.).

—— *The Keys of Industry. A Handbook to the New British and 'Key' Industries Exhibition. Organised by the Industrial Section of the Tariff Reform League* (1918).

—— *A Call to Action* (1921).

I. TARBELL, *The Tariff in Our Times* (New York, 1912).

F. W. TAUSSIG, *Tariff History of the United States* (1st edn., New York, 1888).

—— *Free Trade, The Tariff and Reciprocity* (New York, 1927).

S. E. Thomas, *British Banks and the Finance of Industry* (1931).

E. E. Todd, *The Case Against Tariff Reform* (1911).

S. Turner, *From War to Work* (1918).

C. A. Vince, *Mr. Chamberlain's Proposals: What they Mean and What we shall Gain by Them* (1903).

J. Viner, *Dumping: A Problem in International Trade* (New York, 1966 edn.).

—— 'The Most-Favoured-Nation Clause', *Index*, (*Journal of the Svenska Handelsbanken, Stockholm*), 6 (1931).

S. and B. Webb, *Industrial Democracy* (1st edn., 2 vols., 1897).

J. W. Welsford, *The Strength of Nations* (1909).

P. B. Whale, *International Trade* (Oxford, 1932).

A. White, *Efficiency and Empire* (1901; 2nd edn., G. R. Searle (ed.), Brighton, 1973).

E. E. Williams, *Made in Germany* (3rd edn., 1896).

—— *The Foreigner in the Farmyard* (1897).

—— *The Case for Protection* (1899).

H. G. Williams, *Politics and Economics* (1926).

—— *Through Tariffs to Prosperity* (1931).

H. T. Wills, *Scientific Tariff Making: A History of the Movement to Create a Tariff Commission* (New York, 1913).

G. H. Wright, *Chronicles of the Birmingham Chamber of Commerce, 1813–1913* (Birmingham, 1913).

(I) SECONDARY WORKS (Books, Articles, and Theses)

Anon., *History of Trollope and Colls* (priv. publ., n.d. but 1978).

D. Abel, *A History of British Tariffs, 1923–1942* (1945).

R. J. Q. Adams, *Arms and the Wizard: Lloyd George and the Ministry of Munitions, 1915–1916* (1978).

D. H. Aldcroft (ed.), *The Development of British Industry and Foreign Competition, 1875–1914: Studies in Industrial Enterprise* (1968).

—— and H. W. Richardson, *The British Economy 1870–1939* (1969).

B. W. E. Alford, *Depression and Recovery? British Economic Growth, 1919–1939* (1972).

—— 'New Industries for Old? British Industry between the Wars', in R. Floud and D. N. McCloskey (eds.), *Economic History of Britain since 1700* (Cambridge, 1981), ii.

R. C. Allen, 'International Competition in Iron and Steel, 1850–1950', *Journal of Economic History*, 39 (1979).

—— 'Entrepreneurship and Technical Progress in the Northeast Coast Pig Iron Industry, 1850–1913', *Research in Economic History*, 6 (1981).

R. G. D. Allen and J. E. Ely, *International Trade Statistics* (New York, 1953).

O. Anderson, *A Liberal State at War: English Politics and Economics During the Crimean War* (1967).

D. R. Annett, *British Preference in Canadian Commercial Policy* (Toronto, 1948).

T. Balderston, 'War Finance and Inflation in Britain and Germany, 1914–1918', *Economic History Review* (2nd. ser.), 42 (1989).

T. Balogh, *Studies in Financial Organization* (Cambridge, 1947).

S. BALL, *Baldwin and the Conservative Party: The Crisis of 1929–1931* (New Haven, 1988).

K. D. BARKIN, *The Controversy over German Industrialization, 1890–1902* (Chicago, 1970).

J. BARNES and D. NICHOLSON (eds.), *The Leo Amery Diaries*, i. *1896–1929* (1980).

W. H. BECKER, 'American Manufacturers and Foreign Markets, 1870–1900: Business Historians and the "New Economic Determinists" ', *Business History Review*, 47 (1973).

—— *The Dynamics of Business-Government Relations: Industry and Exports, 1893–1921* (Chicago, 1982).

S. H. BEER, *Modern British Politics* (1965; 1969 edn.).

J. BELLAMY, *The Trade and Shipping of Nineteenth-Century Hull* (East Yorkshire Local History Society, Publication No. 27, 1971).

F. BENHAM, *Great Britain under Protection* (New York, 1941).

L. BENSON, *Turner and Beard* (Glencoe, Ill., 1960).

P. BERCK, 'Hard Driving and Efficiency: Iron Production in 1890', *Journal of Economic History*, 38 (1978).

M. W. BERESFORD, *The Leeds Chamber of Commerce* (Leeds, 1951).

SIR HENRY BESSEMER, *An Autobiography* (1905).

M. H. BEST and J. HUMPHRIES, 'The City and Industrial Decline', in B. Elbaum and W. Lazonick (eds.), *The Decline of the British Economy* (Oxford, 1986).

S. BLANK, *Industry and Government in Britain: The Federation of British Industries in Politics, 1945–65* (Farnborough, 1973).

N. BLEWETT, 'Free Fooders, Balfourites, Whole Hoggers: Factionalism within the Unionist Party, 1906–10', *Historical Journal*, 11 (1968).

—— *The Peers, the Parties and the People: The General Elections of 1910* (1972).

R. W. D. BOYCE, *British Capitalism at the Crossroads, 1919–1932: A Study in Politics, Economics and International Relations* (Cambridge, 1987).

J. BRANDES, *Herbert Hoover and Economic Diplomacy: Department of Commerce Policy, 1921–1928* (Pittsburgh, 1962).

B. H. BROWN, *The Tariff Reform Movement in Great Britain, 1881–1895* (New York, 1943).

K. D. BROWN, 'The Trade Union Tariff Reform Association, 1904–1913', *Journal of British Studies*, 9 (1970).

L. BROWN, *The Board of Trade and the Free Trade Movement 1830–42* (Oxford, 1958).

D. BURN, *The Economic History of Steelmaking, 1867–1939: A Study in Competition* (Cambridge, 1940).

T. H. BURNHAM and G. O. HOSKINS, *Iron and Steel in Britain, 1870–1930: A Comparative Study of the Causes which Limited the Economic Development of the British Iron and Steel Industry Between the Years 1870 and 1930* (1943).

N. K. BUXTON and D. H. ALDCROFT (eds.), *British Industry between the Wars: Instability and Industrial Development, 1919–1939* (1979).

I. C. R. BYATT, 'Electrical Products', in D. H. Aldcroft (ed.), *The Development of British Industry and Foreign Competition, 1875–1914* (1968).

—— *The British Electrical Industry 1875–1914: The Economic Returns to a New Technology* (Oxford, 1979).

P. CAIN, 'Political Economy in Edwardian England: The Tariff-Reform Controversy', in A. O'Day (ed.), *The Edwardian Age: Conflict and Stability, 1900–1914* (1979).

—— and A. G. HOPKINS, *British Imperialism: Innovation and Expansion, 1688–1914* (1993).

—— and A. G. HOPKINS, *British Imperialism: Crisis and Deconstruction, 1914–1990*, (1993).

F. CAPIE, 'The Pressure for Tariff Protection in Britain, 1917–31', *Journal of European Economic History*, 9 (1980).

—— *Depression and Protectionism: Britain Between the Wars* (1983).

—— and M. COLLINS, *The Inter-War British Economy: A Statistical Abstract* (Manchester, 1983).

J. C. CARR and W. TAPLIN, *A History of the British Steel Industry* (Oxford, 1962).

Y. CASSIS, *City Bankers, 1890–1914* (French edn., 1984; Eng. edn., Cambridge, 1994).

E. CHAMBERLIN, *The Theory of Monopolistic Competition* (Cambridge, Mass., 1933).

A. D. CHANDLER, *The Visible Hand: The Managerial Revolution in American Business*, (Cambridge, Mass., 1977).

A. D. CHANDLER, *Scale and Scope: The Dynamics of Industrial Capitalism* (Cambridge, Mass., 1990).

B. CHATTERJI, *Trade, Tariffs, and Empire: Lancashire and British Policy in India, 1919–1939* (Delhi, 1992).

S. G. CHECKLAND, 'The Mind of the City, 1870–1914', *Oxford Economic Papers*, 9 (1957).

R. A. CHURCH, 'The Effect of the American Export Invasion on the British Boot and Shoe Industry, 1885–1914', *Journal of Economic History*, 28 (1968).

—— *The Great Victorian Boom 1850–1873* (Houndmills, 1975).

J. H. CLAPHAM, *An Economic History of Modern Britain*, ii. *Free Trade and Steel, 1850–1886* (Cambridge, 1932).

G. KITSON CLARK, 'The Repeal of the Corn Laws and the Politics of the Forties', *Economic History Review*, 2nd ser., 4 (1951).

P. F. CLARKE, *Lancashire and the New Liberalism* (Cambridge, 1971).

—— 'The End of Laissez-Faire and the Politics of Cotton', *Historical Journal*, 15 (1972).

H. A. CLEGG, *A History of British Trade Unions since 1889*, ii. *1911–1933* (Oxford, 1985).

P. CLINE, 'Winding Down the War Economy: British Plans for Peacetime Recovery, 1916–19', in K. Burk (ed.), *War and the State: The Transformation of British Government, 1914–1919* (1982).

A. W. COATS, 'Political Economy and the Tariff Reform Campaign of 1903', *Journal of Law and Economics*, 11 (1968).

S. COBEN, 'Northeastern Businessmen and Radical Reconstruction: A Re-examination', *Mississippi Valley Historical Review*, 46 (1959–60).

F. COETZEE, 'Pressure Groups, Tory Businessmen and the Aura of Political Corruption before the First World War', *Historical Journal*, 29 (1986).

—— *For Party or Country: Nationalism and the Dilemmas of Popular Conservatism in Edwardian England* (New York, 1990).

D. C. COLEMAN, *Courtaulds: An Economic and Social History* (2 vols., Oxford, 1969).

—— *History and the Economic Past: An Account of the Rise and Decline of Economic History in Britain* (Oxford, 1987).

J. A. C. CONYBEARE, *Trade Wars: The Theory and Practice of International Commercial Rivalry* (New York, 1987).

A. F. COOPER, *British Agricultural Policy, 1912–36: A Study in Conservative Politics* (Manchester, 1989).

W. M. CORDEN, *The Theory of Protection* (Oxford, 1971).

—— *Trade Policy and Economic Welfare* (Oxford, 1974).

J. CORNFORD, 'The Transformation of Conservatism in the Late Nineteenth Century', *Victorian Studies*, 7 (1963–4).

M. COWLING, *The Impact of Labour: The Beginning of Modern British Politics* (Cambridge, 1971).

N. F. R. CRAFTS, S. J. LEYBOURNE, and T. C. MILLS, 'Britain', in R. Sylla and G. Toniolo (eds.), *Patterns of European Industrialization* (1991).

N. CRATHORNE, *Tennant's Stalk* (1973).

M. CULLEN, *The Statistical Movement in Early Victorian Britain: The Foundations of Empirical Social Research* (Hassocks, 1975).

R. P. T. DAVENPORT-HINES (ed.), *Markets and Bagmen: Studies in the History of Marketing and British Industrial Performance 1830–1939* (1986).

P. N. DAVIES, *The Trade Makers: Elder Dempster in West Africa, 1852–1972* (1973).

L. DAVIS, 'The Capital Markets and Industrial Concentration: The US and UK, a Comparative Study', *Economic History Review*, 2nd ser. 19 (1966).

L. E. DAVIS and R. A. HUTTENBACK, *Mammon and the Pursuit of Empire: The Political Economy of British Imperialism, 1860–1912* (Cambridge, 1986).

P. DEANE and W. A. COLE, *British Economic Growth, 1688–1959: Trends and Structure* (Cambridge, 2nd edn., 1967).

C. DEWEY, 'The End of the Imperialism of Free Trade: The Eclipse of the Lancashire Lobby and the Concession of Fiscal Autonomy to India', in C. Dewey and A. G. Hopkins (ed.), *The Imperial Impact: Studies in the Economic History of Africa and India* (1978).

M. DINTENFASS, 'The Politics of Producers' Co-operation: the FBI-TUC-NCEO Talks, 1929–1933', in J. Turner (ed.), *Businessmen and Politics* (1984).

J. A. DOWIE, 'Growth in the Inter-war Period: Some More Arithmetic', *Economic History Review*, 2nd ser., 21 (1968).

I. M. DRUMMOND, *British Economic Policy and the Empire, 1919–1939* (1972).

—— *Imperial Economic Policy, 1917–1939: Studies in Expansion and Protection* (1974).

A. L. DUNHAM, *The Anglo-French Treaty of Commerce of 1860 and the Progress of the Industrial Revolution in France* (Ann Arbor, 1930).

D. DUTTON, 'Unionist Politics and the Aftermath of the General Election of 1906: A Reassessment', *Historical Journal*, 22 (1979).

—— 'Lancashire and the New Unionism: The Unionist Party and the Growth of Popular Politics, 1906–1914', *Transactions of the Historic Society of Lancashire and Cheshire*, 130 (1980).

—— 'The Unionist Party and Social Policy, 1906–1914', *Historical Journal*, 24 (1981).

M. EDELSTEIN, *Overseas Investment in the Age of High Imperialism: The United Kingdom, 1850–1914* (New York, 1982).

B. EICHENGREEN, 'Sterling and the Tariff, 1919–1932', *Princeton Studies in International Finance*, 48 (1981), repr. in *idem.*, *Elusive Stability* (Cambridge, 1990).

H. V. EMY, 'The Impact of Financial Policy on English Party Politics before 1914', *Historical Journal*, 15 (1972).

—— *Liberals, Radicals and Social Politics, 1892–1914* (Cambridge, 1973).

C. ERICKSON, *British Industrialists: Steel and Hosiery, 1850–1950* (Cambridge, 1959).

G. FAIRRIE, *The Sugar Refining Families of Great Britain* (priv. publ., 1951).

D. A. FARNIE, *The English Cotton Industry and the World Market, 1815–1896* (Oxford, 1979).

—— *The Manchester Ship Canal and the Rise of the Port of Manchester* (Manchester, 1980).

G. D. FELDMAN, *Iron and Steel in the German Inflation, 1916–1923* (Princeton, 1977).

M. FFORDE, *Conservatism and Collectivism, 1886–1914* (Edinburgh, 1990).

J. FOREMAN-PECK, 'Tariff Protection and Economies of Scale: The British Motor Industry before 1939', *Oxford Economic Papers*, 31 (1979).

—— 'The British Tariff and Industrial Protection in the 1930s: An Alternative Model', *Economic History Review*, 2nd ser., 34 (1981).

P. FRASER, 'Unionism and Tariff Reform: The Crisis of 1906', *Historical Journal*, 5 (1962).

M. FREEDEN, *The New Liberalism: An Ideology of Social Reform* (Oxford, 1978).

—— *Liberalism Divided: A Study in British Political Thought, 1914–1939* (Oxford, 1986).

D. FRENCH, *British Economic and Strategic Planning, 1905–1915* (1982).

A. L. FRIEDBERG, *The Weary Titan: Britain and the Experience of Relative Decline, 1895–1905* (Princeton, 1988).

W. R. GARSIDE, *British Unemployment, 1919–1939: A Study in Public Policy* (Cambridge, 1990).

A. GERSCHENKRON, *Bread and Democracy in Germany* (New York, 1966 edn).

J. A. GIBBS, *History of Antony and Dorothea Gibbs* (1922).

J. F. GODFREY, *Capitalism at War: Industrial Policy and Bureaucracy in France, 1914–1918* (Leamington Spa, 1987).

A. M. GOLLIN, *Balfour's Burden: Arthur Balfour and Imperial Preference* (1965).

E. O. GOLOB, *The Méline Tariff: French Agriculture and Nationalist Economic Policy* (New York, 1944).

H. F. GOSPEL, 'Employers' Labour Policy: A Study of the Mond-Turner Talks, 1927–33', in R. P. T. Davenport-Hines (ed.), *Business in the Age of Depression and War* (1990). E. H. H. GREEN, 'Radical Conservatism: The Electoral Genesis of Tariff Reform', *Historical Journal*, 28 (1985).

—— 'Radical Conservatism in Britain, 1900–1914', unpubl. Ph. D. thesis, University of Cambridge, 1985.

—— 'Rentiers versus Producers? The Political Economy of the Bimetallic Controversy, *c.* 1880–1898', *English Historical Review*, 103 (1988).

R. GREENHILL, 'Merchants and the Latin American Trades', in D. C. M. Platt, *Business Imperialism, 1840–1930* (Oxford, 1977).

—— 'The Nitrate and Iodine Trades', in D. C. M. Platt, *Business Imperialism, 1840–1930* (Oxford, 1977).

H. G. GRUBEL and P. J. LLOYD, *Intra-Industry Trade: The Theory and Measurement of International Trade in Differentiated Products* (1975).

P. S. GUPTA, *Imperialism and the British Labour Movement, 1914–1964* (1975).

L. F. HABER, *The Chemical Industry during the Nineteenth Century: A Study of the Economic Aspect of Applied Chemistry in Europe and North America* (Oxford, 1958).

—— *The Chemical Industry, 1900–1930: International Growth and Technological Change* (Oxford, 1971).

G. VON HABERLER, *The Theory of International Trade, with its Applications to Commercial Policy* (Eng. edn. transl. A. Stonier and F. Benham, 1936).

D. C. HAGUE, *The Economics of Man-Made Fibres* (1957).

J. HAMILTON, 'Henry Chaplin and English Agriculture, 1875–1895', unpubl. BA thesis, University of Manchester, 1977.

W. K. HANCOCK, *Survey of British Commonwealth Affairs, 1918–1939*, ii. *Problems of Economic Policy, 1918–1939*, Part. 1 (1942).

L. HANNAH, *The Rise of the Corporate Economy* (1976).

L. HANNAH, 'Scale and Scope: Towards a European Visible Hand?', *Business History*, 33, 1991.

G. W. HARDACH, *The First World War, 1914–1918* (1973; Eng. edn., 1977).

P. HARNETTY, 'The Indian Cotton Duties Controversy, 1894–1896', *English Historical Review*, 77 (1962).

N. HARRIS, *Competition and the Corporate Society: British Conservatives, the State and Industry, 1945–1964* (1972).

A. E. HARRISON, 'The Competitiveness of the British Cycle Industry, 1890–1914', *Economic History Review*, 2nd ser., 22 (1969).

G. R. HAWKE, 'The United States Tariff and Industrial Protection in the Late Nineteenth Century', *Economic History Review*, 2nd ser., 28 (1975).

J. R. HAY, 'Employers and Social Policy in Britain: The Evolution of Welfare Legislation, 1905–14', *Social History*, 4 (1977).

—— 'Employers' Attitudes to Social Policy and the Concept of "Social Control", 1900–1920', in P. Thane (ed.), *The Origins of British Social Policy* (1978).

C. HAZLEHURST, *Politicians at War: July 1914 to May 1915* (1971).

R. H. HEINDEL, *The American Impact on Great Britain, 1898–1914: A Study of the United States in World History* (New York, 1968 edn.).

R. D. HERZOG, 'The Conservative Party and Protectionist Politics, 1918–1932', unpubl. Ph. D. thesis, University of Sheffield, 1984.

R. K. HILL, 'Accountancy Developments in a Public Utility Company in the Nineteenth Century', *Accounting Research*, 5 (1955).

R. J. S. HOFFMAN, *Great Britain and the German Trade Rivalry, 1875–1914* (Philadelphia, 1933).

R. F. HOLLAND, 'The Federation of British Industries and the International Economy, 1929–1939', *Economic History Review*, 2nd ser., 34 (1981).

—— 'The End of an Imperial Economy: Anglo-Canadian Disengagement in the 1930s', *Journal of Imperial and Commonwealth History*, 11 (1982–3).

C.-L. HOLTFRERICH, *The German Inflation, 1914–1923: Causes and Effects in International Perspective*, (Eng. edn., transl. T. Balderston, Berlin, 1986).

D. A. HOUNSHELL, *From American System to Mass Production, 1800–1932: The Development of Manufacturing Technology in the United States* (Baltimore, 1984).

J. R. T. HUGHES, *Fluctuations in Trade, Industry and Finance: A Study of British Economic Development, 1850–1860* (Oxford, 1960).

Sir H. HUTCHINSON, *Tariff-Making and Industrial Reconstruction: An Account of the Work of the Import Duties Advisory Committee, 1932–1939* (1965).

F. E. HYDE, *Mr. Gladstone at the Board of Trade* (1934).

—— *Blue Funnel: A History of Alfred Holt and Company of Liverpool, 1865–1914* (Liverpool, 1956).

—— et al., *Shipping Enterprise and Management, 1830–1939: Harrisons of Liverpool* (Liverpool, 1967).

—— and S. MARRINER, 'The Economic Functions of the Export Merchant', *Manchester School*, 20 (1952).

A. R. ILERSIC and P. F. B. LIDDLE, *Parliament of Commerce: The Story of the Association of British Chambers of Commerce, 1860–1960* (1960).

A. H. IMLAH, *Economic Elements in the Pax Britannica: Studies in British Foreign Trade in the Nineteenth Century* (Cambridge, Mass., 1958).

G. INGHAM, *Capitalism Divided? The City and Industry in British Social Development* (Houndmills, 1984).

J. N. INGHAM, *Making Iron and Steel: Independent Mills in Pittsburgh, 1820–1920*, (Columbus, Ohio, 1991).

D. A. IRWIN, 'Welfare Effects of British Free Trade: Debate and Evidence from the 1840s', *Journal of Political Economy*, 96 (1988).

H. JANES, *The Master Millers: The Story of the House of Rank* (priv. publ., 1955).

D. T. JENKINS and K. G. PONTING, *The British Wool Textile Industry, 1770–1914* (1982).

N. JHA, *The Age of Marshall: Aspects of British Economic Thought, 1890–1914* (2nd edn., 1973).

A. H. JOHN, *A Liverpool Merchant House: Being the History of Alfred Booth and Company, 1863–1958* (1959).

H. G. JOHNSON, *Money, Trade and Economic Growth: Survey Lectures in Economic Theory* (1962).

P. B. JOHNSON, *Land Fit for Heroes: The Planning of British Reconstruction, 1916–1919* (Chicago, 1968).

A. E. KAHN, *Great Britain in the World Economy* (New York, 1946).

J. E. KENDLE, *The Colonial and Imperial Conferences, 1887–1911* (1967).

P. M. KENNEDY, *The Rise of Anglo-German Antagonism, 1860–1914* (1980).

W. P. KENNEDY, *Industrial Structure, Capital Markets and the Origins of British Economic Decline* (Cambridge, 1987).

M. KITSON and S. SOLOMOU, *Protectionism and Economic Revival: The British Inter-War Economy* (Cambridge, 1990).

G. M. KOOT, *English Historical Economics 1870–1926: The Rise of Economic History and Neomercantilism* (Cambridge, 1987).

I. N. LAMBI, *Free Trade and Protection in Germany, 1868–79* (Wiesbaden, 1963).

D. S. LANDES, *The Unbound Prometheus: Technological Change and Industrial Development in Western Europe from 1750 to the Present* (Cambridge, 1969).

W. LAZONICK, 'Competition, Specialization, and Industrial Decline', *Journal of Economic History*, 41 (1981).

—— 'Factor Costs and the Diffusion of Ring Spinning in Britain prior to World War I', *Quarterly Journal of Economics*, 96 (1981).

—— 'Competition, Specialization, and Industrial Decline', *Journal of Economic History*, 41, 1981.

C. H. LEE, *Regional Employment Statistics, 1841–1971* (Cambridge, 1979).

—— *The British Economy since 1700* (Cambridge, 1986).

—— 'Corporate Behaviour in Theory and History: I. The Evolution of Theory', *Business History*, 32 (1990).

A. L. LEVINE, *Industrial Retardation in Britain, 1880–1914* (1967).

W. LEWCHUK, *American Technology and the British Vehicle Industry* (Cambridge, 1987).

H. LIEPMANN, *Tariff Levels and the Economic Unity of Europe* (1938).

R. LLOYD-JONES and M. J. LEWIS, 'Personal Capitalism and British Industrial Decline: The Personally Managed Firm and Business Strategy in Sheffield, 1880–1920', *Business History Review*, 68, 1994.

A. F. LUCAS, *Industrial Reconstruction and the Control of Competition: The British Experiments* (1937).

A. M. MCBRIAR, *Fabian Socialism and English Politics, 1884–1918* (Cambridge, 1964).

D. N. MCCLOSKEY, *Economic Maturity and Entrepreneurial Decline: British Iron and Steel, 1870–1913* (Cambridge, Mass., 1973).

D. N. McCloskey, 'Magnanimous Albion: Free Trade and British National Income, 1841–1881', in D. N. McCloskey (ed.), *Enterprise and Trade in Victorian Britain: Essays in Historical Economics* (1981).

N. McCord, *The Anti-Corn Law League, 1838–1846* (1958).

H. W. McCready, 'Alfred Marshall and Tariff Reform, 1903: Some Unpublished Letters', *Journal of Political Economy*, 63 (1955).

O. J. McDiarmid, *Commercial Policy in the Canadian Economy* (Cambridge, Mass., 1946).

A. Maizels, *Growth and Trade* (Cambridge, 1970).

A. J. Marrison, 'Great Britain and her Rivals in the Latin American Cotton Piece Goods Market, 1880–1914', in B. M. Ratcliffe (ed.), *Great Britain and Her World 1750–1914: Essays in Honour of W. O. Henderson* (Manchester, 1975).

—— 'The Development of a Tariff Reform Policy during Joseph Chamberlain's First Campaign', in W. H. Chaloner and B. M. Ratcliffe (eds.), *Trade and Transport: Essays in Economic History in Honour of T. S. Willan* (Manchester, 1977).

—— 'British Businessmen and the "Scientific" Tariff: A Study of Joseph Chamberlain's Tariff Commission, 1903–1921', unpubl. Ph. D. thesis, University of Hull, 1980.

—— 'Businessmen, Industries and Tariff Reform in Great Britain, 1903–1930', *Business History*, 25 (1983); repr. in R. P. T. Davenport-Hines (ed.), *Business in the Age of Depression and War* (1990).

—— 'The Tariff Commission, Agricultural Protection and Food Taxes, 1903–1913', *Agricultural History Review*, 34 (1986).

—— 'Indian Summer, 1870–1914', in Mary B. Rose (ed.), *The Lancashire Cotton Industry: A History since 1700* (Preston, 1995).

W. Mass and W. Lazonick, 'The British Cotton Industry and International Competitive Advantage: The State of the Debates', *Business History*, 33, 1990.

H. C. G. Matthew, *The Liberal Imperialists: The Ideas and Politics of a Post-Gladstonian Elite* (1973).

R. C. O. Matthews, 'Why has Britain had Full Employment since the War?', *Economic Journal*, 78 (1968).

—— C. H. Feinstein, and J. C. Odling-Smee, *British Economic Growth, 1856–1973* (Oxford, 1982).

Sir H. Maxwell, *Half- A-Century of Successful Trade: Being a Sketch of the Rise and Development of the Business of W. & A. Gilbey, 1857–1907* (priv. publ., 1907).

R. C. Michie, 'The Social Web of Investment in the Nineteenth Century', *Revue internationale de histoire de la banque*, 18–19 (1979).

K. Middlemas, *Politics in Industrial Society: The Experience of the British System since 1911* (1979).

W. E. Minchinton, *The British Tinplate Industry: A History* (Oxford, 1957).

—— 'E. E. Williams: "Made in Germany" and after', *Vieteljahrschrift für Sozial-und Wirtschaftsgeschichte*, 62 (1975).

B. R. Mitchell and P. Deane, *Abstract of British Historical Statistics* (Cambridge, 1962).

—— *British Historical Statistics* (Cambridge, 1988).

W. Mock, *Imperiale Herrschaft und nationales Interesse: 'Constructive Imperialism' oder Freihandel in Grossbritanien vor dem Ersten Weltkrieg* (Stuttgart, 1982).

D. E. Moggridge, *British Monetary Policy, 1924–1931: The Norman Conquest of $4.86* (Cambridge, 1972).

E. V. MORGAN, *Studies in British Financial Policy, 1914–1925* (1952).

K. O. MORGAN, *Consensus and Disunity: The Lloyd George Coalition Government, 1918–1922* (Oxford, 1979).

J. H. MORRIS and L. J. WILLIAMS, *The South Wales Coal Industry, 1841–1875* (Cardiff, 1958).

R. J. MUNTING, 'Ransome's in Russia: An English Agricultural Engineering Company's Trade with Russia to 1917', *Economic History Review*, 2nd ser., 31 (1978).

B. K. MURRAY, *The People's Budget, 1909/10: Lloyd George and Liberal Politics* (Oxford, 1980).

A. E. MUSSON, *Enterprise in Soap and Chemicals: Joseph Crosfield & Sons Limited, 1815–1965* (Manchester, 1965).

—— 'The "Manchester School" and Exportation of Machinery', *Business History*, 14 (1972).

—— *The Growth of British Industry* (1978).

D. NELSON, *Managers and Workers: Origins of the New Factory System in the United States, 1880–1920* (Madison, Wis. 1975).

S. NEWTON and D. PORTER, *Modernization Frustrated: The Politics of Industrial Decline in Britain since 1900* (1988).

S. J. NICHOLAS, 'The Overseas Marketing Performance of British Industry, 1870–1914', *Economic History Review*, 2nd ser., 37 (1984).

D. P. O'BRIEN, *The Classical Economists* (Oxford, 1975).

—— 'A. Marshall, 1842–1924', in D. P. O'Brien and J. R. Presley (eds.), *Pioneers of Modern Economics in Britain* (1981).

A. OFFER, 'Empire and Social Reform: British Overseas Investment and Domestic Politics, 1908–1914', *Historical Journal*, 26 (1983).

M. OLSON, *The Economics of the Wartime Shortage: A History of British Food Supplies in the Napoleonic War and in World Wars I and II* (Durham, NC, 1963).

—— *The Logic of Collective Action* (Cambridge, Mass., 1965).

—— *The Rise and Decline of Nations* (New Haven, 1982).

P. L. PAYNE, 'The Emergence of the Large-Scale Company in Great Britain, 1870–1914', *Economic History Review*, 2nd ser., 20 (1967).

—— 'Iron and Steel Manufactures', in D. H. Aldcroft (ed.), *The Development of British Industry and Foreign Competition, 1875–1914* (1968).

—— *British Entrepreneurship in the Nineteenth Century* (2nd edn., 1988).

H. PELLING, *Social Geography of British Elections, 1885–1910* (1967).

G. D. PHILLIPS, *The Diehards: Aristocratic Society and Politics in Edwardian England* (Cambridge, Mass., 1979).

A. C. PIGOU, *Aspects of British Economic History, 1918–1925* (1947).

G. F. PLANT, *Oversea Settlement: Migration from the United Kingdom to the Dominions* (1951).

D. C. M. PLATT, *Latin America and British Trade, 1806–1914* (1972).

—— *Britain's Investment Overseas on the Eve of the First World War* (1986).

—— (ed.), *Business Imperialism, 1840–1930* (Oxford, 1977).

S. POLLARD, 'Laissez-Faire and Shipbuilding', *Economic History Review*, 2nd ser., 5 (1952–3).

—— 'British and World Shipbuilding, 1890–1914: A Study in Comparative Costs', *Journal of Economic History*, 17 (1957).

—— *A History of Labour in Sheffield* (Liverpool, 1959).

S. POLLARD, 'British Capital Exports, 1870–1914: Harmful or Beneficial?', *Economic History Review*, 2nd ser., 38 (1985).

—— *Britain's Prime and Britain's Decline: The British Economy, 1870–1914* (1989).

—— and P. ROBERTSON, *The British Shipbuilding Industry, 1870–1914* (Cambridge, Mass., 1979).

D. PORTER, 'The Unionist Tariff Reformers, 1903–1914', unpubl. Ph. D. thesis, University of Manchester, 1976.

—— 'A Newspaper Owner in Politics: Arthur Pearson and the Tariff Reform League, 1903–1905', *Moirae*, 5 (1980).

G. PORTER and H. C. LIVESAY, *Merchants and Manufacturers: Studies in the Changing Structure of Nineteenth-Century Marketing* (Baltimore, 1971).

A. PROCHASKA, *History of the General Federation of Trade Unions, 1899–1980* (1982).

[SIR ARTHUR PUGH], *Men of Steel* (1951).

M. D. PUGH, 'Asquith, Bonar Law and the First Coalition', *Historical Journal*, 17 (1974).

J. RAMSDEN, *The Age of Balfour and Baldwin, 1902–1940* (1978).

—— *The Making of Conservative Party Policy: The Conservative Research Department Since 1929* (1980).

W. J. READER, *Imperial Chemical Industries: A History*, i (1970).

A. REDFORD, *Manchester Merchants and Foreign Trade* (2 vols., Manchester, 1934, 1956).

J. F. REES, *A Short Fiscal and Financial History of England, 1815–1918* (1921).

R. V. REMINI, 'Martin Van Buren and the Tariff of Abominations', *American Historical Review*, 63 (1957).

R. A. REMPEL, *Unionists Divided: Arthur Balfour, Joseph Chamberlain and the Unionist Free Traders* (Newton Abbot, 1974).

H. W. RICHARDSON, *Economic Recovery in Britain, 1932–39* (1967).

J. H. RICHARDSON, *British Economic Foreign Policy* (1936).

J. RIDLEY, 'The Unionist Social Reform Committee, 1911–1914: Wets before the Deluge', *Historical Journal*, 30 (1987).

L. ROBBINS, *The Theory of Economic Policy in English Classical Political Economy* (1952).

M. ROBBINS, *The Railway Age* (Harmondsworth, 1965).

J. ROBINSON, *The Economics of Imperfect Competition* (1933).

T. RODGERS, 'Sir Allan Smith, the Industrial Group and the Politics of Unemployment, 1919–24', in R. P. T. Davenport-Hines (ed.), *Speculators and Patriots: Essays in Business Biography* (1986).

T. ROOTH, 'The Political Economy of Protectionism in Britain, 1919–32', *Journal of European Economic History*, 21 (1992).

—— *British Protectionism and the International Economy: Overseas Commercial Policy in the 1930s* (Cambridge, 1993).

D. M. ROSS, 'The Clearing Banks and Industry—New Perspectives on the Inter-War Years', in J. J. Van Helten and Y. Cassis (eds.), *Capitalism in a Mature Economy* (Aldershot, 1990).

V. H. ROTHWELL, *British War Aims and Peace Diplomacy, 1914–1918* (Oxford, 1971).

W. D. RUBINSTEIN, 'Henry Page Croft and the National Party, 1917–22', *Journal of Contemporary History*, 9 (1974).

—— 'The Victorian Middle Classes: Wealth, Occupation, and Geography', *Economic History Review*, 2nd ser., 30 (1977).

—— *Men of Property: The Very Wealthy in Britain Since the Industrial Revolution* (1981).

—— *Capitalism, Culture and Decline in Britain, 1750–1990*, (1993).

A. K. RUSSELL, *Liberal Landslide: The General Election of 1906* (Newton Abbot, 1973).

L. G. SANDBERG, 'American Rings and English Mules', *Quarterly Journal of Economics*, 83 (1969).

—— *Lancashire in Decline: A Study in Entrepreneurship, Technology, and International Trade* (Columbus, Oh., 1974).

S. B. SAUL, *Studies in British Overseas Trade 1870–1914* (Liverpool, 1960).

—— 'The Motor Industry in Britain to 1914', *Business History*, 5 (1962–3).

—— 'The Market and the Development of the Mechanical Engineering Industries in Britain, 1860–1914', *Economic History Review*, 2nd ser., 20 (1967).

—— 'The Machine Tool Industry in Britain to 1914', *Business History*, 10 (1968).

G. SAXONHOUSE and G. WRIGHT, 'Stubborn Mules and Vertical Integration: The Disappearing Constraint?', *Economic History Review*, 2nd ser., 40 (1987).

R. S. SAYERS, *The Bank of England, 1891–1944* (3 vols., Cambridge, 1976).

R. J. SCALLY, *The Origins of the Lloyd George Coalition: The Politics of Social-Imperialism, 1900–1918* (Princeton, 1975).

E. E. SCHATTSCHNEIDER, *Politics, Pressures and the Tariff: A Study of Free Private Enterprise in Pressure Politics, as Shown in the 1929–1930 Revision of the Tariff* (New York, 1935).

J. A. SCHMEICHEN, *Sweated Industries and Sweated Labour: The London Clothing Trades, 1860–1914* (1984).

J. A. SCHUMPETER, *Imperialism and Social Classes* (Oxford, 1951).

J. D. SCOTT, *Vickers: A History* (1962).

P. SCRANTON, *Proprietary Capitalism: The Textile Manufacture at Philadelphia, 1800–1885* (Cambridge, 1983).

G. R. SEARLE, *The Quest for National Efficiency: A Study in British Politics and British Political Thought, 1899–1914* (Oxford, 1971).

—— 'The Edwardian Liberal Party and Business', *English Historical Review*, 98 (1983).

—— *The Liberal Party: Triumph and Disintegration, 1886–1929* (1992).

R. C. SELF, 'The Conservative Party and the Politics of Tariff Reform', unpubl. Ph. D. thesis, University of London, 1982.

B. SEMMEL, *Imperialism and Social Reform: English Social-Imperial Thought, 1895–1914* (1960).

G. W. SHANAFELT, *The Secret Enemy: Austria-Hungary and the German Alliance, 1914–1918* (New York, 1985).

F. SHEHAB, *Progressive Taxation: A Study in the Development of the Progressive Principle in the British Income Tax* (Oxford, 1953).

E. SIGSWORTH, *Black Dyke Mills: A History* (Liverpool, 1958).

H. A. SILVERMAN, *Studies in Industrial Organization* (1946).

R. SKIDELSKY, *Politicians and the Slump: The Labour Government of 1929–1931* (Harmondsworth, 1970 edn.).

M. S. SMITH, *Tariff Reform in France, 1860–1900: The Politics of Economic Interest* (Ithaca, NY, 1980).

R. SMITH, 'The Manchester Chamber of Commerce and the Increasing Foreign Competition to Lancashire Cotton Textiles, 1873–1896', *Bulletin of the John Rylands Library*, 38 (1955–6).

R. K. SNYDER, *The Tariff Problem in Great Britain, 1918–1923* (Stanford, Calif., 1944).

D. STEVENSON, *French War Aims against Germany, 1914–1919* (Oxford, 1982).

J. STUBBS, 'Lord Milner and Patriotic Labour, 1914–1918', *English Historical Review*, 87 (1972).

—— 'The Impact of the Great War on the Conservative Party', in C. P. Cook and G. R. Peele (eds.), *The Politics of Reappraisal* (1975).

S. G. STURMEY, *The Economic Development of Radio* (1958).

A. SUMMERS, 'The Character of Edwardian Nationalism: Three Popular Leagues', in P. Kennedy and A. Nicholls (ed.), *Nationalist and Racialist Movements in Britain and Germany before 1914* (1981).

B. SUPPLE, 'Scale and Scope: Alfred Chandler and the Dynamics of Industrial Capitalism', *Economic History Review*, 2nd ser., 44, 1991.

A. SYKES, 'The Confederacy and the Purge of the Unionist Free Traders, 1906–1910', *Historical Journal*, 18 (1975).

—— *Tariff Reform in British Politics, 1903–1913* (Oxford, 1979).

—— 'Konstruktiver Imperialismus in Grossbritannien', in A. M. Birke and G. Heydemann (eds.), *Die Herausforderung des Europäischen Staatensystems: Nationale Ideologie und staatliches Interesse zwischen Restauration und Imperialismus* (Göttingen and Zurich, 1989).

F. TAUSSIG, *Tariff History of the United States* (1st edn., New York, 1888).

P. TEMIN, 'The Relative Decline of the British Steel Industry, 1880–1914', in H. Rosovsky (ed.), *Industrialization in Two Systems* (New York, 1966).

M. THOMAS, 'An Input-Output Approach to the British Economy, 1890–1914', *Journal of Economic History*, 45 (1985).

A. THORPE, *The British General Election of 1931* (Oxford, 1991).

S. TOLLIDAY, 'Tariffs and Steel, 1916–1934: The Politics of Industrial Decline', in J. Turner (ed.), *Businessmen and Politics* (1984).

—— *Business, Banking, and Politics: The Case of British Steel 1918–1939* (Cambridge, Mass., 1987).

J. TOMLINSON, *Problems of British Economic Policy 1870–1945* (1981).

M. TRACHTENBERG, ' "A New Economic Order": Étienne Clementel and French Economic Diplomacy during the First World War', *French Historical Studies*, 10 (1977–8).

M. TRACY, *Agriculture in Western Europe* (1st edn., 1964).

R. J. TRUPTIL, *British Banks and the London Money Market* (1936).

J. TURNER, 'The British Commonwealth Union and the General Election of 1918', *English Historical Review*, 93 (1978).

—— 'State Purchase of the Liquor Trade in the First World War', *Historical Journal*, 23 (1980).

—— 'The Politics of "Organised Business" in the First World War', in *idem*. (ed.), *Businessmen and Politics: Studies of Business Activity in British Politics, 1900–1945* (1984).

—— 'Servants of Two Masters: British Trade Associations in the First Half of the Twentieth Century', in Hiroaki Yamazaki and Matao Miyamoto (eds.), *Trade Associations in Business History*, International Conference on Business History, 14, Proceedings of the Fuji Conference (Tokyo, 1988).

—— 'The House of Commons and the Executive in the First World War', *Parliamentary History*, 10 (1991).

—— *British Politics and the Great War: Coalition and Conflict, 1915–1918* (New Haven, 1992).

R. E. TYSON, 'The Cotton Industry', in D. H. Aldcroft (ed.), *The Development of British Industry and Foreign Competition, 1875–1914* (1968).

H. TYSZYNSKI, 'World Trade in Manufactured Commodities, 1899–1950', *Manchester School*, 19 (1951).

I. UNGER, *The Greenback Era: A Social and Political History of American Finance, 1865–1879* (Princeton, 1964).

M. I. UROFSKY, *Big Steel and the Wilson Administration: A Study in Business-Government Relations* (Columbus, Oh., 1969).

N. VOUSDEN, *The Economics of Trade Protection* (Cambridge, 1990).

D. WALKER-SMITH, *The Protectionist Case in the 1840s* (Oxford, 1933).

P. J. WALLER, *Democracy and Sectarianism: A Political and Social History of Liverpool, 1868–1939* (Liverpool, 1981).

K. WARREN, *The British Iron and Steel Sheet Industry since 1840: An Economic Geography* (1970).

—— 'Iron and Steel', in N. K. Buxton and D. H. Aldcroft (eds.), *British Industry between the Wars* (1979).

S. B. WEBB, 'Tariffs, Cartels, Technology and Growth in the German Steel Industry, 1879–1914', *Journal of Economic History*, 40 (1980).

U. WENGENROTH, *Enterprise and Technology: The German and British Steel Industries, 1865–1895* (Cambridge, 1994).

E. H. WHETHAM, *The Agrarian History of England and Wales*, viii. *1914–1939* (Cambridge, 1978).

R. C. WHITING, *The View from Cowley: The Impact of Industrialization upon Oxford, 1918–1939* (Oxford, 1983).

E. WIGHAM, *The Power to Manage: A History of the Engineering Employers' Federation* (1973).

C. WILKINS, *History of the Iron, Steel, Tinplate and Other Trades of Wales* (Merthyr Tydfil, 1903).

P. WILLIAMSON, ' "Safety First": Baldwin, the Conservative Party, and the 1929 General Election', *Historical Journal*, 25 (1982).

—— 'Financiers, the Gold Standard and British Politics, 1925–1931', in J. Turner (ed.), *Businessmen and Politics* (1984).

—— 'A "Bankers' Ramp"? Financiers and the British political crisis of August 1931', *English Historical Review*, 99 (1984).

—— *National Crisis and National Government: British Politics, the Economy and Empire, 1926–1932* (Cambridge, 1992).

J. F. WILSON, *British Business History, 1720–1994*, (Manchester, 1995).

D. WINCH, *Economics and Policy: A Historical Survey* (1972 edn.).

J. Worrall, Ltd., *The Lancashire Textile Industry* (Oldham, 1956 edn.).

C. WURM, *Business, Politics and International Relations: Steel, Cotton and International Cartels in British Politics, 1924–1939* (1988; Eng. edn., transl. P. Salmon, Cambridge, 1993).

P. YULE, 'The Tariff Reform Movement and Germany, 1900–14', *Moirae*, 7 (1982).

S. H. ZEBEL, 'Fair Trade: An English Reaction to the Breakdown of the Cobden Treaty-System', *Journal of Modern History*, 12 (1940).

—— 'Joseph Chamberlain and the Genesis of Tariff Reform', *Journal of British Studies*, 7 (1967).

Index

[Individual firms are grouped together under 'companies': similarly, individual trade associations are grouped together under 'trade associations', and individual chambers of commerce are grouped together under 'Chamber of Commerce'.]